D0894433

# England before the Conquest

# ENGLAND BEFORE THE CONQUEST

Studies in primary sources
presented to
Dorothy Whitelock

Edited by
PETER CLEMOES
and
KATHLEEN HUGHES

CAMBRIDGE
At the University Press
1971

Published by the Syndics of the Cambridge University Press
Bentley House, 200 Euston Road, London NW1 2DB
American Branch: 32 East 57th Street, New York, N.Y.10022

© Cambridge University Press 1971

Library of Congress Catalogue Card Number: 76-154508

ISBN: 0 521 08191 2

Printed in Great Britain
at the University Printing House, Cambridge
(Brooke Crutchley, University Printer)

# Contents

# Contents

# Illustrations

## Illustrations

ACKNOWLEDGEMENTS

Photographs have been taken by the following: for the frontispiece by B. Gaye;
for plate I by A. D. Phillips; for plate II by R. L. Grew; for plate VIII*a* by
A. Hidalgo; and for plate VIII*b* by N. Lagergren. Those for plate VIII*c* and *d*
are reproduced by courtesy of the Dean and Chapter of Durham Cathedral.
Figures 1–7 are based on the Ordnance Survey Map by permission of the
Controller of H.M. Stationery Office and Crown copyright is reserved. Figures
10–24 have been drawn by H. M. Taylor.

# Preface

This book, intended to represent as many as possible of the various kinds of source material for Anglo-Saxon studies, has been written by some of Dorothy Whitelock's friends to mark the occasion of her seventieth birthday. Not only on our own behalf but also on behalf of other friends whom the plan of the book has inevitably excluded, we are expressing our gratitude for Dorothy's own work, for her concentration on primary materials, her treatment of a wide range of sources, and her accurate, judicious and imaginative scholarship. Like many others we admire not only the qualities of integrity and intellect that are basic to her work but also her powers of expression – the gift to seize an elusive idea and bind it concisely in words, the ability, in a few brilliant sentences, to condense complex considerations into the essentials which the student needs, the capacity to write with breadth of mind, humanity and elegance. These qualities which she has to such an exceptional degree have advanced the study of Anglo-Saxon literature and history, place-names and numismatics; they have educated many students, and, through her Penguin volume, *The Beginnings of English Society*, have reached a much wider public.

Those of us who have written this book, and many others besides, know her generosity as well as her scholarship, and have appreciated her knowledgeable, acute, searching and constructive criticism. More personally, the pleasure and charm of her companionship are valued by a wide circle of friends. We offer this book in gratitude for her friendship as well as for her scholarship and with our good wishes for her present and future work.

PETER CLEMOES

KATHLEEN HUGHES

# Abbreviations

AJ       *Archaeological Journal*
Allen    W. Allen coin sale, Sotheby, 14 March 1898
AntJ     *Antiquaries Journal*
APS      *Acta Philologica Scandinavica*
Archiv   *Archiv für das Studium der neueren Sprachen und Literaturen*
Argyll   Coin collection of the late Duke of Argyll, now dispersed
ASC      *The Anglo-Saxon Chronicle*
Ashdown, *Documents*  *English and Norse Documents Relating to the Reign of Ethelred the Unready*, ed. and trans. M. Ashdown (Cambridge, 1930)
ASPR     *The Anglo-Saxon Poetic Records*, ed. G. P. Krapp and E. V. K. Dobbie (New York, 1931–42)
Asser    *Asser's Life of King Alfred*, ed. W. H. Stevenson (Oxford, 1904; repr. 1959 with contr. by D. Whitelock)
Baldwin  A. H. Baldwin and Sons Ltd
Bd       Bedfordshire
BdaProsa *Bibliothek der angelsächsischen Prosa*, ed. C. W. M. Grein, R. P. Wülker *et al.* (Göttingen, Kassel, Leipzig and Hamburg, 1872–1933; most vols. repr. Darmstadt, 1964–8, in some cases with suppl. material)
Belfast  Ulster Museum, Belfast
Bethurum, *Wulfstan*  *The Homilies of Wulfstan*, ed. D. Bethurum (Oxford, 1957)
Birch    *Cartularium Saxonicum*, ed. W. de Gray Birch (London, 1885–99)
Björkman E. Björkman, *Nordische Personennamen in England* (Halle, 1910)
Bk       Buckinghamshire
Blunt    C. E. Blunt coin collection
BM       British Museum
BMC      *A Catalogue of the Coins in the British Museum. Anglo-Saxon Series* (London, 1887–93)
BM Facs  *Facsimiles of Ancient Charters in the British Museum*, ed. E. A. Bond (London, 1873–8)
BNJ      *British Numismatic Journal*
Brk      Berkshire
Bruun    L. E. Bruun coin sale, Sotheby, 18 May 1925
BT       J. Bosworth and T. N. Toller, *An Anglo-Saxon Dictionary* (Oxford, 1898)
BT *Suppl*  T. N. Toller, *Supplement* to BT (Oxford, 1921)
Bury     *Feudal Documents from the Abbey of Bury St Edmunds*, ed. D. C. Douglas (London, 1932)
C        Cambridgeshire
Campbell A. Campbell, *Old English Grammar* (Oxford, 1959)

# Abbreviations

Carlyon-Britton   P. W. P. Carlyon-Britton coin sales, Sotheby, 17 November 1913, 20 November 1916 and 11 November 1918

*CC*   *Corpus Christianorum Series Latina*

CCCC   Corpus Christi College, Cambridge

Chester hoard   C. E. Blunt and R. H. M. Dolley, 'The Chester (1950) Hoard', *BNJ* XXVII (1952–4), 125–60

*CLA*   E. A. Lowe, *Codices Latini Antiquiores* (Oxford, 1934–)

Co   Cornwall

*Councils*   *Councils and Ecclesiastical Documents relating to Great Britain and Ireland*, ed. A. W. Haddan and W. Stubbs (Oxford, 1869–78)

*CSEL*   *Corpus Scriptorum Ecclesiasticorum Latinorum*

Cu   Cumberland

D   Devon

*DB*   *Domesday Book*, ed. A. Farley and H. Ellis (London, 1783–1816)

Db   Derbyshire

*DBS*   P. H. Reaney, *A Dictionary of British Surnames* (London, 1958)

*DEPN*   E. Ekwall, *The Concise Oxford Dictionary of English Place-Names*, 4th ed. (Oxford, 1960)

*DGP*   *Danmarks Gamle Personnavne* (København, 1936–64)

Douglas   Manx Museum, Douglas, Isle of Man

Douglas hoard   H. A. Grueber, 'The Douglas Find of Anglo-Saxon Coins and Ornaments', *NC* 4th ser. XIII (1913), 322–48

Drabble   G. C. Drabble coin sales, Glendining, 4 July 1939 and 13 December 1943

Dublin   National Museum of Ireland, Dublin

Dymock   Rev. T. F. Dymock, *Saxon Coins*, unpub. MS owned formerly by J. D. A. Thompson and now by C. E. Blunt

Earle, *Charters*   J. Earle, *A Hand-Book to the Land-Charters and other Saxonic Documents* (Oxford, 1888)

Earle and Plummer, *Chronicles*   *Two of the Saxon Chronicles Parallel...*, ed. C. Plummer on the basis of an ed. by J. Earle (Oxford, 1892; repr. 1952 with contr. by D. Whitelock)

*ECW*   H. P. R. Finberg, *The Early Charters of Wessex* (Leicester, 1964)

*ECWM*   H. P. R. Finberg, *The Early Charters of the West Midlands* (Leicester, 1961)

Eddius   *The Life of Bishop Wilfrid by Eddius Stephanus*, ed. and trans. B. Colgrave (Cambridge, 1927)

EEMF   Early English Manuscripts in Facsimile (Copenhagen, 1951–)

EETS   Early English Text Society

*EGS*   *English and Germanic Studies*

*EHR*   *English Historical Review*

eME   early Middle English

eOE   early Old English

*EPNE*   A. H. Smith, *English Place-Name Elements*, EPNS 25–6

EPNS   English Place-Name Society

ERY   East Riding of Yorkshire

xi

# Abbreviations

ES      *Englische Studien*
Ess      Essex
ESts      *English Studies*
F. Baldwin    A. H. F. Baldwin coin collection
Fellows Jensen    G. Fellows Jensen, *Scandinavian Personal Names in Lincolnshire and Yorkshire* (Copenhagen, 1968)
Forssner    T. Forssner, *Continental-Germanic Personal Names in England in Old and Middle English Times* (Uppsala, 1916)
Förstemann    E. Förstemann, *Altdeutsches Namenbuch* 1 (Bonn, 1900)
Forum    C. C. F. Keary, 'A Hoard of Anglo-Saxon Coins found in Rome', *NC* 3rd ser. IV (1884), 225–55
Gl      Gloucestershire
Glasgow    Kelvingrove Museum, Glasgow
Grantley    Lord Grantley coin sale, Glendining, 22 March 1944
H      Division of Holland, Lincolnshire
Ha      Hampshire
Harmer, *SelEHD*    *Select English Historical Documents of the Ninth and Tenth Centuries*, ed. F. E. Harmer (Cambridge, 1914)
Harmer, *Writs*    *Anglo-Saxon Writs*, ed. F. E. Harmer (Manchester, 1952)
HBS      Henry Bradshaw Society
HE      Bede, *Historia Ecclesiastica Gentis Anglorum*
He      Herefordshire
Hildebrand    B. E. Hildebrand, *Anglosachsiska Mynt i Svenska Kongliga Mynt-kabinettet funna i Sveriges Jord*, ny tillökt upplaga (Stockholm, 1881)
Holm    S. Holm, *Studier öfver Uppsala Universitets Anglosaxiska Myntsamling* (Uppsala, 1917)
Holme    *St Benet of Holme 1020–1210*, ed. J. R. West, Norfolk Record Society 2–3
Hrt      Hertfordshire
Hu      Huntingdonshire
Janzén    A. Janzén, *Personnamn* (Stockholm, 1947)
JBAA    *Journal of the British Archaeological Association*
JDANHS    *Journal of the Derbyshire Archæological and Natural History Society*
JEGP    *Journal of English and Germanic Philology*
JEH    *Journal of Ecclesiastical History*
Jost, *Polity*    *Die* Institutes of Polity Civil and Ecclesiastical, *ein Werk Erzbischof Wulfstans von York*, ed. K. Jost (Bern, 1959)
Jost, *Wulfstanstudien*    K. Jost, *Wulfstanstudien* (Bern, 1950)
JRSAI    *Journal of the Royal Society of Antiquaries of Ireland*
JTS    *Journal of Theological Studies*
K      Kent
*Karl der Grosse*    *Karl der Grosse*, ed. W. Braunfels (Düsseldorf, 1965–8)
Kemble    *Codex Diplomaticus Aevi Saxonici*, ed. J. M. Kemble (London, 1839–48)
Ker, *Catalogue*    N. R. Ker, *Catalogue of Manuscripts containing Anglo-Saxon* (Oxford, 1957)
Kest    Division of Kesteven, Lincolnshire

L        Lincolnshire
Leeds    University coin collection, Leeds
Lei      Leicestershire
Levison  W. Levison, *England and the Continent in the Eighth Century* (Oxford, 1946)
*LibEl*  *Liber Eliensis*, ed. E. O. Blake, Camden 3rd ser. 92 (1962)
Liebermann, *Gesetze*  *Gesetze der Angelsachsen*, ed. F. Liebermann (Halle, 1903–16; repr. Aalen, 1960)
Lockett  R. C. Lockett coin sales, Glendining, 6 June 1955, 4 November 1958 and 26 April 1960
lOE      late Old English
Luick    K. Luick, *Historische Grammatik der englischen Sprache* (Leipzig, 1914–40)
*LVD*    *Liber Vitae Ecclesiae Dunelmensis*, ed. J. Stevenson, Surtees Society Publications 13 (1841); facs. ed. Surtees Society Publications 136 (1923)
*LVH*    *Liber Vitae. Register and Martyrology of New Minster and Hyde Abbey, Winchester*, ed. W. de Gray Birch (London, 1892)
*MA*     *Medieval Archaeology*
*MÆ*     *Medium Ævum*
Maish    W. M. Maish coin sale, Sotheby, 25 March 1918
Mann     A. Mann coin sale, Sotheby, 29 October 1917
Mansion  J. Mansion, *Oud-Gentsche Naamkunde* ('s-Gravenhage, 1924)
MDu      Middle Dutch
ME       Middle English
*MED*    *Middle English Dictionary*, ed. H. Kurath and S. M. Kuhn (Ann Arbor, 1952–)
*MGH*    *Monumenta Germaniae Historica*
Migne, *PL*  *Patrologia Latina*, ed. J. P. Migne
MLG      Middle Low German
*MLR*    *Modern Language Review*
Montagu  H. Montagu coin sale, Sotheby, 18 November 1895
Morlet   M.-T. Morlet, *Les Noms de Personne sur le Territoire de l'Ancienne Gaule du 6e au 12e Siècle* I (Paris, 1968)
Napier, *Wulfstan*  *Wulfstan: Sammlung der ihm zugeschriebenen Homilien*, ed. A. Napier I (Berlin, 1883; repr. with app. by K. Ostheeren, Berlin, 1966)
*NC*     *Numismatic Chronicle*
*NED*    *New English Dictionary*
Nf       Norfolk
*NNUM*   *Nordisk Numismatisk Unions Medlemsblad*
*NoB*    *Namn och Bygd*
Nordman  C. A. Nordman, *Anglo-Saxon Coins found in Finland* (Helsingfors, 1921)
NR       North Riding of the Division of Lindsey, Lincolnshire
NRY      North Riding of Yorkshire
Nt       Nottinghamshire
Nth      Northamptonshire
O        Oxfordshire

ODan   Old Danish
OE     Old English
*OET*    *The Oldest English Texts*, ed. H. Sweet, EETS o.s. 83
OFr     Old French
OG     Old Germanic
OIr     Old Irish
OLG   Old Low German
ON     Old Norse
OS     Old Saxon
OSw   Old Swedish
P      Pipe rolls
Plummer, *Bede*  *Venerabilis Baedae Opera Historica*, ed. C. Plummer (Oxford, 1896)
*PMLA*  *Publications of the Modern Language Association of America*
*PN Bd*  A. Mawer and F. M. Stenton, *The Place-Names of Bedfordshire and Huntingdonshire*, EPNS 3
*PN Bk*  A. Mawer and F. M. Stenton, *The Place-Names of Buckinghamshire*, EPNS 2
*PN C*  P. H. Reaney, *The Place-Names of Cambridgeshire and The Isle of Ely*, EPNS 19
*PN Cu*  A. M. Armstrong, A. Mawer, F. M. Stenton and Bruce Dickins, *The Place-Names of Cumberland*, EPNS 20–2
*PN D*  J. E. B. Gover, A Mawer and F. M. Stenton, *The Place-Names of Devon*, EPNS 8–9
*PNDB*  O. von Feilitzen, *The Pre-Conquest Personal Names of Domesday Book* (Uppsala, 1937)
*PN Db*  Kenneth Cameron, *The Place-Names of Derbyshire*, EPNS 27–9
*PN Ess*  P. H. Reaney, *The Place-Names of Essex*, EPNS 12
*PN Gl*  A. H. Smith, *The Place-Names of Gloucestershire*, EPNS 38–41
*PN La*  E. Ekwall, *The Place-Names of Lancashire* (Manchester, 1922)
*PN NRY*  A. H. Smith, *The Place-Names of the North Riding of Yorkshire*, EPNS 5
*PN Nt*  J. E. B. Gover, A. Mawer and F. M. Stenton, *The Place-Names of Nottinghamshire*, EPNS 17
*PN Wa*  J. E. B. Gover, A. Mawer and F. M. Stenton with F. T. S. Houghton, *The Place-Names of Warwickshire*, EPNS 13
*PN We*  A. H. Smith, *The Place-Names of Westmorland*, EPNS 42–3
*PN Wo*  A. Mawer and F. M. Stenton with F. T. S. Houghton, *The Place-Names of Worcestershire*, EPNS 4
*PN WRY*  A. H. Smith, *The Place-Names of the West Riding of Yorkshire*, EPNS 30–7
Pokorny J. Pokorny, *Indogermanisches etymologisches Wörterbuch* (Bern and München, 1959–69)
*PSAL*  *Proceedings of the Society of Antiquaries of London*
QF     Quellen und Forschungen zur Sprach- und Culturgeschichte der germanischen Völker

# Abbreviations

Ready  W. T. Ready coin sale, Sotheby, 15 November 1920

Redin  M. Redin, *Studies on Uncompounded Personal Names in Old English* (Uppsala, 1919)

*RES*  *Review of English Studies*

Robertson, *Charters*  *Anglo-Saxon Charters*, ed. A. J. Robertson (Cambridge, 1939)

Robertson, *Laws*  *The Laws of the Kings of England from Edmund to Henry I*, ed. A. J. Robertson (Cambridge, 1925)

Rom  Romance

*RSV*  *The Holy Bible. Revised Standard Version*

Ru  Rutland

Ruding  Rev. R. Ruding, *Annals of the Coinage of Great Britain*, 3rd ed. (London, 1840)

Ryan  V. J. E. Ryan coin sale, Glendining, 22 January 1952

Sawyer  P. H. Sawyer, *Anglo-Saxon Charters* (London, 1968)

*SBVS*  *Saga-Book of the Viking Society for Northern Research*

*SCBI*  *Sylloge of Coins of the British Isles* (London, 1958–)

Schlaug I and II  W. Schlaug, *Studien zu den altsächsischen Personennamen des 11. und 12. Jahrhunderts* (Lund, 1955) and *Die altsächsischen Personennamen vor dem Jahre 1000* (Lund, 1962)

Searle  W. G. Searle, *Onomasticon Anglo-Saxonicum* (Cambridge, 1897)

Settimane di Spoleto  Settimane di Studio del Centro Italiano di Studi sull'Alto Medioevo (Spoleto, 1954–)

Sf  Suffolk

Shand  F. J. Shand coin sale, Glendining, 8 March 1949

Sigsarve  M. Stenberger and P. Berghaus, *Der Schatz von Sigsarve, Gotland*, Kungliga Vitterhets Historie och Antikvitets Akademiens Handlingar, 83, Antikvariska Studier 5, 119–74

Sisam, *Studies*  K. Sisam, *Studies in the History of Old English Literature* (Oxford, 1953)

Smarmore  C. E. Blunt, 'The Smarmore Hoard of Tenth Century Pennies', *BNJ* xxvii (1952–4), 161–6

Smart  Veronica J. Smart, 'Moneyers of the Late Anglo-Saxon Coinage, 973–1016', in *Commentationes de Nummis Saeculorum IX–XI in Suecia Repertis* ii (Stockholm, 1968)

*SN*  *Studia Neophilologica*

So  Somerset

SR  South Riding of the Division of Lindsey, Lincolnshire

Sr  Surrey

Staf  Staffordshire

Stenton, *A-S England*  F. M. Stenton, *Anglo-Saxon England*, 2nd ed. (Oxford, 1947)

Stenton, *Charters*  F. M. Stenton, *The Latin Charters of the Anglo-Saxon Period* (Oxford, 1955)

Stockholm  Swedish royal coin collection, Stockholm, but not in Hildebrand

Sw      Swedish

*TCWAAS*  *Transactions of the Cumberland and Westmorland Antiquarian and Archaeological Society*

Tengvik  G. Tengvik, *Old English Bynames* (Uppsala, 1938)

Tetney   J. Walker, 'A Hoard of Anglo-Saxon Coins from Tetney, Lincolnshire', *NC* 6th ser. v (1945), 81–95

TRE      tempore regis Edwardi

*TRHS*   *Transactions of the Royal Historical Society*

TRW      tempore regis Willelmi

Uppsala  University coin collection, Uppsala

*VCH*    *Victoria County History*

W        Wiltshire

Wa       Warwickshire

We       Westmorland

Wells    Coin collection of the late W. C. Wells, bought by A. H. Baldwin and Sons Ltd

Whitelock, *Æthelgifu*  *The Will of Æthelgifu*, ed. and trans. D. Whitelock (Oxford, 1968)

Whitelock, *ASC*  *The Anglo-Saxon Chronicle*, trans. D. Whitelock with D. C. Douglas and S. I. Tucker (London, 1961)

Whitelock, *EHD*  *English Historical Documents* i, ed. D. Whitelock (London, 1955)

Whitelock, *Sermo Lupi*  *Sermo Lupi ad Anglos*, ed. D. Whitelock, 3rd rev. ed. (London, 1963)

Whitelock, *Wills*  *Anglo-Saxon Wills*, ed. D. Whitelock (Cambridge, 1930)

Wo       Worcestershire

WR       West Riding of the Division of Lindsey, Lincolnshire

WRY      West Riding of Yorkshire

WS       West Saxon

WW       *Anglo-Saxon and Old English Vocabularies*, ed. T. Wright and R. P. Wülcker (London, 1884)

Y        Yorkshire

*YAJ*    *Yorkshire Archaeological Journal*

*YCh*    *Early Yorkshire Charters*, ed. W. Farrer and C. T. Clay (Edinburgh and Wakefield, 1914–)

ZeN      E. Björkman, *Zur englischen Namenkunde* (Halle, 1912)

# The writings of Dorothy Whitelock

BOOKS AND ARTICLES

1930    *Anglo-Saxon Wills*, Cambridge Studies in English Legal History 6.

1937    'A Note on Wulfstan the Homilist', *EHR* LII, 460–5.

1939    *Sermo Lupi ad Anglos*, Methuen's Old English Library. (Revised editions, 1952 and 1963.)
'*Beowulf* 2444–71', *MÆ* VIII, 198–204.

1940    'Scandinavian Personal Names in the *Liber Vitae* of Thorney Abbey', *SBVS* XII, 127–53.

1941    'Wulfstan and the So-Called Laws of Edward and Guthrum', *EHR* LVI, 1–21.
'The Conversion of the Eastern Danelaw', *SBVS* XII, 159–76.

1942    'Archbishop Wulfstan, Homilist and Statesman', *TRHS* 4th ser. XXIV, 25–45. (Repr. in *Essays in Medieval History selected from the Transactions of the Royal Historical Society on the Occasion of its Centenary* by R. W. Southern [London, 1968].)
'English Language: General Works (1939–40)', *The Year's Work in English Studies, 1940*, pp. 20–31.

1943    'Two Notes on Ælfric and Wulfstan', *MLR* XXXVIII, 122–6.

1944    'English Language: General Works', *The Year's Work in English Studies, 1941*, pp. 18–42.

1945    'English Language: General Works' and 'Old English', *The Year's Work in English Studies, 1942*, pp. 17–49.

1946    'English Language: General Works' and 'Old English', *The Year's Work in English Studies, 1943*, pp. 15–40.

1948    'Wulfstan and the Laws of Cnut', *EHR* LXIII, 433–52.

1949    'Anglo-Saxon Poetry and the Historian', *TRHS* 4th ser. XXXI, 75–94.

1950    'The Interpretation of *The Seafarer*', *The Early Cultures of North-West Europe: H. M. Chadwick Memorial Studies*, ed. Sir Cyril Fox and Bruce Dickins (Cambridge), pp. 259–72.

1951    *The Audience of Beowulf* (Oxford).

1952    *The Beginnings of English Society*, The Pelican History of England 2.
'On the Commencement of the Year in the Saxon Chronicles' and 'Bibliographical Note', in repr. of Earle and Plummer, *Chronicles* II, cxxxix–cxlii*d* and 316*a–e*.

1954    *The Peterborough Chronicle*, EEMF 4.

1955    *English Historical Documents c. 500–1042*, English Historical Documents (gen. ed. D. C. Douglas) I.
'Wulfstan's Authorship of Cnut's Laws', *EHR* LXX, 72–85.

1956–7    A number of articles in *Encyclopaedia Britannica*.

1958    *Changing Currents in Anglo-Saxon Studies* (an Inaugural Lecture delivered in Cambridge on 21 February 1958).

1959 'The Dealings of the Kings of England with Northumbria in the Tenth and Eleventh Centuries', *The Anglo-Saxons: Studies in some Aspects of their History and Culture presented to Bruce Dickins*, ed. Peter Clemoes (London), pp. 70–88.

'Recent Work on Asser's Life of Alfred', in repr. of *Asser's Life of King Alfred*, ed. W. H. Stevenson (Oxford), pp. cxxxii–clii.

1960 *After Bede* (Jarrow Lecture).

1961 *The Anglo-Saxon Chronicle: a Revised Translation*, by D. Whitelock, with D. C. Douglas and S. I. Tucker (London).

'The Numismatic Interest of an Old English Version of the Legend of the Seven Sleepers', *Anglo-Saxon Coins: Studies presented to F. M. Stenton on the Occasion of his Eightieth Birthday*, ed. R. H. M. Dolley (London), pp. 188–94.

1962 *The Old English Bede*, Sir Israel Gollancz Memorial Lecture, *Proceedings of the British Academy* XLVIII, 57–90.

Foreword to *Liber Eliensis*, ed. E. O. Blake for the Camden Society, pp. ix–xviii.

1963 A complete revision of *Sermo Lupi ad Anglos* (see above, 1939).

1965 'Wulfstan at York', *Franciplegius: Medieval and Linguistic Studies in Honor of Francis Peabody Magoun, Jr*, ed. J. B. Bessinger, Jr, and R. P. Creed (New York), pp. 214–31.

1966 'The Anglo-Saxon Achievement', *The Norman Conquest: its Setting and Impact*, ed. C. T. Chevallier (London), pp. 13–43.

'The Prose of Alfred's Reign', *Continuations and Beginnings: Studies in Old English Literature*, ed. E. G. Stanley (London), pp. 67–103.

1967 *Sweet's Anglo-Saxon Reader*, 15th ed., rev. throughout by D. Whitelock (Oxford).

1968 *The Genuine Asser* (Stenton Lecture 1967, University of Reading).

'Wulfstan *Cantor* and Anglo-Saxon Law', *Nordica et Anglica: Studies in Honor of Stefán Einarsson*, ed. A. H. Orrick (The Hague), pp. 83–92.

*The Will of Æthelgifu. A Tenth Century Anglo-Saxon Manuscript*, trans. and examined by Dorothy Whitelock, with Neil Ker and Lord Rennell, for the Roxburghe Club.

'William of Malmesbury and the Works of King Alfred', *Medieval Literature and Civilization: Studies in Memory of G. N. Garmonsway*, ed. D. A. Pearsall and R. A. Waldron (London), pp. 78–93.

'Sir Frank Stenton', *Onoma* XII, 272–4.

1969 'Frank Merry Stenton', *EHR* LXXXIV, 1–11.

'Fact and Fiction in the Legend of St Edmund', *Proceedings of the Suffolk Institute of Archaeology* XXXI, 217–33.

1970 'Florence Elizabeth Harmer, 1869–1967', *Proceedings of the British Academy* LIV (1968), 301–14.

'The Authorship of the Account of King Edgar's Establishment of Monasteries', *Philological Essays in Honour of Herbert Dean Meritt*, ed. J. L. Rosier (The Hague), pp. 125–36.

# The writings of Dorothy Whitelock

REVIEWS

R. W. Chambers, *Beowulf. An Introduction to the Study of the Poem with a Discussion of the Stories of Offa and Finn*, 2nd ed. (Cambridge, 1932): *MÆ* I (1932), 229–31.

O. von Feilitzen, *The Pre-Conquest Personal Names of Domesday Book* (Uppsala, 1937): *History* XXIII (1938), 68–70.

*The Battle of Maldon*, ed. E. V. Gordon (London, 1937): *MLR* XXXIII (1938), 273–6.

*The Battle of Brunnanburh*, ed. A. Campbell (London, 1938): *MLR* XXXV (1940), 78–80.

J. E. B. Gover, A. Mawer and F. M. Stenton, *The Place-Names of Wiltshire*, EPNS 16 (1939): *MLR* XXXV (1940), 223–6.

G. T. Flom, *The Old Norwegian General Law of the Gulathing* (Illinois, 1937): *SBVS* XII (1937–45), 250.

C. E. Wright, *The Cultivation of Saga in Anglo-Saxon England* (Edinburgh and London, 1939): *SBVS* XII (1937–45), 250–2.

*Anglo-Saxon Charters*, ed. A. J. Robertson (Cambridge, 1939): *MLR* XXXVI (1941), 119–21.

*The Parker Chronicle and Laws (CCCC 173). A Fascimile*, ed. R. Flower and H. Smith, EETS o.s. 208 (1941): *EHR* LVII (1942), 120–2.

J. E. B. Gover, A. Mawer and F. M. Stenton, *The Place-Names of Nottinghamshire*, EPNS 17 (1940): *MLR* XXXVII (1942), 81–3.

*Ælfric's De Temporibus Anni*, ed. H. Henel, EETS o.s. 213 (1942): *EHR* LVIII (1943), 494–5.

J. E. B. Gover, A. Mawer and F. M. Stenton with S. J. Madge, *The Place-Names of Middlesex*, EPNS 18 (1942): *MLR* XXXVIII (1943), 44–5.

F. M. Stenton, *Anglo-Saxon England* (Oxford, 1943): *MLR* XXXIX (1944), 293–5; and *Oxford Magazine* LXII.24 (15 June 1944), 303.

M. L. W. Laistner, *A Hand-List of Bede Manuscripts* (Cornell, 1943): *EHR* LX (1945), 121–2.

W. Levison, *England and the Continent in the Eighth Century* (Oxford, 1946): *RES* XXIII (1947), 268–71.

E. S. Duckett, *Anglo-Saxon Saints and Scholars* (New York and London, 1947): *RES* XXIV (1948), 324–5.

*The Thorkelin Transcripts of 'Beowulf'*, ed. K. Malone, EEMF 1 (1951): *EHR* LXVIII (1953), 123–4.

G. K. Anderson, *The Literature of the Anglo-Saxons* (Princeton and London, 1950): *RES* n.s. IV (1953), 149–50.

*The Anglo-Saxon Chronicle*, trans. G. N. Garmonsway, Everyman's Library (1953): *EHR* LXX (1955), 273–4.

*The Peterborough Chronicle*, trans. H. A. Rositzke (Columbia, 1951): *Erasmus: Speculum Scientiarum* VIII (1955), cols. 139–43.

T. Oleson, *The Witenagemot in the Reign of Edward the Confessor* (London, 1955): *EHR* LXXI (1956), 640–2.

K. Sisam, 'Anglo-Saxon Royal Genealogies', *Proceedings of the British Academy* XXXIX (1953): *RES* n.s. VII (1956), 329–30.

P. Hunter Blair, *An Introduction to Anglo-Saxon England* (Cambridge, 1956): *EHR* LXXII (1957), 488–9.

F. M. Stenton, *The Latin Charters of the Anglo-Saxon Period* (Oxford, 1955): *MLR* LII (1957), 92.

N. R. Ker, *Catalogue of Manuscripts containing Anglo-Saxon* (Oxford, 1957): *Antiquity* XXXII (1958), 129–32.

*The Salisbury Psalter*, ed. C. and K. Sisam, EETS 242 (1959): *RES* n.s. XI (1960), 419–21.

E. John, *Land-Tenure in Early England* (Leicester, 1960): *American Historical Review* LXVI (1961), 1009–10.

B. Colgrave, *The Earliest Saints' Lives Written in England*, Israel Gollancz Memorial Lecture (1959): *EHR* LXXVI (1961), 119.

E. Ekwall, *The Concise Oxford Dictionary of English Place-Names*, 4th ed. (Oxford, 1960): *EHR* LXXVI (1961), 673–5.

*Die 'Institutes of Polity, Civil and Ecclesiastical': ein Werk Erzbischof Wulfstans von York*, ed. K. Jost (Bern, 1959): *RES* n.s. XII (1961), 61–6.

P. H. Sawyer, *The Age of the Vikings* (London, 1962): *History* XLVIII (1963), 351–2.

W. Bonser, *The Medical Background of Anglo-Saxon England* (London, 1963): *History* XLIX (1964), 336–7.

*Studies in Old English Literature in Honor of A. S. Brodeur*, ed. S. B. Greenfield (Oregon, 1963): *RES* n.s. XVI (1965), 299–304.

H. P. R. Finberg, *The Early Charters of Wessex* (Leicester, 1964): *EHR* LXXXI (1966), 100–3.

C. R. Hart, *The Early Charters of Eastern England* (Leicester, 1966): *EHR* LXXXIV (1969), 112–15.

# The letters of Pope Boniface V and the mission of Paulinus to Northumbria

## PETER HUNTER BLAIR

Paulinus is named, together with Mellitus, Justus and Rufinianus, as one of the leading members of the mission which left Rome for England in 601. His career in England lasted until his death forty-three years later and was, with the probable exception of that of his deacon, James,[1] by far the longest of any of the Roman missioners known to us by name. Yet nothing has been recorded about that career between 601 and 625, a period four times as long as the duration of his Northumbrian mission. Bede states that he was ordained bishop by Justus on 21 July 625 and went to Northumbria with Æthelberg, baptizing the infant princess Eanflæd in 626 and Edwin in 627 at York. He continued preaching for six years until Edwin's death, spending most of his time in Deira, but also visiting Bernicia. He baptized in the Glen at Old Yeavering and in the Swale near Catterick. He built a church in *Campodonum*, and went on a mission to the kingdom of Lindsey, building a church at Lincoln and baptizing in the Trent at Littleborough. He received a pallium from Pope Honorius, but after Edwin's death he withdrew to Kent, becoming bishop of Rochester, where he died on 10 October 644. All this information is derived from Bede's *Ecclesiastical History* which was completed rather more than eighty-five years after Paulinus's death.[2]

Among Gregory the Great's correspondents were four men called Paulinus, but three of them were already bishops when Gregory was writing to them. The fourth is mentioned in a letter written in February 591 to Anthemius, rector of a papal estate in Campania, and is described as *presbyter monasterii sancti Herasmi, quod in latere montis Repperi situm est.*[3] Since Anthemius was instructed in the letter to give this Paulinus some assistance we may infer that he was personally known to Gregory, but the whereabouts of the monastery itself is unknown save that it lay in Campania. Among the cities of Campania was Naples with whose neighbourhood the English church had connections in the seventh and eighth

---

[1] James survived until the 670s, see below, p. 12, but we do not know the date of his first arrival in England.

[2] *HE* I. 29; II. 14, 16, 17, 19 and 20; III. 14; and v. 24.

[3] *Gregorii I Papae Registrum Epistolarum, MGH, Epistolae* I, 27. For the three bishops called Paulinus, see *ibid.* II, 502.

centuries,[1] but Paulinus is a common name and a conjecture that the Campanian priest was the same as the later Northumbrian missionary would require better evidence than we possess. The notes about Gregory the Great found in the short collection of papal biographies known as the *Liber Pontificalis* make only brief reference to the English mission. They name Mellitus, Augustine and John, in that order, but they do not distinguish between the first group of missioners who set out from Rome under Augustine in 596 and the second group which reached England in 601 under the leadership of Mellitus. They do not mention Paulinus by name, though he may have been included among the *alios plures...  monachos* who were of the party.[2] No reference to the mission is to be found in the biographies of any of Gregory the Great's successors.

There is no strictly contemporary written evidence about the activities of Paulinus in England. The nearest approach consists of letters written by Pope Boniface V and these, unlike Gregory the Great's letters, have not survived independently in the papal archive, but are known to us only from Bede's *History*.[3] There is no evidence for the survival either in Kent or in Northumbria of original documents relating to the earliest days of the Roman mission and it therefore seems probable that Bede's knowledge of Boniface's letters, as of those of Gregory the Great, derived from copies made in Rome in the eighth century by one of the many Englishmen who visited Rome at that time. Although, in his letter to Albinus, Bede refers specifically to Nothelm as bringing him written documents,[4] we should not overlook Hwætberht as a likely bearer to Jarrow of written documents secured in Rome. Hwætberht, who succeeded Ceolfrith as abbot in 716 and was still alive in 735 when Bede died, was in Rome with other monks from Wearmouth and Jarrow in 701, and Bede wrote of him *non paruo ibidem temporis spatio demoratus, quaeque sibi necessaria iudicabat, didicit, descripsit, retulit*.[5] Was it through the agency of Hwætberht, called Eusebius, whose literary interests are witnessed by the Latin riddles which he composed,[6] that the works of Gregory the Great were first brought to Northumbria?

[1] Neapolitan influence on the Lindisfarne Gospels has long been recognized. A scribal note on the Echternach Gospels, 222v, points to earlier connections with a book from the library of Eugippius (d. 535), abbot of Lucullanum near Naples; E. A. Lowe, *CLA* v, no. 578. Marginal additions in an eighth-century insular hand suggest that the *Diatessaron* written for Victor, bishop of Capua 541–54, may have been in England before it went to Fulda; Lowe, *ibid.* VIII, no. 1196.

[2] *Liber Pontificalis, Pars Prior, MGH, Gesta Pontificum Romanorum* I, 161.

[3] William of Malmesbury gives a series of spurious letters written in support of Canterbury's claims vis-à-vis York. Among them is one supposedly written by Boniface V to Justus; *Councils* III, 73–4.

[4] Plummer, *Bede* I, 3.

[5] *Historia Abbatum*, ed. Plummer, *Bede* I, 383; also *De Temporum Ratione*, ch. XLVII, *Bedae Opera de Temporibus*, ed. C. W. Jones (Cambridge, Mass., 1943), pp. 266–7.

[6] *Eusebius (Hwaetherhtus): Aenigmata*, ed. A. Ebert, *Sachsiche Gesellschaft der Wissenschaften* XXVIII (1877), 20–56.

## The letters of Pope Boniface V

The text of the *Ecclesiastical History* contains three letters written by Boniface V – one to Justus, one to Edwin and one to Æthelberg – but it is possible that Bede did not put into the *History* all the letters of Boniface that he had. Recording the appointment of Mellitus to Canterbury after the death of Lawrence, with Justus remaining at Rochester, Bede notes that Mellitus and Justus *susceperunt scripta exhortatoria a pontifice Romanae et apostolicae sedis Bonifatio qui post Deusdedit ecclesiae praefuit anno incarnationis dominicae DCXVIIII.*[1] Bede thus precisely identified the pope in question as Boniface V, 619–25, rather than Boniface IV, 608–15, but it is not quite clear whether we should take the date 619 as referring to the year of Boniface's succession or to the date of the letters, though the point is of little significance since we know nothing of the contents of the letters save that they were exhortatory.

After recording the death of Mellitus on 24 April 624, the succession of Justus to Canterbury and the consecration of Romanus to Rochester by Justus, Bede noted that Justus had received authority to ordain bishops from Pope Boniface – *cuius auctoritatis ista est forma* – and he then gave the text of a letter addressed *Dilectissimo fratri Iusto Bonifatius.*[2] Neither at the beginning nor at the end is there any dating clause and Bede himself does not say when the letter was written. In places the text is difficult to construe and Plummer,[3] noting the variation between *uos* and *uester* in its earlier part and *tu* and *tuus* in its later part, suggested that careless copying might have resulted in the joining together of two originally separate letters, one to Mellitus and one to Justus, but such a conjecture hardly seems necessary. In isolation from its context the letter is primarily one of exhortation and encouragement to Justus, but within the context of the *History* we can see that Bede inserted it in order to show by what authority Justus had consecrated Romanus as bishop of Rochester.

Setting aside the exhortation, the facts which emerge from the letter are that Pope Boniface has received a letter from Justus, that letters received from a king called *Aduluald* have shown him with what depth of scriptural learning Justus had brought that king to a true conversion, that, with the bearer of his letter to Justus, Boniface has sent a *pallium* which Justus may use in *sacrosanctis celebrandis mysteriis*, but not at any other time, and finally that Boniface has given Justus permission to ordain bishops as need might arise. The Moore manuscript of the *History* reads *filii nostri adulualdi regis*[4] and this reading of the king's name is supported with only minor variations by the other eighth-century manuscripts known to Plummer.[5] The Leningrad manuscript, not known to Plummer, also read originally *adulualdi*, but a later hand erased the first *u* and inserted a *b* partly over the second *u*, to

[1] *HE* II. 7.          [2] *HE* II. 8.          [3] *Bede* II, 92–3.
[4] *The Moore Bede*, ed. P. Hunter Blair, EEMF 9 (Copenhagen, 1959), 33r.
[5] See Plummer's critical notes to *HE* II. 8.

give a reading something like *ad Ibaldi*. A different and considerably later hand added *eadbaldi* in the upper margin.[1] These alterations and additions show that at a relatively early date it was assumed by some that *adulualdi* was an error for *eadbaldi* and that the reference in the letter is to that King Eadbald who ruled in Kent after the death of his father Æthelberht. All modern commentators seem to have made the same assumption, though without knowledge of the Leningrad manuscript. Yet the manuscript authority for the form *adulwald* is excellent, the name is a common one and it is quite distinct from Eadbald, as Bede himself undoubtedly knew. Recalling how little we know of the history of south-eastern England in the first decades of the seventh century, we should be wiser to accept the evidence of the letter at its face value and to believe that Justus did in fact secure the conversion of an otherwise unrecorded king called Æthelwald. Before going to Canterbury Justus was bishop in Rochester for twenty years from 604, and it is a fair inference that it was as bishop of Rochester that he secured King Æthelwald's conversion. The existence of the two Kentish bishoprics is part of a considerable body of evidence pointing to a real division between eastern and western Kent.[2] We know that at certain times in the seventh century there were two kings reigning at the same time in Kent, and that there were times when two, three or even four kings ruled together among both the South Saxons and the East Saxons.[3]

The sending of the pallium to Justus ought not to be regarded in the light of the significance attached to this vestment in later times. The pope stated specifically that it was to be used only in the celebration of the eucharist, and it would be unwise to suppose that already at this early date it had come to be regarded as particular to the archbishop of Canterbury. Mellitus, the predecessor of Justus at Canterbury, was a man of poor physical health[4] and it may well have seemed desirable to authorize Justus to consecrate bishops while Mellitus was still alive. We cannot assume that Boniface's letter was not written to Justus until he was already archbishop. Lacking other evidence we can say only that the letter was written in the years 619–25. It has no relevance to the date of King Eadbald's conversion nor to the date at which news of this event reached Rome.

The letters from Boniface V to Edwin and Æthelberg are given consecutively in the *History* and comprise the entire content of II. 10–11, saving only for brief introductory sentences. Each of the two is explicitly stated to be a copy (*exemplar*) of a letter written by Boniface, called in the one letter bishop of the apostolic see and in the other pope of the city of Rome. The letter to Edwin is a long exhortation to the observance of the true

---

[1] *The Leningrad Bede*, ed. O. Arngart, EEMF 2 (Copenhagen, 1952), 35v, col. 2.
[2] H. M. Chadwick, *Studies on Anglo-Saxon Institutions* (Cambridge, 1905), pp. 271–4.
[3] *Ibid.* pp. 270 and 275.  [4] *HE* II. 7.

faith and the abandonment of all idolatry. It contains only one passage relating to specific events in England:

We suppose that your highness, because of the proximity of place, has become thoroughly acquainted with what the mercy of the redeemer has wrought in the enlightenment of our glorious son, King Audubald, and the peoples subject to him. We therefore trust with assured hope that by heavenly long-suffering this wonderful gift is being bestowed upon you; since indeed we have learned that your illustrious consort, who is discerned to be part of your body, has been enlightened with the reward of eternity through the regeneration of holy baptism.

In later passages Boniface urges Edwin to receive the word of the preachers and the gospel of God of which they are the bearers. In his letter to Æthelberg Boniface refers to the gift of faith which has been bestowed upon her and continues: 'For we have learned from those who brought to us the news of the praiseworthy conversion of our glorious son King Audubald that your highness also, after receiving the wonderful sacrament of the Christian faith, perpetually shines forth in good works pleasing to God.' Urging Æthelberg to refrain from idolatry and the allurements of temples and sooth-saying, Boniface continues: 'and when of our fatherly love we had made enquiry of your glorious husband we learned that, hitherto serving the abomination of idolatry, he has delayed in showing his obedience by giving ear to the voice of the preachers.' Boniface was concerned because in this state the marriage could not be a complete union. *Scriptum namque est: Erunt duo in carne una.* Æthelberg must therefore be unceasing in her efforts to turn Edwin from the worship of idols and to kindle in him the warmth of divine faith.

The letters themselves contain no dating clauses and we have no means of knowing whether they were sent on separate occasions or both together. Bede did not attempt to date them more precisely than by introducing them with the indefinite *quo tempore*. Both letters were written after Boniface had heard of the conversion of King Eadbald (*Audubaldus*) and at a time when he believed that Æthelberg of Kent, though herself Christian, was married to Edwin who as yet remained unconverted. Eadbald's conversion is attributed by Bede to Lawrence whose successor, Mellitus, is said to have died on 24 April 624 after holding the archbishopric for five years.[1] On this evidence Eadbald's conversion should fall before April 619. The date of Æthelberg's conversion is unknown and Bede does not give a date in his reference to the marriage of Æthelberg and Edwin. We can say only that the two letters were written some time during Boniface's tenure of the papacy, i.e. between 619 and 25 October 625. Whether Bede knew this last date is uncertain.

---

[1] *HE* ii. 6 and 7.

Familiarity with Bede's account of the mission of Paulinus to Northumbria may lead us to forget that its value as historical evidence is that of a Northumbrian tradition whose oldest manuscript-witness dates from rather more than a century after the events to which it refers. The account is contained in six consecutive chapters of book II of the *History*, but is divided into two parts by the letters from Boniface V to Edwin and Æthelberg which fill two of those six chapters. The chapter preceding the two letters (II. 9) recounts Edwin's courting of Æthelberg, the consecration of Paulinus as bishop and his journey to Northumbria with Æthelberg, the attempt on Edwin's life by an assassin sent from Wessex, the birth and subsequent baptism of Æthelberg's child, Eanflæd, Edwin's punitive expedition against Wessex and his continuing reluctance to accept Christianity. Bede's chronology for this part of the tradition is precise: Paulinus was consecrated bishop *die XII Kalendarum Augustarum anno ab incarnatione Domini DCXXV*, that is 21 July 625 – the attempted assassination of Edwin occurred *anno sequente*, i.e. 626 – Eanflæd was born *nocte sacrosancta dominici paschae* and was baptized *die sancto pentecostes*, i.e. 31 March 626 for the birth and 19 May 626 for the baptism. The second half of the tradition, following the papal letters, occupies three chapters (II. 12–14) of which the first tells of Edwin's experiences in exile at Rædwald's court in East Anglia, the second of the famous debate in the Northumbrian witan and the third of Edwin's baptism at York and of the activities of Paulinus both in Bernicia and in Deira. Bede gives only one exact date in this part of the tradition – the baptism of Edwin which took place in the year *dominicae incarnationis DCXXVII . . . die sancto paschae pridie Iduum Aprilium*,[1] i.e. 12 April 627.

Bede wrote the *History ad instructionem posteritatis*[2] and he would surely find the story of the mission to Northumbria, in which Edwin rather than Paulinus is the hero, excellently suited to his purpose. Analysis of its different elements – exile and misfortune, the celestial comforter, escape from death, triumph in battle, ultimate conversion – is largely irrelevant. In Bede's view the duty of a historian was to give expression to the beliefs of common people – *opinionem uulgi exprimens, quae vera historiae lex est*, he wrote, in his commentary on Luke,[3] slightly adapting a phrase used by Jerome in his tract *Adversus Helvidium*.[4] Yet we must do Bede the justice of supposing him to be fully aware of the differing evidential value of the *opinio uulgi* on the one hand and the contemporary letters of popes on the other. He plainly signifies this awareness by repeating the texts of such letters verbatim and so leaving his readers to reach their own conclusions from their content. The two letters from Boniface V to Edwin and Æthel-

---

[1] *HE* II. 14.   [2] *HE Praefatio.*
[3] *In Lucam*, ed. D. Hurst, *CC* cxx, 67.   [4] Migne, *PL* xxiii, col. 197.

berg are left to speak for themselves and are not intermingled with the content of the *opinio uulgi*. We cannot tell whether Bede himself was aware of a difficulty with which this method has confronted modern historians in the case of the Paulinus mission. We read first that Paulinus, after being consecrated bishop on 21 July 625, went to Edwin with Æthelberg, and we read next that Boniface V wrote letters both to Edwin and to Æthelberg in which he referred to Edwin's continuing refusal to accept Christianity. Knowing, as Bede may or may not have known, that Boniface V died on 25 October 625, we ask how it was possible for Paulinus to travel from Kent to Northumbria, attempt unsuccessfully to convert Edwin, write to the pope of his failure and for the pope himself to reply, all within the period between 21 July and 25 October of the same year. Though not totally impossible, we must admit that time seems short – a remark which may also apply to the birth of Eanflæd on 31 March 626 if Æthelberg did not set out from Kent on her first visit to Edwin until after 21 July 625.

One means of escape from this problem is to suggest that the letters were not written by Boniface V but by his successor Honorius.[1] Another is to assert that Bede was mistaken in bringing Paulinus to Northumbria with Æthelberg for the first time after 21 July 625.[2] In either case we are impugning the veracity of Bede, by supposing on the one hand that he was incapable of seeing that documents were copied accurately and on the other that he was ill-informed about what was for him perhaps the most important single event in the history of his own Northumbria. And we are implicitly accepting the greater reliability of the *opinio uulgi* as against the belief of a careful scholar. The difficulty has arisen from attempting to do what Bede himself was careful not to do, namely to amalgamate the contemporary document with the *opinio uulgi*. We have no right to assume, because Bede placed Boniface's letters after his account of the journey of Paulinus to Northumbria, that Boniface's letters were not in fact written until after 21 July 625. There was a period of fifteen to twenty years during the reign of Æthelfrith when Edwin was in exile. Some of that time he probably spent in Mercia, since he had children by a daughter of the Mercian royal family[3] – an episode which finds no place in the *opinio uulgi* where it would have reflected ill upon the saintliness of Edwin. Some of it he spent in East Anglia. How did it come about that he married into the Kentish royal family unless as a result of a sojourn in Kent? There is an equally long gap in our knowledge of the doings of Paulinus between his first arrival in England in 601 and his mission to Northumbria in 625. As Plummer pointed out,[4] a rational explanation of the celestial visitor at

---

[1] W. Bright, *Chapters on Early English Church History* (Oxford, 1878), p. 114. Plummer, *Bede* II, 97, advances an objection to this view.
[2] D. P. Kirby, 'Bede and Northumbrian Chronology', *EHR* LXXVIII (1963), 552–3.
[3] *HE* II. 14.                         [4] *Bede* II, 93.

Rædwald's court would be to suppose that Paulinus had at some time been on a mission to East Anglia and had made an unsuccessful attempt to convert Edwin there. The *opinio uulgi* represents Paulinus as bringing the virgin Æthelberg to Edwin in Northumbria, but the scene is as much part of hagiography as history. We do not know when or where the marriage took place and it is not difficult to envisage a situation in which, after a marriage in Kent, Edwin returned to Northumbria still pagan. The letters of Boniface V would be wholly apt to such a situation, and the *opinio uulgi* that Paulinus later brought Æthelberg to Edwin in Northumbria would still be acceptable. Sanctified tradition would prefer to represent her as the unspotted virgin rather than as the already wedded wife. Moreover Pope Boniface had been at pains to point out in his letter to Æthelberg that a marriage between a Christian and a pagan could not result in a complete union.

Despite their best endeavours scholars have not been able to reach complete agreement about the exact date of a number of events in seventh-century England. When we reflect upon the formidable difficulties which faced Bede in seeking to establish a uniform chronology for a country divided into several kingdoms, the regnal dates of whose rulers were at best imperfectly known and sometimes not recorded at all, we need hardly be surprised if here and there we find signs of his failure to solve a problem which was in the last resort insoluble. But before we reject his chronology, we ought to consider carefully whether our own solution is likely to be better founded than his. The mission of Paulinus and the conversion of Edwin were events of outstanding importance in the history of Christianity among the English. If Bede had wished to give chronological precision to an *opinio uulgi*, how would he have set about doing so?

After leaving Northumbria on the death of Edwin, Paulinus went to Kent where he became bishop of Rochester. He died there on 10 October 644.[1] He left behind him in York his deacon, James, who was present at the Synod of Whitby in 664 and died *senex ac plenus dierum* after surviving, as Bede writes, *ad nostra usque tempora*.[2] On this evidence James the Deacon was still living when Bede was born and presumably did not die before the 670s. Hild, abbess of Whitby, was baptized by Paulinus at the same time as Edwin, i.e. 627, and she was aged sixty-six when she died at Whitby in 680,[3] when Bede was about nine. Aged about thirteen at the time of her baptism, Hild was old enough to have remembered something of the occasion and to have passed on her memories to the community at Whitby, where King Edwin himself was buried. Eanflæd, baptized by Paulinus on 19 May 626 in infancy, was taken to Kent by Paulinus but later returned to Northumbria as wife of King Oswiu. In 685, when Bede was about four-

---

[1] *HE* iii. 14.     [2] *HE* iii. 25, ii. 20 and ii. 16.     [3] *HE* iv. 23.

teen, she was presiding jointly with her daughter, Ælfflæd, over the abbey of Whitby. Ælfflæd, *quae uixdum unius anni aetatem impleverat* when the battle at the Winwæd was fought in 655, died as abbess of Whitby, having reached the age of fifty-nine,[1] and on this evidence her death occurred *c.* 714 when Bede was aged about forty-two. We know that the works of Gregory the Great, author of the English mission, were studied at Whitby in the seventh century,[2] we know also that traditions about Paulinus were current there, and we may surely infer that the Easter dispute, culminating in the synod, would stimulate chronological studies. It is scarcely conceivable that the events which occurred in York in 626 and 627 were not remembered and discussed by Hild, Eanflæd and Ælfflæd. When we consider that Benedict Biscop, Ceolfrith and even Bede himself (though only as a boy) could have met and talked with James, the deacon of Paulinus, and when we consider also the kind of information which would have been available to Bede at Whitby, we shall not find it easy to believe that we are better placed than he was to know the truth about such an important event as the arrival of Paulinus in Northumbria.

[1] *HE* III. 24.
[2] *The Earliest Life of Gregory the Great*, ed. B. Colgrave (Lawrence, 1968), p. 53.

# Bede's text of the *Libellus Responsionum* of Gregory the Great to Augustine of Canterbury

## PAUL MEYVAERT

Is the *Libellus Responsionum* which Bede inserted into bk 1, ch. 27 of his *Ecclesiastical History* an authentic Gregorian document?[1] Controversy has surrounded this text since Bede's own time. Bede himself did not doubt its authenticity, but Boniface, writing in 735 (the year of Bede's death) to Nothelm, the newly consecrated archbishop of Canterbury, voiced some misgivings:

I earnestly pray you to obtain for me a copy of the letter containing, as they say, the questions of Augustine, first bishop and apostle of the English, and the replies made to them by the holy pope Gregory. In this letter among other things it is stated that marriages between Christians related in the third degree are lawful. Will you have a careful search made to discover whether or not this writing has been proved to be a true work of St Gregory; for the notaries (*scriniarii*) say they cannot find a copy of it in the archives of the church of Rome among the other exemplars of the said pope.[2]

The reasons for Boniface's hesitation are clear: he questions the authenticity of the marriage permissions contained in the document. Unfortunately we do not know what answer Nothelm made to this letter.

Less than a decade later, confirmation comes from Rome itself that the archive version of the *Libellus* had not yet been found. In the Acts of the Roman Council of 743 Pope Zachary (741–52) says:

Nor should we pass over in silence what is spread abroad through the lands of the Germans, a statement, namely, that we have been unable to discover in the

---

[1] I would like at the outset to express my deep gratitude to many good friends who, in one way or another, have given me help, advice or encouragement in the course of my long investigations in the *Libellus* history; in particular I would like to mention Professor Dorothy Whitelock, to whom the present volume is dedicated, Abbot Eligius Dekkers and Professors Giles Constable and Bernhard Bischoff.

*Libellus Responsionum* is the designation used by Bede himself in his *Life of Gregory* (*HE* II. 1, ed. Plummer, *Bede* 1, 76): 'excepto libello responsionum quem ad interrogationes sancti Augustini primi Anglorum gentis episcopi scripsit'.

[2] *Die Briefe des heiligen Bonifatius und Lullus*, ed. M. Tangl, *MGH*, *Epistolae Selectae* 1, 56–8, Ep. 33: 'quia in scrinio Romanae aecclesiae, ut adfirmant scriniarii, cum ceteris exemplaribus supradicti pontificis quaesita non inveniebatur'. The words do not make it clear whether the search was made only in the *Registrum* or in the exemplars of Gregory's other works as well.

archives of our church. Nevertheless we learn from men who come from Germany that the holy pope Gregory when, through the grace of God, he enlightened them in the Christian religion, granted them permission to marry within the fourth degree. But within the degrees of blood kinship (*dum usque se generationem cognoverit*) such marriages are not permissible to Christians. Nevertheless we are prepared to believe that he allowed this because they were as yet uncivilized (*rudi*) and were being invited to the faith; although, as we said above, we have been unable to discover this writing.[1]

Without entering here into the full history of the controversy which has developed around the *Libellus* over the centuries, we may find it useful to recapitulate some of its most recent stages. In 1941 Dom Suso Brechter published a large work entitled *Die Quellen zur Angelsachsenmission Gregors des Grossen*.[2] One of the main purposes of this work was to demonstrate that not only the section concerned with permissions to marry but the whole *Libellus*, from beginning to end, was a vast forgery, reflecting eighth-century theological and canonical preoccupations.[3] The man responsible for this forgery, according to Brechter, was none other than Bede's friend, the London priest Nothelm, who later became archbishop of Canterbury and to whom, as we saw above, Boniface sent his inquiry. Brechter even assigned a precise year, 731, for the production of the

---

[1] *MGH, Concilia* II. 1, 19–21. The index of the *MGH* volume lists this passage under Gregory II (714–31), but there can be little doubt that it refers to Gregory the Great. Pope Zachary, within the space of a few lines, makes a clear distinction between (1) *beatae memoriae praedecessor noster Gregorius huius apostolicae sedis iunior papa* (whose acts of the council of 721 are cited) and (2) *beatae recordationis sanctus Gregorius papa* – the *sanctus* showing that Gregory the Great is intended. This moreover is confirmed by a letter of Leo III, dated 11 April 800, citing the text of the Roman synod of 743 and introducing it with the following words: 'Prelatus vero frater noster...interrogavit nos de incestis coniunctionibus que usque nunc multis in locis non canonice observabantur, quamquam sunt qui dicant sanctum Gregorium scripsisse Augustino episcopo ad Anglorum gentem: tertia propinquitate se posse copulare, quod omnino in scrinio sancti Petri non invenitur.... In concilio vero sanctae recordationis domnum Zachariam papam scripsisse eius synodi invenimus ita: Sed neque hoc silendum [then follows the text cited above].' These documents which Dom Brechter does not cite in his work (see next note) are sufficient by themselves to invalidate his theory of a Roman curial recension of the *Libellus* by Gemmulus, the papal secretary of Zachary. Had such a curial recension existed Zachary and Leo III could hardly have failed to refer to it.

[2] Beiträge zur Geschichte des alten Mönchtums und Benediktinerordens 22 (Munst./West., 1941).

[3] That some of the preoccupations of the eighth-century church have antecedents in an earlier day is proved, in one instance, by a letter of Gregory preserved in his *Registrum*, and directed against those rigorists in his own Roman flock who prohibited baths on Sunday. Since the same prohibition occurs in the Penitential of Theodore it would be easy to build up a case against the letter (on the ground that it reflected 'eighth-century preoccupations', and was an attempt to counteract the over-rigorous injunctions of the penitentials) were its authenticity not assured by its presence in the *Registrum*. See P. Meyvaert, 'Diversity within Unity, a Gregorian Theme', *The Heythrop Journal* IV (1963), 160, n. 1. Similar criticisms of Brechter's approach have been voiced by Raymund Kottje, 'Zum Frage nach dem Verfasser der *Responsa Gregorii papae ad Augustinum episcopum*', *Studien zum Einfluss des Alten Testamentes auf Recht und Liturgie des frühen Mittelalters*, Bonner historische Forschungen 23 (1964), 110–16.

forgery.[1] It was in this year, the year in which Bede completed his *History*, that Nothelm produced the *Libellus* and brought it to his friend at Jarrow, who made a last-minute insertion of it into his *History*. In Brechter's view, therefore, the *History* contains the earliest and most original form of the document.[2]

Brechter's work remained practically unknown, especially among English historians, until 1959, when Professor Margaret Deanesly and Father Paul Grosjean, a Bollandist, published a long article criticizing it.[3] They sought to show that the *Libellus* was not a forgery in the full sense of the term, a document fabricated out of whole cloth. While still holding Nothelm responsible for it, they argued that he had done no more than copy down some authentic letters of Gregory preserved in the Canterbury archives, adding to them two theological disputations (Gregorian in form, but emanating from the school of Theodore of Canterbury), and presenting the whole in the shape of a single work, the *Libellus*, for inclusion by Bede in his *History*. These authors further believed that Nothelm had produced two versions of the *Libellus*: an earlier version, which they term the *capitula* version, whose best surviving witness is a manuscript now preserved at Copenhagen, dating from *c.* 731–50; then a later version, somewhat rearranged, and presented in the form of *Questions* and *Answers*.[4] It was this last version which Nothelm took to Bede. In an appendix the two authors give a list of manuscripts containing the *Libellus*; five are given for the 'earlier' version and twenty-four for the 'later' one.[5]

My own interest in the *Libellus* originated in a close study of the Deanesly–Grosjean article and Brechter's book. A preliminary investigation of the material firmly convinced me that much work still remained to be accomplished before firm conclusions about the genuine or spurious nature of the *Libellus* could be reached. In particular it seemed that two fields needed a much closer examination: (1) the manuscript tradition of the *Libellus* and (2) the relationship of the *Libellus* to Gregory's other works, from the point of view of vocabulary, style and ideas. I became convinced, and still remain so, that these are not peripheral but fundamental investigations, which must precede any attempt to construct elaborate hypotheses about possible forgers and their motives. These

---

[1] *Quellen*, p. 277: 'Est ist somit eine unleugbare Tatsache, dass Nothelm, der Londoner Presbyter und nachmalige Erzbischof von Canterbury, in diesem Jahre [*sc.* 731] die Fälschung in die Welt gesetzt hat.'

[2] *Ibid.* p. 61: 'Wir folgen in unserer Arbeit von nun an diesem ältesten durch die Historia Ecclesiastica Gentis Anglorum (1.27) bezeugten Überlieferungszweige der Ep. xi.56*a* [*sc.* the *Libellus*].'

[3] 'The Canterbury Edition of the Answers of Pope Gregory I to St Augustine', *JEH* x (1959), 1–49.

[4] *Ibid.* p. 37.

[5] *Ibid.* pp. 45–8.

convictions were expressed in a short article which appeared in 1959.[1] This was followed by a further article in 1963 which dealt exclusively with one of the replies in the *Libellus*, that concerning the liturgy.[2] Brechter had stated that no Roman pope could have penned such a reply, which permitted Augustine to borrow liturgical customs from the churches of Gaul. I tried to show that while this reply might not reflect normal papal attitudes, usually bent on bringing other churches into conformity with Roman usages, it did reflect, both in language and in sentiment, the vocabulary and teaching of Gregory himself. Gregory cherished the idea of a certain diversity of customs within the unity of one faith and charity.[3]

Since 1959 I have continued, off and on, to gather material for a full study of the *Libellus*. If this study has not yet appeared it is not because the approach suggested above has proved unworkable or invalid.[4] On the contrary I am more than ever sure that only a thorough-going examination

[1] 'Les Responsiones de S. Grégoire le Grand à S. Augustin de Cantorbéry', *Revue d'Histoire Ecclésiastique* LIV (1959), 879–94. This article elicited a further note from M. Deanesley:I 'The Capitular Text of the Responsiones of Pope Gregory I to St Augustine', *JEH* XI (1961), 231–4, which stressed the fact that the Bedan text is not found in any manuscript earlier than Bede's *History*. This point will be commented on below, p. 29.

[2] 'Diversity within Unity: a Gregorian Theme', *loc. cit.* 141–62.

[3] Others have likewise expressed doubt and hesitations concerning the conclusions of Brechter and Deanesly–Grosjean about the *Libellus*. See, e.g., Hugh Farmer, 'St Gregory's Answers to St Augustine of Canterbury', *Studia Monastica* I (1959), 419–22, and R. Kottje, *loc. cit.* Brechter's views about Bede's untrustworthiness and duplicity have been seriously – and deservedly – questioned by several scholars: e.g. R. A. Markus, 'The Chronology of the Gregorian Mission to England: Bede's Narrative and Gregory's Correspondence', *JEH* XIV (1963), 16–30, and J. M. Wallace-Hadrill, 'Rome and the Early English Church: Some Questions of Transmission', *Le Chiese nei regni dell'Europa occidentale e i loro rapporti con Roma sino all'800*, Settimane di Spoleto 7 (1960), 523–4. See also R. Bruce-Mitford (*ibid.* pp. 497–501) in the discussion that followed Brechter's lecture mentioned below, next note.

[4] In his most recent article, 'Zur Bekehrungsgeschichte der Angelsachsen', *La Conversione al Cristianesimo nell'Europa dell'Alto Medioevo*, Settimane di Spoleto 14 (1967), 194, Brechter writes: 'Die Diskussion um diese Probleme und um die Wiedergutmachung des bedaischen Prestigerverlustes ist noch in vollem Gang. Paul Meyvaert arbeitet zwar schon seit 1954 [read 1959] an der Rehabilitierung der Authentizität von Ep. XI 56a [*sc.* the *Libellus*] und hat schon wiederholt die Widerlegung meiner These angekündigt. Er hat seine Forschungen auf eine breite handschriftliche Basis gestellt, dabei aber, wie mir scheint, in einem Dschungel von Quisquilien die klare Linie aus den Augen verloren.' One might ask whether the *bedaischen Prestigerverlust* exists elsewhere than in Brechter's own mind. He fails to answer any of the serious criticisms brought against this aspect of his work, particularly by R. A. Markus. As far as I myself am concerned, I do not consider that I hold any brief for the 'rehabilitation' of the *Libellus*. I do however believe that in an historical investigation first things must come first. If a text is involved it is the historian's task to investigate fully the history and transmission of that text. The few pages (*Quellen*, pp. 31–4), based on a discussion of only four manuscripts, which Brechter devotes to the problem give the strong impression that he was seeking ammunition for his theory of forgery rather than making a detached examination of a manuscript tradition as a whole. Nevertheless this manuscript tradition remains crucial. Thus, conclusive proof that the text of the *Libellus* as it stands in Bede had a long history of transmission *behind it* would *ipso facto*, and independently of any other evidence, invalidate the theory of a forgery perpetrated in 731. This might still be insufficient in itself to show that the document was fully authentic, but the historian would be able to calculate better how far back he would have to go to find its origins.

of the textual history and the Gregorian affinities of the *Libellus* can provide fully satisfactory evidence.[1] But the amount of material accumulated is such as to demand a book rather than an article. And up to now it has proved impossible to find time to complete this work, although I remain hopeful that it will not be delayed too long.

The scope of the present paper is more limited; to make some comments on the *Libellus Responsionum* as it is found in Bede, postponing for the present the ultimate question of the document's authenticity. The aspects that call for comment are the following: (1) the quality of Bede's text of the *Libellus*, (2) the problem of the date when Bede got to know the *Libellus*, (3) the source from which he obtained it (this last point will involve us in a broad outline of the whole *Libellus* transmission) and (4) the question of whether Bede knew the *Libellus* preface. Finally we can ask whether Bede's *Libellus* text sheds any light on his procedures as a scholar.

Few works of the early Middle Ages have come down to us whose text can be as accurately established as that of Bede's *History*. The manuscript evidence is abundant and of excellent quality. It was very perspicaciously analysed by Charles Plummer whose critical edition, published in 1896, still remains a monument of sound scholarship. No doubt further refinements can be added to Plummer's text, particularly since the publication of the Leningrad Bede,[2] and the extensive investigations of Sir Roger Mynors,[3] who is working on a new edition of the *History* for the Oxford Medieval Series and for *Corpus Christianorum*. The new edition has not yet appeared at the time of writing. Until it does we can still have recourse to Plummer's edition and use it as a sound basis for discussion.

Plummer's text of the *Libellus Responsionum* can be accepted as it stands with the exception of a few readings which he relegated to the footnotes because he considered them obvious mistakes. Nevertheless I believe they should be included in the main text because they are supported by the best and earliest manuscripts of *HE*. Plummer had not made a specialized study of the *Libellus* transmission, and so was not in a position to see the special significance of these readings and the light they might shed on

---

[1] Brechter (*Quellen*, p. 64, n. 155) has only one short note on the question of the vocabulary of the *Libellus*. The material I have gathered on this aspect of the problem is such as to show that if the author of the *Libellus* is a forger he had such an intimate knowledge of Gregory's vocabulary, his style, his use of cursus and his idiosyncrasies, as to make it impossible to distinguish between him and his model. Other grounds than these will have to be found if the document is to be proved a forgery.

[2] *The Leningrad Bede*, ed. O. Arngart, EEMF 2 (Copenhagen, 1952).

[3] Cf. *The Moore Bede*, ed. P. Hunter Blair, EEMF 9 (Copenhagen, 1959). R. A. B. Mynors contributed a section to the preface (pp. 33–7) entitled 'The Early Circulation of the Text' which discusses the relationship between the Moore Bede and the other early manuscripts of *HE*.

Bede's source. The following is therefore a list of proposed restorations to the *Libellus* text in Plummer:[1]

p. 52, n. 1   Gallis M.L.C.B.
p. 52, n. 3   homo dei M.L.C.Rh.N.
p. 60, n. 1   debeat M.L.C.B.N.
p. 60, n. 3   aliquando enim ex crapula, aliquando [ex naturae superfluitate vel infirmitate, aliquando ex cogitatione contingit. Et quidem cum] ex naturae superfluitate vel infirmitate evenerit... The passage in [ ], through homoeoteleuton, is omitted in M.L.Rh.B.N. Its presence in C poses a problem which will be discussed below.[2]
p. 60, n. 4   animus nesciens L.H.W.O$_{1-6}$ or animus nescius C.B.N.
p. 60, n. 8   turpis M2.L.C.Rh.B.

The critical notes which Plummer added to his edition of *HE* show that there were several other instances where he considered the *Libellus* text, despite the unanimous witness of all the best manuscripts, to be corrupt. Here are his observations (in vol. II):

p. 47   *Quaerere*] We should expect *quaerat*, and so the AS version translates: but there is no variation in the manuscripts.
p. 49   *frater et soror*] We should certainly read *fratris et sororis*. But again there is no variation in the manuscripts.
p. 49   *et quidem...debeant convenire*] The text is certainly corrupt. The readings of A$_2$ and O$_3$ improve the sense somewhat, but these and other readings are probably only expedients of scribes and editors to emend a text which they found unintelligible.
p. 53   *si donum...videatur*] It is difficult to get much meaning out of the text as it stands.
p. 54   *oportet...culpam*] A verb is wanting after *oportet*.

These remarks by themselves help to make an important point: there is good *prima facie* evidence for believing that the Bedan text of the *Libellus Responsionum* is not of the highest quality. This impression is reinforced when we contrast the *Libellus*, from the point of view of textual quality, with some other documents cited by Bede, namely the seven other Gregorian letters quoted in *HE* 1. The text of these letters is excellent, as can be proved by comparing them with the critical edition of Gregory's

[1] The *sigla* not found in Plummer are: L = Leningrad Bede; Rh = Zurich, Zentralbibliothek, Rheinau 95, fols. 106–21, *s.* x, which contains the *Libellus* copied from what appears to be an early *HE* manuscript of the C type.

[2] See p. 26, n. 3. On the problem of the *Libellus Responsionum* in the Old English Bede see Dorothy Whitelock, *The Old English Bede*, Sir Israel Gollancz Memorial Lecture 1962, *Proceedings of the British Academy* (1962), pp. 62, 70 and 86, n. 123. In a long letter, dated 25 May 1961, Professor Whitelock kindly reviewed for me in detail the readings of the OE *Libellus*. They do not have much bearing on the problems discussed in this paper, but it is worth noting that, as in C, no omission occurs at this particular place. The OE on the whole uses a C type of text, but better in some respects than our C (BM Cotton Tiberius C. ii).

*Registrum.*[1] We know the channel through which Bede obtained these other Gregorian letters. They were brought to him by his friend Nothelm, who had copied them down in Rome directly from Gregory's *Registrum.*[2] It is therefore not surprising that the quality of the text is so good, since only one or two intermediaries stand between Bede and the *Registrum.*

When did Bede obtain his copy of the *Libellus*? We can be sure that it was not brought to him by Nothelm together with the other Gregorian letters on his second journey north. This journey can be dated close to 731, when Bede had almost completed his *History*, for these letters appear to be a late insertion into it.[3] Bede on the other hand already had the *Libellus* in his possession in 721, when he completed his prose Life of St Cuthbert, for he quotes a *responsum* from the *Libellus* in this work.[4] It is not impossible that a very close and careful scrutiny of Bede's other works might provide further evidence for a *terminus non post quem* of his knowledge of the *Libellus*. There seem to be unacknowledged borrowings from it elsewhere. For example, a clear reminiscence occurs in Bede's sermon on the Beheading of St John the Baptist. The text is worth presenting here since it helps to show not only how closely Bede approximates to the *Libellus*, but also how closely the *Libellus* is paralleled by two other passages in Gregory's works (the *Moralia* and the Homilies on Ezechiel). Bede may also have had these last lines in mind, along with those of the *Libellus*, when he wrote his sermon.

| Bede | Libellus Responsionum |
|---|---|
| Neque enim dubitandum est quia beatus Iohannes pro redemptoris nostri quem praecurrebat testimonio carcerem et vincula sustinuit, pro ipso et animam posuit, *cui non est dictum a* persecutore *ut Christum negaret,* sed ut veritatem reticeret; et tamen pro Christo occubuit. *Quia* enim | Pro qua re etiam Iohannes Baptista capite truncatus est et sancto martyrio consummatus *cui non est dictum ut Christum negaret,* et pro Christi confessionem occisus est: sed *quia* isdem *Dominus noster Iesus* |

---

[1] *MGH, Epistolae* I and II.

[2] Cf. P. Meyvaert, 'The Registrum of Gregory the Great and Bede', *Revue Bénédictine* LXXX (1970), 162–6.

[3] On this question see P. Meyvaert, *Bede and Gregory the Great*, Jarrow Lecture 1964, pp. 8–13 and nn. 30–40.

[4] Ed. B. Colgrave, *Two Lives of St Cuthbert* (Cambridge, 1940), ch. 16, p. 208. Bede repeats this passage in his Life of Cuthbert in *HE* IV. 25 (27): Plummer, *Bede* I, 270–1. The combined evidence of *HE* I. 27 and IV. 25 (27) allows one to see that Colgrave's choice of readings from the manuscripts was not always correct: thus read *auctore Deo* for *deo auctore*; omit *in* before *inicio*; read *eis* for *illis* in the Cuthbert Life. This again confirms M. Laistner's criticism of the way Colgrave handled the manuscript tradition (*A Hand-List of Bede Manuscripts* [Cornell, 1943], p. 89, n. 40).

| | |
|---|---|
| *Christus ipse ait:* ' *Ego sum Veritas*' ideo utique *pro Christo quia pro veritate sanguinem fudit* . . .[1] | *Christus dixerat:* '*Ego sum Veritas*'; *quia pro veritate* Iohannes occisus est, videlicet *pro Christo sanguinem fudit*.[2] |

Gregory (*Moralia* XXIX. 16)

Neque. . .Iohannes Baptista de confessione Christi sed de iustitiae veritate requisitus occubuit: sed quia *Christus est Veritas* ad mortem usque idcirco *pro Christo quia* videlicet *pro veritate*, pervenit.[3]

Gregory (*In Ezech.* II. 3. 21)

Errantibus huius mundi potentibus libere loqui decernimus? Iohannis auctoritas ad animum reducatur, qui, Herodis nequitiam reprehendens, pro verbi rectitudine occidi non timuit. Et quia *Christus est Veritas*, ipse ideo *pro Christo, quia pro veritate*, animam posuit.[4]

Unfortunately we lack a firm date for the composition of the Homilies, although we know they must be earlier than 731, since Bede includes them (*Omeliarum Evangelii libros II*) in the autobiography which closes the *History*, finished in that year.[5] Another reminiscence may be the following, which occurs in his commentary on Genesis:

| *Libellus Responsionum* | Bede |
|---|---|
| quia hanc animus nesciens pertulisse magis dolendum est quam fecisse[6] | tale scelus incesti nesciens pertulit, magis quam fecit[7] |

---

[1] *Opera Homiletica* II. 23, ed. D. Hurst, *CC* CXXII, 354. In his commentary on Luke (*In Lucam*, ed. D. Hurst, *CC* CXX, 375) Bede writes: 'Iohannis Baptista, qui non pro Christi confessione, sed pro defensione veritatis occubuit, ideo tamen pro Christo, quia pro veritate martyrium suscepit.' This passage echoes the *Moralia* (XXIX. 16) of Gregory rather than the *Libellus Responsionum*.

[2] *HE* I. 27: Plummer, *Bede* I, 51.

[3] Migne, *PL* LXXVI, cols. 485–6.

[4] *Ibid.* col. 971.

[5] We do not know whether the Homilies, which cover a liturgical year, represent sermons delivered within one single calendar year, or whether they are a selection made by Bede from a larger group given over a series of years. Laistner in his *Hand-List* (pp. 114–18) does not suggest a specific date. Dom David Hurst, who has recently edited the Homilies (see above, n. 1), proposes 730–5. This can hardly be maintained in view of the evidence mentioned above. Dom Hurst's reasoning runs as follows: if one compares the Homilies with Bede's commentaries on Mark and Luke one can note that whereas the commentaries are no more than a vast compilation of patristic texts, from Ambrose, Augustine, Jerome, Gregory etc., often quoted verbatim, the Homilies have a more personal tone, even though Bede's words may sometimes echo the sentiments or words of these same Fathers. This suggests therefore a more mature thought and consequently a much later date. Now the commentary on Mark dates from about 716, and that on Luke, as Bede himself tells us, was written 'many years afterwards'. This leads Dom Hurst to propose the very late date just mentioned. Some caution however seems necessary here, for in a sermon to be preached in the church a less bookish and more personal tone might seem more appropriate. Only a careful comparison of the Homilies with Bede's other works is likely to provide firm clues as to dating. For example it can be shown that Homily I. 13, on St Benedict Biscop, was written after 716, since the phrasing of the words shows a dependence on Bede's Lives of the Abbots of Wearmouth-Jarrow.

[6] *HE* I. 27: Plummer, *Bede* I, 60, lines 7–8.

[7] Ed. C. W. Jones, *CC* CXVIII A, 229, lines 1258–9.

Jones has shown that this portion of the commentary is a late work although, since it also appears in the autobiographical list, it must be earlier than 731.[1]

If we cannot determine as yet the exact time when Bede obtained his copy of the *Libellus*, can we discover through what source it came to him? Plummer considered Bede's version to be the most ancient and authentic in existence, and he suggested that it might have been transcribed from the original or a copy preserved at Canterbury by Nothelm or Albinus and brought to Jarrow,[2] presumably on the first journey which Nothelm made to the north. I believe that the only solution to this problem lies in the study of the textual history of the *Libellus*. For where a document has a long history of transmission, and where it can be shown that this history is moving in a given direction which is irreversible, it becomes possible to situate a particular branch of the transmission within the transmission as a whole. The following pages therefore aim at presenting in broad outline a summary account of the *Libellus* history, reserving the full details for a larger and separate work.

The *Libellus Responsionum* has been transmitted both through Bede's *HE* and as a separate work. In its separate form it is preserved in more than 130 manuscripts, not all of which, however, are equally important.[3] The early history of the work can be reconstructed from the evidence of only forty-six manuscripts out of this total.

The *Libellus* survives in three different versions which we will term (1) the Letter version, (2) the Capitula version[4] and (3) the Question and Answer (Q/A) version. The distinction is an important one and can best be illustrated by citing the following example:

(1) III (al. III cap.) Obsecro quid pati debeat si quis aliquid de ecclesia furto abstulerit. Hoc tua fraternitas ex persona furis pensare potest...

(2) Tertio quippe capitulo requiris quid pati debeat si quis aliquid de ecclesia furto abstulerit. Sed hoc tua fraternitas ex persona furis pensare potest...

(3) III Interrogatio (Augustini): 'Obsecro quid pati debeat si quis aliquid de ecclesia furto abstulerit.' Respondit Gregorius: 'Hoc tua fraternitas ex persona furis pensare potest...'

---

[1] *Ibid.* p. viii.  [2] Plummer, *Bede* II, 45.

[3] In a few cases the *Libellus* in separate form was copied out from a manuscript of Bede's *HE* (see above, p. 20, n. 1), or Bede's text was used in a revision. Thus, for example, the earliest manuscripts of the Pseudo-Isidore Collection known as the $A_1$ group of Hinschius derived their text from the continental Q/A version, but in one branch the text was revised on Bede and the opening words of *HE* I. 28 (*Hucusque responsiones beati Gregorii ad consulta...Augustini*) came to be included in the text. There will be a separate section on the Pseudo-Isidore transmission of the *Libellus Responsionum* in my full work. I would like however to take this early opportunity to thank Professor Schafer Williams for permitting me to consult the vast store of material (microfilms etc.) he has amassed on this Collection.

[4] My use of the term differs from that in the article by M. Deanesly and P. Grosjean mentioned above, p. 17, n. 3.

The last two present themselves as edited versions, in contrast with the first which retains a more primitive form.[1] In the Letter version the text begins *ex abrupto*, and no device is used to distinguish between the 'question' and 'answer' portions, both of which are integrated into a single unit: Gregory's reply. A simple numbering (like *III* or *III cap.*) in the margin, or in the middle of the page, is all there is to warn the reader that he has passed on from one subject or *capitulum* to another. In common with the Letter version, the Capitula version also does not clearly distinguish between what is 'question' and what is 'reply'. But to underline the transition from one subject to another the opening phrase of each *responsum* has been recast, and it now appears as if Gregory himself is explicitly warning us of the transition. The third version is intent on drawing a clear demarcation between Augustine's 'question' and Gregory's 'answer'.

In addition to the manner in which they introduce the *responsiones*, the three versions also differ in the order in which they list them. The following sequence uses the numbering of the Letter version as basis:

| | | | | | | | | | |
|---|---|---|---|---|---|---|---|---|---|
| Letter | I II III IV | V | *Obsecro*[2] | VI VII | | VIII | | |
| Capitula | I II III VII | VIII VI*a* | | VI*b* IV | | V | | *Obsecro* |
| Q/A | I II III VI*a* | VI*b* IV | | V | *Obsecro* | VII | VIII | |

The single *responsum* on marriage in the Letter version has become two in the Capitula and Q/A versions through the introduction of an interpolated passage. This interpolated passage accounts for all the doubts expressed in early times about the authenticity of the *Libellus*.[3]

The three versions are found in a variety of manuscripts, nearly all of which are canonical or penitential collections. A study of the history of these collections, together with the information that can be obtained about the origin and provenance of the individual manuscripts, allows us to reconstruct the pattern of the early diffusion of the *Libellus* in consider-

---

[1] The title of the *Libellus* in the Letter version reads: 'Rescriptum beati Gregorii papae ad Augustinum episcopum quem saxoniae in praedicatione direxerat. Inter cetera et ad locum.' The phrase *inter cetera et ad locum* is a warning to the reader that what follows is only an extract from a longer document. I have so far been unable to discover this unabridged original, although a passage does survive in a canonical collection which could have belonged to it. It will be discussed at length in the full study.

[2] All the versions of the *Libellus* contain the request for the relics of St Sixtus ('*Obsecro* ut reliquiae sancti Sixti nobis transmittantur...') which was left unnumbered in the Letter version. A few of the manuscripts in the Q/A version have omitted it, including the branch from which Bede obtained his text.

[3] The Capitula version has the least corrupt text of the interpolation and therefore probably brings us closest to its origins. This is not meant to suggest that the Q/A version derives from the Capitula version. What seems more probable is that the interpolation was made in a manuscript of the Letter version, from which, at a later stage, the Capitula and Q/A branched out. In any case the single *responsum* on marriage in the Letter version pleads strongly for the priority of this version.

able detail. This pattern does not confirm the *a priori* suppositions that have been made on this matter.

The Letter version circulated mainly in northern Italy, but also in Septimania. It is represented by ten manuscripts, the oldest of which is Copenhagen Ny Kgl. S. 58, which E. A. Lowe dates at the beginning of the eighth century, giving Septimania as its place of origin.[1] Although it is the oldest surviving manuscript of the *Libellus*, the Copenhagen volume already bears witness, by various small slips and mistakes, that the text it contains must have been in circulation for some time before it was written.

The Capitula version also seems to have been limited to northern Italy, southern Gaul and Switzerland. It has eight manuscript-witnesses whose combined evidence shows that this version too can be dated back to the eighth century.

The Q/A version had the monopoly of circulation in Gaul, England and Germany. The majority of the manuscripts belong to this version and are divided into various groups, canonical collections and penitential collections forming the main channels of transmission. Two types of early text of the Q/A version can be distinguished, one of which circulated in Gaul and parts of Germany, the other in England and then probably through English missionaries in Germany. Both the continental and insular texts ultimately derive from a single exemplar, and all the evidence points to the continent as its place of origin.

In order to situate Bede's text more accurately we must spell out in somewhat greater detail some of the points made in the above paragraph. The earliest witnesses to the continental text of the Q/A version are all manuscripts containing the canonical collection known as the *Collectio Andegavensis*, which G. Le Bras connects with St Leodegar (616–79), bishop of Autun.[2] Of the thirteen manuscripts known to me, most of which belong to the eighth century or the early ninth, all but one contain the *Libellus*. This shows that the *Libellus* had already become connected

---

[1] *CLA* x, no. 1568. Despite Lowe's claim there may still be doubts about the real origin of this manuscript. I hope to discuss it fully in my book. W. Levison was the first to draw attention to this manuscript in connection with the *Libellus Responsionum* (Levison, p. 17, n. 1). Another manuscript belonging to the Letter version is the famous Lucca, Bibl. Capitolare 490, dated by Lowe to the end of the eighth or the beginning of the ninth century (*CLA* iii, no. 303 *b*). The text of the *Libellus* in this manuscript is complete, despite all assertions to the contrary (*MGH*, Brechter, Deanesly–Grosjean etc.); it is written by a single hand, but there has been an inversion of folios at the end, suggesting a gap. The text of the Lucca manuscript remains almost identical with that of the Copenhagen manuscript until half-way through *responsum* vii when it brusquely switches over, completely, to the insular penitential branch. We know from Paul the Deacon's History of the Lombards (v. 30) that Theodore's penitential was known in Italy at an early date. It must be assumed, therefore, that in an ancestor of Lucca 490 an incomplete text of the Letter version was completed from a Q/A text taken from a penitential collection.

[2] 'Sur la Date et la Patrie de la Collection dite d'Angers', *Revue Historique de Droit Français et Étranger* viii (1929), 775–80.

with this collection at a very early date. The *Andegavensis* was the source for the *Libellus* text in many other early continental manuscripts. When we speak of the continental text in the following pages it is therefore to this early text which circulated in Gaul that we refer.

The early insular text is found in the copies of the *Libellus* that accompany the penitential collection of Theodore of Canterbury, and may represent a revision done at Canterbury itself.[1] Two collections in particular are of importance, the one known as the *Discipulus Umbrensium* and the other known under the name of the *Canones Gregorii*. Textual analysis can show that the *Libellus* text transmitted with the *Canones Gregorii* derives from a branch of the *Discipulus Umbrensium* transmission, and the best surviving witness of this branch is Vienna Cod.Lat.2223 from the beginning of the ninth century.[2] Bede's own text comes closest to this particular branch, and in all probability he obtained his copy of the *Libellus* from this penitential collection, which must have circulated fairly widely in England.[3] For this reason there is no necessity to suppose that Bede obtained his copy through the agency of Nothelm.

Since it is impossible to present here all the textual evidence to support step by step the outline of the *Libellus* transmission sketched above, we can limit ourselves to one salient fact. A demonstration that the Q/A version, as such, is a defective and secondary one should be enough to show that Bede's text cannot be considered in any way as the fountainhead of the

[1] In the continental Q/A text the word *Interrogatio* by itself precedes all the questions, including the first. The insular text has *Interrogatio beati Augustini episcopi Cantuariorum ecclesiae* for the first question, and *Interrogatio Augustini* for the others. This suggests a special interest in the person placing the questions. The way Gregory is introduced in the 'answer' portion remains basically the same throughout the whole early Q/A transmission: that is, *Respondit* (*sanctus, beatus*) *Gregorius papa urbis Romae* for the first reply, *Respondit Gregorius papa* for the second, *Respondit Gregorius* for the rest.

[2] Cf. B. Bischoff, 'Panorama der Handschriftenüberlieferung aus der Zeit Karls des Grossen', *Karl der Grosse* II, 248.

[3] Bede shares a series of readings in common with this group against the whole of the Q/A tradition, including both the continental and insular text (*cet.*). For example:

| | | |
|---|---|---|
| p. 48, line 26 | seorsum fieri | *cet.* seorsum vivere |
| p. 49, line 20 | in galliarum | in galliarum ecclesiis |
| p. 50, line 25 | contradicere videatur | contradixisse videatur |
| p. 52, line 15 | facile | facillime |
| p. 54, line 1 | communionis sacrae | sanctus communionis |
| p. 54, line 12 | pro culpa sua | in culpa sua |
| p. 58, line 4 | portat in ramo | portat arbor in rubore |
| | | (insular) in ramo |
| p. 59, line 6 | prius | ante |
| p. 61, lines 1–2 | suggestione...delectatione...peccati consensu | in suggestione...in delectatione...in peccati consensu |

The group to which Bede belongs also lacks the passage on p. 60, lines 3–6, which we spoke of above. Since this omission occurs in all the best manuscripts of *HE* with the exception of C, there is ground for believing that it was lacking in Bede's fair copy, but was supplied in the parent of the C transmission from a manuscript of Theodore's penitential containing the complete insular text.

transmission, despite the assertions of Plummer and Brechter. Such a demonstration would also eliminate the suppositions of M. Deanesly and P. Grosjean, which would make Nothelm responsible for two versions of the *Libellus*.

In matters of textual history, as Paul Maas has accurately pointed out, it is the errors that occur in the course of transcription that are of decisive significance for establishing the relationship between the manuscripts.[1] Errors through homoeoteleuta are of particular importance, since they indicate a direction which is irreversible. Now all the manuscripts of the Q/A version have two such errors in common. This defect must therefore have been present in the exemplar from which the whole Q/A version stems.

(1) The Letter version, which we quote here from the Copenhagen manuscript, has the following passage in *responsum* VII on ritual cleanliness:

Et laudabilis ergo est ira contra vitium et tamen molesta quia turbatum se pro aliquem reatum [sentit. Sic itaque et bonum est coniugium et tamen de voluptate carnis habet apud se aliquem reatum], quia legitima carnalis copula oportet ut causa prolis sit non voluptatis.

In the Q/A version the part indicated by [ ] has dropped out, due to the repetition of *aliquem reatum*. The awkwardness left in the text by this gap was differently emended in the continental transmission and in the insular one:

Continental ...quia turbatum se aliquem reatum *esse indicabat.* quia legitima carnalis copula oportet ut causa prolis sit non voluptatis.
Insular ...quia turbatum se aliquem reatum *incurisse aestimabat.* oportet itaque legitimam carnis copulam ut causa prolis sit non voluntatis.

The continental text supplies some words to complete the meaning, but otherwise does not alter the word order of the Letter (and Capitula)[2] version. The insular text, from which Bede stems, further changes the order of the phrase and presents the obviously erroneous *voluntatis* for *voluptatis*.

(2) Again in the Letter (and Capitula) version we read the following, in the same *responsum* VII:

Quia mulieri vir miscetur quando inlicitae concupiscentiae animus in cogitatione per deliberationem coniungitur [qui, nisi sol occidat ecclesiam non intret] quia nisi prius ignis concupiscentiae a mente deferveat, dignum se congregationi fratrum aestimare non debet qui se gravari per nequitiam pravae voluntatis videt.

---

[1] *Textual Criticism* (Oxford, 1958), p. 42.

[2] The Capitula version reads: 'Et laudabilis ergo est ira contra vitium et tamen molesta *quia turbat animum.* Sic itaque et bonum est coniugium et tamen de voluptate carnis' etc., as in the Letter version. It therefore presents its own independent textual problem at this point with the omission of 'se pro aliquem reatum sentit' of the Letter version.

Due to the repetition of *qui/quia* there is again an omission in the Q/A version, which also gives *per delectationem* for the *per deliberationem* of the Letter and Capitula versions. This last is a *lectio difficilior* which, moreover, responds to the *nequitia pravae voluntatis* in the same passage, and is in full conformity with the teaching of the next *responsum*: *si autem ex deliberatione consentit tunc peccatum cognoscitur perfici*.

(3) Further proof of the derivative or secondary nature of the Q/A version can be drawn from the opening words of the same *responsum*. As was explained above, this version uses an editorial device to distinguish more clearly between what is question and what is answer in the various *responsiones*. The Letter version begins this *responsum* as follows:

Requisisti si praegnans mulier debeat baptizari...vel etiam ad mysterium sanctae communionis accedere: quae omnia apud anglorum gentem (a rudi anglorum gente *Capitula version*) fraternitatem tuam arbitror requisitam, cui iam te responsum redidisse non ambigo, sed hoc quod ipse dicere et sentire potuisti credo quia mea apud te volueris responsione firmari.

In the Q/A version we read:

Interrogatio: 'Si praegnans mulier debeat baptizari...vel etiam ad mysterium sanctae communionis accedere. Quae omnia rudi anglorum[1] genti oportet haberi conperta.' Respondit Gregorius: 'Hoc non ambigo fraternitatem tuam esse requisitam cui iam et responsum redidisse me arbitror. Sed hoc quod ipse dicere et sentire potuisti, credo quia mea apud te volueris responsione firmari.'

The Letter and Capitula versions present no difficulties. Gregory recapitulates some of the points made to him by Augustine, adding that the English must have raised all these questions, that he does not doubt that Augustine has already provided them with answers, but that Augustine is now seeking Gregory's own confirmation of those answers. The Q/A version, in order to distinguish between what is 'question' and what is 'answer', is obliged to cut artificially into this train of thought and make two sentences out of what was originally one. In the process a slip has occurred with the introduction of the word *me* ('cui iam et responsum redidisse *me* arbitror') which makes havoc of the meaning – for Gregory has not yet given an answer! It is Augustine who is seeking an answer from Gregory.

The branch from which Bede obtained his text introduced a further variation by substituting *communionis sacrae* for the *sanctae communionis* which the remainder of the early Q/A manuscripts (both insular and continental) still have in common with the Letter and Capitula versions, and which is furthermore repeated further on in the same *responsum*:

---

[1] On this point of contact between the Capitula and Q/A versions see what was said above, p. 24, n. 3.

'*sanctae autem communionis mysterium* in eisdem diebus percipere non debet prohiberi.'

(4) Two more small examples can be given to show the defective nature of the Q/A version. In the *responsum* on 'nocturnal illusions':

| | |
|---|---|
| Letter and Capitula | vanis imaginationibus in cogitatione inquinatur |
| Q/A | veris imaginibus in cogitatione inquinatur[1] |

The Q/A reading fails to make sense in the context.

| | |
|---|---|
| Letter and Capitula | In suggestione igitur peccati semen est |
| Q/A (continental) | peccati initium est |
| (insular) | peccati simens est[2] |

Here we have an indication that the continental text has tried to emend a faulty reading (probably *simens*) which must already have been introduced at an early stage. It was no doubt already present in the ur-exemplar of the Q/A version.

The widespread diffusion of the Q/A version at an early date and the proof that this version is not the source of the Letter and Capitula versions should be enough to show what a long and complex transmission the *Libellus* must have undergone. A study of the manuscripts helps to clear up many problems – those that had puzzled Charles Plummer, and others that he did not suspect.[3] What consistently emerges is the inferior quality of the *Libellus* text cited by Bede. Nevertheless Bede's testimony remains of the utmost value, since it provides the textual historian with an object lesson. For Bede's *History* fixes for us the state of the *Libellus* text at a precise date, 731, the year when the work was published. Although the surviving manuscripts of the independent *Libellus* transmission, with the exception of the Copenhagen manuscript, are all later than Bede, they nevertheless retain full value for unravelling the history of the text prior to Bede's time: *posteriores non deteriores*![4]

---

[1] Cf. *HE* I. 27: Plummer, *Bede* I, 59, line 31.

[2] All the insular manuscripts of the Q/A version, including all the important manuscripts of Bede's *HE* share this reading. The Old English Bede likewise translates it 'if the mind'!

[3] Thus, for example, *responsum* II on the liturgy ends in Bede with the phrase: 'et haec quasi in fasciculum collecta apud Anglorum mentes in consuetudinem depone' (Plummer, *Bede* I, 49, lines 31–2). In the Letter version we read: 'et haec quasi in vasculo collecta apud Anglorum mensam in consuetudinem depone.' The manuscripts provide all the steps in the transmutation. A branch of the Letter version had the defective reading *mens*[*am*] which was emended to *gentem* (Capitula version) and *mentes*. The *vasculo* became *fasculo* (a Germanic feature) suggesting an error for *fasciculo*, changed to *fasciculum* in the insular text. The whole tenor of the *responsum* is that a certain diversity of things is good, and in the article cited above, p. 16, n. 3, I tried to show how this idea often evoked the image of food with Gregory the Great. The image of the Letter version is certainly a more telling one than that found in Bede.

[4] The *Libellus Responsionum* – if it be an authentic document – is one that was sent from Rome to Canterbury. Therefore one would expect, *a priori*, to discover that either Canterbury or Rome was at the origin of the diffusion. Instead – and this is the surprising element of the investigation – it is northern Italy (with its ancient Lombard kingdom) which appears to

Another question needing comment is that of Bede's introduction to the *Libellus* in *HE* I. 27. Here Bede explains that Augustine sent to Rome Lawrence the priest and Peter the monk to announce to Gregory the good news of the conversion of the English and his own consecration as bishop, and to submit to him certain problems connected with the work of the missionaries.[1] The *Libellus* is then presented as the reply to these problems. As far as surviving sources are concerned only two can be cited in which the names of Peter and Lawrence occur together; they are Gregory's letter to Queen Bertha, King Æthelberht's consort,[2] and the *Libellus* preface.[3]

Now Bede gives no explicit indication that he knew the letter to Bertha, and the Q/A version of the *Libellus* from which he obtained his text did not carry the preface. Hence the problem to which various solutions have been proposed. Brechter maintains that the preface is a forgery, later in date than Bede, concocted by Gemmulus the papal secretary, and prefixed to a 'curial' version of the *Libellus* deposited as authentic in the papal archives.[4] In Brechter's view Bede drew his information from the letter to Bertha which, for some sinister reason, he was unwilling to make use of otherwise or to admit that he knew.[5] M. Deanesly and P. Grosjean hold that it was not Gemmulus but Nothelm who forged the preface to support the Gregorian 'authenticity' of his *Libellus*, and that Bede used it for his own introduction.[6] R. A. Markus, without committing himself to a view that the *Libellus* preface was forged, nevertheless considered the preface, rather than the letter to Bertha, to be Bede's source.[7]

occupy a key rôle in the transmission. Since the Lombards were a Germanic people there would be no problem to explain how the *responsum* on marriage came to be interpolated there. The problem is to explain how the *Libellus* text got there in the first place. To this I have as yet no answer!

[1] In the introduction Bede tells us that Augustine journeyed to Arles to be consecrated bishop, that immediately upon his return to England he sent Lawrence and Peter to Rome with the questions, and that Gregory replied without delay (*nec mora*). The marginal note supplied by Charles Plummer giving 597 as the date of Augustine's consecration has led some historians to think that Bede considered the *Libellus* to have been sent from Rome in 597 or 598. This is, in fact, a pseudo-problem on which I touched in a note to the Jarrow Lecture of 1964 (p. 24, n. 40). For Bede himself provides us with his own date of the *Libellus* in the introduction to *HE* I. 28, where he makes it clear that he considered the *Libellus* to have been written *after* the letter quoted in that chapter, that is, after 22 June of the year 601. The date supplied by Plummer for Augustine's consecration (597) is his own conjecture and is not found in Bede; nor can too much stress be laid on a phrase like *nec mora*, which Bede uses no less than seventeen times in the *History*. In interpreting such passages we must always remember that our own sense of time, geared to a jet age, is very different from that of the eighth century.

[2] *MGH, Epistolae* II, 304: Ep. XI. 35.     [3] *Ibid.* pp. 332–3: Ep. XI. 56*a*.

[4] We said above, p. 16 and n. 1, that the words of Zachary in the council of 743 – which Gemmulus no doubt had a hand in drawing up – together with the letter of Leo III of the year 800 dispose of such an hypothesis.

[5] R. A. Markus, *loc. cit.*, has provided an effective reply to Brechter's implication of duplicity in Bede. Brechter is alone in asserting that Gregory's letter to Bertha implies that King Æthelberht had not yet become a Christian in 601. Both the letters, to Æthelberht and to Bertha, seem clearly to imply that Gregory viewed the king as a Christian.

[6] *Loc. cit.* pp. 32–3.     [7] *Loc. cit.* pp. 20–1.

In a long footnote to the Jarrow Lecture of 1964 I opted for the letter to Bertha as source, indicating the arguments that could be put forward to suggest why Bede must have known it.[1] At present I would be inclined to consider it possible that Bede knew and used both the letter and the *Libellus* preface. The way he links the good news of the conversion with the names of Peter and Lawrence may seem to plead for the letter,[2] but the way in which the *Libellus* is linked with these names pleads for the preface.[3] While it is true that Bede's own *Libellus* source, the penitential collection with its Q/A version, could not provide him with the preface, there is no reason why there should not have been some other canonical collection containing the Letter or Capitula version among the many manuscripts brought from Italy and southern France to Wearmouth-Jarrow by Benedict Biscop and Ceolfrith. It was from such a collection that Bede must have obtained his copy of Gregory's *Libellus Synodicus* (the Acts of the Roman Synod of 695) which he mentions in his Life of Gregory (*HE* II. 1).[4] Another possibility is that on his journey to and from Rome Nothelm somewhere encountered a copy of the Letter or Capitula version of the *Libellus* and transcribed its preface for Bede.

We can finally ask what light Bede's text of the *Libellus Responsionum* sheds on Bede himself and on his working methods. Unlike the other Gregorian letters, which were brought to him by Nothelm at a late date when the *History* was almost completed, the *Libellus* – which Bede already knew in 721 – must have been a document that was part of his plan for the *History* from the start. Being the only Gregorian letter he then knew, it is easy to understand why he chose to quote it in full, despite its length. It must have seemed to him a precious cornerstone on which to build his section on the Gregorian mission. With the advent of all the new material Bede was obliged to make further insertions. He avoided, however, quoting documents that were exceptionally long, like the letter to Augustine, of which he cites only a short section (*HE* I. 31), and it is probable that he refrained from making full use of other material that Nothelm had brought him, in

---

[1] P. 24, n. 40.

[2] The link is less obvious than Brechter (*Quellen*, p. 250) seems to suppose, since, in the letter to Bertha, Gregory does not explicitly refer to the conversion but relates how Lawrence and Peter had told him: 'qualis erga reverentissimum fratrem et coepiscopum nostrum Augustinum gloria vestra extiterit quantaque illi solacia vel qualem caritatem impenderit.' Bede was evidently entitled, as an historian, to make his own deductions about what further news the two missionaries related to Gregory while in Rome.

[3] In the *Libellus* preface we read: 'per dilectissimos filios meos Laurentium presbyterum et Petrum monachum fraternitatis tuae scripta suscepi in quibus me de multis capitulis requirere curasti...' (cf. P. Meyvaert, 'Les Responsiones de S. Grégoire le Grand', *loc. cit.* p. 890); Bede's introduction says: 'Augustinus...misit continuo Romam Laurentium presbyterum et Petrum monachum...simul et de eis, quae necessaria videbantur, quaestionibus eius consulta flagitans' (*HE* I. 27: Plummer, *Bede* I, 48).

[4] 'Bede and the Libellus Synodicus of Gregory the Great', *JTS* n.s. XII (1961), 298–302.

order not to overload book I and thus to preserve a sense of balance between the various books of the *History*.[1]

As far as the *Libellus* text itself is concerned it may seem surprising to us that Bede failed to correct what appear to be fairly obvious mistakes in the text. And this surprise is likely to increase if we are willing to suppose that Bede may have known another version of the *Libellus* (the Letter or the Capitula version) from which to draw the information included in his introduction. If Bede had had another version of the *Libellus* in hand would he not have made a careful comparison between the two texts and produced his own 'critical edition'? It is perhaps a hazardous thing for a modern editor to project his notions of what scholarship implies into a past age and to expect, *a priori*, that an eighth-century writer will conform to them![2] Bede himself seems to have been quite content to transmit the *Libellus* text to us as he had received it, without setting out to polish it up or to correct it in any way. This fact is interesting and worth noting. It is, moreover, not the only piece of evidence that pleads for such an interpretation.[3] A yet fuller picture of Bede's attitude towards his texts may emerge when further work has been done in comparing the long quotations from works of the Fathers against the critical editions of these same works. For here again it may emerge that Bede felt an unwillingness to tamper with texts as he had received them.[4] And if his text of the *Libellus* came to him, as seems very likely, in a penitential collection associated with Theodore, might it not have carried with it, in his eyes, some of the authority of Theodore's (and Augustine's) see?

It is fortunate for us, as far as the question of the document's authenticity is concerned, that Bede transmitted his text to us 'warts and all'.

[1] Cf. my Jarrow Lecture, p. 24, n. 29.

[2] If my own investigations into the *Libellus* manuscripts have taught me anything, it is that one should be ready to encounter the unexpected. Thus, to take but one example, at a given point in the eighth century someone acquired two copies of the *Libellus*, one of the Capitula version and the other of the Q/A version. The ordering of the *responsiones* in the Capitula version seemed more pleasing, so the Q/A text was recopied to conform to this order. At this point, at least, I would have expected some clear signs of contamination in the Q/A text, but none occurs. The interest was in the arrangement of the replies in the Capitula version, not in the text itself, despite the fact that – to the modern editor – the Capitula version helps to clear up some textual problems in the Q/A version.

[3] Bede's citations of the various papal letters in the *History* show that he transmitted to us faithfully what he had received: see P. Meyvaert, 'The Registrum of Gregory the Great and Bede', *loc. cit.*

[4] Bede was undoubtedly conscious that a text could become corrupted through transmission, as is shown by his statements in the Retractation on Acts (ed. Laistner, p. 93): 'In quo etiam quaedam quae in Graeco sive aliter seu plus aut minus posita vidimus...; quae, utrum neglegentia interpretis omissa vel aliter dicta an incuria librariorum sint depravata sive relicta' – here at least he could use the Greek text of Acts as criterion; or again in his autobiography (*HE* v. 24: Plummer, *Bede* I, 359): '...librum vitae et passionis sancti Anastasii, male de Graeco translatum, et peius a quodam inperito emendatum, prout potui, ad sensum correxi...' Is there perhaps a clue in this last phrase: as long as Bede thought he could get meaning out of a text it was better to leave it intact?

These allow us to place it in its own branch of the textual transmission, and to demonstrate that the text was already old and corrupt when Bede transcribed it into his *History*. In that setting its corruptions are thrown into strong relief by the excellence of Bede's own Latin – no wonder Plummer felt obliged to relegate the worst of the errors to his footnotes! He could not have realized that these very errors would later be needed to establish the nature of the *Libellus* text in Bede's own day, and thus to show that it could not have been a forgery by one of his contemporaries. At this point it seems safe to say that, apart from the passage on marriage permissions which alarmed Boniface and others, and which can be shown to be an interpolation, we have at present no more reason to doubt the Gregorian authenticity of the *Libellus* than Bede had himself.[1]

[1] The purely textual evidence of the *Libellus Responsionum* indicates that one would have to go back a considerable time before Bede to find the beginnings of the transmission. The further back we go beyond this time, the more unlikely does any theory of forgery become, although the question of where and by whom the *Libellus* text was first disseminated still remains an open one.

# A background to St Boniface's mission

## J. M. WALLACE-HADRILL

An English scholar in search of a continental background to St Boniface's mission will naturally turn to Wilhelm Levison's Ford Lectures, delivered in Oxford in 1943 and published in 1946.[1] Yet the quarter-century that has since passed has seen much activity in Levison's field, notably among his own pupils; and thus his picture can be modified in some important respects[2] and filled out in others. Generally one may say that it has become more complex, and that the Frankish scene in which Boniface lived out the second half of his long life can no longer be regarded as one of degraded isolation, politically or religiously. The time may be opportune to attempt to reassess some aspects at least of the picture.

The English never forgot their connection with the continental Saxons. For different reasons, the Franks never forgot theirs with the Germans east of the Rhine. It is a thread that runs right through the history of Frankish Gaul. We must take it up – if we wish to understand St Boniface's situation – in the early seventh century, during the reigns of two powerful Merovingian kings, Chlotar II and his son Dagobert I, and the regency of Balthildis. The one tenaciously pursued ambition of the early Merovingians, Robert Latouche has written, 'a été de reconquérir la Germanie dans toute sa profondeur pour l'annexer à leur royaume.'[3] This is to claim rather too much, though Merovingian campaigns against Saxons, Alamans and Thuringians lend some colour to it. What is clear is that Austrasian Francia could never be secure while German tribes over the Rhine were aggressive and some of their neighbours west of the Rhine unsettled and

[1] Levison, ch. 4 and app. 7. The shorter study of S. J. Crawford, *Anglo-Saxon Influence on Western Christendom, 600–800* (Oxford, 1933), though clear and good in some ways, is marred by factual error (for some, see M. L. W. Laistner's review in *History* XVIII (1934), as well as outmoded in interpretation. G. W. Greenaway's *Saint Boniface* (London, 1955) is an excellent introductory sketch, written in the wake of Levison's book. The penetrating résumés of Sir Frank Stenton, *Anglo-Saxon England*, pp. 167–73, and of Professor Dorothy Whitelock, *EHD* I, 88, should not be overlooked. The outstanding recent study of St Boniface is Th. Schieffer's *Winfrid-Bonifatius und die Christliche Grundlegung Europas* (Freiburg, 1954), based on his own researches in *Angelsachsen und Franken* (Akad. d. Wiss. und d. Lit., Mainz, 1950). Also essential is the *Sankt Bonifatius Gedenkgabe* (Fulda, 1954), to which reference is frequently made in this essay; its very full bibliographies should be referred to for well-known studies not cited explicitly here.
[2] I am not here referring to matters of detail on which more recent scholars have taken a different view (e.g. the establishment of sees at Erfurt and Eichstätt) but to problems of interpretation.
[3] *Les Origines de l'Économie Occidentale* (Paris, 1956), p. 155.

independent. A stage in this uneasy relationship was reached in the early seventh century. One indication is that Chlotar and Dagobert provided those tribes they distrusted, but wished to conciliate, with written national laws of their own, firmly based on the Merovingian *Lex Salica* and subordinating them politically to Frankish overlordship: *Lex Ribvaria* for the tribes round Cologne, the *Pactus Alamannorum* for the Alamans, and *Lex Baiuvariorum* for the Bavarians.[1] It is no coincidence that manuscripts of the *Volksrechte* were soon to be found in the libraries of those monasteries most closely associated with Carolingian plans for Germany. Moreover, there is evidence of Frankish colonizing activity at about the same time, notably in the Main–Neckar region. It was spasmodic and unplanned and altogether more modest than what the Arnulfings were later to attempt;[2] yet there is reason to think that it had Merovingian support or approval.[3] It had a religious aspect too. The new Frankish families encouraged by the Merovingians were also monastic founders, both in western Francia and in the Rhineland. Luxeuil and her dependent houses owed their prosperity to this. There is a strong link between the Irish missionaries on the one hand and the Merovingians with their Frankish and Burgundian aristocratic supporters on the other. From these last a new generation of bishops was coming to maturity by the middle of the seventh century: no longer Gallo-Romans of the type to which Gregory of Tours had belonged, but aristocratic and often learned Franks associated with and brought up in the Irish–Frankish monastic tradition.[4] Even after the collapse of Merovingian political authority members of the dynasty can still be found interested in monastic foundations: examples are Chlotar III and his brother, Theuderic III. The last known Merovingian foundation was that of St Peter's at Erfurt by Dagobert III (711–16). In practice, however, Merovingian monastic foundations, or encouragement of such foundations by their supporters, often wilted before local opposition. For example, not much progress was made east of the Vosges, where they came up against the family of the Etichonen, dukes of Alsace and themselves monastic founders.[5] This is about as much as should be said of late Merovingian encouragement of monasticism; for the point is soon reached (long, indeed, before the foundation of St Peter's, Erfurt) where

[1] I summarize this in *The Long-Haired Kings* (London, 1962), pp. 213–14. See also R. Buchner, Wattenbach-Levison's *Deutschlands Geschichtsquellen im Mittelalter: die Rechtsquellen* (Weimar, 1953), pp. 15–33.

[2] On this distinction see R. Sprandel, *Der Merovingische Adel und die Gebiete östlich des Rheins*, Forschungen zur Oberrheinischen Landesgeschichte 5 (Freiburg, 1957), esp. pp. 96–116.

[3] See A. Bergengruen, *Adel und Grundherrschaft im Merowingerreich* (Wiesbaden, 1958), p. 124, and Th. Mayer, *Mittelalterliche Studien* (Konstanz, 1959), p. 297.

[4] The situation is well described by F. Prinz, *Frühes Mönchtum im Frankenreich* (Munich-Vienna, 1965), pp. 488–9.

[5] See Mayer, 'St Trudpert und der Breisgau', *op. cit.* pp. 273–88.

it is hard to know what was being done by others in their name and under their authority; in brief, the Arnulfings and other families advanced to landed power, and so emerged as monastic founders, under Merovingian aegis. Should one ascribe the advancement of the bishopric of Cologne to the Merovingians or to the Arnulfings? The first important bishop was Kunibert, successor to Arnulf of Metz as chief adviser to Dagobert I and Sigebert III, and thus colleague of the first Pippin. Kunibert was a great Merovingian servant, and quite possibly the begetter of *Lex Ribvaria*. Under him the bishopric began to penetrate its pagan surroundings, even as far away as Utrecht and Soest. The effort was premature, but Cologne was from then on a vital point in Frankish control of the north-east. Above all, it was to be an Arnulfing stronghold. From it Bishop Hildegar set out to meet his death on Pippin III's Saxon expedition of 753.[1] The Merovingians made Cologne an outpost of Frankish power: the Arnulfings were to reap the benefit.[2]

It was not the opinion of Levison that Merovingian connections with Rome had much significance. He may have been right in the sense that the connections we know of were informal for the most part and occasional; certainly they were not marked by conciliar activity such as characterized Carolingian–Roman relations. But the evidence, poor as it is, reveals that in important ways the Merovingian church was alive to Roman developments and attached importance to the link.[3] This is clearest in the field of liturgy. A form of the Roman Gelasian sacramentary reached Francia in the first half of the seventh century: there survives a copy of it in MS Vat. Reg. 316, made in Francia about 750.[4] Nor was this the only sacramentary to influence Frankish liturgical practice in the same century; other types were used. So far as is known, they owed their presence in Francia, as well as their dissemination, to private initiative; not until the time of Pippin III do we find unquestionable royal interest in such matters. Nevertheless, the liturgical link was already there. It was supported, moreover, by the circulation of the closely associated *Ordines Romani*; these, too, were in Francia well before the middle of the eighth century. Another symptom of Frankish interest in Rome was the growth of the cult of St Peter, as evidenced in church dedications. In part at least this will have been due to

---

[1] *Geschichte des Erzbistums Köln* i, ed. W. Neuss (Cologne, 1964), 146.

[2] This has been demonstrated by E. Ewig, 'Die Civitas Ubiorum, die Francia Rinensis und das Land Ribuarien', *Rheinische Vierteljahrs-Blätter* xix (1954), 1–29.

[3] The important work in this field is K. Hallinger, 'Römische Voraussetzungen der bonifatianischen Wirksamkeit im Frankenreich', *Bon. Gedenkgabe*, pp. 320–61, the main conclusions of which are accepted by M. Coens, 'S. Boniface et sa Mission Historique d'après Quelques Auteurs Récents', *Analecta Bollandiana* lxxiii (1955), 462–95.

[4] Cf. C. Vogel, 'Les Relations en Matière Liturgique entre l'Église Franque et l'Église Romaine', Settimane di Spoleto 7 (1960), esp. 209 ff.; and H. Frank, 'Die Briefe des hl. Bonifatius und das von ihm benutzte Sakramentar', *Bon. Gedenkgabe*, pp. 58–88.

the influence of St Columbanus and his disciples, Irish and Frankish; in part, to the indigenous tradition of the Gallo-Roman church. Some thirty foundations of the seventh century were dedicated to St Peter, whereas dedications to St Martin, hitherto the favoured Frankish patron, dropped off.[1] If any doubt still existed as to the specifically Roman significance attached to St Peter by the Merovingian church, one need only refer to the *Vitae Patrum Jurensium*.[2] A missionary from Aquitaine, St Amand, who died *c*. 674, dedicated all the northern monasteries of his foundation to St Peter; and his example was followed by others (e.g. Geretrudis of Nivelles). Already in the Merovingian *Formulae* of Bourges St Peter appears as the protector of the Franks.[3] In short, Frankish interest in St Peter long antedated any Anglo-Saxon influence. It may also be noted that the leader of the Petrine party at Whitby, for whom St Wilfrid acted as spokesman, was a Frank.[4] Such interest should not prove surprising when we recall that the Franks were as involved as the English in the Roman pilgrimage; and, unlike the English, had good Roman precedent for being so. In Marculf's Formulary (and others) is plentiful evidence of Frankish pilgrimage to Rome as a normal occurrence of the seventh century;[5] and in the Merovingian *Vitae Sanctorum* there is more.[6] It was not St Boniface who brought the Roman pilgrimage, any more than the Rule of St Benedict with its strongly Roman links, to Francia; they were already part of Frankish life.[7] A diploma of Theuderic IV for St Denis in 724[8] betrays so strong a sense of *missio Romana* that we should also reckon with official Merovingian recognition of Francia's special ties with the papacy. Furthermore, a privilege of Pope Adeodatus (672–6) for Tours[9] (which there is no reason to consider exceptional) makes it clear that the popes were equally conscious of those ties. The background, then, to the Roman missions of St Willibrord and St Boniface is not only English but also Frankish.

The Carolingian family, both in its Arnulfing and its Pippinid branches,[10] was one of several dynasties of Austrasian magnates that owed its early impetus to Merovingian backing, and whose first steps in territorial aggrandizement, on both sides of the Rhine, were associated with control

---

[1] See esp. Th. Zwölfer, *St Peter, Apostelfürst und Himmelspförtner* (Stuttgart, 1929), pp. 74 ff.

[2] *MGH, Script. Rer. Merov.* iii, 151 ff.    [3] *MGH, Formulae*, p. 181.

[4] Bede, *HE* iii. 25; Eddius, ch. 10.    [5] *MGH, Formulae*, pp. 104, 181, 217 and 278.

[6] E.g. *Vitae Columbani* (*MGH, Script. Rer. Merov.* iv, 145); *Fursei* (*ibid.* p. 441); *Audoini* (*Script. Rer. Merov.* v, 559 ff.); *Geretrudis* 2 (*Script. Rer. Merov.* ii, 455); *Amandi* 1 and 2 (*Script. Rer. Merov.* v, 434 ff. and 452 ff.).

[7] On which see Hallinger's comments on the Frankish use of the word *romensis* in relation to the Rule (*Bon. Gedenkgabe*, pp. 343–6).

[8] *MGH, Diplomata* i, no. 93. Schieffer, *Angelsachsen und Franken*, p. 1441, draws attention to its significance.

[9] *MGH, Formulae*, pp. 496–8.

[10] I usually follow normal usage in employing 'Arnulfing' to describe the family before the accession of Pippin III, and 'Carolingian' thereafter.

of churches and monasteries. With Charles Martel, however, a change is discernible; his trans-rhenan activities have more the complexion of planned military conquest than do any of the Merovingian campaigns.[1] Carolingian historiography depicts his conquests rather more as a continuation of what had gone before than they really were. From Charles's time onwards, Carolingian expeditions against the Germans were aimed at Frankish absorption of Germany: Pippin II had shown the way with four campaigns against the Alamans (in 709, 710, 711 and 712); Charles Martel began his series of Saxon expeditions in 718; in 725 he attacked the Alamans and the Bavarians; in 730 he again attacked the Alamans and in 742–3 his son Carloman followed his example; in 745 Pippin III was active in Alamannia while Carloman went for the Saxons; and in 746 Carloman secured a resounding victory over the Alamans at Cannstadt. These were only the more notable campaigns; there were others, and there would have been still more but for Carolingian preoccupation with Aquitaine and the Arabs. They were associated with political reorganization (as with Charles Martel's in Thuringia[2]) and equally with settlements of Frankish families, especially in the Main–Neckar region. A witness to them is the mass of aristocratic *Reihengräber* of the seventh century; warrior-graves, some in hitherto vacant lands, others the result of violent dispossession.[3]

But always these activities had a religious aspect, evident in a modest way long before. Rhineland bishoprics specially involved in missionary or colonizing work (and sometimes both) in the seventh and early eighth centuries were: Cologne (Westphalia and parts of Frisia); Mainz (the Mainland, notably in the direction of Würzburg); Worms (the Neckar valley); Speyer (northern Alamannia and Alsace); and Strassburg (southern Alamannia, i.e. the Black Forest area). With all of these the early Carolingians were associated, sometimes intimately. To start with the most northerly – Cologne: it was the stronghold of Pippin II and, after his death in 714, of his widow, Plectrudis,[4] guardian of their grandson, Theudoald. Pippin's illegitimate son, Charles Martel, found Cologne a centre of legitimist Carolingian resistance to his power, and it did not soon die down. Nevertheless, Cologne became the headquarters of his campaigns against the Westphalian Saxons, who had bitten deep into the Frankish *Gaue* round Cologne between 694 and 714. Charles's counter-offensive was short-lived in its effects, but the hopes that were entertained of it may be gauged from Boniface's anxiety to have the see of Cologne as a centre for missionary work among the Saxons. It is one of several

[1] The point is made, perhaps too forcibly, by Sprandel, *op. cit.* pp. 115–16.
[2] Cf. Mayer, *op. cit.* pp. 128, 133, 303, 320 and 325, for instances of early Carolingian reorganization after conquest.
[3] Sprandel, *op. cit.* p. 98; Bergengruen, *op. cit.* pp. 154–61.
[4] Cf. Ewig, *loc. cit.* p. 26.

indications that Charles and Boniface had a strong common interest in expansion from the northern Middle Rhine.[1] But Cologne has a further interest. In the person of Plectrudis it became linked with Carolingian power further south, in and round Trier. North and east of Trier, between the Mosel and the Maas, lay the nucleus of the family's estates and some of their earliest ecclesiastical endowments. Plectrudis's parents were the Frankish seneschal Hugobert, bishop of Maastricht, and Irmina, probably daughter of Theotar, a duke in western Germany,[2] whose descendants were connected with the Frankish Heteno dynasty of Thuringia. Children of the same pair were Adula of Pfalzel,[3] Chrodelind, Regentrud and Bertrada (to be distinguished from her granddaughter of the same name, who married Pippin III). In the course of a few years this clan founded, or participated in founding, monasteries at Pfalzel, Echternach (which they gave to Willibrord), and Prüm. When we add to these certain nearby foundations, and foundations by neighbouring families (e.g. Mettlach, Hornbach, St Maria ad Martyres at Trier, and the revival of St Eucher and St Paulin, also at Trier), we shall be justified in considering the late seventh and early eighth centuries the first serious revival of religious life in the district of the Middle Rhine–Mosel since the barbarian invasions.[4] Moreover, with the exception of Mettlach, we can claim that these new aristocratic monasteries marked some weakening of episcopal authority; the territory was showing signs of emancipation from the city, at least for a time. What of the bishops of Trier? The period is covered by the rule of Basin, his nephew Liutwin and Liutwin's son Milo. The family were Franks from the Upper Saar.[5] Basin, who died in 705, was on friendly terms with St Willibrord, who put his name in his calendar, perhaps because Basin had played some part in the foundation of Echternach. Not only Basin but also Liutwin were honoured as saints in Trier; both were benefactors of monasteries. Yet Liutwin was also *dux* in Trier; he was trusted by those in power further west, and may indeed have had his own ties with Neustria; he dedicated his monastery of Mettlach to St Denis and

---

[1] It should be noted that the continuator of Fredegar's Chronicle does not confine his association of Charles Martel with the divine purpose to Charles' campaigns against the Arabs. In recording Charles' birth his mind turns to Luke 1. 80, and perhaps also to Hebrews XI. 23 (ch. 6: ed. Krusch, *MGH, Script. Rer. Merov.* II, 172; ed. Wallace-Hadrill, *Fredegarius* [London, 1960], p. 86); it was with God's help that he escaped from Plectrudis's clutches (ch. 8: ed. Krusch, p. 173; ed. Wallace-Hadrill, p. 88); in 738 he was victorious against the Saxons *opitulante Domino* (ch. 19: ed. Krusch, p. 177; ed. Wallace-Hadrill, p. 93).

[2] A good family-tree, showing the connections of the Arnulfings with other houses, is provided by E. Hlawitschka in *Karl der Grosse* (I, 73).

[3] It has been pointed out more than once that Boniface in his early days found no difficulty in associating with this great Frankish lady's household, where he found one of his disciples, her grandson, Gregory, the future bishop of Utrecht. There is no evidence that his feelings towards the family ever changed.

[4] Such is the conclusion of Ewig, *Trier im Merowingerreich* (Trier, 1954), pp. 139ff.

[5] On it see Ewig, *Trier*, pp. 133–5, and 'Milo et Eiusmodi Similes', *Bon. Gedenkgabe*, pp. 415ff.

not to any saint specially honoured by the Irish or Anglo-Saxons. It is another matter to infer that he was more cautious about supporting foreigners than his uncle had been. Milo, then, was heir not merely to large family possessions and official power in the Rhineland and beyond (Charles Martel put Reims and Laon in Liutwin's hands, and afterwards Milo's, as a result of the opposition of Bishop Rigobert) but also to a tradition of generosity to monasteries. Milo stood close to Charles Martel. He was probably not in bishop's orders and very likely secularized some ecclesiastical property; but he was not deprived of office by any reforming council and left a good name behind him locally, in his monastery of Mettlach. It was his hunting that annoyed Boniface; and I know of no evidence that he and the English missionaries were normally hostile to one another. The most one can infer is coldness, and even this will depend on how one interprets a possible friendliness between Milo and St Pirmin. Charles Martel was certainly not hostile to the English in the Mosel–Rhine region: he was himself a benefactor of Echternach; nor was he hostile to St Willibrord, to whom he gave the castle of Utrecht as a base for his resumed operations in Frisia.

A further centre of Arnulfing power (this time well west of the Rhine) was Metz, the see of their ancestor, St Arnulf. The earliest evidence of their awareness of the value to them of St Arnulf's patronage is the gift by Pippin II and Plectrudis, in 691, of a villa at Norroy to the church of Metz, *ubi domnus et avus noster Arnulphus in corpore requiescit*.[1] The church was known as St Arnulf's by about the year 700, and closer Carolingian interest in it is evident. Charles Martel's nine-year-old son, Jerome, wrote a Life of St Arnulf.[2] The more important members of the family were buried in the great Merovingian monastery of St Denis; and it was here that Charles put his sons, Carloman and Pippin III, to be educated. But Metz was still vital to the family. The see was entrusted by them to no less a man than Chrodegang in 742, when he was aged thirty. Chrodegang was a Frank of aristocratic birth from the Maasland, a relation of Chancor (founder of Lorsch) and brother of its first abbot.[3] He was brought up at Charles Martel's court, where he was *referendarius*. He witnessed Charles's last extant deed on 17 September 741.[4] He was, then, very much the man of Charles Martel, though it was to Pippin III that he owed Metz. We know nothing of his education or of the influences that made him the first great Frankish church-reformer; something must have been due to the

[1] *MGH, Diplomata* I, 92, no. 2; and see the important study of O. G. Oexle, 'Die Karolinger und die Stadt des heiligen Arnulf', *Frühmittelalterliche Studien* I (1967), 250–364.
[2] *MGH, Script. Rer. Merov.* II, 429.
[3] See the fundamental work of Ewig, 'Beobachtungen zur Entwicklung der fränkischen Reichskirche unter Chrodegang von Metz', *Frühmitt. Studien* II (1968), 67–77.
[4] *MGH, Diplomata* I, 101 ff., no. 14.

court circle itself, and something also perhaps to the monastery of St Trond, where Charles was later alleged to have found him.[1] Chrodegang was to become, in the 740s, the new representative of Francia's traditional ties with Rome. But it is not by any means certain that he stood for a Frankish tradition of hostility to St Boniface, nor that his master Pippin III was glad to take advantage of it. There was collaboration between him and the Bonifacian bishops of Mainz, Würzburg and Cambrai. He certainly had a link with St Pirmin, whose missionary activity reached at least as far north as Metz. In brief, Chrodegang linked much: not only the Frankish court circle with the followers of Boniface and Pirmin but also with Frankish episcopal interests wider afield, where Boniface was powerless. The reform of the Frankish church outside the Austrasian area of synodal activity owed most to him, and there is evidence that he had something there to build on. Ewig has shown that in the seventh and early eighth centuries there were interesting liturgical developments in Neustria and Burgundy largely independent of Austrasian influence, and has illustrated this from the Soissons Litany.[2] Nor should it be overlooked that both Corbinian of Freising and Emmeram of Regensburg were West Franks.

Mainz had long been the Frankish advance-post for penetration of the Mainland and central Germany generally. How far it was ever an active mission centre is more debatable; in the mid and later seventh century there seems to have been more missionary activity from Trier-Echternach, Speyer-Weissenburg and Worms (the home of the Frankish Bishop Rupert of Salzburg).[3] Not surprisingly, this middle area of the Rhine was a centre of opposition to St Boniface: Gewilib of Mainz was one of the two Frankish bishops who were criticized by name by Boniface.[4] In due course he was deposed for the specific sin of having taken blood-vengeance for the killing of his father (and predecessor as bishop), Gerold. We do not know that any other charge was laid against him; his succession to the see of Mainz was regular, and he may well have been in bishop's orders.[5] What interest he took in the extension of his diocese east of the Rhine is not known; but his opposition to Boniface's activity in Hesse and Thuringia, which may reasonably be inferred, suggests that he took some. His colleague of Worms may well have sympathized with him; but Bishop

---

[1] Early Carolingian relations with St Trond are interesting. Cf. Prinz, op. cit., p. 204.

[2] 'Beobachtungen', loc. cit. pp. 74-7.

[3] See E. Zöllner, 'Woher stammt der hl. Rupert?', Mitt. d. Inst. für Österr. Geschichte LVII (1949), 1-22.

[4] Die Briefe des heiligen Bonifatius und Lullus, ed. M. Tangl, MGH, Epistolae Selectae I, 124, Ep. 60 (of 745), where Pope Zacharius refers to Gewilib as having been mentioned in a letter from Boniface. It is not quite clear from Zacharius's letter of 751 (ibid. p. 198, Ep. 87) that Milo had been mentioned directly by Boniface, but it is a fair assumption.

[5] So Ewig, 'Milo', op. cit. p. 422.

David of Speyer (also abbot of Weissenburg) seems to have been readier to collaborate with the English. From these centres, not so long before, Irish missionaries must have set out with Frankish support for Würzburg,[1] where St Kilian met his death in about 689. There were at least fourteen monasteries in Würzburg diocese alone, founded on the properties of substantial families, some Frankish, some Thuringian. One of them, Kitzingen, was founded by Hadeloga, allegedly a daughter of Charles Martel and in fact very probably connected with him. But the interesting point about St Kilian is not so much his mission as his subsequent career as a saint.[2] In 752, Bishop Burchard of Würzburg translated his relics with much publicity, proclaiming him in effect the symbol and patron of Carolingian *Ostpolitik*.[3] This open championing of an Irish saint in territory peculiarly Bonifacian (Fulda was not far away), and by an English disciple and confidant of Boniface, is indicative of how some English missionaries thought it natural and profitable to work closely with the Carolingians in Germany, as St Willibrord had done. The translation had the full approval of Pippin III. I do not, however, see that it can be represented as a betrayal of Boniface, since the translation took place *mediante Bonifatio archiepiscopo*; it had his approval, too.

Further south, it is possible to argue that Boniface did in practice find himself excluded by Carolingian encouragement of others. In Alamannia and Alsace, for example, from which he was not excluded by his papal brief, there were others at work with Carolingian support. Pre-eminently it was the mission field of St Pirmin,[4] who knew how to make the best of Burgundian-Alsatian family connections and cast his net far afield.[5] Nowhere else can we see so clearly the importance to Charles Martel of church support than in the reorganization of Alamannia; the gifts of land to the missionary centres of Reichenau and St Gallen lay far to their north, in Alamannic territory.[6] From these monasteries, rather than from bishoprics, the early Carolingians planned their control of the approaches to Bavaria. It may well be that in the Christian princess's grave at Wittislingen in eastern Alamannia we have evidence of the seventh- and eighth-century eastward expansion of Frankish Rhineland families into an area

---

[1] See H. Büttner, 'Mission und Kirchenorganisation des Frankenreiches bis zum Tode Karls des Grossen', *Karl der Grosse* I, 458.

[2] Kilian has left no literary traces at Würzburg. Cf. B. Bischoff and J. Hofmann, *Libri Sancti Kyliani* (Würzburg, 1952), p. 5.

[3] See J. Dienemann, *Der Kult des heiligen Kilian* (Würzburg, 1956); Karl Bosl, *Franken um 800* (Munich, 1959), pp. 88 and 98; 'Die Passio des heiligen Kilian und seiner Gefahrten', *Würzburger Diözesangeschichtsblätter* (1952), p. 1.

[4] For a general study see G. Jecker, 'St Pirmins Erden- und Ordensheimat', *Archiv für Mittelrheinische Kirchengeschichte* v (1953), 9–41.

[5] Cf. Ewig, 'Beobachtungen', *loc. cit.* pp. 70–1, and 'Descriptio Franciae', *Karl der Grosse* I, 174–5.

[6] Mayer, *op. cit.* pp. 303–25.

already rich in *Reihengräber*.[1] Perhaps Boniface excused himself from participation through pique or hostility to Pirmin: this might seem the more plausible if Pirmin were an Irishman and not a Spaniard, as he is generally held to have been. But it is just as likely that he felt he had enough to do elsewhere. Pirmin showed no hostility to the English and their known supporters, and none ought to be inferred from his collaboration with Chrodegang of Metz. The only Englishman who certainly had reservations about Chrodegang was Lul,[2] his unsuccessful rival for the succession to Boniface as archbishop. Plainly we cannot infer hostility to Boniface from Chrodegang's reforming colleague at St Denis, Fulrad (a Frankish aristocrat from the Mosel-Saar area),[3] since it was to him that Boniface addressed his plea for official protection of his disciples.[4]

Where, then, did hostility lie? One possible direction that may indicate others is the Irishman, Virgil of Salzburg. He was Pippin III's man in a real sense. He not only owed his see to Pippin's influence with the Bavarian duke, Odilo, but first spent two years at the Carolingian court; his Latin style bears strong traces of Frankish influence.[5] It is mostly in their learning that one sees the wide gulf between him and Boniface. From the so-called Cosmography of Aethicus Ister,[6] now recognized as Virgil's, emerges the proud and prickly mind of a master of the quadrivium, a lover of Greek thought and a geometrician, a despiser moreover of the narrower and more old-fashioned masters of the trivium, of whom the grammarian Boniface was a good example. The book is, among other things, a *reductio ad absurdum* of the traditionalist approach to antique literature that contented itself with Donatus and little else. However, the missionary aims of the two men were not incompatible; for Virgil, too, was a missionary (in Carinthia), and his work had papal approval. Moreover, the Bavarian church, for all its independence and despite its historical ties with the Franks, owed much to Boniface. The Cosmography is rather a cry of despair than of triumph, addressed to friends in Bavaria who thought too highly of the Englishman. There were other than intellectual reasons for mutual antipathy; they differed for example in their conception of the bishop's office. Belonging to the Irish tradition, Virgil preferred to operate as an abbot and left his episcopal functions for as long as he could

[1] See J. Werner, *Das Alamannische Fürstengrab von Wittislingen* (Munich, 1950).

[2] See Ewig, 'Descriptio Franciae', *op. cit.* p. 173.

[3] So Sprandel, *op. cit.* p. 97.

[4] *MGH, Epistolae Selectae* I, 212, Ep. 93.

[5] See H. Löwe, *Ein literarischer Widersacher des Bonifatius: Virgil von Salzburg und die Kosmographie des Aethicus Ister* (Akad. d. Wiss. und d. Lit., Mainz, 1951), p. 966 and *passim*; and B. Bischoff, 'Il monachesimo irlandese nei suoi rapporti col continente', Settimane di Spoleto 4 (1957), 130.

[6] Ed. (in part) by Krusch, *MGH, Script. Rer. Merov.* VII, 517ff.; in full, but unsatisfactorily, by H. Wuttke, *Die Kosmographie des Istriers Aithikos* (Leipzig, 1853).

to his Irish colleague Dobdagrecus.[1] Yet it would be wrong to represent him as an insurance policy taken out by Pippin III against Boniface and the English. The hostility did not stem from the Franks but from Virgil's Irish background; and to the Irish rather than to the Franks I should be inclined to attribute opposition to the English.

When it comes to evidence, there is nothing to show that the Carolingians ever withdrew the special protection accorded to Boniface by Charles Martel in a remarkable document;[2] a *peregrinus* acquires a *patronus*, a protector at law for his life and goods against those who could otherwise enslave or even kill him as a lordless man. Moreover, the Frankish *mundeburdium* implies not merely protection but authority over the protected.[3] It was probably accorded to other missionaries, English and Irish, in the same way. In the political sense, then, Boniface ceased to be a *peregrinus*; in the religious sense, he insisted to the end on the reality of his *peregrinatio*. In this, indeed, may lie something of his basic difficulty in relation to his Frankish masters: he desired always to stand apart. The cries of despair in his correspondence are caused less by specific grievances, though these do occur, than by constant self-reminders that he is an exile in the world, an old man among young men, not by choice a missionary who must make the best of what he finds but a pilgrim whose rôle is and must be to suffer. His idea of himself may well, as Eugen Ewig has suggested,[4] be derived from St Paul, whose apostleship was equally set in a world of pagans, *ignorami* and *falsi fratres*.[5] Boniface's authority was derived from Rome; his interpretation of it came from St Paul. It cannot be shown that his episcopal ordination in 726, which certainly alienated some of the bishops with jurisdiction east of the Rhine, ever alienated Charles Martel. Nor is it clear that Boniface's establishment of sees at Würzburg, Buraburg and Erfurt was possible only after Charles's death in October 741. Much turns on the dating of the *Concilium Germanicum* which Schieffer[6] and others would place in 743 instead of 742; for if the traditional date (supported by the texts) of 742 be correct, then the foundation of the bishoprics will almost certainly have been in the last months of Charles's life. 742 continues to find supporters.[7] Charles had much to gain

[1] Cf. Löwe, *op. cit.* p. 931.

[2] *MGH, Epistolae Selectae* I, 37–8, Ep. 22. See also the comments of F. L. Ganshof, 'L'Étranger dans la Monarchie Franque', *Recueils de la Société Jean Bodin* x (1958), 5–36, and Schieffer, *Winfrid-Bonifatius*, pp. 145–6.

[3] For examples see Marculf's Formulary I. 24 (p. 58) and *Additamenta*, no. 2 (p. 111).

[4] 'Milo', *op. cit.* p. 412.

[5] Boniface's *falsi fratres* were of several nationalities, to judge by their names: Frankish, Irish and English (perhaps Willibrord's men?).

[6] *Angelsachsen und Franken*, pp. 1463–71.

[7] E.g. Löwe in *Deutsches Archiv* xi (1955), 583–4, A. Bigelmair, 'Die Gründung der mitteldeutschen Bistümer', *Bon. Gedenkgabe*, pp. 271–3, and less positively Coens, *loc. cit.* pp. 489–90. It was also the opinion of Levison, pp. 80ff.

by helping Boniface east of the Rhine. They had a common interest in the Saxons, and it may be that Charles's failure in 738 to subdue them, and thus to open up to Boniface the mission field he really sought, caused both to think more seriously of holding-operations on Saxony's southern frontier in Hesse and Thuringia. Would it be going too far to connect this shift of effort with Boniface's disappointment over the see of Cologne?[1] The assumption is made that, at the last minute, Cologne was denied him through the machinations of the Frankish aristocrat-bishops; but an assumption it remains. Mainz, which in fact he obtained, had more to be said for it as a place from which to control the central German sees and to plan future advances into Saxon territory from Thuringia. Mainz was at least as important to Carloman and Pippin as it had been to Charles Martel; and they may in the end have placed Boniface where he could be of most use to them. Perhaps Boniface, too, could see the practical advantages of attempting the conversion of the Saxons from the direction of Thuringia. This also corresponded with the ultimate intentions of the papacy; and if Echternach was originally intended as a mission centre rather than as a retreat, Willibrord too had had some such idea. This, rather than personal animosity or unwillingness to work close with the Franks, is the likeliest reason why Boniface declined to succeed Willibrord in his Frisian mission: there was more to be said for a base in the Middle Rhine area.

In the last resort, the case against Charles Martel as an opponent of Boniface rests on his general reputation as a despoiler of church property. That he was such on a massive scale cannot be disputed. But this is to put the matter too baldly. It may be significant that Boniface himself, who did not hesitate to castigate King Æthelbald of Mercia for the same sin,[2] brought no such charge against Charles.[3] Nor indeed could it easily have been brought so far as the German territories known to Boniface were concerned, since the spoliations were confined to traditional Frankish-controlled territory: Burgundy, Provence, Aquitaine, and the regions of the Meuse, Seine, Loire, and the Austrasian Rhineland. Within these areas, as Lesne has shown,[4] the spoliation was haphazard, affecting both rich and poor communities. It was, in Lesne's words, *sans doute le produit spontané du*

---

[1] *MGH, Epistolae Selectae* I, 235–6, Ep. 109 might suggest that Boniface's interest in Cologne was bound up with the problem of Utrecht. Zacharius's letter to Boniface of 31 October 745 does not state that this was why he had done as the Franks asked in the first place and appointed him to Cologne (*ibid.* p. 124, Ep. 60). On the matter generally see *Geschichte... Köln* I, 144, and Büttner, *Karl der Grosse* I, 465.

[2] *MGH, Epistolae Selectae* I, 152, Ep. 73: 'multa privilegia ecclesiarum et monasteriorum fregisses et abstulisses inde quasdam facultates.' See also *ibid.* p. 169, Ep. 78.

[3] An addition to Boniface's letter (*ibid.* Ep. 73) adds the name of Charles Martel as an example of a spoliator, and this is the earliest known charge against him. The author of the first detailed charge is Hincmar of Reims (*MGH, Script. Rer. Merov.* III, 252).

[4] *La Propriété Ecclésiastique en France* II (2), 263. Lesne's extended treatment of Charles Martel's policy towards church property is *ibid.* II (1).

*désordre*,[1] and as such was resorted to not only by Charles but by many of his contemporaries, to say nothing of Franks of an earlier time. Like them, he was a benefactor as well as a despoiler: many churches and monasteries could have borne witness to this. His problem was that of a conqueror of a land long prone to disorder and self-help. He had not merely to reward his faithful followers[2] but to dispose of close-knit nuclei of secular and church lands held by former opponents. The situation he faced but did not create in Neustria and Burgundy was at every turn bound up with church property: with the collapse of secular local authority, bishops had assumed control of large areas which they ruled in effect as ecclesiastical republics. Just such a situation greeted St Wilfrid when he stayed with the bishop of Lyons.[3] A notable case of a bishop who took every opportunity to feather his own nest was that of Savaric of Auxerre.[4] Other prince-bishops enjoyed a better reputation; for example, Charles Martel's own nephew, Hugo of Rouen, was remembered at St Wandrille as a great benefactor.[5] His successors, Grimo and Ragenfrid, left less savoury local reputations, yet were known elsewhere as friends to reform. As and when Charles Martel overcame huge ecclesiastical communities that were hostile to him, it followed that the conglomerations of secular and church estates that formed them would lose much – and most in the areas where secular power had collapsed longest.[6] He cannot be blamed for seeing the situation politically; indeed, without his ruthless restoration of secular power, the ecclesiastical reforms of his sons could never have taken place. Their very half-heartedness is proof of the difficulty of reversing the slow decline of generations. Carloman himself acknowledged as much when he admitted that he could not carry out the full restitutions anticipated by Boniface.[7] Francia was still on a war-footing, and to have deprived his father's followers of their offices and lands would have been madness – and in many cases unnecessary.[8] In fact, however, Boniface seems to have been less concerned about questions of property than about vacant sees and unworthy holders of church offices.[9] As a firm upholder of the principle of a national church protected by its ruler, he expected the Carolingians to exercise more, not less, authority in the choice of suitable bishops and

[1] *Ibid.* II (1), 2.
[2] There is no evidence for the oft-repeated statement that Charles needed lands to enfeoff cavalry to meet the Arab threat.
[3] Eddius, chs. 4 and 6.
[4] For which see Ewig, 'Milo', *op. cit.* p. 427.
[5] *Gesta Sanctorum Patrum Fontanellensium*, ed. Lohier and Laporte (Rouen–Paris, 1936), ch. 8.
[6] Cf. Ewig, 'Milo', *op. cit.* pp. 434–8.
[7] *MGH, Epistolae Selectae* I, 123, Ep. 60.
[8] W. Goffart, *The Le Mans Forgeries* (Harvard, 1966), pp. 6–22, has argued that Charles Martel's successors pursued a policy of *divisio* based on the actual needs of the churches and monasteries that had suffered deprivation. This may well be true; but it needs further investigation.
[9] The point was made by Lesne, *op. cit.* II (1), 34–5.

abbots; and so, in due course, they did. Thus, reform of the kind Boniface championed was not in principle distasteful to any of the Carolingian princes he knew; but it was impossible as an immediate objective. Its reverberations echoed down the entire ninth century.

Research since the days of Levison has done nothing to dim the splendour of Boniface's achievement; it was greater than that of any other missionary of his time. What research has done is to reveal the complexity of the situation he faced, the varieties of Christian experience already available in the lands of his mission, and the difficulties of the men who supported him. These, and not hostility, were the forces to which he was a martyr.[1]

[1] This article was completed before the publication of D. A. Bullough's '*Europae Pater*: Charlemagne and his Achievement in the Light of Recent Scholarship', *EHR* LXXXV (1970), 59–105, where valuable observations on the Rhineland families will be found.

# Evidence for contacts between the churches of the Irish and English from the Synod of Whitby to the Viking Age

## KATHLEEN HUGHES

Every student of history knows of the close relations which existed between the English and Irish churches before the Synod of Whitby. My readers will be familiar with much, if not all, of the evidence for continued contacts in the late seventh, eighth and early ninth centuries, for all the material I have used is published and most of it has been discussed. Nevertheless, I hope it may be useful to have the references put together. They demonstrate the intimacy and frequency of contacts and serve to put other problems into focus: when, for instance, we see English foundations flourishing in Ireland or an Irishman as master of an English scriptorium, then disputes about the provenance of certain manuscripts appear in a rather different guise. Much of the material relates to Ireland and Northumbria; but there is also a considerable amount about Ireland and the great central area of England, little about the south. This may be partly due to the distribution of historical records during the period under review.

Contacts between England and Ireland were, of course, well established before the Synod of Whitby. Early in the century Laurentius, archbishop of Canterbury, had written to the Irish urging them to conform with the practices of Rome, after an Irish bishop, Dagan, had visited him and refused to eat with him and his clergy.[1] Fursey arrived from Ireland into East Anglia some time after Sigeberht began to reign there in 630 or 631. There must have been an Irish community here, for we read of Fursey's brothers Foillán and Ultán and of the priests Gobbán and Dícuil. King Anna, who died in 654, further endowed Fursey's monastery at *Cnoberesburg*.[2] Oswald and twelve of his thegns in their exile had received Christianity from the Irish and when Oswald became king of Northumbria he sent to Iona for a bishop.[3] Aidán arrived with other Irishmen before the end of 634, and the mission to the English was begun.

---

[1] *HE* ii. 4.        [2] *HE* iii. 19.

[3] *Adamnán's Life of Columba*, ed. A. O. and M. O. Anderson (London, 1961) i. 1, says that Columba prophesied victory in a dream to Oswald the night before his battle with Cadwallon. He also makes it clear that Oswald visited Iona after the battle.

Bede makes it abundantly clear that the decisions in favour of Roman practice at the Synod of Whitby in 664 caused no disruption of communications. The southern half of Ireland had in any case conformed to Roman observance in the early 630s, and the Gaulish bishop Agilbert, who attended the Synod of Whitby as a member of the Roman party, 'had spent a long time in Ireland for the purpose of studying the scriptures' before he became bishop of the West Saxons.[1] There were Englishmen over in Ireland at the time. Young men had been in the habit of going there for study and devotion: their successors were still going later in the century when Aldhelm addressed his defence of English schools to Eanfrith, who had himself just returned home after six years in Ireland, or when he warned Wihtfrith, who was about to set out to Ireland in the pursuit of learning.[2] Egbert was there when the plague broke out in 664 and vowed, if he was spared, never to return home: his friend Æthelhun had gone out with him, and Æthelhun's brother Æthelwine followed them, later to return as bishop of Lindsey.[3] Hygebald, 'an abbot in the province of Lindsey', went there to visit Egbert.[4] Aldfrith was an exile 'among the islands of the Irish for the study of letters', possibly at Iona; he made a considerable impact on Irish traditions, which accorded him the Irish name of Flann Fina.[5] Wihtberht, the two Hewalds and Willibrord all left on their continental missions after long periods of residence in Ireland.[6]

The Irish mission had come not only to Northumbria, but also further south. Diuma and Cellach, the first two bishops of the Middle Angles and Mercians, were both Irishmen; the third, Trumhere, was an Englishman who had received bishop's orders from the Irish;[7] the fifth, Chad, had spent some time as a young man in an Irish monastery.[8] Between 657 and 674 Wulfhere, king of the Mercians, granted land at Hanbury to an abbot with the Irish name of Colmán and to whomsoever he might choose as his heir, if we may trust Patrick Young's record of a charter which was at Worcester in 1622.[9] We hear of Maíldubh founder of Malmesbury, of the Irish students before Theodore,[10] of the Irishman who asked for teaching

---

[1] *HE* III. 7 and 25.
[2] *HE* III. 27. *MGH, Auct. Antiq.* xv, 488 ff. and 479. Cynefrith, brother of Ceolfrith of Jarrow, was one who resigned his abbacy to go to Ireland for sacred studies; Plummer, *Bede* I, 388.
[3] *HE* III. 27.      [4] *HE* IV. 12.
[5] Bede's *Life of Cuthbert* (*Two Lives of St Cuthbert*, ed. B. Colgrave [Cambridge, 1940]), ch. 24. See Plummer's note in *Bede* II, 263–4. Also R. Flower, *The Irish Tradition*, pp. 12–13. Cf. F. Henry, *JRSAI* xcv (1965), 55.
[6] *HE* III. 13 and v. 9 and 10. Alcuin, *Life of Willibrord* (*MGH, Script. Rer. Merov.* VII, 118–19), ch. 4. An Irish monk wrote a Life soon after his death; J. F. Kenney, *Sources for the Early History of Ireland* (Columbia, 1929), p. 233.
[7] *HE* III. 24.      [8] *HE* IV. 3.
[9] Printed by Hearne in his edition of Hemming, p. 567; see Finberg, *ECWM*, p. 86. Since Colmán is a common Irish name, reliable identification is impossible.
[10] Ehwald, *MGH, Auct. Antiq.* xv, 492–3.

and the loan of a book from Aldhelm,[1] of Dicuil following the monastic life with five or six others at Bosham in Sussex.[2]

After the Synod of Whitby Bishop Colmán left Lindisfarne with the Irish and about thirty English monks, went first to Iona, then on to Inishbofin, an island off the coast of Connacht. The English and Irish soon fell out and Colmán obtained a site inland at Mayo, to which the English monks transferred. By Bede's day it had grown very large and it maintained its English connections throughout the eighth century;[3] Conal Mac Geoghagan, who translated the Annals of Clonmacnoise in 1627, says it is called Mayo of the English 'to this day'.[4] The first mention of Mayo in the Irish annals records the death of Garaalt, bishop, in 732. Gerald is not an Old Irish name, but Garuald and Geruald occur in the Durham *Liber Vitae*.[5] Mrs Chadwick suggests that the obit of Gerald is a Norman interpolation;[6] but even if we discard the evidence of the annals he still occurs *cum suis* in the Martyrology of Tallaght of about the year 800 and in a litany of about the same period as *Garald epscop* in *Mag Eo na Saxan*.[7] If Gerald's name in the Irish annals is, as I believe, the Hibernicized form of an Englishman's name we do not need the theory that the name of a thirteenth-century lay patron of Mayo was substituted in several independent texts for that of an early abbot, for all the early evidence fits together in mutual support.

By Gerald's time Mayo, of which Bede wrote so warmly a year earlier, was an episcopal see, presumably in the Roman manner, for Bede declares that 'all things have long since been brought under a better method'. Hadwine, who ruled 768–73, was also a bishop: both Simeon and the Irish annals record him as such, though the Irish annals have Hibernicized his name as Aedán. His successor was Leudfrith, the correspondent of Alcuin.[8] By 786 it seems clear that Mayo regarded itself as under the metropolitan jurisdiction of York, for in that year bishop Ealdwulf was consecrated at Corbridge by Eanbald, archbishop of York, assisted by Tilberht of Hexham and Hygebald of Lindisfarne, and later in the year signed at a great council of the northern province in the presence of the pope's legate George, bishop of Ostia: 'I, Ealdwulf, bishop of the church of Mayo, have subscribed with devout will.'[9] Alcuin clearly regarded Mayo as an English community, living according to English custom.[10]

---

[1] *Ibid.* p. 494.    [2] *HE* iv. 13.
[3] *HE* iv. 4; Symeon of Durham, *Historia Regum*, ed. T. Arnold, Rolls Series (1885), chs. 46, 47 and 53. Mrs Chadwick discussed Mayo in *Celt and Saxon* (Cambridge, 1963), pp. 186–209.
[4] Ed. D. Murphy (Dublin, 1896), p. 9.
[5] As Miss Susan Evans pointed out to me.    [6] *Op. cit.* pp. 197, 201, 203 and 205.
[7] C. Plummer, *Irish Litanies* (London, 1925), p. 56.
[8] *MGH, Epistolae* iv, 19.    [9] *Councils* iii, 460.
[10] 'Ideo, karissimi fratres, confortamini in Domino et viriliter state, locum certaminis vestri non deserentes...Regularem vitam, a sanctis patribus vestris vobis statutam, omni studio con-

Mrs Chadwick has suggested that Mayo became an exponent of the Roman order in Ireland. She means primarily of the Roman Easter and suggests that at the end of the seventh century Egbert, Adamnán and the church of Mayo were in active contact. This may be true, though the English monks had left home as enemies of the Roman Easter; but the real point of interest is that by the 730s Mayo must have been supporting not only the Roman Easter (like the rest of Ireland by this time) but also a bishop who was administrative as well as sacramental head of the church and who later in the century attended a metropolitical council of the province of York. English church councils, from the Synod of Hertford on, were insisting on the diocesan structure of the church; the bishop is to keep to his own diocese, the clergy are not to wander about without letters of introduction from their own bishop, synods are to be held, monks are to remain stable under their own abbots. Theodore denied the validity of orders imposed by Irish or British bishops 'who are not Catholic with respect to Easter and the tonsure' and required reconsecration by a 'Catholic bishop'.[1] The synods of the Irish *Romani* say much the same thing: bishops are not to invade the sees of their fellows, strangers must bring letters of recommendation, synods are to be the court of appeal in ecclesiastical cases.[2] They warn against the Britons 'who in all things are contrary and cut themselves off from Roman custom and the unity of the church'. As late as the early eighth century Irish clerics were collecting and recording such rulings, and, though the diocesan structure of the church was in general superseded by the system of monastic *paruchiae*, such a place as Mayo must have kept a church under an English-style bishop before the eyes of Irishmen at home at least during the eighth century. The early Irish, to whom standardization was never a requirement, seem to have been content to regard Mayo as part of an English *paruchia*.[3]

It is almost certain that Mayo was not the only English foundation in Ireland. Alcuin, in his verse history of the northern province, says that Egbert went to Ireland with Wihtberht as a companion and there 'built for monks of his own race a distinguished fold'.[4] Mrs Chadwick suggests

servare nitimini...luceat lux vestra in medio nationis perbarbarae...Et domnum episcopum habete quasi patrem in omni reverentia et dilectione. Et ille vos gubernet et vestram regat vitam cum omni timore in conspectu Dei' (*MGH, Epistolae* IV, 446).

[1] II *Theod.* IX. 1: *Councils* III, 197.

[2] For these and other Roman rulings see K. Hughes, *The Church in Early Irish Society* (London, 1966), pp. 130–1; cf. pp. 124–6.

[3] Plummer's Litany of Irish Saints 1 (*Irish Litanies*, p. 56) speaks of 'three thousands and three hundreds with Gerald the bishop and fifty saints of Luigne of Connacht who took Mayo of the Saxons'. The name Luigne survives in the modern barony of Leyny, to the north of Mayo. Does this imply that Mayo, at some time after 786, went over to the normal Irish monastic form of organization? It drops out of the English records and, as Mr Smyth points out to me, did not eventually become the centre for an eleventh-century diocese.

[4] *The Historians of the Church of York*, ed. J. Raine, Rolls Series (1879–94) I, 379. I owe this reference to Miss Evans.

that Mayo was Egbert's base, and that he may even have been the founder of that house. But this would really necessitate rejecting Bede's account, and moreover, Alcuin, who was in close touch with Mayo and corresponded with its abbot, gives no hint that Bede's account needs such emendation. It seems much more likely that Colmán founded Mayo, as Bede says he did, and that Egbert built a different house. If so, this must have been governed by a bishop and Egbert was remembered as such in Ireland as well as in England, for his name appears among the signatories of the Synod of Birr (697) as *Ichtbricht epscop*.[1] He is given a stanza in the Martyrology of Oengus, written *c.* 800, at 8 December:

> The triumph of humble Egbert,[2]
> who came over the great sea:
> To Christ he sang a prayer
> in a hideless coracle.[3]

The later glossators could not decide on his house. They offer various suggestions, *vel in alio loco diversi diverse sentiunt*: but they mention places at which there must have been an English community; Tulach Leis of the Saxons in Munster and another house under a brother, Tech Saxan in Huí Echach of Munster. Both these (if they are not one and the same) are in the area which had accepted the Roman Easter in the 630s and are therefore quite possible places in which Romanizing Englishmen might settle. A litany of Irish saints, of about the same period as the Martyrology of Oengus, commemorates 'the Saxons in Rigair', and 'the Saxons in Cluain Mucceda',[4] and we hear of 'the third of the Saxons' among the various areas at Armagh. It looks as if, round about 800, there were various groups of Englishmen in Ireland who were afterwards forgotten. Where were those churches in Ireland to which Alfred, Asser tells us, sometimes sent gifts?[5] There is no evidence that they were English foundations, but they might well have been.

Throughout this period Englishmen went to Ireland, but Irishmen also came to England. Adamnán, the great abbot of Iona who was in constant touch with Ireland, paid two visits to Northumbria. Bede speaks of him in

---

[1] I am not making any claim to the contemporary authenticity of this witness-list, though most of the signatories belong to the right period.

[2] *Ichbrichtán*. The *án* is a diminutive ending. He is in the Martyrology of Tallaght at 18 March, *Ericbirt Saxonis*. See Plummer's note on Egbert, *Bede* II, 285.

[3] A curragh without hides is very odd. Is the poet saying that he came over in a wooden boat, probably of English construction?

[4] For a discussion of the litany see K. Hughes, *Analecta Bollandiana* LXXVII (1959), 305–31, and E. G. Bowen, *Studia Celtica* IV (1969), 68–9, where he provides a distribution map of the sites mentioned showing a mainly south-eastward concentration.

[5] Asser, ch. 102. And where was Bealdhun's community to whose 'southern brothers' Alcuin sent alms via the Irishman Colcu? *MGH, Epistolae* IV, 33–4; Whitelock, *EHD*, pp. 774–5. Was it in England or in Ireland?

a rather condescending way, recognizing him as 'a good and wise man and remarkably learned in holy scripture', but saying that in Northumbria he was 'earnestly admonished by many who were more learned than himself'.[1] This should not blind us to Adamnán's quality, both as scholar and statesman. His first visit to Northumbria, after the battle of Nechtanesmere, was to visit 'our friend King Aldfrith',[2] who had lived among the Irish during his exile, and his purpose was, in part at least, to secure the freedom of captives taken from Ireland in Berht's raid of 684:[3] *Adomnanus captivos reduxit ad Hiberniam* read the Annals of Ulster, and the Annals of Tigernach say there were sixty of them. Persuaded in Northumbria that the Roman Easter was the true and proper date, he put all his efforts towards bringing northern Ireland and Iona to conform with the custom of the rest of western Christendom. Throughout northern Ireland (the south had already conformed) he was largely successful, but the *paruchia Columbae* held out until persuaded by Egbert. It seems very likely that Adamnán inspired the 'Law' which bears his name, though the earliest text is of the eighth century. The annals say it was promulgated in 697 and it was followed by a long series of comparable laws ending in 842; laws requiring the co-operation of provincial kings and ecclesiastics, aimed originally at protecting women, children, clerics and church property from violence. The man who went to Northumbria and brought back the Irish captives may well have had the vision and humanity to institute such measures.

On his second visit to Northumbria Adamnán presented King Aldfrith with his book *De Locis Sanctis*[4] of which Bede strongly approved and from which he quoted at length. The Life of Columba is, however, Adamnán's longer work. Although this is hagiography, written to glorify the patron, it is characterized by accuracy, detailed information and considerable moderation. Adamnán sometimes tried to indicate from whom his evidence came and through how many intermediaries it had passed before it reached him;[5] he did not make untrue claims to enhance the reputation of his hero.[6] He was primarily interested in the saint's prophecies, miracles and visions but he conveys, incidentally, a considerable amount of historical information of great value. Professor Bullough has demonstrated the similarities between Adamnán's Life of Columba and the anonymous Life of Cuthbert written by a Lindisfarne monk a few years later between 699 and 705. Both cite the Life of Antony, the Life of Martin and the Acts of Silvester, both use a similar version of the psalter, both show striking

---

[1] *HE* v. 15. Cf. Ceolfrith's comment, *ibid.* v. 21.
[2] *Adamnán's Life of Columba*, II. 46.
[3] *HE* IV. 26.                     [4] Ed. D. Meehan (Dublin, 1958).
[5] See long footnote, Hughes, *op. cit.* p. 61, for examples.
[6] E.g. he does *not* say that the Pictish king Bruide was converted by Columba's preaching.

parallels of phrasing. Professor Bullough asks whether the texts used by the Lindisfarne monk may not have reached him via Iona.[1] If so, there was Irish influence on our earliest extant piece of original English writing.

It seems very probable, moreover, that Adamnán was responsible for the expansion which took place in the Iona Chronicle from about 672. In a recent article Dr John Bannerman has argued convincingly that an Iona Chronicle was incorporated into the Irish annals *c.* 740, that certain types of entries characterize the Iona material and that records of Pictish, North British and English events between 563 and 740 probably reached the Irish annals via this channel.[2] It is worth adding that after 672 the entries increase in volume and kind. Up to this date nearly all the entries are laconic notices of deaths, battles, burnings and sieges, with the foundation of three churches (Lindisfarne, Rechru and Inishbofin), a wonder (*terremotus in Brittania*) and two voyages.[3] After 672 these entries are carried on in more detail, and further types of entries are added such as the visits of Iona abbots to Ireland. If the presumed 'Iona Chronicle' entries are isolated from the rest of the Irish annals, we find that between 563 and 672 few years have more than one entry and sixty-six years have no entry at all:[4] between 672 and 740 only twelve years are blank, thirty-four years have more than one entry, some have three or four different events recorded for one year. Adamnán became abbot in 679. By 672 he must have held an important position in the abbey, and I regard him as very probably responsible for this developing interest in annal writing at Iona.[5] He was not the last Iona abbot to show an interest in history: the ninth- or tenth-century Chartres manuscript of Nennius, whose text dates from the early ninth century, says, when dating the English arrival in Britain, *sicut Libine abasiae inripum civitate invenit vel reperit*.[6] The man who discovered this date at Ripon is therefore Sléibíne, abbot of Iona 752–67, someone interested, as a historian must be, in chronology.

Ripon is not far from York, and it seems extremely likely that Sléibíne may have visited York also, for at this time the school there was famous. Alcuin became its master in 766 before proceeding to Charlemagne's court, perhaps in 782; his correspondence reveals Irishmen among his friends and pupils. Writing on the continent, he says he had frequently met

[1] D. A. Bullough, *Scottish Historical Review* XLIII (1964), 129–30.
[2] *Scottish Gaelic Studies* XI (1968), 149–70. Cf. T. F. O'Rahilly, *Early Irish History and Mythology* (Dublin, 1946), pp. 253 ff. and Isabel Henderson, *The Picts* (London, 1967), pp. 165 ff.
[3] I am inclined to distrust the exceptions: 574 after the note of Conall's death, *qui obtulit insolam Iae Columbe Cille* and 624 *Nativitas Adomnani abbatis Iae*.
[4] Though fifteen of these should probably be discounted, since there is a complete blank between 606 and 621.
[5] There is another extant work attributed to Adamnán, which belongs to the right period, a commentary on Virgil for use in the monastic schools. See Kenney, *Sources*, pp. 286–7.
[6] F. Lot, *Nennius et l'Historia Brittonum* (Paris, 1934) I, 228.

Irishmen while he was in his own land.[1] One of his correspondents was an Irish teacher named Colcu, who seems to have been at York in the year 790.[2] Another was Joseph, a pupil both of Colcu and of Alcuin himself, almost certainly to be identified with the *Joseph abbas Scottus* who wrote several poems.[3] Alcuin wrote two stanzas commemorating certain Irish saints, Patrick, Ciarán, Columba, Comgall, Adamnán and the two women Brigit and Íte,[4] but his information here may have come not via York but directly from Irishmen on the continent.

Some Irishmen came to stay in England. Early in the eighth century one named Ultán was scribe at a cell of Lindisfarne.[5] 'He was a blessed priest of the Irish race', says Æthelwulf in a poem composed between 803 and 821, 'he could ornament books with fair marking, and by this art he accordingly made the shape of the letters beautiful one by one, so that no modern scribe could equal him.' He entered the monastery 'and mingled with the blessed bands and moulded the monks in holy living, being keen of intellect and chaste in feelings, words, body and mind. He taught the brothers, so that they might seize the light above...' Ultán sounds like the master of the scriptorium. His house remained in contact with Ireland. Towards the end of the century the poet, in a dream, saw the face of his former teacher, Eadfrith, 'a face from Ireland...He was a priest, who was seen as I then saw him with head bent in prayer, venerating in piety the blessed tomb of Cuthbert.'[6] Eadfrith was either an Irishman who had taken an English name, or, more probably as it seems to me, an Englishman trained in Ireland in one of the English foundations there. We can see a very probable illustration of a manuscript written in England by an Irish scribe in the eighth-century Pauline Epistles, now split up in Cambridge, Trinity College B.10.5 and BM Cotton Vitellius C.viii, where numerous interlinear glosses and marginalia have been added by contemporary and somewhat later Anglo-Saxon hands.[7]

Mercia also seems to have had its Irish residents, for between 793 and 796 Charlemagne wrote to Offa asking him to recall an Irish priest to his home diocese for judgement. This must presumably have been somewhere under Offa's control, for the letter asks Offa to order the priest 'to take himself to his own country that he may be judged there, from whence he came', and it is difficult to see what control Offa could have had over a priest in Cologne who was Irish, had come from Ireland, and was to be

[1] *MGH, Epistolae* IV, 445.
[2] *Ibid.* pp. 32–4.
[3] *Ibid.* pp. 483–4 and 33–4; *MGH, Poetae* I, 150–9. See Kenney, *Sources*, pp. 534–6.
[4] *MGH, Poetae* I, 342.
[5] *Æthelwulf De Abbatibus*, ed. A. Campbell (Oxford, 1967), p. 19.
[6] *Ibid.* p. 59.
[7] *CLA* II, no. 133. This manuscript was at Durham in 1391.

ordered to return there.[1] However, much the best evidence for the activity of Irish clerics in Mercia in the early ninth century comes from the rulings of the Council of Chelsea, held in 816 and attended by the Southumbrian bishops and the king and aristocracy of the Mercians.[2] This levels a very heavy attack against Irish bishops and thereby proves conclusively that they had been ministering in sufficient force to provoke strong opposition.

At the end of the tenth century Dunstan's biographer and disciple describes a colony of Irish scholars at Glastonbury, scholars by whom Dunstan had been taught early in the century. They were well established, with books, which Dunstan diligently studied, and they 'cherished that place of Glastonbury...with great affection, especially in honour of the blessed Patrick the Younger (*Patricii Junioris*), who is said to rest there happily in the Lord.'[3] When this Life was revised at Canterbury some time before 1050 Patrick *Senior* was substituted, and it is he who appears in the tenth-century Glastonbury Missal, commemorated at 24 August with a proper mass, while Patrick the bishop occurs at 17 March with a common.[4] Patrick Senior is also commemorated in the Irish Martyrology of Oengus, written *c.* 800, with a later gloss saying that he is 'in Glastonbury of the Gaels, that is a city in the south of England, and Irishmen used to dwell there.'[5] How far back this Irish connection with Glastonbury goes it is impossible to say. The archaeological evidence is difficult to interpret, but Mr Philip Rahtz sees the early settlement on Glastonbury Tor, with its meat bones, not as a hermit site but as the stronghold of a local chieftain.[6] Dr Raleigh Radford dates the foundation of the Christian settlement in the valley to the period before the Saxon conquest in the mid seventh century, on the evidence of wattled oratories and two mausolea.[7] He may well be right, but the closest parallels for the mausolea are with seventh-century Gaul, and how does one decide whether the post-holes of wattled buildings (for which no full plan can be recovered) were made by English or Irishmen? Dr Radford finds it difficult to believe that the cult of St Indracht, a rare saint, was introduced after the Saxon conquest, but Dr Finberg has shown good reason for believing that it was,[8] for Indracht may well be the coarb of Columcille of that name who was martyred among the Saxons.[9] Medieval historians elaborated the Glastonbury legend[10] and by the four-

---

[1] *MGH, Epistolae* IV, 131. Quoted by J. M. Wallace-Hadrill in *Karl der Grosse* (I, 691); cf. Kenney, *Sources*, p. 529.
[2] *Councils* III, 581; see below, p. 64.
[3] W. Stubbs, *Memorials of St Dunstan*, Rolls Series 63 (1874), 10; Whitelock, *EHD*, p. 826.
[4] F. A. Gasquet and E. Bishop, *The Bosworth Psalter* (London, 1908), p. 18.
[5] *The Martyrology of Oengus the Culdee*, ed. Whitley Stokes, HBS 29 (1905), 188.
[6] *The Quest for Arthur's Britain*, ed. G. Ashe (London, 1968), p. 148.
[7] *Ibid.* p. 131.    [8] *Irish Ecclesiastical Record* 5th ser. CVII (1967), 358.
[9] In 854, which is the date derived from the Annals of Ulster, not 852 as Dr Finberg says.
[10] See J. Armitage Robinson, *Somerset Historical Essays* (London, 1921) and *Two Glastonbury Legends* (Cambridge, 1926).

teenth century Glastonbury owned a considerable number of relics of Irish saints. The unpublished relic list in BM Titus D.vii, fols. 1–15 names Patrick, Benén (and a disciple), Indracht *cum sociis*, Ultán, Fursey *cum sociis*, Brigit and Columcille as well as Welsh and Cornish saints; but it is quite possible that the early Irish element was small and that relics of Celtic saints were discovered and acquired after the age of Dunstan, or even after the great fire of 1184. So much hypothesis, medieval and modern, has been written about the Irish at Glastonbury, that one is tempted to sweep the whole away as inadequately founded. Dr Finberg's conjecture is that the Irish school at Glastonbury was opened under Alfred the Great.[1] We should, however, remember that tenth-century Irish scholars were drawn there by the cult of Patrick and that some early Irish monk at Glastonbury is a likely possibility. Moreover archaeological evidence, though so far inconclusive, may yet prove a decisive factor.

Since there was frequent contact between Irish and English it is not surprising to find some similarity between the accepted ideas and expressions of both peoples. We have already noted Adamnán's interest in visions and prophecies. The best known of the early visions is that of Fursey, the Irishman settled in East Anglia, who had been trained from boyhood in the ecclesiastical schools of Ireland, and had taught there for 'many years' before coming to England.[2] Bede had the Life of St Fursey and gave a short account of his two visions. Another Irishman, Adamnán of Coldingham, who had been under the spiritual direction of a priest of his own people who subsequently returned to Ireland, received a prophetic vision of the disaster which was to overtake that monastery.[3] The Englishman, Dryhthelm, a man 'of such simplicity and indifferent wit', after his vision, retired to lead the ascetic life at Melrose; his neighbouring hermit Hæmgisl subsequently went to live in Ireland.[4] Æthelwulf in his poem recounts three visions, and Professor Campbell comments on the important part which birds play as the messengers of heaven, drawing parallels with the Irish voyage of the Uí Corra and the Voyage of Brendan.[5] This poem also uses the phrase *castra beorum*,[6] the Irish *tír na mbéo* or land of the *semper viventes*.

Many of these travellers demonstrate in practice the idea of pilgrimage, so finely expressed in the sermons of Columbanus. For the pilgrim abandoned the security of his kin and the privileges which status gave in aristocratic society to become 'a guest of the world'.[7] A similar idea of

---

[1] *Loc. cit.* p. 351.　　　　　　　　　　　　　[2] *HE* III. 19.
[3] *HE* IV. 25. It was destroyed by fire.　　　　[4] *HE* V. 12.
[5] *Op. cit.* pp. xxxiff.; cf. Hughes, *op. cit.* p. 186 for the delightful glosses on the Martyrology of Tallaght.
[6] Wulfsige 'accompanied by shining birds...entered the blessed dwellings of the living' (*op. cit.* p. 47).
[7] Cf. Hughes, 'The Changing Theory and Practice of Irish Pilgrimage', *JEH* XI (1960), 143–51.

pilgrimage recurs by implication in *The Seafarer* (as Professor Whitelock has shown), in the name Oftfor, 'the much journeyed', and in Boniface's description of himself as *exul Germanicus*. One of the most typical of the ascetic writings of Columbanus on the theme of rejecting all the amenities of the world is his third sermon: *Ne parcas caducis, ne aeterna perdas; alienus tibi totus mundus est, qui nudus natus nudus sepeliris.*[1] This sermon is quoted at length, with a fragment of the seventh sermon, in a letter of Alhfrith the anchorite to Hygelac, lector of the cell of Lindisfarne under abbot Sigewine, who began his rule probably in 771.[2] It must have made a strong appeal to the minds of Hiberno-Saxon pilgrims.

The pilgrims sometimes took their books with them, as we can see from the glosses and commentaries in their manuscripts. The script and decoration of the incomplete psalter in MS Vatic. Palat. Lat. 68 'point to Ireland',[3] and it has eighth-century glosses in both Irish and English: the English commentator is named, *Edilberict filius Berictfridi*, and the commentary seems to be derived in part from a Latin summary of Theodore of Mopsuestia attributed to Columbanus.[4] The Rushworth Gospels were written by the Irishman MacRegol and glossed in tenth-century Anglo-Saxon.[5] The Gospels of MacDurnan, most probably to be associated with Mael-Brigte mac Tornáin, who died in 927 'head of the piety of all Ireland', were subsequently given to Canterbury by King Athelstan.[6]

Since books travelled with people it is possible to cite examples of Irish texts influencing English writings. Professor Cross has drawn my attention to several such instances. The Old English Martyrology, the Latin exemplar of which was written in Mercia before 800,[7] quotes Arculf's account of the church of the Ascension on the Mount of Olives.[8] It also uses the *De Ordine Creaturarum*, a work which was produced in a scriptorium with strong Irish connections:[9] Professor Cross cites verbal and conceptual correspondences in an article soon to be published. The provenance of the *De Ordine Creaturarum*, Irish or Northumbrian, is not certain, but it uses a text which was assuredly Irish, the mid-seventh-century pseudo-Augustine's *De Mirabilibus Sacrae Scripturae*,[10] and in its turn was used by Bede in his

[1] Ed. G. S. M. Walker, *Sancti Columbani Opera* (Dublin, 1957), pp. 76–8.
[2] Levison, p. 297ff., regards this as an original composition of Hygelac, but a considerable part of it comes word for word from Columbanus.
[3] *CLA* I, no. 78.
[4] Ramsay, *Zeitschrift für celtische Philologie* VIII (1912), 428.
[5] *CLA* II, no. 231. MacRegol is most probably the abbot of Birr who died in 822.
[6] Kenney, *Sources*, pp. 644–5; J. Armitage Robinson, *The Times of St Dunstan* (Oxford, 1923), pp. 55–9.     [7] C. Sisam, *RES* n.s. IV (1953), 212–14.
[8] Ed. G. Herzfeld, EETS o.s. 116 (London, 1900), 74–6; cf. *Adamnani De Locis Sanctis*, ed. Meehan, pp. 64–8. See also J. E. Cross, *Neuphilologische Mitteilungen* LXX (1969), 235–8.
[9] M. C. Diaz y Diaz, *Sacris Erudiri* V (1953), 147–66. This article is in Spanish, and I am indebted to Professor Cross for an indication of its contents.
[10] *Ibid.*

*De Natura Rerum.*[1] Another seventh-century Irish tract, *De Duodecim Abusivis Saeculi*, seems to have been current in England. There appears to be an allusion to the ninth abuse, that of the unrighteous king, in the Englishman Cathwulf's letter to Charlemagne.[2] Cathwulf's letter is a very interesting one elaborating his theory of kingship, and he attributes this passage on the unjust king to St Patrick. There is a much closer verbal parallel with the *De Abusivis*, also attributed to Patrick, in the *Collectio Canonum Hibernensis*, which was put together from earlier canonical collections towards the beginning of the eighth century.[3] It would therefore appear that at least part of the *De Abusivis* was attributed to Patrick and was known in England in the ninth century. Professor Leslie also sees parallels to its contents in *The Seafarer*.[4] Specialists in literature may be able to add other such examples.

Irish influence certainly helped to propagate texts of the bible. The Codex Amiatinus used to be considered a direct copy of Cassiodorus's Vulgate, but it is now recognized that the English manuscript is heterogeneous, in fact a 'hotch-potch'. Its psalter is based on a corrupt Irish text and its catholic epistles contain a substantial Irish element.[5] Professor Julian Brown has argued persuasively that the Echternach Gospels and Durham, Cathedral Library, A.II.17 are by the same scribe, written either at Lindisfarne or by someone trained in the Lindisfarne tradition; the transmission of Irish texts may be seen in both these manuscripts, for the gospels in Durham A.II.17 are Irish in type, while the Echternach prefaces are Irish and its gospels are a mixture of Irish and Italo-Northumbrian elements.[6] The division of the psalter into the three fifties is mentioned by Hilary and Cassiodorus and is implicit in a set of sixth-century Coptic manuscripts.[7] It is not found in the Cathach of St Columba, but is common in late-eighth- and early-ninth-century Irish references.[8] The first English reference to the division is in a Kentish charter of 805–10.[9] The practice was probably introduced into England from Ireland first into private

---

[1] Professor Cross has sent me a number of parallels, which will be noted when the edition by Professor C. W. Jones appears in *CC*.

[2] *MGH, Epistolae* IV, 503; cf. S. Hellmann, *De Duodecim Abusivis Saeculi* (Leipzig, 1909), pp. 52–3. It is not a close verbal parallel. It is noted by J. B. Bury, *The Life of St Patrick* (London, 1905), p. 245.

[3] Ed. H. Wasserschleben, *Die irische Kanonensammlung* (Giessen, 1874), pp. 91–2. For a discussion of the *Collectio* see Hughes, *op. cit.* ch. 12.

[4] *The Wanderer*, ed. R. F. Leslie (Manchester, 1966), p. 29.

[5] R. Loewe in *The Cambridge History of the Bible* II, ed. G. W. H. Lampe (Cambridge, 1969), 116–19. For the external features of Amiatinus see R. L. S. Bruce-Mitford, *JBAA* XXXII (1969), 1–25.

[6] *Codex Lindisfarnensis* (Olten and Lausanne, 1956–60) II, bk II, pp. 95–103.

[7] See *The Vespasian Psalter*, ed. D. H. Wright, EEMF 14 (Copenhagen, 1967), 47–8.

[8] See F. Henry, *Proceedings of the Royal Irish Academy* LXI (1960), 25, n. 1.

[9] *Sweet's Anglo-Saxon Reader*, rev. D. Whitelock (Oxford, 1967), no. XXXIIIA; trans. Harmer, *SelEHD*, p. 40.

devotion and then becomes common in English psalters until the end of the eleventh century.[1]

Similar textual influence may be seen in the penitentials. Bede does not mention the Penitential of Theodore, yet most scholars are now agreed that this is a genuine work compiled from answers given by Theodore to the priest Eoda and subsequently edited by a 'disciple of the Humbrenses'; Theodore's answers were compared with a *libellus Scottorum* which is referred to in the text.[2] This is the first of the English manuals of penance and by the time it was written Ireland and Britain had had at least a century's experience of private penance. By far the most sophisticated of the Irish penitentials up to this date is that of Cummean, who died in 662 and whose work is quoted in later penitential writings.[3] Cummean is the first Irish penitential writer to distinguish minutely between the sorts and conditions of men. Before him, Vinnian and Columbanus had usually distinguished between the cleric and the layman in assigning penance, but Cummean names a number of different grades, the bishop, priest, deacon, the monk not in orders, the boy. Circumstances and motive are carefully considered in the Irish penitentials. As Cummean says in his epilogue:

This is to be carefully observed in all penance, the length of time anyone remains in his faults, what learning he has received, by what passion he is assailed, how great is his strength, with what intensity of weeping he is afflicted and with what oppression he has been driven to sin. For Almighty God who knows the hearts of all and has bestowed diverse natures will not weigh the weights of sins in equal scale of penance.[4]

The principle of Cummean's penitential is that the eight chief vices (almost certainly taken from Cassian) are to be healed by their contrary virtues, so he arranges his 'medicine for the salvation of souls' under the headings of gluttony, fornication, avarice, anger, dejection, accidie, vainglory and pride, adding sections on petty offences, on boys and on the host. He is also aware of the practice of commutation of penance, though he makes comparatively little use of it.

Throughout the seventh century ecclesiastical synods seem to have met fairly frequently in Ireland, and some drew up penitential canons. Commutation was a recognized custom. The third canon of the Alleged Second Synod of St Patrick maintains that 'more fitting for pardon...is a short penance with weeping and lamentation and a garment of grief, under control, than a long and lax one with a lukewarm mind', while the

---

[1] K. Sisam in *The Paris Psalter*, EEMF 8 (Copenhagen, 1958), 16.

[2] *Councils* III, 173–204; trans. J. T. McNeill and H. M. Gamer, *Mediaeval Handbooks of Penance* (Columbia, 1938), pp. 182–215.

[3] For identification see L. Bieler, *The Irish Penitentials* (Dublin, 1963), p. 6, and for discussion of this penitential in relation to that of Columbanus, Hughes, *op. cit.* pp. 57–61.

[4] Bieler, *op. cit.* p. 132.

text known as *Canones Hibernenses* has a section entitled *De Arreis*. The title itself suggests that the practice is of Irish origin, for the word comes from the verbal noun of *ar-ren*, 'pays for, pays instead of'.[1]

The Penitential of Theodore shows acquaintance with some, at least, of this Irish legislation. The first part begins like Cummean with sections on gluttony, fornication, avarice and manslaughter, though it subsequently departs from this plan. As previous writers have noted, a few of Theodore's rulings are similar to those in the *Canones Hibernenses*, in particular the penance for homicide, of either ten or seven years.[2] Here the Irish ruling quotes an otherwise unknown Irishman for the second opinion: 'The penance for homicide is seven years on bread and water, or, as Monochoma says, ten.'[3] Theodore is also familiar with the practice of commutation, and one specific passage has sufficient verbal similarity with Cummean to be worth quoting:

| *Cummean* VIII. 25 | I *Theodore* VII. 5 |
|---|---|
| Some give the ruling that twelve *triduana* (three-day periods) are the equivalent of a year, which I neither praise nor blame. Others, a hundred days with half a loaf of dry bread and an allowance of water and salt, and the penitent shall sing fifty psalms during each night. Others, fifty special fasts, with one night intervening. Others determine that the penance of the sick shall consist in the giving of alms, that is, the price of a manservant or maidservant, but it is fitting if anyone gives the half of all the things which he possesses, and if he has wronged anyone that he restore him fourfold. | Further, Theodore approved reckoning the twelve *triduana* as the equivalent of a year. Also in the case of sick persons, the price of a manservant or maidservant for a year, or to give the half of all the things which he possesses, and if he has wronged anyone to restore fourfold, as Christ judged. These are the proofs of what we said in the preface about the *Libellus Scottorum*, in which, as in other matters, sometimes he determined these things therein more strictly in the case of those who are very bad, but sometimes more leniently as seemed best to him; it set the measure of penance for the weak. |

Even this does not prove decisively that the *Libellus Scottorum* was the Penitential of Cummean, though it proves familiarity with some similar ruling.

The Penitential of Theodore, in its turn, gained currency in Ireland. It is quoted in the *Collectio Canonum Hibernensis*, a collection of rulings by patristic authorities and Irish synods put together early in the eighth

---

[1] *Ibid.* p. 50. Professor Binchy edits the Irish treatises.

[2] I *Theod.* IV. 3. Cf. *Can. Hib.* I. 3, ed. Bieler, *op. cit.* p. 160.

[3] The eighth-century Old Irish Penitential gives seven years for homicide (except for bishop and priest) and penances ranging from ten to twenty-one years for kin-slaying, depending on the nearness of the kin: 'this rule is followed to the seventh man both of the mother's and father's kin...as far as the finger nail' (*ibid.* p. 271). This ruling shows the influence of secular law.

century,[1] and again later in the century by the Old Irish Penitential, on two occasions alongside different rulings from Cummean.[2] English penitentials of the eighth century continued their familiarity with Celtic penitential literature: that ascribed to Bede used Cummean and other Celtic writers. Bede's penitential has a long and rational introduction, urging that the penance must be suited to the person as well as to the sin; a principle stated by Cummean but here much more fully expressed. Both Bede and Egbert are concerned with commutations, so it is interesting to find an Irish table of commutations drawn up at much the same period, or perhaps slightly later.[3] By this time the penitential writings of both countries were proceeding independently on somewhat similar lines.

Most interesting are the very detailed prayers of confession which occur in English private prayer-books of the late eighth and early ninth centuries, for they provide the spiritual application of the legislation on penance we have touched on.[4] Some of these list a detailed specification of sins. One in the Book of Cerne[5] enumerates exactly the kind of sins which occur in the penitentials: murder, sodomy, adultery, fornication, greed, anger, masturbation, false witness, perjury, slander. The penitent is trying to confess all his sins 'from my infancy to the present day'. Even so, he could hardly have committed all these and is presumably confessing everything he can think of in case he ever does, 'that the devil may not seize me, nor may I depart on the day of my death or the day of judgement without confession of sins'. This suggests that in practice some people actually anticipated their sins by confession.[6] The twenty-seventh canon of the Council of *Clovesho* held in 747 shows that in England men were even vicariously trying to anticipate penance: one rich man was claiming that if he were to live 300 years more the requirements of penitential fasting would have been met by the penance which had been already performed on his behalf.[7] The prayer already mentioned from the Book of Cerne specifies in intimate detail the parts of the body through which the penitent may have sinned, even enumerating such things as teeth and hair and finger nails, taking care to mention everything *intus vel foras*. This seems to show the influence of the *loricae*, prayers for protection on every named

---

[1] Ed. H. Wasserschleben (Leipzig, 1885) LIV. 12, 13b and 14. For discussion of contents see Hughes, *op. cit.* pp. 123–33.

[2] II. 21 and III. 2; cf. I. 4.

[3] Professor Binchy says 'none of the verbal forms is later than the eighth century' (Bieler, *op. cit.* p. 277), and associates the table with the culdee reform movement in the second half of the eighth century.

[4] Discussed in more detail in my O'Donnell Lecture of 1969, *Studia Celtica* v (1970), 55–7.

[5] Ed. A. B. Kuypers (Cambridge, 1902), no. 8; see below, p. 66.

[6] Chad, educated in Ireland, used to go to the church in a storm to confess (*HE* IV. 3).

[7] *Councils* III, 373. The rational purpose behind commutation is well expressed in the *Old Irish Table of Commutations*, §6 (Bieler, *op. cit.* p. 278), but this canon demonstrates its abuse.

part of the body. The Lorica of Laidcenn,[1] presumably the Irish *sapiens* of the mid seventh century, has a place of honour in the Book of Cerne, and there are other prayers asking for physical and spiritual protection on the various parts of the body. One such specifies hands, inward parts, knees, head, eyes, ears, nose, mouth, lips, tongue, heart, calling Christ the *medicus*.[2] The prayer of detailed confession, regarded as the medicine for souls, is often incorporated into the lorica-like prayer for protection, which was popular in both England and Ireland.[3] By the late eighth and ninth centuries aspects of Irish spirituality had been firmly grafted on to the English stock.

Close and frequent contact between Irish and English clerics up to the early ninth century thus seems to be fairly well proven. Does this contact halt after the Synod of Chelsea in 816? The great liturgist, Edmund Bishop, thought that it did,[4] and certainly the fifth canon of this council is comprehensive in its prohibitions. No Irishman is to be allowed to minister in any diocese, no one is to accept baptism or the celebration of the eucharist or hearing of mass from him: this is because 'it is unknown to us whence and by whom they are ordained' and because the Irish lack a metropolitan. It is a wholesale indictment of the Irish system. This can hardly be the result of Canterbury's re-assertion of primacy and jurisdiction, stated in the Synod of *Clovesho* in 803, nor can it arise from the quarrel between King Cenwulf of Mercia and Archbishop Wulfred of Canterbury which broke out in 817 and lasted until 821. The anti-Irish ruling is much more likely to have been enacted under the influence of Carolingian legislation. Canon 43 of the Second Council of Chalon-sur-Saône, held in 813, reads:

In some places there are Irishmen who say they are bishops and ordain many irresponsible persons as priests and deacons without licence of their lords or masters. The ordination of these men, since it very frequently results in the heresy of simony and is liable to many abuses, we have all unanimously decreed ought to be regarded as null and void.[5]

Sections of the English church had, since Theodore's day, been suspicious of Irish orders, not without reason (as Adamnán's story of the bishop

---

[1] It is attributed to Laidcenn in all the early manuscripts, Nunnaminster, Cerne and a ninth-century Verona manuscript. In the fourteenth-century *Leabhar Breac* it is attributed to Gildas, and Laidcenn is said to have brought it to Ireland. Laidcenn died in 661 according to the Annals of Ulster. He was the author of an abridgement of Gregory the Great's *Moralia*, and he is cited among five Irishmen as an authority in the commentary on the catholic epistles. See P. Grosjean, *Sacris Erudiri* VII (1955), 92–6.

[2] *Book of Cerne*, no. 17.

[3] Cf., e.g., the prayer in Cerne (no. 6), BM Royal 2.A.xx, 22r, and BM Harley 7653, no. 2 with the Irish verse prayer, *Early Irish Lyrics*, ed. G. Murphy (Oxford, 1956), pp. 54–7, though here the detailed confession is omitted.

[4] *Liturgica Historica* (Oxford, 1918), pp. 172–3.

[5] *MGH*, *Concilia* II, 282; Kenney, *Sources*, p. 529. The Carolingians at this time were very aware of the annoyance and abuses caused by *clerici vagantes*.

persuaded to ordain an unsuitable favourite of the abbot's shows[1]), and from its Roman beginning the English church had enjoyed metropolitical rights. During the seventh century Irish *Romani* tried to protect the bishop's rights and Armagh attempted to assert metropolitical authority, but without much success.[2] In 816 English criticism seems to have flared up once more.

Though Carolingian legislation was probably the main influence, Irish church policy may also have played its part in this renewed opposition, for from the later eighth century the Irish attitude to pilgrimage was changing. The culdees seem to have been discouraging pilgrimage oversea: 'Thus Máel-ruain heard the elders say of the desertion of the land: "Anyone who deserts his country except to go from the east to the west or from the north to the south is a denier of Patrick in heaven and of the faith in Ireland."'[3] The eighth-century saint Samthann taught her disciples that the way to the kingdom of heaven is the same distance from every land, so there is no need to go abroad, and the Old Irish Rule of Ailbe enjoins 'the non-desertion of thy monastery'.[4] The devout ascetic by the ninth century seems to have been retiring to a reformed house or to a hermitage: 'All alone in my little cell,' as a poet says, 'such a pilgrimage would be dear to my heart.'[5] Pilgrims to the continent either went on a special journey *ad limina* or were often ambitious clerics, scholars who would grace a bishop's entourage. If the most ascetic and devout now often stayed at home the other elements, which had always existed among pilgrims, might have become increasingly evident to responsible ecclesiastical administrators both in England and on the continent.

Yet it seems very dangerous to assume that the Council of Chelsea brought about any cessation in Irish–English relations. The source material for the ninth century is very sparse, yet in the tenth century, when the picture again fills in, we find Irish scholars at the court of King Athelstan and Irish connections with some of the centres of English monastic reform.[6] The Viking raids must have made voyages more difficult, but they probably did not cease altogether. In the 830s an Anglo-Saxon Pehtred and an Irish deacon Niall and 'other liars' were disturbing the English church with an account that Niall had died and come to life again and with various 'mendacious ravings concerning the Old and New Testaments'.[7] This

---

[1] *Adamnán's Life of Columba* I. 36, *carnaliter amans.*
[2] Hughes, *op. cit.* pp. 111–20.
[3] 'Teaching of Maelruain', *Proceedings of the Royal Irish Academy* XXIX (1911), 133.
[4] For these and other references see Hughes, *JEH* XI, 147ff.
[5] Murphy, *op. cit.* p. 18.
[6] I am most grateful to Dr Denis Bethell who has shown me his paper on this subject, to be published in *Historical Studies.*
[7] *Councils* III, 615; Whitelock, *EHD*, pp. 806–7.

report may not be very creditable to the Irish church but it shows that contacts were continuing, and at a period of acute Viking pressure in Ireland. At much the same period the Book of Cerne was copied in part from a hymnar of Æthelwald, bishop of Lichfield 818–30.[1] This and the related prayer-books, the fragment Harleian 7653 and the Book of Nunnaminster, both probably written at the turn of the eighth and ninth centuries, contain a lot of material of Hiberno-Saxon character, of which we have already mentioned the loricae and prayers of confession.[2] Æthelwald of Lichfield saw no incongruity in using these prayers. Alfred had known enough of Irish houses to send occasional alms. The three Irishmen from the boat washed up in Cornwall in 891 were sufficiently confident of the royal welcome to proceed 'immediately' to the king.[3] During his reign the metrical calendar which survives in BM Cotton Galba A.xviii was, in Edmund Bishop's opinion, produced by an Irishman at his court.[4] Early in the tenth century the boy Dunstan was studying Irish books at Glastonbury and meeting the Irish pilgrims who came there. Dubinnsi, bishop of Bangor, learned a game of gospel dice at 'the house of Athelstan king of the English',[5] while Symeon of Durham has various references to tenth-century contacts between England and Ireland.[6] The cross slab from Alnmouth, now in the Newcastle Museum and probably dating from the tenth century, carries a relief of the crucifixion with the lance- and sponge-bearer of Hiberno-Saxon tradition (not the Mary and St John of the Winchester School), with an inscription in ordinary letters and runes as on the ninth- and tenth-century coins of Northumbria.[7] This reads *Myredah meh wo-*, with a name in its genitive form, *Eadvlfes*. Thus an epigrapher with an Irish name, Muiredach, was working in Northumbria.

The ninth century may have seen a change in the extremely intimate ecclesiastical relations which existed between English and Irishmen before

---

[1] The identification is Sisam's, *RES* n.s. VII (1956), 1–10 and 113–31, and rests on the spelling of the name. (Bishop thought he was bishop of Lindisfarne 721–40.)

[2] The fourth book of this group, BM Royal 2.A.xx, belongs to the second half of the eighth century.

[3] It was presumably these men who brought news of the death of Suibhne, anchorite and scribe of Clonmacnoise (Annals of Ulster, 891) whose obituary notice is entered in *ASC* as 'the best scholar among the Irish'.

[4] 'It is in the highest degree interesting as the only liturgical document that comes down to us from Alfred's times or the early days of Edward the Elder' (*op. cit.* p. 256); cf. Robinson, *Times of St Dunstan*, pp. 64ff.

[5] *Ibid.* pp. 69ff.; Kenney, *Sources*, pp. 647–8.

[6] The bearers of St Cuthbert's relics intended to go to Ireland and embarked at the mouth of the Solway, only to be driven back by a storm (*Historia Dunelmensis Ecclesiae* II.11); a woman healed in Durham (hence after 995) went on pilgrimage to Rome and, on her return, went to Ireland (*ibid.* III.3).

[7] W. G. Collingwood, *Northumbrian Crosses of the Pre-Norman Age* (London, 1927), p. 62. By this time Hiberno-Norsemen must have been filtering across from Ireland.

the Synod of Chelsea. The attitude to pilgrimage overseas was altering at home in Ireland, and the opportunities provided by the Carolingians diverted some scholars who might have made England their home.[1] No doubt the Viking attacks further weakened communication; but if there was interruption it was temporary and by the reign of Athelstan contacts were again frequent. Nevertheless the time of greatest mutual influence between the two churches was the seventh and eighth centuries. In spite of differences in ecclesiastical organization clergy seem to have moved freely between the two countries and settled permanently and happily in each others' lands, so that many of their penitential and devotional ideas and their literary expressions were drawn from a common stock, while their books passed into each others' scriptoria, influencing the transmission of texts, and their scribes developed handwriting so similar in style that it has to be designated as 'insular'.[2] Thus, in these centuries the Celtic and Germanic civilizations enriched each other in what may well be called a Hiberno-Saxon age.

[1] Though many of these must have gone via England; e.g. in 796 the news of King Æthelred's murder was brought to Alcuin by men travelling from Ireland to Gaul via England.
[2] *CLA* II, xii. The fusion of artistic motifs lies outside the scope of this paper.

# The development of military obligations in eighth- and ninth-century England

## NICHOLAS BROOKS

It is well known that when Anglo-Saxon royal diplomas granted immunities to an estate, they normally excepted three obligations: service in the army, the building of fortresses and the construction of bridges. These services, as many of the extant charters insist, were obligatory on the whole people, were never excused, and were therefore described as 'common'.[1] In Wessex at least from the time of King Ine a fine (*fyrdwite*) was exacted by the king from any ceorl or man of higher rank who neglected his duty to serve in the army,[2] and in the tenth and eleventh centuries English kings were concerned to regulate and reiterate in their law-codes the triple obligation of army-service, fortress- and bridge-work.[3] On the continent we have comparable evidence: law-codes, capitularies and diplomas provide details of the fine for failure to serve in the army,[4] and the Frankish kings of the eighth and ninth centuries made clear in their capitularies that all free men, both proprietors and tenants on the lands of ecclesiastical and lay lords, might be required to serve in the host, to build bridges and to perform watch-duty.[5] In studying the development of military obligations in England therefore, it is essential to keep in mind that similar problems were receiving similar solutions in different parts of Europe because of contemporary contacts in times of danger and because the origins of these obligations, difficult though they may be to trace in particular regions, lay in a common Germanic and Roman past.

[1] The references were all collected by W. H. Stevenson in his seminal study of the three obligations, 'Trinoda Necessitas', *EHR* xxix (1914), 689, n. 3.

[2] Ine 51: Liebermann, *Gesetze* I, 112.

[3] II Athelstan 13, V Æthelred 26, VI Æthelred 32 and II Cnut 10 and 65: Liebermann, *Gesetze* I, 156, 242, 254, 314 and 352.

[4] *Lex Ribuaria*, ch. 68 (ed. F. Beyerle and R. Buchner, *MGH, Legum*, sect. I, III.2, 119); and *Capitulare Bononiense* (811), ch. 6 (*MGH, Capitularia* I, 192); only two Merovingian diplomas specify the *heriban* among the payments normally due to the fisc that were to pass to the beneficiary. See M. Kroell, *L'Immunité Franque* (Paris, 1910), pp. 108–9.

[5] *Pippini Italiae Regis Capitulare* (782–7), ch. 4: *MGH, Capitularia* I, 192; *Capitulare Mantuanum Secundum* (?813), ch. 7: *ibid.* p. 197; *Capitula de diversis causis* (806), ch. 2: *ibid.* p. 136; *Memoratorium* (807), ch. 2: *ibid.* p. 134; *Capitulare missorum de exercitu promovendo* (808), ch. 1: *ibid.* p. 137; *Karoli ad Fulradum epistola* (806): *ibid.* p. 168; *Capitulare Aquisgranense* (802–3), ch. 8: *ibid.* p. 171; and *Constitutio de Hispanis prima* (815), ch. 1: *ibid.* p. 261. Compare also the diploma of 775 to the church of Metz (*MGH, Diplomata Kar.*, no. 91, p. 132).

Though the 'common burdens' in England as elsewhere were general obligations falling in some degree upon the whole *folc*, it is likely – as is suggested by the reservation of the three burdens in landbooks – that they were also connected with the possession of land. Occasionally the books themselves make this clear; a charter of King Cenwulf of Mercia granting land in Kent to the archbishop of Canterbury in the year 814 states '[terra]...inlaesa et inconcussa permaneat nisi his tribus tantummodo causis id est expeditionem et arcis munitionem contra paganos et pontis instructionem communiter sicut tota gens illa de suis propriis hereditariis consuete faciunt.'[1] The obligation is compulsory upon *tota gens*, yet is done by each from his hereditary lands. How many men were required to serve in the army, at bridge and at fortress is not specified in the diplomas of the pre-Conquest period.[2] But the regularity with which English diplomas record the assessment of each estate in hides indicates that, as on the continent, the hide – the single peasant family holding – was being used for assessing primitive rents, taxes and services at least from the second half of the seventh century,[3] and would provide a convenient and flexible means of defining military obligations.

On the continent in the eighth and ninth centuries kings regulated not only the weapons and armour that their free subjects had to possess,[4] but also the extent of their obligation to serve in the host, in terms of the number of *mansi* or *casae* that each possessed. One man from every four *mansi* was defined as the rule in Charlemagne's kingdom in 808, though on occasion he might demand more and in the event of invasion the whole people were called out (*lantweri*).[5] To what extent comparable regulations

---

[1] Birch, no. 348; the charter survives in contemporary form (BM Cotton Augustus II.74: BM Facs II, no. 13).

[2] The only exception is the document that forms the dorse of Birch, no. 201 (Cotton Augustus II.27: BM Facs I, no. 9), where five men are required to serve in the host from an estate of thirty, or perhaps thirty-six, hides. It may well be that the number was specified because it represented an exception from the norm.

[3] For the continental equivalents of the hide, the *mansus*, *casa*, *hoba* etc., see D. Herlihy, 'The Carolingian *Mansus*', *Economic History Review* XIII (1960–1), 79–89. Already in Ine's laws the food-rent from a fixed number of hides is defined (Ine 70. 1: Liebermann, *Gesetze* I, 118–20).

[4] *Ahistulfi Leges de Anno I* (751), chs. 2 and 3: *Die Gesetze der Langobarden*, ed. F. Beyerle (Weimar, 1947), p. 360; and *Capitulare missorum in Theodonisvilla* (805), ch. 6: MGH, *Capitularia* I, 123.

[5] For the *lantweri*, see *Adnuntiatio Karoli* (847), ch. 5: MGH, *Capitularia* II, 71; and *Capitula de diversis causis* (806), ch. 2: MGH, *Capitularia* I, 136. For the four *mansi* rule, see *Capitulare missorum de exercitu promovendo* (808), ch. 1: *ibid.* p. 137. In some areas the king had preferred to call up one free man out of every five or six, or one free man from every three *mansi*; in all these arrangements those who did not serve had to help support the men who did. The best discussions of Carolingian military organization are: J. F. Verbruggen, 'L'Armée et la Stratégie de Charlemagne', *Karl der Grosse* I, 420–35, and F. L. Ganshof, 'L'Armée sous les Carolingiens', Settimane di Spoleto 15 (1968), 109–30. The attempt of H. Dannenbauer ('Die Freien im karolingischen Heer', in *Aus Verfassungs- und Landesgeschichte: Festschrift Th. Mayer* [Konstanz, 1954] I, 49–64) to limit the meaning of free man in these capitularies to the

were in force in the contemporary English kingdoms we cannot be certain, since the administrative orders of English kings were probably never written and were certainly not collected like the Carolingian capitularies. But when we begin to have evidence in the tenth and eleventh centuries, we find borough-work and bridge-work levied at a rate of one man from every hide,[1] and army-duty at a rate of one man from every five hides.[2]

The 'common burdens' were merely three out of a whole range of services and payments which were incurred with the possession of land and which are sometimes set out in detail in the immunity clauses of English royal diplomas, particularly those of the eighth and ninth centuries. These obligations included labour on public works, on royal vills and palaces[3] and on churches,[4] fines imposed by the popular courts[5] and other profitable legal rights,[6] and above all the rendering of royal *tributum* or *vectigal* which might be a food-rent or the actual feeding and housing of the king and his companions (nobles, bishops, reeves, officials and the keepers of his hounds, hawks and horses).[7] All such 'secular' obligations might be remitted when an estate was made into bookland except army-duty, bridge-work and fortress-work. These three common necessities were unique in being exacted on all land, even on bookland.[8]

It is worth considering why these three in particular were never remitted. Service in the army and the repair of fortresses were clearly essential for the safety of a kingdom, but bridge-work might seem less vital. Unbridged rivers could seriously delay the efforts of local forces to drive out an enemy army,[9] but if the kings' concern had been with the mobility

so-called *Königsfreien*, military settlers bound closely to the king and of semi-free origin, involves very forced readings of the capitularies and could scarcely accommodate the related English evidence.

[1] In the Burghal Hidage of the early tenth century (Robertson, *Charters*, pp. 246–8), one man from every hide was required for the repair (*wealstilling*) and defence (*waru*) of the West Saxon boroughs; the same ratio was in use for bridge- and borough-work at Chester in 1086 (*DB* I. 262v); by the thirteenth and fourteenth centuries bridge-work had frequently been commuted into a tax (pontage) on every hide in the shire. See R. Stewart-Brown, 'Bridge-Work at Chester', *EHR* LIV (1939), 83–7.

[2] The evidence has been ably assembled and discussed by C. W. Hollister, *Anglo-Saxon Military Institutions* (Oxford, 1962), pp. 38–58.

[3] *Ab omni opere puplico aedificiorum* (Birch, nos. 321 and 341); *ab omni constructione regalis ville* (Birch, no. 416); and *ab omni aedificiorum opere* (Birch, no. 544).

[4] Work on churches, frequently exacted on the continent, appears not to be recorded in England until II Cnut 65. 1: Liebermann, *Gesetze* I, 352.

[5] *Ab omnium...popularium conciliorum vindictis* (Birch, no. 201).

[6] *Liber et securus...poenalium causarum furisque comprehensione* (Birch, nos. 451, 431, 438, 459, 506 etc.).

[7] Birch, nos. 370, 395, 443, 450, 488 etc.

[8] This point needs emphasizing since it has recently been mistakenly suggested that possession of bookland increased a man's military duties (M. Powicke, *Military Obligation in Mediaeval England* [Oxford, 1962], p. 17).

[9] See the comments of Hincmar on Charles the Bald's campaign of 862, *Annales de Saint-Bertin*, ed. F. Grat, J. Vielliard and S. Clemencet, Société de l'Histoire de France 470 (1964), 88.

of their armies and with ease of communications, we might expect to hear in the English sources of *corvées* for the upkeep of roads. The solution may lie in the fact that in England bridges were linked with the fortresses; an early-ninth-century charter from Worcester which speaks of bridge-work and fortress-work as a single obligation[1] and phrases such as *pontis arcisve coaedificatione*[2] suggest that, as at Chester in 1086,[3] the same man normally performed the two services in the same place. Bridge and fortress were a single military unit; together they secured the river crossing for the armies of the kingdom and together they prevented the movement of enemy troops either by land or by river. This feature of English defensive organization became of paramount importance in the English resistance to the Vikings. A Kentish charter of the year 811 which reserves the three common burdens thus: 'exceptis tribus tantum debitis, id est expeditionem et arcis munitionem et pontis instructionem adversus paganos',[4] makes clear that the importance of using bridges to block the main rivers to the Viking ships was appreciated in England at least a half century before Charles the Bald sought to erect fortified bridges on the rivers Seine, Marne and Oise in order to protect the heart of his kingdom.[5] Fortified bridges countered the chief strength of the Vikings, their mobility. Thus in 895 Alfred was able to force a Danish army to abandon its ships after he had blocked the river Lea by building a bridge with a fortification at each end;[6] and the accounts of the siege of Paris in 885–6 or of the destruction of London bridge by Olaf Haroldson[7] leave no doubt of the importance of bridges as military works.

Bridge-work, fortress-work and army-service occur so frequently together in the charters that we are tempted to suppose that they shared a common origin. Indeed W. H. Stevenson regarded them as 'such primitive requirements of any organized state that it is unlikely that they were suddenly imposed in the eighth century',[8] and he cited comparative evidence from the continent to support his view that ecclesiastical estates in England had probably always been liable for these services.[9] We may wonder, however, how far back into the Dark Ages organized states may be held to have existed in England, and the archaeologist may look

---

[1] *Preter tamen his duobus causis arcis et pontis constructione et expeditione* (Birch, no. 360).

[2] Birch, nos. 753, 758, 763, 764, 770, 775, 777, 789, 793 etc.

[3] *DB*, I. 262v.

[4] Birch, no. 332, which survives in contemporary form (Cotton Augustus II.47: *BM Facs* II, no. 11).

[5] *Annales de Saint-Bertin, op. cit. s.a.* 862 and 865. See F. Lot, 'Le Pont de Pitres', *Le Moyen Age* 2nd ser. IX (1905), 1–27.

[6] *ASC*, 896 A: Earle and Plummer, *Chronicles* I, 89.

[7] For the part of the bridges in the defence of Paris, see Abbo's *De Bello Parisiaco*, ed. H. Wacquet (Paris, 1942), *passim*; for London bridge, see Ashdown, *Documents*, pp. 154–6.

[8] *Loc. cit.* p. 698. The statement is made in connection with army-service and fortress-work only.

[9] *Ibid.* pp. 700–1.

in vain for the fortifications which generations of early Anglo-Saxons had laboured to keep in repair. More recently Mr E. John, without discussing the antiquity of the three obligations, has argued (against Stevenson) that church lands were originally immune from military obligations, that the Mercian king, Æthelbald, imposed bridge-work and fortress-work on ecclesiastical estates in, or shortly before, 749, and that King Offa added army-service to these burdens about a generation later.[1] Such a development, as Stevenson saw, would be in contrast to that of the Frankish kingdoms where, until the ninth century, grants of immunity did not normally exempt the men on church estates from military burdens.[2] Moreover an important and intended result of the imposition of military burdens in Mr John's interpretation was that by establishing a right to exact military services from bookland, English kings were henceforth able to grant books to laymen without diminishing their military resources. Yet it is remarkable that few of the earliest grants to laymen reserve the three military obligations;[3] we would expect kings to have taken more care to insist that a grant by charter no longer included immunity from military services.

In the century from 750 to 850 less than one fifth of the extant royal diplomas reserve any or all of the three military obligations. It was not apparently of great importance to donor or donee, lay or ecclesiastical, whether the reservation was included or not. A scribe might reserve the common burdens in one charter, and omit them in his next.[4] The diplomas from the Canterbury archives of Christ Church and St Augustine's record the three obligations with increasing frequency from the early ninth century, whilst charters from Rochester nearly always omit them.[5] It is not

[1] E. John, *Land Tenure in Early England* (Leicester, 1960), pp. 64–79; repr. from *Bulletin of the Institute of Historical Research* XXXI (1958), 117–29.

[2] The essential work remains that of M. Kroell, *L'Immunité Franque* (Paris, 1910), pp. 107–14 and 181–90. See also L. Levillain, 'Note sur l'Immunité Mérovingienne', *Revue Historique de Droit Français et Étranger* 4th ser. VI (1927), 38–67, and K. F. Drew, 'The Immunity in Carolingian Italy', *Speculum* XXXVII (1962), 182–97. The assertion of John (*Land Tenure*, p. 66) that the lands of the Frankish church were free of military service until the Carolingian rulers imposed these burdens is a misunderstanding of the section of the work of E. Lesne to which he refers (*Histoire de la Propriété Ecclésiastique en France* II. 2 [Lille, 1926], 456–72); the passage is concerned only with the personal obligation of bishops and abbots to serve in the army. When Lesne (*ibid.* pp. 472–90) goes on to discuss the obligations of the men on church lands, he repeats and reinforces Kroell's conclusions. The church of Tours in the late sixth century claimed exemption from military service for the men on its estates, but only exceptionally were kings disposed to admit the claim, and it is clear from Gregory of Tours' account that there was no general immunity for the men on ecclesiastical property (*Historia Francorum* v. 26 and VII. 42, ed. B. Krusch and W. Levison, *MGH, Script. Rer. Merov.* I).

[3] Of eighth-century grants to laymen only Birch, no. 274, includes the clause reserving the three burdens, whilst it is not found in Birch, nos. 218, 225, 230, 232, 247, 254, 277–8 and 289.

[4] Compare two diplomas of 822 and 823 written by the same scribe: Birch, no. 370 (Cotton Augustus II. 93: *BM Facs* II, no. 15), which reserves the burdens, and Birch, no. 373 (Cotton Augustus II. 75: *BM Facs* II, no. 16), which does not despite a most extensive immunity.

[5] The only Rochester charters of the eighth and ninth centuries to include reservation clauses are Birch, nos. 395 and 460, both of which are of very doubtful authenticity.

likely that there were significant legal differences between East and West Kent concerning military obligations, and we must therefore suppose that the omission of this clause was simply the normal form of the Rochester *scriptorium*. All this suggests that we are dealing with customary or willingly accepted obligations which were not affected by the drafting of individual charters, rather than with recently abrogated immunities of the English churches. Where the whims of individual scribes and the habits of ecclesiastical *scriptoria* are concerned, it would be dangerous to argue from the silence of the charters of a particular region or period that certain obligations did not yet exist or were not yet imposed on church lands.

In the early eighth century the military companions (*gesithas, comites*) of successful kings hoped to be rewarded with land rather than, or in addition to, treasure. But if a king granted land to a monastery, that land was no longer available for endowing a warrior.[1] Bede, indeed, urged Bishop Egbert of York to cancel, with the aid of the Northumbrian king, the charters by which so much land had been alienated to monastic foundations, which knew little of the religious life, that there was insufficient to endow the sons of nobles and warriors; as a result these youths either lived unsettled degenerate lives or left the *patria* to seek their fortune elsewhere.[2] Land, therefore, without being the source of the military obligation, was the expected reward for loyal military service, and this

[1] After the Battle of the Winwæd, King Oswiu founded twelve monasteries: 'donatis insuper etiam xii possessiunculis terrarum, in quibus ablato studio militiae terrestris ad exercendam militiam caelestem supplicandumque pro pace gentis eius aeterna, devotioni sedulae monachorum locus facultasque suppeteret' (*HE* III. 24: Plummer, *Bede* I, 178). John (*Land Tenure*, p. 74) takes this as proof 'that the granting of land to a monastery in Bede's Northumbria implied the freeing of the land from any liability for military service'. Certainly land which was now to provide food-rent and housing for monks could no longer supply the same needs for warrior lords, but we should not assume that the men on the land had no military obligations. As Sir Frank Stenton pointed out (*A-S England*, p. 287, n. 2), St Cuthbert served in the army before he entered religion; yet he kept his lord's sheep, made long journeys unaccompanied, and was armed only with a spear when he entered Melrose. Neither of his early biographers claim noble rank for him. See *Two Lives of St Cuthbert*, ed. B. Colgrave (Cambridge, 1940), pp. 65–72 and 155–72, and cf. p. 344. The experiences of Imma after the Battle of the Trent (678) show that in a campaign beyond the frontiers of the kingdom *rustici* who were impoverished and married were not expected to fight, but only to bring supplies for the soldiers (*HE* IV. 22).

[2] *Epistola Bede ad Ecgbertum Episcopum*, Plummer, *Bede* I, 414–15. Bede goes on to explain how the founders of these sham monasteries who received the tonsure and called themselves abbots were *liberi exinde a divino simul et humano servitio*. It should be noted that this passage does not refer to the lands of the monasteries, as John assumed (*Land Tenure*, p. 73), but to the men who actually secured bookright from complacent kings. As monks they were free from military obligations. There was a comparable situation in Visigothic Spain in the late seventh century where the popularity of the monastic vocation threatened to cause a serious shortage of warriors (E. A. Thompson, *The Goths in Spain* [Oxford, 1969], pp. 262–4). I owe this reference to Professor D. A. Bullough. In the Frankish kingdom the early Carolingians extended their military resources by seizing church estates and granting them as benefices to their vassals.

may in part explain why in the eighth century landbooks begin to refer to military obligations.

But the appearance of the clause insisting on the performance of the three military duties is more particularly linked with the appearance in English diplomas of immunity clauses. So long as charters did not claim that the land was free from secular services, there was no occasion to reserve the king's right to demand the military services. The earliest grant of an immunity in English charters occurs in a general privilege to the churches of his kingdom made by King Wihtred of Kent in 699.[1] It grants freedom *ab omni exactione publici tributi atque dispendio vel laesione*, but nothing further. The earliest authentic charter granting an immunity for a particular estate is a well-known grant of King Æthelberht II of Kent in 732;[2] what has not hitherto been remarked is that this charter includes not only an immunity clause but also a reservation clause: 'Et ius regium in ea deinceps nullum repperiatur omnino, excepto dumtaxat tale quale generale est in universis ecclesiasticis terris quæ in hac Cantia esse noscuntur.' We cannot be certain what 'royal right' was general in all ecclesiastical estates in Kent, but we have here proof that such rights could exist without their being recorded in previous charters. Moreover unless we suppose that Æthelberht II exacted rents or services from church lands that were abandoned by later kings, the presumption must be that the reserved royal right of 732 is none other than some or all of the military obligations which are more precisely reserved and stated to be 'common' or 'general' in later charters.

Seven years later we have a clearer statement of the right that a king might demand from ecclesiastical property in a grant of King Æthelheard of Wessex to Bishop Forthhere of Sherborne.[3] Unfortunately the charter only survives in an eleventh-century copy; but whilst we cannot rule out the possibility of interpolation,[4] the immunity and reservation clauses do

---

[1] Birch, no. 99. The earliest manuscript (Maidstone, Kent County Record Office, U.140) of *s*. ix was not known when Haddan and Stubbs (*Councils* III, 245–6) and Stevenson (*loc. cit.* p. 703) rejected it as spurious. The presence of Bishop Gefmund of Rochester among the witnesses does not condemn this as a text of 699, for the entry recording his death in 693 in *ASC* D and E is based on a misunderstanding of Bede (*HE* v. 8: Plummer, *Bede* I, 295). The formulae of Birch, no. 99 – notably the invocation, corroboration, dating clause and attestations – can all be paralleled in authentic diplomas of the period, and the witness-list could scarcely be invented. Birch, no. 109 purports to be a similar privilege by Ine to the West Saxon churches; the immunity is again very brief, and it is possible that the privilege is in substance authentic, although its date (704, 2nd indiction) is impossible since Aldhelm did not become bishop until 705.

[2] Birch, no. 148 (Cotton Augustus II. 91: *BM Facs* I, no. 6).

[3] Birch, no. 1331 (Oxford, Bodleian Library, Eng. hist. A. 2, no. 1). For comment and translation, see Whitelock, *EHD*, no. 69, and the works there cited.

[4] The lengthy statement of the bounds in Old English is probably a later interpolation, but the Latin text of the rest of the charter is brief and has no obvious anachronisms. See A. S. Napier and W. H. Stevenson, *The Crawford Collection of Early Charters and Documents* (Oxford, 1895),

not resemble those of later periods. The land is granted 'ut omnium causarum fiscalium et rerum regalium ac secularium operum sit inmunis, sempiternaliterque secura, nisi tantum expeditionalium rerum.' If we may accept this charter, it would seem that church lands were already required to provide men for the West Saxon army in the first half of the eighth century and that this restriction of the immunity was parallel and perhaps identical to the royal right that contemporary Kentish kings exacted from ecclesiastical estates.

The earliest specific reservations of the 'common burdens' that are undoubtedly genuine all occur in Mercian, rather than in Kentish or West Saxon, charters. The first is a general grant of privileges by King Æthelbald of Mercia enacted at the Synod of Gumley in 749.[1] The charter is attested by the bishops of Lichfield and Leicester, but not by any other bishops; there is no indication that the privilege extended beyond the limits of the Mercian kingdom itself to the various kingdoms and sub-kingdoms which Æthelbald had brought under his hegemony.[2] It is a detailed statement of immunities for the Mercian churches and monasteries which 'ab omnibus operibus oneribusque...absoluti maneant nisi sola quae communiter fruenda sint omnique populo edicto regis facienda jubentur, id est instructionibus pontium vel necessariis defensionibus arcium contra hostes non sunt renuenda. Sed nec hoc praetermittendum est cum necessarium constat æcclesiis Dei.' The privilege goes on to guarantee the churches full enjoyment of the produce of their properties, to forbid officials to make exactions for the 'secular feeding of kings and princes', though offerings for this purpose might be made voluntarily, and finally the king warns his *principes* to remove all the tribulations which were harming and impeding the house of God.

It is possible that individual Mercian churches may have secured immunities for some or all of their estates from royal food-rents and works before the Synod of Gumley, though the extant charters provide no certain

---

pp. 37–46; and P. Chaplais, 'The Authenticity of the Royal Anglo-Saxon Diplomas of Exeter', *Bulletin of the Institute of Historical Research* xxxix (1966), 10. For comparable immunities in other West Saxon diplomas of the eighth century, see below, p. 80, n. 5.

[1] Birch, no. 178. Birch and earlier editors took their text from H. Spelman, *Concilia Ecclesiarum Orbis Britannici* I (London, 1639), 256. But it escaped their attention and that of all commentators on this charter that Spelman's text was taken from BM Cotton Otho A. i, fol. 40, which has survived among the charred fragments of Otho A. i, and is now fol. 7. The hand is of *s.* viii (2) (see Lowe, *CLA* II, no. 188), and enough can still be read to establish the reliability of Spelman's text. For the various texts in this important manuscript, see N. R. Ker, 'Membra Disiecta', *British Museum Quarterly* xiv (1940), 79–80.

[2] Thus neither John's comparison of the reservation of the common burdens in this charter with the unrestricted liberty of Birch, no. 162, which purports to be a grant by Æthelbald to the churches and monasteries of Kent in 742, nor his conclusion that the common burdens were imposed between 742 and 749 are valid (*Land Tenure*, pp. 70–1). Moreover Birch, no. 162 is a forgery of the early ninth century; I hope to explain its rôle in the struggles of the see of Canterbury with the Mercian kings in my forthcoming work, *The Early History of Christ Church, Canterbury*.

indication.[1] But there is no reason to assume that the churches and monasteries of the Mercian kingdom, any more than their Frankish counterparts, had hitherto automatically enjoyed a general immunity throughout their properties. There was therefore a need for a detailed statement of ecclesiastical immunities, more particularly so since we know that in 745 Æthelbald had been roundly criticized by Boniface and seven other bishops of the Frankish church not only for his lascivious life but also because he had 'violated many privileges of churches and monasteries, and stolen many revenues from them', and because his 'reeves and gesiths had imposed greater violence and servitude on monks and priests than any other Christian kings before'.[2] These are powerful words not lightly used, for Boniface and his companions had ample experience of the abuse of secular power over the church, in particular of the appropriations of ecclesiastical property by Charles Martel to which they refer a little later in the same letter. What they objected to most of all is made more clear in Boniface's letter of 747 to Archbishop Cuthbert of Canterbury: 'De violentia quoque monachorum servitute operibus et aedificiis regalibus, quae in toto mundo non auditur facta nisi tantum in gente Anglorum.'[3] Evidently Æthelbald and his officials had been compelling monks to join the work-parties on royal halls and vills, and perhaps also, if these public services had yet been demanded in England, on bridges and fortresses.[4] Whilst some of these monks may, like those Bede speaks of in his letter to Bishop Egbert, have been little more than laymen in disguise, the Mercian king was here contravening the earliest privileges of the church which freed priest and monk from secular concerns to leave them free for the service of God.[5]

---

[1] The only grants of land in Mercia before 749 which include immunity clauses and command any credence are Birch, nos. 77, 138, 139 and 165. None of them is free from suspicion, and all are concerned with estates in the territory of the Hwicce which may well not have been covered by the Synod of Gumley since it is not attested by the bishop of Worcester (Birch, no. 178).

[2] *MGH, Epistolae Selectae* I, Ep. 73. The letter is translated in Whitelock, *EHD*, no. 177. I follow the version as it was sent to England rather than Boniface's earlier drafts from which the continental manuscripts are derived. See Levison, pp. 280–1.

[3] *MGH, Epistolae Selectae* I, Ep. 78. This passage is not 'probably a contemporary English gloss' (John, *Land Tenure*, p. 72), but part of the final version as sent by Boniface to England. It survived in Cotton Otho A. i.

[4] John (*ibid.*) argues that Boniface was thinking of the compulsion of the men on ecclesiastical estates to work on bridges and fortresses. But in both letters Boniface clearly refers to the compulsion of monks. There would be nothing 'unheard of' in the compulsion of their men, for bridge-work had been demanded from church lands since 423 in the late Empire (*Codex Theodosianus* XV. 3. 6, ed. T. Mommsen and P. M. Meyer [Berlin, 1905], p. 818) and was stated to be the *antiqua consuetudo* from which no immunity provided exemption in Pepin's earliest capitularies in Italy (*Pippini Italiae Regis Capitulare* [782–7], ch. 4: *MGH, Capitularia* I, 192; *Capitulare Mantuanum Secundum* [?813], ch. 7: *ibid.* p. 197).

[5] See Constantine's letter of 313 quoted by Eusebius, *Historia Ecclesiastica* x. 7: ed. K. Lake and J. E. L. Oulton (London, 1926) II, 464; and also the mass of early-fourth-century legislation in *Codex Theodosianus* XVI. 2, 1, 2, 6, 7, 9, 10, 14, 15, 17, 36 etc.: *op. cit.* pp. 835–47.

The Synod of Gumley may therefore be seen as an attempt to meet some of Boniface's criticisms. The churches and monasteries must no longer be harmed and impeded by the king's officials, their revenues are to be inviolable, and they are to be freed from all works and burdens except 'the building of bridges and the necessary defence of fortresses against enemies'. The reservation of bridge-work and fortress defence should not be taken as a defiance of Boniface, for there is no suggestion that these works were to be done by the monks. The wording of the reservation is important. We do not hear of any obligation to serve in the army (*expeditio*), but on the other hand *necessariis defensionibus arcium contra hostes* seems to imply rather more than the *arcis munitio* of later charters, namely an obligation to garrison the fortresses.[1] Moreover Æthelbald's privilege speaks of a 'royal edict' by which he had ordered these obligations to be done 'by the whole people'; this edict may have been a new imposition on the Mercian people, though we cannot rule out the possibility that it was merely a reinforcement of existing law. The statement that the two burdens were 'agreed to be necessary for the churches of God' also suggests that they were new, but they may have been reserved only because the king was for the first time granting immunity from all other secular labours and burdens.

After the Synod of Gumley the reservation of the common burdens occurs very irregularly in diplomas. Two charters of King Uhtred of the Hwicce of 767 and 770 reserve bridge-work and the defence of fortresses in words identical with those of the Æthelbald privilege.[2] Then there is another long gap until a diploma in which King Offa granted land to thegn Æthelmund between 793 and 796, free from all works: 'preter expeditionalibus causis et pontium structionum et arcium munimentum quod omni populo necesse est, ab eo opere nullum excussatum esse.'[3] Here as in Æthelbald's privilege of 749 it is emphasized that the burdens are to be done by the whole people without exception. By 796 at the latest, therefore, all three burdens were obligatory in the Mercian kingdom.

If we turn from Mercia to the diplomas concerning lands in Kent, we find a different development. We have more authentic charters of the eighth and ninth centuries, both in contemporary form and in reliable copies, from Kent than from any other region. Moreover some 'royal right' had already been known to be general in church estates in Kent as early as 732.[4] Yet only five other eighth-century diplomas granting

---

[1] *Defensio* is glossed by OE *waru* (see BT, *s.v. waru*), the term used in the Burghal Hidage for the obligation of defending the West Saxon boroughs.

[2] Birch, nos. 202 and 203.

[3] Birch, no. 274 (BM Add. Ch. 19790: *BM Facs* II, no. 5). Two charters dated 779 and (730 for) 780 which survive only in later form (Birch, nos. 229 and 234) reserve all three burdens, but are both of doubtful authenticity.   [4] Birch, no. 148; see above, p. 75.

lands in Kent include any immunity clause;[1] they claim no more than the freedom from 'royal tribute' that had been conceded by King Wihtred in 699, and make no mention of military obligations. There has survived, however, in a late text that seems to be reliable, a neglected record of a synod held at *Clofeshoh* in 792 in which Offa granted extensive immunities to all the Kentish churches, but reserved the three common burdens.[2] The churches are free from secular services, from payments to the king and to lesser persons, from the obligation of feeding the king, the men called *fæstincmenn* and the keepers of the king's hounds, horses and hawks, also from any burden on their woods, fields and meadows, and from all work at royal vills: 'nisi expeditione intra Cantiam contra paganos marinos cum classis migrantibus vel in australes Saxones si necessitas cogit, ac pontis constructionem et arcis munitionem contra paganos itemque intra fines Cantwariorum.' Finally Offa is made to say that it is his *petitio atque doctrina* that they (the Kentish churches) should consent to these three obligations, so that his grant of liberty should be the more stable.

The limitation of the military obligations to Kent might arouse our suspicion of this text, but a forger would scarcely mention an obligation to serve in Sussex in an emergency. If it is genuine, Offa's privilege is of great importance. Although some 'royal right' (perhaps army-service) had already been customary in ecclesiastical estates in Kent in 732, Offa's request for the churches' consent suggests that some or all of the three burdens were being imposed on the Kentish churches for the first time in 792; we cannot know whether or not they were also being newly imposed on estates in secular hands. But the reason (or perhaps the excuse) for the imposition of the common burdens is the new threat from sea-borne Viking armies, and here the privilege receives support from the fact that all the earliest authentic Kentish charters to include reservation clauses also specifically state that the three burdens are to be done *contra paganos*.[3] Although *The Anglo-Saxon Chronicle* records the first arrival of Vikings in England in the time of King Beorhtric of Wessex (786–802), it does not

[1] In contemporary form, Birch, nos. 247 and 254; in cartulary copies, Birch, nos. 192, 194 and 195.

[2] Birch, no. 848, which survives only in the thirteenth-century St Augustine's cartulary, BM Cotton Julius D. ii, 105v. Like the other texts from this cartulary, the record has been shorn of its witness-list, which makes it difficult to establish its authenticity. It claims to be a confirmation of earlier privileges to the Kentish churches by Wihtred and Æthelbald; whilst it naturally has a more detailed statement of immunities than the extant privilege of Wihtred (Birch, no. 99), it does not make any of the spurious claims found in the forged privileges attributed to Wihtred and Æthelbald (Birch, nos. 91 and 162). Archbishop Æthelheard is stated to have requested the confirmation; he was certainly elected in 792, though probably not consecrated until the following year. The formulae of the immunity anticipate those of ninth-century charters (cf. Birch, nos. 370, 395, 416, 443 and 450) in much the same way as the privileges of Wihtred (Birch, no. 99) and Æthelbald (Birch, no. 178) anticipate the formulae of somewhat later texts.

[3] Birch, nos. 332 (of 811), 335 (811), 348 (814) and 370 (822).

mention Vikings in Kent until 835. But its silence is misleading; chance references in charters establish that the community of Lyminge needed a refuge within the walls of Canterbury in 804,[1] and that before 811 Viking armies had not only been campaigning in Kent but even building themselves fortresses there.[2] It is therefore by no means impossible that in the last years of his reign Offa reacted vigorously to the new Viking danger and brought Kent into line with Mercia by insisting that all estates, even church lands, should contribute men for service in the army and for the building of bridges and of fortifications. Certainly by the second decade of the ninth century these obligations were customarily due from the hereditary estates of the whole Kentish folk, lay and ecclesiastical.[3]

Outside Kent and Mercia we are on less firm ground. For Northumbria and East Anglia we have no charters of the eighth and ninth centuries, whilst South Saxon charters of this period include neither immunity clauses nor the reservation of the military burdens.[4] It would be unwise to conjecture how much this might be due to differences of military organization rather than to the habits of the Selsey *scriptorium*. In Wessex we are hampered by the fact that only a single charter of the eighth and ninth centuries survives in contemporary form, and we therefore lack adequate criteria for distinguishing the genuine texts from the many forgeries in the cartularies of West Saxon houses. A major study of the diplomatic of the early West Saxon charters is an urgent *desideratum*. However, a pattern does seem to emerge among the few charters upon which some reliance may be placed. Already by 739, if we may accept Birch, no. 1331, service in the host was demanded from men on church estates. The charters of Cuthred (740–56) and Cynewulf (757–86) have neither immunity clauses nor the reservation of military burdens. But a charter dated 794 of Beorhtric, the protégé of Offa of Mercia, which survives only in a late and very corrupt text, has a very remarkable immunity;[5] 'ut libertatem habeat omnium fiscalium negotiorum et operum regalium et omnium rerum quae ad villam regiam pertinent, nisi unquam[6] expeditione sola quam omnes comites ad tutelam totius provinciae et maxime ecclesiarum Dei adire

---

[1] Birch, no. 317.

[2] Birch, nos. 332 (811) and 370 (822) refer to the obligation of destroying forts built by the pagans.      [3] Birch, no. 348; see above, p. 70.

[4] The single exception is Birch, no. 208, a grant of Offa of 772 of uncertain authority; it has a brief immunity *ab omni regale exaccione libera*. None of the South Saxon charters is later than 825.

[5] *ECW*, no. 398. It should be noted that there are verbal similarities between the immunity clauses of this charter and of Birch, nos. 108 and 1331. *ECW*, no. 398 is a grant of ten hides to a *praefectus*, named Wigferth. It is unlikely that the Athelney community would forge a grant to a layman dated a century before the foundation of their house. The modernized spelling of the bounds and the corruptions of the text should mostly be attributed to the

[6] Athelney cartularist rather than to the eighteenth-century transcriber.
MS *aquam*.

debent.' Here as in the record of the Synod of Gumley the reservation is associated with the safety of the churches. But as in Æthelheard's grant of 739 we hear nothing of bridge-work or fortress-work which were already enforced in Mercia and Kent, only of service in the army which all *comites* are to do for the defence of the province. So far as men of comital rank were concerned, it would seem that in Wessex service in the host was an obligation inherent in their status.

It is not until 846 that we have a West Saxon charter of undoubted authenticity with a reservation clause. This is the famous diploma by which Æthulwulf granted twenty hides at South Hams (Devon) to himself;[1] the land is freed from all secular burdens *sine expeditione et pontis instructione*. The absence of any mention of fortress-work may be significant, for there are only three other West Saxon charters of the first half of the ninth century which reserve the common burdens and which command any credence, and two of these mention only army-service and bridge-building.[2] It is possible that it was not until the reign of Æthelbald (855–60) when all three burdens begin to be reserved in West Saxon charters,[3] that an obligation to build fortifications was first regularly exacted in Wessex. Such a development would be closely parallel to that of the Frankish Empire where bridge-work and military service were ancient obligations, but the rebuilding of town-walls and the construction of new fortresses were not begun until the 860s when Charles the Bald began a programme of fortification *iuxta...aliarum gentium consuetudinem*.[4] In the first half of the ninth century by contrast we hear of Frankish bishops destroying city-walls in order to use the stone for cathedral and chapter buildings.[5] Moreover there is some English archaeological evidence to support the suggestion that fortress-work was a late introduction in Wessex. The ramparts of four West Saxon boroughs (Wareham, Cricklade,

---

[1] Birch, no. 451 (BM Cotton Charter VIII. 36: *BM Facs* II, no. 20).

[2] Birch, nos. 282 and 389. Birch, no. 438 (dated 842), which reserves all three burdens, is preserved in the Glastonbury cartularies; it is possible that fortress-work has been added by the cartularist in accord with later forms. Otherwise we must place the introduction of this obligation in Wessex before 842.

[3] Birch, nos. 495 (of 858), 500 (860), 504–5, 508, 550 etc.

[4] *Edictum Pistense* (862), ch. 27 (*MGH, Capitularia* II, 321): '...ut illi qui in hostem pergere non potuerint iuxta antiquam et aliarum gentium consuetudinem ad civitates novas et pontes ac transitus paludium operentur, et in civitate atque in marca wactas faciant; ad defensionem patriae omnes sine ulla excusatione veniant.' The parallel with English military obligations is clear. Work and watch-duty in the *civitates* however was new in the Frankish empire, as comparison with earlier capitularies establishes. For the development of defensive fortifications from the 860s, see F. Vercauteren, 'Comment s'est-on défendu dans l'Empire Franc contre les Invasions Normandes', *Annales du XXXᵉ Congrès de la Féderation Archéologique et Historique de Belgique* (1935–6), pp. 117–32, and J. Hubert, 'L'Abbaye de Déols et les Constructions Monastiques de la Fin de l'Époque Carolingienne', *Cahiers Archéologiques* IX (1957), 155–72.

[5] See the texts cited by F. Vercauteren (*op. cit.* pp. 119–20) for Langres, Rheims, Beauvais and Melun.

Lydford and Wallingford) have received systematic excavation, and in every case the rampart associated by the excavators with the borough of the Alfredian period was the primary defence on the site.[1] By contrast, in the two Mercian boroughs that have been recently excavated, Tamworth and Hereford, the earthworks that have been attributed to the period of Æthelflæd, Lady of the Mercians, were preceded by one or more earlier defences.[2] It may be no coincidence that Mercian charters first refer to borough-work from the middle of the eighth century, whilst in Wessex it was not until the middle of the ninth century that kings began to demand in their diplomas work on the building of fortifications.

The evidence therefore suggests that the development of military obligations may have varied in the different English kingdoms and that we should not assume that bridge-work and fortress-work were necessarily as ancient as the obligation of serving in the army. Royal government in the eighth and ninth centuries became more sophisticated and more powerful, and this development is reflected somewhat tardily and unevenly in the written immunities of growing precision which churches secured for their estates. But at the moment when kings first conceded immunities from secular services and royal works, they also began to reserve their right to demand certain military burdens;[3] and this argues that some at least of these burdens had been levied even from ecclesiastical estates long before they are first mentioned in the charters.

Army-service indeed is likely to have been an ancient obligation in every kingdom. In Wessex, if we may trust the charters of 739 and 794, service in the host was already required from church lands and from bookland in lay hands in the eighth century. The same obligation was probably the royal right that was customary in Kent in ecclesiastical estates as early as 732. The evidence of the immunity on the continent does not encourage belief in the prescriptive exemption of men on church property from military service. But they may not have been called upon very frequently in the eighth century. The military needs of the kingdom are met in Bede's letter to Bishop Egbert by the *milites et comites* of the secular powers,[4] and in Beorhtric's charter of 794 by *omnes comites*. In Mercia and the kingdoms under Mercian control specific reservations of army-service occur in charters from the 790s and great emphasis is laid on

[1] For Wareham, see 'Wareham West Walls', *MA* III (1959), 120–38. For Cricklade, see *Wiltshire Archaeological Magazine* LVI (1955), 162–6. For Lydford, see the brief reports in *MA* VIII (1963), 168; *ibid.* IX (1965), 262–3; and *ibid.* X (1966), 168–9. For Wallingford, see the similar reports *ibid.* X (1966), 168; and *ibid.* XI (1967), 262–3.

[2] For Tamworth, see J. Gould, 'Excavations at Tamworth, 1967', *Transactions of the Lichfield and South Staffordshire Archaeological and Historical Society* IX (1967–8), 18–23. For Hereford, see the report of P. Rahtz in *Current Archaeology* XIX (July, 1968), 242–6.

[3] Birch, nos. 148 and 848 for Kent; Birch, no. 1331 and *ECW*, no. 398 for Wessex; and Birch no. 178 for Mercia.   [4] Plummer, *Bede* I, 414.

the fact that the whole people were to perform this and other obligations. To sustain the Mercian military supremacy it may well be that Offa had to make greater and more regular demands upon his noble and free subjects than previous rulers, just as Charlemagne was at the same time emphasizing the universal obligation of all his free subjects and defining their duties more precisely to meet the military needs of a swollen kingdom. We should expect that in England too kings were already able to vary the composition of their armies, and to demand a more select and better-armed force from the land, with those who did not serve contributing to the expenses of those who did. From the 790s also Viking raids were putting a premium on local defence and on the obligation of all to resist invasion, and there can be no doubt that the Viking danger was foremost in the minds of the scribes who first recorded the triple obligation in Kentish charters.

Among the rights which kings had long exacted from men on the estates of their subjects was labour on royal buildings and vills. Already in the time of King Ine the residence of the king (like that of a noble) was fortified in some degree, and was called a *burh*.[1] Such private strongholds with their gatehouses figure occasionally in the narrative sources.[2] A decisive stage, however, is reached when the king decides to build fortifications not merely for the convenience of his family and followers, but as places of refuge for his people and for the church. We cannot be certain that this happened only when the obligation to construct fortresses first appears in the charters, but *volksburgen* play little part in early English history.[3] The threat from the Welsh caused the eighth-century Mercian kings to build the great linear earthworks known as Wat's Dyke and Offa's Dyke. Extensive administrative arrangements must have been necessary to spread the burden of building and maintaining these works, but it is uncertain whether in border areas work on the dyke replaced fortress-work.[4] The Welsh threat may also have been responsible for Æthelbald's edict in 749 or somewhat earlier by which he imposed bridge-work and fortress defence upon all his people, or at least reorganized a burden that had hitherto been very occasional and sporadic into a general obligation on

---

[1] Ine 45 (Liebermann, *Gesetze* I, 108) defines the penalties for breaking into the burh of a king, bishop, ealdorman, king's thegn or gesith.

[2] See the account of the fight by Cyneheard and his companions at the royal burh of *Merantune* after the slaying of King Cynewulf (786), *ASC*, 755 (Earle and Plummer, *Chronicles*, p. 48).

[3] The name of Canterbury (*Cantwara-burh*) suggests such a rôle for the town in early times. The small seventh-century fort at Yeavering (see *The King's Works*, ed. H. M. Colvin [London, 1963] I, 2) seems to have been a private royal fort. For *volksburgen* on the continent see R. v. Uslar, *Studien zu frühgeschichtlichen Befestigungen zwischen Nordsee und Alpen* (Cologne, 1964), pp. 26–47.

[4] Birch, no. 416 speaks of *vallis…constructionem* rather than the usual *arcis constructionem*, and a spurious St Albans charter purporting to date from 795 has *fossam adversum inimicos faciendam* (Birch, no. 264).

the whole *folc*. In Kent bridge- and fortress-work would seem to have been introduced by Offa in 792 in an attempt to meet the Viking threat. In Wessex the evidence of the charters suggests that bridge-work was already enforced in the opening years of the ninth century, but that the building of fortifications may not have been exacted until about a half-century later. It is noteworthy that it was in Wessex, despite this late start, that the Viking invasions were successfully resisted; and it should be emphasized that the development of royal authority in England was directly connected with the successful enforcement of public works and general military obligations so that an adequate defence against the Vikings was provided. On the continent the failure of the Frankish rulers to maintain the programme of Charles the Bald led to the fragmentation of their public authority and the rise of feudal princes.

# Ælfric and the Old English version of the Ely privilege

## JOHN POPE

Some years ago, in his lecture on the prose style of Wulfstan, Professor Angus McIntosh described for comparison the so-called rhythmical prose of Ælfric, and called attention incidentally to the appearance of the characteristic features of this prose in an unexpected place: namely, the Old English version of the Ely privilege, which he argued might very well have been composed by Ælfric himself.[1] This Old English version purports to be a translation prepared at the command of King Edgar to accompany the official Latin charter, in which the king grants both privilege and numerous gifts to the newly restored abbey at Ely.[2] The Latin version is dated 970, more than twenty years before the supposed invention of this rhythmical prose by Ælfric,[3] who seems to have tried it out for the first time in some of the homilies of his Second Series.[4] There is no need, however, to conjure up an otherwise unknown genius who anticipated the characteristic features of Ælfric's style and diction a generation earlier. The earliest extant copy of the document is Stowe Charter 31 in the British Museum, a single sheet of parchment containing both Latin and Old English, of which the handwriting belongs to the second half of the eleventh century.[5] Though it has recently been persuasively argued that the Latin version, long treated as dubious, is a substantially accurate copy of an original charter of 970,[6] the Old English version could well have been added, or substituted for a less satisfactory version, in Ælfric's time or later. If we take the stylistic evidence at all seriously, the real question is whether this version is to be attributed to Ælfric himself or to some unknown imitator of his style.

My own study of the document, undertaken while I was preparing

---

[1] *Wulfstan's Prose*, Sir Israel Gollancz Memorial Lecture 1949, *Proceedings of the British Academy* (1949), p. 113 and n. 8 and pp. 128–9 (sep. ptg. London, pp. 7 and 22–3).

[2] Latin and Old English in Birch, nos. 1266 and 1267; Kemble, no. 563; and B. Thorpe, *Diplomatarium Anglicum Aevi Saxonici* (London, 1865), pp. 237–44. Best edition of the Old English in Robertson, *Charters*, no. 48.

[3] On the development and peculiarities of Ælfric's rhythmical prose see my edition, *Homilies of Ælfric: a Supplementary Collection*, EETS 259–60 (London, 1967–8), I, 105–36.

[4] The two series of Ælfric's *Catholic Homilies* are in *The Homilies of the Anglo-Saxon Church,... the Sermones Catholici, or Homilies of Ælfric*, ed. B. Thorpe (London, 1844 and 1846).

[5] McIntosh gives this date on the authority of Dr N. R. Ker.

[6] See below, pp. 96–7.

a fresh treatment of Ælfric's rhythmical prose for my edition of his homilies, led me to concur in Professor McIntosh's opinion, and indeed to feel that the stylistic evidence in favour of Ælfric's authorship was considerably stronger than it had been shown to be. Accordingly I recommended the inclusion of the Old English version in the Ælfric canon.[1] But while my edition was still in proof, Professor Whitelock drew my attention to the objections for which she was primarily responsible in a recent publication.[2] There the parallels adduced by Professor McIntosh are called unconvincing, and it is objected that 'so skilled a translator would hardly have produced the clumsy rendering of the Latin proem found here', though 'the Old English reads more like the language of Ælfric's time or later than that of 970'. An exchange of letters made it appear that she did not consider her objections insuperable and would gladly withdraw them if the stylistic argument could be sufficiently strengthened, as I thought it could be. But since there was no room for discussion of the matter in my edition, I was obliged to reserve it for such an occasion as has now presented itself. Whether or not the argument and the additional evidence here set forth turn out to be sufficient to allay her doubts, I offer them as to the 'only begetter' of the enterprise, and as a well deserved tribute to the exacting standards she has set for us all, and constantly exemplified, in matters of literary and historical speculation.

Since the attribution to Ælfric depends on style, and in the first instance on the presence of the distinctive features of Ælfric's rhythmical prose, it has seemed best to exhibit the Old English version in such a way as to bring out its basic rhythmical structure. Accordingly it is printed below in lines like verse, according to the loosely metrical groups into which, like Ælfric's undoubted compositions in this kind, it naturally falls by the rhythms of its syntactical phrases and its prevailing alliterative patterns. Most of Ælfric's *Lives of Saints* are so arranged by Skeat, and so are most of the homilies in my edition, besides others elsewhere.

But rhythm, however important, is only one aspect of style. A minor yet not insignificant part of the stylistic problem is the relation of the Old English to the Latin. I shall therefore present, together with the Old English, that part of the Latin version to which it corresponds. The Old English renders, though sometimes very inexactly, the sentiment and the several provisions of the charter from the beginning up to and including the anathema and an asseverative *amen*. It does not continue, as does the Latin, with the date and place of issue, the list of witnesses and a final

---

[1] *Op. cit.* I, 105, n. 2, and 145, n. 1.

[2] *LibEl*, p. 415. Professor Clemoes had previously called Ælfric's authorship 'altogether doubtful' in 'The Chronology of Ælfric's Works', *The Anglo-Saxons, Studies...presented to Bruce Dickins*, ed. Peter Clemoes (London, 1959), p. 219, n. 1.

corroboration in which is contained, as introduction to the Old English, the king's command that a translation be made and entered on the same sheet as the Latin.[1]

THE TEXT[2]

My text of the Old English version, with the corresponding Latin, is based on Stowe Charter 31 in the British Museum (abbreviated Stowe). It has been reproduced photographically in *Facsimiles of Anglo-Saxon Manuscripts*, Ordnance Survey, Part III, no. 32. I have used the facsimile, but at several points the Old English is obscure because of creases in the parchment or torn places that have been mended with loss of portions of letters. I am indebted to Dr Faulkner for verifying the readings of the original at these points. For the Old English I have also reported a few readings of interest from three much later manuscripts, which are abbreviated as follows in the footnotes:

Aug = BM Cotton Augustus II. 13, a single parchment presenting the charter, Latin and Old English, as confirmed by Henry VI in 1423. It appears not to be derived from Stowe, which, despite many blunders, it helps to confirm at most points. It shares with 9822 (next below) a mistaken emendation (line 9) and an omission due to homoeoteleuton (lines 49–50), but these two copies supply an essential word (line 18) omitted by Stowe.

9822 = BM Add. 9822, 13v–14v (Latin, 13r–v), an Ely cartulary of the late fourteenth or early fifteenth century described by G. R. C. Davis, *Medieval Cartularies of Great Britain* (London, 1958), p. 44. This copy of the charter purports to be derived from a confirmation by Edward the Confessor, reciting the original. It has many blunders, including frequent miswriting of OE insular *g* as *d*, but it supplements Aug helpfully.

5819 = BM Add. 5819, 4v–5r (Latin, 3v–4v), a copy of Stowe made by William Cole in the eighteenth century and used by Kemble and Thorpe before Stowe was available. Valuable, if at all, only where Stowe is hard to read.

I have used photostats of 9822 and 5819, and Dr Faulkner's collations of Aug. My text, though I think it is adequate for the present purpose, should not be considered definitive. Sawyer, pp. 247–8, lists eight other manuscripts containing both Latin and Old English, ranging in date from the late fourteenth to the seventeenth century, in the British Museum, the Public Record Office and the Bodleian, none of which I have seen. He also lists twenty-five manuscripts containing the Latin alone.

---

[1] The Stowe charter gives this final corroboration as follows: 'His igitur testibus et aliis compluribus de omnibus dignitatibus et primatibus regni mei hæc constituta et peracta noscuntur, quæ etiam nostra usitata sermocinatione describi mandauimus hac eadem sceda, quo possint in auribus uulgi sonare, ne aliqua scrupulositate admisceri uideantur; sed regia auctoritate seu potestate nobis a Deo donata omnis contradictio funditus adnulletur.' The Old English then follows directly.

[2] I wish to thank my colleague, Dr D. R. Faulkner, for his examination of the manuscripts, and especially for the very helpful reports mentioned below. Thanks are due likewise to the authorities of the British Museum for their help to us both and for permission to make use of their manuscripts.

87

References to previous editions, which are cited, like the supplementary manuscripts, only when a variant reading has seemed of interest, are abbreviated as follows:

K = Kemble, no. 563 (Latin and Old English), based selectively on 5918 and Aug.

T = Thorpe, *Diplomatarium*, pp. 237–43 (Latin and Old English), based, with differences from K, on 5819 and Aug.

B = Birch, no. 1266 (Latin) and 1267 (Old English), based on Stowe, with some inaccuracies.

R = Robertson, *Charters*, no. 48 (Old English only), based on Stowe, with variant readings from 5819, K, T and B.

The Latin, being of secondary concern here, is treated more simply. Besides the edition in Birch, no. 1266, based on Stowe, there is an excellent edition with variant readings from several manuscripts including Stowe and 9822 in *LibEl*, pp. 76–8. To avoid needless confusion in footnotes I have given the text as in Stowe (accepting Birch's expansions of the abbreviations and modernizing the punctuation), and placed in square brackets after the relevant words the few preferable readings in Dr Blake's text. Minor inaccuracies in Birch's text are similarly indicated. Line references to the Old English version are entered before corresponding segments of the Latin.

> Gode ælmihtigum rixiende, ðe ræt and gewissað
> eallum gesceaftum þurh his agenne wisdom –
> and he ealra cininga cynedom gewylt –,
> Ic EADGAR cining, eac þurh his gife
> ofer Engla þeode nu up aræred –      [5
> and he hæfð nu gewyld to minum anwealde
> Scottas and Cumbras, and eac swylce Bryttas,
> and eall þæt ðis igland him on innan hæfð,
> þæt ic nu on sibbe gesitte minne[1] cynestol –,
> hohful [eom][2] embe þæt, hu ic his lof arære,   [10
> ðe læs ðe his lof alicge to swyðe
> nu on urum timan þurh ure asolcennysse;
> ac ic wille nu þurh Godes wissunge
> þa forlætenan mynstru on minum anwealde gehwær

1–3] Omnipotentis Dei, cunctorum sceptra regentis moderamine regum, immo totius sæculi creaturæque cunctæ indissolubili regimine æquæ [æque] gubernantis habenas, 4–5] ipsius nutu et gratia suffultus, Ego Eadgarus basileus dilectæ insulæ Albionis, 6–9] subditis nobis sceptris [B *wrongly* sceptri] Scotorum, Cumbrorumque, ac Brittonum, et omnium circumcirca regionum, quiete pacem [pace] perfruens, 10–12] studiosus sollicite de laudibus creatoris omnium occupor addendis, ne nostra inertia nostrisque diebus plus æquo seruitus eius tepescere uideatur; 13–18] sed greges monachorum et sanctimonilium [sancti-

---

[1] *on minne* Aug, 9822, K, T.   [2] Supplied by conjecture. See below, p. 99.

mid munecum gesettan, and eac mid mynecenum,   [15
and Godes lof geedniwian ðe ær wæs forlæten,
Criste wissiendum, ðe cwæð þæt he wolde
wunian mid us oð þissere worulde[1] geendunge;
and þa munecas libban heora lif æfter regole
þæs halgan Benedictes, us to þingunge,   [20
þæt we þone hælænd[2] habban us glædne,
and he us gewissige and urne eard gehealde,
and[3] æfter geendunge þæt ece lif us forgife.

   Nu is me on mode, æfter mynegungum
Atheluuoldes biscopes, þe me oft manode,   [25
þæt ic wille góódian,[4] ðurh Godes silfes fultum,
þæt mynster on Elig mid agenum freodome
and sinderlicum wurðmynte, and siððan mid æhtum,
þam to bigleofan þe we gelogiað þær
to Godes ðeowdome, þe ðær simble wunion.   [30
Seo stow wæs gehalgod iu fram ealdum dagum
þam halgan Petre to wyrðmynte, ðæra apostola yldost,
and heo wæs geglengd þurh Godes sylfes wundra,
þe gelome wurdon æt Atheldrythe byrgene
þæs halgan mædenes, þe ðær gehal lið oð þis   [35
on eall-hwittre[5] ðryh of marmstane geworht.
Be hyre we rædað hu heo her on liue wæs,
and hu heo Gode ðeowode on godre drohtnunge,
and be hyre geendunge, and hu heo up adon wæs
ansund of hyre byrgene, swa swa Beda awrat,   [40
Engla þeodæ[6] lareow, on his larbocum.

monialium] hac nostra tempestate, ipso opitulante qui se nobiscum usque in finem sæculi manere promittere dignatus est, ubique in regno nostro desertis monasteriis antiquitus Dei famulatu deficiente, nunc reuiuiscente, adsurgere cupimus, 19–23] sub Sancti Benedicti abbatis regula uiuentes, quatinus illorum precatu et uigente religione sancta seruitus Dei nos ipsum placatum rectorem habere queamus.

24–32] Unde frequentes monitus uenerabilis Athelwoldi episcopi cordetenus pertractans, cupio honorare hoc priuilegio rebusque copiosis monasterium quod in regione ELIG situm dinoscitur antiquitus, ac Sancti Petri apostolorum principis honore dedicatum, 33–41] decoratumque reliquiis et miraculis almæ uirginis Ætheldredæ [B Ethel-, *overlooking initial hooked* e], cuius uita uenerabilis nobis modernis historia Anglorum promitur, quæ etiam incorruptibili corpore hactenus condita mausoleo marmoreo albo perdurat.

[1] *worulde* Aug, 9822, K, T; om. Stowe, 5819, B, R.
[2] *hælend* Aug, K, T; *haelend* 9822.   [3] *ge* Aug; *de* (for *ge*) 9822.
[4] *gegoodian* Aug, K, T; *de Goodian* (for the same) 9822.
[5] *-hwitre* Aug, 9822, K, T.   [6] *ðeode* Aug, 9822, T; *þeoda* K.

Nu wæs se halga stede yuele forlæten,
mid læssan ðeowdome þonne us gelicode,
nu on urum timan, and eac[1] wæs gehwyrfed
þam cyninge to handa – ic cweðe be me sylfum;　　　[45
ac Atheluuold bisceop, þe his[2] min rædbora
and soð Godes freond, sealde me to gehwærfe[3]
þone ham Heartingas, on sixtigum hidum,
wið þam mynster-lande þe lið into Helig,[4]
and ic þa geeacnode into Elig-mynstre　　　　　[50
þas ðry hamas ðe þus sind gehatene:
Meldeburna, Earningaford,[5] Norðwold;
and he þær-rihte mid minum ræde and fultume
mid munecum gesette þæt mynster æfter regole,
and him ealdor gesette us eallum ful cuðne,　　　[55
Brihtnoð gehaten,
þæt he under him þane halgan regol
for Gode geforðade æfter mynsterlicum þeawe.
　　Ða gelicode me þæt he hit swa gelogode
mid Godes þeowum Gode to lofe,　　　　　　[60
and ic þa geeacnode to þære ærran sylene
tyn þusenda ælfixa[6] ælce geare þam munecum,
þe me for fyrdinge[7] gefyrndagum aras

42–5] Locus denique predictus deficiente seruitio Dei nostra ætate regali fisco
subditus erat, 46–52] sed a secretis noster Atheluuoldus Deique amator
diocesi Uuintoniensis ciuitatis fungens, datis nobis sexaginta cassatis in uilla quæ
ab accolis Heartingas nuncupatur, mutuauit locum predictum cum appendiciis
eius, augmentauique mutuationi tres uillas quæ his nominibus uocitantur:
Meldeburna, Earmingaford, Northuuold, 53–8] et ipse ilico monachos meo
consilio et auxilio Deo fideliter regulari norma seruientes perplures inibi
collocauit, quibusque Brihtnothum quendam sapientem ac bene morieratum
[morigeratum] uirum præpositi iure præfecit.

59–61] Cui effectui admodum ego congaudens letabundus pro amore Christi
et Sancti Petri quem patronum michi sub Deo elegi et Sancte Ætheldredræ [*sic*]
uirginis Deo dilectæ et eius prosapiæ sanctæ illic quiescentis, et pro animabus
patrum meorum regum antiquorum augmentare largiter mutuationem illam his

---

[1] *eac* Aug, 9822, K, T, R (by emendation), and originally Stowe, which is torn and mended,
hence misread as *uc* 5819 and R, and as *ac* B.　　[2] *is* Aug, 9822, K, T (rightly).
[3] *-hwerfe* Aug, K; *-whearfe* 9822; *-hwearfe* T (the normal spelling).
[4] *Helig...into* (next line) om. Aug, 9822.
[5] *Earniga-* B (misreading due to a crease). Except for the Latin version in Stowe, the manuscripts
consulted have *n* rather than *m*, despite modern *Armingford*. Obviously the pronunciation
varied, but *n* is etymologically correct: see *PN C*, p. 50.
[6] Stowe is damaged, leaving only part of *e* visible at the beginning of the word, but the spacing
suggests original *æ*, not *e* as read by 5819, B and R; *ælfixa* Aug, K, T; *aelfixa* 9822.
[7] The translator properly understood Latin *expenditione* as *expeditione*.

binnan þam iggoðe of þam folce æt Wyllan,
and ealle¹ þa socna eac ofer þæt fennland                [65
into þam twam hundredum him to scrudfultume;
and on East-Englan² æt Wichlawan eac
ealle þa socna ofer fif hundredum,
and ofer ealle þa land gelice þa socna
þe into þam mynstre nu synd begytene,               [70
oððe ða þe him gyt becumað þurh Cristes foresceawunge,
oððe þurh ceap oððe þurh gife,
habban hi æfre on eallum þa socne,
and þone feorðan pening on folclicre steore
into Grantanbricge³ be minre unnan;                 [75
and gif ænig mann þiss awendan wylle,
þonne gange eall seo socn þe to anre niht feorme gebyreð
into þære stowe.⁴

And beo þis priuilegium, þæt is sindorlice wyrðmynt
oððe agen freodom into þære stowe,⁵               [80
mid eallum þissum ðingum,
Gode geoffrod mid urum góodum willan,

donis, testibus consiliariis meis uolo.    62–4] Hoc est, decem millia anguillarum quæ æt Uuyllan dicitur pro expenditione redduntur fratribus ad uictualia, modo et deinceps concedo,    65–6] et intra paludes causas seculares duorum centuriatuum,    67–8] et extra paludes quinque centuriatuum in Uuichlauuan in prouincia Orientalium Saxonum benigne ad fratrum necessaria sanctiendo [B *emends to* sanciendo] largior,    69–70] quin etiam omnes causas seu correptiones transgressionum iuste legis in sermonibus secularibus omnium terrarum siue uillarum ad monasterium predictum rite pertinentium,    71–3] et quas in futurum æuum Dei prouidentia loco prefato largitura est, siue emptione, seu donatione, aut aliqua iusta adquisitione, stent cause seculares emendandæ tam [*some MSS* tamen] clementi examine fratrum loco manentium uictui uel uestitui necessaria ministrantes,    74–5] adhuc insuper omnem quartum nummum reipublicæ in prouincia Grantaceaster fratribus reddendum iure perpetuo censeo.

79–84] Et sit hoc priuilegium liberum quasi munus nostrum Deo deuote oblatum et sanctis eius predictis, ad remedium animarum nostrarum sicuti

---

¹ *ealla* R (wrongly).
² By the time of the Conquest the Wicklow hundreds were on the Suffolk side of the boundary between that county and Essex, so that the OE *East-Englan* looks right and the Latin *Orientalium Saxonum*, though it persists in later copies of the Latin, looks wrong. But Eric John, *Orbis Britanniae and Other Studies* (Leicester, 1966), pp. 220–5, in a defence of the authenticity of the Latin version to which I refer below, p. 96, shows the likelihood that the Suffolk–Essex boundary was fluid in Edgar's reign, so that Essex was right in 970 though wrong later.
³ The Latin version's *Grantaceaster* is simply the more archaic name for Cambridge (not the modern Grantchester). See *PN C*, pp. 36–8.
⁴ On lines 76–8, which have no counterpart in the Latin, see below, pp. 93–4.
⁵ On lines 79 b–80, which interrupt the rhythmic movement of the passage, see below, pp. 94–5.

Gode æfre frig and Godes halgum,
for minre sawle and minra yldrena, us to alysednysse,
swa þæt nan þæra cyninga ðe cumað æfter me,     [85
oððe ealdorman, oððe oðer rica,
mid ænigum riccetere oððe unrihte
þiss ne awende oððe[1] gewanige,
be þam þe he nelle habban Godes awyrgednysse,
and his halgena, and mine, and minra yldrena,     [90
þe þas ðing fore synd gefreode on ecum freote on ecnysse.

AMHN.

prefati sumus, 85–91] ut nullus regum nec principum aut ullius ordinis quis-
libet prepotens inposterum [B im-] obstinata tyrannide aliquid horum infringere
presumat, si non uult habere omnipotentis Dei maledictionem, et sanctorum eius,
et meam, et patrum meorum, pro quibus ista omnia libera haberi uolumus
æterna libertate in æternum. amen.

### RHYTHMIC AND PHONETIC RESEMBLANCES TO
### ÆLFRIC IN THE OLD ENGLISH VERSION, AND SOME IRREGULAR
### LINES THAT SUGGEST INTERPOLATION

My arrangement of the Old English version will already have brought out
its most obviously Ælfrician characteristics. The lines in this arrangement
consist of roughly symmetrical pairs of phrases, each generally having two
prominent stresses. A caesura between the two phrases can almost always
be clearly recognized by the syntactical grouping even when there is no
call for punctuation. I prefer not to introduce an extra space, as is usual in
the printing of Old English poetry, because this exaggerates the independence of the half-line phrases and may seem to impede the flow of the
sentences. About nine times out of ten, each pair of phrases is bound
together by fairly conspicuous alliteration of the sort more strictly called
initial rhyme. For instance, in the first two lines, *rixiende* alliterates with
*ræt*, *eallum* with *agenne* – for, as in the poetry, any two initial vowels in
stressed syllables alliterate, whether they are the same or different.
Occasionally there is repetition of an entire syllable with change of suffix,
as in line 3, where *cyning* (in normal spelling) is matched with *cynedom*; or in
line 41, *lareow* with *larbocum*; or in line 12, *urum*, a mere possessive, with
*ure*. Occasionally, too, the alliteration is strengthened by plays on words.
These may be etymological, as in line 19 (*libban*, *lif*) or 54 (*munecum*,
*mynster*), or they may involve etymologically distinct words with associated meaning and partial similarity of sound but difference of gram-

---

[1] The scribe of Stowe forgot to cross his ðs, but he used his habitual form for *ð* rather than *d*.
The word is reported as *odde* in 5819, B and R.

matical function. The obvious example of this is the play on *God* and *gōd* in lines 26 and 38, a play frequently exploited by Ælfric, doubtless because the combination is theologically prescribed. Alliteration may also be supplemented by suffix-rhyme, especially when there is genuine parallelism of grammatical form and function. The most conspicuous example is in line 59 (*gelicode, gelogode*). Suffix-rhyme may even take precedence as a binder when alliteration is weak or lacking. In line 7 the translator had to deal with three proper names that do not alliterate. He balanced his phrases by adding *eac swylce* before the third name, and this gave him a weak alliteration with the first name, *Scottas*. But the three names had the same number of syllables and belonged to the same declension, so that the most obvious binder of the line is the repeated suffix. Equally conspicuous at the opposite extreme in position is the repetition that enforces the parallelism of alternatives in line 72 (*oððe þurh, oððe þurh*).

All these devices can be found in Ælfric's writings, and so can occasional lines with scarcely recognizable alliteration or none at all, and no phonetic substitute for it.[1] In this category I should put lines 34, 41, 52, 58, 64, 68 and 70. In all but one of these lines the rhythm is so regular and well balanced that one hardly notices the lack. Line 52 is unique. Here the translator encountered, in the three place-names, totally intractable but essential material. Since the names contained, in sum, approximately the right number of syllables, he placed them in asyndetic series, letting their three dissimilar rhythmic units take the place of the usual two.

Occasionally in Ælfric's writings we find two-stress phrases that lack mates.[2] A clear example here is line 56, *Brihtnoð gehaten*, which seems to stand alone naturally enough as a parenthetical explanation. We may notice, however, that, as often in Ælfric's practice, this phrase alliterates with the next line (*gehaten, he, him, halgan*).[3]

So far I have drawn illustrations from various and widely separated lines in the Old English version as if it were entirely homogeneous in style. But there is one passage, lines 76–81, that is irregular enough to arouse suspicion. On grounds of content as well as style I think this passage contains two separate interpolations, different in intent but similarly disruptive to the style. In lines 76–8 we find the king threatening to exact a compensatory payment in case his grant of the fourth penny from Cambridge is not honoured. Threats of this pecuniary sort, in contrast to threats of damnation such as we encounter in the closing anathema, are common in

---

[1] For repetition, word-play and suffix-rhyme in Ælfric see my edition I, 131–3, and for irregular and altogether lacking alliteration, pp. 124–30.

[2] See my edition I, 120–1.

[3] Possibly a half-line has been lost, for the Latin adjectives, *sapientem* and *morigeratum*, are not translated.

continental but not in Anglo-Saxon charters,[1] and this threat has no counterpart in the Latin version.[2] Moreover, the threat is entirely out of
keeping with the spirit of the Old English version at other points. Elsewhere, as will be clear when we examine more closely the relation between
Latin and English, the translator is concerned to render the sentiment and
the main provisions of the charter without much regard for legal precision.
Here alone we descend to litigious practicality, and this discrepancy of tone
and matter is matched by the lack of conformity in style. My arrangement
of these 'lines' accords with their syntax, and the resulting irregularity in
their length suggests that they should really be treated as ordinary prose.
Line 76 would, indeed, pass muster in spite of the confinement of the
alliteration to the second half, and the next line, if there were some
assignable reason for the sudden expansion, might be taken as a three-
stress pair (like the expansive concluding line, 91) with weak vocalic
alliteration on *eall* and *anre*, but this leaves us with a dangling, nondescript
*into þære stowe* for the concluding line. I am strongly inclined to believe that
these lines were inserted by someone at Ely who found that the lay
authorities of Cambridge were not disposed to honour the grant of the
fourth penny.[3]

A much less important but stylistically troublesome problem arises in
lines 79–81. Here alliteration is uncertain and a two-stress phrase is left
over at line 81. If, however, we omit the definition of *priuilegium* (*þæt
is...stowe*, 79 b–80), we have a single satisfactory line with alliteration of
*þis* with *þissum ðingum*:

> And beo þis priuilegium, mid eallum þissum ðingum,
> Gode geoffrod *etc.*

The definition, aside from what seems to me a slight awkwardness in the
application of the phrase *into þære stowe*, is natural enough and harmless,
but is it necessary? When, near the beginning of the Latin version, the

[1] See Pierre Chaplais, 'Some Early Anglo-Saxon Diplomas on Single Sheets: Originals or
Copies?', *Journal of the Society of Archivists* III. 7 (April, 1968), 322.

[2] Miss Robertson (*Charters*, p. 347) suggests that this threat is somehow connected to a passage
in a related Latin charter, Birch no. 1265, in which Edgar grants to Æthelwold, on behalf of
Ely, some sort of profits having to do with the king's food-rent for one night. There may
indeed be some connection, but as Miss Robertson is aware, the threat here is not at all the
same as the grant in no. 1265, however that is to be understood.

[3] Miss Robertson (*ibid.*) calls attention to a suit brought by the abbey at some time between
1072 and 1075 against Picot the sheriff of Cambridge, who was accused of usurping the fourth
penny. It is tempting to see a connection between that suit and this suspicious passage, but
although Stowe, our earliest witness to the text, may be later than the date of the suit, that is
by no means a certainty, and there is a further reason for caution. Add. 9822, though written
at a late date, purports to be derived from a confirmation of Edward the Confessor. Since
9822 contains the passage in question, we ought perhaps to assume that it had already been
incorporated in the charter some years before the Conquest. Quite possibly there was dispute
about the fourth penny before Picot's time.

translator encountered the ablative *priuilegio*, he translated it freely, *mid agenum freodome and sinderlicum wurðmynte* (lines 27b–28a). I cannot help suspecting that, when he came to the same word later, he kept the Latin form without translating it, and that someone else, thinking it needed explanation, reverted to the earlier translation and produced this stylistically intrusive clause.[1]

If the translator was Ælfric, there is support for this conjecture in his Life of St Maur, where he is describing how a Frankish nobleman named Florus persuaded the king to let him found a monastery for the saint. The whole passage is interesting as showing Ælfric's familiarity with the language and the legal process of founding and endowing monasteries:

> Florus ða cydde þam cyninge his willan,
> and be his leafan arærde on his agenum lande
> mynster, and munuc-lif, swa swa Maurus him dihte,
> and mid micelre are þæt mynster gegodode,
> and priuilegium sette on swutelre gewitnysse,
> and Maure betæhte þæt mynster mid ealle
> to fullum freodome, for his sawle ðearfe.[2]

Here Ælfric has introduced the word *priuilegium* as if it had already been sufficiently naturalized to be understood, and unless his copy of the Latin Life differed at this point from ours, he introduced it independently of his source.[3]

Aside from these two bits of suspected interpolation, which differ sufficiently from one another in function to have been added by different persons, the Old English version shows the same technique throughout. Rhythm, alliteration and the supplementary phonetic devices are thoroughly characteristic of Ælfric. Superficially, this is his kind of rhythmical prose, nor do I know of another writer who imitated even these superficial features so closely in a passage of comparable length.[4] Yet such imitation would very likely have been possible. Several other aspects of the style must be considered before we can form a reasonable judgement, and some of these will be more clearly distinguished if we compare the Old English version with the Latin.

---

[1] The grammatical fault, *sindorlice* for *sindorlic*, is perhaps scribal.

[2] *Ælfric's Lives of Saints*, ed. W. W. Skeat, EETS o.s. 76, 82, 94 and 114 (London, 1881–1900, repr. 1966), no. VI, lines 144–50. I have modernized Skeat's punctuation. At this time Ælfric was presumably at *Cernel* (Cerne Abbas), in the monastery which had been somewhat similarly founded by the nobleman Æthelmær.

[3] The supposed source has only this: 'Tunc clarissimus vir Florus, scripto, juxta consilium beati viri, testamento, tradidit ei omnia, et de suo jure in ejus delegavit potestatem atque dominium.' *Acta Sanctorum Bollandiana*, 15 Jan., p. 329. See J. H. Ott, *Über die Quellen der Heiligenleben in Aelfrics Lives of Saints* (Halle a. S., 1892), pp. 21 ff.

[4] I have commented on some possible imitations in my edition, I, 72, n. 1, and 309, but these are brief introductions to genuine homilies, and I have judged them to be imitations because of irregularities and ineptitudes.

### THE RELATION OF THE OLD ENGLISH TO THE LATIN

A minor but troublesome problem must be dealt with at the very outset of this discussion. Although it is obvious that the Old English version is presenting at most points the substance of the Latin charter as it has come down to us, there are a number of very striking differences of detail, especially in the opening lines. These differences have awakened doubt as to whether the translator had precisely this version of the Latin charter before him. For example, the attributive phrases applied to God and the king at the beginning of the proem are by no means the same, and somewhat closer parallels to those applied to the king in the Old English version have been quoted from other charters by Professor Whitelock.[1] It is possible, as she suggests, that the Latin charter was rewritten at some points after the translation had been made. Yet I am inclined to believe, because of certain correspondences to be mentioned, that the translator was working with the text exactly as we have it, aside from mere scribal variations. This belief has been strengthened by a recent defence of the authenticity of the Latin version.

For many years the experts in Anglo-Saxon diplomatic have been suspicious of the charter,[2] primarily, one may suppose, because many of its formulae, including the regnal style and the anathema, are unparalleled in other charters of Edgar's reign. This and other possible causes for suspicion, mainly a number of discrepancies between the account of the transactions in the charter and what can be gathered from other Ely records, have been summarized by Dr Blake on the basis of Professor Whitelock's careful and acutely critical study of the documents.[3] In terms of traditional assumptions about the form to be expected in Edgar's charters, the novelty of the formulae immediately arouses suspicion, and the various discrepancies, if not necessarily proof of forgery, nevertheless require explanation. But recently a very powerful argument on behalf of the charter has been put forward by Mr Eric John, who admits the accuracy of nearly all the observations I have mentioned but puts them in a new light.[4] He points out that the strangeness of the formulae in this charter is a characteristic shared by several other foundation charters of Edgar and argues that this is a sign, not that they are forgeries, but that they were drafted by the

---

[1] *LibEl*, p. 415.

[2] See the digest of comments on its authenticity in Sawyer, pp. 248–9.

[3] *LibEl*, p. 414. The resemblance there alluded to between the phrase *regali fisco subditus* in the charter and *regali fisco deditus* in the *Life of Æthelwold* (both Ælfric's and Wulfstan's versions), with reference to precisely the same situation, certainly suggests borrowing, but not necessarily by the author of the charter; for if Ælfric translated the charter he was very likely the borrower. I agree with Professor Whitelock in believing that his version of the *Life of Æthelwold* preceded Wulfstan's.

[4] *Op. cit.* pp. 210–33.

beneficiaries in the restored monasteries rather than in the king's scriptorium, as had been the rule in the immediately preceding reigns.[1] He also shows that the several discrepancies can be explained in such a way as not to discredit the charter.[2] Although I am not competent to pass final judgement in such a matter, I find Mr John's argument convincing,[3] and shall therefore assume, for the purposes of this paper, that our version of the Latin charter is substantially the same as an authentic charter of Edgar issued in 970. This assumption need not exclude the possibility that minor changes were introduced after the date of the translation, but it makes changes in the ceremonial portions of the charter, such as the proem, particularly improbable.

As I have already intimated, a close comparison of the Old English version with the Latin seems to me to make against the notion that the translator had a substantially different text before him. Some of his most startling deviations from the Latin are counterbalanced by small correspondences that would not be likely to occur if the Latin had been significantly different. At the very beginning, for instance, although the translator changes the construction, substituting a dative absolute that suggests a very common ablative absolute formula in other Latin charters, beginning with *regnante*, it is almost always *Iesu Christo* that follows, and I have seen no instance of *regnante* (or *regente*) *Deo omnipotente*.[4] The *Omnipotentis Dei...regentis* of the present charter, though in the genitive case, has apparently influenced the translator's *Gode ælmihtigum rixiende*.[5] Again, though the praise of God in the first few lines is varied in grammatical form, order of ideas and metaphor, the basic notions of God's governance of all creation and his control of all kingly power are preserved. The

[1] On this development, see the generalization by Chaplais in 'The Origin and Authenticity of the Royal Anglo-Saxon Diploma', *Journal of the Society of Archivists* III. 2 (October, 1965), 60.

[2] One such explanation is mentioned above, p. 91, n. 2. Mr John has anticipated the inference drawn above (p. 96, n. 3) about the direction of the borrowing between the charter and the *Life of Æthelwold*, if there was any borrowing, but I think he is unnecessarily sceptical about the probability of it.

[3] It is accepted without question by C. R. Hart, *The Early Charters of Eastern England* (Leicester, 1966), p. 43.

[4] Miss Robertson (*Charters*, p. 278), annotating a charter in which the Latin formula, *Regnante in perpetuum domino nostro Iesu Christo*, is translated literally by *Ricsiendum urum dryhtne hælendum* [*sic*] *Criste in ecnisse*, cites a number of instances of virtually the same formula in Birch, and there are many others.

[5] The form *rixiende*, where one would expect the ordinary participial dative *rixiendum* (cf. the translator's *Criste wissiendum*, line 17), may be scribal, either an instance of levelling (as in the much later text printed Robertson, *Charters*, p. 22, *Rixiende ure dritte hælende Crist*) or a reminiscence of Latin *regnante*, but I hesitate to emend, because if Ælfric was the translator he may have deliberately used an ending corresponding to a participial noun *rixiend* (recorded only for the *Durham Ritual*) in order to avoid a suffix-rhyme with *ælmihtigum*. Elsewhere, in the combinations *eallwealdend God* and *þrymwealdend God*, he uses the nominal form *-wealdend* as an adjective. See BT and the glossary in my edition, II, 821 and 928. Note, however, the normal participle in the nominative case in the line, *an ælmihtig God æfre rixiende*, homily no. IV, line 170 and homily no. XI, line 86 in my edition.

expression *ipsius nutu et gratia suffultus* is passed over at the point where it occurs, but is partially recognized a bit later by *þurh his gifu...nu up aræred*. Amid the many differences of expression that occur in lines 5–12 there is nevertheless an exact rendering of the *Scotorum, Cumbrorumque, ac Brittonum*, a comparable emphasis on peace and on the king's anxious concern for the glorification of God, and a relatively close correspondence in the final clause of the sequence, lines 11–12, where the Latin *ne, nostra inertia* and *nostris diebus* have natural counterparts in *ðe læs ðe, ure asolcennysse* and *nu on urum timan*, while *his lof alicge to swyðe* is a skilful simplification of the ponderous *plus æquo seruitus eius tepescere uideatur*. Almost as striking is the fact that the next clause in the Latin, corresponding only roughly to the syntactically very different clauses in lines 13–21 of the Old English, is nevertheless introduced by *ac*, an exact rendering of the vaguely adversative and transitional *sed* of the Latin.

Furthermore, if we assume provisionally that the translator was working with the Latin text as we know it, we can account for nearly all[1] the additions, omissions and substitutions, radical though some of them are, as resulting in part from his preferences as a writer of English, in part from the demands of his peculiar rhythmical style, in part from his response to the subject-matter and his apparent purposes in making the translation.

The translator's preferences as a writer of English account, I think, for most of the syntactical differences. Although he is willing to use a dative absolute in imitation of the Latin ablative absolute, and even to introduce it where the Latin has a different construction, as he does in line 1, he consistently avoids the extreme hypotactic construction of the long Latin sentences, breaking them up into a series of paratactic clauses with brief subordinate appendages. This can be seen very clearly in lines 13–41, as well as at later points in the document. A different but not wholly dissimilar strategy is discernible in lines 1–12, although this strategy is partially obscured by a grammatical flaw which is attributable, I think, to a mere oversight, probably on the part of a scribe. In view of the importance of the passage, this flaw is serious enough to require special attention.

As the text of these lines has come down to us, it comprises a disconcerting sequence of phrases and subordinate or parenthetical clauses without a main verb and with no clear indication where such a verb ought to be. One's first impression is certainly of a very clumsy performance. Yet when the rhythmic structure has been clearly set out, it is evident that, line by line, we are dealing with a well built and rhetorically accomplished passage. And when we examine the Latin, we notice how much – again

---

[1] Excluded are lines 76–8 and 79b–80, the two passages discussed above (pp. 93 ff.) as probable interpolations, and the grammatical flaw which has prompted the emendation in line 10. This is discussed below, in the next paragraph but one.

line by line – has been done to reduce its turgidity and simplify its syntax. But we also notice that the translator seems to be striving to retain some of the grandiloquence and periodical suspense of the original. The Latin clause is not only periodic; it is also a hypotactic labyrinth out of which one escapes ultimately by the almost too unobtrusive verb *occupor*. I think the translator was sufficiently impressed by the stately progress of this complicated period to want to capture something of its elevation without its laborious intricacy. This could be done by breaking down the interocking minor phrases and clauses into a syntactically looser sequence with parenthetical shifts of construction, but preserving the periodic effect by lputting the main verb in approximately the same position as the Latin *occupor*. Consequently I have inserted *eom* after *hohful* in line 10. I had considered inserting it before *nu* in line 5. This would have made an easier sequence with no protracted suspense, but it would have constituted a rejection of the central design of the Latin and it would have blurred the meaning. For if we put *eom* in line 5, *hohful embe þæt* will seem to depend directly on *ic gesitte* in line 9. In the Latin, the king's anxiety to show his gratitude to the Lord arises, as according to good sense it should, not simply from the fact that he is allowed to reign in peace, but from the whole series of blessings of which that is the last and best. *Hohful eom* is a satisfactory simplification of the prolix *studiosus sollicite...occupor*, and it supplies the necessary resolution of the grammatical suspense with complete faithfulness to the spirit and essential meaning of the Latin.[1] I think we must credit the translator with having had the intelligence and the skill to complete his clause in this way, or in a better way if such can be found, for whether he was Ælfric or not, he shows at other points in this very sentence, and in the rest of the translation, a more than adequate command of grammar and rhetoric.

The prolonged suspense of this passage as emended helps to set the elevated tone appropriate to a royal diploma, but once it has served its turn it is not repeated. In general, the Old English version moves onward easily from one idea to the next without forcing the reader to hold several ideas, some of them only half expressed, in his head for a long time before the final unravelling. Concurrently, there is a marked tendency to simplify ornate or complicated expressions. I have already directed attention to one such simplification in line 11, and a combination of verbal and syntactic simplification is obvious in lines 1–3. In line 13 the translator anticipates *hac nostra tempestate* by a simple *nu*, and line 16 reduces to balanced ease and clarity a heavily freighted sequence extending from *antiquitus* to the

---

[1] In the sequence *eom embe* it would have been easy for a scribe to omit *eom*, both because of the similarity of the letters and because *hohful embe* makes good sense locally. The mistake must have arisen very early in the textual history of the translation.

grammatically unrelated *adsurgere*. Comparable simplification may be observed in lines 24–5 and 35–6.

As we move from the proem into the section dealing with Edgar's specific grants, we notice that the translator is careful to state each one faithfully, though sometimes without legal flourishes, and it may seem that he is taking fewer liberties with the Latin. Yet here too we find him avoiding prolixity and ready to expand or abridge or rearrange. In lines 42–58, where the Latin is simpler and more straightforward than usual, he changes very little until he comes to the mention of Brihtnoth, where his alterations have nothing to do with style.[1] But in the next paragraph, lines 59–75, he performs almost a miracle of condensation, at least partly in the interest of style, and here too he does not hesitate to rearrange. The Latin mentions the king's desire to provide food for the monks (*ad uictualia*) in the passage corresponding to lines 62–4, where eels are granted, but the translator had already mentioned this desire in an elaboration at line 29 (*þam to bigleofan*), and he does not repeat it here. On the other hand he supplies immediately afterwards, at line 66, where the first grant of jurisdictional revenue is introduced, the desire to provide for clothing (*to scrudfultume*). This anticipates the mention of *uestitui necessaria* in a later passage which would normally have been translated after line 73 in the Old English, but the whole passage (*emendandæ...ministrantes*), which seems both complicated and superfluous, is there left untranslated. The result of all this is a much shorter, clearer, and more vigorous paragraph.

The simplified syntax that prevails must have been encouraged by the translator's rhythmical style with its prevailingly end-stopped pairs of phrases. In Ælfric's rhythmic homilies (in partial contrast to some of those in ordinary prose) such long sentences as we encounter tend to be composed of a paratactic series of relatively brief clauses, with only such subordinate members as will fit the rhythmic pattern of a line or two and not greatly impede the forward movement of the thought.

Metrical considerations would also have encouraged additions and abridgements, and the search for alliteration would have led to freedom in the choice of words. In line 2, for instance, the phrase *þurh his agenne wisdom*, which has no counterpart in the Latin, serves to complete the line with proper stress and alliteration at the same time that it introduces a no doubt welcome allusion to the second person of the Trinity. Again, in lines 4 and 5, the adaptation and displacement of *ipsius nutu et gratia suffultus* was presumably as much a consequence of metrical and alliterative requirements as of idiom or syntax. The *eac* of line 4 serves as a link with the preceding statement and is to some extent comparable to *ipsius*, but it also supplies alliteration and a needed stress. The phrase *ofer Engla þeode*,

---

[1] These alterations are considered below, p. 112.

which sounds more natural in Old English than any literal rendering of *dilectæ insulæ Albionis*, is also of just the right length and alliteration to match *nu up aræred*. The translator's repetition of *lof* in line 11 in preference to introducing a variation comparable to that of *seruitus* upon *laudibus* serves the alliterative scheme as well as providing a good pivot for the contrast between *arære* and *alicge*. In line 26, the phrase *ðurh Godes silfes fultum*, though appropriate, is not in the Latin and has clearly been added to fill out the line. These are only a few conspicuous examples of a process of adjustment which continues throughout the Old English version.

Prevailingly, however, while making these adjustments, the translator keeps the broad significance of the charter foremost. The Latin version makes much of Edgar's zeal as the restorer of monasteries, of his enthusiastic compliance with the counsel of Æthelwold, of the special sanctity conferred upon Ely by the relics and the miracles of Æthelthryth and finally, of course, of the thoughtfulness and liberality with which Edgar and Æthelwold together have provided for the material needs of the monks, their spiritual leadership and their adherence to the rule of St Benedict. The translator gives full attention to all this, often increasing the emphasis of the Latin, sometimes by suppressing needless complications, sometimes by elaboration. Allusions – to Trinitarian doctrine in line 2, to God's guidance in line 13, to his help in line 26 and to his responsibility for the miracles at Æthelthryth's tomb in line 33 – make the king seem even more pious than does the Latin. Two lines, 22 and 23, added to the proem, bring it to a close on a strongly religious note. The first of these lines, prompted by the untranslated *rectorem*, emphasizes the king's concern for God's help in governing and protecting his realm. The second, with its hope of eternal life, balances this and at the same time complements the mention of Christ's promise to be with us here on earth in lines 17–18.

The translator's concern with these themes shows itself not simply in direct statement but also in the organization of his sentences and the repetitions that give them coherence and emphasis. Thus, in the proem, the change in the order of ideas in lines 2 and 3 brings *ealra cininga* close to *Eadgar cining* and enforces Edgar's recognition of divine authority. In a larger way, the repetition of forms of *wissian* and *wissung* increases the emphasis on God's guidance, while the recurrence of *nu*, several times added without prompting from the Latin, helps to focus all the king's thoughts about his power, his good fortune, his desires and anxieties on the urgency of the present. Thus the *Nu* that ushers in the grant of the privilege at line 24 is much more heavily charged than the *Unde* it replaces. It seems to assure us of the king's sincerity. Presently, at line 31, the mood and the interest shift to a venerable antiquity introduced by *iu*, and the past is dwelt upon with a loving attention that goes beyond the Latin. The movement from the miracles that have made Ely sacred, to the recollections of St Æthelthryth's life, to reverence for Bede as the great teacher of the English not only elaborates the suggestions of the Latin but gives them the effect of a naturally unfolding reminiscence, almost an artless digression, from which we are brought back at the beginning of the next paragraph to a sharp sense of the recent desolation of the site. In short, the translation is so far from being perfunctory that it is animated throughout by the translator's active re-creation of the thought.

The image of the translator that emerges from this comparison is not so sharply delineated that we can be certain it is Ælfric's, but nonetheless it accords with what we otherwise know of him. Nearly all his writing is founded on Latin originals, and his treatment of them varies from the faithful but never slavish translations of biblical passages to the exceedingly free adaptations of numerous expositors. It would have been like him to assert his independence of a regnal formula that did not suit his taste or his stylistic exigencies, to draw upon his own knowledge of Æthelthryth and Bede, and yet to remain utterly faithful to the essential spirit and the specific provisions of the charter. For he would have taken the charter to heart as this translator did, and displayed in the process both his own mastery of Latin and his command of English rhetoric. In interests, knowledge, craftsmanship, habits of mind and seriousness of purpose, insofar as these have become apparent, the translator cannot easily be distinguished from Ælfric.

### THE DICTION OF THE OLD ENGLISH VERSION AND SOME ÆLFRICIAN PARALLELS[1]

I turn now, after this survey of the broadly Ælfrician character of the translation, to a close inspection of the details of expression. Professor

[1] In this section the following abbreviations are used for references to Ælfric's works:

Assmann *Angelsächsische Homilien und Heiligenleben*, ed. B. Assmann (Kassel, 1889; repr., with supplementary introduction by Peter Clemoes, Darmstadt, 1964). Cited by number of article and line.

CH *Catholic Homilies*, ed. Thorpe (as above, p. 85, n. 4). Cited by volume, page and line.

EpJ Epilogue to Ælfric's translation of *Judges*, cited by line, in *The Old English Version of the Heptateuch*, ed. S. J. Crawford, EETS o.s. 160 (repr. 1968, with the text of two additional manuscripts transcribed by N. R. Ker), 414–17.

*Grammar Ælfrics Grammatik und Glossar*, ed. J. Zupitza (Berlin, 1880; repr., with a pref. by H. Gneuss, Berlin, 1966). Cited by page and line.

HÆ *Homilies of Ælfric*, ed. Pope (as above, p. 85, n. 3). Cited by number of article and line.

LS *Ælfric's Lives of Saints*, ed. Skeat (as above, p. 95, n. 2). Cited by number of article and line.

ONT Ælfric's *Letter to Sigeweard, On the Old and New Testament*, cited by line, in *The Old English Version of the Heptateuch* (as above, EpJ), pp. 15–80.

McIntosh, in his brief note,[1] declared his conviction that the diction was thoroughly characteristic of Ælfric, but the parallels he assembled were not very numerous, and some of them, as he confessed, were very weak, being stylistically inert and the more or less inevitable consequences of similar subject-matter. This aspect of the problem will bear fuller analysis and stronger evidence.

Most of Professor McIntosh's parallels were drawn from Ælfric's treatment of three conspicuous themes of the charter: Edgar's kingly virtues, his concern for the monasteries and the wondrously manifested sanctity of Æthelthryth. The first two of these themes Ælfric had elaborated in three passages of great importance for the present discussion. One of these, a nine-line outburst prompted by Moses' use of prayer to gain a miraculous victory over the Amalekites,[2] does not mention Edgar himself but looks back wistfully on his reign as a time of peace founded on a combination of military power and piety:

> Wel we magon geðencan hu wel hit ferde mid us
> þa þa þis igland wæs wunigende on sibbe,
> and munuc-lif wæron mid wurðscipe gehealdene,
> and ða woruldmenn wæron wære wið heora fynd,
> swa þæt ure word sprang wide geond þas eorðan.

It is the subsequent overthrow of monasteries and contempt for divine worship that is blamed for current evils:

> Hu wæs hit ða siððan ða þa man towearp munuc-lif,
> and Godes biggengas to bysmore hæfde,
> buton þæt us com to cwealm and hunger,
> and siððan hæðen here us hæfde to bysmre.

At about the same period of his career, Ælfric began his Life of St Swithun with praise of the days of Edgar, and concluded it with twenty lines in elaboration of the theme:[3]

> We secgað to soðan þæt se tima wæs gesælig
> and wynsum on Angelcynne, þa ða Eadgar cynincg
> þone cristendom gefyrðrode, and fela munuclifa arærde,
> and his cynerice wæs wunigende on sibbe,
> swa þæt man ne gehyrde gif ænig scip-here wære
> buton agenre leode þe ðis land heoldon,
> and ealle ða cyningas þe on þysum iglande wæron,
> Cumera, and Scotta, comon to Eadgare,
> hwilon anes dæges eahta cyningas,
> and hi ealle gebugon to Eadgares wissunge.
> Þær-to-eacan wæron swilce wundra gefremode

[1] See above, p. 85, n. 1.    [2] *LS* XIII. 147 ff.    [3] *LS* XXI. 444–63.

þurh þone halgan Swyðun, swa swa we sædon ær,
and swa lange swa swa we leofodon þær wurdon gelome
wundra.
On ðam timan wæron eac wurðfulle bisceopas,
Dunstan se anræda æt ðam erce-stole,
and Aþelwold se arwurða, and oðre gehwylce,
ac Dunstan and Aþelwold wæron Drihtne gecorene,
and hi swyðost manodon menn to Godes willan,
and ælc god aræron, Gode to cwemednysse:
þæt geswuteliað þa wundra þe God wyrcð þurh hi.

This is the fullest of the three passages. Ælfric returned to the theme in
a broader context in the elaborate epilogue to his translation of *Judges*.
After noting that the rule of judges in Israel was succeeded by a period of
monarchy, he takes a brief look at political history, considering the character of the rulers, chiefly kings, who have contributed to the power and
prosperity of nations. After a review of Roman history he turns to his
own country, extols the victorious reigns of Alfred and Athelstan, who,
after defeating Anlaf, *on sibbe wunude siþþan mid his leode*, and concludes with
the glories of Edgar:[1]

Eadgar, se æðela and se anræda cining,
aræde Godes lof on his leode gehwær,
ealra cininga swiðost ofer Engla ðeode,
and him God gewilde his wiðerwinnan a,
ciningas and eorlas, þæt hi comon him to
buton ælcum gefeohte friðes wilniende,
him underþeodde to þam þe he wolde,
and he wæs gewurðod wide geond land.

It is obvious that these passages can furnish several parallels to the charter,
and the more significant of these are included in the list of parallels below;
but the passages are more important as testimony to Ælfric's deep commitment to the themes themselves, the greatness of Edgar and his bene-
ficent concern for the monasteries.

Ælfric's Life of Æthelthryth[2] has a similar importance, outweighing its
value for parallels, as exhibiting his familiarity with and enthusiasm for
another of the prominent themes of the charter. Even so it does contain
some very suggestive parallels. Both Ælfric and the author of the Latin
charter depended on Bede's account of the saint,[3] so that all three have
some correspondences, yet those between the Old English version of the
charter and Ælfric's Life are particularly close. Since the relevant parts of
the Life are of some length, and not consecutive, quotations from it are

---

[1] *EpJ* 81–7 according to the editor's arrangement.
[2] *LS* xx.    [3] *HE* IV. 19.

limited to the most important parallels in the list shortly to be presented. First, however, we must look in a more general way at the diction of the Old English version.

When we compare the vocabulary of this piece with that of Ælfric's accredited writings, its general conformity is obvious. A number of the words that have to do with order, with creative activity and government on the one hand, obedience and service on the other, whether in the universe or in human society, are among Ælfric's favourites. Such, for example, are the various inflected forms of *rixian* 'to reign' (line 1), *wissian* or *gewissian* 'to guide, direct' (1, 17 and 22) and its verbal noun *wissung* (13), *gewealdan* 'to rule' (3), *gewyldan* 'to subdue, subject' (6), *anweald* 'authority, sway' (6), *aræran* 'to raise, advance, establish' when applied to abstractions such as *lof* (10), *geedniwian* 'to renew' (16), *mynegung* 'prompting' (24) and *manian* 'to admonish' (25), *þeowdom* 'service' (30), *þeowian* 'to serve' (38), *geforðian* 'to promote' (58), *foresceawung* 'providence' (71) and *steor*, 'guidance, discipline, correction' (74). Equally familiar in his works are the specifically doctrinal terms *þingung* 'intercession' (20) and *alysednyss* 'redemption' (84), the sin of *asolcennyss* 'sloth' (12), the barely naturalized *regol* 'rule' (19, 54 and 57) with its specific reference to St Benedict and to *mynsterlic þeaw* 'monastic custom' (58). These words were of course common property among the clergy. All that one can say is that the selection and emphasis are characteristic of Ælfric if not necessarily distinctive.

Several other words, not quite the staples of discourse but ideologically neutral and relatively familiar, are of very frequent occurrence in Ælfric: for example, *wurðmynt* 'honour' (28 and 32), *geglengan* 'to adorn' (33), *drohtnung* 'way of life, conduct' (38) – not neutral indeed when modified by *god*, *bigleofa* 'food, sustenance' (29), the impersonal *gelician* 'to please' (43 and 59) and *geendung* 'ending' as applied to a person's death (23 and 39). In fact nearly all the words in the translation can be found in Ælfric's writings with similar construction and meaning, though some are so common as to be beneath notice and others so rare as not to seem characteristic.

As might be expected, however, one or two of the familiar words have meanings not recorded for Ælfric, and there are a few words that have not been observed in his writings. Five of these words are legal or political terms indispensable in charters and not often required in sermons: *hid* as a measure of land (48), *socn* as revenue from judicial proceedings (65, 68, 69, 73 and 77), *hundred* as a territorial entity (66 and 68), *freot* as freedom in a legal sense (91), and *gehwearf* 'exchange' of property (47). Closely related to this last is the specialized use of *gehwyrfan* (a word Ælfric uses occasionally in other senses) in the sense 'to transfer' property (44). Three other words are nonce-compounds of which the elements were obviously familiar to everyone and can be found in Ælfric: *mynster-land* (49), which needs no comment, *scrud-fultum* 'provision for clothes' (66) and *æl-fisc* 'eel-fish' (62), of which the first element, *æl*, translates *anguilla* in the fish section of the glossary appended to Ælfric's *Grammar* (308/6). These three compounds occur nowhere else, according to the dictionaries. An adverbial compound, *gefyrn-dagum* 'in former times' (63), is on record apart from this charter only once, in the non-Ælfrician account of the Seven Sleepers included in Skeat's edition of Ælfric's *Lives of Saints*.[1] The phrase *in* or *on fyrndagum* appears several times in the poetry, and *gefyrn* 'formerly, of old' is used often by Ælfric, but *gefyrndagum* is surprisingly rare. Alliteration and rhythm must have helped to elicit it here. Finally, there are two words of somewhat greater interest. The intransitive *alicgan* 'to decline, fail', here rendering *tepescere* (11), is recorded not at all for Ælfric and only once for Wulfstan,[2] although both use the corresponding transitive *alecgan* 'to suppress, impair, diminish' very often. The other word is *rædan* 'to rule' in the form *ræt* (1), which is not recorded for Ælfric in this not uncommon sense, though it appears frequently in his works in the senses 'to advise' and 'to read'. If Ælfric was the author of the translation, his exceptional use of the word can probably be attributed to the stylistic desire to multiply words for ruling (he has also used three of his customary words for it at this spot: *rixian*, *gewissian* and *gewealdan*) and to provide alliteration.

These exceptions seem no more than what one would expect in the translation of a document so different in style and content from the literature with which Ælfric was accustomed to deal. They are easily outweighed by a number of usages, including several collocations of words, to which Ælfrician parallels can be found. In the following list I have combined these parallels with comments on some individual words that seem of more interest than those already mentioned as familiar in Ælfric's works. The order is that of occurrence in the Old English text, as indicated by the line numbers:

1–3 *gewissað...gewylt*. These words have already been mentioned as of frequent occurrence in Ælfric's writings. He used the two together at *CH* I, 78/15: *se Heretoga seðe gewylt and gewissað Israhela folc*, a parallel already noted by McIntosh.

2 *þurh his agenne wisdom*. This phrase, not suggested by the Latin, alludes to God the Son in a manner habitual with Ælfric. Cf. *CH* I, 10/5: *þurh his wisdom he geworhte ealle þing*; *HÆ* VI. 243: *Se wisa Fæder...geworhte ðurh his halgan Wisdom, þe his Sunu is, ealle gesceafta*; Assmann I. 8: *Se ælmihtiga God...gesceop ealle þing...þurh his soðan wisdom. And se wisdom is witodlice his Sunu*.

5 *ofer Engla þeode*, partially replacing, in a different construction, *dilectæ*

[1] *LS* XXIII. 588.
[2] In one of the laws he framed, V Æthelred 32 (Liebermann, *Gesetze* I, 244). On the attribution, see Whitelock, *Sermo Lupi*, p. 23.

*insulæ Albionis.* At *EpJ* 83, Edgar is described as *ealra cininga swiðost ofer Engla ðeode.* Noted by McIntosh.

6 *he hæfð nu gewyld to minum anwealde,* enlarging upon the Latin *subditis nobis.* The idea and the first verb correspond to what is said of Edgar at *EpJ* 84: *and him God gewilde his wiðerwinnan a, cyningas and eorlas* (noted by McIntosh), but the verbal play had been used a few lines earlier with reference to the Romans, *EpJ* 24–5: *hi mid heora wisdome gewyldon. . .ealne middaneard to heora anwealde.*

9 *þæt ic nu on sibbe gesitte minne cynestol,* a free rendering of *quiete pace perfruens.* The *on sibbe,* though the phrase itself and the idea are present in the three passages on Edgar (and Athelstan) quoted above, is hardly to be avoided in view of the Latin. More striking are parallels to the construction with *gesittan* and to the rhythmic balance of the line. Cf. *LS* VII. 95, *He gesæt þa his dom-setl dreorig on mode*; *LS* XVIII. 384, *þine suna gesittað þæt cynesetl on Israhel*; and especially *CH* II, 306/1, *He mid sige gesæt siððan his cynestol.* This last example was quoted by McIntosh, but the word *sige* was inadvertently omitted, spoiling the rhythmic balance as well as the sense, and the rhythmic parallel between *on sibbe* and *mid sige.*

10 *hohful. . .embe. . .hu.* The word *hohful* occurs several times in Ælfric and less frequently elsewhere. It is found at *CH* II, 152/6 and 10, and 324/5; *LS* XII. 84 (and Napier, *Wulfstan,* p. 142, line 6, in an extract from the same piece); *LS* XXXI. 1084; Napier, *Wulfstan,* p. 152, line 19 (in a uniquely preserved passage by Ælfric identified as his by McIntosh). The construction with *embe* occurs at *HÆ* XI. 154, and that with *hu* at *LS* II. 121–2.

10 *hu ic his lof arære,* corresponding to *de laudibus creatoris addendis.* Inflected variations occur at least three times in Ælfric: *EpJ* 83, *arærde Godes lof* (of Edgar, noted by McIntosh); *LS* XXV. 382, *Godes lof arærdon*; and *LS* XXVI. 137, *Godes lof arærende.* K. Jost observed this expression in Wulfstan's panegyric on Edgar, *ASC,* 957 D, *He arærde Godes lof,* and regarded it as a borrowing from Ælfric, since Wulfstan does not normally use *Godes lof.*[1]

11 *his lof alicge to swyðe.* The lack of parallels for *alicge* and the frequency of *alecgan* in Ælfric have already been mentioned.[2] An otherwise close parallel is *ONT* 790, *Godes lof alecgan.* For *to swyðe,* a type of intensive less common in Ælfric than in Wulfstan, compare nevertheless *ONT* 1071–2, *to lufienne leahtras to swiðe.*

12 and 44 *nu on urum timan,* translating *nostris diebus* and *nostra ætate.* Cf. *CH* I, 292/15, *Nu eac on urum timan,* and *LS* XVI. 219, *Nu on urum dagum.* Possibly a widespread turn of phrase, but at any rate congenial to Ælfric.

15 *mid munecum gesettan,* and similarly 54. The construction *gesettan mid* 'to people with, fill with' is not common in Ælfric, but cf. *CH* II, 466/23, *þæs dæges godspel. . .is eal mæst mid haligra manna naman geset.*

16 *Godes lof geedniwian,* partially suggested by *reuiuiscente.* Cf. *LS* XXVII. 134–5, which bears on lines 26 and 29 also: *Godes cyrcan gegodode mid landum and bigleofum, and Godes lof geedniwode.*

17–18 *ðe cwæð þæt he wolde wunian mid us oð þissere worulde geendunge.* Ælfric translates and refers to this promise (Matthew XXVIII. 20) on several occasions.

---

[1] *Anglia* XLVII (1923), 117.  [2] Above, p. 106.

Cf. *CH* I, 310/18–19, *Ic beo mid eow eallum dagum, oð þisre worulde geendunge* (slightly varied at *CH* I, 600 and *CH* II, 368); and *HÆ* VIII. 225–6, *ac he wunað swaðeah, oþ þissere worulde ende, mid his halgum mannum.*

22–3 *and he us gewissige...and...þæt ece lif us forgife.* These lines, expanding the sentiment of the Latin with no direct warrant, are adapted to the king by *urne eard gehealde*, but otherwise they bring to mind the closing formulae of some of the homilies. Cf. Assmann III. 595–6, *Gewissige us se hælend to his willan a, and he us gelæde to þam ecan life*; and similarly *LS* XVII. 268–9 and *HÆ* XIII. 235. The phrase *to his willan a* may suggest the sentiment of line 21.

26–7 *ic wille goodian...þæt mynster on Elig mid agenum freodome.* Cf. *CH* I, 452/23, *þæt mynster gegodode*; and especially *LS* VI. 147–50, *þæt mynster gegodode,...and... betæhte...to fullum freodome.*[1] The form *gegodian* is usual in Ælfric and is probably the better reading here. Ælfric has *godode* at least once, *CH* II, 468/12 (according to Thorpe's manuscript), but with a different application and directly after *gegodod.*

28 *and sinderlicum wurðmynte.* This definition of *priuilegium* is found in a gloss to Aldhelm's prose *De Virginitate*[2] and Ælfric uses *synderlic wurðmynt* to designate the peculiar honour accorded by Christ to virgins, Assmann III. 431.

29 *þe we gelogiað þær* and 59 *hit gelogode mid Godes ðeowum.* The verb *gelogian* as construed in the first example is very common in Ælfric. The construction *gelogian mid* is rarer, but it occurs at *CH* I, 344/11 and 506/15, *Ðæt mynster he gelogode mid wellybbendum mannum*, and *LS* XXXII. 256.

31 *iu fram ealdum dagum*, rendering *antiquitus* at a slightly different place. Cf. *HÆ* XXI. 525, *fram ealdum dagum*, and XVIII. 281, *Iu on ealdum dagum.*

33–4 *þurh Godes sylfes wundra, þe gelome wurdon æt Atheldrythe byrgene.* Cf. the Life of Æthelthryth, *LS* XX. 4, *swa swa þa wundra geswuteliað þe heo wyrcð gelome.* Similar expressions concerning the miracles of other saints are found at *CH* II, 152/28, *LS* XXI. 456,[3] *LS* XXXVI. 418 and *LS* XXXII. 172: *gelome wundra wurdon æt his byrgene.*

35–6 *þe ðær gehal lið oð þis on eall-hwittre ðryh of marmstane geworht.* McIntosh has quoted *LS* XX. 111–12, *seðe hire lic heold hal on ðære byrgene git oð þisne dæg*; and 79–81, *ane mære þruh...geworht of marmstane eall-hwites bleos.* Cf. also 100, *þær ðær heo lið oð þis.* Ælfric's use of *eall-hwit, eall-god, eall-niwe*, and *eall-sweart* is illustrated in the glossary to my edition. For *gehal* see *CH* II, 20/23, 154/22, 166/11 and 352/22 and *LS* XXXII. 176.

38 *and hu heo Gode ðeowode on godre drohtnunge.* That expressions of this sort have a long history is suggested by *The Old English Version of Bede's Ecclesiastical History of the English People*, ed. T. Miller, EETS o.s. 95, 96, 110 and 111 (London, 1890–8), 242, lines 3–4: *Sume in mynsterlicre drohtnunge in regollicum life getreowlice Drihtne þeowodon.* But at *LS* XX. 32–4 Ælfric expresses similarly Æthelthryth's request *þæt heo Criste moste þeowian on mynsterlicre drohtnunge.*

39–40 *and hu heo up adon wæs ansund of hyre byrgene.* Cf. *LS* XX. 73–4, *Þa wolde seo Sexburh...don hire swustor ban of ðære byrgene up*; 93–5, *Þa wæs seo wund gehæled,...*

---

[1] The entire passage is quoted above, p. 95.
[2] A. S. Napier, *Old English Glosses* (Oxford, 1900), no. 211.
[3] Quoted above, p. 104.

*eac swilce þa gewæda...wæron swa ansunde swylce hi eall-niwe wæron.* Also of Edmund, *LS* XXXII. 184, *he liþ swa ansund oþ þisne andwerdan dæg,* which except for *ansund* resembles the expression in line 35.

40–1 *swa swa Beda awrat, Engla þeodæ lareow, on his larbocum.* The parallels here are so important that they have been reserved for separate discussion below.

46 *rædbora.* Ælfric uses this word for counsellors, *CH* II, 522/32, and for Roman consuls, *EpJ* 17.

58 *for Gode geforðade æfter mynsterlicum þeawe,* a free elaboration of the Latin. Cf. Assmann VIII. 83, *And he hi geforðode on fægerum þeawum.* The verb *geforþian* appears elsewhere in Ælfric, and also in Wulfstan: Bethurum, *Wulfstan,* no. XVIII, lines 17 and 18.

61 *sylene.* Ælfric uses this word occasionally, e.g. *CH* II, 500/33, 502/5 and 556/26 and *HÆ* XXX. 36.

63 *fyrdinge.* Ælfric uses *fyrding* for an army or a military campaign several times, e.g. *CH* II, 66/2 and 194/13, Assmann IX. 46, 55 and 67 and *HÆ* XXII. 53 and XXIX. 42 and 44.

64 *iggoðe.* This not very common word for a small island appears at *CH* I, 58/31 and *ONT* 1034.

75 *be minre unnan.* The noun *unne* 'grant', though particularly frequent in charters, appears also in *CH* I, 506/27 and *LS* III. 556.

77 *feorme.* The word *feorm* is used by Ælfric, though I think the passage including it here is not by Ælfric.

79 *priuilegium.* As I have already mentioned,[1] Ælfric uses this Latin loan-word without explanation in the Life of St Maur, *LS* VI. 148.

87 *riccetere.* Ælfric uses this word frequently for power, especially if tyrannical, or arrogance: e.g. *CH* I, 82/21 and 242/4 and II, 592/27, *HÆ* XXVI. 110, *LS* XXXII. 233 and *ONT* 92.

88 *gewanige.* The verb *wanian* or *gewanian* 'to diminish' is not very common, but appears in Ælfric at *CH* II, 466/6 and *HÆ* X. 168 and 169 and XI. 264, as well as in Whitelock, *Sermo Lupi,* line 29.

91 *gefreode.* Cf. *HÆ* XXIII. 40–1, concerning the liberation of prisoners, *he gefreode ealle and mid æhtum gegodode.* The last phrase may remind us of key words in lines 26 and 28.

Most of the parallels in the foregoing list are probably of more value for their cumulative power than for anything unquestionably distinctive about them as individuals. They serve mainly to assure us that we are dealing with a piece of writing that is well within the range of Ælfric's habits of expression, and to make us wonder whether any other writer would so consistently have come within that range. I think there may be something truly distinctive in the use of *priuilegium* at line 79 (especially if the explanation of it in lines 79b–80 is an interpolation) taken in conjunction with the earlier translation of this word as *sinderlic wurðmynt* at line 28. The most telling parallel of all, however, is one that I have reserved for special consideration here.

[1] Above, p. 95.

In lines 40–1 the translator recasts the Latin allusion to the *historia Anglorum* as follows:

swa swa Beda awrat,
Engla þeodæ lareow, on his larbocum.

There are two features of line 41 that are of interest, the characterization of Bede, and the verbal play of *lareow* and *larbocum*. There is only one other occurrence on record of *Engla þeode lareow*, and it is applied by Ælfric to Bede in the homily on St Cuthbert, *CH* II, 132/5. I think Ælfric invented this characterization in order to suggest that Bede, in a more limited sphere, was comparable to St Paul. Paul, as apostle to the Gentiles, is very properly called *ealra þeoda lareow* by Ælfric on several occasions: for example, at *CH* I, 384/23, *LS* XVII. 1 and Assmann III. 152; and sometimes just *þeoda lareow*, as in some passages to be quoted presently. This may have been a long established way of referring to Paul, although the dictionaries have not helped me to find an earlier example. But *Engla þeode lareow* is an honorific adaptation that, however appropriate to Bede, would not occur to everyone. If it was not invented by Ælfric, it is at least the sort of compliment that only a writer of his sentiment and sensitivity would know how to value. And it would seem that in this passage the association with St Paul was stylistically infectious. At Assmann VI. 108 is the line, *Paulus, þeoda lareow, cwæð on his larbocum*; and at *ONT* 1213–14 we read, *swa swa Paulus sæde, se þeoda lareow, on his lareowdome*. I will not shake the reader's confidence further than I have already done by telling him which of these lines, the two just quoted and the line in the charter, came first, although all three probably belong among compositions later than 1005, the year when Ælfric became abbot of Eynsham; but my guess would be that the lines on Paul preceded the line in the charter. In any case the parallels are striking, and we may fairly ask, who but Ælfric himself would have referred to Bede in this fashion or combined the reference with a play on words that he uses elsewhere in connection with the very saint whose example inspired the characterization of Bede?

SOME TENTATIVE CONCLUSIONS

The argument for Ælfric's authorship of the translation must rest on the kind of evidence, necessarily internal, that has now been presented. It should be clear that, if he was not the author, we must postulate a very extraordinary imitator, one who was not only capable of composing rhythmical prose of a precisely Ælfrician sort, but one whose mind was so completely attuned to Ælfric's writings that he could think in Ælfric's words and idioms without once betraying his own idiosyncrasy or reaching out for some other writer's expressions. He must have been able to invent

Ælfrician variations upon Ælfric's earlier inventions. He must have had Ælfric's command of Latin and Ælfric's seasoned readiness to assert his own independence as a writer without betraying the spirit of his original. And he must either have shared Ælfric's concerns and enthusiasms wholeheartedly, or have been one of the subtlest and most talented of impersonators. And to what end would he have laboured? Would he have admired Ælfric's way of writing so fervently that it would have seemed to him the only way to do justice to the charter? If his purpose had been to strengthen its authority by a translation that would pass for an original part of the document, he would hardly have chosen to imitate so brilliantly the most accomplished writer of a later generation. Under the circumstances it seems best to conclude that the translator was Ælfric himself.

As Professor McIntosh saw, there is little difficulty in supplying Ælfric with motives for the translation, or with an occasion for it. It is evident, from Ælfric's celebrations of Edgar, that the charter would have appealed to him as a confirmation of his own idealized image of the king. It emphasizes not only Edgar's readiness to attribute his unrivalled power and security to God's grace, and his grateful resolve to increase God's praise by restoring the monasteries, but also his particular regard for the counsel of Bishop Æthelwold, who had actually been the prime mover in the restoration. Ælfric had studied under Æthelwold at Winchester, had introduced himself as his pupil in the Latin preface to the first series of homilies, and was eventually, in about 1006, to produce a Latin Life of the man.[1] What more natural than that he should espouse Æthelwold's cause? Moreover, his interest in Ely had already been aroused by Bede's account of Æthelthryth, upon which he had based his own version of her Life, and this interest would presumably have been strengthened by the ties between Winchester and Ely which the charter itself makes evident.

Professor McIntosh has suggested that Ælfric might have translated the charter at about the time, 1006, when he was at work on Æthelwold's Life, and this is an attractive hypothesis. His preparation of the Life would have been an occasion for gathering what information he could about his hero's career. The charter would have appeared as one of the primary sources, and indeed there is a wisp of evidence to show that it was used. The Life includes an account of the restoration of Ely that accords roughly with what the charter has to say, and there are two expressions, one within that account and one soon after it, that may have been borrowed from the charter.[2] Ælfric might very well have visited Ely and studied the charter

[1] *Vita S. Æthelwoldi*, in *Chronicon Monasterii de Abingdon*, ed. J. Stevenson, Rolls Series II (1858), 253–66.

[2] Compare what is said in the *Vita* (*ibid.* p. 262), first about Ely prior to Æthelwold's efforts to restore it: *erat tunc destitutus et regali fisco deditus*, and then, a few sentences later, about

there, or a copy might have been sent to him. His own position, after 1005, as abbot of Eynsham would have made him all the more interested in it, and all the more concerned to support the monastic cause. It is possible, certainly, that he did not set about making the translation till some time after he had completed the Life of Æthelwold, but this is a matter of no particular moment.

I am inclined to doubt, however, that Ælfric intended his translation to be incorporated in the charter. There is indeed every reason to suppose that he meant it to serve as a piece of propaganda, not only for the monks of Ely but for the monasteries in general. Yet besides the freedom of the translation, which weakens its value as testimony to the exact content of the Latin, there is a possibly significant substitution in the passage about the first abbot, Brihtnoth. In the Latin he is described in a distantly complimentary way as *quendam sapientem ac bene morigeratum uirum*. For this the translator has substituted the warmer but much less specific phrase, *us eallum ful cuðne*.[1] Literally, this friendly commendation is the king's, but as an invention of the translator's it looks like an affectionate gesture toward an old Winchester man who had been kindly remembered both there and at Ely. Brihtnoth was apparently still alive in 996,[2] so that Ælfric himself could have known him, though he might merely have been paying tribute to the feelings of the older generation. In any case the translator appears to be thinking more of his own contemporaries or elders at Winchester and Ely than of posterity, a sign, as it seems to me, that he did not have distinctly in mind the perpetuation of his translation as part of an official document.

Whether or nor Ælfric intended it, however, the translation came to be treated not only as official but as a translation produced at King Edgar's behest.[3] I was for a long time inclined to regard the Latin passage containing Edgar's command as altogether spurious, and the consequent misrepresentation of the Old English version as a deliberate piece of deception. With such deception, however venial it might have been, I was altogether unwilling to associate Ælfric, for it is out of keeping with everything else we know about him,[4] and there would have been so little need to charge him with complicity that to do so would have been irresponsibly cynical.

But once again Mr Eric John has opened the way to a more satisfactory

---

Æthelwold: *Erat autem Athelwoldus a secretis regis Eadgari*, with the sentence in the charter corresponding to lines 41–5 in the Old English: *Locus. . .regali fisco subditus erat, sed a secretis noster Athelwoldus* etc. See above, p. 96, n. 3, and p. 97, n. 2.

[1] Line 55. As I remarked above, p. 93, n. 3, something more like the Latin may have been lost from the incomplete line 56, but in any case the familiar tone of line 55 would remain.

[2] *LibEl*, p. 411.    [3] See above, p. 87, n. 1.

[4] See, for example, his outburst against lies in my edition, homily no. XXII, lines 95–103.

explanation.[1] He points out that Edgar's command has a parallel in Edgar's confirmation to Winchester Cathedral of land at Chilcomb, Birch no. 1147. The Old English version of this confirmation, Birch no. 1148, is in language that seems entirely appropriate to Edgar's reign, and there is no reason that I am aware of to question its authenticity. Mr John suggests that a contemporary translation may very well have been made for the Ely charter and subsequently replaced by the one we have. The suggestion is by no means unreasonable. A glance at the Chilcomb translation will show that it is a thoroughly pedestrian performance, omitting the Latin proem altogether, and doing less than justice to the remainder of its not particularly distinguished original. If such a translation had been made of the Ely charter in Edgar's time, it would have struck Ælfric as hopelessly inadequate, for it would have omitted or cheapened the very passages he most valued. The mere sight of it, once his interest in the Latin version had been aroused, would very likely have inspired him to attempt something more satisfactory. He would have employed his own characteristic style, wishing simply to make the translation as eloquent as possible, and not at all concerned to conceal his authorship of it, for he would have had no thought of pretending that it had been composed in Edgar's time. Even the monks of Ely, when their awareness of its superiority induced them to substitute it for the earlier translation, would scarcely have been chargeable with intent to deceive, though the effect of their action was to befuddle many a learned head in times to come. I propose, therefore, until a likelier interpretation is offered, to consider the Latin charter genuine in its entirety, the Old English version Ælfric's, its position in the charter the result of a simple substitution, and the monks of Ely, if we shut our eyes for the moment to the doings of that meddlesome interpolator at line 76, guilty for once of nothing more than a little carelessness and an indifference to the as yet unwritten laws of copyright.

[1] *Op. cit.* p. 231.

# Towns in late Anglo-Saxon England: the evidence and some possible lines of enquiry

## HENRY LOYN

England, though well blessed with evidence relating to urban development, has never produced a school of urban history on the model of some continental countries. This is not to denigrate the value of the contribution of many historians who have devoted much time and energy to urban studies: the names of F. W. Maitland, Miss Mary Bateson and J. Tait come instinctively to mind from an earlier generation. But it is significant that Tait's book on the *Medieval English Borough*, published in 1936, remains the last general book of consequence to appear on the topic of urban development through the whole sweep of the Middle Ages.[1] Important work in detail over the last generation, by the very fact that it has increased awareness of complexity, may have helped to inhibit attempts at a general account. It nevertheless remains surprising that so obviously worthwhile a subject should have eluded its synthesizer for so long.

Hesitations are more intelligible about the earlier phases of our medieval urban history, about the period that lies before the Norman Conquest. Evidence exists, but it is patchy, spasmodic and lacking in continuity in time and space. The bearing of this evidence on the master-problem of urban origins is clear-cut, but it is impossible to make firm propositions about the moment of transition from non-urban to urban community, or to tell whether military, administrative, merchant or artisan elements predominated at such a moment. Yet great advance has been made, notably in the work of Sir Frank Stenton and Professor Dorothy Whitelock.[2] One general result of recent investigation is a growing sense of wonder that scholars could ever seriously have held that the Anglo-Saxons, outside London, had no town worthy of the name. From Alfred's establishment of burhs and the work of his children, Edward and Æthelflæd, through the plentiful diplomatic, legal and ancillary material of the tenth and early eleventh centuries to the great storehouse of Domesday Book, there is evidence enough for the existence of towns, and firm and conclusive indication of varied and subtly complex urban growth. The controversy that

---

[1] J. Tait, *The Medieval English Borough* (Manchester, 1936; repr. 1968).
[2] Stenton, *A-S England*, esp. pp. 518–35, and Dorothy Whitelock, *The Beginnings of English Society* (London, 1952), pp. 126–33.

vexed the 1930s between Tait and Stevenson has been resolved in Tait's favour: we are all Taitians now.[1] Work on coinage alone, with all its bearing on urbanization, has been enough to establish the existence of towns beyond all reasonable doubt.[2]

A further effect of recent work has been to give us a better idea of the widespread distribution of urban effort in England south of the Humber and of the considerable variation in the nature of that effort. Appreciation of the importance of trade with the continent, especially Frankia and the Rhineland, has sharpened, and of trade back to Scandinavia. Respect has grown for the multitude of small market-towns in Wessex as well as for the substantial Anglo-Danish towns of the Danelaw. Conscious guard has been taken and continues to be taken against distortion which has occurred because of the heavy weight of evidence in the last generations before the Norman Conquest from the east, notably from the great abbeys of Peterborough and Bury St Edmunds.[3] The south and west are no longer neglected in favour of the east. Winchester, Exeter, Cricklade and Lydford receive their proper due as well as Thetford, Stamford and Peterborough. On the internal organization of the town a better knowledge of the surviving guild statutes has enabled us to recognize clear moves towards corporate action notably in social matters, though it is of course recognized that even at the end of the Anglo-Saxon period there was some way to go before the characteristic exaction of rights through charters was achieved. The sneaking suspicion has grown that townsmen played a greater part in national politics as well as in social and economic life than used to be thought, and that the distribution of population in the ratio of about one to ten, townsmen to country-dwellers, a figure normally accepted for the England of Domesday Book, is probably a modest estimate, and even so significantly high for the age.[4]

Some tentative general conclusions may therefore be advanced in favour of a relatively well advanced urban order in Anglo-Saxon days. What types of evidence are available for such investigation and how best may they be classified? Three main divisions of material are immediately evident: charters, laws and guild statutes. Ancillary evidence from coinage and archaeology must also be taken into account. There remains one

[1] The controversy is best followed in the article by Carl Stephenson, 'The Anglo-Saxon Borough', *EHR* XLV (1930), 177–207, and the rejoinder by J. Tait, *ibid.* XLVIII (1933), 642–8 (substantially ch. 6 of *The Medieval English Borough*).

[2] *Anglo-Saxon Coins*, ed. R. H. M. Dolley (London, 1961), a set of essays presented to Sir Frank Stenton in honour of his eightieth birthday, provides a compact introduction to this difficult but rewarding topic.

[3] C. R. Hart, *The Early Charters of Eastern England* (Leicester, 1966), p. 11, emphasizes the weight and mass of the evidence from Peterborough, Thorney, Ely and Ramsey from the time of their second foundation in the later tenth century. Bury St Edmunds increases the eastern weight after its eleventh-century foundation.

[4] A point made by P. H. Sawyer, *EHR* LXXIX (1964), 579.

document, essential to our understanding of the early stages of urban development and difficult to classify: the Burghal Hidage.[1] Nearest in form to a charter it is yet not a charter. It is best regarded as a very early government memorandum, drawn up initially in the reign of Alfred, elaborated and brought up-to-date in the reign of his son Edward the Elder, a necessary instrument to remind the king and his advisers of acts taken fundamental for the defence of the community.

The Burghal Hidage stands alone in importance, and it is doubtful even now whether we have realized its full significance in relation to the development of royal government as well as in the more purely urban field. The document has a dramatic quality, not in the sense of the chance of its survival – there are no fewer than seven known manuscripts – but in the sense of the fitness of its survival.[2] The Hidage is a coherent document setting out to show how defensive works were centrally planned and how defensive works were locally manned. It is a record of an effective answer to the barbarian raids of the ninth and tenth centuries. English defensive effort was directed by a true king of Greater Wessex. The immediate purpose was to hold the frontier but there was a capacity for development outside to Kent and to Mercia. The Mercian Register with its record of burhs fortified or refortified by Æthelflæd and her husband Æthelred in the Mercian lands is a natural sequel to the Burghal Hidage. The poem in *The Anglo-Saxon Chronicle, s.a.* 942, is a further natural and proper consequence as the fortifications built by the Danes themselves were absorbed.[3] It seems very likely that the general principles behind the Burghal Hidage, allowing for local variations in practice, were recognized throughout the kingdom subject to the House of Cerdic. The combination of ultimate royal responsibility and supervision and effective action on the part of local landowners came to apply to Derby and Leicester as well as to Tamworth and Watchet. The framer of the Burghal Hidage knew precisely how to express this combined effort. In stating his general principles he betrays a sometimes underestimated degree of sophistication in the arts of government:

For the maintenance and defence of an acre's breadth of wall, sixteen hides are required. If every hide is represented by one man, then every pole of wall can be

[1] The most convenient edition and translation of the Burghal Hidage appears in Robertson, *Charters*, pp. 246–9. There is a valuable article by Nicholas Brooks on 'The Unidentified Forts of the Burghal Hidage', *MA* VIII (1964), 74–90. Also Robin Flower, 'The Text of the Burghal Hidage', *London Medieval Studies* I (1937), 60.

[2] The manuscripts are discussed by David Hill, 'The Burghal Hidage: the Establishment of a Text', *MA* XIII (1969), 84–92. Also Miss Robertson, *op. cit.* p. 494, who prints from the Nowell transcript (BM Add. 43703) of the early-eleventh-century BM Cotton Otho B. xi (almost totally destroyed in the fire of 1731).

[3] Earle and Plummer, *Chronicles* I, 93–105 (C with variants from B), and a note on pp. 92–3 for the Mercian Register; also Whitelock, *ASC*, p. xiv and pp. 59–68. The poem in the annal for 942 appears in Earle and Plummer, *Chronicles*, p. 110, and, in translation, Whitelock, *ASC*, p. 71.

manned by four men. Then for the maintenance of twenty poles of wall eighty hides are required, and for a furlong 160 hides are required by the same reckoning I have stated above...for the maintenance of a circuit of twelve furlongs of wall 1,920 hides are required. If the circuit is greater, the additional amount can easily be deduced from this account, for 160 men are always required for one furlong, then every pole of wall is manned by four men.

The arrival at the general principle after a long succession of sums, culminating in the duodecimal complexities of 12 × 160, is no mean triumph. It implies the existence of strong-minded practical royal servants, capable of issuing practical instructions in the vernacular, and capable too of framing rules which could be extended throughout the kingdom. And, as we shall see, the royal control of burhs was a matter of great moment to the development of towns. Not all burhs grew into towns; but no town could flourish without fortifications in the tenth and eleventh centuries. And some, such as Oxford and Wallingford, bear trace of urban planning virtually *ab initio*.[1] This direct royal concern with fortifications, openly expressed in the Burghal Hidage, is to be found also in the so-called *trinoda necessitas* of Anglo-Saxon charters.[2] The three royal rights almost invariably reserved, even in grants made to the greatest franchise holders, were the rights over the army, the *fyrd*, over bridges and over burhs. In this respect royal authority and the often still tentative urban element in society grew together.

It is fair to say that recent work on the Burghal Hidage is bringing about slowly but surely a new evaluation of the growing complexity of late Old English society, and a new appreciation of the connection between burhs and towns. Archaeologists and historians are increasingly conscious that the physical features of English recovery in the first quarter of the tenth century brought into being institutions of continuous and permanent significance. The recovery of the Danelaw was closely associated with an elaborate burghal policy. *The Anglo-Saxon Chronicle* has many references to the building of fortifications, the refurbishing of older fortifications and even, in relation to Towcester, the provision of a stone wall to an existing fortified burh.[3] An intense series of repairs and restorations, for example, took place at Huntingdon, Colchester, Stamford, Tamworth, Thelwall

[1] Whitelock, *The Beginnings of English Society*, p. 127, draws attention to Asser's testimony that some burhs were founded on places of little previous importance, and suggests that Oxford and Wallingford, founded on eight yardlands of land, probably fell into this category.

[2] The most acute discussion of this institution is that of W. H. Stevenson, 'Trinoda Necessitas', *EHR* xxix (1914), 689–703.

[3] Earle and Plummer, *Chronicles*, p. 102, and, in translation, Whitelock, *ASC*, p. 66. Dr Florence Harmer refers to the *burhwealles sceating* of Worcester in her perceptive article, a key discussion of Anglo-Saxon markets and fairs, 'Chipping and Market: a Lexicographical Investigation', *The Early Cultures of North-West Europe*, ed. Sir Cyril Fox and Bruce Dickins (Cambridge, 1950), p. 344.

and Manchester. Powerful corporate effort was made to provide fortifications which would give protection to substantial populations. Strategic reasons often, though not always, coincided with economic needs. After 942 and the reabsorption of the Danish Five Boroughs, even more so after 954 with the removal of the last Viking king of York, a network of strong points, a great number of which held urban content or potential, existed throughout the English kingdom, close in their ties with the king, and big with promise of development in the social and economic life of the community.

The tenth-century borough may in this sense be identified as a conspicuous product of successful resistance to barbarian invasion, peculiarly royal in an England where king and community were welded together in the fire and force of the Scandinavian onslaught. Borough walls did not exhaust the possibilities for fortified defence, and attention has been focused recently on other more humble manifestations of effective defensive works. In particular a text from the private compilation associated with Wulfstan of York, and known as *Geþyncðo*, has received fresh appraisal. It reads: 'If a ceorl throve so that he had full five hides of his own land, a church, a kitchen, a bell-house, a *burhgeat*, a *setl* and special office in the king's hall, then was he thenceforth worthy of the rights of a thegn.'[1] The key expression is *burhgeat*, innocuously translated in the twelfth century as *ianua* or *porta*.

The nineteenth century, until disillusioned by Stevenson in a famous article in 1897, tended to run *burhgeat* and *setl* together into one horrendous compound *burhgeatsetl* with a root meaning of duty at the guard-room of a borough, by no means foolish institutionally, though alas, stylistically impossible.[2] All now agree that we have a simple *burhgeat* on our hands, but the meaning is far from clear. Maitland, with later charter evidence in mind, associated it with right of jurisdiction.[3] It may also be linked with our Burghal Hidage burhs in the sense that duty at the borough-gate was connected with the landowner's responsibility for defence of the burh. The present tendency, however, is to move from the public to the private sector and to look to the origins of the private fortress. The text can be interpreted formally as invoking ownership of land assessed at five hides, a territorial church, rights over oven, altar, crops, a *burhgeat* (or fortified residence), a seat and an office in the king's hall. Concern with the origin of the Norman motte has led to a realization that the ring-work with strong gatehouse existed side by side with the motte: that in early Norman

---

[1] Liebermann, *Gesetze* I, 4. Trans. Whitelock, *EHD*, p. 432, from CCCC 201 which omits 'church and kitchen'.

[2] W. H. Stevenson, 'Burh-geat-setl', *EHR* XII (1897), 489–92.

[3] F. W. Maitland, *Township and Borough* (Cambridge, 1898), pp. 209–10, where he draws attention to the term *burgiet* in the FitzHarding Berkeley charter.

England there existed not a simple sequence of type of fortification but a duality of type. The limitations of *Geþyncðo* as a private text have to be recognized, but at very least the urban historian must take notice of the recognized coincidence of economic advance with possession of some rights or duties over a fortified centre.[1]

The Burghal Hidage and the complex burh tradition of the tenth and eleventh centuries can take us so far along the paths of urban development and can suggest incidentally the growth of prosperous private individuals. What now of the more traditional classes of evidence, and, to begin with, what of the charters? They are certainly not borough charters in the commonly accepted sense of the term but together in all their variety they constitute an important corpus of material, though often intractable, and extend in temporal range from the Worcester charter of Alfred to the London charters of the Confessor. Much of the information they give about town life is incidental, but enough to add considerably to our knowledge of towns and town life. Careful investigation of familiar material can still lead to fresh topographical precision, as for example in Dr Hart's reconstruction, from a privilege of King Edmund, of the bounds of Bury St Edmunds. 'First south by the eight trees, up by Ealhmund's trees, and so to Osulf's lea. Then to the right of many hills. Then up *Hamarlunda*, to four *hogas*, so to the way to *Litlandtune*. Then over the river, following the way to Barton valley, and so eastwards to Holegate, a furlong eastwards to *Bromleage*. Then south to *Niwantune meaduwe*.'[2] Dr Hart's reconstruction is based on exact local knowledge and an ingenious appreciation of the fact that the framer of the bounds was consistently 90° out in his reckoning (for south we must read west and for east we must read south). It is important in telling us that the Old English bounds were substantially identical with the medieval *banleuca* of the abbey and indeed to a significant extent with the modern borough boundary.

The Bury St Edmunds bounds give a good example of the way in which the development of a particular town may be illuminated by Anglo-Saxon charter evidence. More general conclusions may also be teased out of the body of such evidence. Peterborough documents give us a better understanding of the process of *team*, of vouching to warranty and also of the allied processes connected with the exaction of sureties.[3] The *Liber Eliensis*, preserving tenth-century documents from the muniments of the great abbey of Ely, gives us our clearest indication of the care taken to safe-

---

[1] B. K. Davison, with these problems in mind, has recently drawn attention to the importance of this text in 'The Origins of the Castle in England', *AJ* CXXIV (1967), 202–11, esp. 204. A very important note by A. H. Smith on *burh* in *EPNE* I, 58–62, includes a shrewd semantic observation (3(*e*), p. 59) on the development of the meaning of the term to denote a 'manor house' or the 'centre of an estate'. He defines *burhgeat* (p. 62) as 'a town-gate, a manor gate'.

[2] C. R. Hart, *op. cit.* pp. 56–8.

[3] Robertson, *Charters*, nos. 39 and 40.

guard publicly the rights of buyers and sellers of land *coram tota civitate* at Cambridge.[1] Cnut's grant of the haven of Sandwich to Christ Church, Canterbury, illustrates royal concern to protect the rights and customs of the king and the community in the ports of the realm.[2] Anxiety over rights of property, marketing and legal perquisites within the towns is a feature of many of our surviving charters, helping to fill out the general picture of towns as important units in economy and defence and linking directly with the Domesday evidence.[3] Thegns, dwelling habitually and by inclination in the country, own their town houses. Defence of the town walls is intimately linked with the possession of tenements in the country-side.[4] Overall royal rights persist, but already by 1066 a complicated pattern of ownership exists within the big boroughs and many of the small – in London and in Cricklade, for example, at both ends of the navigable stretch of the Thames.

Charter evidence helps to build a picture of complicated urban institutions at work. Legal evidence, in some respects even more valuable to the historian, helps to make deeper analysis possible. There are obvious dangers in the theoretical nature of such evidence. It is only too easy to sort out towns, once their existence is accepted, into various categories and then to make the categories too rigid and inflexible. The stone walls at Cricklade, and now at Cadbury, lead to emphasis on their military reasons for being. An administrative element emerges with realization of the importance of the royal hand, the geld, mints, and the presence, perhaps the permanent presence, of royal officers. The borough court, the *burh-gemot*, provides a sharp reminder of the legal responsibilities of a town. Traffic in iron, salt and agrarian products indicates the underlying economic motives behind their appearance. A balance must be kept among possibilities, an awareness of chronological variation. At one stage military emphasis is to be expected in the nature of the town, at another administrative, legal or economic emphasis. Massive holes exist in the web of evidence which alone makes generalization feasible. Yet some general truths emerge to face the test of available primary material.

Of first importance was perhaps the growth of a clearer idea of a

---

[1] *LibEl*, p. 100.

[2] Robertson, *Charters*, no. 82. The officers were to receive dues from both sides of the river from 'as far inland as can be reached by a small axe thrown from a ship'. There is an important discussion of subsequent disputes between Christ Church, Canterbury, the recipient of Cnut's gift, and St Augustine's, the principal landowner in Thanet, in Lady Stenton's *English Justice, 1066–1215* (London, 1965), pp. 19–21 and 115–23, where the Sandwich plea of 1127 is printed in full with translation.

[3] A recent attempt to give the factual bones of the Domesday evidence has been made by J. F. Benton, *Town Origins: the Evidence from Medieval England* (Boston, 1968), pp. 67–79.

[4] Effective diagrams of 'tenurial tentacles' at Chichester and at Wallingford are given by R. P. Beckinsale, *Urbanization and its Problems*, ed. R. P. Beckinsale and J. M. Houston (Oxford, 1968), pp. 17 and 18.

borough-right which was separate and distinct from simple land-right. The early-eleventh-century tract *Episcopus* gives the most precise statement when it divides all legal right[1] into the two elements of land-right and borough-right. The distinction it makes, however, is implicit throughout the period, in relation to trading regulations, the rights of *burhwaru* to take corporate action against men who infringe a truce, rights of exculpation, or in the simple phrase 'within or without the borough', which becomes enshrined in the common form of many medieval charters.

This borough-right was naturally very closely associated with chaffering and bargaining. The code, known generally as IV Æthelred, reveals the complicated state of affairs which existed in London in the early eleventh century.[2] The gates at Aldersgate and Cripplegate were to be manned. Toll was to be paid at Billingsgate by merchants and traders from within and without the kingdom. The discipline involved in collecting toll was to be enforced by a system of vouching to warranty with the royal authority in reserve. Special care was taken over the coinage and the issue of the currency, a care which extended from the particular London example to apply to the whole of the kingdom. A very important and somewhat neglected social truth emerges from this code and from other legal statements: that towns were places where good witnesses could be gathered, key institutions in the process of vouching to warranty. Edward the Elder had commanded at a very early stage that 'every man shall have a warrantor to his transactions, and that no one shall buy or sell except in a market town with the witness of the port reeve and of other men of credit.'[3] This was part of the involved and ultimately unsuccessful attempt to confine trade to market towns under pain of fines and penalties. Compromise was needed on this issue in the reign of Athelstan when attempt was made to limit purchases outside towns to goods valued at 20 d.[4] Cnut finally recognized that such attempts were dead letters, but also isolated the principle behind them when he ordered that 'no one is to buy anything worth more than four pence, neither livestock nor other goods, unless he has the trustworthy witness of four men, whether it is in the borough or in the country (*binnan byrig, sy hit upp on lande*)'.[5] True witness is the heart of the matter, most conveniently found within a borough. It is no accident that

[1] Liebermann, *Gesetze* I, 477, *Episcopus*, ch. 6: *æghwylc lahriht, ge burhriht ge landriht*.
[2] *Ibid.* pp. 232–7. Trans. Robertson, *Laws*, pp. 71–9.
[3] Liebermann, *Gesetze* I, 139, I Edward 1: *nan man ne ceapige butan porte*. Infringement was to be treated as disobedience to the king.
[4] *Ibid.* p. 156, II Athelstan 12: *þæt mon nænne ceap ne ceapige buton porte ofer XX penega*. This is contradicted almost immediately by 13.1 (*ibid.* p. 158): *þæt ælc ceaping sy binnon port*, and some of the feeling of uncertainty is reflected in the *Thunresfelda* decrees (*ibid.* p. 171, IV Athelstan 2): 'ut observentur omnia iudicia, que apud Grateleiam posita fuerunt, preter mercatum civitatis et diei dominice' (i.e. II Athelstan 24.1 which forbade Sunday markets).
[5] *Ibid.* p. 326, II Cnut 24. Trans. Whitelock, *EHD*, p. 422.

Edgar, when he wished to distinguish larger boroughs from small, made his line of demarcation according to the number of witnesses the borough could provide.[1] Cnut's association of boroughs with witness, and so with the whole process of vouching to warranty, provides a final valuable clue to English urban development.

Which brings us to the last of our group of records, somewhat neglected recently because initially overrated; that is to say, to evidence relating to the existence of guilds in pre-Norman days. Neglect has come about on two principal grounds, the belief that no urban manifestations before the Conquest were worthy of study and the further vague idea that the origins of the guilds should be sought in a purely social context, indeed in the eyes of some continental scholars in what were virtually primitive drinking-clubs.

English records are undoubtedly important and need to be fitted into the general European pattern of urban development. London had its *cnihten-gild*, an organization capable of owning property, including churches, with rights of jurisdiction within and without the borough over its lands and men. Knowledge of the guild comes to us from writs of the Confessor's reign, but reference back takes us to the time of Cnut, Æthelred and Edgar.[2] An Ely gospel book has preserved the elaborate rules framed by a comparable thegns' guild at Cambridge. What are virtually guild statutes have survived from Exeter. Similar developments were taking place in smaller urban communities as well as in greater. Statutes have survived from Bedwyn and Abbotsbury, the former more specifically social, concerned with rudimentary death and fire insurance, the latter of more general significance. We are told in it that Urki (a housecarl of Cnut) gave the guildhall and the site at Abbotsbury for the praise of God and St Peter to the guildship to own in his lifetime and after it. In return the guildship was to offer one penny and one pennyworth of wax to the minster together with other contributions. The arrangement was closely concerned with the foundation of the new little Dorset abbey at Abbotsbury, but the chief interest of the transaction lies in the acknowledged corporate existence of the guild in this somewhat remote community. The reason for the existence of the fellowship appears heavily social. An entrance fee was exacted; social protection was offered in return. If any member were taken ill within sixty miles a posse of fifteen of his fellow-members was pledged to ride to fetch him home. If he died, his fellow-

---

[1] *Ibid.* p. 210, IV Edgar 3. 1–5. Trans. Whitelock, *EHD*, p. 399. Witnesses were to be appointed in boroughs and in hundreds, thirty-six in boroughs and a minimum of twelve in small boroughs and in hundreds.

[2] There is a valuable selection of documents relating to London in *EHD* II, ed. D. C. Douglas and G. W. Greenaway (London, 1953), 944 ff., esp. 948–53 for documents relating to the *cnihtengild*.

members took on the responsibility, this time thirty strong, of transporting his body back to Abbotsbury. Two days' hard labour were surely involved on behalf of the sick or the dead.[1] The impression is given of an active, mobile group of traders. Social duties were also heavy at home. A man who undertook a brewing and did not do so satisfactorily was to be fined the equivalent of his entrance fee with no remission. A proper emphasis was placed on corporate action, on social duties and on ownership of property. We are still an appreciable way from the time when a town charter will involve corporate rights and attempt to exclude outside officers. But the germs of the matter are here in the actions undertaken by these modest guild fellowships.

Enough has been said to suggest that we have in our Anglo-Saxon towns structures of varying complexity and centres of urban activity, with military, administrative, legal and economic aspects. These towns grew in complexity as society and government grew in complexity in late Anglo-Saxon England, bearing the potential of yet further growth with yet firmer government, which the Normans were quick to exploit. In no field is this complexity, this growing together of town and other not inevitably urban institutions, more conspicuous than in the ecclesiastical. To some measure this is true of pre-Conquest England. Worcester and York are both closely knit with their sees; Abbotsbury, Peterborough and Bury St Edmunds – to hint at the range and variety – with their abbeys. In 1050 the chief diocese of the south-west moved its headquarters from Crediton to the flourishing town of Exeter. But all of this was intensified and the very work itself overshadowed by systematic royal policy under William and Archbishop Lanfranc which resulted in a full-scale urbanization of bishoprics.[2] Early Norman England was a much governed land in church and state. Well protected urban communities and well protected great churches were among the most typical of their institutions. Chichester not Selsey, Salisbury not Sherborne, Chester not Lichfield, ultimately Norwich not Elmham, and Lincoln in place of Dorchester on Thames became their favoured cathedral centres. St Albans and later Reading may be taken as representative of their view of seemly Benedictine order. But urbanization is no pious abstraction. Norman systematization would not have been possible if system had not already in part existed. The towns of Chichester, Thetford, Norwich and Lincoln were well fitted to take on their new Norman burdens.

[1] Guild regulations (Cambridge, Exeter, Bedwyn and Abbotsbury) trans. Whitelock, *EHD*, pp. 557–60. The Cambridge, Exeter and Abbotsbury documents ed. B. Thorpe, *Diplomatarium Anglicum Aevi Saxonici* (London, 1865), pp. 605–14, and the Bedwyn frag. ed. M. Förster, *Der Flüssname Themse und seine Sippe* (Munich, 1941), pp. 791–2.
[2] Stenton, *A-S England*, pp. 658–9. F. Barlow, *Feudal Kingdom of England* (London, 1955), p. 123, who properly associates the movement with a greater respect for canon law.

Finally a word is needed on the wider framework into which this particular set of urban problems can fit and on the fields of activity which are most likely to be fruitful in the near future. There is general agreement that the early tenth century represents a critical phase in the development of western Europe, the beginning of a period which was to culminate in the Ottonian triumph at the Battle of the River Lech in 955, a period when resistance to barbarian invasion becomes successful. Raids in western Europe by Magyars, Vikings and Moslems had been local and sporadic. Defence had also been substantially local and sporadic. Fortified strong-holds proved the key to success, and so to the historian the development of fortifications, of town-gates or of private fortresses in the countryside, takes on a special significance. By 1100 success against the barbarians was complete, and the west was everywhere on the offensive, against Moslems and Slavs. Scandinavia and Hungary had been absorbed into Christendom; Poland was a Christian kingdom. Fortified towns, mottes and ring-works were widespread throughout the west. Urban revival was conspicuous; the progress of the medieval town and urban institutions was continuous from that date forward.

Exploration of the nature of the urban revival in depth – and Anglo-Saxon towns have a vital part to play in such revival – brings many vexing problems to light. Was revival limited to specified great trade routes? Was it general among the smaller markets of the west? In fact both movements existed side-by-side and England provides a useful field for the sorting out of the gradations and variations in emphasis common to both processes. London, York, and to some measure Winchester benefited from the wider movements. Towns of the second rank, Chester, Exeter, the eastern boroughs were also not unaffected. Knowledge of the physical make-up and of the internal structure of, for example, Winchester and Canterbury in the eleventh and twelfth centuries has increased enormously over the last decade, and is already helping to sharpen awareness of our complex urban structures.[1] But the strongest trends were those operating in the lesser boroughs, communities empowered to set up one mint, drawing their sustenance from a multiplicity of yet smaller vills and many in direct contact with the agrarian heart of the matter. The most promising lines of approach seem to be associated with the lesser and medium-sized boroughs and with the development of fortification in town and in countryside, lines of approach which increasingly involve the archaeologist

---

[1] Martin Biddle has conducted a series of valuable excavations at Winchester (interim reports in *AntJ*, notably the sixth interim report, XLVIII [1968], 250–84). For Canterbury the work of W. Urry, *Canterbury under the Angevin Kings* (London, 1967) is indispensable. An article by Biddle, 'Archaeology and the History of British Towns', *Antiquity* XLII (1968), 109–16, indicates work in progress, and points to the special challenge and difficulties facing the archaeologist working on medieval towns.

as well as the historian. Three spheres of activity seem to offer more at the moment than any others.

First there should be continuation and intensification of work at our known boroughs, at Cricklade, Cadbury, Oxford and Wareham. Much is already becoming plain which used to be doubtful. At Thetford a fortunate eleventh-century movement of site has left much of the Saxon borough snug beneath later medieval farms. Patient work, made increasingly difficult and urgent by the spread back of the modern town over its Saxon site, is establishing the lines of its defensive banks and ditches and its street-pattern.[1] Some of Harold's work in fortifying the town has been identified at Hereford.[2] Probable pre-Conquest work has been disclosed at Northampton and at Tamworth.[3] At Lydford Saxon town defences underlie the Norman fort; at Wallingford the north gate of the Saxon burh lies beneath the outer bank of the castle. The evidence is partial but important. We are presented with a continuity problem with a difference. Lines of investigation converge on towns and fortifications, on burhs and mottes, and such investigation helps us further to understand the complexity that surrounds the origins of our towns. Every hint, and there are many, that implies the existence of a trading centre within or alongside a fortified settlement, is particularly valuable and needs to be rigorously assessed. Some of the burhs of the Burghal Hidage withered after performing their defensive function to be replaced by adjoining or nearby marketing centres, themselves capable of fortification and further growth.[4] The possible

[1] Davison, 'The Late Saxon Town of Thetford', *MA* xi (1967), 189–95, with its interesting suggestion (p. 190), valuable as a reminder of the fluidity of the situation even in the larger boroughs, that 'the great Norman motte, most probably a work of the 1070s,...is...likely to have been a cause, rather than an effect, of the abandonment of the s[outh] bank'.

[2] Philip Rahtz, 'Hereford', *Current Archaeology* xi (November 1968), 1–7, reports on the succession of timber walls, ramparts and stone walls uncovered at Hereford as a result of excavations conducted in 1967 and 1968. On p. 6 he adds a note on parallel work by J. Gould on the Saxon rampart at Tamworth. Gould has interim notes on the 'Excavations at Tamworth, Staffs. 1967 – the Saxon Defences' in *Transactions of the Lichfield and South Staffordshire Archaeological and Historical Society* ix (1967–8), 16–29, and on 'The Western Entrance to the Saxon Borough', *ibid.* x (1968–9), 32–42.

[3] Recent excavations at Lydford under P. V. Addyman and at Wallingford under Nicholas Brooks have proved fruitful. Regular reports appear in *MA*; see x (1966), 168–9 and 196–7 (on Lydford) and 168 (on Wallingford) and xi (1967), 262–3 (on Wallingford). Traces which imply that the defences were erected in a series of individual sections have been discovered at Lydford together with some evidence for a systematic internal physical arrangement. At Wallingford, as at Cricklade and Wareham, clear evidence has been found of a replacement of timber fortifications by a stone wall during the Anglo-Saxon period.

[4] The burhs of Chisbury, Pilton and Halwell were Iron Age hill-forts refortified for the emergency which prompted the Burghal Hidage; urban development took place at Bedwyn, Barnstaple and ultimately Totnes. Bredy lacked the economic essentials for a town; Dorchester, Abbotsbury and Bridport (a *-cester*, a *-bury* and a *-port*) came to provide a medieval urban triangle for the district. The island *Sceaftesege* (Shaftsey or Sashes) supplied a defensive position, but Cookham the town. Brooks, *loc. cit.*, gives a valuable account of Chisbury and Sashes. The hill-fort at Cadbury had to all appearance a short life as a late Saxon burh but, as

Southampton pattern of early suburban development with subsequent complex growth both of the original -*ton* and the suburban -*wic* may yet turn out to be the model for other favoured urban areas, though it must be admitted that English legal concentration on marketing within boroughs points to a contrast between insular and much continental development in this respect.[1] Then secondly full encouragement must be given to any work that promises to tell us more of the homes of Anglo-Saxon thegns, or for that matter of Welsh princelings of the eleventh century at Dinas Powys or Llantrithyd.[2] Special difficulties abound here. Where the superstructure is twelfth-century it is not always easy to look at the substructure. Hints are occasionally given of continuity; but for the most part the view that mottes were erected *de novo* seems dominant. But while this may be true of the exact site it is not necessarily true in the wider context, and archaeologists are increasingly aware of the need to contribute every scrap of physical evidence possible to our knowledge of Norman additions to existing communities. Some very complicated sites – Richard's Castle and Rayleigh come to mind – may, it is true, prove difficult to fit into any new synthesis of settlement problem and fortification that we attempt to effect. Sulgrave is proving one of the most rewarding of all sites and recent excavation suggests strongly that the plan of the late Saxon enclosure differed radically from that of the Norman ring-work.[3] The removal of existing buildings to make way for Norman castles, so much a feature of so many Domesday towns, may well have been paralleled also in the countryside.

Last of all, and closely linked with the question of fortification in

the excavator has said after recent work on the site, it is hard to believe that a township enclosed with about 1,200 yards of well laid masonry was intended to be merely temporary: Leslie Alcock, 'Excavations at South Cadbury Castle, 1967: a Summary Report', *AntJ* XLVIII (1968), 6–17.

[1] L. A. Burgess, *The Origin of Southampton* (Leicester, 1964), pp. 5–7. He suggests that the phenomenally low hidage of Southampton, a mere 150 hides, implying a defensive perimeter of only just over 200 yards, may be explained on topographical grounds, the defensive centre, possibly on the site of the later windmill, being highly and exceptionally concentrated into an area roughly equivalent to the size of the later Norman motte. A note of caution against full acceptance of Burgess's interesting thesis in relation to Southampton itself is sounded by the archaeologists P. V. Addyman and D. H. Hill in their important paper 'Saxon Southampton: a Review of the Evidence, Part One, History, Location, Date and Character of the Town', *Proceedings of the Hampshire Field Club* XXV (1968), 63–5.

[2] Alcock, *Dinas Powys, an Iron Age, Dark Age and Early Medieval Settlement in Glamorgan* (Cardiff, 1963). For the Henry I coins discovered at Llantrithyd, see Dolley, 'The 1962 Llantrithyd Treasure Trove', *BNJ* XXXI (1962), 74–9, and XXXIII (1964), 169–71. Also T. F. R. Jones, *Morgannwg* VI (1962), 98–105.

[3] Davison gives a useful, condensed and up-to-date account of Sulgrave in *Current Archaeology* XII (January 1969), 19–20. He shows that a pre-Conquest gateway had been the entrance to a free-standing tower, blocked when incorporated by the Normans into the ring-work. Also *AJ* CXXV (1968), 305–7, where it is suggested (p. 306) that either the later Norman ditch removed all trace of the Saxon perimeter or the plan of the perimeter differed radically from that of the later ring-work at the point excavated.

general, must be placed encouragement of any work which adds to our knowledge of the early history of castles, in or outside towns, traditional mottes with their pudding-basin effect, or ring-works. Spirited discussion at the time of the 1966 celebrations brought many fruitful ideas forward. Some, sceptical of Norman antecedent, were inclined to follow Mr Davison in claiming England as a possible seed-bed for the type of the motte.[1] Von Uslar in a monumental discussion would draw us further to the Rhineland as a possible source: square earthworks and ring-works in early Carolingian times, mottes with or without baileys in late Carolingian times.[2] All recognize that mottes and ring-works are coincidental types, existing side by side; that the motte did not evolve from the ring-work and supersede it. Ring-works with strong gatehouses have long, clear, and possibly direct Carolingian Rhenish precedents. Mottes are still elusive: Anjou, Normandy, the Rhineland, England, even the Celtic west, all receive attention as possible sources. But fortified townships, walls, gates and earth mounds are commonplace in the troubled world of north-western Europe in the tenth and eleventh centuries.

It is hard to end on a questioning note, but in this field symbolic and right. There are so many unsolved problems. The ring-works with strong gatehouses may in small compass mirror the towns with strong gatehouses at large. Where treasure was stored and councils held there was need for strong defence. It may well have been the supreme achievement of Alfred, Edward and their successors, English and Danish, to encourage defensive points, the best placed of which, their potential for trade as well as for war well in evidence, could develop into the powerful little town of late Anglo-Saxon England, an integral and vital element in the economic and administrative strength of the realm.

[1] Davison, *AJ* cxxiv (1967), 205, with reference to a possible hypothesis that 'a sudden and late development of the motte could be attributed to the special circumstances attending the [Norman] Conquest itself'.

[2] R. v. Uslar, *Studien zu frühgeschichtlichen Befestigungen zwischen Nordsee und Alpen* (Cologne, 1964). Reviewed by M. W. Thompson, *MA* ix (1965), 224–7.

# *Regnum* and *sacerdotium* in the early eleventh century

## DOROTHY BETHURUM LOOMIS

There is a certain irony in the fact that Wulfstan, the foremost statesman of the early eleventh century, whose explicit programmes for bringing order to a chaotic society all invoked the past with nostalgia, should really have been an innovator, anticipating some of the attitudes of a later time. Though he recalls King Edgar's practices and sees his reign as the Golden Age, Wulfstan's own political slant is that of the second half of the eleventh, not the tenth, century. This attitude is perhaps more pragmatically fortuitous than consciously philosophical. Circumstances forced upon him a magnification of the rôle of the church and of its hierarchy that Gregory VII would have found very congenial if he had known it. Something of the bent of Wulfstan's political ideas becomes apparent from a comparison of his own statements with those of the sources from which he borrows.

The documents upon which to base an understanding of the archbishop's ideas are the codes he drew up – V–X Æthelred, I and II Cnut, *Hadbot, Að, Geþyncðo, Mircna laga, Norðleoda laga, Grið*, the Peace of Edward and Guðrum – and the *Institutes of Polity*. The last, upon which Wulfstan probably worked for many of his last years, is the most considered of his statements and will receive most attention in this article.

*Polity*, though it takes its place with all the many *Via Regia*s, to borrow Smaragdus's title (which he took from Numbers XXI. 22[1]), both before his time and extending to *The Prince* or *The Bok of the Gouvourner*, is not primarily a mirror for magistrates. It belongs to an even older tradition, one going back to Paul. It is a kind of estates literature, a *norma recte vivendi* setting out the duties of most of the classes of society. As Ullmann points out,[2] the *ecclesia*, which was the whole of society, was a closely integrated body in which the welfare of all depended upon each member's knowing his proper function and proper conduct and observing it.[3] Ullmann cites as an early example of this type of instruction the Order of

---

[1] See J. M. Wallace-Hadrill, 'The *Via Regia* of the Carolingian Age', *Trends in Medieval Political Thought*, ed. Beryl Smalley (Oxford, 1965), p. 22.

[2] Walter Ullmann, *Principles of Government and Politics in the Middle Ages* (London, 1961), pp. 33–4.

[3] Wulfstan was very aware of this. See I *Polity* 30 (Jost, p. 57): *And awacige heora ænig, sona se stol scilfð*. See also V Æthelred 4 and I Cnut 6 and 6a, which say that all estates must fulfil their proper duties, and especially ecclesiastics of all kinds.

Hippolytus (pope *c.* 215) which gives regulations for laymen. Even earlier, at the very beginning of Christianity as a new way of life, Paul found it necessary to define the duties of people in all sorts of relationships.[1] These are largely familial relationships, but not entirely, and as Christianity became more widely disseminated it was necessary to regulate for a wider and wider nexus of society. The task was a congenial one to Wulfstan, for he spent a good part of his long and active life trying to rebuild the structure of a society whose foundations, he felt, were crumbling but which could be cemented up again with a proper idea of *ordo* and a real sense of responsibility throughout society, from king to serf.

Wulfstan was faced with the central problem of early medieval life: what authority will keep the peace and encourage the pursuit of righteousness in all citizens? The answer provided by his Carolingian sources is clear – the king. The answer given at the end of the eleventh century by the triumphant papal party was equally clear – the pope. Neither answer was possible for England in the first two decades of the eleventh century. The king under whom Wulfstan had the longest experience, Æthelred, was notoriously unable to protect his kingdom, and Cnut, though he grew into what the English considered a model Christian king, could not have appeared at the beginning of his reign as reliable defence for a Christian society. What Wulfstan's attitude was toward Æthelred's connivance at the murder of the thegns of the Seven Boroughs by Eadric Streona in 1015 and the seizing of their lands or to the cruel slaughter of the Danes on St Brice's Day in 1002[2] we can well imagine. He may have still been bishop of London in the autumn of 1002 or he may have moved to his northern see, but in any case he began his archiepiscopal life in one of the darkest moments of the century under an unstable, even treacherous, king. Again, in Cnut's reign, what must have been his attitude toward Cnut's bigamous marriage to Emma or to his murder of Eadwig (Æthelred's son) and other early acts of violence?[3] When Louis the Pious in 882 appeared to his bishops to be unworthy to reign, they deposed him, or at least declared the throne vacant,[4] but the English bishops had no such power over Æthelred. Wulfstan set about to increase their authority, and though he really had to break new ground to do it, he had also to make his statements seem traditional, and perhaps he really thought they were.

It is the Carolingians who are the principal source for Wulfstan's ideas, both in *Polity* and in the laws. Their interest in political theory was very strong, for the circumstances demanded a definition of the limits of power,

---

[1] Ephesians v. 22–5 and vi. 1–9; Colossians iii. 18–22 and Titus ii. 2–10; also I Peter ii. 17–18 and iii. 1–9.
[2] *ASC* C, D and E, *s.a.* 1002 and 1015.   [3] See Stenton, *A-S England*, p. 391.
[4] *Cambridge Medieval History*, ed. H. M. Gwatkin *et al.* iii (Cambridge, 1964), ch. 1. For a slightly different reading of events see the essay cited in the first note.

both in the time of Charlemagne himself and in the tempestuous break-up of the empire after his death. Smaragdus wrote a *Via Regia* for Charles himself, followed a generation later by Sedulius Scotus in a similar treatise, *De Rectoribus Christianis*. Cathwulf addressed a letter to Charlemagne dealing with kingly power and duties, and Alcuin also wrote important letters to him, besides setting forth his views of kingly virtues in *Disputatio de Rhetorica et de Virtutibus*. Bishop Jonas of Orleans in 831 wrote *De Institutione Regia* for the instruction of Pippin of Aquitaine; Hincmar somewhat later wrote *De Regis Persona et Regio Ministerio*. Rabanus Maurus and the Pseudo-Cyprian (really Irish) *De XII Abusivis Seculi* add to the list.[1] Exactly which of these works Wulfstan knew is uncertain. He drew upon either Smaragdus or Sedulius Scotus for some passages in *Polity*, and some of Alcuin's letters appear in the collections of manuscripts assembled under his direction.[2] *Polity* is much more under the influence of Alcuin than Jost's notes would indicate. Even where the exact phraseology is not parallel in the two writers – and it often is – the temper and direction of Wulfstan's thought are strikingly like Alcuin's.[3] Apart from these works Wulfstan was widely read in ninth-century literature and borrowed elsewhere from some of Charlemagne's capitularies, from Jesse of Amiens, Theodulf, Amalarius, Rabanus, the *Capitulare Episcoporum*, Alcuin and Atto of Vercelli. In fact, his inspiration was as largely Carolingian as English – more so if measured by the bulk of his borrowing.

In the Carolingian view the king, the anointed of God, his vicar on earth, has all power in his kingdom, a power given him to protect the church and promote righteousness. Charlemagne so understood his office; his capitularies govern church affairs, and in the light of that responsibility he carried his supervision of the church so far as to reform the liturgy and to clarify matters of doctrine.[4] Sedulius Scotus, as well as Alcuin and Smaragdus, makes clear that he could not himself decide doctrinal issues, but he felt himself responsible for the morals and faith of his people, and his care for their moral health extended even to the small details in which

[1] These works will be found in Migne, *PL* cii, cols. 933–70; Migne, *PL* ciii, cols. 291 ff.; *MGH, Epistolae* iv, 84, 157–9, 173, 176–8 and 205–10; *Disputatio*, ed. and trans. L. Wallach (Princeton, 1941); Migne, *PL* cvi, cols. 285–306; Migne, *PL* cxxv, cols. 833–56; *MGH, Epistolae* v, 406–8; and *CSEL* iii. 3, 152 ff.

[2] See D. Whitelock, 'Archbishop Wulfstan, Homilist and Statesman', *TRHS* xxiv (1942), 30, 32 and 43; and D. Bethurum, 'Archbishop Wulfstan's Commonplace Book', *PMLA* lvii (1942), 929. The letters are listed in the article cited below, p. 135, n. 1.

[3] See especially *MGH, Epistolae* iv, 49–52, one of the letters in BM Cotton Vespasian A. xiv, which is, like *Polity*, a *modus recte vivendi* for all people; and *ibid*. pp. 46–7, from which Wulfstan borrowed in the *Sermo Lupi* and which might have suggested several passages in *Episcopus*.

[4] See especially *Capitulare missorum generale*, chs. 3–9 (*MGH, Capitularia* i, 92–3). For the emperor's part in the reform of the baptismal rite see his letter of 812 to his metropolitans, *Bibliothek Rerum Germanicarum* vi, 403.

his *iudices* were instructed as overseers of the royal villas.[1] The question of papal power versus the king's is certainly present in the minds of the Carolingian writers, but as long as the kingdom (which is only the secular arm of the *ecclesia*) is ruled by a just king, the king does not submit his judgments to papal approval. On the contrary, in the tenth century it is the Emperor Otto I who has Pope John XII tried before a synod, convicted of treason and deprived of his office.

Alcuin and Sedulius Scotus are at one in stating that the emperor's power comes from God and that it is given him to protect the church, extend its borders and secure Christian peace; and Wulfstan had doubtless read the letter of Alcuin to Charlemagne in which he congratulates the emperor on the defeat of the Huns.[2] (What a contrast to Æthelred!) These writers made few direct statements about the relative powers of *rex* and *sacerdotes*, probably because they felt little need for it, for they saw society under Charles as a unit with Christ as king and priest. But Alcuin at one point stated that the Frankish king is superior to the pope;[3] and though he said in another letter that sacerdotal power is superior to secular power, he was there speaking of the sacerdotal power of the king. Cathwulf's letter called the emperor *vicarius Dei* and quite explicitly said that the bishop as *vicarius Christi* is in the second place.[4] From the point of view of the ninth-century writers on political theory the anointed king, ruling *gratia Dei*, though he could be admonished and rebuked by his confessor or his bishop, could be held accountable to no one but God.[5]

The theory of kingship which Wulfstan inherited did not differ greatly from the Carolingian view. Schramm suggests that the ceremony of anointing the king was brought to England by Alcuin,[6] for four years after Charles's two sons were anointed by the pope as successors to the emperor, Offa had his son Ecgfrith anointed to mark him as heir to the throne, and the Legantine Synod of 787 refers to the king as *christus Domini*.[7] His power came from God, not from the people, for all the appearance that the witan chose the king. Ælfric says in an oft-quoted passage: 'Ne mæg nan man hine sylfne to cynge gedon, ac þæt folc hæfð cyre to ceosenne þone to cyninge þe him sylfum licað; ac syððan he to cyninge gehalgod bið, þonne

---

[1] Capitula *De villis*.

[2] *MGH, Epistolae* IV, 156–9; see also *ibid.* pp. 280–3, 288–9 and 292–3.

[3] *Ibid.* p. 413.

[4] *Et episcopus est in secundo loco, in vice Christi tantum est* (*MGH, Epistolae* IV, 282).

[5] For recent statements on Carolingian views see the works cited above, p. 129, nn. 1 and 2; W. Ullmann, *The Growth of Papal Government in the Middle Ages* (London, 1955); and Ernst Kantorowicz, *Laudes Regiae* (Berkeley, 1946) and *The King's Two Bodies* (Princeton, 1957), ch. III.

[6] P. E. Schramm, *A History of the English Coronation*, trans. L. G. W. Legg (Oxford, 1937), p. 15.

[7] *Councils* III, 453. Æthelred in a charter quotes ps. CIV. 15, *nolite tangere cristos meos*, referring to himself (Whitelock, *EHD*, p. 532).

hæfð he anweald ofer þæt folc, and hi ne magon his geoc of heora swuran asceacan.'[1] As Schramm said,[2] the real elector is God, as the coronation prayer in Edgar's *Ordo* shows: *Deus qui te voluit super populum suum constituere regem*. And the Legantine Synod says: 'Ideo omnes generaliter admonuimus ut consona voce et corde Dominum rogent, ut qui eligit eum in regnum, ipse ei tribuat regimen disciplinae sanctae suae, ad regendum plebem suam.' Ælfric's statement would probably be interpreted by his contemporaries to mean that God directed the choice of the witan, for certainly the form of aristocratic election is preserved. It shows also that by the time of Æthelred the sense of theocratic kingship is so strong that no idea of deposing a ruler, no matter how great his crimes, can be tolerated. To Wulfstan, Æthelred's expulsion from his kingdom in 1013 seemed a crime heinous enough to account for the ills with which God was punishing the English. When the witan disagreed about the choice, as it did after Æthelred's death in 1016, God might be supposed to be on the side of the heavy artillery, wielded, in theory, by the bishops.

Whatever may have been the impulse behind Offa's having his son anointed as his successor, there can be little doubt that by the time of Edgar and Dunstan, when, according to Schramm, the history of the English coronation really begins,[3] it is under continental influence that Dunstan's *Ordo* makes of the coronation ceremony a religious rite in which Edgar is made priest and king, his secular powers reinforced by divine sanction. As Stenton pointed out,[4] Edgar's delaying the actual coronation until he was thirty years old may have been dictated by the fact that a priest could not be ordained at an earlier age. From Edgar's time on the king is rightly *rex et sacerdos*, though in Wulfstan's time Æthelred showed little awareness of the latter functions.

On the continent in the second half of the eleventh century the ecclesiastical power began to minimize the parallels between priest and king. Kings were anointed not with the oil of consecration used for a bishop, but with the less sacred oil with which candidates for baptism were anointed; and the oil was applied not to the head, as in the case of priests, but to arms and shoulders. No longer was the rite considered one of the sacraments. But these changes did not take place in Anglo-Saxon England, if the evidence of Abbo's *Vita S. Eadmundi* can be trusted, for the *Vita* lists the sacring of the king along with baptism and confirmation as one of the sacraments.[5] And the royal unction is applied to the king's head in Dunstan's and Edgar's *Ordo*. Ælfric's meticulous and legalistic description

---

[1] *The Homilies of the Anglo-Saxon Church,...the Sermones Catholici, or Homilies of Ælfric*, ed. B. Thorpe 1 (London, 1844), 212.   [2] *Op. cit.* p. 148.
[3] *Ibid.* p. 19.   [4] *A-S England*, p. 363.
[5] Migne, *PL* cxxxix, col. 512; cited by Schramm, *op. cit.* p. 119.

in his second Latin letter for Wulfstan[1] of the three oils used by priests makes no mention of the anointing of a king, for these are directions issued to the lower clergy. But it is likely that if the matter were currently in dispute he might have spoken of it. Furthermore, the principal argument of the Norman Anonymous as he examines Edgar's *Ordo* phrase by phrase in the tractate *De Consecratione* is that the king was made *sacerdos* by sacramental anointing; and since the sacraments are indelible he cannot be deposed.[2] The idea of theocratic kingship remained secure in England in spite of the poor example Æthelred offered of the divine choice.

Wulfstan's treatment of the relation of the two powers does not reflect the emphasis of his sources – and of other documents known to him, such as the decrees of the Legantine Synod – upon the superiority of royal power. Several things besides conditions in England may have influenced his shift in emphasis, for change it he surely did, to give to bishops the powers the Carolingian documents gave the emperor.

First it must be noted that *Polity* and Wulfstan's other statements that define or infer the relation between the two powers, unlike continental treatments, never deal with papal power at all. In spite of claims often made that relations between England and the papacy were uniformly good, and in spite of isolated examples, such as that of Edward the Confessor, of kings who venerated the papacy unreservedly, there is not much evidence that at Wulfstan's time the see of Peter evoked much reverence, or indeed had much influence on affairs. Peter's Pence, to be sure, seems to have been paid regularly, and the laws Wulfstan shaped never fail to mention it. It is also true that at an earlier time both Ine and Æthelwulf (accompanied by his young son Alfred) had made pious journeys to Rome, that the *scola Anglorum* was early established there, and that Cnut made a pilgrimage to Rome in 1027. Throughout the Anglo-Saxon period Rome was a great object of pilgrimage, but this does not imply a continuous respect for the papacy. What significance should be given to the fact that Edgar's very severe penalties for withholding Peter's Pence (II Edgar 4) are in Wulfstan's Laws of Edward and Guðrum (6.1) greatly reduced and left vague is uncertain. It may have been that the heavy penalties proved unenforceable, but it may anticipate a later reluctance to see so much money leaving England to go overseas. In any case *Polity* takes no account of the pope, never mentions him. But we probably should not over-emphasize this fact, for the pope does not play a large rôle anywhere in the tenth century or the early eleventh. Burchardt's *Decretals*, for example, have little to say of him. In theory, however, he remained the head of the church.

The only explicit evidence of the attitude of Wulfstan to his superior is

---

[1] *Die Hirtenbriefe Ælfrics*, ed. B. Fehr (Hamburg, 1914; repr. Darmstadt, 1966), pp. 58–60.
[2] *MGH, Libelli* III, 641–87.

the letter he addressed to the pope protesting against the necessity of archbishops' going to Rome to receive the pallium,[1] a protest which Cnut repeated and strengthened,[2] probably under Wulfstan's influence. The letter is made up of excerpts from Bede and Alcuin, but Wulfstan's own addition is a sharp warning to the pope against the sin of simony. The tone does not indicate much reverence for the Holy See. It is significant, too, in the light of the literature he knew well,[3] that he so seldom alludes to the source of episcopal power, Matthew XVI. 18–19, which comes to bishops from the pope. There is one reference in a brief sentence in his sermon on the consecration of a bishop,[4] and here he omits any reference to the pope but simply says, *And nu syndan biscopas Petres gespelian.* I am not arguing that Wulfstan was markedly anti-papal, but simply that he could not rely on the pope as the source of authority in his reorganization of the church.

There was certainly little reason in the tenth century, either moral or political, for holding the successor of Peter in reverence. With the collapse of the Frankish monarchy, the power that had kept the papacy strong, decline set in, until papal depravity and political weakness made a mockery of the earlier claims of a Nicholas I that the pope is divinely constituted prince over all the earth, superior to all other rulers. Though the emperor still had to be anointed by the pope, real power rested with the emperor. Perhaps Wulfstan saw with dismay the usurpation of ecclesiastical powers by secular rulers. Otto III in 1001 improved on the pope's title of *servus servorum Dei* and called himself *servus apostolorum*, and his successors went even further. Henry II's title was 'Henricus servus servorum Christi et Romanorum imperator augustus secundum voluntatem Dei et salvatoris nostrique liberatoris.'[5] Even Conrad II, whose abuse of the clergy was notorious, was called in a papal privilege *divus rex augustus*, but this, fortunately, Wulfstan could not know. Otto I's action against Pope John XII is mentioned above.

What would have been the attitude of a man of Wulfstan's interests and beliefs to such developments? He need not have been anti-royalist to see, against the background of his own experience, great danger in the weakening of ecclesiastical control, and it may have been reaction against the imperial usurpation of power that led him to the statements of *Polity* and of some of the laws. Few statesmen have been more concerned with authority and the necessity for order than Wulfstan. Some recognized

---

[1] See Bethurum, 'A Letter of Protest from the English Bishops to the Pope', *Philologica: the Malone Anniversary Studies*, ed. T. A. Kirby and H. B. Woolf (Baltimore, 1949), pp. 97–104.

[2] Cnut's letter to the English people after his journey to Rome is in Liebermann, *Gesetze* I, 276.

[3] For example, Alcuin's letter to Archbishop Æthelheard of Canterbury (*MGH, Epistolae* IV, 46–9), which was among the letters that Wulfstan had assembled for his own use, places a good deal of emphasis on the fact that the bishop holds the keys of the kingdom of heaven.

[4] Bethurum, *Wulfstan*, p. 243, lines 28–32.

[5] See Ullmann, *Growth of Papal Government*, pp. 240 and 246–7.

source of authority there must be, and before 1020 in England it could hardly have been the king. Wulfstan, then, to meet the chaos left by thirty years of war and under the strong impulse of his own convictions, set about to stabilize the authority of the church, principally by frequent appeals to the clergy to live exemplary lives and to discharge their clerical functions faithfully, but also by writing into the laws sanctions against laymen who did not properly honour the church, and, in *Polity* and elsewhere, by defining the duties of each class of society and by clarifying their relations to each other.

*Polity* begins with the heavenly king and proceeds to the earthly king. This section is relatively short and is mainly devoted to the king's duty to protect the church. To be sure, this is conventional advice to magistrates, and the Carolingian writers all make it clear that the king's principal function is to rule in such a way that the church can exercise full control over all spiritual matters. What is absent in Wulfstan's treatment is the context in which the Carolingians make this point, a context in which in nearly all cases eulogy of the king plays a large part. Sedulius Scotus, for example, from whom Wulfstan borrows, writes a treatise that is dignified, formal, rhetorically polished and filled with praise of a just ruler. Beside it Wulfstan's treatment is stark and, though not wanting in rhetorical skill, certainly not marked by warmth. He says little that is laudatory about the office of kingship, and in it we do not see, as we do in Sedulius and Alcuin, the reflection of the heavenly king in his earthly representative. Alcuin could think of Charles in his great palace at Aachen, but Wulfstan would find little to suggest God in his glory in the figure of Æthelred.[1] In the first version of *Polity* he says the king is *Cristes gespeliga*, but Sedulius would make him *Dei vicarius*, as do other Carolingian documents. In fact, Cathwulf's letter to Charlemagne cited above[2] says that the king is God's vicar and the bishop is in the second place, that of the vicar of Christ – 'Et episcopus est in secundo loco, in vice Christi tantum est.' I think that Wulfstan, who in rewriting the code *Geþyncðo* in sec. 8 altered the earlier form, *cyng...7 bisceop* to read *bisceope 7 cinge*[3] knew what he was doing when he made the king *Cristes gespeliga*.

The differences in this section in the various versions of *Polity* are remarkable. Jost thinks the D2 version (CCCC 201) closest to Wulfstan's original form of the work[4] and that G1 (BM Cotton Nero A.i) is Wulfstan's rewriting of it. This would be in line with the general relationship of

---

[1] Kantorowicz, *Laudes Regiae*, pp. 44–50, examines some tenth-century ivories which represent the king attended by angels and archangels, as is the heavenly sovereign. See also the same author's study of the representation of Otto II in the frontispiece of the Aachen Gospels (*c.* 973) in *The King's Two Bodies*, pp. 61–78.

[2] P. 135, n. 1.

[3] Bethurum, 'Six Anonymous Old English Codes', *JEGP* XLIX (1950), 458.

[4] *Op. cit.* pp. 18–19.

the versions of the homilies that appear in the two manuscripts, particularly marked in the *Sermo Lupi*.[1] The X version (Oxford, Bodleian Library, Junius 121) Jost regards as a rewriting of *Polity* done at Worcester after Wulfstan's death, and though the additions are genuine Wulfstan material, they were not included by the archbishop in *Polity*. Of the opening section there are two versions in Nero A.i, the second like the first but more finished. It is quite significant that in the later versions Wulfstan removed the phrases that echo the Carolingian view of kingship, both *Cristes gespeliga* and *þæt he sy on fæder stæle cristenra þeode*. These phrases are replaced by '*þæt he sy, ealswa hit riht is, folces frofer and rihtwis hyrde ofer cristene heorde.*' The later version has lost whatever divine aura surrounded the king in the first form, and, with the omission of *cristene*, might be said at present of the Prime Minister of England or of the President of the United States. To be sure, Wulfstan would certainly not apply these words to the head of a secular state, for his treatment continues with stating in strong terms the principal duty of kings, to protect the church and further its interests. The first version is very short and makes no distinction between the king's religious and secular duties, under the older assumption, I believe, that there is no difference between them. The revised version three times adds *for Gode and for worolde*, a phrase which I have elsewhere claimed[2] shows Wulfstan's growing awareness of separate secular and ecclesiastical spheres. It specifies in sec. 7 that the king must apply severe secular punishments (*mid woroldlicre steore*) to criminals; sec. 12 speaks of a just king's strengthening *cristendom and cynedom*, which cannot be a redundant phrase, since the kingdom was not co-extensive with Christianity; and finally sec. 14 says the king must punish those who *Godes lage wyrde oððe folclage myrre*. Otherwise the virtues becoming to a king are here not unlike those described by the Carolingians – a love of righteousness, vigour in punishing evil-doers, mercy, a regard for learning. The section ends in G with a strong statement: 'And do swa his þearf is: clænsige his þeode for Gode and for worolde, gif he Godes miltse geearnian wylle.'

An obvious explanation for the changes Wulfstan made in his treatment of the king is that he wrote the first version fairly early in his archiepiscopate – Jost places the terminus *a quo* of the D version at 1008–10 – and that the events of Æthelred's reign, and even of the early years of Cnut's, caused him to modify his view of the king's sanctity and unique position.[3]

---

[1] Bethurum, *Wulfstan*, pp. 22–4.       [2] *Ibid.* pp. 74–6.

[3] Edgar was Wulfstan's ideal king, whose *fiat* protected the church and her officers. Wulfstan's many laudatory references to him indicate that if he had been king when *Polity* was written there would have been no change in its earlier statement. Strangely enough Wulfstan never mentions Alfred, though Ælfric does, and though Dr Ker has found Wulfstan's own hand in alterations to the preface to Alfred's version of Gregory's *Pastoral Care* in Oxford, Bodleian Library, Hatton 20, the copy at Worcester. The sections in *Polity* on the three orders (D 2, 25–31 and X, 31–8) he probably took from Ælfric, as Jost's note says.

The same phrase, *Cristen cyning is Cristes gespelia on cristenre þeode*, occurs in VIII Æthelred 2.1, a code written in 1014. This was issued after Æthelred's return from exile on condition that he rule his kingdom more justly than before, and perhaps the phrase is intended to remind the king as well as his subjects of his position and responsibility. There is nothing to forbid the assumption that the late versions of *Polity* were written after 1014. In that year Wulfstan wrote the *Sermo ad Anglos* with its reference to Æthelred's expulsion. The change in this phrase is the only significant one in the whole of *Polity*, for, while the different versions vary in length, X being the longest, and while there are passages in D also which are not in the other versions, in no other case are there important differences in the same passage. The only notable one is in a section dealing with clerical chastity,[1] where X includes deacons among those who may not marry, while D does not. Otherwise the differences are minor ones of phraseology.

There are two phrases in the revised versions in the section on the king that suggest, though certainly do not prove, that they are a topical English reference rather than the abstract general treatment of the Carolingian documents and of most of *Polity*. Sec. 14 says that if there are stubborn criminals anywhere among the people who corrupt God's law and obstruct secular law, and they are reported to the king, he must at once consider what amends are to be made and exact them, however the evil-doer objects, if he cannot otherwise correct him. This sounds as if, in the many deeds of violence in Wulfstan's time, on the part of English or Danes, the ruling king had failed to bring the order he should.[2] There is nothing like this in Wulfstan's sources. A second passage is the end of this section in G quoted above. The word *clænsige* suggests a time of disorder when sin was rife. The Carolingians exhort the king to keep peace or bring peace but do not tell him to cleanse the land. These are slender clues, but taken with the specificity of the later treatment of bishops and with the general direction of Wulfstan's total activities they indicate that in part *Polity* is a *modus recte vivendi* for his own land in his own time, though based on what he believed to be immutably right.

If the king could not be relied upon as the source of authority to keep the state in order, who could? Wulfstan's answer is pretty clear: the

---

[1] *Op. cit.* p. 116.

[2] Whether the monks of Glastonbury had attempted to get royal punishment for the ealdorman Ælfric for his depredations to their church before they appealed to the pope we do not know. But the pope wrote to Ælfric and threatened excommunication if he did not restore their property (Whitelock, *EHD*, p. 824). The whole career of the ealdorman Ælfric is an illustration of unpunished treachery, as is that of Eadric of Mercia. There is a curious reference in V Ethelred 32.1 to 'crafty rogues in the west' – *swicigende manswican þe westen* – who attach property not belonging to them, an exact description of Ælfric's theft at Glastonbury. Æthelred punished Wulfbald for his crimes but not very promptly (*ibid.* pp. 532–3), and took no action against Æthelric, who was accused of treason, until after his death (*ibid.* p. 535).

church and especially her highest officers, the bishops. It is a revolutionary answer coming in the first quarter of the eleventh century, for it is in implication anyway both anti-royalist and anti-papal. Though it is clear enough that Gregory VII's attack on royal supremacy at the end of the century grew out of beliefs long held by priests and laymen alike, yet there had been before 1050 little disposition to question royal sanctity.[1] The fact that the king had 'two bodies', as the pope always had had,[2] in one of which he embodied kingship and was *rex et sacerdos*, in the other of which he was an individual of varying degrees of imperfection, made it possible for the people to accept him as God's anointed even when he proved to be the scourge of God. Wulfstan makes no overt challenge to such a view; he simply substitutes another authority. He certainly would not have agreed with Hildebrand very far, for he held that the king could not be deposed, and there is no sign of his defection in the troubled years of Swein's seizure of power, Æthelred's return after Swein's death, Æthelred's death or Edmund's short reign.[3] And, though he probably found little to be happy about in Cnut's succession to power, he early supported him as king and began to instruct him. If Wulfstan knew Isidore's distinction between a king and a tyrant – and he could scarcely have failed to know it, both from his own knowledge of Isidore and from the fact that it is quoted so often in the literature he knew – he would not have called either Æthelberht or Cnut a tyrant. But when he wrote the second version of *Polity* he did not rely very far on the king to keep England in order.

The direction of his shift can be seen at the end of the section on the three orders of society which support the throne, a commonplace of medieval thought, when he says, 'Forðam soð is þæt ic secge: awacige se cristendom, sona scylfð se cynedom.'[4] The language is familiar, and Wulfstan could have got the form of his sentence from one of Alcuin's letters.[5] But he makes a significant change: the Carolingians make the health of the state depend upon the health of the king, Wulfstan of the church.

Indeed, the clergy and the church's needs occupy the greater part of *Polity*, and since it is a form of estates literature, it is their duties and the sins that beset them that are chiefly dealt with. On these Wulfstan is very eloquent. A long passage identical with another in one of his homilies states in strong language the familiar exhortation to preach – *clama, ne cesses* – and makes the priests responsible for the souls of the people.

[1] For statements on this point see the works cited above, p. 129, nn. 1 and 2, and R. F. Bennett's introduction to and translation of Tellenbach's *Church, State, and Christian Society at the Time of the Investiture Contest* (Oxford, 1948).
[2] For a recent summary see Ullmann, *Principles of Government*, ch. 2, and Kantorowicz, *The King's Two Bodies*, esp. ch. III.
[3] On this point see Whitelock, *Sermo Lupi*, pp. 15–16.
[4] *Op. cit.* p. 58.
[5] *MGH, Epistolae* IV, 281 and 49–52.

Similarly the bishops are made responsible for the clergy under them, and their duties are specified in detail. But throughout *Polity* the necessity of heeding the bishops is emphasized and the rôle of responsible laity to honour and protect the church.

Throughout his career Wulfstan had devoted himself to strengthening the position of the church, and since he realized that it is upon the priesthood that the honour of the church depends, he did everything he could, both by threats of eternal damnation to the unfaithful and by promise of rewards both temporal and eternal to the faithful, to hold them to the responsible exercise of their duties. The most conspicuous of his changes is the claim that celibate priests are entitled to the rank of thegns. This provision occurs in V Æthelred 9.1f., VI Æthelred 5.3f., VIII Æthelred 28f., I Cnut 6.2a, *Hadbot* 68.3, *Geþyncðo* 7 and *Að* 2. It was something he insisted on, and his Pastoral Letter is addressed to *þegnas on þeode, gehadode and lærwede*. Priests normally go from their clan (*mæg*) into the church and are ruled not by the laws of the clan but by canon law. But with the constant temptation to defection in the late tenth and early eleventh centuries the civil position of the clergy needs definition, for civil protection was called for.[1] Besides, the respect of society was certainly greater for a thegn than for a ceorl. Hence the provision of these laws, and whether their heightened *kudos* kept the clergy more faithful than they otherwise would have been to their vow of celibacy we do not know. It probably did. There is no evidence in extant documents that this provision antedates V Æthelred; it was a part of Wulfstan's constant attempt to strengthen the clergy.

A good part of Wulfstan's attention was given to codification, to making explicit the rights of the church. The seven codes referred to above are better evidence than the laws on which to base the archbishop's views because they were not the action of the witan but are his own compilation. *Norðleoda* 5 equates the wergeld of a priest and a thegn; *Að* 2 states that their oaths are of equal value. *Norðleoda* 2 equates the wergeld of the archbishop and the atheling. *Hadbot* 1.2 states that injuries to the church or to the clergy are to be compensated sevenfold. *Grið* 6–8 recall the laws of Kent, though not exactly as they have come down to us, saying compensation for violation of the king's and archbishop's *mund* were the same; that damage to the archbishop's property must be repaid elevenfold, to the king's ninefold; that violation of the king's and of the church's peace required equal compensation. Actually Æthelberht 1 says that a *bishop's* property must be repaid elevenfold and does not mention the king's. Obviously these codes are aimed at elevating the status of the upper clergy.

---

[1] VIII Æthelred 36–8 speaks of the need the church has of the civil protection it formerly enjoyed.

VIII Æthelred deals almost exclusively with the rights of the church and of the clergy, and of all the laws that Wulfstan framed this code is probably most exclusively his. Again he specifies clearly what these rights are, repeating earlier legislation and adding new sections. He reintroduces the equal division of fines between the church and the king (2, 15 and 36) and decrees that the bishop and lord of the manor divide the fine for the non-payment of tithes. He writes into law the threefold division of tithes which he took from the Carolingian *Capitulare Episcoporum* (known as *Excerptiones Egberti* in Wulfstan's manuscripts); he specifies the amount of all church dues and the dates at which they are payable; and he differentiates carefully the fines that must be paid to churches of different rank (5 and 5.1). For the first time homicide within a church is declared *botleas* unless the criminal manages to escape to put himself under the king's *mund* and the king allows him to pay the heavy penalty – he must give his *wer* to both the king and to the church (1, 1.1 and 1.2). It is the specificity of the code that is important, for rights can be claimed and penalties exacted when it is known exactly what they are. Again, the church and its servants are put in the highest position.

Wulfstan did not make all these claims lightly. The clergy must earn their rights, and most of *Polity*, as well as many of the homilies and even the laws, lays great stress in equal detail upon their duties. The bishops' daily work is laid out for them (*Polity*, 77–84), their responsibility emphasized, and their sins relentlessly exposed.[1] Similarly with priests and monks. But there is never any doubt about the authority of the clergy, which is absolute. It rests upon one thing: by virtue of their consecration they can administer the sacraments and save their people from damnation. I Cnut 4.1 and 4.2, part of which is in *Polity*,[2] state with awe the unique power of the priesthood:

Forþam, understande se ðe cunne, mycel is and mære þæt sacerd ah to donne folce to þearfe, gif he his Drihtne gecwemeð mid rihte. Mycel is seo halsung and mære is seo halgung þe deofla afyrsað and on fleame gebringeð, swa oft swa man fullað oððe husel halgað; and halige englas þær abutan hwearfiað and þa dæda beweardiað and þurh Godes mihta þam sacerdon fylstað, swa oft swa hig Criste ðeniað mid rihte.[3]

An interesting point about this statement is the fact that it does not speak of the indelible character of the sacraments but twice implies that their efficacy is bound up with the priest's own character – *gif he his Drihtne gecweme mid rihte* and *swa oft swa hig Criste þeniað mid rihte*, though the last phrase could mean 'as often as they perform the rite canonically'. Yet in his sermon on baptism Wulfstan inserted a clear statement on the indelible

[1] Jost, *op. cit.* pp. 262ff.   [2] *Ibid.* pp. 162–3.   [3] Leibermann, *Gesetze* I, 284.

character of baptism and the eucharist,[1] and at that point certainly he believed it. But he mentions only these two sacraments, and since the question was being debated in the eleventh century, he may later in his life have changed his view of it. If he did, as this passage indicates, he again takes his place with the controversialists of the latter part of the century. It was in 1075 that Gregory VII declared the office of incontinent priests invalid.

Priests could baptize, say mass, hear confession, impose penance, give extreme unction; but only a bishop could administer confirmation and consecrate priests. Therefore it should come as no surprise that finally Wulfstan gave to bishops what amounts to the highest position in the secular-ecclesiastical hierarchy. The most extreme of his statements is in the chapter entitled *Episcopus* which Thorpe printed as a part of *Polity* (sec. VII), since it occurs in the X version between sec. VI, *Item de episcopis*,[2] and a section on the bishops' daily work.[3] It is pertinent at just that point and Jost does not doubt Wulfstan's authorship, but from the facts that it appears in *Quadripartitus* and that the latter part (10–15) relates to priests and not to bishops, even to lords who own slaves, Jost thinks that it was inserted into *Polity* at Worcester after Wulfstan's death. Liebermann also, who edits it,[4] argues from its appearance in *Quadripartitus* that it was originally an independent piece. I agree with Jost and Liebermann, and for the further reason that Wulfstan might have hesitated to put into a work on the orders of society which probably represented his mature thought so extreme a statement. Yet at Worcester where episcopal power remained strong even after the Conquest, where the holdings of the bishop constituted a sort of ecclesiastical palatinate, the claims of this chapter would be neither shocking nor unwelcome, and a reviser of *Polity* might well include it. It might have been inserted under Ealdred's episcopacy. It shocked Liebermann, however, and he protested[5] that while it might apply to Worcester, it was not a general statement about bishops.

It begins with a statement that sounds like a call to battle of the late eleventh century: 'Bisceope gebyreð ælc rihting, ge on godcundan þingan ge on woruldcundan.' This claim to the direction of all affairs, ecclesiastical and secular, Wulfstan makes particular. The bishop shall instruct men in orders both as to what they should know and what they should tell laymen to do. Then in a phrase that recalls *kingly* duties in *Polity*[6] he says, 'He sceal beon symle ymbe some and ymbe sibbe, swa he geornost mæg.' And this becomes particular in the following sections that direct that he join forces with just judges to settle litigation, that he direct the administration of

---

[1] Bethurum, *Wulfstan*, pp. 177 and 315–16.
[2] Jost, *op. cit.* pp. 67–74.
[3] *Ibid.* pp. 75–6.
[4] *Gesetze* I, 477–9.
[5] *Ibid.* III, 270.
[6] Sec. 4 in D 2 and G and sec. 6 in X and G 3: *op. cit.* pp. 42–3.

oaths and ordeals of exculpation, that he be responsible for just weights and measures,[1] that all laws, *ge burhriht ge landriht*, shall be administered according to his counsel, that he vigorously apply himself to everything – *þy he sceal on æghwæt hine þe swyðor teon* – to shield his flock from the devil's snares, that he take part in cases before secular judges – *mid worolddeman domas dihtan* – to make sure that justice is done. In other words, the bishop is to engage himself completely in secular affairs; and though such a position goes counter to the view of a strict constructionist like Ælfric and to the early medieval church's conception of its duty, it is in line with the practices of a German bishop like Burchardt or of the Irish bishops[2] and with the Hildebrandine claim for the papacy in the latter part of the century. It is probable that political conditions in England, quite unlike those on the continent or in Ireland, had delayed the secularization of the English church and that it was left to Wulfstan to state a position that met the realities of his own time.[3]

Wulfstan certainly did not take this position out of ignorance. On the conduct of the borough court he had borrowed in II Cnut 18.1 a decree of III Edgar 5 which says the court is to be administered by the diocesan bishop and the ealdorman to secure the observance of ecclesiastical and secular law. Does he ignore the position of the ealdorman here because he had found the ealdorman unreliable in too many cases? Or opposed to the bishop's counsel? Or does he wish the bishop to get the perquisites belonging to this jurisdiction? Or is he simply asserting the overall primacy of bishops? We do not know the answer to these questions, but it looks as if this is only one illustration of the first sentence of *Episcopus*. Nor could Wulfstan have been ignorant of the explicit prohibition against a cleric's involving himself in secular affairs. Sec. 10 of the Legantine Synod of 787, whose record he knew and used, is unequivocal: 'Vidimus etiam ibi Episcopos in conciliis suis secularia judicare, prohibuimusque eos voce Apostolica: "Nemo militans Deo implicet se negotiis secularibus, ut ei militet cui se probavit."'[4] Some time ago Professor Whitelock raised the question whether Ælfric's similar warning in his Latin letter to Wulfstan were not dictated by disapproval of Wulfstan's secular activities.[5] The section is fairly long, quotes Paul's words, as does the synod above, and

---

[1] Sec. 12 makes clear that the bishop's oversight of weights and measures was not to be exercised in person, for the parish priest is to keep the standard weight and measure. Nevertheless the standards bore the bishop's name until after the Conquest, for Liebermann cites an inventory of the property of Canterbury cathedral which lists cheese weighed 'by Lanfranc's weight'; see *ibid*. Glossary, *s.v. Gewicht* 11 b.

[2] See Kathleen Hughes, *The Church in Early Irish Society* (London, 1966), chs. 20 and 21.

[3] Alcuin's letter to Æthelbald (*MGH, Epistolae* IV, 49–52), may have influenced Wulfstan in the statements of *Episcopus*.

[4] *Councils* III, 452.

[5] 'Archbishop Wulfstan, Homilist and Statesman', p. 44; Ælfric's letter is in Fehr, *op. cit.* pp. 222–7, and the pertinent sentences in sec. xv, p. 226.

states clearly, 'Seculares iudices debent iudicare de furibus et latronibus, quia canones prohibent episcopos uel clericos de his iudicare.' I think Wulfstan's whole career, as well as his outspoken words in *Episcopus*, indicates that he did not share the view of the early Middle Ages about the church's function in the world, and I think that the events of his own time forced upon him this modification of the orthodox position.

It is in this point that Wulfstan shows himself most akin to the thinking of the last quarter of the century, but the influences that moved Gregory VII to assert ecclesiastical jurisdiction over all affairs had little to do with Wulfstan's position except that both Gregory and Wulfstan responded to the changing conditions of society. The teaching of the church in the first centuries that involvement with secular affairs was in the first place useless and, more important, a distraction from the real business of a Christian might have yielded earlier to participation in worldly affairs had not Augustine given his powerful sanction to the belief that a good life could not be lived in the world, though he wished the church to make use of the earthly city for its own purposes. While *The City of God* looked forward to the all-embracing *ecclesia* which should encompass the kingdoms of the world, that perfect *unitas* had not come, the world was indeed full of sin, and man's essential concern was with the Heavenly City, not the Earthly.[1] A second influence to reinforce the separation of spheres was of course Pope Gelasius's classic statement of the theory of the two powers, both of which rule the world, each in his separate realm.[2] If Gelasius was more given to telling the emperor that his authority did not extend to the church than to telling pope and bishops not to take part in secular affairs, that was not because he thought the latter less important.

In one important respect Wulfstan takes his place with Gregory VII's adversaries, and that is in his belief that all bishops, not only the pope, were Peter's successors and in the pure episcopalism of his statement in *Episcopus*. In his sermon on the consecration of a bishop occurs the sentence quoted above, *And nu syndan biscopas Petres gespelian*, with no indication of papal instrumentality. We have no evidence of how the archbishop would have reacted to a papal attempt to usurp jurisdiction over his own dioceses like Gregory's in Germany, but he did voice one protest to the papal see,[3] and the tenor of *Polity* and of *Episcopus* makes it likely that he might have ranged himself with the bishops who joined Henry IV in protesting against papal infringements of their rights. It is the Norman

---

[1] Augustine's position cannot be thus briefly stated, for it is too subtle and too dependent on his idea of nature. But see *De Civitate Dei* XVIII. 54 or XIX. 17. Here, as in his treatment of *caritas*, he distinguishes between use (*usus*) and enjoyment (*fructus*) of the earthly state, and urges the former but deplores the latter. See also the chapter on Augustine in Smalley, *Trends in Political Thought*.

[2] A letter to the Emperor Anastasius I in *Epistolae Romanorum Pontificum*, ed. A. Thiel I (1868), 349.         [3] See above, pp. 134–5.

Anonymous who argues the case most eloquently. He attacked the claim that Christ made Peter supreme over the other apostles; each apostle is equal to Peter, all churches are equal and all its bishops are equal. He came near the Protestant interpretation of 'upon this rock I will found my church' as he claimed that the rock is Christ and that to each of the apostles he gave the power to bind and to loose. Wulfstan would probably not have agreed with the royalism of the Norman Anonymous's tracts,[1] as he certainly would not have agreed with Hildebrand's claims for papal supremacy; but he is in accord with both in certain points.

It seems unlikely that Wulfstan for any considerable part of his life accepted the ideal of clerical withdrawal from the affairs of the world. Though no one could have seen the conditions of his time as more stained with sin than did Wulfstan, yet the word *worold*, which he uses with great frequency, never has the pejorative force of Augustine's *saeculum*. The world's evils he seemed to regard as in part meliorable, and he thought it the duty of God's servants to labour unceasingly and in every place to make things better. Whether he sought it or not he was in a position of great responsibility, and besides being a very zealous churchman, he was also an ardent patriot. He had the power and the ability to bring authority to bear on things secular and ecclesiastical, as his mark on the diplomata of the eleventh century shows. He was a public man, and apparently he did not find that rôle unbecoming to a soldier of God.

---

[1] It is tractates III and v that deal with this question (*MGH, Libelli* III, 656ff. and 680). See also H. Böhmer, *Kirche und Staat in England and in der Normandie im 11 und 12 Jahrhundert* (Leipzig, 1899), pp. 437ff.

# Scandinavian settlement in the territory of the Five Boroughs: the place-name evidence Part III, the Grimston-hybrids

## KENNETH CAMERON

Grimston-hybrid is a term which has been given to those place-names in which the first element is a Scandinavian personal name and the second element is OE *tūn* 'a farmstead, village'. In a classical discussion of this type Sir Frank Stenton[1] drew attention to their distribution in Nottinghamshire, noted their geographical situations, and pointed out that it is unlikely that the villages with such names denoted new settlements of the Danish period. He admitted that their historical background was uncertain, but suggested that it was at least possible that they denoted English villages 'acquired by a Danish owner at the time when the Great Army of the Danes divided out the land which it had chosen for settlement'. He added that we have no reason to suppose that the English peasantry had been deliberately expropriated by the new Danish lords. Sir Frank argued further that whether a village acquired in this way became known as a *tūn* or a *bȳ* was decided by local circumstances, in particular by the relative number of Danes and English in the neighbourhood.

Dr F. T. Wainwright[2] accepted this general interpretation. He noted that the great majority of Grimston-hybrids appear in Domesday Book, and he asserted that they are characteristic of an early phase of Scandinavian settlement, though not quite so early as the *bȳs*, but he did not quote or even refer to relevant evidence. Wainwright drew attention to what he called their 'curious distribution' – that these hybrids are very rare in districts where there are concentrations of *bȳs*, but are common on the fringes of such concentrations. He also pointed out that they are usually the names of large and important villages.

Wainwright's interpretation of the historical significance of the Grimston-hybrids is, therefore, very much in line with that of Stenton. He saw them as characteristic of areas outside those where Scandinavian

---

[1] *PN Nt*, pp. xviii–xix and, further, 'The Historical Bearing of Place-Name Studies: the Danish Settlement of Eastern England', *TRHS* 4th ser. xxiv (1942), 1–24.
[2] For the argument in this and the following paragraph, see 'Early Scandinavian Settlement in Derbyshire', *JDANHS* lxvii (1947), 105–10 and 115.

influence was 'most potent'. Though there may have been many Danes in the districts in which these hybrids occur, there was also a powerful English element in the local population, and this is in fact an extension of an argument put forward long before by Ekwall.[1] Wainwright saw the Grimston-hybrids as perhaps representing, by 'their chronological relation to the *bys*', the movement of Danes from their initial settlements into areas 'where they met and mingled with a considerable English population'. Here, 'linguistically, they were strong enough to influence but not strong enough to dominate the English population with which they mingled'. And to Wainwright this linguistic balance is strikingly illustrated by names which appear with -*bi* in Domesday Book, but with -*ton* later.

Professor Hugh Smith[2] reported Sir Frank Stenton's interpretation with implied approval, but went on to suggest that the names of the new Danish owners of these villages replaced those of the disposed English owners. In fact, however, all we *could* reasonably deduce, if we follow this general interpretation, is that the names of the new Danish owners replaced the earlier first element of the names, whatever those happened to be.

In a discussion of the Grimston-hybrids in Derbyshire,[3] I supported Stenton's arguments, pointing out that they were found particularly near the Dove and the Trent on excellent agricultural land – so bringing choice of site into the argument for the first time.

The importance of the Grimston-hybrids as evidence for Scandinavian settlement has been challenged by Mr P. H. Sawyer.[4] Though accepting Stenton's assessment in part, that some may 'stand for the replacement of an Englishman by a Dane as lord of an existing village', he objected that 'Scandinavian personal names were borne by men of English descent' in England, and, 'it would perhaps be best not to consider these hybrid names as evidence of Scandinavian settlement'. An implication of his argument certainly seems to be that at least some of the Grimston-hybrids were the names of *new* settlements founded in the period between the first Danish settlements in England and the compilation of Domesday Book, though Sawyer does not expressly say so. None the less, he clearly wishes to omit them *entirely* from any discussion of Danish settlement in England.

Now, it is perfectly true that, in the subsequent history of the English Danelaw, Scandinavian personal names were adopted into general use.

[1] E.g. 'The Scandinavian Settlement', *An Historical Geography of England before 1800* (Cambridge, 1936), p. 139.   [2] See *EPNE* II, 192–3.
[3] 'The Scandinavians in Derbyshire: the Place-Name Evidence', *Nottingham Mediaeval Studies* II (1958), 91–2.
[4] 'The Density of the Danish Settlement in England', *University of Birmingham Historical Journal* VI (1958), 14, and *The Age of the Vikings* (London, 1962), p. 161.

Their occurrence, therefore, is no indication of the racial origin of the men and women who bore them. It is, of course, entirely possible that some of the hybrids contain names of this type, and represent new settlements in the strict sense. But, if we can demonstrate that they fall into well defined topographical patterns, that they show correlations to other names in the same areas, and that they are not distributed in an apparently sporadic way, then Sawyer's argument loses much of its force and pertinence. We can, in fact, demonstrate precisely this. Grimston-hybrids do fall into well defined patterns, as we shall see.[1]

It must be pointed out, however, that there was by the side of OE *tūn* a cognate ON *tún* 'an enclosure, a farmstead', but this word is rare in East Scandinavian place-names. Hugh Smith has commented, 'The evidence for the use of ON *tún* in English place-names is slight', and this is indeed the generally accepted view.[2] It is certainly not reckoned with at all by Ekwall in *The Concise Dictionary of English Place-Names*. We can, therefore, be confident that the Grimston-hybrids are what they have always been considered to be, hybrids, part Scandinavian, part English.

The relevant figures of Domesday Grimston-hybrids, with the corresponding numbers of *by*s and *thorp*s in brackets, in the territory of the Five Boroughs are

| | | |
|---|---|---|
| Db | 10 (one transferred to Leicestershire) | (9, 4) |
| Nt | 19 | (21, 16) |
| Lei | 21 (1 doubtful) | (56, 18) |
| L | | |
| NR | 1 | (52, 1) |
| SR | 0 | (86, 20) |
| WR | 1 ? | (28, 17) |
| Kest | 8 | (51, 28) |
| H | 1 | (0, 0) |
| Ru | 1 ? | (0, 5) |

a total of sixty, of which one, Aylestone Lei, is perhaps doubtful. Two others, Glaston Ru and Scampton L WR, are extremely doubtful and should no doubt be excluded at this stage.

Forty-six different Scandinavian personal names occur in the sixty Grimston-hybrids, eleven being found in more than one place-name. These are *Barkr* (Barkestone Lei, Barkston L Kest), *Fótr*, with an -*s* genitive (Foston Db, L Kest, Lei), *Gamall* (Gamston two Nt), *Grímr* (Grimston

---

[1] Below, pp. 154–9.
[2] *EPNE* II, 193. Professor J. Kousgård Sørensen and his colleagues at the Institut for Navneforskning, Copenhagen, have confirmed that *tún* was no longer a living place-name formative element in Denmark in the period of the Danish settlement of England.

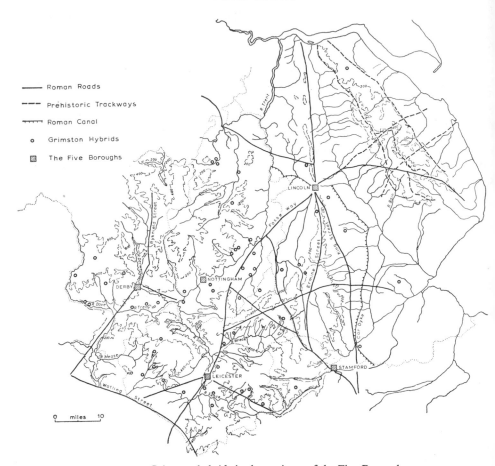

FIG. I   Grimston-hybrids in the territory of the Five Boroughs

Lei, Nt), *Kolr* (Colston two Nt), *Krókr* (Croxton two Lei, L NR), *\*Roðulfr*, *Rolf* (Rolleston Lei, Roolton Nt, Rowston L Kest), *Þorfrøðr* (Thoroton Nt, Thurvaston Db) and *Þormóðr* (Thrumpton Nt, Thurmaston Lei), while partially Anglicized forms of *Ásbjǫrn, Esbjorn* (*Osbern*) and of *Þorleifr* (*-láf*) are the first elements of the pairs Osbaston Lei, Osberton Nt, and Thurlaston Lei, Tollerton Nt. It will be noted that there are two pairs of Domesday Grimston-hybrids in Nottinghamshire and one in Leicestershire.

In addition to the two examples quoted above, there are two further instances of Anglicized Scandinavian personal names: *Þorgeirr*, with *-gār* for *-geirr*, is the first element of Thurgarton Nt, and *Þorsteinn*, with *-stān* for *-steinn*, occurs in Thrussington Lei.

A further feature of these personal names is that no less than nineteen are not recorded independently in Domesday Book: *Bak* (Baston L Kest),

FIG. 2    Place-names in *by* and *thorp* and the Grimston-hybrids in the territory
of the Five Boroughs

*Bíldr* (Bilston Lei), *Egill* (possibly in Ayleston Lei), *Fótr* (Foston Db,
L Kest, Lei), *Gjafvaldr* or *\*Gjǫfull* (Gelston L Kest), *Hermóðr* (Harmston
L Kest), *Jǫlfr* (probably in Illstone Lei), *Kátr* (Coston Lei), *Klyppr* (Clip-
stone Nt), *Krókr* (Croxton two Lei, L NR), *Oddr* (Odstone Lei), *Skopti*
(Scofton Nt), *Skropi* (Scropton Db), *Slagr* (Slawston Lei), *Sprok* (Sproxton
Lei), *Sváfi* (likely in Swaton L Kest), *Swerkir* (Swarkeston Db), *Þorleifr*
(Thurlaston Lei) and *\*Þrǽingr* (probable in Thringstone Lei). In addition,
*Barkr* (Barkestone Lei, Barkston L Kest), *Brandr* (Branston L Kest),
*Gunnulfr* (Gonalston Nt), *Hróaldr* (Rolleston Nt), *Klak* (Clawson Lei),
*Kolr* (Colston two Nt) and *Styrr* (Sturston Db) are found only rarely in
Domesday Book.[1]

[1] For the evidence, see *PNDB*.

Some Scandinavian personal names common in England are certainly found as first elements of this type of hybrid, e.g. *Gamall* (Gamston two Nt), *Grímr* (Grimston Lei, Nt) and *Ketill* (Kedleston Db); but, as we have seen, the number absent from or rare in Domesday Book forms well over half the total personal names involved. This may well point to the Grimston-hybrids, as a group, belonging rather to a comparatively early than to a later stage of Scandinavian settlement here. Further, though there are only four,[1] the fact that some have Anglicized forms fits in well with their general distribution on the fringes of areas where there are concentrations of *by*s, but where there are numerous English-named villages.

Some support for the argument that local circumstances played their part in deciding whether a place was called a *bý* or a *tún* is perhaps afforded by the forms of two of these hybrids. Thringstone Lei is recorded as *Trangesbi* in Domesday Book but later it is always -*ton(e)*,[2] while Scofton Nt is *Scotebi* in Domesday Book but *Skofton* when its next recorded form is found.[3] The reverse process, however, occurs too. Bleasby Nt is first recorded as *Blisetun* in 958, but the second element in all its later forms is *by(e)* etc.[4] Thringstone is the northernmost in the group of four lying to the west of Leicester; Scofton is the most northerly example in Nottinghamshire, in the group of three on the R. Ryton (see fig. 1); and Bleasby is the isolated *by* in the Trent valley above Nottingham (see fig. 2).

A different variation occurs in the forms of Ravenstone Db, now Lei,[5] which is recorded as *Ravenestun* and apparently also as *Ravenestorp* in Domesday Book, but the precise interpretation of such a variation is not apparent, unless it is a parallel to Bleasby.

It has often been pointed out that the vast majority of Grimston-hybrids are recorded in Domesday Book, but as far as I am aware no attention has been paid to the fact that some are recorded a good deal earlier. Goverton Nt is recorded as *Sofertune* in a document dated 958, admittedly in a poor fourteenth-century copy.[6] Tolleston Staf, however, is recorded even earlier, as *Roðulfeston* in a thirteenth-century copy of a charter dated 942, and again as *Rólfestun* in Wulfric Spot's will of 1002.[7] Nor is this the only example in this district of a personal name of Scandinavian origin appearing in a hybrid place-name at this date, for Croxall Db, now Staf, is also recorded in 942 as *Crokeshall*.[8] And this area is not one rich in Anglo-Saxon charters. Clearly, at least some of the Grimston-

---

[1] See above, p. 150.
[2] See *DEPN*, p. 470, *s.n.* This is confirmed by the large collection of forms now in the EPNS collection for Lei.
[3] See *PN Nt*, pp. 108 and xix–xx.    [4] See *ibid.* p. 155.
[5] See *PN Db*, p. 652. The reverse may be seen in Oglethorpe (*PN WRY* iv, 83–4), which has forms in -*tun* and -*torp* in DB, but only -*t(h)orp(e)* later.
[6] See *PN Nt*, pp. 155–6.    [7] See *DEPN*, p. 391, *s.n.*    [8] See *PN Db*, pp. 631–2.

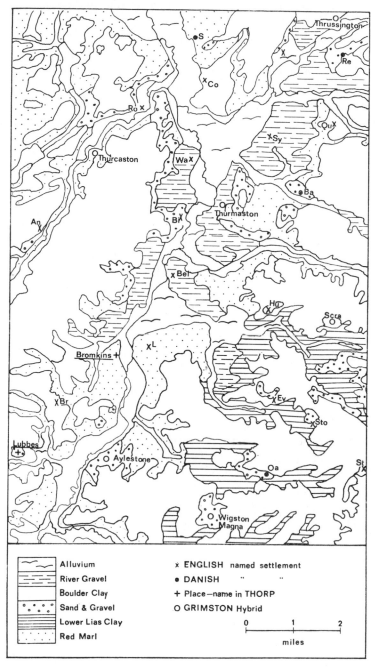

FIG. 3    Settlements around Leicester (L)

hybrids had been formed at latest before the middle of the tenth century.

The most striking feature of the actual figures of the Grimston-hybrids is that, as compared with 217 names in *by* and sixty-six in *thorp*, there are only eleven examples in Lincolnshire, of which one, Scampton in the West Riding, is extremely doubtful, and another, Asperton, is in Holland, where there are no Domesday *by*s or *thorp*s. On the other hand, in Nottinghamshire there are almost as many of these hybrids as there are *by*s, and in Derbyshire the hybrids are just in the majority.

Put another way, where Danish settlement, in terms of names in *by*, is thickest, Grimston-hybrids are rare. There is not a single example in the South Riding of Lincolnshire, a district with over a hundred *by*s and *thorp*s; in the West Riding, as we have just seen, it is again unlikely that there are any of these hybrids, as compared with forty-five *by*s and *thorp*s; in the North Riding there is only one, Croxton, in an area dominated by settlements with names in *by*. In Kesteven the proportions are only a little higher with eight as compared with nearly eighty, and only one of them, Baston, is in the south – on the fringe of the *by*s and *thorp*s. These are precisely areas, as I have suggested elsewhere,[1] which could have been settled in large measure by Danish immigrants who entered the country from the east coast, the estuary of the Humber and the Wash.

There are only five Grimston-hybrids in the northern half of Nottinghamshire, all on the *southern* fringes of the parts where *by*s are found – again a district which I have argued could have been settled by Danish immigrants coming up the rivers which flow into the Humber.[2]

The contrast in Nottinghamshire between these and others in the Vale of Trent is clear enough from fig. 1. Indeed, in the valley of the Trent and its tributaries there are comparatively few *by*s, though rather more *thorp*s. But it is precisely here that over 25 % of all the Grimston-hybrids in the territory of the Five Boroughs are located. They are restricted to the Vale itself above Newark, and the valleys of its tributaries the Devon and the Dove. Here, English-named sites, containing the elements *tūn*, *cot*, *hām*, *wīc* and *worð*, are very common.[3]

Six of the Grimston-hybrids in Derbyshire form part of this pattern, and it is worth noting that the one *by* there is Ingleby 'the village of the English'. Three of the other four in this county are in the excellent agricultural area east of Derby. The fourth is Ravenstone, the name of a place since transferred to Leicestershire, and which fits into the pattern of hybrids in the west of that county. These are situated between two small

---

[1] *Scandinavian Settlement in the Territory of the Five Boroughs: the Place-Name Evidence* (Nottingham, 1965), pp. 14, 15 and 19.
[2] *Ibid.* p. 15.  [3] See also fig. 4.

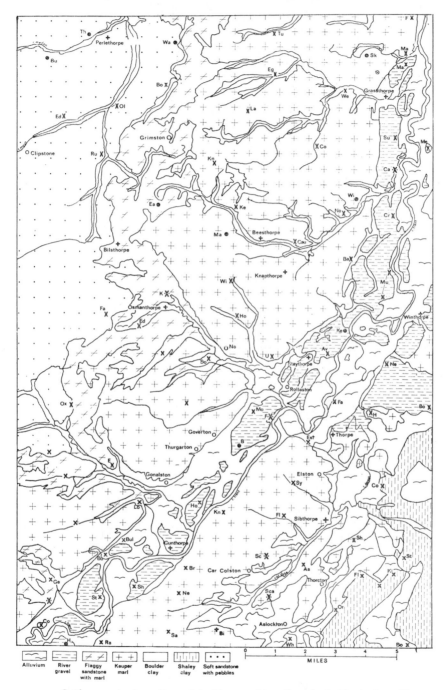

FIG. 4 Settlements in the valleys of the Trent and its tributaries in Nottinghamshire

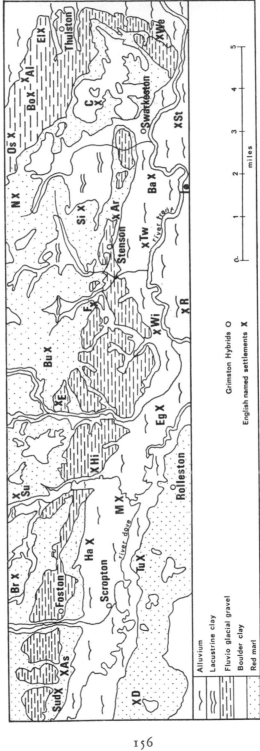

FIG. 5   Settlements in the valleys of the Trent and Dove in Derbyshire

Alluvium

Lacustrine clay

Fluvio glacial gravel

Boulder clay

Red marl

Grimston Hybrids O

English named settlements X

0    1    2    3    4    5
miles

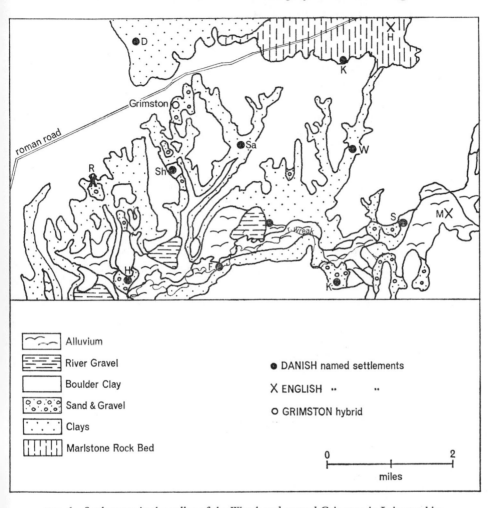

groups of *by*s, in a district, once more, where English-named places are common. We need have no doubt, therefore, that the English were well established over the whole of this area before Scandinavian settlers appeared. As with the Trent valley it would seem that comparative numbers of English and Danes must enter into any assessment of the historical implications of this group of hybrids.

Even in the valley of the Wreak, where the large number of Scandinavian names testifies to the strength of Danish settlement, there are four hybrids. Near the confluence of the Wreak and the Soar are four English-named sites and a hybrid, Thrussington, which has an Anglicized Scandinavian personal name, situated a little further up, on the right bank of the Wreak itself (see fig. 3). Grimston lies on much higher ground at the head of a tributary valley (see fig. 6). Then further to the east towards the source of the R. Eye, the English name for the upper reaches of the Wreak, there is an interesting pattern consisting of a *by*, Saxby, a *thorp*, Garthorpe, two hybrids, Coston and Sproxton, and a further *by*, Saltby (see fig. 2). A little further north is another hybrid, Croxton, on the edge of an area where again English-named sites are common. The three Scandinavian personal names in these hybrids are not recorded in Domesday Book. The impression gained from the names in the Wreak valley is clearly one of intensive Scandinavian settlement in a district apparently not already heavily developed. I suspect this took place at an early stage in Danish settlement here.

Now, immediately to the north of Leicester there is a further pair of hybrids, Thurmaston in the valley of the Soar and Thurcaston in the valley of one of its tributaries (see fig. 3). Though Leicester was the headquarters of a division of the Danish army, there are many English-named villages around. Less than two miles from Thurmaston, however, is Barkby (Ba)[1] 'the village of Bjǫrkr'. My explanation of the historical relationship of these places is simple: Barkby is a new Danish settlement, Thurmaston is not; it is an earlier English settlement partially renamed by the Danes; and an examination of their sites suggests that this is the correct interpretation, as we shall see.[2]

The pattern in the Wreak valley discussed above is a complex one. To the west and to the east are numerous English-named villages. Two others, Melton and Stapleford, occupy important sites where route-ways must have crossed the river and where the names in *by* are thickest. The pattern of settlement here seems to me to be similar to that north of Leicester: in general the *by*s represent new settlements, as I have already suggested elsewhere, and the hybrids represent earlier English villages taken over and partially renamed by the Danes.

To the south-east of Leicester the pattern is one of less concentrations of Scandinavian names in *by* and *thorp*, and where the Grimston-hybrids occur there are numerous English-named villages in the neighbourhood. This does not at first sight seem to be the case with Foston,[3] south of the R. Sence, since the nearest villages are Kilby and Countesthorpe (not recorded in Domesday Book). Kilby, however, is a Scandinavianized form of an earlier English name, so the situation is more apparent than real.

There is little to be said about the distribution of the hybrids in much of

---

[1] The abbreviation given in brackets after a place-name is that used on the relevant map.
[2] Below, p. 159.
[3] Foston is the most southerly Grimston-hybrid, almost due south of Leicester; see figs. 1 and 2.

Lincolnshire, except to draw attention again to the fact that there is one example in Holland, where not a single Domesday *by* or *thorp* is found. As we have seen, Baston in south Kesteven is just beyond the *by*s and *thorp*s, which occur in numbers to the north.[1] Of the rest, two are closer to Lincoln itself than any of the *by*s; three more are located in the fertile Witham and Brant valleys, again beyond the areas where *by*s are found; another, Rowston, is between two *by*s in an area which otherwise shows considerable evidence of intensive English settlement, with numerous names in *tūn*, and others in *hām* and *wīc*.

The Grimston-hybrids, therefore, occur in various districts where English-named sites are common, and they are extremely rare in others where names in *by* occur frequently. In fact, it is only in north Nottinghamshire and near the Wreak in Leicestershire that the two groups seem to be associated. In the latter they are at the fringes of concentrated Danish settlement as suggested by the many names in *by*, while in north Nottinghamshire they are situated upstream beyond the *by*s.

The suggestion has been made, as I have already pointed out,[2] that local circumstances, and in particular the relative numbers of English and Danes in the neighbourhood, played an important part in deciding whether a village taken over by the Danes became known as a *by* or a *tūn*. From the evidence I have presented so far, at least this can be said, that so many of the hybrids are in areas where English-named villages are common that it seems a reasonable deduction that there was a much larger English than Danish element in the racial complex of these districts.

We have also seen that English-named sites are common in the valley of the Soar. These are frequently situated on gravel terraces or on compact sand and gravel spreads (see fig. 3). The sites of three hybrids near Leicester, Wigston Magna, Aylestone (a doubtful case) and Thurmaston, have precisely the same characteristics and cannot be distinguished on these criteria from English-named villages. I have already claimed that Thurmaston was not a new settlement made by the Danes and the Geological Drift map suggests the reason. A comparable example is certainly Thrussington, a little way up the Wreak from its confluence with the Soar.

Similarly, many of the English-named villages in the valley of the Trent are situated on river gravel terraces, or on the slopes above the river on the edge of the Keuper Marls (see fig. 4). Further to the west, on the left bank of the river, as along its tributary the Dove, some are situated on the alluvium of the valley. The Grimston-hybrids follow patterns so similar that in almost every case they cannot be distinguished from English-

---

[1] See above, p. 154. Baston is the isolated example just east of Car Dyke and north-east of Stamford; see figs. 1 and 2, as also for the other examples in Kesteven.
[2] Above, p. 147.

named villages. Rolleston, south-west of Newark (Ne), is a typical river gravel terrace settlement; Goverton and Thurgarton are equally typical settlements on the edge of the marl; and Gonalston is not so dissimilar from either or from other adjacent villages as to be considered 'out of line'.

Across the Trent, settlement is on the marl, and the sites of Elston and Car Colston are again as typical of this area as are those of any English-named villages. The same is true of Thoroton further to the east. Only Aslockton is in any way different, on boulder clay, above the alluvium of the Smite valley.

Toton[1] is situated close to the Derbyshire boundary above the left bank of the river on the alluvium, and its site can be compared with that of the nearby Attenborough. Indeed, in some ways its situation has decided advantages, since it is set higher on the slopes of the valley.

The sites of the Derbyshire hybrids in the valleys of the Trent and Dove once more share the characteristics of neighbouring English-named villages (see fig. 5). Thulston is on a river gravel terrace like the nearby Elvaston (El); Swarkeston and Scropton, which lies further to the west, are on the alluvium close to the Trent and Dove respectively, as is a whole series of English-named places; and Stenson and Foston are on the gravels, strictly comparable to other adjacent sites. Across the river, in Staffordshire, Rolleston is on gravel and marl, beside a tributary of the Dove and so compares excellently with Draycott (D) to the west.

The pattern of settlement seems fairly clear. The similarity of the sites of the Grimston-hybrids in this region to neighbouring English-named villages is in general so close that we can hardly distinguish between them. The consequence of this is equally clear. We must, in general, agree with Stenton that these hybrids represent earlier English villages, partially renamed by the Danes. One or two may well be new settlements, as Sawyer apparently assumes, but this does not seem to be at all usual.

Indeed, if we examine closely the site of Grimston Lei (see fig. 6), we can see that it shares the characteristics of many English-named villages in Leicestershire. It is situated on the largest and most compact spread of sand and gravel in the district, set high about the 450′ contour, just below a Roman road and near the source of one of the many streams which feed the Wreak. It is thus close to an important route-way, is at the head of a protected valley with a ready water supply, yet the sand and gravel spread affords a drier site, less densely wooded than the adjacent clays. Many English-named villages in Leicestershire are situated on similar sand and gravel spreads which lie on top of the boulder clay. There can, therefore, be little doubt that Grimston is identical in origin with these,

---

[1] Toton is shown on figs. 1 and 2, south-west of Nottingham, north of the Trent and close to the boundary with Derbyshire.

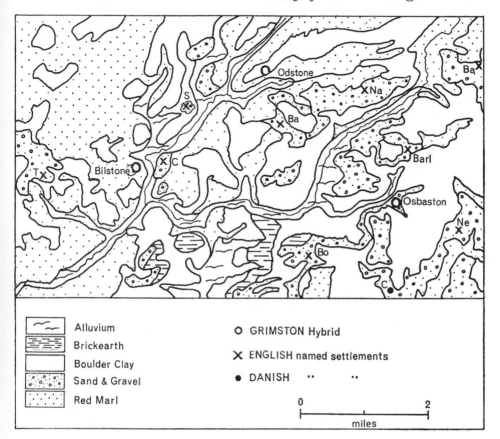

FIG. 7    Settlements north and west of Cadeby in Leicestershire

even though it is a hybrid name, and so represents an English village taken over and partially renamed by the Danes.

To the west of Leicester beyond Cadeby (C) is a district dominated by English-named villages (see fig. 7). North of Market Bosworth (Bo) is a group of *-tūn*s, two of which, Carlton (not in Domesday Book or shown on map) and Congerston (XC), have forms which are partially Scandinavianized. Three others, Bilstone, Odstone and Osbaston, are hybrids, and the Scandinavian personal name in the last has an Anglicized form. The villages in this area are situated in the river valleys or on the slopes above the rivers on spreads of sand and gravel or on the Keuper Marl. Only Odstone of the hybrids is 'out of line', on the slopes of a hill-spur on boulder clay, between two tributary valleys.

Time and again, with only rare exceptions, we can demonstrate that the Grimston-hybrids, as a group, share the topographical characteristics of neighbouring English-named villages, so that it seems extremely likely that they do in fact represent earlier settlements taken over by the Danes.

The Danish settlement of the territory of the Five Boroughs was for long looked upon simply and solely as military in character, and the settlements themselves were seen as resulting directly from members of the settling army. An immigration element was never considered relevant. Because of this, Stenton assumed – and his views have been shared by many other scholars – that these hybrid names arose 'at the time when the Great Army of the Danes divided out the land which it had chosen for settlement'.[1]

Elsewhere I have suggested that an immigration element *was* involved in this settlement.[2] The evidence I have brought together here certainly shows that the Grimston-hybrids are very rare indeed in precisely those areas I suggested were settled principally by immigrants who entered the country by way of the east coast, the Humber estuary and the Wash. Not more than a dozen or so altogether occur in such areas, and two-thirds of these are in Kesteven. Even so, only one is found in south Kesteven, where I have assumed substantial settlement by immigrants.

Nearly fifty of these hybrids are in more westerly districts, and more than half of these are in the valleys of the Trent and its tributaries, where names in *by* are rare and where English-named villages abound. It could well be, therefore, that we should look upon these Grimston-hybrids as resulting from the activities of early, but small, groups of Danish settlers pushing out beyond the areas where place-names in *by* are common. Indeed, it could also well be that, *in general*, it is the hybrids rather than the *by*s which represent the places where Danes took over earlier English settlements. Of course, some of the *by*s belong to this category as the forms of names like Bleasby and Kilby indicate; and I have suggested other place-names in *by* where the topographical and geological characteristics of the village seem to indicate that this could in fact have happened, even though there is no documentary evidence to substantiate it.[3]

In the development of the forms of the place-names themselves, local conditions, including comparative numbers of Danes and English, were no doubt important. But I suggest that this is not the whole story and I point to the patterns of settlement in the Wreak valley, in particular, to support me. Indeed, I am convinced that this area had not been exploited much before the arrival of the Danes, though there was some English settlement in various areas near this river.

There can be no certainty with problems of this type, but there seems to be ample evidence to suggest that the Grimston-hybrids, in general,

[1] *PN Nt*, p. xix.　　　　　　　　　　　[2] *Scandinavian Settlement*, pp. 14, 15 and 19.
[3] *Ibid.* pp. 12–13, 14, 15, 17 and 19.

represent English villages taken over and partially renamed by Danes, as most scholars have supposed. I suggest further that on the balance of probabilities this belongs to an early rather than to a later phase of Danish settlement into areas already heavily settled by the English: after all, two are recorded by the middle of the tenth century, and half of the Scandinavian personal names occurring in these place-names are rare, or are not found independently, in Domesday Book. Finally, it seems at least possible that *in general* it is the Grimston-hybrids which represent English settlements taken over by the Danes, and not the *bys*, the great majority of which on topographical and geological grounds appear to represent colonization in the strict sense.[1]

[1] The theme of this article provided the basis of a lecture given at the Institut for Navneforskning, Copenhagen, in April 1969. I am greatly indebted to Professor J. Kousgård Sørensen and the staff of the Institut for their generous help and criticism.

# How long did the Scandinavian language survive in England?
## The epigraphical evidence[1]

### R. I. PAGE

It is forty years since Professor Eilert Ekwall published his 'How long did the Scandinavian language survive in England?', the substance of a lecture given three years earlier.[2] In answering his question Ekwall used three types of evidence: inscriptions, place-names, loan-words. The last two I do not consider here: several English Place-Name Society Danelaw volumes have come out since Ekwall wrote, adding to his a wealth of material for careful sifting, while Dietrich Hofmann has re-examined the loan-words in *Nordisch-Englische Lehnbeziehungen der Wikingerzeit* (Copenhagen, 1955). Only very recently, however, has the work of collecting and evaluating this country's early English and Norse inscriptions been taken in hand, and already it is clear that we need more precise description and analysis of the epigraphical material than Ekwall gave in 1930.

Ekwall used epigraphical evidence in two ways. He took three Old English inscriptions, all from Yorkshire, and argued that Scandinavians had commissioned them: the Kirkdale and Aldbrough sundials and the St Mary Castlegate, York, foundation stone. These he claimed showed Scandinavians leaving their native tongue for English. He then examined five inscriptions in Scandinavian which showed native speakers keeping to that tongue. In order of decreasing importance these are the Pennington, Lancashire, tympanum and the Carlisle graffito, both of which Ekwall studied in detail, and the Skelton in Cleveland, Thornaby on Tees and Harrogate stones which he mentioned only briefly. He listed also, but rejected as irrelevant, the Lincoln comb ('there is nothing to prove that the

---

[1] In this paper I use lower-case bold for inscriptions in Norse runes, lower-case roman between single inverted commas for Anglo-Saxon runes, and upper-case roman for texts in Roman characters. I use my own readings for runic texts. I have also examined some of those in Roman characters, but here I rely too on the work of Dr Elisabeth Okasha, acknowledged in greater detail below. In a general account like this I cannot give such precise transcripts as would be expected in an epigraphical study, so that in minor points my transliterations may be incorrect or may differ from Dr Okasha's rigorous ones. For convenience I have adopted the practice of dividing texts into their individual words even if they are undivided in the original. For help on archaeological matters I wish to thank Mr D. M. Wilson.

[2] *A Grammatical Miscellany offered to Otto Jespersen...* (London and Copenhagen, 1930), pp. 17–30.

comb was made in England') and the St Paul's, London, stone ('purely Scandinavian...probably commemorates some Dane who came over with Cnut'). It is a thin collection, and Ekwall felt obliged to apologize for it, comparing England's poverty with Manx plenty. 'I am inclined to believe ...that the rare occurrence of Scandinavian runic stones in England is partly due to the quality of the stone used', for it is 'soft...easy to work but does not offer strong resistance to the effects of time and weather'.[1]

Ekwall's list of Scandinavian runic monuments in England was incomplete when he published it. The late Professor Hertha Marquardt's *Bibliographie der Runeninschriften nach Fundorten* I (Göttingen, 1961) adds Bridekirk (known since about 1600), Conishead (found 1928, recorded the following year) and Dearham (published in the nineteenth century), all from north-west England. It misses the York spoon, which the Yorkshire Museum catalogued in 1891, and which has two runes, possibly Norse but rather more likely to be English.[2] Also absent is the Settle slate, found in 1870 but not published until 1962.[3] One further fragment has appeared more recently, a small piece of magnesian limestone discovered under York Minster, having traces of two runes so slight that we cannot tell which type they belong to.[4]

Even with these additions it is a small field, so right at the beginning it is worth facing Ekwall's argument that many Scandinavian rune-stones failed to survive in this country because they were cut on poor quality material. Ekwall cites in contrast the plentiful Viking rune-stones of the Isle of Man, but I doubt if this is a valid comparison. L. Musset's summary of the rune-stones (up to the year 1300) in the various northern lands gives 2,400 to Sweden, rather more than 300 to Denmark and the neighbouring coastal areas, fifty to Norway and ninety to the Norwegian colonies overseas, a figure which includes the forty-seven Icelandic ones which do not belong to this period at all.[5] Publishing the newly found Kirk Maughold, Man, stone, A. M. Cubbon listed the inscriptions in the British Isles:

---

[1] *Ibid.* p. 23.
[2] J. Raine, *Yorkshire Museum: Handbook to the Antiquities* (1891), pp. 216–18, republished in D. M. Waterman, 'Late Saxon, Viking, and Early Medieval Finds from York', *Archaeologia* XCVII (1959), 85–6.
[3] *PN WRY* VII, 62.
[4] I thank Dr B. Hope-Taylor for telling me of this find. So far (August 1969) all other inscriptions from this site have been non-runic and in either Latin or Old English. For completeness I note here a few more inscriptions to be rejected out of hand. Smith, *loc. cit.*, records 'the name "kuni Onlaf" on a stone at Leeds', but these runes are Anglo-Saxon and the name *Onlaf* not at all certain. Marquardt's *Bibliographie* lists two Swedish stones at Oxford which are modern imports. There is a second stone from St Paul's, London, on which G. Stephens, following G. F. Browne, identified runes; certainly there is a rough mark on its edge which looks like **k**, but the identification is doubtful. For other uncertain references to rune-stones see my 'Runes and Non-Runes', *Medieval Literature and Civilization*, ed. D. A. Pearsall and R. A. Waldron (London, 1969), pp. 28–54.
[5] L. Musset and F. Mossé, *Introduction à la Runologie* (Paris, 1965), p. 241.

thirty-one in the Isle of Man, forty-two in the Orkneys and Shetlands, eleven in the Western Isles, four in mainland Scotland, nine in England and Wales and three in Ireland.[1] Of course, not all these are from the Viking Age. Only 170–180 of the Danish examples come from that period.[2] Few runic inscriptions of any kind occur in early Viking Age Norway, and it seems that Norwegian Viking Age rune-stones are generally rare, though there are two groups of some size, those from Jæren which link to the Manx examples, and those in the Ringerike style which date from the last century of Viking activity. Surprising is the dearth of inscriptions in areas of intensive Scandinavian settlement. Iceland has no Viking Age runic monuments. Normandy has no runes at all. There are only three examples from the Faroe Islands. The Vikings who travelled *i austrveg* cut, as far as yet we know, only the *Aldeigjuborg* rune-inscribed stick, the Berezanj stone and the carving on the Piraeus/Venice lion. Greenland has as many as fifteen inscriptions, but all relatively late and several on wood which survived there in the frozen ground. The three Irish specimens apparently include the Nendrum, Co. Antrim, stone which is doubtfully runic and doubtfully Scandinavian. Otherwise the only Irish rune-stone is the runic-ogham cross from Killaloe, Co. Clare.

Compared with these numbers the English corpus does not look inadequate, which suggests that it has not suffered excessively from loss or decay through the years. On the contrary, it is the plenty of Manx inscriptions which needs accounting for, rather than the dearth of English ones. In any case, it is unlikely on practical grounds that Viking rune-stones have suffered more from poor quality material in England than elsewhere. The north of England is rich enough in stone, easy to obtain and cut, yet resistant to weathering, as the surviving Anglo-Saxon monuments show. Dr Elisabeth Okasha's *Hand-list of Anglo-Saxon Non-Runic Inscriptions*[3] gives over eighty inscribed stones in Old English or Latin in the northern part of the Danelaw, and of the thirty-seven Anglo-Saxon rune-stones thirty-four come from a region north of the Dee–Wash line. There must be thousands of fragments of carved, uninscribed, Dark Age stones from the same area.

A preliminary corpus of Scandinavian inscriptions in England thus consists of five stones in the north-west coastal area (Carlisle, Bridekirk, Dearham, Conishead and Pennington), two from near the north-east coast (Thornaby on Tees and Skelton in Cleveland), two in the Pennines (Settle

---

[1] A. M. Cubbon, 'Viking Runes', *Journal of the Manx Museum* VII (1966), 25–6. It is hard to arrive at exact figures in the absence of an adequate corpus of these inscriptions. M. Olsen gives slightly different statistics in 'Runic Inscriptions in Great Britain, Ireland and the Isle of Man', *Viking Antiquities in Great Britain and Ireland*, ed. H. Shetelig (Oslo, 1940–54) VI, 153. Cf. also K. Düwel, *Runenkunde* (Stuttgart, 1968), pp. 86–7.

[2] L. Jacobsen and E. Moltke, *Danmarks Runeindskrifter: Text* (Copenhagen, 1942), col. 1020.

[3] Cambridge, 1971.

and Harrogate),[1] the London stone and the Lincoln comb. The two York inscriptions I exclude from the start since neither is clearly Scandinavian. Two of those provisionally accepted also look doubtful, Thornaby on Tees and Harrogate.

Stephens was the first to publish the Thornaby stone, and it is worth reproducing in full his rather naive account: 'Thornaby, Yorkshire, England. Slightly scribbled in, below a small stone Sundial in the wall of the Church, which is of early Norman date. Carvd about A.D. 1100. It was communicated to me by M. Fallow, Esq. In spite of many accidental-scratches, we can read: IT BISTR IS AN BI-UIK. *This is the best at Bi-wik.* Where BI-WIK is, I do not know. It is not in Philip's Atlas of the counties of England.'[2] I do not know if Fallow's drawing, from which Stephens worked, still exists. Fallow's own description appeared posthumously, in 1911, and is vaguer about the textual details: the stone 'appears to have been inscribed with a sentence in runes, as well as some other marks'.[3] Certainly, Stephens's reading is convincing neither as Old Norse nor as a useful comment to cut on a stone. W. G. Collingwood also saw the Thornaby runes: at least he published a drawing of them in 1907, claiming to read BISTR with traces of letters on either side, but without room for the whole sentence that Stephens found. His picture shows B and, less clearly, R, either runic or Roman, either English or Norse. There is a possible runic 's', either Anglo-Saxon or Danish, but no other identifiable letters.[4] Collingwood's accounts of the stone present a further problem. Fallow, whose description is the most detailed, reported that the stone was 'near the ground at the east end of the south wall'. Collingwood said it was 'under E. window outside', which sounds like a different place, unless Collingwood was misreading his notes.[5] Could there have been two faintly marked stones, on one of which Collingwood identified runes as a consequence of reading Stephens's account of the other? Collingwood said that the inscription had been lost since 1904, the date the church was restored, and it is certainly not to be found now. If there were runes they were very faint, and we cannot be sure they were Scandinavian. But can we even be sure there were runes?

The Harrogate case is quite different. This stone survives for examination, in the Pump Room Museum, Harrogate. Though it is sometimes

---

1 To be precise, six miles south-west of Harrogate.
2 G. Stephens, *The Runes, Whence Came They* (London and Copenhagen, 1894), p. 15. It may be significant that Professor S. O. M. Söderberg did not include the Thornaby runes in the fourth volume of G. Stephens, *The Old-Northern Runic Monuments of England and Scandinavia* (London, Copenhagen and Lund, 1866–1901) which appeared after Stephens's death.
3 'The Fallow Papers', *YAJ* xxi (1911), 238.
4 W. G. Collingwood, 'Anglian and Anglo-Danish Sculpture in the North Riding of Yorkshire', *YAJ* xix (1907), 402–3.
5 *VCH, Yorkshire* ii, 127.

called a hogback, it is an untypical specimen, for it looks like a plain boulder broken away at the back and one end. On the face where the 'runes' are, I can see no signs of tool-marks, of shaping or decoration. The 'runes' are a group of deep, coarse scores, somewhat weathered but quite distinct. W. J. Kaye found and published the stone, and there is an excellent photograph and a more detailed find-report, based on Kaye's evidence, in G. Baldwin Brown, *The Arts in Early England* (London, 1903–37) VI, 265–7. Brown noted that the stone had deteriorated in condition since it was discovered, and that early photographs did not show the deep scar which now runs obliquely across the face below the last two 'letters'. Kaye sent photographs of his find to Fowler and Kermode who identified the 'runes', and the identification has persisted. The marks on the stone were, and still are, ' ⌐ ⊦ ⅄. Kermode suggested SUNA, a form of ON *sunr*, 'son' (Brown agreeing), but he was unsure of the second letter, and so gave the alternative STNA, an abbreviated form of *steinn*, 'stone', perhaps as a personal name element.[1] Neither of these fragments of text is helpful as it stands, for each needs a fair amount supplied to give a useful meaning, and the present size, shape and state of the stone preclude much addition, while the rough marks on the battered back of the boulder are not likely to be the remains of an inscription. Clearly the 'runes' need re-examination. They are unlike any other Scandinavian runes in this country, being large (no. 3, for example, is 21 cm. high), rough, widely spaced and ill-disciplined, and the lines which form them are not markedly different from the modern score across the face. The first is a half-length vertical which could be Swedo-Norwegian **s**. Brown even claimed that it ended with a terminal dot, but this I cannot confirm. To me it looks as though the shortness of the stroke is due to the lower part of the stone face breaking away. The second 'rune' may have lost its left-hand base in the same way, though I am less sure of that. It now looks little like **t** and less like **u**. Its top is a wide curve such as rune-masters usually avoid, certainly in these two letters. The third could be Swedo-Norwegian **n** and the fourth Danish **a**, though each is simply two lines meeting or crossing at an acute angle. As a group the marks on this stone do not much resemble runes, though equally they do not seem accidental marks cut into the surface and then damaged by breaking.

Kaye's find-report shows that the stone, 'runes' uppermost, lay near a long barrow, and could have rolled from its top. There was no chance of a careful examination of the site, but a number of artifacts are somehow linked to the discovery: glazed pottery, remains of oak beams, an iron axe-head and two small horseshoes, a saw blade, flints and bones. Brown

[1] *PSAL* 2nd ser. XIX (1901–3), 55.

thought the axe-head, badly corroded as it was, to be Viking, and suggested that the Harrogate stone marked an intrusive Viking burial in the long barrow. If this were true it would tend to confirm the identification of the marks on the stone as Viking runes, but modern archaeologists have ignored this find and confirmation is lacking. For the moment we must suspend judgment. These do not look like Scandinavian runes to me. Even if they are, they are too fragmentary to tell us what language they record.

This last point may seem a quibble, for most people would assume that Scandinavian runes give a text in a Scandinavian tongue. The Bridekirk font shows this to be a false assumption. Reginald Bainbrigg, the sixteenth-century Appleby antiquary, reported that this font came from the neighbouring site of Papcastle, Cumberland, but throughout modern times the parish church of Bridekirk has sheltered it, and hence it survives in excellent condition, its surface lightly plastered and recently painted. It is a single block of stone with elaborate carving, which art historians date to the twelfth century. Across its east face a curling ribbon runs between two capitals, and here is cut a text in mixed runes and bookhand characters, for the most part intelligible: ⑂ **ricarþ : he : m̄e : iwrocte : 7 : to þis : me : rÐ : ꝣer : [..] : m̄e : brocte**, '⑂ Ricarth he made me, and... brought me to this splendour', the obscure sequence **ꝣer[..]** perhaps representing a second personal name.[1] The runes are Scandinavian, supplemented by *eth*, *yogh* and *wynn* and the nota for *and*. The language is late Old English or early Middle English, its form fitting admirably the art historians' twelfth-century dating of the decoration. There is no clear sign of Norse influence on the language, and the name form *Ricarþ* could equally well be ON *Ríkarðr* or Continental Germanic *Ricard* which appeared in England as early as the mid-eleventh century.[2]

Since the Bridekirk font shows that Norse runes do not necessarily record a Norse legend, it follows that, where we cannot interpret a group of these runes, we can draw no conclusions about the language their rune-master spoke. The point is significant with regard to the Dearham stone, from a site some four miles from Bridekirk. This is an elaborately carved grave slab, ascribed by art historians to the twelfth century.[3] It records the name ADAM in decorative Roman capitals. A plain border surrounds the design, and across its lower part (at the opposite end to the name and probably added to the finished stone) runs a line of runes, rather roughly cut and damaged at the beginning. The clearly readable

---

[1] There are excellent pictures of the font in M. D. Forbes and Bruce Dickins, 'The Inscriptions of the Ruthwell and Bewcastle Crosses and the Bridekirk Font', *Burlington Magazine* xxv (1914), 24–9.  [2] Forssner, pp. 213–14.

[3] This date, which Collingwood suggested (*VCH, Cumberland* I, 281) is confirmed in a private communication by Mr R. Bailey of the University of Newcastle upon Tyne.

part of the legend is • ᚼ ᚿ ᛁ ᛅᚱ ᛘ , **·hniar͡m** or **·hniær͡m**, with three staves or lines preceding the point. This group has no obvious meaning, and a sequence **hn** is suspect at this date, since in all Norse dialects but Icelandic initial *hn* became *n* before the twelfth century. It is worth noting that the second *ætt* of the later futhark begins with the group **hnia**, so the Dearham runes may preserve a casual memory of the futhark scratched in the stone by some chance visitor to the grave.

The rest of the west coast inscriptions are meaningful, at any rate in part. The twelfth-century tympanum at Pennington on which Ekwall relied so heavily is poorly preserved. Part of its surface looks chiselled away, perhaps when later medieval masons re-used it as building material. For about a century after the new church was built in 1826 the stone was set into the wall of an outhouse, attacked by the weather. Only part of its text can be made out, some of this disputed. Ekwall's reading, '. . . kial (*or* mial) seti þesa kirk. Hubert masun uan m.', seems, from the two aberrant forms given for the first word and from the reading *þesa*, to derive from W. G. Collingwood's early attempts.[1] Independent is Bruce Dickins's 'KML : SETE : ThES : KIRK : HUBIRT : MASUN : UAN : M....', 'Gamal built this church. Hubert the mason carved...', with *Gamal* taken as the name of the later twelfth-century lord of Pennington.[2] I read: **–kml : [ . ]et[ . ] : þe[ . ] : kirk : hub[ . ]rt : m[ . ]sun : u[ . ]n : m–.** Initial **k** is suspect for it is much bigger than other runes and is different in quality. Moreover there could have been up to two letters preceding it, now lost with the stone surface. The second word seems to begin with **l** not **s**, as indeed Collingwood showed. Certainly it could not have the **s**-form, ᛋ, used later in the text. The ending of the third word is damaged, but looks to me like two vertical staves with lines between them, perhaps **na**. Of **hub[ . ]rt** the fourth rune has a vertical set rather far from **b**, and in some lights this letter looks like ᚭ, **o**. A sloping gash cuts across the vertical which forms the second letter of **m[ . ]sun**. Collingwood, who examined the inscription when it was in the open air, thought this mark accidental, and he may well be right.

It is worthwhile here summing up the objections to the earlier readings of this legend. Certainly **kml** could represent *Gamal*, with **k** used for a voiced stop and the vowels omitted in the personal name,[3] but such abbreviation is odd if the purpose of the inscription was to commemorate the church's founder, and, as we have seen, **kml** may not be a correct, or at

[1] See, e.g., 'Runic Tympanum at Pennington, Furness', *SBVS* III (1903), 139–41.

[2] A. Fell, *A Furness Manor: Pennington and its Church* (Ulverston, 1929), pp. 217–19.

[3] Cf. such Danish parallels as **þurlf** for *Þorulf*, **askl** for *Askil* (Jacobsen and Moltke, *Danmarks Runeindskrifter*, col. 1010).

least a complete, reading. *Seti* or *sete*, 'established, set up', is meaningful, but no other Old Norse inscription uses *setja* for 'found (a church)', *gera* being preferred. In any case, *sete* could be as well Old English as Old Norse. ON *setja*, OE *settan* are often found for 'set up (stones, memorials)', and the Old English St Mary Castlegate stone has *settan* in the context 'set up (this minster)'. Unfortunately I cannot find *seti/sete* on the Pennington tympanum, and the alternative *leti/lete* makes no sense. The demonstrative looks like *þena* which is acceptable as a masculine acc.sg. form, but not as the feminine which ON *kirkja* would require. We could here assume confusion of grammatical gender, just as we must assume loss of the distinctively ON inflexional ending in *kirk*. Further, in such a sentence as this a word order *þena kirk* would be unusual for Old Norse where commonly the demonstrative follows its noun.[1] Some form of a personal name *Hubert* is probably acceptable, but a title *masun* would be strange at this early date, and a spelling with medial -*s*- also seems anachronistic. Perhaps we should accept here Ekwall's suggestion that this word is the patronymic *Másson*.

In this uncertainty it is hard to define the language of the Pennington inscription. Suggestive of Old Norse are (i) the runes, (ii) ? the name *Gamal* and the ? patronymic *Masun* and (iii) the word *kirk*. Characteristic of Old English are (iv) the word order *þena kirk* and (v) ? the use of *seti/ sete*. Neither specifically Old Norse nor Old English are (vi) the form of the verb *seti/sete*, (vii) the grammatical forms of *þena kirk*, (viii) the personal name *Hubert* and (ix) ? the verb *uan*. (i) is, as I have shown, inconclusive, while I argue below that (ii) the possession of an Old Norse name does not stamp a man as of Scandinavian stock nor need he use a Scandinavian tongue. (iii), *kirk*, is interchangeable with English *cirice* in place-name forms probably as early as the twelfth century. Though Anglo-Norman spellings are ambiguous since scribes use *ch* for front and back stop alike, it looks as though a name like Whitkirk, Yorkshire – *Witechirche* 1154–66, *Withekirke* 1185, with runs of -*church*(*e*) and -*kirk*(*e*) forms down to modern times – shows the two elements used side by side through the Middle English period. If the Pennington legend is Old Norse, it is markedly corrupt Old Norse, presumably influenced by English. If it is Old English or Middle English it has been much affected by Old Norse. From it I would hesitate to argue what language the people of the area spoke in the twelfth century.

The Carlisle graffito has a few unusual features, but the find-report, recording its discovery 'on removing the plaster and white-wash from the interior of the south transept' of the cathedral, is convincing enough to

---

[1] *Ibid.* col. 887. See also K. M. Nielsen, 'The Position of the Attribute in Danish Runic Inscriptions', *APS* XVI (1942–3), 227–9.

guarantee its authenticity.[1] Nor, despite some points which need more detailed attention, is there reason to dispute the general tenor of the transcription, **tolfin: urait ͡þasi runr a þisi ͡stain**, 'Dolfinn engraved these runes on this stone.' Such features as the retention of the diphthong in *urait* and *stain*, and of the labial before *r* in *urait* link the text tentatively with southern Norway. But Dolfinn is a name comparatively rare in Scandinavia yet widespread in this country and well recorded in Cumberland in post-Conquest times,[2] so the carver may be a local man or at least a man from the British Isles. The word order *þasi runr*, with the demonstrative preceding its noun, also suggests this.[3] The runes are quite carefully, though freely scratched on the stone, presumably by someone who visited the church after the block was laid or who was in the mason's shop after it was dressed. Carlisle cathedral was begun in the last years of the eleventh century, which gives the earliest possible date for the inscription.

From Conishead priory comes a stone which formed part of a thirteenth-century altar.[4] It has incised symbols, presumably mason's marks, and the runic text **dotbrt** on an inner face where it would be invisible when the structure was assembled. **d** is ⿃, a late type which occurs first on Svein Estridsson's coins of *c.* 1065–75 and rather later on rune-stones where it is rare. This rune links the inscription specifically with Denmark, rather than Norway, Sweden or the other rune-using areas of the British Isles. *Dotbrt* seems to be a personal name with the second element *-bert*, its vowel omitted. The name is not in G. Knudsen and M. Kristensen, *Danmarks gamle Personnavne* (København, 1936–64). There are the simplex forms *Dota, Dot*, the latter occurring in Domesday Book where von Feilitzen regards it as likely to be of Norse origin.[5]

The other two northern stones give little information, though they seem to have held Scandinavian legends. In 1870 excavators at Victoria Cave, Settle, Yorkshire, found an irregular fragment of slate, very roughly 8.5 cm. square, bearing a group of Norse runes. This is now kept in the Pig Yard Club Museum, Settle, together with the manuscript journal of Joseph Jackson, director of the dig, which preserves the only find-report. The entry for 23 April runs, '3 Men at work all day at the Cave. found a flat stone (slate) with grooves scored upon it in various directions. under datum line 12 Inches deep in cave earth.' There were no associated finds, and the cave yielded material from widely differing dates, so there are no external dating features. The rune staves are quite clear and in the main

[1] E. Charlton, 'On an Inscription in Runic Letters in Carlisle Cathedral', *Archaeologia Æliana* n.s. III (1859), 66.

[2] *PN Cu*, p. 191.

[3] It is worth recording a similar word order in **[I]uan·brist·raisti·þisir·runur**, '[I]óan the priest cut these runes', on the Maughold, Man, I stone: see Olsen, *op. cit.* p. 202.

[4] P. V. Kelly, 'Excavations at Conishead Priory', *TCWAAS* n.s. xxx (1930), 156–7.

[5] *PNDB*, p. 226.

unambiguous, though the tops of all letters are broken away with the slate edge. They read afralfr, or perhaps, though less likely, afraufr or afraulfr. This looks like a personal name with a second element -*álfr* (which is rare) or -*úlfr*, perhaps with the spelling -*aulfr* for -*ólfr*. *Farúlfr*, recorded in Sweden though not in West Norse, would fit.[1] The retention of inflexional -*r* in the Settle form suggests that the language is still Old Norse, uninfluenced on this point by English.

Little of the Skelton in Cleveland sundial survives: part of the dial itself, with, below it, the ends of four lines in Roman capitals, and to their right part of a vertical line of runes with a tiny fragment of a second. The Roman text is -S·[.]T· | -NA·G[.]ERA | -C·HWA | -A·COMA; the runic line reads -iebel·ok.[2] I cannot make much of this, though the individual word *ok* shows the text to be Scandinavian, and this may be confirmed by such words as g[.]era (could this be *giera* for ON *gera*?) and *coma* (? = ON *koma*).

To sum up. Of the seven northern stones admitted to the corpus, four seem to preserve casual graffiti, which, being casual and so personal, may be in a language untypical of the place and time in which they were cut: these are Carlisle (Scandinavian, though perhaps by a native of the British Isles), Settle (probably Scandinavian), Conishead (probably Scandinavian) and Dearham (as yet undeciphered). Foreign workmen or perhaps visiting tourists or worshippers could have cut Conishead and Carlisle. Settle is not from a settlement site and may be the work of a passer-by camping out in the cave above the town. Three, Bridekirk, Pennington and Skelton in Cleveland, are major monuments, using runes in formal inscriptions. Here we must assume their language is in some way representative of the region where they are found. Bridekirk is in English, Pennington in a mixed English and Scandinavian, and Skelton in Cleveland perhaps in Scandinavian though there is little to go upon.

Of these seven stones two are undated. The other five, Carlisle, Conishead, Dearham, Bridekirk and Pennington, are post-Conquest. I doubt if such western texts represent a continuity of Scandinavian usage from pre-Conquest and Viking times: they are more likely to show a new influx of Scandinavian speakers from areas such as Man where the language persisted at least until the twelfth century. The Bridekirk and Conishead rune-masters certainly had contacts with the Scandinavian runic world outside, for from there they must have got their late rune types ⵉ for **e** and ⵉ for **d**.

Ekwall's assessment of the last two examples, the gravestone from St

---

[1] Fellows Jensen, *s.n.*

[2] There is a good drawing of the dial, showing slightly more of the text than is now visible, in Stephens, *Runic Monuments* IV, 50.

## How long did the Scandinavian language survive in England?

Paul's churchyard, London, and the Lincoln comb or rather comb-case, is adequate. Unlike the monuments treated so far, these two are included in Jacobsen and Moltke's splendid corpus of Danish runes.[1] The design of the London stone links it firmly to Scandinavian, perhaps even Swedish, work of the first half of the eleventh century, and its text, **k[i]na:let:lekia:st|in:þensi:auk:tuki**, 'Ginna and Toki had this stone laid', fits such a date and provenance. The Lincoln comb has a legend in good Scandinavian: **kamb:koþan:kiari:þorfastr**, 'Thorfastr made a good comb', with rune-forms of the Danish type. Jacobsen and Moltke date it to 1050–1150. As Ekwall pointed out, this is a portable object which may have strayed far from its place of manufacture.[2] Both these pieces suggest that the Scandinavian tongue was known in this country, but not necessarily used by its permanent inhabitants.

On this showing the Scandinavian runic inscriptions in England tell us little of the continued use of the Norse tongue in the lands the Vikings settled. They may, as Ekwall claimed, 'offer the utmost interest', but it is an interest aroused more by their ambiguity and scarcity than by their evidential value. They contrast with the other vernacular inscriptions of northern and eastern England during the Viking Age, which show a clear continuity of English used in formal style from the eighth century to the eleventh. The Anglo-Saxon runic examples are well listed in Marquardt's *Bibliographie*, but the non-runic ones are less well known, and in what follows I lean heavily on, without quoting precisely from, Dr Okasha's Cambridge dissertation, 'Anglo-Saxon non-runic inscriptions', and the material of her published hand-list. I ignore a large group of texts which are probably pre-Viking Age but which cannot be precisely dated, as the Carlisle, Dewsbury, Gainford, Hexham, Thornhill, Wycliffe and Yarm stones, and the Aberford and Lancashire rings, and I also omit several from the later Anglo-Saxon period whose texts are obscure or uncertain. This leaves a collection of legends containing clearly identifiable material, and securely dated to the tenth, eleventh or perhaps the twelfth century on linguistic, artistic or historical grounds. In the Roman character are the legends of the Aldbrough, Great Edstone and Kirkdale sundials, all in Yorkshire, the Ipswich stone, the St Mary-le-Wigford, Lincoln, and the St Mary Castlegate, York, dedication stones, the All Hallows, Barking, cross and the Sutton, Isle of Ely, brooch.[3] The Alnmouth and Chester-le-

---

[1] Jacobsen and Moltke, *Danmarks Runeindskrifter*, nos. 412 and 418.

[2] I correct the Jacobsen and Moltke entry which describes the comb as *fra en samling i Lincoln; nøjere oplysninger om dens herkomst savnes*. The comb was found in Lincoln in 1851: see *PSAL* 2nd ser. III (1864–7), 382.

[3] On the Old Byland, Yorkshire, sundial D. H. Haigh read SVMARLEÐAN HVSCARL ME FECIT, with the Scandinavian name *Sumarliði*, and the name or title *huskarl* ('Yorkshire Dials', *YAJ* v [1879], 141). The inscription has long been illegible (cf. J. Romilly Allen's

Street stones mix runic and Roman scripts. From the Anglo-Saxon runic corpus I include here the Monkwearmouth 'tidfirþ', the Overchurch, Cheshire, the Crowle, Lincolnshire, and the Collingham, Yorkshire, stones.

Some show not the least sign of Scandinavian linguistic influence. Among these are the two name-stones, Chester-le-Street with EADmVnD and Monkwearmouth with 'tidfirþ'. The Ipswich carved slab has a simple title: HER:$\overline{\text{SCE}}$ MIHAEL:FEHT WIÐ ÐANE:DRACA (or perhaps DRAC$\overline{\text{A}}$ for *dracan*), 'Here St Michael fights with the dragon', which again is fairly consistent Old English. The Alnmouth cross has the fragmentary maker signature MYREDaH·MEH·wO-, and the genitive name form EADVLFES. The Overchurch stone reads 'folcæ arærdon bec-|[.]biddaþ fote æþelmun-', which, despite its two errors, must be Old English for 'The people set up a monument: pray for Æthelmund'. Perhaps most significant of this group is the Sutton, Isle of Ely, brooch, whose design is so influenced by Norse style that D. M. Wilson describes it as 'pseudo-Viking'.[1] The extensive text on the brooch back runs: ✠ÆDVWEN ME AG AGE HYO DRIHTEN DRIHTEN HINE AWERIE ÐE ME HIRE ÆTFERIE BVTON HYO ME SELLE HIRE AGENES WILLES, '✠ Ædwen owns me, may the Lord own her. May the Lord curse the man who takes me from her unless she give me of her own free will.' Despite its strong stylistic influence from Scandinavia, there is no corresponding effect on the language. The Crowle and Collingham stones present similar, though less striking, examples. On Crowle the rune-master set out his text on a curving ribbon of stone in the Norse manner. Little of the legend survives, but one word, 'licbæcun' is readable. Though this word does not occur elsewhere, its two elements *lic-* and *-bæcun* are common in Old English, and the compound, with the meaning 'gravestone', is a plausible one. The Collingham inscription is likewise fragmentary. Only 'æft[.]|[.]swiþi' remains, presumably a memorial formula with the preposition *æfter* followed by a name with the second element *-swiþ*. The runes are Anglo-Saxon and the surviving text Old English despite the fact that the decoration of the stone shows strong Scandinavian influence.[2]

A small number of stones have Old English inscriptions incorporating names of a Norse type. One of these is the dedication stone of St Mary-le-

rubbing, now BM Add. 37581. 31 and 32, which shows traces of SVMAR-, perhaps -AN, and very little else). Haigh was an unreliable reader of Old English inscriptions, and in this case was working from a cast, though indeed with the help of J. T. Fowler, a more sober scholar in the field.

[1] D. M. Wilson, *Anglo-Saxon Ornamental Metalwork 700–1100 in the British Museum* (London, 1964), pp. 50 and 86–8.

[2] G. Baldwin Brown, *The Arts in Early England* (London, 1903–37) VI, 154–7.

Wigford, Lincoln, which has stood outside the church, affixed to its west tower, at least since the eighteenth century. Comparing its present condition with drawings and a photograph taken earlier this century Dr Okasha notes considerable modern deterioration. The versions of J. Wordsworth (1879) and R. G. Collingwood (1923), together with Bruce Dickins's report of 1946, enable us to restore the text: ✠EIRTIG ME LET WIRCE[*A*]N·7 FIOS GODIAN CRISTE TO LOFE 7 SCE MARIE, '✠ Eirtig had me made and endowed with property in honour of Christ and St Mary.'[1] There are two points of difficulty. A construction *godian* + genitive of the thing given seems otherwise unrecorded in English, but neither is its equivalent found in Old Norse and it may be simply an individual or local peculiarity. Earlier readers of the legend record the builder's name as *Eirtig* though it is no longer clear on the stone. There is no such name in Old English. Bruce Dickins suggested it was a Norse name with an ending *-ig* representing ON *-i*, as in *Tostig*, *Pallig* etc.[2] It could perhaps be a form of the rare *Eitri* which has been identified in the lost village name *Eterstorp*, Yorkshire.[3]

The Great Edstone sundial has two texts, one the Latin ORLOGIV[*M VIA*] TORIS (or [*VIA*]TORVM as commonly read in the past).[4] The other is ill-arranged and probably incomplete, ✠LOÐAN ME WROHTEA; perhaps it was to have been a double makers' signature, ✠*Loðan me wrohte a*(*nd* + a second name). The legend is Old English, but the name *Loðan* Scandinavian, ON *Loðinn*, ODan *Lothæn*. The St Mary Castlegate, York, stone is fragmentary, with a good part of the text remaining. It begins in Old English, continues in Latin, and may revert to Old English in a damaged ending. Dr Okasha reads [.]:M[*I*]NSTER SET[.]ARD 7 GRIM 7 ÆSE:O[.]MAN DRIHTNES HÆ[.], continuing in Latin.[5] The original was presumably something like *þis minster setton*...*ard and Grim and Æse on naman drihtnes hælendes*, '...ard and Grim and Æse established this church in the name of Our Lord and Saviour.' Accepting a tenth-century date for the church Ekwall argued that 'in York the Scandinavian language was given up early, for the persons mentioned in the inscription were clearly Scandinavians.' *Grim* is indeed a common Scandinavian name. *Æse* may be an Anglicization of the Scandinavian *Ási*, *Esi*,[6] but it could also be a native Old English name, perhaps related to the recorded *Æsica*. In any case Ekwall's comment begs an important question. He assumes that people with Scandinavian names need necessarily be Scandi-

---

[1] R. G. Collingwood and R. P. Wright, *The Roman Inscriptions of Britain* I (Oxford, 1965), no. 262, where there is an excellent drawing and an extensive bibliography.
[2] Bruce Dickins, 'The Dedication Stone of St. Mary-le-Wigford, Lincoln', *AJ* CIII (1946), 163–5.     [3] Fellows Jensen, p. 76.
[4] A. R. Green, 'Anglo-Saxon Sundials', *AntJ* VIII (1928), 510.
[5] Illustrated in *VCH, York*, facing p. 333.     [6] Fellows Jensen, p. 24.

navian, though this is palpably untrue, and it is hard to see quite what 'Scandinavian' need mean in such a context. To take an example, the Englishman Earl Godwine had by his Danish wife a number of children, some of whom had Scandinavian names, as Swein, Tostig and Harold, and others of whom had English names, as Leofwine and Wulfnoth. By his English wife Harold Godwineson had sons whose names were Godwine, Edmund, Magnus, Ulf and Harold. Despite their names Magnus and Ulf could hardly be thought Scandinavians. Even in the highly Scandinavian-ized York, people with Norse names need not be of Norse descent. Surviving English inhabitants may have given their children fashionable Norse names in imitation of a Norse dominant class.

There remain three inscriptions where the language may be affected by Norse usage. In the case of the All Hallows, Barking, cross the effect is minimal and uncertain. The legend, being badly damaged, is obscure, but it seems to contain a formula naming the man who put up the cross and the deceased it commemorated: *NN let settan ofer Here-*.[1] The word *ofer* is incomplete but likely. Its use rather than *æfter* in such a formula is unparalleled in Old English, but there are a few cases of *yfir* in similar contexts on Danish and Norwegian rune-stones, and in the British Isles on the newly found Iona specimen. Thus All Hallows shows possible influence from Old Norse.

The Aldbrough sundial is a more important case. The text is quite well preserved and reads: ✠VLF LET (?*HET*) ARŒRAN CYRICE FOR HÆNVM 7 FOR GVNWARA SAVLA, usually translated, '✠Ulf had this church built for his own sake and for Gunnvǫr's soul.'[2] There is some trace of late Anglo-Saxon work in Aldbrough church, and certainly the inscription contains corresponding late linguistic forms, seen in the collapse of the classical Old English inflexional system. So, *cyrice* for acc.sg. *cirican* shows loss of final *-n* and has confusion of the unstressed vowel as does *savla* for *saule*. *Gvnwara* is presumably genitive. The Old Norse form should be *Gunnwarar* but the Aldbrough name may be Anglicized, its second element a borrowing of OE *-waru* which should have the genitive *-ware*. Loss of definition in the vowel ending is common in late Anglian texts and shows a breakdown of the Old English inflexional system which is not necessarily a result of Old Norse admixture. Aldbrough has also the difficult form *hanvm*, which is usually taken as dat.sg. of the 3.personal pronoun, since attempts to derive it from OE *hean*, 'poor, desolate', seem semantically misguided. *hanum* is certainly the ON dat.sg. of such a pronoun, but of course Old Norse would use the reflexive *sér* in this context.

[1] E. Okasha, 'An Anglo-Saxon Inscription from All Hallows, Barking-by-the-Tower', *MA* XI (1967), 249–51.

[2] There is an excellent photograph of this dial in A. L. Binns, *East Yorkshire in the Sagas* (York, 1966), p. 20.

The Old English equivalent is *him*, and Old English has no reflexive. It looks as though the Aldbrough dialect has a pronominal system influenced but not superseded by the Old Norse one. Both *Vlf* and *Gvnwara* represent Scandinavian names, one with loss of inflexional *-r* (which suggests English affection), the other with a second element probably Anglicized. Whether these people spoke a Scandinavian dialect is impossible to say, for the evidence of the inscription is inconclusive, and we cannot identify them from other sources. According to Domesday Book one Ulf owned land at Aldbrough in Edward the Confessor's reign, and this could be the man named on the dial. But Ulf is one of the commonest of Scandinavian names in this country, and any identification is perilous.[1]

Finally there is one of the longest and most famous of early English inscriptions, that which accompanies the Kirkdale sundial, excellently preserved within the porch and above the south doorway of that church.[2] The main text reads: ✠ORM·GAMAL·SVNA·BOHTE:$\overline{\text{SCS}}$ GREGO-RIVS·MINSTER ÐONNE HIT WES ÆL:TOBROCAN·7 TOFALAN· 7 H$\widehat{\text{E}}$ HIT LET MACAN NEWAN·FRO$\underline{\text{M}}$ GRVNDE $\overline{\text{XPE}}$:7 SCS GREGORIVS·IN EADWARD:DAGVM·$\overline{\text{CNG}}$ 7N TOSTI:DAGVM· EORL✠, '✠ Orm Gamal's son bought St Gregory's church when it was quite broken down and ruined, and he had it built anew from the foundations in honour of Christ and St Gregory in the days of King Edward and of Earl Tosti.' There are two others, the double maker formula, ✠7 HAWARÐ·ME WROHTE·7 BRAND $\overline{\text{PRS}}$, and the comment on the dial itself, ✠ÞIS IS DÆGES SOLMERCA✠ ÆT ILCVM TIDE✠, 'This is the day's sun-marker at every hour.' The references to King Edward and Earl Tosti allow us to date the inscription 1055–65, and so to identify Orm with the man who held *Chirchebi*, apparently Kirkdale, in Edward the Confessor's reign. Again the texts are recognizably English, but not classical Old English. They show typical late features, as the weakening of unstressed vowels in *svna*, *tobrocan*, *tofalan*, the loss of the distinctive 2. weak conjugation infinitive ending in *macan* and of the inflexional endings in *Gamal svna*, *Eadward...cng*, *Tosti...eorl*, and the imprecision in the use of grammatical gender in the concord *ilcvm tide*. But again these are not the effects of a Norse admixture. Scholars have traditionally pointed to three specifically Norse features of the texts: (i) the admittedly Scandinavian names *Orm*, *Gamal*, *Hawarð* and *Brand* where however there is Anglicization in the loss of the nominative *-r*, (ii) the patronymic type *Gamal svna* and (iii) the use of the word *solmerca*. As I have shown above, (i) is an

---

[1] Binns, *ibid.* p. 21, confidently identifies him with Ulf Thorvaldsson who gave his estates to York Minster. This seems to be one of the few men called Ulf who it cannot be, for the Domesday survey shows Aldbrough owned, not by St Peter's, York, but by Drogo de Bevrere.

[2] There is an excellent picture in P. Hunter Blair, *An Introduction to Anglo-Saxon England* (Cambridge, 1956), pl. XII.

invalid criterion. Nor is (ii) acceptable since Tengvik pointed to Old English patronymics of this type from parts of England and from times in which Norse influence is unlikely.[1] (iii) is less clear than commonly supposed. *Solmerca* occurs nowhere else in Old English, whereas there is an ON *sólmerki*, apparently rare, having the sense 'sign of the zodiac'. The difficulty is the meaning of *solmerca* in the Kirkdale context. Scholars have usually glossed it 'sundial', presumably taking this part of the inscription as equivalent to the explanatory ORLOGIV[*M VIA*]TORIS of Great Edstone, or the fragmentary word on the broken Orpington, Kent, dial which should probably be supplied OR[*ALOGI*]VM.[2] The second element of ON *sólmerki* is presumably *merki*, 'a mark', where *solmerca*, 'sundial', needs a second element meaning 'marker, something which marks (the position of the sun)'. -*merca* would then be a -*jan*-stem nomen agentis related to the verb *mearcian* (cf. *dema*, 'judge' or *brytta*, 'distributor'), and could be a native Old English word. There seems to be a parallel in *inmerca, onmerca* which the Lindisfarne and Rushworth scribes use to gloss *inscriptio*, 'superscription, legend which marks a coin as belonging to a particular emperor'. Since *sol*, 'sun', is very rare in Old English but common in Old Norse, we must then assume *solmerca* to be a hybrid compound. The alternative, possible but less likely, is to translate the Kirkdale sentence as 'This is the mark of the sun for each hour', referring, not to the dial as a whole, but to the rays which give the times of the canonical hours. In this case *solmerca* could be a loan of the Old Norse word, with a weakening of the unstressed ending.

In this paper I have dealt with inscriptions only from the Danelaw, assuming it unlikely that those from the south and west show Scandinavian influence on the language. As a generalization this is acceptable, but there is an exception, a coped memorial stone found recently at Winchester.[3] This has an inscription reading ✠HER LIÐ GV[*N*]NI EORLES FEOLAGA, '✠ Here lies Gunni, earl's (or possibly, with a personal name, Eorl's) comrade'. OE *feolaga* ( < ON *félagi*, but with Anglicization of the first element) is not otherwise recorded before the eleventh century, and the 'here lies' formula is unusual in Anglo-Saxon contexts but common enough after the Conquest, which also suggests a late date for this text. *Gvnni* is a Scandinavian name recorded elsewhere in England, and the use of *eorl* as a title (if that is the correct interpretation) derives from Old Norse practice. It is likely that the Winchester slab dates from the late period of Danish control in England, and shows its linguistic effect even in Wessex.

[1] Tengvik, pp. 147 ff.
[2] H. M. and J. Taylor, *Anglo-Saxon Architecture* (Cambridge, 1965), pp. 476–7.
[3] M. Biddle, 'Excavations at Winchester 1965', *AntJ* XLVI (1966), 325.

## How long did the Scandinavian language survive in England?

The extant epigraphical evidence for my subject is slight. What survives shows little use of the Scandinavian tongues, and a small effect on English epigraphical practice, facts to be noted in discussing the size and importance of Viking settlements in this country. Yet we cannot assume that because there are few Norse-influenced inscriptions there were few Norse speakers. It is easy enough to suggest other reasons for this epigraphical dearth: the Norse settlers may have belonged in the main to social classes with no tradition of setting up memorial stones, or the English church to which so many inscriptions are linked may have exerted influence against the use of an alien tongue and in favour of the language traditionally employed for vernacular texts. The inscriptions, like the Old English written sources, show surprisingly little Old Norse admixture compared with the Middle English material from many areas. They suggest a number of lines of investigation which might prove fruitful: the possible importance of Middle English epigraphy, of which we know practically nothing: the contrast between the situation in the Isle of Man where Old Norse inscriptions are plentiful, and that in related regions of England: continuing links between parts of England and the Viking North in post-Conquest times. In turn, these may add their quota of evidence to the debate about the nature, size and significance of the Viking influx into northern and eastern England.

# Personal names on the coinage of Edgar

## OLOF VON FEILITZEN and CHRISTOPHER BLUNT

Sir Frank Stenton, in one of his last publications, wrote of the value to the historian of the personal names of moneyers which are found as a regular feature of the Anglo-Saxon penny coinage, and remarked that 'the names of moneyers recorded on the coins of the period often appear in forms which would compromise any charter displaying them.' He notes however that this evidence has not yet been marshalled systematically in print.[1]

Since Stenton wrote, a first step has been taken to filling this need by the publication of Mrs V. J. Smart's important study of the names of moneyers found on coins struck from c. 973 to 1016.[2] The present article lists the names found on Edgar's coins and the various forms in which they occur. It has not been possible to follow Mrs Smart's plan of arranging the names according to the areas in which they are found, because the bulk of Edgar's coins, before the reform which was carried out towards the end of his reign, do not give the mint at which they were struck. Where the mint name is found, it is noted in the lists that follow, and, below, certain geographical indications of the general areas in which some types were issued are given.

The types have been arranged according to the *British Museum Catalogue of Anglo-Saxon Coins* (*BMC*),[3] an arrangement which, it must be emphasized, makes no claim to be chronological. The various types will be found conveniently illustrated in the most recent study of Edgar's coinage as a whole by Mr R. H. M. Dolley and Dr D. M. Metcalf.[4]

The *BMC* types may be summarized as follows:

*Type I.* Obverse, a small cross pattée with the inscription around between two circles.

Reverse, moneyer's name in two lines, divided by three crosses pattée; above and below a triangle of dots.

This type was struck over a wide area with seemingly a preponderance in the north-eastern part of the country. The hoard evidence is, however, uneven, and the scarcity of surviving coins likely to have come from southern mints is probably due to a dearth of hoards from the south.

[1] Stenton, *Charters*, pp. 24–5.
[2] In *Commentationes de Nummis Saeculorum ix–xi in Suecia Repertis* II (Royal Swedish Academy, Stockholm, 1968).  [3] II, 165–7.
[4] *Anglo-Saxon Coins*, ed. R. H. M. Dolley (London, 1961), pp. 136–68.

*Type Ia–b.* Two slight variants of type I; the first replaces the triangle of dots on the reverse by a single dot; the second by a cross pattée.

Both are southern types.

*Type Ic–g.* Similar to type I, but, on the reverse, rosettes of dots are found variously placed. *f* and *g* have rosettes on the obverse.

This group is confined to Mercia, with emphasis on the north-western portion.

*Type II.* The obverse remains the same. The reverse, which continues the use of rosettes of dots noted on the previous group, now adds an abbreviated form of a mint name – Chester (most commonly), Derby, TE (Tamworth?) and NE (Newark?). The type is a late one.

*Type III.* Same obverse type. Reverse type similar to obverse.

This type is found on mint-signed coins issued widely over the country, with the notable exception of East Anglia (Bedford however is recorded on a single coin) and the area on the east of the country to the north. No mint-signed coins are found of Lincoln or Stamford and only two of York. Hoard evidence supports the view that a large number of the coins without mint-signature come in fact from this area.

*Type IV.* Similar to type III, but a rosette of dots replaces the small cross pattée in the centre on both sides. Essentially, like other rosette-marked coins, a Mercian type.

*Type V.* The obverse of this type is completely different. It shows a crowned bust of the king facing right. The reverse continues the type of III, with a small cross pattée in the centre.

A number of mint-signed coins are found, mostly from places in the eastern part of the country – Bedford, Hertford, Huntingdon, London and Thetford; but isolated specimens of Bath and Totnes are also known. Many of the coins without mint-signature are likely to have originated from the eastern area.

*Type VI.* The so-called Reform type. This also shows the king's bust, this time diademed and facing left. The reverse is very similar to the preceding type.

With this type mint-signatures become a regular feature, and the importance of York as a mint, which had been shrouded in anonymity since the reign of Athelstan, emerges. Coins of thirteen York moneyers are recorded for this type, compared with five of London. This should not, however, be taken to mean that the York mint was necessarily two-and-a-half times as productive as London; the incidence of hoards can distort the picture. It does, however, bring out the importance of the Northumbrian mint.

In the lists that follow, an attempt has been made to bring together the various forms under which a single name appears and to relate them to normalized forms. The *BMC* type is given in Roman numerals and the mint is given where known.

Some of the forms listed are of rare occurrence and readers who wish to check the frequency of any particular form can most conveniently do so by consulting *BMC*,[1] the various volumes of the *Sylloge of Coins of the British Isles*, especially the Edinburgh fascicule, which is rich in tenth-century material, and some of the reports on major hoards such as Chester, 1950,[2] Iona, 1950[3] and Tetney, 1945.[4] The authority for the form cited is given after the type. In many cases it would have been possible to give a number of references and, where this is so, we have sought, wherever practicable, to select one where the coin in question may be found illustrated. For this purpose the *Sylloge* has been found particularly useful.

We are indebted to the many writers whose works we have quoted and, in particular, to Professor Kenneth Jackson of Edinburgh University who has most kindly advised us on Celtic problems produced by names such as *Cawelin* and *Demence*.

### LIST OF NAMES

**Abenel** Hertford V BM[5] ex Chester hoard 493. – Cf. *Abunel* 901 (14/15) Birch 585, a witness to a Wiltshire charter, and the moneyers *Abenel*, Athelstan II, East Anglia, *BMC* 90 and *SCBI Cambridge* 456 and *Oxford* 63, Alfred, *BMC* 190, and Edmund, Forum 286; *Abonel*, Athelstan, Wessex, *SCBI Copenhagen* 1, 694 (Hertford) and *Edinburgh* 118; and *Abunel*, Edmund, *SCBI Edinburgh* 200. Note also *Abonel*, *Abonello*, *Abbonoe*, St Edmund memorial coinage, *BMC* 118, 126–7, 119–25 and 128 (with numerous blundered variants).[6] Perhaps an *-el* derivative of *Ab(b)un*, recorded as the name of a moneyer under Athelstan (*BMC*, p. 101) and Edmund (*BMC* 5), but for which no etymology can at present be suggested. It may be non-Germanic. An alternative etymon would be OG (Rom) *Abbonel*, a diminutive of OG *Abbo*.[7] In either case the vowel variation in the second syllable is due to lack of stress.

**Ācwulf,** see **Agulf.**

[1] II, 168–90.

[2] *BNJ* xxvii (1952–4), 125–60.

[3] *NC* 6th ser. xi (1951), 68–90.

[4] *Ibid.* 6th ser. v (1945), 81–95.

[5] Throughout this article BM signifies 'in the British Museum, but not in *BMC*'.

[6] *Abenel*, mon. Eadwig, *BMC* II, 156 (not in BM), could not be verified.

[7] *Abbonellus*, 886, a manciple at Fins near Péronne in French Flanders, son of Folcard and Oderna (Morlet 13). It survives in the modern French surname *Abonneau*; see A. Dauzat, *Dictionnaire Étymologique des Noms de Famille et Prénoms de France* (Paris, 1951), p. 2. Note also the Norman pl.n. [Ascelinus] de *Abonelvilla*, 1079–83 (12), in a charter printed by L. Musset, *Mémoires de la Société des Antiquaires de Normandie*, xxxvii (Caen, 1967), 101, and tentatively identified with Béneauville (Calvados). *Abbanae* (gen.), 604–16 (12), Birch 8, *Abonis* (gen.) *principis*, 664 (13), Birch 22 (cf. also *Abon aeldorman, ASC,* 656 E) in spurious charters are scribal genitives of *Abba*; see Forssner, pp. 3 f. and 266.

**Adelaver** I; **Aðelaver** I; **Adeloverd** I. – The first form is by far the most common one: *BMC* 57–60, *SCBI Cambridge* 607, *Edinburgh* 349–57 and *Reading* 55, Chester hoard 375–6, Smarmore 29–30, and Tetney 123–7 and 133–44; also Edward II, Lincoln, *SCBI Glasgow* 743.[1] *Aðelaver* occurs *BMC* 61, *SCBI Copenhagen* 1, 784 and *Edinburgh* 358–60, and Tetney 128, and *Adeloverd* once only, *BMC* 62. The first el. is probably OG *Adel-* rather than OE *Æðel-*, but the second cannot be identified. The persistent occurrence of final *-r* and of medial *-a-*, which looks like an epenthetic vowel but would be unparalleled in ordinary compounds with *Adel-*, seems to rule out both *-ward* (Anglicized *-weard, -werd*) and *-frid* (Anglicized *-frið, -ferð*).[2]

**Adelger** I *BMC* 63. – OG *Adelger* (Förstemann 166f. and Schlaug I, 65 and II, 49f.).

**Aden** I *SCBI Copenhagen* 785. – Obscure.

**Ælfgar** Thetford VI *SCBI Glasgow* 726. – OE *Ælfgār*.

**Ælfnoð** London III Douglas, V *SCBI Cambridge* 619, VI *SCBI Copenhagen* 778, Winchcombe VI *BMC* 51. – OE *Ælfnōð*.

**Ælfred** Id *SCBI Edinburgh* 580, Newark (?) II *SCBI Edinburgh* 617; **Ælfredes** (gen.) Ic BM ex Chester hoard 379; **Ælferd** Thetford (?) V BM; **Elfred** Id *BMC* 148. – OE *Ælfrēd*.[3]

**Ælfsige** I BM ex Chester hoard 381, Id *SCBI Edinburgh* 582, IV *BMC* 198, V BM ex Chester hoard 497, Newport III BM, Wilton VI *BMC* 49, Winchester VI *SCBI Glasgow* 728; **Ælfsig** Id *SCBI Copenhagen* 788, III Blunt, IV Chester hoard 468, V Carlyon-Britton 1017, Chester II *SCBI Chester* 79, III Carlyon-Britton 452, Bedford V *BMC* 2; **Ælfsie** Stafford VI Hildebrand 39; **Ealfsige** Id *SCBI Edinburgh* 591. – OE *Ælfsige*.

**Ælfstan** Ia Ruding, pl. 28. 2, Bedford VI Allen 234, Chester II *SCBI Edinburgh* 619–20, VI Hildebrand 18, Exeter VI *SCBI Copenhagen* 769, 'Weardburh' III *BMC* 6; **Elfstan** Ic *SCBI Glasgow* 692, IV *BMC* 201; **Ead Ælfstan**[4] Exeter (?) III Chester hoard 459. – OE *Ælfstān*.

**Alfwold** Lymne VI *SCBI Copenhagen* 776; **Elfwald** I *ibid.* 798; **Elfval** I *BMC* 88. – OE *Ælfwald*.[5]

**Æscman** Stamford VI *SCBI Cambridge* 622; **Ascman** Lincoln VI BM; **Asma** Lincoln VI Hildebrand 26. – OE *Æscmann*; see *PNDB* 182. The last form is blundered; cf. *Asman*, Æthelred II, Lincoln, Hildebrand 1674, by the side of frequent *Æscman, ibid.* 1635–41. See also **Asmaned**.

---

[1] The form *Adelavern* (?) is found once on a coin of this Lincoln moneyer (*SCBI Oxford* 427).

[2] R. E. Zachrisson, *ES* LXIV (1929), 227, would explain *Adelaver* as the outcome of a French die-cutter's attempt to render OE *Æðelweard*, but this is clearly improbable.

[3] In giving the normalized spellings of names with this second el., *-rēd*, which is by far the most common form in OE sources, has been used throughout instead of *-ræd*.

[4] On this legend, see below, pp. 194 and 210.

[5] In the present paper *-wald* has been adopted as the standard form instead of *-weald*; cf. *PNDB* 59.

**Æsculf** I *SCBI Glasgow* 679. – OE *Æscwulf*.

**Ætferd**, see **Ead-**.

**Æðelbrand** V BM ex Chester hoard 498. – OG *Adelbrand* (Forssner 14). The first el. has been Anglicized.

**Æðelferð** Ilchester VI Hildebrand 10, London V *SCBI Glasgow* 708; **Æðelfed** 'Weardburh' III BM ex Chester hoard 458. – OE *Æðelfrið*.

**Æðelm** Id *SCBI Edinburgh* 583; **Eðelm** Chester II *SCBI Chester* 85. – OE **Æðelhelm**.

**Æðelnoð** Exeter VI Stockholm. – OE *Æðelnoð*.

**Æðelred** London III Lockett 3710, VI *BMC* 39; **Æðered** I Argyll, Ic *SCBI Cambridge* 614, Ig *BMC* 166, London V *SCBI Edinburgh* 646. – OE *Æðelrēd*.

**Æðelric** Bath III *SCBI Edinburgh* 511, London VI Stockholm. – OE *Æðelrīc*.

**Æðelsige** Bath III *SCBI Edinburgh* 512, London III Hildebrand 28, Shrewsbury VI *SCBI Oxford* 422; **Æðelsie** I *SCBI Copenhagen* 786; **Æðelsig** I Douglas hoard 36; **Æðelsge** SW mint III BM; **Ædelsie** I *BMC* 68. – OE *Æðelsige*.

**Æðelstan** I Douglas, London VI BM; **Æðestan** Canterbury VI Hildebrand 2, Gloucester VI *SCBI Glasgow* 712, Lymne VI Lockett 633, Winchester III Drabble 432. – OE *Æðelstān*.

**Æðelwald** London VI Lockett 3711; **Aðelwold** London III *BNJ* xxxv (1966), pl. xiv. 19, VI *SCBI Glasgow* 717. – OE *Æðelwald*.

**Æðelwine** Oxford III *SCBI Oxford* 408, VI *SCBI Glasgow* 723; **Adlvine** I *SCBI Edinburgh* 363; **Adlvne** I Blunt; **Adlvini** I Carlyon-Britton 1710a; **Eðelvine** I Tetney 219; **Eðelaine** I *SCBI Glasgow* 683. – OE *Æðelwine*. The last five forms are clearly due to incompetent engravers.

**Æðelulfes** (gen.) Ic Douglas hoard 72; **Eðelulfes** (gen.) I Chester hoard 383; **Aðulf** London V *SCBI Glasgow* 709. – OE *Æðelwulf*.

**Agulf** I Tetney 153. – OG *Agulf* (Morlet 22).[1] If, however, *g* stands for *c*, a common error on coins, we have OE *Ācwulf*; cf. *Aculf*, mon. Eadwig, Tetney 54.

**Albart** Cambridge VI Hildebrand 13. – OG *Albert* (Forssner 19f.). In -*bart* for -*bert* the engraver has mistakenly repeated the initial vowel of the first el.

**Albutc** I *SCBI Copenhagen* 791. – The form is well authenticated and shows no variation.[2] Obscure.

**Aldewine** Ic Maish 39, Id *SCBI Edinburgh* 585–6, IV *BMC* 199; **Aldewin** Chester II *SCBI Edinburgh* 622. – OE *Ealdwine*.

---

[1] Well evidenced in French sources as *Agulfus, Agolfus, Aggulfus*, from *c*. 650 to the late tenth century.

[2] *BMC* 70–2 and *SCBI Copenhagen* 1, 790–1, *Edinburgh* 368–74, *Glasgow* 680 and *Oxford* 386.

**Alhmund** I d *SCBI Edinburgh* 587–8. – OE *Ealhmund*.

**Amund** IV Carlyon-Britton 1047a. – ON *Amundr*, ODan *Amund*; see Björkman 4, Janzén 62 and Fellows Jensen 10.

**Ana** I *SCBI Copenhagen* 792. – OE *An(n)a* (Redin 60).

**Andreas** I *SCBI Cambridge* 608. – This moneyer seems to be the first bearer of the name in England and may actually have been a foreigner.[1]

**Ascman**, see **Æscman**.

**Asferð** I *BMC* 74; **Asferd** I *SCBI Copenhagen* 793, III *SCBI Glasgow* 698. – ON *Ás(f)røðr*, ODan *Asfrith* (*PNDB* 165).

**Asma**, see **Æscman**.

**Asmaned** I Lockett 3706; **Asmneda** I *SCBI Edinburgh* 375; **Asmin** I Tetney 161. – Possibly OE *Æscmann* (*q.v.*), but final -*ed*, -*eda* is obscure. In *Asmin i* might be an engraver's error for *a*.

**Aðulf**, see **Æðelwulf**.


**Balddic** Bedford VI Hildebrand 1. – This could be an error for *Baldric* (*q.v.*), as suggested by Redin (p. 149) and Mrs Smart (p. 246), but it is noteworthy that on the Bedford coins of the following reigns the name is consistently spelled without an *r*: *Baldic*, Edward II (*BMC* 3 and *SCBI Glasgow* 735 and *Oxford* 426), *Balddic*, Æthelred II (*SCBI Glasgow* 768). Hence possibly a short form in -*ic* of OE names in *Beald-*, though the suffix is admittedly archaic and unproductive,[2] or an OLG *\*Baldic*, a variant of *Baldicho* (Schlaug I, 175), -*ik* being a common suffix in early OS names.[3]

**Baldric** Northampton III Carlyon-Britton 1039, VI *SCBI Glasgow* 719. – OG *Baldric*, a common continental name,[4] rather than OE *Bealdrīc*, which is not well evidenced.[5]

**Baldwin** V Chester hoard 499–502. – OG *Baldwin* (Forssner 41 f.).[6]

**Beneðiht** I *SCBI Glasgow* 681. – Latin *Benedictus*. Medial *ð* for *d* in the coin-spelling may reflect the Vulgar Latin spirant. Final -*ht* for [kt] is due to an OE sound-change.[7]

[1] Cf. E. G. Withycombe, *The Oxford Dictionary of English Christian Names*, 2nd ed. (Oxford, 1950), p. 22.

[2] See the survey in Redin, pp. 149–52. Note also *Domic*, *c*. 990, Whitelock *Æthelgifu*, line 18.

[3] Schlaug I, 26f. and II, 14f.

[4] *PNDB* 191, Morlet 50 and *DBS*, *s.n.* *Baldree*.

[5] The only bearers of the name in pre-Conquest sources are the Northampton moneyer under notice, who also worked under Eadwig (*SCBI Cambridge* 603 and Chester hoard 282) and may be identical with *Baldric* on coins of Athelstan, Edmund and Eadred (*BMC* 151, 157 and 14 respectively), *Balderic*, Athelstan (Blunt), and the man who figures in the boundary-mark *into Baldrices gemæran*, eleventh-century, Kemble 612 (Wolverton, Wo). In both cases we may be concerned with the OG name. The cleric mentioned by Searle (p. 84) was a monk of Salzburg; see *MGH*, *Epistolae* IV, 309.

[6] The corresponding native name occurs in *LVD* (*Balduini* 5 x) and in the bds of Bedwyn, W: *Baldwines healh*, 778 (contemp.), Birch 225.

[7] Campbell, §§ 484, 530 and 534.

**Beorht-:**

**Brrehtferð** SW mint III Chester hoard 452; **Britfer** I *SCBI Cambridge* 610; **Bitfer** I Carlyon-Britton 1711b; **Byrhtefrd** Malmesbury (?) VI Hildebrand 29. – OE *Beorhtfrið*.

**Byrhtnoð** Leicester (?) (type not in *BMC*) *SCBI Edinburgh* 645; **Borhtnoð** SW mint III Dublin. – OE *Beorhtnoð*.

**Beorhtric** Ib *BMC* 139, Wallingford III Lockett 623; **Byrhtric** Lymne (?) VI Hildebrand 25. – OE *Beorhtrīc*.

**Bircsige** London V Ryan 798. – OE *Beorhtsige*.

**Biorhtulf** Bath V Chester hoard 490. – OE *Beorhtwulf*.

**Byrhtwold** Shaftesbury VI Hildebrand 38. – OE *Beorhtwald*.

**Beornstān, see Burhstan.**

**Bernard** Ic Carlyon-Britton 447a; **Bernardes** (gen.) III Douglas; **Berenard** Ic Carlyon-Britton 1031, Derby III Grantley 1102.–OE *Beornheard* or OG *Ber(e)nard* (Forssner 46). The absence of forms in *Beorn-, Byrn-* and the medial vowel in *Berenard* favour the second alternative.

**Bernferð** I *BMC* 76; **Byrnferð** Ib Chester hoard 384, V *ibid.* 503, V var. *SCBI Glasgow* 711, Bath III BM. – OE *Beornfrið*.

**Bernulf** I Chester hoard 385. – OE *Beornwulf*.

**Birc-, see Beorht-.**

**Biorht-, see Beorht-.**

**Boia** IV Chester hoard 453, Canterbury III *SCBI Edinburgh* 514, Chester II *SCBI Chester* 80, Derby II Ryan 787, III Chester hoard 443, Wilton III Private Collection; **Boiga** Derby IV *SCBI Edinburgh* 572, Wilton VI Hildebrand 43; (Fastolf) **Boiga** III *SCBI Glasgow* 702;[1] **Boigaes** (gen.) Ic Blunt; **Bogea** Canterbury VI Drabble 435, Chester VI Hildebrand 19; **Boga** Canterbury VI *BMC* 5; **Boge** V Baldwin 1952. – This name was borne by a great number of moneyers from the reign of Alfred to that of Edward the Confessor[2] and is also found in charters and other records during the tenth and eleventh centuries.[3] In most cases contemporary variants with medial *i, ig, ge, gi* from the same mint prove that the spellings *Boga, Boge* on

---

[1] On this legend, see also below, pp. 195 and 210.
[2] Note, in addition to the variant spellings shown above, *Boie*, Æthelred II (Lincoln); *Boigea*, Edward II (Chester); *Bogia*, Æthelred II (Wilton); and *Boiai*, Æthelred II (Hertford). In *Boigalet*, Athelstan (Chester), a Rom diminutive suffix seems to have been added.
[3] To the pre-Conquest instances listed *PNDB* 205 and by E. J. Dobson in an appendix to his important article on 'The Etymology and Meaning of Boy', *MÆ* ix (1940), 147–8, we may add the following examples: *Boge mes(s)epreost* 3 x, *c.* 960, Durham, Cathedral Library, A.11.17 (Ker, *Catalogue*, no. 105); *filii Boge de Hemmingeford*, *c.* 975, *LibEl* 98 (Hemmingford, Hu); *filii Bogan, a filiis Bogan, ibid.* 99; *Bogan* (acc.), a serf in Langford (Bd), *c.* 990, Whitelock, *Æthelgifu*, p. 9, line 18; *Bogan* (acc.), a serf in Munden (Hrt), *ibid.* line 23; and *Bogan* (dat.) *hire preoste, ibid.* p. 15, line 56. An early example is probably *Bogia*, a mass-priest (from Mercia?), mentioned in a letter from Wynfrith to Eadburh, 716–17; see Sisam, *Studies*, pp. 206, n. 1 and 223. He is, however, called *Beggan* (dat.) in the Latin original of the letter. For post-Conquest examples of *Boia*, see *PNDB* 205 and *DBS* 43.

coins stand for *Boia, Boie*, and this is probably true even when such parallel forms are not recorded, examples being *Boga*, Alfred (no mint), Æthelred II (London and Southwark), Cnut–Edward the Confessor (Dover) and Harold I (Norwich), *Boge*, Æthelred II (Thetford), and the forms from documentary sources listed above, p. 189, n. 3. In some of the latter cases we may, however, be concerned with an OE *Boga*, an original byname from *boga* 'bow', which is apparently evidenced in that function in *Edwig boga*, *c*. 970, Birch 1244 (D); cf. Tengvik 238–9 and von Feilitzen, *SN* XL (1968), 7.

*Boia* has been explained as a continental loan from OS *Bŏio, Băio*,[1] and some of the bearers may actually have been foreigners. However, in view of the frequent occurrence of the name in various OE sources and in place-names it seems reasonable to assume, as is done by Mawer, Stenton and Reaney, that it could be native and identical with the supposed OE ancestor of ME *boie* 'boy'.[2] The existence of an OE common noun *\*boia* appears in fact to be attested by the place-name *boiwic*, 785 (11–12), Birch 245 (in the bds of Aldenham, Hrt),[3] which cannot of course contain the personal name. Additional evidence for the existence of a native word is provided by the byname *Aluuinus boi*, 1066, *DB* 31 (Sr), clearly a strong variant of *\*boia*.[4] The meaning would be 'servant, young man', the same as that recorded in ME texts, where the word turns up *c*. 1300 (*MED, s.v.*), semantic cognates being OE *cnapa, swān* and *\*ladda*,[5] which are also used as first elements in place-names. According to K. Roelandts the

---

[1] See *PNDB* 205 with references and Dobson in the paper mentioned above, p. 189, n. 3. On the OS name, which is recorded from *c*. 825 onwards but whose ultimate etymology and vowel quantity are uncertain, cf. Schlaug I, 179 and 176, and II, 63 f., and H. Kaufmann, *Altdeutsche Personennamen*, Ergänzungs-Band (München, 1968), p. 66.

[2] For surveys of the relevant place-name material and discussions of the etymological problems see *PN Wo* 303–4, *PN D* 600, *PN Ess* 426 and *EPNE* I, 40. The following names are evidenced before *c*. 1200: *Boicote, DB*, Boycott Fm (Bk); *Boicote, c*. 1189, Boycott Fm (Wo); *Boicroft, c*. 1180, in Peasenhall (Sf; Pipe Roll Society Publications 76 [1962], 74); *Boieham, c*. 1165, in Wolvercot (O); *Boielund, DB*, Boyland (Nf); *Boiemilne*, 1107, *Chron. Monast. de Abingdon* II (1858), 106 (Brk; in Abingdon ?); *Boiemulna, c*. 1185, Boymill, lost (O; cf. *PN D* 600); *Buitorp, DB*, Boythorpe (Db, ERY); *Boientone, DB*, Boyton (W); *Boituna, DB*, Boyton Hall (Ess), Boyton End (Sf); *Boietone, DB*, Boyton (Co); *Boiwiche* 1122–36, Boyke Wood (K); and *Boiwrde*, 1171–81, field-name (WRY: *PN WRY* VII, 160). Additional early examples will no doubt come to light as the place-name survey progresses. In several of the cases listed above the absence of a medial vowel suggests that the 1st el. is OE *\*boia* as in *boiwic*, Birch 245.

[3] The authenticity of the charter as a product of Offa's reign is doubtful; cf. Sawyer, no. 124. In any case the bounds have probably been added later.

[4] Cf. Tengvik 238. Later instances of the word in a byname function are listed in *MED, s.v. boie*; note also *Hugo Boia*, 1157–8, *YCh* I, 402 (Y), and *Willelmus boie forestarius*, 1165–6, P 40 (Y). *Maneboia*, 963–92 (12), Robertson, *Charters* 40 (Nth), may be ON *Máni* or ODan *Manni* with the added byn. *boia*. On *Edwig boga*, see above.

[5] *\*ladda* is a kind of parallel to *\*boia*. It occurs as the byn. of *Godric Ladda*, 1050–1100, Earle, *Charters* 270 (Bath); *Richard Ladde, c*. 1175 (Nth); and *Walter le Ladd*, 1242 (K), on which see Tengvik 256–7 and *DBS, s.n. Ladd*, but is not evidenced in ME texts until *c*. 1300 (*NED*). The etymology is obscure.

word *boia* may have originated in children's speech as a hypocoristic form of *brōðor* with [i̯] as a substitute for [r].[1]

Dobson derives ME *boie* from OFr *buié, an aphetic variant of *embuié*, the past participle of *embuiier, emboiier* 'to put in irons, shackle, fetter'.[2] However, this etymology, which has been proposed to account for certain irregular pronunciations of the word *boy* recorded by sixteenth- and seventeenth-century orthoepists and found in modern dialects, seems, even if phonologically admissible, most improbable on grounds both of chronology and semantics.[3]

**Breht-**, see **Beorht-**.

**Brentinc** York VI BM. – OE *Brenting*, an *ing*-derivative of OE *Brant*[4] or the identical adjective *brant* 'steep, high'. Other examples are *uncer Brentinges* (gen.), 944 (contemp.), Birch 792 (Nth); *Brenting*, 963–92(12), Robertson, *Charters* 40 (Nth); and *Bræntinc*, mon. Sudbury, Cnut, Hildebrand 3395. Cf. also the unmutated variant *Branting* (Redin 172f.).

**Broðer** I Chester hoard 387; **Broðar** I *ibid.* 388. – ON *Bróðir*, ODan *Brothir* or OE *Brōðor* 'brother' used as a pers.n. (*PNDB* 208 and Fellows Jensen 65).

**Bruninc** V *BMC* 206. – OE *Brūning* (Redin 165).

**Burhstan** III BM, Totnes V Chester hoard 496. – OE *Burgstān*.[5]

**Byrht-**, see **Beorht-**.


**Carðen**, see **Farðein**.

**Cawelin** I *SCBI Copenhagen* 795. – Note also *Cawelin*, Cnut, Stamford, Hildebrand 3239–42, Nordman 224–5, with the variants *Cawlin*, Hildebrand 3243, and *Cwalin*, Hildebrand 3244. Not native, as is shown by the suffix.[6] Professor Kenneth Jackson thinks it should be associated with the sixth-century Anglo-Celtic name *Ceawlin*, which Arngart explains as a hypocoristic derivative of *Ceadwalla*.[7]

---

[1] 'Familiarismen met anorganische Konsonant', K. *Vlaamse Akad. voor Taal- en Letterkunde, Verslagen en Mededelingen*, 1966, pp. 271 and 279.

[2] See his articles in *MÆ* IX (1940), 121–54 and XII (1943), 71–6, and cf. A. J. Bliss's notes, *EGS* IV (1951–2), 22–9, on the complicated phonology of the supposed OFr etymon.

[3] It is a matter for surprise that it should have been adopted without reservation both by C. T. Onions in the *Oxford Dictionary of English Etymology* (Oxford, 1966) and in the 3rd ed. of the *Shorter Oxford Dictionary* (1967), and by H. Kurath in *MED*. G. W. S. Friedrichsen, on the other hand, in the 5th ed. of the *Concise Oxford Dictionary* (1964), drily remarks that the origin of *boy*, 'subject of involved conjectures, remains unascertained'.

[4] Recorded as the 1st el. of *Branteswyrð*, 937 (14), Birch 712 (bds of Water Newton, Hu) and other pl.ns; cf. *DEPN*, *s.n. Brandeston*.

[5] These legends have also been read *Burnstan*. This could be *Byrnstan < Beornstān* with *u* for *y* by an engraver's error.

[6] *Cawe*, Æthelred II, London, Hildebrand 2288, is irrelevant, the coin being a Scand. imitation; see Smart, p. 251. *Caua*, *LVD*, stands for *Cawa*, not *Cafa < OE cāf*, as Redin thinks (p. 88); see Tengstrand, *NoB* XXXI (1943), 174, who compares MDu *cauwe* 'jackdaw'.

[7] O. S. Anderson [Arngart], *Old English Material in the Leningrad Manuscript of Bede's Ecclesiastical History* (Lund, 1941), p. 92, n. 1.

**Cnapa** Stamford VI *BMC* 42; **Cnape** I *BMC* 81–2. – OE *Cnapa*, an original byname from OE *cnapa* 'child, youth, servant' (Redin 74–5).[1]

**Colenard**, see **Folchard**.

**Colgrim** Ia BM. – ON *Kolgrímr* (Björkman 84).

**Copman** I *BMC* 83. – ON *Kaupmaðr*, ODan *Køpman* byn. (Björkman 86 and *DGP, Tilnavne* 644).

**Cylm** North/Southampton VI *SCBI Glasgow* 720. – He continued to work under Edward II (*SCBI Glasgow* 753). A variant of the same name is probably *Cilm*, Eadwig, Newark, Chester hoard 278–9, *Cillm*, *ibid.* 317 (no mint). As Redin points out (p. 28), this is scarcely a contraction of OE *Cyn(e)helm*, an explanation later proposed by the editors of *PN Wo* (p. 102) and *PN Bd* (p. 53) and by Mrs Smart (p. 248). It is true that as a first el. in place-names *Cynehelm* is sometimes reduced to *Cylm*-,[2] but we are hardly entitled to assume that this form which arose as the result of phonetic development in polysyllabic compounds could have existed independently. A hypocoristic formation *\*Cylma* from *Cynehelm* with a hypothetic strong variant *\*Cylm* would be difficult to parallel in OE nomenclature.[3] The boundary-mark *on cylman stane, of cylman stane*, 956 (12) Birch 963 (bds of Welford, Brk), seems to contain an el. *\*cylme, \*cylma*, but the evidence for a Germanic stem with which it could be associated is slight.[4]

**Cynsige** Chichester (?) III Belfast, Chichester VI Hildebrand 5. – OE *Cyn(e)sige*.

**Daniel** IV Chester hoard 472. – The biblical name; borne by several clerics from the seventh century to the tenth.

**Deal** Winchester III.[5] – OE *deall* 'proud, bold'. Not previously recorded as a pers.n. in independent use but has been inferred from the

---

[1] ON *knapi*, ODan OSw *knape* 'servant of a knight', which was occasionally used as a byn. (14th and 15th c.), is a MLG loan-word.

[2] *to Cylmestuna*, 984–1001 (12), Harmer, *Writs* 107, beside *æt Chenelmestune, to Cenelmestune*, 961 (12), Birch 1077, and *æt Cenelmestune*, 981 (12), Robertson, *Charters* 33, Kilmeston, Ha. Other cases in point are *on cylmes gemære*, 978 (11), Kemble 618 (bds of Smite in Hindlip, Wo), and *on cylmæscumb*, 973 (12), Birch 1292 (bds of Harwell, Brk); see also *DEPN, s.nn. Kilmeston, Kilmington* and *Kinsham*. Cf. also *Cyrdes leah* 1016–35, Robertson, *Charters* 78, *Curdeslege* DB, *Kynardesle* 1242, Kinnersley (He), 1st el. OE *Cyneheard*; see *DEPN, s.n.*

[3] Note that the drastic shortening seen in *Ceolf < Ceolwulf* (*Chronicle of Æthelweard*, ed. A. Campbell [London, 1962], pp. lvii, 21, 26, 28 and 41) is due to haplology, and that *\*Wilma* which has been inferred from *Wilman lehttune*, 956, Birch 946 > Wormleighton (Wa) is best explained as a pet form of *Wilmund*; see *PN Wa* 275.

[4] Cf. Sw dial. *kalm* 'heap of stones, cairn' (Blekinge, Gotland), on which see E. Hellquist, *Svensk Etymologisk Ordbok* (Lund, 1948), *s.v. Kalmar*, and Pokorny 357. Smith, *PN WRY* vii, 298 somewhat rashly postulates a pers.n. *\*Culm* from the ME field-name *Colmesholm*.

[5] The coin itself has not been seen; it is described in the Carlyon–Britton sale catalogue, 11 November 1918, lot 1722.

place-name Dalston (Cu) (*PN Cu* 130–1 and *DEPN*, *s.n.*). As an el. it occurs in the compounds *Cynedeall* fem.[1] and *Dealwine*.[2]

**Demence** I c *SCBI Edinburgh* 504. – This moneyer turns up under Athelstan and continues working under his successors. The form shown here is the most common one.[3] Other variants include *Demenec*, Edmund, *BMC* 39–40; *Domences* (gen.), Athelstan, *BMC* 102 and *SCBI Edinburgh* 127 and Edmund, *BMC* 41; and *Dominic*, Athelstan, *BMC* 103. The last form suggests that we are concerned with the Latin name *Dominicus* (also *Domnicus*, *Domenicus*, *Domenecus*),[4] of which this would be the earliest example in English sources. It also occurs as *Domnicus* in *DB* TRW 212b(Bd). The forms with *e* in the first syllable are curious; they can hardly be explained by the rare type of *i*-mutation occasionally found in late Latin loan-words, such as *oele*, *ele* < *\*oli* (Luick, § 213. 1 and Campbell, § 502). However, Professor Kenneth Jackson informs me that *Demenec* might go back to an Old Welsh form of *Dominicus* with the *e* < *o* by internal *i*-affection.[5] Final *-ce* for *ec* in *Demence*, which is after all the predominant form, remains unexplained.

**Deorlaf** Chester II *SCBI Edinburgh* 623–5; **Diurlaf** Chester II Glasgow; **Dyurlof** Chester VI Hildebrand 20. – OE *Dēorlāf*. The last form could stand for *Dyurolf* < *Deorulf* (*q.v.*).

**Deorulf** I d *SCBI Edinburgh* 589, IV Chester hoard 475, Chester II Douglas hoard 23, Tamworth (?) II *SCBI Edinburgh* 641, Tamworth III Carlyon-Britton 1721, IV BM; **Deorulfes** (gen.) IV *SCBI Glasgow* 706. – OE *Dēorwulf*.

**Dudeman** III *BMC* 167; **Dudæmones** (gen.) III Carlyon-Britton 1043 a. – OE *Dudemann*.

**Dudinc** Huntingdon (?) V Lockett 629. – OE *Dud(d)ing* (Redin 169 f.).

**Dun** York VI *BMC* 10. – OE *Dunn* (Redin 12 f.).

**Durand** I *SCBI Oxford* 388, III Carlyon-Britton 456b; **Durandes** (gen.) III *BMC* 168; **Durandies** (gen.) III *BMC* 169; **Duran** Chester II *SCBI Chester* 82. – OFr *Durand* (Forssner 62).[6]

---

[1] In the boundary-mark *on Cynedealle rodæ*, 990 (12), Kemble 673 (bds of Wootton St Lawrence, Ha).

[2] *Dealuuino* (dat.), 743–6 (9), MGH, *Epistolae Selectae* I, 144; varr. *ad dealbuuinum, dealbuuino*.

[3] Eadred, *BMC* 26; Edmund, Chester hoard 75 and 389; Eadwig, Chester hoard 322 and *SCBI Cambridge* 600; Edgar, *SCBI Edinburgh* 504, Chester hoard 389 and *BMC* 140.

[4] *Thesaurus Linguæ Latinæ, Onomasticon, s.n.* Cf. also the popular forms found in French sources: *Domenchius* in an Angevin charter of *c.* 1075 cited by H. Drevin, *Die französischen Sprachelemente in lateinischen Urkunden des 11. und 12. Jahrhunderts* (Halle, 1912), p. 53, and the modern surnames *Demanche* (Paris region) and *Demange* (Lorraine), listed by Dauzat, *op. cit.* p. 190.

[5] Cf. on this sound-change (7th–8th-c.) K. Jackson, *Language and History in Early Britain* (Edinburgh, 1953), §§ 171 (2), 166 (2) and 176. Note also that *Domnicus* is recorded in a British inscription from *c.* 500 (Jackson, *ibid.* p. 621).

[6] No satisfactory Germanic etymology has ever been suggested for *Durand* (in continental sources also *Durantus, Durannus*), and the name is no doubt a Medieval Latin formation from *durare* 'to be patient, to persevere; to endure; to last, remain', as has recently been

**Ead Ælfstan** Exeter (?) III Chester hoard 459. – If the legend is to be taken at its face value we are concerned with two names, the second being OE *Ælfstān*. The first would be a previously unrecorded *\*Ēad*, a short form of compounds in *Ēad-* which has been inferred from place-names; see *DEPN, s.nn. Adisham* and *Eddisbury*. Or did the die-maker start to cut *Eadstan* and then realizing that this was the wrong name go on to incise the correct one without deleting the traces of his first attempt?

**Ætferd** I *BMC* 67; **Ætfer** I *BMC* 66; **Atverd** I Carlyon-Britton 1711 d; **Etfer** I Dublin. – OE *Ēadfriŏ*. These unorthodox phonetic spellings are probably due to an inexperienced engraver.

**Eadmer** V *BMC* 14. – OE *Ēadmǣr*.

**Eadmund** I d *SCBI Edinburgh* 590, IV *BMC* 200, Chester II *SCBI Edinburgh* 628, IV *BMC* 33; **Eadmun** I d *BMC* 152. – OE *Ēadmund*.

**Eadnoŏ** North/Southampton VI Chester (1920) hoard 11. – OE *Ēadnōŏ*.

**Eadstan** Wilton III Lockett 625, Winchester III Lockett 626; **Eatstan** Winchester III *BMC* 52, VI Hildebrand 48. – OE *Ēadstān*.

**Eadwine** Wallingford III *SCBI Cambridge* 617, Wilton VI *BMC* 50. – OE *Ēadwine*.

**Ealfsige**, see **Ælfsige**.

**Eanulf** I *SCBI Oxford* 389, Lincoln VI *SCBI Glasgow* 715. – OE *Ēanwulf*.

**Elf-**, see **Ælf-**.

**Eoferard** III Chester hoard 461, IV *SCBI Edinburgh* 573; **Eaferard** III Chester hoard 460, IV *SCBI Glasgow* 707. – Probably OG *Everhard*, Anglicized *Eoforheard* (Forssner 63 f. and Schlaug II, 81 f.).

**Eofermund** III Lockett 622, IV Carlyon-Britton 459, Tamworth III Dublin, IV *SCBI Glasgow* 705. – OG *Evermund* (Förstemann 444 and Morlet 77) or OE *Eoformund*.[1]

**Efeorolf** I *SCBI Edinburgh* 399; **Efrolf** I *ibid.* 400; **Eofrlf** Tamworth (?) II *BMC* 46. – OG *Everulf* (Forssner 64) or OE *Eoforwulf*.

**Eoroŏ** I d *SCBI Edinburgh* 592-3, IV/III Chester hoard 478, Chester II *SCBI Edinburgh* 629–30. – Note also *Eoro*, Eadred, Smarmore 14, and *Eoroŏ*, Eadred, Wells, and Eadwig, Chester hoard 296.[2] Possibly from an unrecorded ON *\*Iór(f)røŏr*[3] with *eo* for initial *ió* as in *Eola*, mon. Edward

plausibly argued by O. Brattö, *Nuovi Studi di Antroponimia Fiorentina* (Stockholm, 1955), pp. 85–7; cf. also A. Dauzat, *Les Noms de Famille de France*, 2nd rev. ed. (Paris, 1949), pp. 17 f., and Morlet 76.

[1] With the exception of *Eoforhuæt* and *Eoforuulf* (once each), *c.* 800–40, *LVD*, names with this 1st el. are found only on coins, but some of them may well be native. See further Ekwall, *PN La*, p. 115, n. 1, and Reaney, *Studier i Modern Språkvetenskap* XVIII (1953), 91 f. (with ME material). The 1st el. of Erwarton (Sf) < DB *Eurewardestuna* may be OE *\*Eoforweard*.

[2] The spellings *Erod*, Edmund I, Blunt, and *Eroŏ*, Eadred, *BMC* 43, may perhaps represent the same name.

[3] On the el. *Iór-*, see Janzén 83 f.

the Confessor, York, *BMC* 268 and Hildebrand 124, by the side of *Iola*, *BMC* 305 and 346 and Hildebrand 130.[1] Loss of interconsonantal *f* is regular in ON, and the simplification of *rr* would have a parallel in *Þoreð*, *Þureð* < *Þor(f)røðr* (*ASC* and charters, from 966 onwards; Björkman 148–9). The use of the graph *o* for *ø* is attested by late-tenth- and eleventh-century Anglo-Scand. forms like *Asforð*, *Osforð* and *Þurforð* < *-frøðr*; see *PNDB* 51f.[2]

**Erconbold** Norwich VI Hildebrand 30. – OG *Ercanbald* (Forssner 76).

**Etfer,** see **Ead-.**

**Eðel-,** see **Æðel-.**

**Farman** I *SCBI Edinburgh* 405–6. – ON *Farmann*, ODan *Farman* (*PNDB* 250).

**Farðein** I *SCBI Oxford* 391; **Farðen** I *BMC* 93; **Fardein** I *SCBI Glasgow* 684; **Carðen** I *SCBI Copenhagen* 796. – ON *Farþegn*, ODan *Farthin* (*PNDB* 250).

**Fastolf** III *SCBI Glasgow* 700, York VI *BMC* 11; **Fastolf Boiga** III *SCBI Glasgow* 702; **Fastolf Oda** III *BMC* 183; **Fastolf Rafn** III *SCBI Edinburgh* 548–50; **Fastolfes** (gen.) III *SCBI Glasgow* 699. – ON *Fastulfr*, ODan *Fastulf* (*PNDB* 250). The second names in some legends, which evidently refer to partners of Fastolf (see below, p. 210), are dealt with separately in their proper alphabetical places.

**Flodger** Chester II *SCBI Edinburgh* 631. – OG (Rom) *Flodger* < *Hlodger*, with Rom *fl-* < *hl-*[3] (Morlet 133 and Forssner 89f.).

**Flodulf** Chester II Douglas hoard 24. – OG (Rom) *Flodulf* < *Hlodulf* (Morlet 133).

**Flodvin** Chichester (?) III BM; **Flodfin** Chichester VI Carlyon-Britton 1705. – OG (Rom) *Flodwin* < *Hlodwin* (Morlet 133).

**Folchard** V BM; **Colenard** V *BMC* 207. – OG *Folchard* (Förstemann 551

---

[1] Note also *Eresbi* 12th-c. > Eresby, L ( < ON *Ióarr*; *DEPN*, *s.n.*). As a rule, however, initial Scand. *ió* is adopted as *io* in OE; cf. A. S. C. Ross, *APS* XIV (1939–40), 2–4, and B. Sandahl, *SN* XXXVI (1964), 266 ff.

[2] In OE sources Scand. *-frøðr* is usually treated like the corresponding OE *-frið*, but the loss of *f*, which took place in the 2nd half of the 10th c., is reflected in forms like *Aseret* (DB) < *Ásrøðr*, *Gu(d)ret* (DB) < *Guðröðr*, and *Þoreð* (see above). *Sihroð dux*, 1050 (13), Kemble 792 and 793 (*PNDB* 52) is identical with Earl Siward of Northumbria (ODan *Sigwarth*, ON *Sigurðr*), but since the charter form clearly goes back to ON *Sigrøðr*, this is evidently an instance of the occasional confusion of the two names discussed by C. J. S. Marstrander, *Bidrag til det Norske Sprogs Historie i Irland* (Kristiania, 1915), pp. 156f.; cf. esp. *Sicurt* by the side of *Siefredus*, *Sieuert* on York coins, *BMC* I, 1048–9. *Syhrod dux*, 1019, Kemble 729 (14th-c., spurious), should probably be identified with *Siræd dux*, 1023, Kemble 739, and *Sired eorl*, 1036, Robertson, *Charters* 89, and if the first spelling is at all reliable, it suggests that the name of the earl was in reality *Sigrøðr* with OE *-ræd*, *-red* for *-reð* in the 2nd and 3rd forms.

[3] On this sound-change, see, e.g., H. Kaufmann, *Untersuchungen zu altdeutschen Rufnamen* (München, 1965), pp. 202 ff.

and Morlet 95).[1] The second form is badly blundered. Forssner's comments on it (p. 283) are not to the point.

**Forŏgar** Bedford V Lockett 628. – OE *Forðgār*. This is the only known example of the name.

**Freoðeric** III/IV *SCBI Edinburgh* 570–1, IV *ibid.* 575, Chester III *SCBI Chester* 74; **Freoðerci** IV Chester hoard 481; **Freoŏric** I d *SCBI Glasgow* 693; **Froŏric** I d *SCBI Edinburgh* 594–7, Chester II *SCBI Chester* 90; **Froŏrc** Chester II *BMC* 26. – OE *Friðurīc, Freoðorīc* (*PNDB* 254, n. 6).[2] Cf. **Freŏic**.

**Freŏic** Derby III Douglas, IV *BMC* 7; **Freŏices** (gen.) Ic *BMC* 141. – Cf. also *Freðices*, Eadred, *BMC* 42, and Eadwig, *BMC* 24, and, with metathesis, *Ferðices*, Eadred, *SCBI Glasgow* 651. Perhaps best explained as a curtailed form of *Freoðeric* (*q.v.*). A possible alternative might, however, be OG *Fredic*[3] with *ð*[4] by association with OE *Friðu-*.

**Friðemund** Winchester (?) III *SCBI Edinburgh* 551; **Fryŏemund** Winchester VI *SCBI Glasgow* 729. – OE *Friðumund*.

**Froŏald** IV BM. – OG (Rom) *Frodald* < *Hrodwald*[5] (Förstemann 544). *ð* on the coin may reflect OFr intervocalic [ð].

**Fugetat** I *SCBI Edinburgh* 404. – Cf. perhaps *Fuheltae*, the name of a Thetford moneyer under Æthelred II (Hildebrand 3744, *SCBI Copenhagen* II, 1217 and Igelösa hoard),[6] which is evidently an original byname, OE *\*fugeltā* or ON *\*fugltá* 'bird's toe'.[7] Semantic parallels are the ON bynames *gulltá, langtá* and *leirtá*.

**Garwig** Canterbury VI *SCBI Copenhagen* 768. – OE *Gārwīg*. This is the only pre-Conquest instance of the name; for later examples see von Feilitzen, *NoB* XXXIII (1945), 80.

**Gillys** I d *SCBI Edinburgh* 600, Chester II *SCBI Chester* 91–2; **Gilys** IV *SCBI Edinburgh* 576; **Gyllis** Chester II *ibid.* 632, Hereford VI Hildebrand 16. – Perhaps to be associated with Hiberno-Norse *Gilli* < OIr *gilla* 'young man, servant'; cf. *PNDB* 261 and Fellows Jensen 100 f. The final

---

[1] The name is found on English coins from Alfred onwards, the only example in a written source being *Folcardus, c.* 975, *LibEl* 92, probably a cleric, who witnesses a transaction at Haddenham (C). The existence of a native *Folcheard* is thus seen to be somewhat uncertain.

[2] *Froðric*, which also occurs on coins of Eadred (*BMC* 44–6) and Eadwig (*BMC* 10), may alternatively represent OG *Frodric* (Morlet 90).

[3] Förstemann 528 and Morlet 94.

[4] *ð* may of course have been present in the continental Rom or OLG parent form.

[5] On Rom *fr-* < *hr-*, see Kaufmann, *Untersuchungen*, p. 203. As H. Knoch has recently suggested, *Frodald* in West Frankish sources may, however, go back to a genuine OG *Frod-(w)ald* < *\*frōda-*; cf. *Beiträge zur Namenforschung*, Beiheft 11 (Heidelberg, 1969), 96 ff.

[6] U. Ericsson, *The Personal Names of the English and Irish Coins in the Igelösa Hoard* (unpub. thesis, Lund), pp. 34 f. and 59.

[7] The Thetford coins have *h* for *g* by unvoicing before syllabic *l*, but final *-e*, if phonologically relevant, is difficult to explain. It could hardly reflect eOE *tā(h)e*.

*-is* is curious. Dolley, *BNJ* XXXVI (1967), 42 derives the name from an OIr *\*Gilla Ísu* 'servant of Jesus', but this etymon would hardly account for the forms under notice.

**Ginand** Northampton III Douglas hoard 30. – OG *Ginand* (Förstemann 642).[1]

**Godeferð** I Carlisle Museum. – OG *Godefrid* (Forssner 118f.).

**Goldstan** Lewes VI *SCBI Cambridge* 621. – OE *Goldstān*.

**Grim** Bedford III *SCBI Edinburgh* 513, V *SCBI Cambridge* 618, VI *BMC* 4, Derby II BM; **Grimes** (gen.) I Chester hoard 402–4. – ON *Grímr*, ODan *Grim* (*PNDB* 276).

**Grimter** Ic Blunt. – This legend which is found on one coin only may be a blundered form of OG *Grimbert*, on which see Forssner 131f.

**Grind** Lincoln VI *SCBI Copenhagen* 777. – The form is well attested. It also occurs on Lincoln coins of Edward II (*BMC* 14, Hildebrand 12 and *SCBI Glasgow* 744) and Æthelred II (*BMC* 151 and Hildebrand 1789–90). Perhaps, as Björkman tentatively suggests,[2] an original byname from ON, ODan *grind* 'field-gate, lattice-door; enclosure'; hence possibly 'man who lived at a *grind* or came from a place called *Grind*'.[3]

**Grið** I Douglas hoard 46; **Grid** I *SCBI Cambridge* 611, III *BMC* 186. – Probably to be connected with ON *grið* 'domicile, home (with the notion of service)', OE *grið* n. (from ON) 'truce, asylum, sanctuary', which is recorded as a byname in ME, *Willelmus Grith*, 1222 (*MED, s.v.*). The meaning is not obvious, but the word may be used elliptically for ON *griðmaðr* 'a free man serving in a household', which also occurs as a byname in ON.

**Gunar** Ic BM, Id Argyll; **Gunares** (gen.) III Carlyon-Britton 457d. – ON *Gunnarr*, ODan *Gunnar* (*PNDB* 277).

**Gunfred** I *SCBI Edinburgh* 423; **Gunverd** I *SCBI Copenhagen* 800. – ON *Gunn* (*f*)*røðr*, on which see *PNDB* 277, or OG *Gundfrid* (Forssner 133). The OG name is borne by a moneyer under Edmund (*Gundferð*, *BMC* 72; *Geundfeð*, *BMC* 71).

**Gunnulf** York VI Montagu 735. – ON *Gunnulfr*, ODan *Gunnulf* (*PNDB* 278).

---

[1] On the 1st el., see Kaufmann, *Personennamen*, p. 147 and *Untersuchungen*, p. 73. Cf. also *Ginard*, mon. Athelstan, *SCBI Glasgow* 638 < OG *Ginard* (Morlet 109). OG (Rom) *Guinand* < *Wi(g)nand* would not be an acceptable etymon. The earliest spelling with Central French initial *Gu-* for *W-* appears on a coin of Edward the Confessor: *Guolfwine*, *BMC* 466. Moreover, the OFr reduction of *gw- > g-* does not take place until the 12th c.

[2] *ZeN* 39.

[3] *Grind, Grinden* is a common pl.n. in Norway; see O. Rygh, *Norske Gaardnavne, Forord* (Kristiania, 1898), p. 52. In OSw, *grind* is actually recorded as a byn. (E. Hellquist in *Xenia Lidéniana* [Stockholm, 1912], p. 98). Cf. also ON *Dalr* (byn.), ON *Skógr*, ODan *Skogh*, ON *Vikr* (byn.). An ODan pers.n. *\*Grindir* (*ja*-stem) is taken by the editors of *Danmarks Stednavne* IX (København, 1948), 25, to be the 1st el. of Grinderslev (Viborgs Amt). They also refer to the name dealt with here but offer no further comment.

**Hacuf** I. – The form is certainly authentic; see *BMC* 98, Chester hoard 405, *SCBI Cambridge* 612 and *Edinburgh* 424,[1] and Tetney 242. Perhaps an Old Cornish name with the second el. -*cuf* ' dear, amiable' found in *Bleyðcuf* and *Wincuf* (Bodmin manumissions),[2] but the first is obscure.

**Harcer**, see **Heriger**.

**Herebert** I *BMC* 99. – OG *Herebert* rather than OE *Herebeorht*, as indicated by the form of the second el.; cf. Forssner 148.

**Hereman** I *SCBI Oxford* 392. – OG *Hereman* (Forssner 149 f.).

**Heremod** Wallingford III *SCBI Oxford* 412–13. – OE *Heremōd*.

**Heriger** I *SCBI Glasgow* 688; **Harger** I Tetney 243–6; **Harcer** I Carlyon-Britton 1030. – OG *Heriger, Harger* (Forssner 143). The third form has *c* for *g* by a common engraver's error.

**Herolf** III *BMC* 187–91; **Herolfes** (gen.) III *BMC* 192–3, York III BM; **Herulf** I a Hildebrand 58. – OE *Herewulf*. In the first three cases, with -*olf* for -*ulf*, we may alternatively have ON *Heriolfr*, ODan *Herulf*; see below, pp. 212–13.

**Hilde** I *BNJ* XXIII (1938–40), 17. – OE *\*Hilda*, a short form of names in *Hild*-; cf. *Hild* (Redin 7).[3]

**Hildic** Shrewsbury VI BM. – Probably OE *\*Hilding*, an *ing*-derivative of names in *Hild*-, which is found in *Hildingeslei*, DB, Hildenley (NRY), rather than OE *\*Hildic*.[4] There is little safe evidence for the use of the rare suffix -*ic* with ordinary pers.n.els.; cf. however **Balddic** and **Teoðic**.

**Hildulf** IV Chester hoard 483.[5] – ON *Hildolfr*, ODan *Hildulf* or OE *Hildewulf* (Björkman 68 f.).[6]

**Hiltwine** London V Carlyon-Britton 436. – OE *Hild(e)wine*. For the unvoicing of *d*, see below, p. 213.

**Hingolf, Higolf**, see **Ingolf**.

**Hrodulf** I d Lockett 615. – OG *Hrodulf* (Förstemann 918 f. and Morlet 138) or the corresponding native *Hrōðwulf*, which occurs in *LVD* and perhaps as the first el. of Rolleston (Lei, Staf, W; *DEPN, s.n.*).[7] A possible alternative would be ON *\*Hróðulfr* > *Hrólfr*, on which see *PNDB* 294.

---

[1] In the Edinburgh *Sylloge* the name is incorrectly transcribed and indexed as *Haculf*, a reading that is also adopted in the Cambridge volume.

[2] Jackson, *op. cit.* p. 417.

[3] The authenticity of the name *Hild*, which is borne by a Stamford moneyer under Edward II, is questioned by Redin on the ground that it happens to coincide formally with the fem. noun *hild*. But the name occurs as an el. in pl.ns., e.g. *Hildeshlæw*, 979 (12), Kemble 621 (bds of Olney, Bk); see further *PN Bk* 62 f. and *PN Gl* III, 30.

[4] On -*ic* for -*inc*, -*ing*, see Redin 149, n. 6.

[5] See also *BNJ* XXXI (1962), pl. III. 16.

[6] The OE name is not too well authenticated. It seems to enter into the pl.ns. *Hildoluestone*, 1047–70, Whitelock, *Wills* 35, Hindolveston (Nf); *Hildulvestune*, DB, Hilderstone (Staf); and perhaps *Heldovestun*, DB, Hilston (ERY). But *Hildulf* on coins from Athelstan onwards could be the Scand. name.

[7] In the case of *Hrodolf Sewies sune an Alfintune*, c. 1100, Earle, *Charters* 258 (D), we may also have the native name.

**Hunbein**, see **Unbein**.

**Hunred** I Dublin, I var. Dublin. – OE *Hūnrēd*.

**Igenc** I Tetney 346. – Obscure.

**Ingelbert** I Tetney 418; **Ingelberd** I c *BMC* 142. – OG *Ingelbert* (Forssner 71f.).

**Igolferðes** (gen.) III *SCBI Edinburgh* 565–6. – OG *Ingelfrid*, *Ingolfred* (Förstemann 965 and Morlet 145).

**Ingolf** I *SCBI Oxford* 396, Newark VI Sotheby 23 May 1966 123; **Hingolf** I Tetney 344; **Higolf** I *BMC* 112. – ON *Ingolfr*, ODan *Ingulf* (*PNDB* 298).

**Ingolries** (gen.) I c BM. – OG *Ingelric* (Forssner 74).

**Iohan** York VI *SCBI Glasgow* 731; **Iuhan** Exeter VI *BMC* 9. – The biblical name usually appears in the Latinized form *Iohannes* (Searle 319), but cf. *Johan presbyter*, 904, Birch 604, 612 and 613, and 969, Birch 1239–41.

**Iole** Derby IV Chester hoard 445; **Ioles** (gen.) I c *BMC* 143. – ON *Ióli*, ODan *Iuli*, Anglicized *Iola* (*PNDB* 300). *Ioles* may alternatively be the genitive of the strong variant *Iol*, perhaps an Anglo-Scand. formation, for which there is good evidence in ME sources.[1]

**Isembert** I *BMC* 113. – OG *Isen-*, *Isembert* (Forssner 165 f.).

**Ismala** I *SCBI Edinburgh* 460. – Probably OE *Smala* (Redin 78) < OE *smæl* 'small'. A moneyer of that name worked under Athelstan (*BMC* 154 and *SCBI Cambridge* 581).[2]

**Isulf** York VI Grantley 1097. – ON *Ísolfr*, ODan *Isulf*; cf. Björkman 194.

**Ive** I *SCBI Oxford* 397. – OE *Ifa* (Redin 99 and 135). Cf. *Iua*, mon. Edward the Elder, *BMC* 47; *Ive*, Edmund, The Hermitage, Leningrad, Eadred, *BMC* 115, and Eadwig, Smarmore 22 and Tetney 110–12.

**Landbriht** 'Hamwic' VI Bruun 118. – OE *Landbeorht* or OG *Landbert* (Forssner 172 and *PNDB* 308, n. 4).

**Landferð** I c Douglas hoard 73; **Loandferð** I Blunt, I c *SCBI Edinburgh* 505, I f Carlyon-Britton 448. – OE *Landfrið*. On the second form, see below, p. 211.

**Lenna** I *BMC* 119–20. – Perhaps an OE *\*Le(o)nna*, a hypocoristic form of *Lēofnōð*. Redin (p. 99) suggests no etymology.

**Leofgar** Dover VI BM. – OE *Lēofgār*.

---

[1] See the material collected by Fellows Jensen, p. 157.

[2] The initial *I* is no doubt a vertical stroke inadvertently made by the engraver; cf. *Iscula*, Harold I, York, Hildebrand 189 by the side of *Scula*, Hildebrand 195–200. The legend *Mala*, Athelstan, *SCBI Glasgow* 639, which clearly refers to a man of the same name, must be a die-maker's error for *Smala*. Note incidentally that (*Goisfridus filius*) *Malæ*, DB (Redin 68), is a misreading for (*Goisfridus filius Rogeri*) *Malae Terrae*; see Tengvik 349.

**Leofhelm** III *BMC* 195. – OE *Lēofhelm*.

**Leofinc** III *SCBI Edinburgh* 567–8; **Leofinces** (gen.) III *BMC* 196; **Lefinces** (gen.) I c *BMC* 144; **Lyfingc** Ipswich VI Hildebrand 11; **Lyfinc** Norwich VI *SCBI Glasgow* 722; **Lifinc** Cambridge VI Uppsala; **Levic** I Tetney 371–4, Lincoln VI Dymock. – OE *Lēofing, Lȳfing* (Redin 167 f.).[1]

Lefmanes (gen.) I c *SCBI Copenhagen* 806. – OE *Lēofmann*.

Leofric Ipswich VI *SCBI Glasgow* 713–14. – OE *Lēofric*.

Leofsige North/Southampton VI *SCBI Glasgow* 721, Oxford III *SCBI Oxford* 409, Wilton III Ryan 789; **Leofsig** North/Southampton VI *BMC* 16–17; **Leofsi-i** North/Southampton VI Lockett 635. – OE *Lēofsige*.

Leofstan I c Chester hoard 427, I d Blunt, Chester II *SCBI Edinburgh* 633, Shaftesbury III Chester hoard 456; **Liofstan** V *ibid.* 504–6, Bedford V *BMC* 3 and *SCBI Oxford* 417. – OE *Lēofstān*.

Leofwine Lymne VI *SCBI Glasgow* 718, Tamworth (?) II Shand 331; **Leofwin** Tamworth (?) II *SCBI Edinburgh* 643. – OE *Lēofwine*.

Leofwold Wilton III Blunt, VI Hildebrand 45. – OE *Lēofwald*.

Loandferð, see Landferð.

**Macus** I BM. – OIr *Maccus*; cf. *PNDB* 323.

**Mægerd** Winchester VI Hildebrand 49. – OE *Mǣgrēd*[2] with metathesis of *r* or OE *Mægenrēd* with loss of unstressed *n* before *r*.[3] The latter alternative is supported by the variant spelling *Megered* on Winchester coins under Edward II (Hildebrand 24 and *SCBI Glasgow* 765), which clearly refers to the same moneyer. The loss of the second *e* would be due to the die-cutter. The full form of the name is found at Derby under Athelstan: *Mægenredes* (gen.), *SCBI Edinburgh* 152 and *Glasgow* 624.[4]

**Mælsuðan** Chester II *SCBI Chester* 93–4; **Mælsuðon** Chester VI *ibid.* 107; **Melsuðan** Chester II *SCBI Glasgow* 678. – OIr *Máel-suthain*; see *PNDB* 377, *s.n. Sudan*, with references.

**Mærtin** I d *SCBI Edinburgh* 601, Chester II *ibid.* 634. – Latin *Martinus*, *æ* being due to Anglicizing.[5]

---

1. *Levic* is evidently identical with the Lincoln moneyer *Le(o)finc, Lefing* under Æthelred II (Hildebrand 1793–1801).
2. Cf. also *Megred*, Athelstan, Chester, *BMC* 50, and Edmund, *BMC* 110, with normal non-WS *ē* for *ǣ*[2]. The name is found only on coins.
3. See E. Tengstrand, *A Contribution to the Study of Genitival Composition in Old English Place-Names* (Uppsala, 1940), p. 296, and Campbell, § 474.
4. The editor of the Edinburgh volume incorrectly emends to *Megenfreðes*. Searle (p. 345) takes *Mægerd* to be *Mægheard* for which there is no other evidence, but this is clearly improbable.
5. Cf. *Mærtene*, Athelstan, Chester, *BMC* 31 and *SCBI Chester* 20–1, and Edmund, *BMC* 99–100; *Mærten*, Edmund, *BMC* 98, and Eadred, Chester hoard 201; *Martin*, Edmund, *BMC* 101; *Mærtin*, c. 950, Whitelock, *Wills* 3, p. 14; and *Mærtines* (gen.), c. 990, Whitelock, *Æthelgifu*, line 32. Cf. *ibid.* p. 60.

**Mamolet** I BM; **Mamoiet** I *BMC* 121. – A Rom diminutive of OG *Mam(m)o* (Förstemann 1088)?[1]

**Man** Stamford VI *BNJ* xxiii (1938–40), 21, Winchester VI Hildebrand 50–1, York VI *SCBI Glasgow* 732; **Manes** (gen.) Derby (?) IV Chester hoard 447. – OE *Mann* (Redin 8).

**Mangod** Exeter III Dublin. – OG (Rom) *Mangod* (Morlet 167.[2] Cf. Forssner 186 ff., *PNDB* 324 and *PN Gl* iii, 98 f.).

**Mani** Leicester VI Hildebrand 22; **Manai** I Tetney 384–6; **Mania** I *SCBI Edinburgh* 477. – ODan *Manni* (Björkman 95). The two blundered forms may stand for *Manna*.

**Manna** York VI *BMC* 12; **Manne** I *SCBI Oxford* 399, V Chester hoard 507; **Mannees** (gen.) I c *BMC* 145; **Mana** I *SCBI Copenhagen* 807; **Manan** I *ibid.* 808;[3] **Monna** Chester II *SCBI Edinburgh* 636, Tamworth (?) II *ibid.* 644. – OE *Manna* (Redin 52). In some cases we may have ODan *Manni*, Anglicized.

**Manning** I Tetney 400; **Maning** I *BMC* 127; **Manin** I Carlyon-Britton 1716c, I c *SCBI Copenhagen* 810, I g *SCBI Edinburgh* 510. – OE *Manning* (Redin 168).

**Manntat** III *SCBI Copenhagen* 811; **Mantat** V Ryan 795, Northampton III Drabble 431, VI *SCBI Copenhagen* 771; **Mansat** Northampton VI *BMC* 18. – The Northampton moneyer continued under Edward II: *Mantat*, Hildebrand 8. Other examples of the name are *Mantat*, a manumitted serf in Langford (Bd), *c.* 990, Whitelock, *Æthelgifu*, line 10; *Mantat ancer*, temp. Cnut, Whitelock, *Wills* 23 (C); and *Mantat*, 1087–98, *Bury* 27 (Sf); also, as Reaney points out,[4] in the Nf place-name *Mantatestona*, DB (lost), and in *Mantotescroft*, a thirteenth-century L field-name. The name has been regarded as a continental loan, an Anglicized form of OLG *Mantēt*,[5] but Reaney may be right in taking it to be a native compound of *Man*- and the el. *\*tāt* 'glad, cheerful'. On evidently native fem. names in -*tāt*, -*tēt*, -*tāta*, see von Feilitzen, *SN* xl (1968), 11, and Whitelock, *Æthelgifu*, p. 59.

**Manticen** V *BMC* 209. – Cf. also *Manticen*, Athelstan, Norwich, *BMC* 76 and Chester hoard 31, and Edmund, Lockett 590; *Mantieen*, Edmund, Norwich, *BMC* 4 and *SCBI Copenhagen* 1, 719. Possibly a diminutive in -(*i*)*kīn* of the OLG (Flemish) name *Manto*,[6] but *e* for *i* in the final syllable is difficult to explain. Low German names in -*kin*, of which several are recorded in OE and eME sources, invariably retain the original vowel

---

[1] The legend *Manolet* listed *BMC* 11, 156 under Eadwig may refer to the same man. If this is the correct form, we are probably concerned with a Rom derivative of OG *Man(n)o*.
[2] With several examples from French cartularies during the period 756–1068.
[3] *Manan* is represented by at least two dies and may be a different name. Dolley, *BNJ* xxxvi (1967), 44, thinks it is Irish but suggests no definite etymology.
[4] *Studier i Modern Språkvetenskap* xviii (1953), 97 f.      [5] See *PNDB* 153, n. 3.
[6] See Mansion, pp. 29 and 34, and W. de Vries, *Friese Persoonsnamen* (Assen, 1952), pp. 97 f. On the suffix cf. A. Bach, *Deutsche Namenkunde* i (Heidelberg, 1952), §108, and Mansion, p. 99.

of the suffix, e.g. *Mannecin*, mon. Eadred, *BMC* 117; *Erlechin*, *Hardekin* and *Tepekin*, *DB* 1066; and *Fresechinus*, 1130–1, P 136.[1]

**Marcer** I *BMC* 128. – OG *Marcher* (Forssner 286f.).

**Marscale** Winchester VI *SCBI Copenhagen* 783. – OG *Marscalc* (Forssner 188).

**Meinard** I var. BM. – OG *Meinard* (Forssner 181).

**Monna**, see **Manna**.

**Morgna** I *SCBI Edinburgh* 497 and *BMC* 129–31; **Morne** I *SCBI Edinburgh* 498. – Probably OE *Morgna*, not previously recorded, from OE *morgen* 'morning'. For a semantic parallel cf. the OE names in *Ūht-* < *ūht(e)* 'twilight, dawn'.[2] The second form shows loss of interconsonantal *g*, as in *morna*, gen. pl. of *morgen*.[3]

**Norŏberd** Norwich VI Hildebrand 31; **Norbert** V Lockett 630. – OG *Nordbert*.[4]

**Oda** York VI Lockett 2756; (Fastolf) **Oda** III *BMC* 183. – OE *Od(d)a*, a short form of names in *Ord-* (*PNDB* 333). On the second legend, which refers to two persons, see below, p. 210.

**Ogea** Stamford VI *SCBI Glasgow* 724. – OS *Oio* (Förstemann 1178, Schlaug II, 139, G. Müller, *Niederdeutsches Wort* VII [1967], 131, and von Feilitzen, *SN* XL [1968], 10); note also *Oge*, mon. Eadwig, Tetney 121.

**Ogeman** I *BMC* 132. – OE *Ocgemann*, first el. OE *Ocga* (Redin 103),[5] or, if *g* should be read *c*, *Occemann*, a compound with OE *Occa* (Redin 103).[6]

**Osbearn** Wilton III Douglas, VI Malvern Museum. – ON *Ásbiǫrn*, ODan *Esbiorn* or OLG *Osbern*; see *PNDB* 165 and 338f. and Fellows Jensen 18f. The second el. has been identified with OE *bearn*.

**Osferŏ** V Ryan 796–7; **Osferd** I c *SCBI Edinburgh* 507, I g Ruding, pl. 30. 23. – OE *Osfrið*. This and the following compounds in *Os-*, except of course *Oswine*, may to some extent be Anglicized forms of the corresponding Scand. names in *Ás-*.

---

[1] In OLG sources *-ken* < *-kin* is not found until the first quarter of the 12th c. (Schlaug I, 36). The existence of a corresponding OE suffix is attested by the pers.n. *Cynicin*, *LVD*, and by the diminutives *tyncen* 'little tub' (with early reduction of unstressed *i* > *e*) and *þyrncin* 'a kind of thorn'.

[2] On these see Searle 465 f., and for additional material my paper, *NoB* XXXIII (1945), 90 f.

[3] Campbell, § 477. 6.

[4] Cf. von Feilitzen, *Early English and Norse Studies presented to Hugh Smith*, ed. A. Brown and P. Foote (London, 1963), p. 55.

[5] Apart from some early and probably fictitious characters in the royal genealogies the name is borne by *Ogga æt Suthwycan*, 963–92 (12), Robertson, *Charters* 40 (Southwick, Nth), and *Ogga de Mildenhale*, c. 975, *LibEl* 94 (Mildenhall, Sf). The 10th-c. name is evidently a short form of *Ordgār*.

[6] A formal parallel is *Dudemann* (q.v.). *Hudeman*, 963–92 (12), Robertson, *Charters* 40, the name of a landowner in Thorpe Achurch (Nth), which is taken to be OG by Forssner (p. 156) and Redin (p. 98), may be a similar formation with OE *Hud(d)a* as 1st el.

**Oslac** Ig Dublin, Norwich VI *SCBI Copenhagen* 779. – OE *Ōslāc*.

**Osmund** York VI *SCBI Glasgow* 733. – OE *Ōsmund*.

**Osulf** Derby IV Chester hoard 448–9, VI *BMC* 8; **Osulfes** I c Blunt. – OE *Ōswulf*.

**Oswald** III *SCBI Edinburgh* 569, Northampton III *BNJ* xxi (1931–3), 51; **Oswold** Northampton VI Lockett 3713. – OE *Ōswald*.

**Oswardes** (gen.) I c *SCBI Glasgow* 696; **Oswards** (gen.) I c *ibid.* 695; **Oswerd** Warwick VI *BNJ* xxxiv (1965), 73. – OE *Ōsweard*.

**Oswine** *BNJ* xxxi (1962), pl. iii. 17. Halfpenny. – OE *Ōswine*.

**Oðelries** (gen.) I c *SCBI Copenhagen* 812; **Oðelrie** Derby IV Chester hoard 450. – OG *Othelric* (Forssner 196 and Schlaug I, 133 and II, 141). *ð* reflects the OLG spirant.


**Pirim**, see **Prim**.

**Prim** Huntingdon V Chester hoard 494; **Pirim** Huntingdon V *BMC* 19. – Perhaps a nickname from OE *prīm* 'the first hour, six o'clock, the service held at that hour'. Cf. also Primethorpe (Lei), *Torp DB*, *Prymesthorp* 1316 (*DEPN, s.n.*).[1]


(Fastolf) **Rafn** III *SCBI Edinburgh* 548–50. – ON *Hrafn*, ODan *Rafn* (*PNDB* 292f.). On the double name, see below, p. 210.

**Ranvvwin** I *SCBI Edinburgh* 499–500. – OG *Ranwin* < *Hrabanwin* (Morlet 135) or *Randwin*[2] (Förstemann 1247 and Morlet 187); see also *PNDB* 346.

**Raðulf** III Blunt. – OG *Radulf*; cf. *PNDB* 345. *ð* may be due to Scand. influence or reflect OFr [ð] from intervocalic [d].

**Redwine** I c Carlyon-Britton 1717c. – OE *Rǣdwine*[3] or possibly OS *Redwini*, on which see Schlaug II, 143.

**Regenold** Winchester VI *SCBI Glasgow* 730. – OG *Regenold* (Forssner 208 and Morlet 185 f.).

**Regenulf** Winchester VI Hildebrand 55; **Rægnulf** Winchester VI *ibid.* 52. – OG *Reg(i)nulf* (Forssner 211).

**Regðeres** (gen.) I c Blunt. – ON *Hreiðarr*, ODan *Rether* (*PNDB* 293).

**Reinad** I Blunt; **Rernart** I Tetney 417. – OG *Reinard* (Forssner 208f.).

**Richtmund** III Dublin. – Probably OE *Wihtmund* with R for *wynn* by engraver's error. A moneyer of that name worked under Athelstan (Stafford, *SCBI Glasgow* 635) and Edmund (*SCBI Copenhagen* I, 732 and *Oxford* 351).

**Riculf** Stamford VI *BNJ* xxiii (1938–40), 21; **Ricolf** I *BMC* 134;

---

[1] On the ME surname *Prim(m)e* from OFr *prim(e)* 'fine, delicate', see *DBS, s.n.*

[2] For a Flemish example of *Randwin*, see C. Tavernier-Vereecken, *Gentse Naamkunde van ca. 1000 tot 1253* (Brussels, 1968), p. 18.

[3] A rare name; for instances, see my note, *NoB* xxxiii (1945), 87.

Olof von Feilitzen and Christopher Blunt

**Riccolf** I *BMC* 133. – OG *Riculf* (Förstemann 1271, Morlet 189 and von Feilitzen, *Early English and Norse Studies*, 56).
**Rodbriht** Winchester III BM. – OG *Rodbert* (Forssner 216f.).

**Saydtine** V *BMC* 210. – Obscure.
**Selewold** III *BNJ* xxvIII (1955–7), pl. xxvI. 14, Oxford VI *SCBI Oxford* 419. – OE *Selewald*. This name has not been recorded before.
**Serclos** Ia Ryan 784. – An original byname from ON *\*serklauss* 'shirtless' (*ZeN* 73 and Smart 231). Cf. also *Broclos DB* < ON *\*bróklauss* 'breek-less' (*PNDB* 208).
**Sexbyrht** Lewes VI Hildebrand 17. – OE *Seaxbeorht*. The only known bearer of the name is this moneyer who also worked under Edward II (*SCBI Glasgow* 742).
**Sideman** Chichester VI Stockholm, Rochester VI *SCBI Reading* 59; **Sydyman** Rochester VI Hildebrand 37; **Sedeman** I *SCBI Copenhagen* 813, Ib *BNJ* xxxv (1966), pl. xIV. 12, York VI Stockholm. – OE *Sidumann*. The last two forms go back to OE *Siodu-, Seodumann* with back-mutation, *y* in *Sydyman* being a Kentish inverted spelling for *e*.
**Siferð** Id *SCBI Edinburgh* 603–5, IV *ibid.* 577. – OE *Sigefrið*.
**Sigares** (gen.) Ic Chester hoard 432. – OE *Sigegār*.
**Sigewald** Gloucester VI Stow-on-the-Wold Museum; **Sigewold** Shrewsbury VI Sigsarve 242. – OE *Sigewald*.
**Siulf** Stafford VI Lockett 2755. – OE *Sigewulf*.
**Smala**, see **Ismala**.
**Spereman** Tamworth IV Tamworth Castle Museum. – OE *Speremann* < *\*speremann* 'warrior armed with a spear'; not previously recorded. For its use as a byname in ME see *DBS* 303.
**Styrcar** Leicester VI Hildebrand 23. – ON *Styrkárr*, ODan *Styrkar* (Björkman 132 and Janzén 90f. and 119f.).
**Sumerleda** Ia *SCBI Copenhagen* 814. – ON *Sumarliði*, Anglicized *Sumerlida* (Björkman 133f.).

**Teoðic** Chester II *SCBI Edinburgh* 638; **Teoðuc** Chester II *ibid.* 637. – Perhaps a derivative of names in *Þeod-*, with *-ic* by the side of *-uc* by suffixal variation, and identical with OE *\*Teodic* or *\*Teoduc* in the place-names *Teodeces leage* and *Teodeces broc*, 963 (11), Birch 1111 (Wa), and *Te(o)dekesberie, DB*, Tewkesbury (Gl); cf. *PN Gl* II, 61f. and *DEPN, s.n.*[1] Medial *ð*, unless an error for *d*, may be due to Scand. influence.
**Tuholf** V Chester hoard 509. – For *Tunolf* < OE *Tūnwulf*. One *Tunulf*

[1] Cf. also *Teoda* (Redin 55). T for initial *þ* in the parent name is normal in hypocorisms. A variant *Þeoda* is evidenced in *Goduuine Thede filius*, 1087–98, *Bury* 25 (Sf). A clear case of suffixal variation in the name of the same person is *Ufuc cl[ericus]*, 984 (contemp.), Earle, *Charters* 208, by the side of *Ufic clericus* in numerous charters, 965–85.

worked at Buckingham under Edward II (Hildebrand 1) and Æthelred II (*BMC* 14).

**Tumma** York VI *SCBI Oxford* 424; **Tuma** York VI *BMC* 13. – OE *Tum(m)a* or ODan *Tum(m)i* (Redin 72, *PNDB* 388 and Fellows Jensen 293).

Þ**eodgar** Lewes VI *BMC* 20. – OE *Þēodgār*[1] or OG *Theodger*; cf. *PNDB* 383, E. Ekwall, *Early London Personal Names* (Lund, 1947), pp. 2 and 66, and Smart 262.

Þ**urcetel**, see **Wyrcetel**.

Þ**urferð** I e *BMC* 164, III *SCBI Cambridge* 616, Northampton VI Sotheby 23 May 1966 121; **Durefrö** Northampton III Chester hoard 454. – ON *Þor(f)røðr*, ODan *Thor(fri)th* (*PNDB* 392 and Fellows Jensen 303f.).

Þ**urmod** I d *SCBI Oxford* 406, IV *SCBI Copenhagen* 770, Chester II *SCBI Chester* 101–3, III *ibid.* 75–7, IV *ibid.* 78, VI Hildebrand 21; Þ**urimod** Chester II *SCBI Chester* 100. – ON *Þormóðr*, ODan *Thormoth* (*PNDB* 395 and Fellows Jensen 311).

**Ugelberd** I c Leeds, I g Grantley 1101. – Cf. also *Uglebart*, Edmund, *SCBI Glasgow* 644; *Ucelberd*, Eadred, Chester hoard 232, and Eadwig, *ibid.* 366; perhaps the same man. Later examples are *Ugle-*, *Ugelbert*, *DB* TRE (Croom and Kirkby Grindalythe, ERY), and the first el. of Ugglebarnby (NRY), *DB Ugleberdesbi*, ME *Ugel-*, *Uglebardeby*, *Uggelbardebi* etc., on which see *PN NRY* 121. The name seems to survive in the We surname *Oglebird*.[2] The *DB* forms have been derived from an ON *Uglu-Bárðr*[3] or *Uglubarðr*,[4] i.e. *Bárðr*, pers.n.[5] or *-barðr* 'beard' with the prefixed genitive of *ugla* 'owl' (also byn.), hence 'Owl-Bárðr' or 'Owl-Beard', *-bert* being explained as due to association with the common el. *-beorht* (*DB -bert*). The coin-spellings listed above clearly represent the same name; in most of them the second el. has been replaced by OE *-beard* which was reduced to

---

[1] Only recorded as borne by the Lewes moneyer, who continued to work under Edward II and Æthelred II, and by some TRE landowners in *DB*. In both cases continental origin will have to be considered. The abbot *Theotgar* mentioned by Searle was a Frank; see *PNDB* 383, n. 5. For additional lOE and ME names in *Þeod-*, many of which may well be native, see von Feilitzen, *NoB* xxxiii (1945), 90, Reaney, *Studier i Modern Språkvetenskap* xviii (1953), 103 f., and Whitelock, *Æthelgifu*, line 33 and p. 59.

[2] Cf. Ogleburg Scarr, 1651; the manor of Oglebird 1777; Oglebird Plantation etc. (*PN We* ii, 125 and 131).

[3] *PNDB* 397f. and Fellows Jensen 320; cf. also *ZeN* 89. The *DB* forms, esp. the genitival *-es* in the pl.n., point to *-Bárðr*, *-barðr* rather than *-Barði*, the alternative preferred by Ekwall, *DEPN*, s.n., who thinks *-s-* is redundant; see his *Etymological Notes* (Lund, 1959), p. 99.

[4] H. Lindkvist, *Middle English Place-Names of Scandinavian Origin* (Uppsala, 1912), p. lxii.

[5] Cf. *Barð*, *LVH* 59 and Thorney Liber Vitae, 101, both early-11th-c.; *Barað*, a festerman, c. 1023–51 (Björkman 24f.); and *Bared*, *Baret*, *DB* (*PNDB* 192). The disyllabic forms reflect earlier *Barøðr*.

-*berd* as in -*weard* > -*werd*.[1] In view of the occurrence of the name in the tenth century,[2] at least ninety years before it turns up again in *DB*, ON *\*Uglu-Bárðr*, a typical nonce-formation, seems a less likely etymon than *\*Uglubarðr*, an original nickname, which may have enjoyed some currency although its precise meaning is not obvious. Moreover, it is doubtful whether the pers.n. *Bárðr* could really appear as -*berd* in the middle of the tenth century, whereas in -*berd* for -*barðr* we are merely concerned with the substitution of an OE synonym.[3]

**Unbein** I *SCBI Edinburgh* 454–5; **Hunbein** I *ibid.* 453; **Unbin** I *ibid.* 457. – ON *Úbeinn* (*PNDB* 397).

**Unspac** York VI BM. – ON *Óspakr* (Björkman 170f. and *PNDB* 340).

**Werstan** I d *SCBI Edinburgh* 613–16, IV Dublin. – OE *Wǣrstān*.

**Wiferö** I *BMC* 136; **Vwiferö** I *SCBI Copenhagen* 819. – OE *Wīgfrið*.

**Wīgstān**, see **Wistan**.

**Wihtmund**, see **Richtmund**.

**Wihtsige** Winchester III *SCBI Edinburgh* 516, VI BM and Hildebrand 56. – OE *Wihtsige*.

**Wilsige** IV Carlyon-Britton 1048b; **Wilsig** IV *SCBI Copenhagen* 815.- OE *Wilsige*.

**Wine** III *BNJ* xxvii (1952–4), pl. vi. 53, Canterbury VI Mann 163; **Winees** I f *BMC* 165. – OE *Wine* (Redin 9f.).

**W[i]nebirht** V Chester hoard 492. – OE *Winebeorht*[4] or OG *Winebert*.

**Winemes** I c Blunt, I f F. Baldwin; **Winenr** I *BMC* 137–8. – Perhaps OG *Winemer* (Forssner 258).[5] A native *Winemǣr* is not on independent record but may enter into the place-names *Winemeresham*, *DB*, Wilmersham (So), and *Wynemerislega*, 1212, Winmarleigh (L); see *DEPN*, *s.nn.*

**Wistan** I *SCBI Edinburgh* 382.[6] – OE *Wīgstān*.

---

[1] See below, p. 211, and note also *Ealdabeard*, mon. Cnut, Exeter, Hildebrand 373–4, by the side of *Ealdeberd*, *ibid.* 375 (Nordman 32), an original byn., (*se*) *ealda beard* 'Old Beard'.

[2] The coin forms are not in Searle and have not previously been noted. *BMC* ii, 123 only lists an *Ulgebert* (in italics; among the moneyers of Edmund), which the editors tentatively identify with *Ingelbert* (!).

[3] It should perhaps be added that there is no evidence for an OG *Hugil-*, *Ugilbert*. The form *Ochelbert* (Förstemann 1175), bp of Belluno, stands for *Othelbert*; see *Regesta Pontificum Romanorum, Italia Pontificia*, ed. P. F. Kehr vii (Berlin, 1923), 90. *Chuglibert* (Förstemann 926), quoted from J. M. Pardessus, *Diplomata* ii (Paris, 1849), 108, is a misreading for *Chagliberct*; see *MGH, Diplomata* i, 32.

[4] *Uiniberct*, *LVD* 6x, and *Winiberht*, mon. Osberht of Northumbria, *BMC* 670–4 and *SCBI Cambridge* 350, *Copenhagen* 1, 378–80 and *Glasgow* 260. The remaining examples in Searle (p. 500) all represent OE *Wynbeorht*. *Winebreht*, mon. Eadred, *NC* 5th ser. v (1925), 363, is probably identical with the Edgar moneyer.

[5] To the forms adduced by Forssner we may add *Winemerus*, *DB* ii, 105 (Colchester 1086); *Winemeri* (gen.) *monachi*, 1162–8, *Holme* 51 (Nf); and *Winemer*, 12th-c., *LVD* 5, col. 2.

[6] The editor reads *Christian* with a question mark. The coin may actually have P for *wynn*.

**Wulfbald** Bath III Montagu 710. – OE *Wulfbald*.

**Wulfgares** (gen.) I c *SCBI Edinburgh* 508–9; **Wulgar** Chester II *SCBI Chester* 104, Stamford VI *SCBI Glasgow* 725. – OE *Wulfgār*.

**Wulfmær** V Chester hoard 510, Hertford VI Ready 107. – OE *Wulfmǣr*.

**Wulfred** Oxford VI *SCBI Oxford* 420–1. – OE *Wulfrēd*.

**Wulfric** York VI Hildebrand 9; **Welfric** York VI Drabble 437; **Wlfric** Malmesbury III Drabble 854. – OE *Wulfrīc*.

**Wulfstan** I Lockett 614, Leicester VI *SCBI Copenhagen* 775; **Wulstan** I c Blunt, V Chester hoard 511–12, Wallingford VI *SCBI Oxford* 423; **Wulftan** III *BMC* 197; **Wulestan** V Ryan 800; **Wulsan** Oxford III *SCBI Oxford* 410. – OE *Wulfstān*.

**Wynnelm** Oxford III *SCBI Oxford* 411. – OE *Wynhelm*.

**Wynsige** Gloucester VI Hildebrand 12, Winchester III *BMC* 53. – OE *Wynsige*.

**Wynstan** Totnes VI Montagu 730; **Wunstan** SWmint III *BMC* 54, Totnes III Lockett 621. – OE *Wynstān*. *u* for *y* in the second form is due to a slip of the die-cutter.

**Wyrcetel** V *SCBI Cambridge* 620. – A blundered form of Đ*urcetel* < ON Þ*orke(ti)ll*, ODan *Thorkil* (*PNDB* 394f. and Fellows Jensen 309ff.).[1]


## GENERAL OBSERVATIONS

Of the native names the majority conform to the usual dithematic pattern and call for no special comment. In the cases of *Forðgār*, *Gārwīg*, *Ogeman* and *Sexbyrht* the moneyer in question is the only known pre-Conquest bearer of the name. *Selewold* has not been recorded before, nor has *Spereman*, an original by-name. *Fugetat*, if from OE *\*fugeltā*, would be another instance of a nickname used as a personal name. *Goldstan* is the earliest known compound with the lOE element *Gold-*.[2]

Uncompounded names are *Ana*, *Bald(d)ic* (?, OG),[3] *Boia*, *Brentinc*, *Broðer* (ON), *Bruninc*, *Cnapa*, *Deal*, *Dudinc*, *Dun*, *Ead* (?), *Hilde*, *Hildi[n]c*, *Ive*, *Lenna*, *Leofinc*, *Man*, *Manna*, *Manning*, *Morgna*, *Oda*, *Prim*, *Smala*, *Teoðic* (*Teoðuc*), *Tumma* (ON) and *Wine*.

*Deal*, *Ead*, *Hildi[n]c*, *Morgna* and *Teoðic*, *-uc* have not been recorded before in independent use. *Hilde* ( < *\*Hilda*) and *Lenna* are the only known bearers of their respective names.

---

[1] If *y* is phonologically relevant and not a mere error for *u*, the coin spelling could reflect the ODan variant Þ*yrkil* with *y* < *u* by *i*-mutation (*DGP*, col. 1395). Another Anglo-Scand. example would be *Thirkillus*, 12th-c. (L); see *DBS*, *s.n. Thurkell*.

[2] The el. *Gold-* was popular in lOE and eME times; see von Feilitzen, *NoB* xxxii (1945), 81f. and 95, n.

[3] Where alternative etymologies have been suggested, this is indicated in the following lists by the addition in parentheses of the abbreviations OE, OG or ON. Doubtful cases, apart from those listed below among obscure names, are followed by a question mark.

The foreign element falls into four categories: (1) Scandinavian names, (2) continental Germanic names, (3) Celtic names and (4) Latin and biblical names.

(1) The Scandinavian element is represented by *Amund, Asferð, Broðer* (OE), *Colgrim, Copman, Eoroð* ( < *Iórfrøðr* ?), *Farman, Farðein, Fastolf, Grind, Grið, Gun[n]ar, Gunfred* (OG), *Gunnulf, Herolf* (OE), *Hildulf* (OE), *Hrodulf* (OE, OG), *Ingolf, Iole, Isulf, Manni, Osbearn* (OG), *Rafn, Regðer, Serclos, Styrcar, Sumerleda, Tumma* (OE), *Þurferð, Þurmod, Þurcetel, Ugelberd, Unbein* and *Unspac*.[1] Of these *Iórfrøðr, Grind, Grið, Serclos* ( < *Serklauss*) and *Ugelberd* ( < * *Uglubarðr*) are not found in Scandinavian sources. The last four, which are clearly original bynames, may have originated among the Scandinavian settlers in England.

Most of these names can be either Old Norse or Old Danish. *Colgrim, Gunfred, Sumerleda, Unbein* and *Unspac* are recorded only in ON, *Manni* is only in ODan.

(2) Many of King Edgar's moneyers were immigrants from the continent and names of continental Germanic provenance are correspondingly numerous in our material. They are *Abenel* (?), *Adelger, Æðelbrand, Agulf, Albart, Bald(d)ic* (?, OE), *Baldric* (OE), *Baldwin, Bernard* (OE), *Durand*,[2] *Eoferard, Eofermund* (OE), *E(o)ferolf* (OE), *Erconbold, Flodger, Flodulf, Flodvin, Folchard, Freðic* (?, OE), *Froðald, Ginand, Godeferð, Grimbert* (? *Grimter*), *Gunfred* (ON), *Herebert, Hereman, Heriger* (*Harger*), *Hrodulf* (OE, ON), *Ingelbert, I[n]golferð, Ingolri[c], Isembert, Landbriht* (OE), *Mamolet* (?), *Mangod, Manntat* (OE), *Manticen* (?), *Marcer, Marscalc, Meinard, Norðberd, Ogea, Osbearn* (ON), *Oðelric, Ranwin, Raðulf, Redwine* (OE), *Regenold, Regenulf, Reina[r]d, Riculf, Rodbriht, Þeodgar* (OE), *W[i]nebirht* (OE) and *Winemer* (OE).

The continental Germanic names form a rather heterogeneous group. On general historical grounds it seems reasonable to assume that many of them are Old Low German, more specifically Old Saxon or Old Flemish (Old Low Franconian), whereas others are undoubtedly of West Frankish origin. A great number were, however, current over a wide area[3] and adequate linguistic criteria for assigning individual names to a specific region are seldom available. On the basis of a comparison with the tenth-century (and earlier) material collected by Schlaug for Old Saxon, Mansion for Old Flemish[4] and Morlet for the names in French sources, the following provisional classification may perhaps be attempted:

---

[1] Note also that most of the names in *Os-* listed as OE may alternatively be Anglicized forms of the corresponding Scand. names in *As-*.

[2] *Durand* is probably a Medieval Latin name; cf. above, p. 193, n. 6.

[3] Cf. Mansion's useful list of *overal voorkomende namen*, pp. 63–4.

[4] Supplemented for the early eleventh century by C. Tavernier-Vereecken, *Gentse Naamkunde van ca. 1000 tot 1253* (Brussels, 1968).

(*a*) Common to the three dialect areas: *Adelger, Albert, Baldric, Bernard, Eoferard, Folcard, Godeferð, Gunfred, Herebert, Heriger, Hereman, Hrodulf, Landbriht, Norðberd, Raðulf, Riculf, Rodbriht* and *Þeodgar.*

(*b*) Old Saxon and West Frankish: *Æðelbrand, Baldwin, Eoferolf, Grimbert, Marcer, Meinard, Oðelric, Redwine, Reinard, Regenold, Regenulf* and *Winebert.*

(*c*) Flemish and West Frankish: *Erconbold, Ranwin* and *Winemer.*

(*d*) Old Saxon and Flemish: *Osbern.*

(*e*) Old Saxon only: *Marscalc* and *Ogea.*

(*f*) Flemish only: *Manntat* and *Manticen* (?).

(*g*) West Frankish only: *Abenel* (?), *Agulf, Flodger, Flodulf, Flodvin, Froðald, Ingelbert, -ferð, -ric, Isembert, Mamolet* (?) and *Mangod.*

In the last group the names in *Flod-* and *Froð-* have initial *fl-, fr-* < *hl-, hr-* as a result of Romance sound-substitution.

Some of the OG names in our material may be of Middle or South German provenance. *Ginand* is only recorded once, in a Fulda charter. Since there exist no satisfactory collections of early Frisian names, the possible presence of a specifically Frisian element could not be ascertained.

(3) Celtic origin has been suggested, usually with great hesitation, for *Cawelin, Demence* (ultimately Latin?), *Gillys, Hacuf, Macus* and *Mælsuðan.* The only safe cases are the last two, both of Old Irish provenance.

(4) Latin or biblical are *Andreas, Beneðiht, Daniel, Demence* (if < *Dominicus*), *Iohan* and *Mærtin.* Some of these may well, as Mrs Smart points out (pp. 226 f.), have been borne by persons of Celtic ancestry. *Andreas* is the earliest known example of the name in England.

Of obscure origin, finally, are *Adelaver, Aden, Albutc, Asmaned* (*Asmneda*), *Cylm, Igenc* and *Saydtine.* Some of these may of course be blundered forms of known names.

Several of the foreign names listed above exhibit some degree of Anglicization, usually by assimilating an element to the form of its OE counterpart. Examples are *Æðel-* for *Adel-* in *Æðelbrand*; *-bearn* for ON *-biǫrn* (or OG *-bern*) in *Osbearn*; *-briht* for *-bert* in *Landbriht* (if OG) and *Rodbriht*; *Eofor-* for OG *Eber-, Ever-* in *Eoferard, -mund* (OE) and *-olf* (OE); and *-ferð* for OG *-frid* and ON *-frøðr* in *Asferð, Godeferð, Gunverd, I[n]golferð* and *Þurferð.* ON *ó-* has been replaced by the corresponding OE prefix *un-* in *Unbein* and *Unspac.* Note also *Mærtin* with *æ* for *a*; *Beneðiht* with OE *-ht* < [-kt]; and *Copman* and *Serclos* with *o* for the Scandinavian diphthong *au*.

On the coins of Edgar and his predecessors the moneyer's name often appears in the genitive.[1] The relevant instances for the reign under notice

---

[1] Genitives are first recorded on some coins of Athelstan: *Domences, BMC* 102; *Mægen-, Megenredes, SCBI Edinburgh* 152 and *Glasgow* 624; *Paules, BMC* 33–4 and 52; *Sælces, SCBI Chester* 26, *Salces, SCBI Copenhagen* 1, 696; and *Tiotes, ibid.* 716, *Totes, SCBI Chester* 44. The

are *Ælfredes, Æðelulfes, Eðelulfes, Bernardes, Boigaes, Deorulfes, Dudæmones, Durandes, Durandies, Fastolfes, Freðices, Grimes, Gunares, Herolfes, Igolferðes, Ingolri[c]es, Ioles, Leofinces, Lefinces, Lefmanes, Manes, Mannees, Oswardes, Oswards, Osulfes, Oðelrices, Regðeres, Sigares, Winees* and *Wulfgares*.

It should be noted that the strong ending is used even with weak names (*Boigaes* and *Mannees*). There are in fact no safe instances of weak genitives on coins.[1]

An important aspect of our material which unfortunately cannot be satisfactorily elucidated is the local distribution of the names. Most coins have no mint-signature and although we can now, thanks to the recent work of British numismatists, usually assign the different types to approximate geographical areas,[2] these are as yet far too vaguely defined to be very helpful in an attempt to classify the material on regional lines. It is to be hoped that future research on coin types and hoards will enable numismatists to identify more precisely the output of the various English mints in the pre-reform period.

A special problem is raised by the occurrence of double names on some coins. B. E. Hildebrand in the introduction to his catalogue (pp. vii–viii) lists the examples recorded in his material, from Cnut to Edward the Confessor. To these we can now add *Ælfwine Tosti* (Cnut, Oxford, *SCBI Oxford* 720), and for the Confessor's reign *Arngrim Coa* (York, *SCBI Glasgow* 1048), *Ælfsie Alda* (Chester, *SCBI Chester* 299) and *Lifwine Horn* (Rochester, *BMC* 1140 and *SCBI Cambridge* 948). While Hildebrand is no doubt right in taking the majority of second names to be ordinary bynames, there remain a few instances where this interpretation is definitely improbable or impossible. Such cases are *Aðelmod Arnulf* (Athelstan, *BMC* 150), *Ælfwine Tosti* (see above), *Wulfwi Ubi* (Cnut (?), Ilchester, Holm 664)[3] and the examples in our material, *Fastolf Boiga, Fastolf Oda, Fastolf Rafn* and *Ead Ælfstan*, if that legend should indeed be taken at its face value. In these cases it seems an inevitable conclusion that we are concerned with two persons who shared the privilege of striking coins. Fastolf was no doubt the same man in all three cases, a great entrepreneur who was working in partnership with Boiga, Oda and Rafn. Additional proof of such an arrangement is furnished by a series of Winchester coins from Cnut to Edward the Confessor with the legend *Godwine Widia* alternating

---

fashion became increasingly common under Edmund, Eadred and Eadwig and culminates under Edgar. Edward the Martyr's brief reign yields no examples, and there are only two under Æthelred II: *Ælfrics*, Norwich, Holm 295; and *Oddas*, York, Hildebrand 798–9, and *SCBI Copenhagen* II, 279–80.

[1] *Oban*, mon. York, Æthelred II, which has been explained as a gen. of *Oba*, could perhaps, as Professor Jackson kindly informs me, be OIr *opunn* [obun:] 'quick, swift, prompt', later *obonn, obann*. It cannot be derived from ON *úbeinn* as Smart suggests (p. 231).

[2] See above, pp. 183-4.

[3] Also mentioned by Hildebrand (p. viii) but without details.

with *Godwine* and *Widia* occurring separately.[1] A parallel case is probably *Leofred Brun* (Harthacnut, London, Hildebrand 127-8) by the side of *Brun* (*ibid.* 111) and *Leofred* (*ibid.* 124-6).

## PHONOLOGY

### *Vowels and diphthongs*

Occasional *e* for *æ* in *Elfred, -stan, -wald, Eðelm, Eðelvine* and *Eðelulf* has probably no phonological significance, since, as Mrs Smart points out (pp. 201 f.), the die-cutters often failed to distinguish properly between the two letters.[2] *Ealfsige*, if a reliable form, could be an inverted spelling indicating the incipient lOE change *ea > æ*.

*Alfwold, Aðelwold* and *Aðulf* have *a* for *æ* before a second element containing a velar vowel.[3] Initial *a* for *æ* in *Ascman* and *Asma* (Lincoln), could, if phonologically relevant, be due to Scandinavian influence. *Adlvine, -vne, -vini* are blundered forms and clearly worthless.

Before nasals we find *o* for *a* in *Dudæmones, Mælsuðon* (Chester), *Monna* (Chester and Tamworth?) and in the compromise spelling *Loandferð* by the side of *Landferð*. After *c.* 950 this is mainly a West Midland feature, which agrees with the distribution of the coins under notice.[4]

Breaking of *æ* before *l* + consonant is evidenced in *Deal*[*l*], the name of a Winchester moneyer, but other relevant forms show Anglian *a*: *Aldewin(e)* and *Alhmund*; note also *Balddic, Baldric* and *Baldwin*, all probably OG loans. Irrespective of dialect, absence of fracture is normal in the weakly stressed second elements *-bald* (only in *Wulfbald*)[5] and *-wald*. The latter frequently appears as *-wold*, examples being *Alfwold, Aðelwold, Byrhtwold, Leofwold, Oswold, Selewold* and *Sigewold* by the side of *Elfwald, Æðelwald, Oswald* and *Sigewald*.[6]

Breaking did not take place in the second element of *Osward*, and the diphthong is reduced to *e* in *Oswerd*; cf. also *Ugelberd*.[7] In *Sexbyrht < Seaxbeorht* we have an instance of late WS smoothing of *ea > e* before *hs*.

---

[1] Cnut: *Godwine Widia*, Hildebrand 3760, *Godwine Widii, ibid.* 3761 and *Widia, ibid.* 3837; Harold I: *Godwine Widi*, Hildebrand 1019, *Widia, ibid.* 1038-41, *Wudia, BMC* 100 and *Widig, ibid.* 104; Harthacnut: *Godwine Wudi*, Hildebrand 208 and *BMC* 24; and Edward the Confessor: *Godwine Widia, BMC* 1426-8, *Widia, ibid.* 1438 and *Wida, ibid.* 1436-7. Redin (pp. 159 f.) correctly concluded that we are concerned with two different persons. This view is also held by Grueber who transcribes the legends in question *Fastolf* and *Boiga, Godwine* and *Wudia*, etc.

[2] Note for example that the form *Elfred* is extremely common on the obverse of King Alfred's coins (*BMC passim*).

[3] *PNDB*, § 5; Campbell, § 329. 3, n. 2; and Whitelock, *Æthelgifu*, p. 53.

[4] *Ibid.* p. 56.

[5] In *Erconbold o < a* in the 2nd el. is due to an OG or OE change.

[6] *PNDB*, p. 59.

[7] *PNDB*, § 24 and Campbell, § 338 and n. 1; note also *Æðelerd*, mon. Athelstan, *SCBI Edinburgh* 191 and *Ecgherd*, mon. Athelstan, *SCBI Oxford*, 337.

8-2

In *Copman* < ON *Kaupmaðr* and *Serclos* < ON *\*Serklauss o* has been substituted for the Scandinavian diphthong.[1]

Anglian *ē* for *ǣ*[2] appears in *Redwine* and *Werstan*. There are no cases of WS *ǣ* in our material unless *Mægerd* (Winchester) stands for *Mǣgerd*. The el. *-rǣd* is *-red* throughout, whilst the variants *-mǣr*, *-mēr* are found in *Wulfmǣr* and *Eadmer* respectively.

The element *Beorht-* exhibits the usual range of forms: *Beorht-, Biorht-, Byrht-, Birc[t]-, Breht-* and *Bri[h]t-*; note also *Landbriht, Rodbriht, Sexbyrht* and *W[i]nebirht*.[2] *Biorhtulf* (Bath) is noteworthy on a WS coin of this date. The change *beor- > byr-* is also seen in *Byrnferð* < *Beornfrið*.[3] In *Bernferð* and *Bernulf* < *Beornfrið, -wulf* we may have early examples of the change *eo > [ø, e]*.

Back-mutation of *e* accounts for the diphthong in *Eoferard, -mund*. The variant *Eaferard* has *ea* for *eo*, a mainly Northumbrian feature, which also appears sporadically in other dialects.[4]

The spellings *Ætfer(d)* and *Etfer* would seem to furnish the earliest evidence at present available for the incipient monophthongization of *ēa*, which is abundantly attested on the coinage of Æthelred II; see the forms in *Ed-* by the side of *Ead-* listed in Hildebrand, pp. 177f.

The phonological significance of the spellings *Diur-, Dyur-* by the side of *Deor-* is difficult to assess; they could scarcely represent a survival of archaic *iu* for *ēo, īo*.[5] *Liofstan* (Bedford) reflects the interchange of the graphs *io* and *eo* in various OE sources, and *Lefman* and *Lefinc* (both Mercian mints) and *Levi[n]c* (Lincoln) may be early instances of the change *ēo > [ø̄, ē]*.[6]

Rounding of *i > y* is seen in *Fryðemund* by the side of *Friðemund* (Winchester). As an unstressed second element *-frið* regularly appears as *-ferð* with lowering of *i > e* and metathesis of *r*.[7] *Sedeman* and the second element of *Sumerleda* have *e < eo*, earlier *io*, from *i* by Anglian back-mutation.[8] *Sydyman* (Rochester) looks like an inverted spelling for *Sedeman* prompted by the Kentish change *y > e*.

The element *-(w)ulf* appears as *-ulf* in native and continental Germanic names, as *-ulf* or *-olf* in Scandinavian ones. Exceptions are *Ef(eo)rolf* (Staf?), *Ric(c)olf* and *Tuholf* ( < *Tūnwulf*), but in these cases *-olf* may be due to local

---

[1] Luick, § 384. 2.

[2] *Borhtnoð* has *o* for *eo* owing to a slip of the die-cutter.

[3] On the development of *Beorht-, -beorht, Beorn-* see the detailed discussion in *PNDB*, §§ 31–2. *-bert, -berd* is usually a criterion of OG provenance, as in *Albart* (for *Albert*), *Herebert, Ingelbert, Isembert* and *Norðberd*, unless the el. has been Anglicized as in *Rodbriht*.

[4] Campbell, §§ 278 and 280–1; cf. also *eafor, Beowulf* 2152.

[5] Campbell, § 275.

[6] Campbell, §§ 294–7; on *ēo > ē*, see *PNDB*, p. 63, n. 5 and Campbell, § 329. 2.

[7] Also in the Anglicized names *Asferð, Godeferð, I[n]golferð* and *Þurferð*, the only form without metathesis being *Gunfred* (ON or OG) by the side of *Gunverd*.

[8] Cf. *Siademan*, mon. Eadmund, *BMC* 127, and *sæleoda* by the side of *sælida* (BT).

Scandinavian influence. The extensive material available for the reign of Æthelred II confirms this observation; here *-olf* occurs only in Scandinavian names, whereas *-ulf* is found in both native and Scandinavian ones, a distinction which affords a useful etymological criterion.[1]

Final *-a* is levelled to *-e* in *Boge, Cnape, Hilde, Iole* (from Anglicized *Iola*), *Ive, Manne* and *Morne*, but is retained in the majority of cases: *Ana, Boia* (and variants), *Cnapa, Lenna, Manna, Morgna, Oda, Ogea, Smala* and *Tumma*.[2]

Apocope of final *-e* in the elements *-sig* and *-win* by the side of *-sige*, *-wine* is evidenced in the pairs *Ælfsig/-sige, Æðelsig/-sige, Leofsig/-sige, Wilsig/-sige, Aldewin/-wine* and *Leofwin/-wine*.[3]

The interchange of *e* and *a* in the second syllable of *Broðer, Broðar* exemplifies the variation in the quality of unstressed vowels which is a common feature of lOE.[4] Medial *e* in *Aldewin(e)* is inorganic. In *Berenard* and *Godeferð* it is probably a continental feature.[5]

### Consonants

The element *Æðel-* exhibits occasional loss of *l* in *Æðered* and *Æðestan*, and is further reduced in *Æðelm* < *Æðelhelm* and *Aðulf* < *Æðelwulf*.[6] Metathesis of *r* has taken place in *Ælferd* < *Ælfred* and *Mægerd* if < *Mǣgred*. It is regular in *-ferð* < *-frið*.

The occasional use of *v* for voiced *f* seen in *Atverd* < *Ēadfrið, Gunverd* < ON *Gunnfrøðr* (or OG *Gundfrid*), *Ive* < *Ifa* and *Levi[n]c* < *Lēofing* is due to the influence of Latin or continental usage.[7]

In the elements *Sig-, -sige* and *Wīg-* the combination *ĭg* tends to become *ī*, examples being *Siferð, Sigar, Siulf, Ælfsie, Æðelsie, Wiferð* and *Wistan*.[8] *Farðen* by the side of *Farðein* reflects the OE loss of *g* before *n* with lengthening of the preceding vowel. In the combination *eg* the palatal consonant is written *g* or *i*: *Farðein, Meinard, Regenold, Regenulf, Rægnulf, Reina[r]d* and *Regðer*. Intervocalic [i̯] is spelled *i, ig, ge, g* in *Boia, Boiga, Bogea, Boga* and *Ogea*.

Occasional *d* for *ð*, as in *Asferd, Ædelsie, Ætferd, Atverd, Gunverd, Osferd, Farden, Grid* and *Durefrð* is phonetically irrelevant, the die-cutter having omitted the small horizontal bar on the letter *D*.

Unvoicing of *d* occurs in *Ætfer(d), Atverd, Eatstan, Hiltwine* and *Rer-*

---

[1] A doubtful case is *Dreolf*, London, Hildebrand 2307 and *SCBI Copenhagen* II, 739, which may be a blundered form of *Deorulf*; cf. *Dærul*, London, Hildebrand 2298–9.

[2] The change *-a* > *-e* probably began about 950; cf. *SCBI Reading*, p. 11, n. 8.

[3] Cf. *PNDB*, §§ 47–8. Campbell, § 348, n. 5 thinks *-sig* may be an *a*-stem but in view of the evidence a phonetic explanation is surely preferable.

[4] See also Whitelock, *Æthelgifu*, pp. 55 f.

[5] Cf. *SCBI Reading*, p. 10. The inorganic *i* in *Pirim* (for *Prim*) and *Þurimod* is evidently due to the engraver who inadvertently added a redundant vertical stroke.

[6] *PNDB*, § 62.

[7] For additional early examples see *PNDB*, p. 88, n. 2.

[8] *PNDB*, § 133; Whitelock, *Æthelgifu*, p. 55.

*nart,* and conversely *d* stands for final *t* in *Ingelberd* and *Norðberd.* The suffix *-ing* appears as *-inc* in *Brentinc, Bruninc, Dudinc, Leofinc* (*Lyfinc*) and *Hildi*[*n*]*c.*

The final consonant is lost in *Elfval, Britfer, Ætfer, Duran* and *Eadmun,* but whether any of these spellings is phonologically significant and not merely due to negligence on the part of the engraver cannot be determined. *Bircsige, Morne* < *Morgna, Wulgar* and *Wulstan* exemplify the well-known loss of medial consonants in triple clusters.

An inorganic initial *h* has been added in *Hingolf* and *Hunbein.*

Interchange of single consonant and geminate is seen in *Mana, Maning, Mantat, Ricolf* and *Tuma* by the side of *Manna, Manning, Manntat, Riccolf* and *Tumma.* Double consonants are simplified in *Æðered* ( < \**Æðerred* < *Æðelred*), *Gunar* and *Macus.*

# The narrative mode of *The Anglo-Saxon Chronicle* before the Conquest

## CECILY CLARK

With a few exceptions,[1] scholars have paid more attention to the syntax of *The Anglo-Saxon Chronicle*[2] than to its style. True, stylistic observation has at least once thrown light upon its compilation, by identifying the author of the additional entries at 959 DE and 975 D as the homilist Wulfstan.[3] In general, however, the *Chronicle*'s standing as an anthology of three centuries' prose writing has gone unacknowledged.[4] Yet stylistic study of the *Chronicle* is rewarding, for it reveals not only how prose style developed within a single genre and a single tradition but also how the very concept of annal writing shifted beween the ninth century and the twelfth.

### THE INITIAL ALFREDIAN COMPILATION

Shifts of style in the *Chronicle* must be related to stages in its compilation, some of which are revealed by changes of hand and ink in surviving copies. The earliest such change in any extant text occurs between the recto and the verso of fol. 16 of the Parker manuscript (A, Cambridge, Corpus Christi College 173), and involves also a change of layout, with annal-numbers assigned to a column of their own up to 16r but from there onwards being variously placed. This change, then, which occurs at the annal-number 892, may mark the end of a compilation in some respects unified by common principle. Does the unifying principle embrace style as well as layout?

As a rule, *Chronicle* entries up to this point (common, broadly speaking,

---

[1] These exceptions include G. C. Donald, *Zur Entwicklung des Prosastils in der Sachsenchronik* (Diss. Marburg, 1914) and F. Viglione, *Studio critico-filologico su l' 'Anglo-Saxon Chronicle', con saggi di traduzioni* (Pavia, 1922); see also Ashdown, *Documents*, pp. 13–16 and D. Whitelock, 'The Prose of Alfred's Reign', *Continuations and Beginnings: Studies in Old English Literature*, ed. E. G. Stanley (London, 1966), pp. 97–9.

[2] Editions consulted include *The Anglo-Saxon Chronicle*, ed. B. Thorpe, Rolls Series, vol. 1 (1861); Earle and Plummer, *Chronicles*; Ashdown, *Documents*, pp. 38–70, for 978–1017 C; and *The Parker Chronicle (832–900)*, ed. A. H. Smith (London, 1935). The customary sigla are used to indicate the different versions. In quotations I supply my own punctuation, both for the sake of consistency and to bring out the points under discussion.

[3] K. Jost, 'Wulfstan und die angelsächsische Chronik', *Anglia* XLVII (1923), 105–23; see also Bethurum, *Wulfstan*, p. 47 and Whitelock, *Sermo Lupi*, pp. 27–8.

[4] Viglione did make this point (*op. cit.* pp. 3 and 64–5), but his study is superficial.

to all the main versions) are terse: hence the high relief in which the more expansive entry at 755 stands out. A typical early-ninth-century annal reads:

833. Her gefeaht Ecgbryht cyning wiþ xxxv sciphlæsta æt Carrum, 7 þær wearþ micel wæl geslægen, 7 þa Denescan ahton wælstowe gewald. 7 Hereferþ 7 Wigþen, tuegen biscepas, forþferdon; 7 Dudda 7 Osmod, tuegen aldormen, forþferdon.

Adjectives are sparse, and adverbs rare or (as happens here) absent; nor is there any complexity of syntax, just a chain of simple sentences rendering a series of simple propositions. Furthermore, with the events noted all falling within a narrow range, vocabulary and phrasing are correspondingly restricted, annal after annal using the same semi-formulaic language. Compare, for instance, the entry for 837:

Her Wulfheard aldormon gefeaht æt Hamtune wiþ xxxiii sciphlæsta, 7 þær micel wæl geslog 7 sige nom. 7 þy geare forþferde Wulfheard. 7 þy ilcan geare gefeaht Æþelhelm dux wiþ Deniscne here on Port mid Dornsætum, 7 gode hwile þone here gefliemde, 7 þa Deniscan ahton wælstowe gewald 7 þone aldormon ofslogon.

Except for the use of the descriptive adverbial phrase, *gode hwile*, that annal hardly varies in vocabulary or phrasing from that at 833; and those at 838, 839, 840 and 845, for instance, observe the same conventions. Nor do longer entries necessarily show any greater range either of subject-matter or of style: thus the annal for 851 lists several campaigns all in the same standard, factual terms, departing from these only with a closing flourish of pride: '7 þær þæt mæste wæl geslogon on hæþnum herige þe we secgan hierdon oþ þisne ondweardan dæg, 7 þær sige namon'; and in the annal for 871 the account of the Battle of Ashdown and of the related campaign, although fuller than usual, likewise keeps to the conventional chain of simple sentences.

Now this restricted prose style was by no means the only one current in ninth-century English. Although no early literary prose is extant, there survive from the early ninth century, and before, vernacular charters, wills and laws,[1] and these show as much and as varied subordination and qualification as the matter requires, laws being rich in conditional clauses and jussive subjunctives, 'Gif hwa oðrum his eage oðdo, selle his agen fore',[2] and charters likewise: 'Gif hit ðonne festendæg sie, selle mon uuege cæsa, ond fisces, ond butran, ond aegera ðaet mon begeotan maege, ond xxx ombra godes Uuelesces aloð ðet limpeð to xv mittum, ond mittan fulne huniges, oðða tuegen uuines, suę hwaeder suae mon ðonne begeotan

---

[1] Although surviving law-codes date back to the early seventh century, none, unfortunately, has been preserved in a pre-Alfredian text; for this reason I prefer not to explore the stylistic detail of the earlier codes.
[2] Liebermann, *Gesetze* I, 32.

maege.'[1] Nor is this, from a Kentish charter of the first decade of the ninth century, exceptional for the date.[2] The early *Chronicle* style, then, shows limitations peculiar to itself.[3]

Closer definition of this style may be reached through comparison with that of the Old English Orosius, which, as well as being comparable with this part of the *Chronicle* both in date and as historical narrative, also happens to be the only Old English work still extant which the compiler of the early *Chronicle* certainly knew.[4] The style of the Old English Orosius is simple, admittedly, with little subordination other than temporal and relative clauses; but, instead of being terse as that of the early *Chronicle* is, it ranges freely both into description and into explanations of motive, thus, for instance:

> Swa egefull wæs Alexander þa þa he wæs on Indeum, on easteweardum þissum middangearde, þætte þa from him ondredan þe wæron on westeweardum. Eac him coman ærendracan ge of monegum þeodum, þe nan mon Alexandres geferscipes ne wende þæt man his naman wiste, 7 him friþes to him wilnedon. Þagiet þa Alexander ham com to Babylonia, þagiet wæs on him se mæsta þurst monnes blodes. Ac þa þa his geferan ongeatan þæt he ðæs gewinnes þagiet geswican nolde, ac he sæde þæt he on African faran wolde, þa geleornedon his byrelas him betweonum hu hie him mehten þæt lif oþþringan...[5]

The ampler narration derives, of course, from the Latin original; but it is noteworthy that the translator, although rendering his original loosely, makes no attempt to reduce this amplitude to a *Chronicle*-like simplicity. Indeed, his additions from contemporary vernacular sources, such as the narratives of Ohthere and of Wulfstan, admit not only circumstantial description: '7 þær is mid Estum ðeaw, þonne þær bið man dead, þæt he lið inne unforbærned mid his magum 7 freondum monað, ge hwilum twegen; 7 þa kyningas, 7 þa oðre heahðungene men, swa micle lencg swa hi maran speda habbað, hwilum healf gear, þæt hi beoð unforbærned 7 licgað bufan eorðan on hyra husum';[6] but also hypothesis: 'Þyder he cwæð þæt man ne mihte geseglian on anum monðe, gyf man on niht wicode, 7 ælce dæge hæfde ambyrne wind.'[7] Clearly, the Old English Orosius and the *Chronicle* are obeying different stylistic principles.

[1] *Sweet's Anglo-Saxon Reader*, rev. D. Whitelock (Oxford, 1967), p. 198.

[2] See *OET*, pp. 441–2, 443–4, 445, 447–9 and 449–50, for several comparable documents all dated before 840.

[3] This has sometimes been insufficiently recognized by investigators concerned with the *Chronicle* as evidence for chronological development of syntax; see, e.g., G. Rübens, *Parataxe und Hypotaxe in dem ältesten Teil der Sachsenchronik (Parker HS. bis zum Jahre 891)* (Diss. Göttingen, 1915), pp. 51–3 and A. Rynell, *Parataxis and Hypotaxis as a Criterion of Syntax and Style*, Lunds Universitets Årsskrift n.f. avd. 1. bd 48. nr. 3 (1952), p. 26.

[4] See D. Whitelock, *Continuations and Beginnings*, pp. 73–4. The entry at 81, 'Titus...se þe sæde þæt he þone dæg forlure þe he noht to gode on ne gedyde', is derived from the Old English Orosius: *King Alfred's Orosius*, ed. H. Sweet I, EETS o.s. 79 (London, 1883), p. 264, line 2.

[5] *Ibid.* p. 136.     [6] *Ibid.* p. 20.     [7] *Ibid.* p. 19.

The origins of the *Chronicle*'s special stylistic principles are not, at first sight, obvious. The arts of rhetoric current in the early Middle Ages, being mainly concerned with oratory (or preaching) or with letter-writing, do not, as far as I know, specify styles for the various genres of historiography. Such hints as they give imply that for most narrative purposes some form of *stilus humilis* should be used: thus *Rhetorica ad Herennium* illustrates *oratio adtenuata* (i.e. *stilus humilis*) by a specimen of *narratio*,[1] and in *De Doctrina Christiana* Augustine prescribes *stilus humilis* for instructional use, that is, for factual, non-emotive writing.[2] Indeed, as Auerbach pointed out, plain Latin prose is best exemplified during the Dark Ages in the narrative parts of the bible, in the early saints' lives, and in the *Historia Francorum* of Gregory of Tours.[3] But the terse formulas of the early *Chronicle* are not simply *stilus humilis* in English, not 'the humblest sort of everyday speech',[4] but, as the contrast both with the charters and with the Old English Orosius shows, constitute in their own way a highly artificial manner, especially in their avoidance of descriptive elements of all kinds.

The origins of this manner may lie in the *Chronicle*'s origins. Annals evolved from notes in the margins of Easter tables.[5] Necessarily brief, such notes, being adjuncts to the calendar rather than contributions to literature, were also factual and objective, remaining so as long as they continued to be made: witness, for instance, this sequence from a twelfth-century Peterborough table, '1087 *Obiit* Wille*l*mus rex. 1089 *Obiit* Land-franc*us* archie*piscopu*s. 1096 Iter incepit ierosolimitanum. etc.'[6] The objective manner of the primitive annals abstracted from such tables (although not their extreme brevity) was imitated in annals independently composed: Dr C. W. Jones has remarked how Bede's specimen chronicles, in contrast with his work in other historical genres, are 'mundane and factual', eschewing all miraculous elements.[7] Similarly with the vernacular. What the sources of the *Chronicle* to 891 may have been is matter for conjecture, as no surviving text contains annals antedating it; analysis has suggested that as far as the early part of Æthelwulf's reign the compiler was drawing upon, amongst other things, various earlier sets of annals, but that from

---

[1] Ed. and trans. H. Caplan (Loeb, 1954), pp. 260–3.
[2] *On Christian Doctrine*, trans. D. W. Robertson (New York, 1958), pp. 145–7, 153–4, 159 and 162.
[3] E. Auerbach, *Literary Language and its Public in Late Latin Antiquity and in the Middle Ages* (London, 1965), pp. 52, 53, 60 ff., 87–8 and 103–11.
[4] *Infimum et cotidianum sermonem* (*Rhetorica ad Herennium*, p. 260).
[5] R. L. Poole, *Chronicles and Annals: a Brief Outline of their Origin and Growth* (Oxford, 1926), pp. 26, 42 and 58 ff.; C. W. Jones, *Saints' Lives and Chronicles in Early England* (Cornell, 1947), pp. 7 ff. and 16 ff.
[6] *Ungedruckte Anglo-Normannische Geschichtsquellen*, ed F. Liebermann (Strasbourg, 1879), p. 13; cf. *MÆ* xxiii (1954), pl. facing p. 71.
[7] Jones, *op. cit.* pp. 20, 22 and 27.

the latter part of that reign onwards he composed the annals himself.[1] At all events, many of the seventh- and eighth-century annals consisting of only one line (see, for instance, 7v of the Parker manuscript) could have been derived from Easter table notes; and there must have been some written record to preserve for over two centuries such entries as *671. Her wæs þæt micle fugla wæl.*

In spite of variations in origin, however, stylistic continuity is (with exceptions such as the entry at 755) well maintained: with the annals for 833 and 837 already quoted compare these across the centuries:

568. Her Ceaulin 7 Cuþa gefuhton wiþ Æþelbryht, 7 hine in Cent gefliemdon, 7 tuegen aldormen on Wibbandune ofslogon, Oslaf 7 Cnebban.

675. Her Wulfhere Pending 7 Æscwine gefuhton æt Biedanheafde; 7 þy ilcan geare Wulfhere forþferde, 7 Æþelræd feng to rice.

845. Her Eanulf aldorman gefeaht mid Sumursætum, 7 Ealchstan biscep 7 Osric aldorman mid Dornsætum gefuhton æt Pedridan muþan wiþ Deniscne here, 7 þær micel wæl geslogon 7 sige namon.

Although the compiler evidently knew Bede's *History*, he set down under 627, as the equivalent of six of Bede's chapters,[2] the single simple sentence, 'Her Edwine kyning wæs gefulwad mid his þeode on Eastron.' Contemporary events too he transmuted into his terse, timeless formulas, thus:

886. Her for se here eft west þe ær east gelende, 7 þa up on Sigene, 7 þær wintersetl namon. Þy ilcan geare gesette Ælfred cyning Lundenburg, 7 him all Angelcyn to cirde, þæt buton Deniscra monna hæftniede was, 7 he þa befæste þa burg Æþerede aldormen to haldonne.

His sense of continuity is a living one which allows creation of fresh conventions: that opening, *Her for se here*, appears in the entries for 867, 869, 872–5, 879–84 and 886–7, and is the basis for variants in 868, 870–1, 876–8 and 885.

Study thus suggests that, whether or not the distinction were as yet consciously formulated, 'annals' were felt to be a separate genre requiring a style of their own. Practice speaks for itself. For theory – and even then confined to the formal, superficial level – we have, however, to wait until the late twelfth century, when Gervase of Canterbury described the differences observable between chroniclers and historians:

Historici autem et cronici secundum aliquid una est intentio et materia, sed diversus tractandi modus est et forma varia. Utriusque una est intentio, quia uterque veritati intendit. Forma tractandi varia, quia historicus diffuse et eleganter incedit, cronicus vero simpliciter graditur et breviter. 'Proicit' historicus 'ampullas et sesquipedalia verba;' cronicus vero 'silvestrem musam

---

[1] See A. J. Thorogood, 'The Anglo-Saxon Chronicle in the Reign of Ecgberht', *EHR* XLVIII (1933), 353–63, and also Whitelock, *ASC*, pp. xxi–xxiii.
[2] *HE* II. 9–14.

tenui meditatur avena.' Sedet historicus 'inter magniloquos et grandia verba serentes,' at cronicus sub pauperis Amiclæ pausat tugurio ne sit pugna pro paupere tecto. Proprium est historici veritati intendere, audientes vel legentes dulci sermone et eleganti demulcere, actus, mores vitamque ipsius quam describit veraciter edocere, nichilque aliud comprehendere nisi quod historiæ de ratione videtur competere. Cronicus autem annos Incarnationis Domini annorumque menses computat et kalendas, actus etiam regum et principum quæ in ipsis eveniunt breviter edocet, eventus etiam, portenta vel miracula commemorat. Sunt autem plurimi qui, cronicas vel annales scribentes, limites suos excedunt, nam philacteria sua dilatare et fimbrias magnificare delectant. Dum enim cronicam compilare cupiunt, historici more incedunt, et quod breviter sermoneque humili de modo scribendi dicere debuerant, verbis ampullosis aggravare conantur.[1]

Broadly understood, that could apply to the differences between the Old English Orosius and the *Chronicle*: as a history, the Old English Orosius uses some amplitude of narration (although to describe its style as *ampullas et sesquipedalia verba* would be exaggeration), whereas the *Chronicle*, in its different genre, *simpliciter graditur et breviter*, intent on chronology and on fact, rather than on personality or on verbal ornament.

Gervase, however, deals only with the surface. In a deeper sense, the difference between annalists and historians is not that the latter discard chronological frameworks and indulge in rhetorical flourishes, 'making broad their phylacteries and enlarging the borders of their garments'; nor that they deal with the *mores vitamque* of their personages as well as with their *actus*, using for this purpose physical description, direct speech, even anecdote; nor even that, as medieval writers maintained, they described good men's good deeds so as to excite emulation but evil men's evil deeds so as to inspire revulsion;[2] but much more that on both personal and national levels they relate motive, causation, and consequence. Annalists, on the other hand, simply record events as they occur.

For this function of plain record the early *Chronicle* style is well adapted, enabling events to be set forth with minimum interference from any author's personality. The absence of adjectives and adverbs allows the record to stand clear, unclouded by subjective impressions; the absence of subordination keeps it uncontaminated by conditions, concessions or speculations. To speak of 'meditating with a scrawny oatstalk a rustic muse' misses the mark: on its own level this unadorned, unqualified record is as near absolute fact as history can get; and, aesthetically, it has the dignity of utter plainness.

But objectivity is hard to sustain: feelings and opinions will break in.

---

[1] *The Historical Works of Gervase of Canterbury*, ed. W. Stubbs, 2 vols., Rolls Series (1879–80) I, 87–8; cf. Poole, *op. cit.* pp. 7–8.
[2] See, e.g., *HE Praefatio*.

Even in early annals an adjective or an adverb sometimes betrays the annalist's point of view, as when Æthelhun is called *þone ofermedan aldormonn* (750), or when it is noted, not without pride, how, faced by Hengest's forces, *þa Brettas...mid micle ege flugon to Lundenbyrg* (457) and how *þa Walas flugon þa Englan swa fyr* (473); and, dealing with matters of living memory, the annalist calls Ceolwulf II of Mercia *anum unwisum cyninges þegne* (874) and notes that when Æthelwulf returned home with his Frankish bride his people *þæs gefægene wærun* (855) and that his son Æthelberht reigned *on godre geþuærnesse 7 on micelre sibsumnesse* (860). More elaborately, a relative clause or a causal one may lend character or motive to a personage of the record, as with the borrowing from the Old English Orosius, 'Titus...se þe sæde þæt he þone dæg forlure þe he noht to gode on ne gedyde' (81),[1] or with such notes as 'Hæfde hine Penda adrifenne 7 rices benumenne, forþon he his swostor anforlet' (658), 'se gerefa þærto rad 7 hie wolde drifan to þæs cyninges tune, þy he nyste hwæt hie wæron' (787), and 'Þy fultomode Beorhtric Offan, þy he hæfde his dohtor him to cuene' (836). Such touches bring both gain and loss: gain in that they put events into a contemporary, human perspective; loss in that they adulterate fact with impression, hearsay, and opinion.

### THE LATER ALFREDIAN ANNALS

At the top of 16v, beginning with what seems to be (in spite of the annal-number 892 entered at the foot of the recto) an addition to the annal for 891, a new hand takes over in the Parker manuscript, continuing probably, although not with perfect regularity, to 924.[2]

The opening entries in the new hand, those from 892 to 896 especially,[3] contrast markedly with those of the early Alfredian compilation.[4] Not only are they longer and fuller of detail, but their syntax, in contrast with the scarcely varied co-ordination of the preceding entries, shows free use of subordination: for instance, compare with the entries previously quoted this sentence from 893: 'Ond þa gegaderade Ælfred cyning his fierd, 7 for þæt he gewicode betwuh þæm twam hergum, þær þær he niehst rymet hæfde for wudufæstenne ond for wæterfæstenne, swa þæt he mehte ægþerne geræcan gif hie ænigne feld secan wolden.' The novelty of style must not be exaggerated; for, on the one hand, these annals still show

---

[1] See above, p. 217, n. 4.  [2] Ker, *Catalogue*, pp. 57–9.

[3] Stylistically the break is not sharp: syntax is complex and description ample in 891 A, both in the section by the first scribe and in that by the second, but the subject-matter there is unrelated to that of the following group of annals, 892–6, which form a unit because of their narrative continuity. A simple style relying on co-ordination reappears in 897. Note further that, although the entries for 891 and for 893–9 are common to A, B, C and D, E is blank for these years.

[4] See Whitelock, *Continuations and Beginnings*, pp. 97 and 99.

many passages of purely co-ordinate structure – thus, for instance, 'Þa forrad sio fierd hie foran, 7 him wið gefeaht æt Fearnhamme, 7 þone here gefliemde, 7 þa herehyþa ahreddon' (893) – and, on the other, as we have seen, there had appeared from time to time throughout the earlier annals clauses of condition (755), of result (716 and 867), of purpose (2, 48, 430, 853 and 867), of comparison (734, 797, 874, 877 and 885) and of reason (658, 661, 680, 694, 787, 823, 836 and 887). But, compared with previous entries, these later Alfredian annals do offer both a wider range of connectives for types of clause already used, for instance, *þa hwile þe* and *swa oft swa* for temporal clauses, and also some new types of clause, notably the concessive, *þeh ic ða geðungnestan nemde* (896); and, above all, they show subordination used in far greater density.

This new annalist does indeed wear his phylacteries a thought broader. His more complex syntax is accompanied, although to nothing like the same degree as in homiletic style, by rhetorical patterning. Doublets and triplets occur: *ægþer ge of East Englum, ge of Norþhymbrum* (893); *ægðer ge þæs ceapes, ge þæs cornes* (894); *ge on feo, ge on wifum, ge eac on bearnum* (893); and *ægðer ge swiftran, ge unwealtran, ge eac hieran* (896). The doublets are often antithetical, usually only in the simplest way – *oþþe on dæg, oþþe on niht* (CD); *ge of þære fierde, ge eac of þæm burgum*; *healfe æt ham, healfe ute*; *þiderweardes...hamweardes*; and *suð ymbutan...norþ ymbutan* (all from 893) – but sometimes more elaborately, as in 'tuwwa: oþre siþe þa hie ærest to londe comon, ær sio fierd gesamnod wære, oþre siþe þa hie of þæm setum faran woldon' (893), where the balanced clauses have similar structure and almost the same number of syllables (*isocolon*). Patterns so simple, often seemingly dictated by the material itself, would be unremarkable, were it not that in the earliest entries they had been very rare and had remained uncommon even in those from the 860s, 870s and 880s (*Ær wærun Romanisce biscepas, siþþan wærun Englisce* [690]; *oþer heold Daniel, oþer Aldhelm* [709]; *ge þa Walas, ge þa Deniscan* [835]; *sume binnan, sume butan* [867]; *on twæm gefylcum: on oþrum wæs...7 on oþrum wæron...* [871]; and *oþer dæl east, oþer dæl to Hrofesceastre* [885]: these are almost the only examples of such patterning in the earlier annals).[1] Feeling for rhetoric comes out more strongly in the phrase, *manige eac him, þeh ic ða geðungnestan nemde* (896), with its touch of *occultatio*, and especially in the antithesis, combined with progression from positive to superlative: 'Næfde se here, Godes þonces, Angelcyn ealles forswiðe gebrocod, ac hie wæron micle swiþor gebrocede on þæm þrim gearum mid ceapes cwilde 7 monna, ealles swiþost mid þæm þæt manige þara selestena cynges þena...forðferdon' (896).

---

[1] Rhetorical description being so all-embracing, it is often hard to decide whether an apparent 'trope' may not be accidental, e.g. *his tungon forcurfon 7 his eagan astungon* (797: ? *isocolon* and *similiter cadens*) or *þa he þæt hierde 7 mid fierde ferde* (835: ? *similiter cadens*).

As that phrase, *Godes þonces*, shows, what has changed here is not simply syntax, or taste for word patterns, but the view of chronicling: objectivity is partly discarded. Whereas the earliest annals recorded facts, excluding condition, concession, comparison and causality, these late Alfredian annals go some way towards interpreting the facts they record: that is what the more complex syntax and the rhetoric are there for. Subordination gives insight, if only of an elementary kind, into purpose and motivation, usually those of King Alfred himself: 'Hæfde se cyning his fierd on tu tonumen, swa þæt hie wæron simle healfe æt ham, healfe ute' (893); 'Þa wicode se cyng on neaweste þære byrig, þa hwile þe hie hira corn gerypon, þæt þa Deniscan him ne mehton þæs ripes forwiernan' (895); 'Rad se cyng up bi þære eæ 7 gehawade hwær mon mehte þa ea forwyrcan, þæt hie ne mehton þa scipu ut brengan' (895); and 'Næron nawðer ne on Fresisc gescæpene ne on Denisc, bute swa him selfum ðuhte þæt hie nytwyrðoste beon meahten' (896). Indeed, for such effects subordination is essential: compare 'For þæt he gewicode betwuh þæm twam hergum, þær þær he niehst rymet hæfde for wudufæstenne ond for wæterfæstenne, swa þæt he mehte ægþerne geræcan gif hie ænigne feld secan wolden' (893) with this version in which the same points are expressed through co-ordination plus one temporal clause, with the result that all sense of purpose is lost: '*Þa for he 7 gewicode betwuh þæm twam hergum. Þær hæfde he niehst rymet for wudufæstenne 7 for wæterfæstenne, 7 mehte ægþerne geræcan, þa hie ænigne feld secan woldon.' So, syntax is here being used to give an illusion of insight into the motives underlying King Alfred's various acts, a touch of 'historical' interpretation.

Another sign of 'historical' technique is the deliberate linkage between the annals. Whereas the earlier annals each stood alone, linked at most by an occasional cross-reference such as *Her for se ilca here* (868), here cross-reference is systematic. The entry for 892 describes how *se micla here, þe we gefyrn ymbe spræcon* (note how the annalist, instead of effacing himself, now presents himself as *we* or *ic*) landed *on Limene muþan*; that for 893, after referring to some other events, goes on to speak of *se micla here...þe ær on Limene muþan sæt*; that for 894, which begins *Ond þa sona æfter þæm*, referring back to the destruction of corn and cattle described at the end of 893, closes with 'Þæt wæs ymb twa ger þæs þe hie hider ofer sæ comon'; and the entry for 895, which opens by referring to *se foresprecena here*, ends with 'Þæt wæs ymb þreo ger þæs þe hie on Limene muðan comon hider ofer sæ.' Apart from this formal linkage, this block of annals from 892 to 896 is also united by some common themes, especially interest in tactics, expressed in concern with topography, with conditions of military service and availability of supplies, and also with the king's own ideas and methods. Thus, the campaign, occupying several years, is recorded as a single whole.

But the 'historical' virtues of this group of annals must not be exaggerated. To begin with, as there is no reason to suppose King Alfred himself their author, the insights into his motives cannot be more than conjectural. Further, although his mind is suggested behind many individual developments, there is little sense of any control of events as a whole, nor is the formal continuity controlled by any real plan of exposition; indeed, at times the mere sequence of events is unclear. The movement away from 'annals' towards 'history' is only relative. This is reflected by the use of adjectives and adverbs: the latter remain rare, and the former are still almost confined to definition, thus, *se micla here, anre westre ceastre, þara niwena scipa* and so on, with only an occasional phrase, such as *þara selestena cynges þena*, carrying even a hint of subjective evaluation. The chief virtue here remains the annalistic one of objectivity.

### THE ANNALS FOR THE REIGN OF ÆTHELRED II

During the tenth century greater divergences appear between the surviving versions of the *Chronicle*, divergences which are by no means closely related to the make-up of the extant manuscripts. A shows three hands at work between the entry for 925 and that for 1001; but its version is no longer the primary one. The other manuscripts show no significant changes of hand in this period: B breaks off at 977; C is in a single hand from the entry for 491 to that for 1045 or 1048; none of the several hands of D is to be dated before the mid eleventh century;[1] E is in one hand to 1121. As for the character of the entries, this ranges from the objective brevity of, for instance, those for 909, 912, 944 and 955, to the setting down under 937 of the whole poem on *The Battle of Brunnanburh*.

What divergences there can now be between the manners of the main versions of the *Chronicle* is well illustrated by the notices of Æthelred's accession in 978. A shows a laconicism worthy of an Easter table: 'Her wearð Eadweard cyning ofslegen. On þis ilcan geare feng Æðelred æðeling his broðor to rice.' C also uses the classic manner, departing from objectivity only with the one word, *gemartyrad*, to describe Edward's end, and is no less restrained in the following entry, where a fearful portent, *blodig wolcen...on fyres gelicnesse*, is noted but not explicitly linked with Æthelred's consecration as king, the only other event recorded there. D and E, by contrast, although they give no details of the horrid deed,[2] add an impassioned commentary, heavy with antitheses:

Ne wearð Angelcynne nan wyrse dæd gedon þonne þeos wæs, syþþan hi ærest Britenland gesohton. Menn hine ofmyrþredon, ac God hine mærsode. He

---

[1] Ker, *Catalogue*, pp. 57–9, 252–3 and 254.
[2] For the various stories current about Edward's murder, see C. E. Wright, *The Cultivation of Saga in Anglo-Saxon England* (Edinburgh and London, 1939), pp. 162–71.

wæs on life eorðlic cyning: he is nu æfter deaðe heofonlic sanct. Hyne noldon his eorðlican magas wrecan, ac hine hafað his heofonlic Fæder swyþe gewrecan. Þa eorðlican banan woldon his gemynd on eorðan adilgian, ac se uplica Wrecend hafað his gemynd on heofonum 7 on eorþan tobræd. Þa ðe noldon ær to his libbendan lichaman onbugan, þa nu eadmodlice on cneowum gebugað to his deadum banum. Nu we magan ongytan þæt manna wisdom 7 heora smeagunga 7 heora rædas syndon nahtlice ongean Godes geþeaht.

As is clear, both from the references to Edward's established sainthood and to the accomplishment of divine vengeance and also from the incongruous description immediately following of Æthelred's consecration *mid micclum gefean*, this must be a later interpolation in the annal. But, even as a later interpolation, it remains a remarkable sign of how far the *Chronicle* is coming to admit elements foreign to its original terse objectivity.

Indeed, the tone of the main record itself is shifting. Throughout the 980s, in spite of the fierce Viking raids recorded, the impersonal manner persists; but, from about 991, the annalist, enlarging the borders of his garments, begins to offer explanations of the events he records, and also comments on them. Thus he ascribes the decision taken after Maldon, to pay the Danes £10,000, to *ðam miclan brogan þe hi worhton be ðam særiman* (991). Further, as well as imputing motives to his personages, he allows himself to be far more openly partisan than the Alfredian annalists ever were: 'Ac hi (*sc.* the Danes) þær geferdon maran hearm 7 yfel þonne hi æfre wendon þæt him ænig buruhwaru gedon sceolde. Ac seo halige Godes modor on þam dæge hire mildheortnesse þære buruhware gecydde, 7 hi ahredde wið heora feondum' (994 C). From the mid-nineties until the end of the reign, this tone, imaginative and personal, dominates the entries.

In contrast with the earliest annals, where the personages are only names and ranks, and even with the later Alfredian ones, where only the king himself is presented from inside, these annals show much interest in personalities, their *mores* as well as their *actus*, and also some readiness to pass judgment on them, as when they tell of Ealdorman Ælfric of Hampshire, one of the generals, who 'sende...7 het warnian ðone here; 7 þa on ðære nihte þe hy on ðone dæig togædere fon sceoldan, þa sceoc he on niht fram þære fyrde, him sylfum to myclum bysmore' (992). Another general, Ulfcytel, is both prudent and brave, first advising (unlike the dead hero of Maldon) 'þæt hit betere wære þæt mon wið þone here friðes ceapode, ær hi to mycelne hearm on ðam earde gedydon, forðæm hi unwæres comon 7 he fyrst næfde þæt he his fyrde gegaderede', yet, in the event, impressing the Danes by his prowess (1004). Byrhtric is vain: 'ðohte þæt he him micles wordes wyrcan sceolde þæt he Wulfnoð cucone oþþe deadne begytan sceolde' (1009). The Danes, though arrogant, 'wendon him þa andlang Æscesdune to Cwicelmeshlæwe, 7 þær onbidedon beotra gylpa' (1006), yet acknowledge the valour of Ulfcytel and his men, 'sædon þæt hi næfre wyrsan handplegan on Angelcynne ne gemitton' (1004) – not so much character drawing, perhaps, as a neat way to emphasize English merit. Lively as these portraits are, they are necessarily impressionistic and so diminish rather than enhance the absolute veracity of the recital. By contrast with the later Alfredian annals, the king himself is left undefined, with the massacre on St Brice's Day explained detachedly, 'forðam þam cyninge wæs gecyd þæt hi woldan hine besyrwan æt his life...7 habban siþþan þis rice' (1002), and with his epitaph understated, 'he geheold his rice mid myclum geswince 7 earfoðnessum þa hwile ðe his lif wæs' (1016).

Circumstantial descriptions likewise enliven the narrative. The times and scenes of Ealdorman Ælfric's treacheries are indicated with economical brush-strokes, making moral points as well as visual ones, 'þa on ðære nihte þe hy on ðone dæig togædere fon sceoldan, þa sceoc he on niht...' (992) and 'sona swa hi wæron swa gehende þæt ægðer here on oþerne hawede...' (1003). The mastery of the Danes and the helplessness of the English, of the very citizens of the West Saxon capital, who see no confident army other than a Danish one, are ironically pictured: 'Ac þær mihton geseon Wincesterleode rancne here 7 unearhne, ða hi be hiora gate to sæ eodon, 7 mete 7 madmas ofer .l. mila him fram sæ fetton' (1006). In the account of Ælfheah's murder one phrase indicates not only the condition of the Canterbury Vikings but also the trade routes they dominated: *swyþe druncene, forðam þær wæs broht win suðan* (1012).

In association with these shifts in tone, style in the narrower sense has also evolved. Although grammatical resources are only a little richer than those of the later Alfredian annals, use of them is suppler, the range of clause-types wider. Hypothetical conditions, quite alien to the factual early annals, now add an extra dimension to the narrative: 'oft man cwæð, gif hi Cwicelmeshlæw gesohton, þæt hi næfre to sæ gan ne scoldon' (1006); 'ða buruh raðe geeodon, gif hi ðe hraðor to him friðes ne gyrndon' (1009); and, combined with supposed quotation of enemy testimony, 'Ac gif þæt fulle mægen ðær wære, ne eodon hi næfre eft to scipon: swa hi sylfe sædon þæt hi næfre wyrsan handplegan on Angelcynne ne gemitton, þonne Ulfcytel him to brohte' (1004). This speculative turn gives the narrative new depth, partly because events are no longer seen as absolute and, as it were, predestined, partly because contemporary opinion and reaction are invoked; but at the same time it reduces its factual value.

Diction too has become richer and suppler, giving a coloured and shaded effect that contrasts with the line-drawing of the earliest annals.

Adjectives and adverbs, although still sparse, are more emotive, helping to set events against the background of contemporary reaction: the Danes, *se ungemætlica unfriðhere*, now do *unasecgendlice yfel, þæt mæste yfel þæt ænig here don mihte*, taking *unasecgendlice herehyðe*; betrayed seamen are *þæt earme folc* (999), the army marching past Winchester is *ranc 7 unearh* (1006) and the famine of 1005, *se micla hungor*, is *swylce nan man ær ne gemunde swa grimne*; the Danes murder Ælfheah *bysmorlice* and Eadric Streona slays Sigeferth and Morcar *ungerisenlice*; and in 'forleton þa scipu ðus leohtlice, ...7 leton ealles þeodscypes geswinc ðus leohtlice forwurðan' (1009) the reiterated *ðus leohtlice* stresses the magnates' frivolity in sacrificing the new fleet to a private quarrel. Vocabulary now comes from a wider range of registers. Colloquialism brings out the black comedy of Ealdorman Ælfric's second treachery: 'Þa sceolde se ealdorman Ælfric lædan þa fyrde, ac he teah ða forð his ealdan wrencas: sona swa hi wæron swa gehende þæt ægðer here on oþerne hawede, þa gebræd he hine seocne 7 ongan hine brecan to spiwenne, 7 cwæð þæt he gesicled wære...' (1003). *To spiwenne* conveys Ælfric's loss of dignity as well as of honour, while *ealdan wrencas* implies a complicity between the annalist and his audience, whom he assumes not only to know what he knows but also to share his view of it. Elsewhere it is poetic language which extends the emotional range. The kennings in *þær he wiste his yðhengestas* (1003) and in *næfre wyrsan handplegan...ne gemitton* (1004)[1] momentarily raise the war to an heroic plane; and in 1016 the doom overhanging Edmund Ironside's accession is implicit in the phrase '7 he his rice heardlice werode, þa hwile þe his tima wæs'.

These poetic snatches, with the further dimension of feeling they bring into the *Chronicle*, could be reminiscences of current lays; but, even if they are, they have nonetheless a stylistic function. Apart from the heightened emotion they convey, most of them form rhetorical codas to the entries they occur in. This is so with *þær he wiste his yðhengestas*, and also with the two most elaborate passages of this kind: 'Þonne æt ðam ende ne beheold hit nan þing, seo *sc*ipfyrd*ing* ne seo land*f*yrd*ing*, buton *f*olces ge*s*winc, 7 *f*eos *sp*ylling, 7 heora *f*eonda *f*orðby*ld*ing' (999); and '7 hi þær togædere fæstlice fengon, 7 micel wæl ðær on ægðre hand gefeol. Ðær wearð East-Engla *f*olces seo *y*ld ofslagen. Ac, gif þæt *f*ulle mægen ðær wære, ne *e*odon hi næfre *e*ft to scipon: swa hi sylfe sædon þæt hi næfre wyrsan handplegan on *A*nge*l*cynne ne gemitton, þonne *U*lf*c*ytel him to brohte' (1004). The rhyme and alliteration used here belong no less to rhetorical prose than to verse. Elsewhere alliteration may add emphasis, or perhaps echo a legal formula: '*m*ete 7 *m*admas ofer .l. [*f*iftig] *m*ila him fram sæ fetton' (1006) and 'man þa *f*ulne *f*reondscipe ge*f*æstnode mid *w*orde 7 mid

---

[1] Cf., e.g., 'Næfre he on aldordagum, ær ne siþðan, / heardran hæle healðegnas fand' (*Beowulf*, 718–19).

wedde on ægþre healfe, 7 æfre ælcne Deniscne cyng utlah of Englalande gecwædon' (1014); in 'ge fyrðon on þa wildan fennas hi ferdon' (1010) alliteration is combined with emphatic word-order, and in 'seo fyrding dyde þære landleode ælcne hearm, þæt him naðer ne dohte, ne innhere ne uthere' (1006), the unexpected innhere[1] instead of fyrd is stressed by the vocalic alliteration as well as by the antithesis; doublets are thrown into relief by rhyme and alliteration: 'þæt scyp genaman eall gewæpnod 7 gewædod' (992) and 'þa scypo ða ealle tobeot 7 toþærsc 7 on land awearp' (1009); and an exclamation, itself unusual enough in annalistic style, is reinforced by rhyme (similiter cadens): 'Ac wala þæt hi to raðe bugon 7 flugon!' (999).

Other rhetorical devices also occur, for this annalist's passionate feelings could not be expressed without verbis ampullosis. In 'Þonne wearð þær æfre ðuruh sum þing fleam astiht, 7 æfre hi æt ende sige ahton' (998) and in '7 á swa hit forðwerdre beon sceolde, swa wæs hit lætre fram anre tide to oþre, 7 á hi leton heora feonda werod wexan, 7 á man rymde fram þære sæ' (999), the repetition (traductio) of æfre and that (repetitio) of 7 á, the latter coupled with the antithesis forðwerdre/lætre, stress the permanence of the situation. The same point is later made by a series of antitheses, ending in a balanced pair: '7 þonne hi to scipon ferdon, þonne sceolde fyrd ut eft, ongean þæt hi up woldan: þonne ferde seo fyrd ham. 7 þonne hi wæron be easton, þonne heold man fyrde be westan, 7 þonne hi wæron be suðan, þonne wæs ure fyrd be norðan' (1010). Another chain of antitheses reflects on the capture of Ælfheah: 'Wæs ða ræpling, se ðe ær wæs heafod Angelkynnes 7 Cristendomes; þær man mihte ða geseon yrmðe, þær man oft ær geseah blisse, on þære earman byrig, þanon us com ærest Cristendom 7 blis for Gode 7 for worolde' (1011); and a combination of antithesis and isocolon describes his murder: 'sloh hine...þæt mid þam dynte he nyþer asah, 7 his halige blod on þa eorðan feol, 7 his haligan sawle to Godes rice asende' (1012). With the style of the *Chronicle* developing in this direction, the impassioned interpolation in 979 DE, so loaded with antitheses, can now be given its due place in the tradition.

Literary craft appropriate to history rather than to annals appears not only in this emotive rhetoric but also in the devices used to weld the whole group of annals into a single narrative. These include forward glances, as when 1011 closes with a reference to Ælfheah's martyrdom the next year, and 1013 (which, exceptionally, opens not with Her but with On ðam æftran geare þe se arcebiscop wæs gemartyrod) with one to Swein's death, likewise in the next year. Sometimes the interval, although vague, seems longer: '7 him þa Anlaf behet, swa he hit eac gelæste, þæt he næfre eft to Angelcynne mid unfriðe cuman nolde' (994: one of the few examples here

---

[1] The DE reading; C inghere.

of a man of honour); and 'hine bebyrigdon on Sc̄e Paules mynstre, 7 *þær nu God sutelað þæs halgan martires mihta*' (1012). Under 991 the repeated *ærest* in 'on þam geare man geræedde þæt man geald *ærest* gafol Denescum mannum...þæt wæs *ærest* .x. ðusend pund' implies all the further, larger, tributes to come, by 1017 reaching £72,000.[1] Even more, continuity appears in phrases which recur like refrains, each tied to its own theme, with an effect wholly unlike that of the earlier formulaic repetitions. In 999 the new fleet 'æt ðam ende ne beheold...nan þing, ...buton folces geswinc 7 feos spylling...'; in 1006 the summoning of the fyrd 'naht ne beheold þe ma ðe hit oftor ær dide'; again in 1009 'we ða gyt næfdon þa gesælða ne þone wyrðscype þæt seo scypfyrd nyt wære þissum earde, þe ma ðe heo oftor ær wæs.' The measure of English demoralization is given by the frequency of the keywords *fleam, fleah, flugon: Þa onstealdan þa heretogan ærest þone fleam* (993), *Þonne wearð þær æfre ðuruh sum þing fleam astiht* (998), *Ac wala þæt hi to raðe bugon 7 flugon!* (999), *sona þæt wered on fleame gebrohton* (1006) and 'Þa sona flugon East-Engle. ... Þone fleam ærest astealde Þurcytel Myranheafod. ... Æt nextan næs nan heafodman þæt fyrde gaderian wolde, ac ælc fleah swa he mæst mihte; ne furðon nan scir nolde oþre gelæstan æt nextan' (1010). Complementary to English incapacity are the mastery and barbarity of the Danes. Time and again they overrun the country *swa swa hi sylf woldan* (1001; compare 994, 998, 999, 1006, 1009 and 1010), staying *swa lange swa hi woldon* (1011) and burning *swa mycel swa hi sylfe woldon* (1010). They observe what customs they please: *hi á dydon heora ealdan gewunan, atendon hiora herebeacen* (1006); *dydan eal swa hi bewuna wæron, slogon 7 bærndon* (1001); *dydon eal swa hi ær gewuna wæron, heregodon 7 bærndon 7 slogon* (1006); and *heregodon 7 bærndon, swa hiora gewuna is* (1009). Harrying, burning and slaying form, indeed, the most constant refrain: *on bærnette 7 heregunge 7 on manslyhtum* (994); *on bærnette 7 on mannslihtum, bærndon 7 slogon* (997); *mid bryne 7 mid heregunge* (1006); and *geheregodon 7 forbærndon* (1003; compare 1004 and 1010). In 1013 a new turn of events is reflected by new keywords: *beah, gislas, bugon, gisludon* and *beah 7 gislude*; with the old refrains nevertheless returning, 'for eallon þam, hi heregodon swa oft swa hi woldon.' The next entry completes the pattern: Æthelred it was (for once) who 'hergode 7 bærnde 7 sloh eal þæt mancynn þæt man ræcan mihte', and Cnut saw to it that the English *gislas* paid the price. In 1016 all the strands are finally woven together: 'Com Cnut mid his here...7 heregodon 7 bærndon 7 slogon eal þæt hi to comon. ... Þa hi (*sc.* the fyrd) ealle tosomne comon, þa ne beheold hit nan ðinc, þe ma ðe hit oftor ær dyde. ... Slogon 7 bærndon (*sc.* the Danes) swa hwæt swa hi oferforan, swa hira gewuna is...Þa dyde Eadric ealdorman swa swa he ær oftor dyde,

[1] 994, £16,000; 1002, £24,000; 1007, £36,000; 1009, £3000 (East Kent only); 1012, £48,000; 1014, £21,000; and 1017, £72,000.

astealde þæne fleam...' In spite of the momentary shift when Edmund Ironside *geflymde* the Danish *here*, events followed the old patterns until Edmund's death left the way open for Cnut to take peaceful possession of England.

For all the attempts at characterization and at continuity, and the free rhetorical comment, these annals cannot be called 'history' in the full sense. There is no sense of perspective or of causation; events may be commented on, moralized on even, but they are not explained even at the personal level. When the annalist says 'Man ne mihta geþencan 7 ne asmeagan hu man hi of earde adrifan sceolde, oþþe ðisne eard wið hi gehealdan' (1006), he does not transcend the helplessness he records but shares it. His diagnosis of the country's ills is pragmatic, and, for one who was probably a monk, oddly indifferent to metaphysical possibilities: 'Ealle þas ungesælða us gelumpon þuruh unrædas, þæt man nolde him a timan gafol beodan...ac þonne hi mæst to yfele gedon hæfdon, þonne nam mon frið 7 grið wið hi' (1011).[1] Whereas the value of the early annals had lain in objectivity, that of these annals lies in rendering, with literary skill, but without intellectual sophistication, the feelings of an ordinary observer of the events recorded.

## THE ANNALS FOR THE CONFESSOR'S REIGN

For most of Cnut's reign the *Chronicle* reverts to classic terseness, the several versions showing a general agreement. With the reigns of Cnut's two sons, Harold Harefoot and Harthacnut, the annalists not only begin again to expand their material and to comment on it, but also show some independence of one another, C and D being regularly more outspoken than E. Thus, in the entries for the year 1035, while E (*s.a.* 1036) remarks how 'Sume men sædon be Harolde, þet he wære Cnutes sunu cynges 7 Ælfgiue Ælfelmes dohtor ealdormannes, ac hit þuhte swiðe ungeleaflic manegum mannum', C and D impute the claim to Harold himself, adding roundly *þeh hit na soð nære*. E remains blank while C and D, under 1036, relate the shocking murder of *Ælfred se unsceððiga æþeling*, in a quasi-Laʒamonic verse which could be that of a popular lay.[2] Under 1037, although all three versions note how the ageing, widowed Emma was expelled, only C and D add *butan ælcere mildheortnesse ongean þone weallendan winter*. Under 1040 and 1041 (= 1039 and 1040E) only C and D condemn the king, for doing

---

[1] Compare not only the diagnosis in the contemporary *Sermo Lupi*, 'Nis eac nan wundor þeah us mislimpe, forþam we witan ful georne þæt nu fela geara mænn na ne rohtan foroft hwæt hy worhtan wordes oððe dæde' (ed. Whitelock, p. 60), but also 1087 E, 'Ac swylce þing gewurðaþ for folces synna, þet hi nellað lufian God 7 rihtwisnesse.'

[2] F. Holthausen, 'Zu dem ae. Gedichte von Ælfreds Tode (1036)', *Beiblatt zur Anglia* L (1939), 157 has shown that behind the *Chronicle* versions there probably stood one with better rhymes.

*naht cynelices*, as *wedloga*, and for throwing his predecessor's body *on fenn*; and under 1042 ( = 1041 E) only they record the exact manner of his death in such terms as to make of this an implicit judgment: 'Her gefor Harða-cnut swa þæt he æt his drince stod, 7 he færinga feoll to þære eorðan mid egeslicum anginne.'

How great a change has come over the *Chronicle* appears both in this free criticism of the kings and, at least equally, in the discrepancies between the various versions. Discrepancies there had always been, in plenty, but earlier ones seemed due to varying access to information, not to varying party allegiance. Now, however, although access to information still varies (whereas, for instance, 1046*E [ = true date 1049] lists several bishops attending the synod of Rheims, the corresponding entry in D [dated 1050] complains that it is *earfoð to witane þara biscopa þe þærto comon*), what determines the differences between the versions of the *Chronicle* is party allegiance. Thus E's silence about Alfred's murder, in which C (but not D) implicates Earl Godwine, seems due not so much to lack of information as to the Godwinist sympathies which later become patent in E's account of Godwine's banishment in 1051 (*s.a.* 1048 E).[1] Godwine's banishment is, indeed, a touchstone for the party allegiances of the chroniclers. C records it briefly, without explanation. D (*s.a.* 1052) depicts a hotheaded and arrogant man first challenging established authority, then fleeing from confrontation by it. E, in contrast, shows a good man first misunderstood in his endeavours to protect his own earldom and avenge *þæs cynges bismer...7 ealles þeodscipes* and at the last denied a fair hearing. Indeed, forgetting that respect for plain fact which had dignified the early *Chronicle*, D and E make assertions so irreconcilable that Sir Frank Stenton considered the story to be garbled beyond reconstruction.[2]

Stylistically, the means by which these partisan impressions are conveyed differ from any previously noted. Among earlier styles, the one which those of both D and E here most resemble is that of the later Alfredian annals: modestly complex and without obvious rhetorical ornament. But, with the earlier annals impartial and these eleventh-century ones tendentious, the resemblance is not only superficial but misleading. Whereas, for instance, the later Alfredian annals eschewed descriptive elements, especially adverbial ones, these annals exploit such elements to impart bias to their narratives. This is partly how the E annalist gives his picture of Eustace of Boulogne and his men its hostile colouring. Some

---

[1] See Earle and Plummer, *Chronicles* II, 211–15; cf. below, p. 233, n. 3. Independent accounts of this murder, both insisting on Godwine's complicity, occur in *Encomium Emmae Reginae*, ed. A. Campbell, Camden Third Series 72 (1949), 40–6 (cf. pp. lxiv–lxvii) and in *Guillaume de Poitiers: Histoire de Guillaume le Conquérant*, ed. and trans. R. Foreville (Paris, 1952), pp. 6–12.

[2] *A-S England*, p. 553; see also B. Wilkinson, 'Freeman and the Crisis of 1051', *Bulletin of the John Rylands Library* XXII (1938), 368–87.

underhandedness in Eustace's original mission seems implied in the phrase, *spæc wið hine þet þet he þa wolde*, and then in the Dover episode all the adverbial phrases have a moral ring: *þa woldon hi innian hi þær heom sylfan gelicode*; *wolde wician æt anes bundan huse his unðances*; *ofslogon hine binnan his agenan heorðæ*; and *cydde be dæle hu hi gefaren hæfdon*. D, on the other hand, shows Eustace's men starting the affray stupidly, *dyslice*, rather than viciously, and notes Godwine's flight in a phrase like the one that the earlier annalist had used of Ealdorman Ælfric: *For ða on niht awæg*. This shows the danger inherent in the *Chronicle*'s shift away from plainness and impartiality: once comment on motive and character was acceptable, indeed, once subjective description was admitted, the way was open for biased interpretation.

Yet, biased as it is, interpretation here shows an enhanced sense of causation. Events are not happening willynilly, as in the annals for Æthelred's reign, but are determined by previous acts. In E, everything hinges on that phrase, *cydde be dæle*, for from Eustace's one-sided report arises all the king's anger and misunderstanding of Godwine; and the same motif reappears when the French 'castlemen' of Herefordshire 'wæron...ætforan mid þam cynge 7 forwregdon ða eorlas, þet hi ne moston cuman on his eagon gesihðe': consistently, if not always clearly, Godwine is being shown as a victim of duplicity and of calumny. With the Frenchmen at his ear, the king continues to refuse his earl a fair hearing and so comes to banish him out of hand. D, too, traces events back to individual actions and so to personal character, but to Godwine's own irascible arrogance rather than to Eustace's mendacity: 'Þa undernam Godwine eorl swyðe þæt on his eorldome sceolde swilc geweorðan; ongan þa gadrian folc...' D indeed displays its chain of causation better than E does, better perhaps than any previous annals had done. Whereas E, perhaps advisedly, skips some of the steps in the narrative, D offers a tale apparently complete (although not for that necessarily truer to the facts).[1] Godwine assembles forces *ealle gearwe to wige ongean þone cyng*. That said, it needs no further explanation why the king summons his loyal earls to bring their forces to his aid or why Godwine is summoned to answer for his deeds before the court.

In both narratives this sense of human causation is underlined by reference to the thoughts and feelings of the protagonists. In E it is Godwine's heart which is laid bare: he finds it *lað to amyrrene his agenne folgað*, and *lað...þet hi ongean heora cynehlaford standan sceoldan*. In D insight is shown rather into the minds of the loyal earls. Having come to the king with token forces, they appraise the situation, and 'siððan hy wiston hu

---

[1] Wilkinson, *ibid.* p. 385 describes D as the best of the extant accounts of the crisis; but see below, p. 233, n. 3, for some omission from it.

hit þær be suðan wæs, þa...leton beodan myccle fyrde heora hlaforde to helpe.' But, unlike the hotheaded Godwine, these earls think before acting:

Wurdan þa ealle swa anræde mid þam cynge, þæt hy woldon Godwines fyrde gesecan, gif se cyng þæt wolde. Þa leton hy sume þæt þæt mycel unræd wære, þæt hy togedere comon, forþam þær wæs mæst þæt rotoste þæt wæs on Ænglalande on þam twam gefylcum, 7 leton þæt hi urum feondum rymdon to lande 7 betwyx us sylfum to mycclum forwyrde.

Such an explanation why *no* battle took place shows how the concept of annal writing has shifted since those strictly factual records of two centuries earlier, 'Her gefeaht se cyning, 7 micel wæl geslog 7 sige nam.'

For all that, causation is not yet seen in any but short and personal perspectives. Some naïveté of outlook is indeed betrayed by D's comment on Godwine's fall: 'Þæt wolde ðyncan wundorlic ælcum men þe on Englalande wæs, gif ænig man ærþam sæde þæt hit swa gewurþan sceolde, forðam þe he wæs ær to þam swyðe upahafen, swylce he weolde þæs cynges 7 ealles Englalandes.' Neither D nor E offers the wider view of events that history in the modern sense requires. Indeed the Eustace–Godwine clash, which personified the clash at the Confessor's court between Norman and Anglo-Danish interests and which 'through its results became one of the ultimate causes of the Norman invasion of 1066',[1] gets little more attention than episodes with few repercussions such as Swein Godwinsson's murder of his cousin Beorn.[2] True, the 'Frenchmen' are seen as a party: '...7 geutlagedon ealle þa Frenciscean þe ær unlagon rærdon 7 undom demdon 7 unræd ræddan into ðissum earde' (1052 CD) and '...7 cweð man utlaga Rotberd arcebiscop fullice, 7 ealle þa Frencisce menn, forðan þe hi macodon mæst þet unseht betweonan Godwine eorle 7 þam cynge' (1052 E). But there is no sign that either motives or consequences were understood in political rather than in personal terms; and, even on the personal level, the rôle of Robert of Jumièges is left obscure.[3] Not even the E annalist, partisan as he is, has expressed what issues his partisanship involves.

Yet, although these annals thus show objectivity replaced by rather short-sighted partisanship, the change is not all loss. To know how differently events were seen by chroniclers apparently based respectively at York (D) and at Canterbury (E) is itself a gain.

[1] Stenton, *loc. cit.*
[2] 1049 C, 1050 D and 1046* E.
[3] Neither version mentions the story that Robert of Jumièges had helped to bring about Godwine's fall by accusing him of Alfred's murder; see *The Life of King Edward*, ed. F. Barlow (London, 1962), pp. 18–23 and cf. Wilkinson, *loc. cit.* pp. 371 and 379–82.

### THE CONQUEST

7 þa hwile com Willelm eorl upp æt Hestingan on Sancte Michaeles mæsse-dæg; 7 Harold com norðan, 7 him wið gefeaht ear þan þe his here come eall; 7 þær he feoll, 7 his twægen gebroðra, Gyrð 7 Leofwine. And Willelm þis land geeode, 7 com to Westmynstre, 7 Ealdred arcebiscop hine to cynge gehalgode, 7 menn guldon him gyld 7 gislas sealdon 7 syððan heora land bohtan.

In defeat E recaptures the lapidary dignity of the earliest annals, refraining from either lament or recrimination. Behind all the passion and partisan-ship of the preceding century, the old tradition of objective recording still flowed strong.

The D annalist, in contrast, uses a voice not unlike that of his pre-decessor in Æthelred's reign, not hiding his scorn, whether for the supporters of Edgar the Ætheling as laggards alike in war and in peace: 'Ac swa hit æfre forðlicor beon sceolde, swa wearð hit fram dæge to dæge lætre 7 wyrre[1]...Bugon þa for neode, þa mæst wæs to hearme gedon; 7 þæt wæs micel unræd þæt man æror swa ne dyde, þa hit God betan nolde for urum synnum', or for the Conqueror as a hypocrite: '7 he heom behet þæt he wolde heom hold hlaford beon – 7, þeah, onmang þisan, hi hergedan eall þæt hi oferforon...7 he sealde him on hand mid Cristes bec, 7 eac swor...þæt he wolde þisne þeodscype swa wel haldan swa ænig kyngc ætforan him betst dyde, gif hi him holde beon woldon – swa þeah, leide gyld on mannum swiðe stið...'

Nevertheless, it is D, not E, which to express the outcomes of the two battles, Stamford Bridge and Hastings, reverts to the ninth-century for-mula:[2] 'Engle ahton wælstowe geweald...7 þa Frencyscan ahton wæl-stowe geweald.' This formula, so characteristic of the *Chronicle* although not peculiar to it,[3] is not recorded again in any of the extant texts, as though, once used of the Conquest, it could never again be used of any punier victory.

Thus the narrative mode of the *Chronicle* sways continually between the austere objectivity of the original Easter table entries and a more emotive utterance, sometimes as of the pulpit, sometimes as of every day. This oscillation will continue to the very end; for the Final Continuation, best known for its moving account of the Anarchy, can also be classically objective: '7 te eorl of Angæu wærd ded, 7 his sune Henri toc to þe rice. 7 te cuen of France todælde fra þe king; 7 scæ com to þe iunge eorl Henri, 7 he toc hire to wiue, 7 al Peitou mid hire. Þa ferde he mid micel færd into

---

[1] Compare especially the extract from 999 quoted above, p. 228.
[2] First used in the *Chronicle* in the annal for 833 quoted above, p. 216. Note that 1066 C says of the Battle of Fulford 7 *Normen ahton wælstowe gewald*.
[3] See BT, *s.v. wælstow*.

Engleland, 7 wan castles' (1140 E). For all the occasions when rhetoric – not to mention human nature – breaks in, there remains nevertheless an underlying sense of annals as a genre of their own, requiring a special diction and a special attitude of mind: the feeling which Gervase of Canterbury tried to express when he warned chroniclers against 'making broad their phylacteries'. But what Gervase failed to see was that the modest style, the 'scrawny oatstalk', expressed a respect for absolute truth in the record.[1]

[1] I am deeply grateful to Professor Clemoes for having read this article several times in draft and having suggested many improvements in my argument.

# The classical additions in the Old English Orosius

## JANET BATELY

Although it came to be used as a standard history textbook in the Middle Ages, Paulus Orosius's *Historiarum adversus Paganos Libri Septem*[1] was intended not so much to provide a comprehensive survey of world history as to answer the charge that the times in which its author lived were unusually beset with calamities and that this was due to the adoption of Christianity and the neglect of idols.[2] Orosius accordingly tended to select only those details that would illustrate and reinforce his case and did not hesitate to confine himself to the briefest allusions to people and events that would have been well known to his classically educated fifth-century audience. It is therefore not surprising that the author of the Old English version of OH,[3] free from the restrictions imposed upon Orosius by his polemic aim[4] and writing for a late-ninth- or early-tenth-century audience[5] with little or no classical knowledge, found it both desirable and possible to expand and comment on certain features of his source. Of the numerous classical additions[6] to be found in Or. some are explanatory, rendered necessary by the change of audience, while others provide additional information about people and incidents neither essential to an understanding of the text nor relevant to the apologist's theme but of some interest historically. Thus, for example, allusions to stories well known in Latin literature but presumably unfamiliar to the majority of Or.'s readers are

[1] Ed. K. Zangemeister, *CSEL* v; cited henceforth as OH.
[2] Cf., e.g., OH I, prol. 9.
[3] Ed. H. Sweet I, EETS o.s. 79 (London, 1883) under the misleading title *King Alfred's Orosius*; cited henceforth as Or., references being to page and line.
[4] For the translator's theme cf. D. Whitelock, 'The Prose of Alfred's Reign', *Continuations and Beginnings: Studies in Old English Literature*, ed. E. G. Stanley (London, 1966), p. 90.
[5] Since William of Malmesbury's attribution of the Old English Orosius to King Alfred would appear to be unfounded (cf. J. Raith, *Untersuchungen zum englischen Aspekt. I. Grundsätzliches, Altenglisch* [München, 1951], pp. 54–61 and J. M. Bately, 'King Alfred and the Old English Translation of Orosius', *Anglia* LXXXVIII [1970], 433–60), it is no longer possible to provide a *terminus ad quem* for the translation other than the date of the earliest surviving manuscript, i.e. the first quarter of the tenth century.
[6] Biblical additions are not included in this study; nor are those 'classical' ones for which I can find no support in classical texts, e.g. the erroneous assumption (Or. 220, 1–2) that Mancinus was left outside the Numentine camp until he died, or the claim (Or. 240, 23) that Pompey had the support of thirty kings at Dyrrachium. Geographical additions will be discussed in a separate paper.

expanded; passing references to the outwitting and defeat of an enemy – OH being more interested in the frequency and extent of war than in the way in which it was waged – are replaced by details of the military stratagems employed.

Or.'s explanations of unfamiliar terms are generally brief, concerned mainly with Roman institutions and shedding little light on the possible extent of the translator's classical knowledge. We are told, for instance, that consuls were *ladteowas*,[1] each man holding office for one year; that the dictator was likewise a *ladteow*, but higher in rank than the consuls; that the senate was a body first constituted by Romulus and consisting originally of 100 men, whose function it was to remain in Rome, to act as counsellors, to appoint consuls, to have authority over all the Romans and to control the treasury; that the Capitol was the Romans' *heafodstede* and housed their gods and idols; that a cohort was a *truma* of 1500 men; that a talent was worth eighty pounds; that the gold ring was a badge of the nobility; and that centaurs were creatures half horse, half man.[2] This is information which could have been derived from a wide variety of Latin sources, both classical and post-classical, but for most of it the translator need have looked no further than to a work most influential in the early Middle Ages, Isidore's *Etymologies*.[3] Occasionally, however, the details that are given can be traced back to no more than one or two possible sources. Thus, although the observation that the term Pharaoh was a title not a personal name is to be found in a number of Latin texts, the phraseology of Or.'s comment that 'on Egyptum...hiora þeaw wære þæt hi ealle hiora cyningas hetan Pharaon' suggests that it is derived from *Ægyptiorum reges omnes tunc Pharaones dicebantur* in Jerome's *Interpretatio Chronicae Eusebii*.[4] The information in the comment on the term *senatum* that the number of senators was increased to 300 would seem to have been derived from either Livy or Festus.[5] The definition – prompted by OH's description of Minucia as a *virgo Vestalis* – of a Vestal Virgin as a kind of

---

1 So BM Add. 47967 (the Lauderdale manuscript); BM Cotton Tiberius B. i, *underlatteowas*.

2 Or. 68, 2–3; 70, 1–2; 190, 28–9; 70, 36–72; 86, 30–1; 268, 29–30; 240, 32–4; 170, 27–8; 190, 13–16; and 44, 1.

3 Cf., e.g., *Isidori Hispalensis Episcopi Etymologiarum sive Originum Libri XX*, ed. W. M. Lindsay (Oxford, 1911) IX. iii. 6–7, IX. iii. 11, IX. iv. 8–9, XV. ii. 31, IX. iii. 52 and XI. iii. 37. Also *Servii Grammatici qui Feruntur in Vergilii Carmina Commentarii*, ed. G. Thilo and H. Hagen (Leipzig, 1884), *Aeneid* II. 319, VIII. 652 and VIII. 105; Augustine, *De Civitate Dei*, ed. E. Hoffman, *CSEL* XL, III. 19; etc. For the talent of eighty pounds cf. the *Leiden Glossary*, ed. J. H. Hessels (Cambridge, 1906) XXXIII. 1 and Eucherius, *Instructionum Libri Duo*, ed. C. Wotke, *CSEL* XXXI, 158; though Or.'s *LXXX* may well be an error for *LXX*: cf. Isidore XVI. xxv. 22; Servius, *Aeneid* V. 112; etc.

4 Or. 34, 25–7; Jerome, *Interpretatio Chronicae Eusebii Pamphili*, Migne, *PL* XXVII, cols. 150–2. Jerome, like Or., is referring to the *Dynastia Diospolitanorum*.

5 Or. 72, 1; Livy, *Ab Urbe Condita*, ed. W. Weissenborn and M. Müller (Leipzig, 1902 etc.) II. 1; Festus, *De Verborum Significatu*, ed. W. M. Lindsay (Leipzig, 1913), p. 304.

nun, making a vow of chastity to Diana, is apparently the result of a misunderstanding of the reference in Jerome's *Adversus Jovinianum* to the same
Minucia as being one of the innumerable *sacerdotes Dianae Tauricae et
Vestae*.[1] The comment on OH *Iani portae*, with its account of a building
with doors facing north, south, east and west, the opening of one of which
was a signal to the Romans to hitch their clothes above their knees in
readiness for war in that quarter and the closing of which was a sign of
peace and a signal to the Romans to let their clothes down to their feet
once more,[2] seems to have been inspired by a sequence of three entries in
Servius's commentary on the *Aeneid*. These entries, which deal with a description by Virgil of Roman preparations for war, not only include
references to a temple of Janus with four doors[3] and to a theory that
Janus has four faces *secundum quattuor partes mundi*[4] but also define *Gabinus
cinctus* as 'toga sic in tergum reiecta, ut una (ima?) eius lacinia a tergo
revocata hominem cingat. Hoc autem vestimenti genere veteres Latini,
cum necdum arma haberent, praecinctis togis bellebant.'[5]

Only one explanatory comment with a classical basis presents any
serious problem, that dealing with the triumph.[6] Here Or. begins ortho-
doxly enough by distinguishing between the triumph and the ceremony
that followed victory without bloodshed.[7] However, all other details apart
from the references to captives preceding the triumphal chariot (which
could have been derived from OH itself[8]) and to the senate following it
(which could have been derived from either Vopiscus or more probably
Valerius Maximus[9]) contain striking deviations from the extant Latin
descriptions of the two ceremonies. Thus the senate is said to meet the

---

[1] Or. 108, 15–17; Jerome, *Adversus Jovinianum Libri Duo*, Migne, *PL* XXIII, col. 270. That
Vesta is Proserpina and Proserpina Diana could with some difficulty be discovered from
Isidore VIII. xi. 58–9 and *Mythographus I*, ed. A. Mai, *Classicorum Auctorum e Vaticanis Codic-
ibus Editorum* (Rome, 1828) III, ccxii.

[2] Or. 106, 11–19; OH III. viii. 2.

[3] Servius, *Aeneid* VII. 607, 'inventum est simulacrum Iani cum frontibus quattuor, unde…
quattuor portarum unum templum est institutum.' Cf. Augustine, *Civ. Dei* VII. 8, 'Non
habent omnino unde quattuor ianuas, quae intrantibus et exeuntibus pateant, interpretentur
ad mundi similitudinem.'

[4] Servius, *Aeneid* VII. 610; cf. also Augustine, *Civ. Dei* VII. 8, Remigius, *Commentum in Martia-
num Capellam*, ed. C. E. Lutz (Leiden, 1962) I. vi. 1 etc.

[5] Servius, *Aeneid* VII. 612; cf. also Festus, *op. cit.* p. 67. Or.'s account may be influenced by
pictorial or sculptural representations of Roman soldiers.     [6] Or. 70, 22–35.

[7] I.e. the *ovatio* or *minor triumphus*. Cf. Festus, *op. cit.* p. 213, *ovalis corona*, and (for triumph and
*tropaeum*) Servius, *Aeneid* X. 775, Isidore XVIII. ii. 3–4 etc.     [8] OH V. i. 2.

[9] *Scriptores Historiae Augustae*, ed. E. Hohl (Leipzig, 1965) II, *Flavi Vopisci Syracusii Divus
Aurelianus* XXXIV. iv. 2; Valerius Maximus, *Factorum et Dictorum Memorabilium*, ed. C. Kempf
(Leipzig, 1888) VII. v. 4. Cf. Aulus Gellius's reference to such an order in the *ovatio*, *Noctium
Atticarum Libri XX*, ed. C. Hosius (Leipzig, 1903) V. vi. 27, and Honorius's refusal to let the
fathers march before his chariot in the *Panegyricus de Sexto Consulatu Honorii Augusti* of
Claudian, *Carmina*, ed. J. Koch (Leipzig, 1893) XXVIII. 551. Servius, *Aeneid* IV. 543, however,
states that the senate preceded the chariot. That the senators ride back to Rome in carriages
may well be Or.'s own assumption.

consuls six miles from Rome, although in actual fact the procession of the triumpher (a person holding the highest magisterial power) seems to have started from the Campus Martius.[1] The welcoming party brings with it a chariot adorned with gold and jewels and, as the text stands, two white quadrupeds,[2] although Latin accounts refer to a triumphal chariot of gold[3] drawn by four white horses.[4] As for the lesser ceremony, Or. relates how the consuls are brought a chariot adorned with silver and 'one of each kind of four-footed cattle', although in fact the ovator either walked or rode on horseback.[5] The source of these deviations, whether a lost Latin text or scribal error, faulty recollection, misunderstanding, or even the translator's imagination, cannot be determined. However, it is possible that the four-footed cattle owe their presence in the ceremonies to a reference – perhaps Servius's – to bulls or oxen as well as horses preceding the triumpher.[6]

Of the additions concerning people to be found in Or., the majority are again accurate but contain insufficient detail to enable us to identify the precise sources used. Thus the information that the Amazons were so called because of their seared breasts,[7] that Liber Pater was held to be a god after his death and to be *ealles gewinnes waldend*,[8] that Cecrops was first king of Athens, Darius the kinsman of Cyrus, Cincinnatus a poor man, Seleucus king of the east, one of the Scipios *vir optimus*, Caesar renowned for his clemency, Antony ruler of all Asia, Cleopatra the mistress of Caesar and Dido the founder of Carthage,[9] has its counterpart in many Latin texts –

[1] Cf. the entry *Triumphus* in Pauly-Wissowa, *Real-Encyclopädie der classischen Altertumswissenschaft* (Stuttgart, 1939).

[2] Or. 70, 27, *feowerfetes twa hwite* (Lauderdale MS, *hwit*) is surely corrupt. Cf. Or. 70, 34, *ælces cynnes feowerfetes feos an.* Did the translator originally refer to 'two white specimens of each kind of four-footed cattle'?

[3] Cf. Livy x. vii. 10; Florus, *Epitomae Libri II*, ed. O. Rossbach (Leipzig, 1896) I. i. 5; and Freculph, *Chronicon*, Migne, *PL* cvi, col. 985.

[4] Cf. Livy v. xxiii. 5; Ovid, *Ars Amatoria*, ed. R. Merkel, *Opera* I (Leipzig, 1852), I. 214; Servius, *Aeneid* iv. 543; Apuleius, *Apologia*, ed. R. Helm, *Opera* ii Leipzig, 1959), xxii; etc. Claudian, however, writes of two white horses (*Panegyricus* xxviii (369–70).

[5] Cf. Gellius v. vi. 27.

[6] Cf. Servius, *Georgics* ii. 147, '*Perfusi* autem tauri, qui ante triumphantes usque ad templa ducebantur: aut certe *perfusi greges* intellegamus, quod ad equos triumphales potest referri.' Also possible is a source using an expression such as the *niveis quadriiugis* of Statius, *Thebaid* xii. 521, ed. A. Klotz, *Opera* ii (Leipzig, 1908), or the *quadrigas albas* of Apuleius, *Apologia* xxii.

[7] Or. 46, 14, 'For þon hi mon hæt on Crecisc Amazanas, þæt is on Englisc *fortende*.' Here, as in the case of the comment on Cleopatra's asp (Or. 246, 24–7), the translator may well have derived his information from a gloss in his manuscript of OH. Cf. J. M. Bately, 'King Alfred and the Latin Manuscripts of Orosius's History', *Classica et Mediaevalia* xxii (1961), 69–105.

[8] Or. 36, 20–1. Cf. Isidore ix. ii. 64 and ix. ii. 32, Augustine, *Civ. Dei* xviii. 12 etc. Professor Simeon Potter's suggested emendation of *gewinnes* to *wines* ('Commentary on King Alfred's "Orosius"', *Anglia* lxxi (1953), 391) is attractive, particularly in view of Isidore xvii. v. 1, where Liber's discovery of wine and his posthumous deification are referred to together. However, the connection of Liber with war is widespread in Latin literature.

[9] Or. 36, 5–6; 78, 8–9; 88, 7; 144, 1; 148, 35; 242, 19–20; 244, 31; 246, 2; and 252, 17. The reference to Deucalion as *moncynnes tydriend* (Or. 36, 13; cf. Servius, *Aeneid* i. 743 etc.) is excluded here since its source could be OH i. ix. 2, *a quo...genus hominum reparatum ferunt.*

though it is worth noting that it could have been provided by a total of not more than four works, all of which achieved considerable popularity in the early Middle Ages: Jerome's version of Eusebius's *Chronicle*, Isidore's *Etymologies*, Augustine's *De Civitate Dei* and Bede's *De Temporum Ratione*.[1] However, there are five notable exceptions. The knowledge that Nectanebus the sorcerer was the man supposed to be Alexander the Great's father is derived from Julius Valerius, though possibly via Fulgentius.[2] The comment that Marius was Julius Caesar's uncle has no Latin equivalent and it is probable that the source was the now missing opening of Suetonius's *Life of Caesar*.[3] The remark about Titus's goodwill is, as Professor Whitelock has demonstrated, to be derived from either Jerome's version of Eusebius or his commentary on Galatians.[4] The identification of the deathplace of the consul Cinna as Smyrna is an error based ultimately on an association of the names Cinna and Smyrna to be found in the works of Catullus, Quintilian, Servius and Acron – though there the Cinna referred to is a poet and Smyrna the name of his poem.[5] The description of Julian the Apostate as a man *ær þæm to diacone gehalgod* is likewise erroneous and would seem to have as its only 'justification' a paragraph in Bede's *De Temporum Ratione* referring first to Julianus the emperor and then to a *Julianum diaconum*.[6]

Incidents about which Or. produces additional information fall into three groups: famous episodes from Roman history, battles in which noteworthy stratagems were employed, and miscellaneous events, mainly, but not exclusively, Roman. Of the famous episodes from Roman history allusions to which are expanded by Or. four – the rape of the Sabines, the rape of Lucretia, the burning of Mucius Scaevola's hand and Regulus's mission to Rome – are referred to so frequently in Latin literature that it is often difficult if not impossible to determine the sources actually used by Or. Thus the Romans' request for wives, the Sabines' refusal and the intervention of the women in the ensuing war are features of the rape of

---

[1] Cf., e.g., Jerome-Eusebius, cols. 52, 538 and 299; Isidore xv. i. 44 and xv. i. 14; Augustine, *Civ. Dei* v. 18 and ix. 5; and Bede, *De Temporum Ratione*, Migne, *PL* xc, A.M. 2798, 3389, 3629, 3966, 3925 and 2930. Although the Scipio of Augustine, *Civ. Dei* i. 30, *ille Scipio... iudicio totius senatus vir optimus*, is in fact Scipio Nasica, Or. 224, 24 (Cotton MS), *se besta 7 se selesta Romana witena 7 þegena* refers to Scipio Aemilianus.

[2] Or. 126, 25–6; Julius Valerius, *Res Gestae Alexandri Macedonis*, ed. B. Kuebler (Leipzig, 1888) i. 2–6; Fulgentius, *De Aetatibus Mundi et Hominis*, *Opera*, ed. R. Helm (Leipzig, 1898), p. 164 (extant MSS, *Dictanabo*).

[3] Or. 236, 4; cf. Plutarch, *Lives*, ed. B. Perrin (London, 1919) vii, *Caesar* i; and *ibid.* ix, *Marius* vi.

[4] Cf. *Continuations and Beginnings*, p. 74. Jerome is quoted by Freculph, col. 1146.

[5] Or. 236, 24–5. Cf. Catullus, *Carmina*, ed. M. Schuster (Leipzig, 1949) xcv. 1; Quintilianus, *Institutionis Oratoriae Libri XII*, ed. L. Radermacher (Leipzig, 1965) x. 4; Servius, *Bucolics* ix. 35 and *Georgics* i. 288; and Acron, *Art. Poet.* 388 in *Acronis et Porphyrionis Commentarii in Q. Horatium Flaccum*, ed. F. Hauthal (Berlin, 1864). See further, below, p. 250. Cinna the consul in fact died near Ancona.

[6] Or. 284, 27–8; Bede, *De Temporum Ratione*, A.M. 4316.

the Sabines[1] to be found in the accounts not only of Ovid, *Fasti* and Livy, but also of Servius, Florus, Augustine and others.[2] The references to great slaughter in the war and the duration of hostilities for many years (if not Or.'s own invention) could be derived the one from either Augustine, *De Civitate Dei* or an Orosius commentary,[3] the other from either Ovid, *Fasti* or scholia on Juvenal.[4] Ultimately from Ovid comes the observation that when the Sabine women interposed themselves between husbands and fathers they had their children with them;[5] however, this detail is also to be found in scholia on both Lucan and Juvenal[6] and Or.'s source could equally well have been one of these.

Similarly, in adding to OH *adulteratae Lucretiae* that Lucretia was wife of (Col)latinus,[7] that she was raped by Tarquin's son and that Brutus and Collatinus were responsible for driving out the Tarquins, Or. is using details given by a number of writers, including Livy, Cicero, Ovid, Eutropius (followed by Paulus Diaconus), Servius (followed by Mythographus I) and Augustine.[8] The absence of Brutus and Collatinus with the army is a feature of the accounts of Livy, Ovid, Paulus Diaconus, Servius and Mythographus I. Only the surprising claim that Lucretia was Brutus's sister has no more than three possible sources:[9] Augustine's reference to Brutus as *propinquus* of Lucretia; the description in *De Viris Illustribus* of first Collatinus then Brutus as *sorore Tarquinii superbi genitus*; and a misreading of Eutropius, *Brutus, parens et ipse Tarquini, populum concitavit* as *parens et ipsae* (sc. *Lucretiae*) *Tarquini populum concitavit*.[10]

As for the interrogation of Mucius Scaevola, when Mucius, having refused under torture to say how many men had declared hostility towards Tarquin and being then asked how many there were like him, replies that 'ðær fela þara monna wære, 7 eac gesworen hæfdon ðæt hie oþer forleosan

---

[1] Or. 64, 25–66, 3. The deceitful invitation, the seizing of the Sabine women as wives and subsequent slaughter are details given by OH II. iv. 2.

[2] Cf. Livy I. ix; Ovid, *Opera* III, *Fasti* III. 189–228; Servius, *Aeneid* VIII. 635; Florus I. i; Augustine, *Civ. Dei* II. 17; etc. For the interpretation of the *ludis* of OH II. iv. 5 as a sacrifice to the gods cf. references to *ludi* as honours paid to the gods (*Civ. Dei* II. 27; Festus, *op. cit.* p. 109; etc.) or to the occasion as being a feast for Neptune or Consus (Livy, Ovid, Servius etc.).

[3] Augustine, *Civ. Dei* III. 13; fragmentary Orosius Commentary in Rome, Vatican Library, Codices Reginenses Latini 1650, 7v.

[4] Ovid, *Fasti* III. 204; *Scholia in Iuvenalem Vetustiora*, ed. P. Wessner (Stuttgart, 1967) VI. 163. 2.

[5] Ovid, *Fasti* III. 217–24.

[6] *Adnotationes super Lucanum*, ed. J. Endt (Leipzig, 1909) I. 118; *Scholia in Iuvenalem* VI. 163. 2.

[7] Both manuscripts of Or. read *Latinus*.

[8] Or. 66, 30–68, 1. Cf. Livy I. lvii–lx; Cicero, *De Re Publica*, ed. C. F. W. Mueller, *Opera* IV. 2 (Leipzig, 1878), II. 25; Ovid, *Fasti* II. 721–852; Eutropius, *Breviarium Historiae Romanae*, ed H. R. Dietsch (Leipzig, 1849) I. 8; Paulus Diaconus, *Historia Miscella*, Migne, PL XCV, col. 750; Servius, *Aeneid* VIII. 646; *Mythographus I* lxxiv; Augustine, *Civ. Dei* I. 19; etc.

[9] It may be no more than coincidence that Or., like Florus and Augustine, omits all reference to Lucretia's father.

[10] Augustine *Civ. Dei* I. xviii; *Liber de Viris Illustribus* 9. 1 and 10. 1 (ptd in Aurelius Victor, *Liber de Caesaribus*, ed. F. Pichlmayer [Leipzig, 1911]); Eutropius I. 8. -*e* for -*ae* is common in Latin manuscripts of the early Middle Ages.

woldon, oþþe hira agen lif, oþþe Porsennes þæs cyninges,'[1] the details of this are ultimately based on Livy II. 12, where Porsenna, having been told by Mucius 'Nec unus in te ego hos animos gessi: longus post me ordo est idem petentium decus', orders him to be burnt alive, 'nisi expromeret propere, quas insidiarum sibi minas per ambages iaceret'. Mucius, having then placed his hand in the fire of his own accord and been told that he may go free, tells Porsenna, as it were in gratitude, what he could not force from him by threats, 'trecenti coniuravimus principes iuventutis Romanae, ut in hac via grassaremur', a speech which is echoed by several versions of the story.[2] However, the vague reply given in Or., that there were *many* such as Mucius who had sworn to kill Porsenna, could have been derived from either Augustine or the Statius commentary of Lactantius Placidus[3] and the other details could be Or.'s own invention, arising from the (erroneous) supposition that the burning of Mucius's hand was a torture inflicted by Porsenna, not a voluntary act of courage.[4]

Again, in its version of the Regulus story,[5] when Or. narrates how Regulus had sworn in the gods' names to carry the Carthaginians' message and bring back a reply,[6] how part of his mission was to arrange an exchange of prisoners, how he urged the Romans not to accept[7] and how the grounds for refusal were the shamefulness and inequality of such an exchange,[8] it may be drawing on one or more of a wide variety of Latin texts. Only Regulus's reply to the Romans' insistence[9] that he should remain in Rome has apparently no more than two possible sources: 'cwæð þæt hit na geweorþan sceolde þæt se wære leoda cyning se þe ær wæs folce þeow' could be echoing either Augustine, *De Civitate Dei*, 'respondisse fertur, postea quam Afris servierat, dignitatem illic honesti civis habere non posset' or an almost identical statement in Eutropius.[10]

---

[1] Or. 68, 21–9. According to OH II. v. 3 Mucius moved the enemy *constanti urendae manus patientia*.  [2] E.g. Florus I. 4; Freculph I. iv. 2; *De Viris* 12. 4.

[3] Augustine, *Civ. Dei* v. 18, 'Mucius [dixit] multos tales, qualem illum videret, in eius exitium coniurasse'; Lactantius Placidus, *Commentarii Statii Thebaida*, ed. R. Jahnke, P. *Papinius Statius, Opera* III (Leipzig, 1898), II. 703, *plures.*

[4] The immediate withdrawal of Porsenna (Or. 68, 30) is a feature of the accounts of Livy, Augustine and *De Viris*.

[5] Or. 178, 5–25. OH IV. x. 1 relates merely how Regulus was sent to Rome to arrange a peace and how, when he returned without having done so, he was put to death by the Carthaginians.

[6] According to Livy, *Periochia* XVIII, Cicero, *De Officiis*, ed. R. Klotz, *Opera* IV. 3 (Leipzig, 1876), III. 26, *De Viris* 40. 4, Augustine, *Civ. Dei* I. 15 etc. Regulus swore to return if unsuccessful.

[7] So Livy, Cicero, *De Viris* and Augustine. Other possible sources include Eutropius II. 25; Florus I. 18; Silius Italicus, *Punica*, ed. L. Bauer (Leipzig, 1890–2) VI. 346–9; Horace, *Carmina*, ed. F. Vollmer (Leipzig, 1912) III. v, and Porphyrio's scholia on this ode (ed. F. Hauthal, *op. cit.*); Valerius Maximus I. i. 14; and Tertullian, *Liber ad Martyres*, Migne, PL I, col. 625.  [8] See below, p. 251.

[9] Cf. Augustine, *Civ. Dei* v. 18; Eutropius II. 25; and Horace, *Odes* III. v. 53, and Porphyrio's comment on this line.

[10] Or. 178, 20–1; Augustine, *Civ. Dei* v. 18; Eutropius II. 28, followed by Paulus Diaconus, col. 774.

A fifth famous episode from Roman history of which Or. gives additional details is Cato's suicide. While OH states merely that Cato killed himself at Utica, Or. relates first how Cato urged his son to go to meet Caesar and seek his protection, '"for þon", cwæð he, "þe ic wat þæt nan swa god man ne leofað swa he is on þeosan life, þeh þe he me sie se laþesta, 7 for þon eac ic ne mæg findan æt me seolfum þæt ic hine æfre geseo"', and second how Cato then went to the town wall and *fleah ut ofer, þæt he eall tobærst.*[1] The details of Cato's speech before suicide are most probably to be derived from Augustine's *De Civitate Dei*, where it is said that Cato commanded his son to hope for Caesar's clemency but refused it for himself, possibly because he envied Caesar the glory he would win by sparing him.[2] However, *De Viris Illustribus* also tells how Cato urged his son *ut clementiam Caesaris experiretur*, while Valerius Maximus reports Caesar as saying of the dead Cato *et se illius gloriae invidere et illum suae invidisse* – using the same verb as Augustine, *invidere*, the possible meanings of whose root include not only 'envy' but also (as in Or.) 'hate'.[3] As for the details of the suicide itself, these would appear to be derived, as the result of misunderstanding or careless reading, from a text in which the suicide of Cato is linked with the suicide by leaping from a wall of a certain Cleombrotus. Such a text is Firmianus Lactantius's *Divine Institutions.*[4]

Of the military stratagems which Or. supplies only three are unconnected with the Punic wars: those purportedly used by Philip against the Scythians, by Fulvius against the Gallograeci and by Marius against the Numidians. According to Or., the 'trick' that Philip of Macedon used against the Scythians[5] was the concealing of a third of his forces and the ordering of the remainder when battle commenced to flee towards this body, 'þæt he siþþan mid þæm ðriddan dæle hie beswican mehte, þonne hie tofarene wæron' – an ambush of a type not infrequently reported in Latin literature.[6] However, there is no evidence whatsoever that Philip used such a stratagem. Or.'s source here would appear to be a passage from Frontinus's *Stratagems* in which are described Philip's

---

[1] Or. 242, 30–244, 5; OH VI. xvi. 4.

[2] Augustine, *Civ. Dei* I. 23.

[3] *De Viris* 80. 4; Valerius Maximus V. i. 10.

[4] Migne, *PL* VI, col. 408, 'Cato...antequam se occideret, perlegisse Platonis librum dicitur, qui est scriptus de aeternitate animarum, et ad summum nefas philosophi auctoritate compulsus est; et hic tamen aliquam moriendi causam videtur habuisse, odium servitutis. Quid Ambraciotes ille, qui cum eumdum librum perlegisset praecipitem se dedit, nullam aliam ob causam, nisi quod Platoni credidit?' The suicide of Cleombrotus the Ambraciot is linked with that of Cato also in a (spurious?) epistle of Jerome (Migne, *PL* xxx, col. 263), but here Cato is correctly described as stabbing himself with a sword. In Augustine, *Civ. Dei* the two suicides are referred to in adjacent chapters, I. 22 and I. 23, the manner of only 'Theobrotus's' death being described.

[5] Or. 116, 25–30; OH III. xiii. 6, *fraude.*

[6] Cf., e.g., Frontinus, *Strategematon Libri IV*, ed. G. Gundermann (Leipzig, 1888) II. v. For the convention of dividing an army into three parts cf. also Or. 52, 32–3 and 76, 20–2.

precautions against flight by his own men during battle with the Scythians, the king being said to have placed his trustiest cavalry in the rear to kill any one who should attempt to leave the battlefield.[1] Or.'s account of Fulvius's battle against the Gallo-Greeks on Mount Olympus in 189 B.C. is also derived from Frontinus's *Stratagems*, though as the result of a somewhat different misapprehension. According to Or., Fulvius, hoping to entice the enemy out of their stronghold, ordered some of his men to withdraw and the others to flee towards them when battle was at its height. In their subsequent flight back to their stronghold 40,000 of the townsfolk were slain.[2] This corresponds to Frontinus's account of the strategy employed by a commander named Fulvius, who, discovering that whenever his cavalry withdrew in pretended flight the enemy habitually followed in hot pursuit and left their camp exposed, concealed himself with a body of men behind the camp and captured it when the enemy poured forth after the cavalry as usual.[3] However, although the name of the commander is in each case the same, the occasions are different. The Fulvius of Frontinus is fighting not the Gallo-Greeks but the Cimbrians. As for the 'outwitting' of the Numidians at Capsa,[4] when Or. explains that Marius achieved this by making for a certain town as though intending to attack it, but as soon as Jugurtha had led his army there marching off to another and taking that, it is again oversimplifying and misrepresenting a classical source, this time Sallust's *Bellum Jugurthinum*.[5] According to Sallust, Marius, in order to conceal his real objective, is said to have made out that he was going to Lares. Then, marching by night until he was close to Capsa, he kept his army hidden until the Numidians, unsuspecting, came out of the town in force.

The majority of stratagems elaborated on by Or., however, are associated with the Carthaginian wars. From Frontinus come the details of Xanthippus's fight against Regulus,[6] of the battle of Trasimene[7] and of

---

[1] Frontinus II. viii. 14.

[2] Or. 206, 15–20; OH IV. xx. 25, 'usque ad congressum hostium perruperunt: quadraginta millia Gallograecorum eo proelio interfecta referuntur.'

[3] Frontinus II. v. 8.

[4] Or. 230, 1–6; OH v. xv. 8, *Marius urbem Capsam dolo circumvenit et cepit.*

[5] Sallust, *Bellum Iugurthinum*, ed. A. Kurfess (Leipzig, 1957), xci.

[6] Or. 174, 32–176, 3, '[Exantipus] gesette twa folc diegellice on twa healfa his 7 þridde beæftan him; 7 bebead þæm twam folcum þonne he self mid þæm fyrmestan dæle wið þæs æftemestan fluge, þæt hie þonne on Reguluses fird on twa healfa þwyres on fore.' Frontinus II. iii. 10, 'Xanthippus...adversus M. Atilium Regulum levem armaturam in prima acie conlocavit, in subsidio autem robur exercitus praecepitque auxiliaribus, ut emissis telis cederent hosti et, cum se intra suorum ordines recepissent, confestim in latera discurrerent et a cornibus rursus erumperunt; exceptumque iam hostem a robustioribus et ipsi circumierunt.' This is the second of Frontinus's two references to the battle.

[7] Or. would seem here to be combining Frontinus and OH. Or. 188, 8–16, 'Mid þæm þe Hannibal to ðæm londe becom, swa gewicade he an anre diegelre stowe, neah þæm oþrum folce. 7 sum his folc sende gind þæt lond to bærnanne 7 to hergenne, þætte se consul wæs wenende þæt eall þæt folc wære gind þæt lond tobræd, 7 þiderweard farende wæs, 7 þencende

Claudius Marcellus's attack on Hannibal, 216 B.C., though once again distorted by oversimplification and misunderstanding and, in the last instance, misapplication, the Claudius Marcellus referred to by Frontinus being an officer of Marius engaged against the Teutons in 102 B.C.[1] Or.'s description of Scipio's act of arson at Utica as directed against only one of the enemy's two camps could likewise be taken from Frontinus, though, like the claim that Scipio took Carthagena by coming upon it *on ungearwe*, it could equally well have been derived from Livy.[2]

Material from Livy certainly seems to have been used by Or. Thus, when Or. describes Hanno as coming upon Scipio *unwærlice*, it appears to have some knowledge of the ambush into which the Carthaginians on that occasion were drawn, an account of which I have found only in Livy.[3] When it relates how Fabius Maximus took a fleet to Tarentum *swa Hannibal nyste* and attacked the town by night *swa þa nyston þe þærinne wæron*, it seems to be echoing Livy's detailed account, in which Hannibal is said not to have heard of the attack until it was too late for him to intervene, Fabius having asked Marcellus to detain him *acerrimo bello...dum ipse Tarentum oppugnaret*, and in which Fabius is said to have made a sudden attack at first watch, using ships and reaching the market-place at about daybreak.[4]

It is from Valerius Maximus, however, that Or. seems to have derived its knowledge of one stratagem used in the Punic Wars – that devised by Hannibal at Cannae. Or. relates how Hannibal tricked the Romans in the same way as he had done before and also in a new way: 'þæt wæs, ðæt he on fæstre stowe let sum his folc, 7 mid sumum for angean þa consulas; 7 raðe

þæt he hie on þære hergunge beswice, 7 þæt folc buton truman lædde, swa he wiste þæt þæt oþer wæs, oþþæt Hannibal him com þwyres on mid þæm fultume þe he ætgædere hæfde.' Frontinus II. v. 24, 'Idem ad Trasumennum...simulata fuga per angustias ad (*mistakenly read a*?) patentia evasit ibique castra posuit ac nocte dispositis militibus et per collem, qui imminebat, et in lateribus angustiarum prima luce...aciem direxit. Flaminius velut fugientem insequens (*cf. Or.* buton truman *etc.*), cum angustias esset ingressus, non ante providit insidias, quam simul a fronte, lateribus, tergo circumfusus ad internecionem cum exercitu caederetur. OH IV. xv. 4, 'Ubi vero proximus castris Flaminii consulis fuit, vastatione circumiacientium locorum Flaminium in bellum excitavit.' Cf. Livy XXII. iv, *in frontem lateraque pugnari coeptus est.*

[1] Or. 192, 11–13, 'He (*sc.* Claudius Marcellus) for dearnenga mid gewealdene fultume on þone ende Hannibales folces þe he self on wæs 7 fela þæs folces ofslog.' Frontinus II. iv. 6, 'Marius ...Marcellum cum parva manu equitum editumque nocte post terga hostium misit.' Cf. OH IV. xvi. 12, *Claudius Marcellus...Hannibalis exercitum proelio fudit.* Frontinus goes on to describe his Marcellus as using campfollowers to give the appearance of a large force, which is precisely what the other Marcellus is said to have done (cf. Livy XXIII. xvi. 8 and Frontinus II. iv. 8), and it is tempting to suppose a manuscript gloss or note to the effect that similar tactics were used by Marcellus against Hannibal.

[2] Or. 200, 14–15; Frontinus II. v. 29; Livy XXX. v and vi; and Or. 196, 25; Frontinus III. ix. 1; Livy XXVI. xlii. 5. The reference to the guards at Utica being far from the camp (Or. 200, 12) perhaps owes something to the accounts in Frontinus I. ii. 1 or Livy XXX. iv. 1–3 of spying by Scipio's men.

[3] Or. 200, 4; Livy XXIX. xxxiv.

[4] Or. 198, 6–9; Livy XVII. xii, xv and xvi. Cf. OH IV. xviii. 5, *Fabius...Tarentum...iterum expugnavit et cepit.*

þæs þe hie tosomne comon, he fleah wið þara þe þær beæftan wæron, 7 him
þa consulas wæron æfterfylgende, 7 þæt folc sleande, 7 wenden þæt hie on
ðæm dæge sceoldon habban þone mæstan sige. Ac raðe þæs þe Hannibal to
his fultume com, he gefliemde ealle þa consulas...' This corresponds to
Valerius Maximus's account of how Hannibal ordered part of his forces
to simulate flight in the middle of battle, 'quam cum a reliquo exercitu
abrupta legio Romana sequeretur, trucidandam eam ab his, quos in insidiis
collocaverat, curavit.'[1]

Of the other additions concerning incidents only six[2] are unconnected
with Roman history. OH's allusion to the rape of Helen is expanded by
a brief comment informing the reader who Helen was and who abducted
her, the numerous possible sources of which include the fragmentary
Orosius commentary.[3] The meeting of the Amazons for the *externos concu-
bitus* referred to by OH I. xv. 3 is said to be annual, a detail presumably
ultimately derived from Julius Valerius, though it may have reached the
translator via Jordanes or the Orosius commentary or Servius.[4] Theseus
replaces Miltiades as leader at Marathon and is said to have achieved
*micelne dom* in that battle – an alteration to the text which could be based
either on a misconstruing of Pomponius Mela, 'Marathon magnarum
multarumque virtutem testis iam inde a Theseo, Persica maxime clade,
pernotus', as Professor Whitelock has pointed out, or on Lactantius
Placidus, 'Marathon...quam cum Persae invasissent, ab Atheniensibus
Theseo duce caede magnorum virorum liberati sunt', if not on a combination of the two.[5] Philip of Macedon's reason for attacking the Thessali
is said to have been that they were the first to fight on horseback and the
best at it, a claim which must be linked with Or.'s earlier explanation that
the Thessali were called Centaurs by the Lapiths 'for þon hie on horse
feohtan ne gesawon ær þa',[6] and which would appear to have as its source
Pliny's comment that the Thessali called Centaurs were said to have

---

[1] Or. 188, 32–190, 7; Valerius Maximus VII. iv. ext. 2. Livy XXII. xlvii and Frontinus II.
iii. 7 are less close here.

[2] I exclude the reference to Alexander as drunk when he killed Clitus (Or. 130, 25; cf. Justinus,
*Epitoma Historiarum Pompei Trogi*, ed. F. Ruehl [Leipzig, 1886] XII. 6, Quintus Curtius Rufus,
*Historiae Alexandri Magni*, ed. E. Hedicke [Leipzig, 1908] VIII. i. 43–4 and Seneca, *Epistulae
Morales*, ed. O. Hense, *Opera* III [Leipzig, 1898], LXXXIII. 19) and the suggestion of a
vengeance motive at Thermopylae (Or. 80, 19–22; cf. Justinus II. xi. 3), since these could
be Or.'s own deduction from OH II. ix. 4 and III. xviii. 8.

[3] Or. 50, 6–8; cf. Commentary, 71.

[4] Or. 46, 8–9; Julius Valerius III. 45; Jordanes, *De Gothorum Origine*, Migne, PL LXIX, col. 1258;
Commentary, 71; Servius, *Aeneid* XI. 659.

[5] Or. 78, 26–8 (both MSS, *Htesseus*); Pomponius Mela, *Chorographia*, ed. C. Frick (Leipzig,
1880) II. 3 (cf. *Continuations and Beginnings*, p. 91); Lactantius Placidus, *Commentarii in Statii
Thebaida* V. 531. This comment includes a reference to Marathon as a mountain; cf. Or.
78, 25, ðære dune...Morotthonie.

[6] Or. 112, 3–4 and 42, 32–44, 2. OH's explanation (I. xiii. 4) is that man and horse seemed to be
one body.

invented fighting on horseback.[1] Finally Darius is said to have been found pierced by spears and Alexander to have been stoned, details for which the only parallels that I know of are in Quintus Curtius.[2]

As for the Roman additions, these are concerned mainly, but not exclusively, with the Punic wars and Caesar's struggle for power.[3] Often there is more than one possible source. Thus, that Manlius Torquatus had his son executed because he engaged in single combat against orders is a detail to be found in Livy, Valerius Maximus, Florus, Augustine, Jerome and others.[4] The information that Caesar demanded a triumph on his return from Gaul is common to Servius, Lucan scholia and *De Viris*,[5] that Pompey sought help from Ptolemy is common to Caesar, Eutropius (followed by Paulus Diaconus) and Bede,[6] and that Hadrian rebuilt Jerusalem 'in another place' is common to Gregory the Great, the *Liber Nominum Locorum ex Actis* and Christian of Stavelot.[7] Or.'s description of Julius Caesar's behaviour at Munda, when Caesar, fearing that he might be taken prisoner, *for þære ondrædinge þæs þe swiþor on þæt weorod þrong*,[8] could be based either on Frontinus *in primam aciem pedes prosiluit* or on similar statements in Florus and Velleius Paterculus, though in the latter Munda is not mentioned by name.[9] The theory that Scipio Aemilianus was smothered in his bed could have been derived from either Velleius Paterculus or Sidonius.[10] However, in three instances there appears to be only one extant

[1] *Naturalis Historiae Libri XXXVII*, ed. C. Mayhoff (Leipzig, 1906) VII. lvi. 202. Less close is the explanation that the Thessali were called Centaurs because they were the first to break in horses: cf. Isidore XIV. iv. 12; *Mythographus I* clxiii; and Servius, *Georgics* III. 115.

[2] Or. 128, 14 and 134, 15–16; Quintus Curtius V. xiii. 16 (*tela*) and IX. iv.

[3] I exclude references to Scipio's son placing himself in front of his wounded father at Ticinum (Or. 186, 23–6; cf. Valerius Maximus V. iv. 2), to Scipio persuading the Romans to let him invade Hannibal's land (Or. 198, 36–200, 1; cf. Livy XXVIII. xl) and to the peace terms of the Second Punic War (Or. 202, 20–3; cf. Livy XXX. xxxvii, but note Or. 180, 12–14), since these could be Or.'s own deductions.

[4] Or. 108, 7–11; Livy VIII. vi. 16 and vii; Valerius Maximus VI. ix. 1; Florus I. ix; Augustine, *Civ. Dei* I. 23 and v. 18; Jerome-Eusebius, col. 474. According to Livy, the disregarded command was that no man should quit his place to attack the foe. See further, below, p. 250.

[5] Or. 240, 1–2; Servius, *Aeneid* I. 286; *Adnotationes super Lucanum* I. 202; *De Viris* 78. 5.

[6] Or. 242, 15–16; Caesar, *Commentarii Belli Civilis*, ed. A. Klotz, *Opera* II (Leipzig, 1952), III. 103. 3; Eutropius VI. 21; Paulus Diaconus, col. 847; Bede, *De Temporum Ratione*, A.M. 3925.

[7] Or. 266, 17; Gregory the Great, *Homilia XIII in Evangelia*, Migne, *PL* LXXVI, col. 1294; *Liber Nominum*, Migne, *PL* XXIII, col. 1301; Christian of Stavelot, *Expositio in Matthaeum*, Migne, *PL* CVI, col. 1454.

[8] Or. 244, 11–13. Or. mistakenly interprets OH VI. xvi. 7, *praevenire morte futurum victi dedecus cogitavit* as referring to death in battle not suicide.

[9] Frontinus II. viii. 13; Velleius Paterculus, *Historiae Romanae Libri II*, ed. C. Stegman de Pritzwald (Stuttgart, 1965) II. lv. 3; Florus II. xiii. 82.

[10] Or. 224, 34; Velleius Paterculus II. iv. 5; Sidonius, *Opera*, ed. P. Mohr (Leipzig, 1895), *Epistulae* VIII. xi. Or.'s claim (172, 1–2) that Diulius's ships were the first ever built by the Romans may be a garbled version of the information that Duilius was the first to win a naval triumph (so Valerius Maximus III. vi. 4, Jerome, *Adversus Jovinianum*, col. 255 etc.). Cf., however, Eutropius II. 20, 'Primum Romani C. Duilio et Cn. Cornelio Asina coss. in mari

possible source. Or.'s comment that the title Augustus was given to Octavianus because his victory over Antony took place in the month of August[1] is based on a misunderstanding of Bede's 'Augustus mensis Sextilis antea vocabatur, donec honor Augusto daretur ex senatusconsulto, eo quo ipse die primo hujus mensis Antonium et Cleopatram superavit.'[2] The reference to Nerva (and his aide Trajan) deciding to change all Diocletian's decrees is paralleled only by Jerome's version of Eusebius's *Chronicle*,[3] while, as Professor Whitelock has pointed out, the treatment of the portents in Augustus's reign[4] appears to owe something to this work and to pseudo-Jerome's commentary on Luke.[5]

It would seem, then, that the classical additions to be found in Or. are to be traced back to a variety of Latin sources, including Livy, Sallust, Pliny the Elder, Quintus Curtius, Frontinus, Valerius Maximus, Servius,[6] Jerome,[7] Bede and (though the evidence is not conclusive) probably also Augustine, Firmianus Lactantius and Suetonius. In one instance details added by Or. appear to be derived from either Pomponius Mela or Lactantius Placidus, in another from either Velleius Paterculus or Sidonius.[8] A handful of additions use material from Ovid's *Fasti* and Julius Valerius, but in the case of the former this may have reached Or. via scholia on Juvenal or on Lucan, and in the case of the latter via Fulgentius and any one of Jordanes or Servius or the Orosius commentary.[9] Other possible sources include Isidore, Eutropius (direct or via Paulus Diaconus), Florus, Festus and *De Viris*,[10] though of these only Festus, *De Verborum Significatu* contains material in common with Or. that is not also to be

---

dimicaverunt paratis navibus rostratis...' and the comment in a Greek source (Polybius, *Histories*, ed. T. Büttner-Wobst [Leipzig, 1904] I. xxii. I) that up to that time the Romans had no fleet of their own, first building one to fight the Carthaginians.

[1] Or. 246, 16–18; OH VI. xix. 16, *kalendas Sextilibus.* OH VI. xx. 2 assigns the title-giving to 6 January.

[2] *De Temporum Ratione*, col. 351. For a somewhat different rendering of this comment cf. *An Old English Martyrology*, ed. G. Herzfeld, EETS o.s. 116 (London, 1900), 134f.

[3] Or. 264, 18–21; Jerome-Eusebius, col. 603, *Nerva: Senatus decrevit ut omnia quae Domitianus statuerat, in irritum deducerentur.*

[4] Or. 248, 15–29. Or.'s comment on the census may owe something to Bede's commentary on Luke, Migne, *PL* xcii, cols. 328–9.

[5] Or. 248, 6–13; Jerome-Eusebius, col. 542; *Expositio in Evangelium Secundum Lucam*, Migne, *PL* xxx, cols. 587f. (cf. *Continuations and Beginnings*, p. 91). With Or.'s allusion to a golden ring round the sun (pseudo-Jerome on Luke, *circulus aereus*, presumably misread *aureus*) cf. *Die Vercelli Homilien*, ed. M. Förster (Hamburg, 1932), p. 115.

[6] On the *Aeneid*, less certainly on the *Georgics* and *Bucolics.*

[7] *Adversus Jovinianum, Interpretatio Chronicae Eusebii Pamphili* and (pseudo-Jerome's) commentary on Luke, less certainly the commentary on Galatians.

[8] Lactantius Placidus elsewhere provides an alternative to Augustine, Velleius Paterculus to Frontinus and Florus.

[9] The Orosius commentary elsewhere provides an alternative to Augustine, the Lucan scholia to Servius and *De Viris.*

[10] For the possible use of Horace, see below, p. 251. Less likely sources include Caesar, Vopiscus, Acron, Catullus and Quintilian.

found in two or more other Latin works of which at least one is apparently elsewhere an actual source of material in Or.

However, Or.'s immediate source may have been none of these works. Some of the additions may have been present in the manuscript of OH used by the translator.[1] Others may have been derived from a Latin-Latin[2] or Latin-Old English glossary,[3] from oral communications with scholars or from a (Latin?) commentary.[4] There are a number of features that would appear to support second-hand derivation of this kind. First of all, the translator frequently shows ignorance of incidents or people described in the texts from which he is apparently quoting and sometimes incorporates a relevant comment in an irrelevant or even ludicrous manner. Thus, for example, the Minotaur is half man, half lion,[5] Cincinnatus is no more than 'a certain poor man', Smyrna, the title of a poem, becomes the deathplace of a consul,[6] the story of Torquatus with its additions is attached to Decius Mus.[7] Numitor becomes Romulus's uncle, most probably because of a gloss or comment on OH *avo Numitore* pointing out that Romulus in fact killed not his grandfather but his (great)-uncle.[8] Tarquin is said to have been challenged by Brutus but to have sent *Arrunses sunu ðæs ofermodgan* in his stead,[9] most probably because of a gloss or comment *pro Tarquinio* intended to refer to the *Superbi* of OH *cum Arrunte, Superbi filio, congresso*. Again, the description of Philip of Macedon as wounded in the thigh by a woman is surely most plausibly accounted for if we assume a gloss *femine* for OH *femore*,[10] while Or.'s claim that Valerianus was *mid Emilitum þæm folce* would appear to depend on a gloss or comment such as *a militibus* on OH *ab exercitu*.[11]

[1] For additions certainly present in that manuscript, e.g. the Aeacida quotation from Ennius and the reference to the Dead Sea Fruit, cf. Bately, 'King Alfred and the Latin Manuscripts of Orosius's History'.

[2] Cf., e.g., the *Glossarium Ansileubi*, ed. W. M. Lindsay *et al.*, *Glossaria Latina* (Paris, 1926–31) I, with its extensive quotation from Isidore, Augustine, *Civ. Dei* etc.

[3] Cf. Bately, *loc. cit.* p. 99.

[4] For King Alfred's apparent use of a Latin commentary in translating the Boethius, cf. K. Otten, *König Alfreds Boethius* (Tübingen, 1964), pp. 119–57.

[5] Or. 42, 29–30. For the correct definition cf. Isidore XI. iii. 38 and many other popular Latin sources.

[6] See above, pp. 240 and 241.

[7] Or. 108, 4–14; see above, p. 248. The origin of this most surprising error is probably the wording of OH III. ix. 1, *unus consul interfectus est, alter exstitit parricida*, following as it does immediately on the naming of the consuls in the order Torquatus and Mus.

[8] Or. 66, 5 and 66, 9; OH II. v. 2. For the killing of the *avunculus* or *patruus* Amulius cf. Livy, Servius, Florus, Ovid, Jerome etc. A second apparent instance of 'confusion' of the words *avus* and *avunculus* (Or. 54, 8) is in fact due to a variant reading in the Latin manuscripts.

[9] Or. 68, 17–18; OH II. v. 2. The translator may have intended accusative singular *Arruns*. Cf genitives such as Or. 240, 26, *Pompeius* (Lauderdale MS; Cotton, *Pompeiuses*).

[10] Or. 118, 2; OH III. xiii. 8. Cf. the *femine: femore* of Latin glossaries such as *Abstrusa*. For *-e* = *-ae* see above, p. 242.

[11] Or. 274, 18; OH VII. xxii. 1. Cf. Or. 286, 15, *Actesifonte* (OH *a Ctesiphonte*) and 188, 30 *Amilius* (OH MSS, *Emilius*).

Yet another addition combines themes found in certain Latin texts in a way which suggests ignorance or at least independence of those texts. In its version of the Regulus story, Or., in making Regulus oppose the exchange of prisoners because 'him to micel æwisce wære þæt he swa emnlice wrixleden, 7 eac þæt hiora gerisna nære þæt hie swa heane hie geþohten þæt hi heora gelican wurden',[1] seems to be elaborating on a source stating merely that the opposition was on the grounds of shamefulness and inequality and not to be using directly any of the Latin texts still extant. In these the themes of shamefulness and inequality certainly appear, but in a different guise: the terms are shameful,[2] the Romans have become disgraced and degraded by their captivity,[3] there is inequality between the prisoners on the two sides as regards numbers, age and vigour.[4] Again, although on the one hand the use of certain passages from Livy, Frontinus, Sallust and Valerius Maximus suggests great interest in military stratagems, on the other hand the translator's rendering of them shows an indifference to the manœuvres involved and a naiveté in handling them which cannot be explained away on the grounds of faulty recollection, the inadequacies of Old English as a language or the translator's ignorance of Latin.[5]

Unfortunately, these features, while strongly suggesting that the translator learned of at least some of the classical additions in Or.[6] in the form of a gloss or commentary on OH, do not in themselves prove that he did. Nonetheless, even though we can do no more than guess at the channels through which the translator's information reached him, and even though if a commentary was used this could well have been continental not English in origin, a study of the sources of the classical additions in Or. sheds considerable light on the quality of the translator's classical knowledge as displayed in this work and explains a number of peculiar features in the translation. To this extent it may be claimed to contribute a little to our knowledge of learning in England before the Conquest.

[1] Or. 178, 15–18.  [2] So Horace, *Odes* III. v.
[3] So Horace, *Odes* III. v. 26–7 and scholia.
[4] So Valerius Maximus I. i. 14; Eutropius II. 25; Silius Italicus VI. 479. 81; Tertullian, *Apology*, Migne, *PL* I, col. 532; etc. For Or.'s apparent ignorance of the elephant cf. J. E. Cross, 'The Elephant to Alfred, Ælfric, Aldhelm and Others', *SN* XXXVII (1965), 367–73.
[5] Equally suggestive, though not conclusive, is the passing over of material when it appears in OH and its insertion elsewhere: cf. the loss of 400,000 books at Alexandria, casually referred to in connection with the burning of the Capitoline library (Or. 270, 2), but omitted from the translation of OH VI. xv. 31; also the echo of Suetonius (Or. 252, 25) omitted from the translation of OH VII. vii. 7.
[6] The fragment of a Latin commentary on OH that is still extant has only a handful of details in common with Or. See above, pp. 242 and 247 and (for the comment on Helen), Bately, *loc. cit.* p. 99.

# The orientation system in the Old English Orosius

## RENÉ DEROLEZ

Many a beginner in the field of Anglo-Saxon studies will have wondered why the Norwegian Ohthere, who was undoubtedly familiar with the intricacies of seafaring, told his lord King Alfred that he sailed 'due north' along the coast of northern Norway, when he was actually following a north-easterly course. If the young Anglo-Saxonist, after having found his way through the mild intricacies of Ohthere's narrative, has had the courage to do some further exploring of his own, he will have discovered other strange deviations in the system of orientation: Britain is said to extend SW–NE instead of S–N, the continental home of the Angles is located NW of the Old Saxons instead of N or even NE etc.

These deviations in the first chapter of the Old English translation of Orosius's *Historiarum adversus Paganos Libri Septem* have claimed the attention of scholars for almost two centuries now, and although it is only forty years ago that the first systematic study of the problem appeared, it is hardly possible to examine here in detail the various attempts that have been made to solve it.[1] I shall be concerned mainly with two important contributions to the discussion, and those mainly with a view to their basic assumptions. Some material that seems to have been unduly neglected in this context will also be surveyed, and by way of a conclusion a different approach will be suggested – not as a panacea with which to resolve all uncertainties, but in an attempt to place the problem in its chronological context. As I cannot hope to discuss what implications, if any, my suggestion may have for the authorship of the text, I shall refer to it as the Old English Orosius and call the author simply 'the translator'.[2]

Although the essentials of the problem will be known to any student of Old English, it may not be superfluous to remind the reader of a few points

---

[1] The merits of Henrik Gabriel Porthan, Professor of Eloquence at Åbo Akademi 1777–1804, as an editor of 'Alfred's Geography' have been duly stressed by Nils Erik Enkvist, 'Porthans "Försök at uplysa Konung Ælfreds Geographiska Beskrifning öfver den Europeiske Norden"', *Årsskrift utg. av Åbo Akademi* XXXI (1956–7).

[2] All references are to, and all quotations from, *King Alfred's Orosius*, ed. H. Sweet I, EETS o.s. 79 (London, 1883); cited henceforth as Or., references being to page and line. For an up-to-date discussion of the work see D. Whitelock, 'The Prose of Alfred's Reign', *Continuations and Beginnings: Studies in Old English Literature*, ed. E. G. Stanley (London, 1966), pp. 67–103.

which have sometimes been overlooked in the heat of the debate on the puzzling orientation. First, it will be safe to keep always in mind that the geographical chapter, and indeed the whole Old English Orosius, can be called a translation only up to a point.[1] Where it is possible to compare the Old English with the Latin original, it will often be found to have been profoundly changed and reorganized, shortened or expanded. At times – and this is not unimportant in a discussion of orientation systems – it becomes very difficult to decide which Latin word or phrase in a given context has been rendered by which Old English word or phrase; and as far as the geographical introduction is concerned, long stretches do not correspond to anything in the Latin.

Second, it is only since Miss Janet Bately's pioneering study of the Latin Orosius that we have become fully aware of the inadequacy of the eclectic text which Sweet printed on opposite pages with the Old English.[2] To be sure, misgivings had been expressed as to the way in which Sweet had cut and rearranged the Latin, but it was not known how remote the Latin original used for the translation may have been from the text in Zangemeister's edition.[3] The translator must have used an inferior, and in places perhaps even a very bad text, and until the whole of the Old English has been confronted with surviving representatives of the Latin prototype, we cannot hope to undertake a definitive study even of such subsidiary matters as the orientation problem.

Third, the Old English text that has come down to us is not always above suspicion either. For one thing, the major part of the geographical introduction has disappeared from the practically contemporary Tollemache or Lauderdale manuscript (BM Add. 47967) and so BM Cotton Tiberius B. i of the first half of the eleventh century becomes our sole witness (Or. 18, 3–42, 24).[4] Though some of its errors may well be due to a faulty Latin model or to misunderstanding of the Latin, some passages look suspiciously like scribal corruptions. When *Libia Cirimaica* (i.e. *Libya Cyrenaica*) has to the north *Wendelsæ, þe man hæt Libia Æthiopicum* (Or. 26, 1) there is decidedly something wrong with the text. The Latin has *a septentrione mare Libycum...a meridie Aethiopicus oceanus* (OH 1. ii. 89), but also *post se habet usque ad oceanum meridianum gentes Libyoaethiopum* (OH 1. ii. 88). It is not unlikely that at one stage *Libyoaethiopum* had become *Libya aethiopicum* and that the second word was understood as an adjective defining *oceanum*, upon which the whole paragraph was conflated to produce

[1] *Ibid.* p. 89 f.
[2] Janet M. Bately, 'King Alfred and the Latin Manuscripts of Orosius's History', *Classica et Mediaevalia* xxii (1961), 69–105.
[3] *CSEL* v; cited henceforth as OH, references being to book, chapter and paragraph.
[4] Ker, *Catalogue*, nos. 133 and 191. *The Tollemache Orosius*, ed. A. Campbell, EEMF 3 (Copenhagen, 1953).

the nonsense of Or. Again when we read that *Narbonense* has 'be eastan him Profentsæ; and be westan him Profentsæ ofer ða westenu seo us nearre Ispania' (Or. 22, 29 ff.) it is difficult to reject the suspicion that the second *Profentsæ* is superfluous.[1] This state of affairs also obliges us to be cautious in our study of indications of orientation which, by their very repetitiveness, must have been even more subject to corruption than the rest of the text. Thus, when the 'Britannic ocean' is said to be south-west of *Gallia Bellica* (Or. 22, 24; OH I. ii. 63, *a circio*) instead of north-west, or Constantinople has Macedonia to the east, instead of to the west (Or. 22, 8; OH I. ii. 56, *ab occasu et Africo Macedoniam*), and the Balearic Islands have Africa north of them (Or. 28, 22), it will be safe to consider the 'deviation' simply a mistake, at whatever stage of the tradition it may have occurred.

Finally, it may be useful to distinguish four or five parts in the geographical introduction. The first and the last are those where the translator was obliged to follow Orosius fairly closely because he was not likely to have better information at his disposal, viz. the descriptions of Asia (Or. 12, 3–14, 26), Africa (Or. 30, 7–35, 6) and the islands of the Mediterranean (Or. 35, 8–40, 5) – which does not exclude his treatment of the text being very free, e.g. in the section devoted to Asia Minor (Or. 10, 36 ff.).[2] Then there are those parts of Europe for which the translator had more adequate information than could be found in Orosius, and in which the political divisions had changed appreciably since Orosius's times (Or. 14, 26–35 and 22, 1–24, 23).[3] Next, there is the description of the part of continental Europe north of the Danube and east of the Rhine, about which he knew so much more (Or. 14, 28–16, 36) than Orosius, who had had to be satisfied with the statement that it included *Alania, Dacia ubi et Gothia* and *Germania, ubi plurimam partem Suebi tenent; quorum omnium sunt gentes LIIII* (OH I. ii. 53). And, finally, there is the account of the voyages of Ohthere and Wulfstan, from whom he had first-hand information (which could not be recast into the descriptive patterns of the rest of the chapter). It should be obvious that these various sections will require different approaches, if only because the descriptive procedure varies.

Orosius's technique for describing the geographical structure of an area was fairly simple: each country was taken in turn and the territories, seas, mountain ranges etc. by which it was bounded were enumerated, starting from the east and moving clockwise. Theoretically, and also in practice, this procedure was to lead to a large amount of repetition; some of the

---

[1] Kemp Malone's attempt to save the reading of the manuscript can hardly be considered successful (see below, p. 256, n. 2).

[2] See below, p. 257.

[3] Contemporary interest in Moravia, e.g., may have been stimulated by reports of the Great Moravian kingdom under Swatopluk I (871–94).

translator's abridgements are precisely the result of an attempt to do away with such repetitive matter. There was of course some danger that simplifications would leave gaps and would even upset the system of orientation, but the gain in space compensated for this inconvenience. For the *Germania* the translator proceeded even more economically: instead of repeating the procedure for each single tribe, or for a large number of them, he selected a few 'pivotal' areas (the East Franks, the Saxons, the Moravians) and enumerated the surrounding territories in clockwise or anti-clockwise order (which obliged him to insert as best he could those territories which did not abut on any of his pivotal areas).[1]

We owe the first large-scale discussion of the problem of orientation to Kemp Malone.[2] Having become convinced that Or. contained a number of instances 'of a 45° clockwise shift' of the north, he set out to prove that 'Alfred' in an impressive number of cases wrote 'north-east' when he meant north etc. Malone believed that this shift was due to the influence of an Old Scandinavian system of orientation which had its north in the astronomical NE. We shall not be concerned here with this hypothetical system of orientation, nor with the interpretation of the numerous passages from which he collects his arguments; but it will be expedient to summarize briefly some of the explicit and implicit assumptions on which he built his demonstration.

To begin with, he assumed that Orosius's terminology, and also that of the Old English, reflects an eight-point orientation system such as we know nowadays: N, NE, E etc. Moreover, he treated the terms indicating bearings very much as if they indicated precise points on a 360° horizon. Nor does he seem to have entertained any doubt as to the equivalence of such OE terms as *suðaneastan, eastansuðan, suðan and eastan* and *eastan and suðan*, all four of which he takes to mean precisely SE.[3]

Then he seems to have treated bearings and geographical features very much as if Anglo-Saxons in the ninth century had access to maps that did not differ fundamentally from the products of modern cartography. To be sure, his paper is accompanied by plates showing Konrad Miller's reconstruction of 'the world according to Orosius', and the same scholar's 'restoration' (whatever that may be) of 'the world according to Brit. Mus.

---

[1] A systematic account of this procedure was given by E. D. Laborde, 'King Alfred's System of Geographical Description in his Version of Orosius', *Geographical Journal* LXII (1923), 133–8. Except as far as its economy is concerned, the procedure was perhaps rather less systematic and original than would appear from Laborde's text and maps. As becomes apparent e.g. in the description of Moesia, the translator was following his model fairly closely: 'Moesia ab oriente habet ostia fluminis Danuuii, ab euro Thraciam, a meridie Macedoniam, ab Africo Dalmatiam, ab occasu Histriam, a circio Pannoniam, a septentrione Danuuium' (OH I. ii. 55).

[2] 'King Alfred's North: a Study in Mediaeval Geography', *Speculum* V (1930), 139–67.

[3] See below, p. 263.

MS. Cott. Tib. B v, fol. 58v',[1] but in practice he hardly ever confronted his findings with the data of these maps.

It is somewhat surprising that Malone should have looked for instances of an Old Scandinavian system of orientation in Or.'s description of other parts of the world than Europe, or even NW Europe. The implication seems to be that the translator was so much influenced by this system that he went so far as to change Orosius's data for regions such as Asia Minor or the Mediterranean. This does not sound very likely, nor are all of Malone's examples of a 45° clockwise shift equally convincing. Thus, when he sees the statement in Or. that *Cilia* (i.e. *Cilicia*) and *Issaurio* (i.e. *Isauria*) were situated between *Capodocia* and *seo læsse Asia* (Or. 12, 10f.) as another instance of 'a genuine, though indirectly expressed, displacement of the term of direction 45 degrees clockwise',[2] the displacement, if any, ought rather to be called counter-clockwise. The translator placed *Asia Minor* (the Roman province) west of Cappadocia and inserted *Cilicia* and *Isauria* between the two, consequently east of *Asia Minor*, whilst in reality they were south-east (shift from SE to E = counter-clockwise). The same applies to the description of Sicily: if the *Pelorus* (Or. *Polores*) corner of the island is said to point north instead of north-east (Or. 28, 3; cf. OH I. ii. 99, *aspicit ad aquilonem*), this again is a counter-clockwise shift, and so is the location of the Straits of Messina north of Sicily instead of *a borea*, 'to the north-east'[3] – unless the translator took both *Aquilo* and *Boreas* to mean north.

On the other hand, Malone noted that several of his clockwise shifts could be found not only in Or., but also in OH: 'in the description of Upper Egypt, Orosius himself exhibits a displacement of the terms of direction', and 'this is not the only passage in which Orosius has the same shift of 45° clockwise which we have come to associate with Alfred.'[4] In the case of Britain, which is said to extend SW–NE instead of S–N, the shift is even older than Orosius: it is to be found in Ptolemy (and in other ancient geographers: Eratosthenes, Pliny and Strabo). Strangely enough, Malone does not seem to have drawn any conclusion from this finding, nor did he examine the vocabulary of orientation in Latin and Old English before undertaking his study. Yet some of his assumptions in this matter are rather less than obvious. When he stated that 'Alfred' correctly takes *Aquilo* to mean north-east, not north,[5] and treated the rendering of *Aquilo* by 'north' in the description of Sicily as an instance of shift, he omitted to mention that the 'north' in *Be norþan þæm porte (Samera) is se muþa þære ie þe mon nemneþ Ottorogorre* (Or. 10, 12f.) corresponds to *Aquilo*

---

[1] See below, p. 267.       [2] *Loc. cit.* p. 164.
[3] *Ibid.* p. 165. The 'southern corner', corresponding to OH *ad euronotum*, would represent a clockwise shift (but only one of 22° 30, if *euronotus* meant SSE).
[4] *Ibid.* p. 164.       [5] *Ibid.* p. 149, n. 1.

in Orosius (OH i. ii. 14), and that similarly *be norþan Capodocia is þæt gefilde þe mon hæt Temeseras* (Or. 12, 9) renders *Cappadocia... habet...ab aquilone Themiscyrios campos* (OH i. ii. 25), whilst in three instances *Aquilo* is not translated (OH i. ii. 59, 66 and 104). There remains only the one instance of *westansuþan* corresponding, by a reversal in the description, to *ab aquilone* in Orosius.[1]

Rudolf Ekblom's attempt to disentangle the orientation of the geographical chapter showed some progress over Malone's, both because he set out from a systematic analysis of the text and because he restricted his study to the description of Europe, the only area about which the translator could be expected *a priori* to know much more than Orosius and hence to deviate freely from his model.[2] Ekblom adopted the idea of the pivotal points (apparently without knowing Laborde's paper) and set out to prove 'Alfred's and his informants' use of Old Scandinavian orientation'. Of the sixty-two indications of orientation in the passage in question, he found that twenty-three deviated considerably clockwise in precisely the same way as a number of similar indications in Adam of Bremen's *Historia* and in the *Knytlingasaga* (an earlier study of these texts had convinced him of the existence of this shift, but he had also found traces of a 'transition to the use of normal orientation... obviously by the influence of Christianity and continental orientation').[3] The average deviation he calculated as 60°, O. Scand. 'north' being N 60° E etc.

The method by which Ekblom arrived at such precise results was deceptively simple. Proceeding in what he described as 'a strict and rather mechanical way', he obtained his bearings by drawing lines from the central point of a pivotal area to the central points of the surrounding territories and measuring the angles relative to meridians and parallels.

For the rest Ekblom's basic assumptions differed little from Malone's. Although he did raise the question whether phrases such as *be eastan and be norþan* meant 'east and north' or simply north-east (depending on the situation he was prepared to admit one or the other translation),[4] he seems to have had no misgivings as to the meaning of *eastnorþ, norþanwestan* etc. Yet he noted that the terms used in an eight-point orientation system did not refer to points of the compass but to 'sectors, so that, as eight directions were used, each sector (i.e. each "point") strictly speaking included

---

[1] *Ibid.* p. 149.

[2] 'Alfred the Great as Geographer', *SN* xiv (1941–2), 115–44. Ekblom's thesis was attacked by Alvar Ellegård, 'De gamla nordbornas väderstrecksuppfattning', *Lychnos* (1954–5), 1–19; cf. Ekblom's reply (published posthumously), 'King Alfred, Ohthere and Wulfstan', *SN* xxxii (1960), 3–13, and Ellegård's rebuttal 'The Old Scandinavian System of Orientation', *ibid.* 241–8. Ellegård's views, viz. 'that the itinerary model underlay practically all medieval geography' (p. 242) and that the Icelandic system of orientation (244 ff.) will help to solve the problems of Or., are also open to question.

[3] Ekblom, 'Alfred as Geographer', p. 123, n. 1.    [4] *Ibid.* p. 127.

45°, i.e. 22° 30 to either side of the centre of each sector'.[1] In practice, however, he ignored even this source of errors, on the assumption that in a large number of indications of orientation the deviations from the centre would cancel each other out.

Although Ekblom avoided some of the pitfalls which weakened Malone's argument, his procedure too is debatable. For one thing, his choice of the central points of his pivotal areas sometimes gives the impression of being prejudiced. He may well have been right in locating the centre of the Old Saxons' territory near Verden, but when he located that of the Frisian area somewhere between the Elbe and the Weser, he added in a footnote: 'The Frisian area stretched roughly from present-day Cuxhaven to Bruges in Alfred's time.'[2] More generally, one may doubt whether the calculation of central points for the purpose of establishing the relative positions of territories can ever have entered the head of a ninth-century geographer. The question, then, is not whether Ekblom's twenty-three deviated bearings stand up to close examination, but rather whether his procedure can be applied at all to an early medieval geographical treatise. Theoretically there are two ways of describing the relative positions of territorial units (states, provinces, tribes): (*a*) by setting out from a pivotal unit as a *centre* and indicating the general direction of the surrounding units relative to this pivot; and (*b*) by following the *boundaries* of the pivotal unit and enumerating the abutting territories. The two methods need not produce the same results. Thus, in describing present-day France, one could say that Spain is *south-west* of it (comparing the relative positions of the two areas); but one could equally well describe France as having Spain and the Mediterranean *south* of it. Similarly, Italy, together with Switzerland and Germany, is on France's *eastern* border, but lies *south-east* of it etc. These two examples, for which parallels from other areas could easily be found, also show how easily a shift from the one method of surveying to the other could produce 45° clockwise or anti-clockwise deviations. This is not to suggest, of course, that Orosius or his translator was conscious of the difference between the two procedures and of the possible consequences. The words and phrases which they used to describe the positions of geographical entities were comfortably ambiguous as far as this distinction was concerned. If they wrote 'A has north of it B, east of it C etc.,' these indications could refer to boundaries as well as to relative positions on a map. There can be little doubt, I believe, that the central-point pro-

---

[1] *Ibid.* p. 123.

[2] *Ibid.* p. 127, n. 1. In the text of his paper he argues: 'Here he (Alfred) cannot mean the centre of the Frisians, which must have been somewhere round the mouth of the Ijssel; he must mean the easternmost Frisian area round present-day Cuxhaven, near the Elbe estuary.' But 'somewhere round the mouth of the Ijssel' was definitely west of the Saxons and the mouth of the Elbe was just west of the Northalbingian Saxons (Or. 16, 5 f.).

cedure as suggested by Ekblom will hardly have occurred to an 'earth-bound' observer, nor will it have proved practicable to the owner of a map. For it also presupposes the existence of maps showing fairly accurate territorial divisions – but did such maps exist in Orosius's days, or in ninth-century England, for that matter? Before examining this angle of the problem, let us briefly return to the question of the terms of orientation, for the fate of Malone's and Ekblom's theories in some measure depends on it.

The Latin terms for the four *cardinales* leave no space for doubt. The equinoctial (or average) directions of sunrise and sunset, and the highest point of the sun in the sky provided the observer with the points *ortus* or *oriens*, *occasus* or *occidens* and *meridies*, whilst the constellation constituting the polar star, the 'seven plough-oxen' (*septem triones*), gave him the *septentrio*. This basic compass with its astronomical basis could easily be established and was valid for any inhabited place north of the Tropic of Cancer. It corresponded perfectly to the OE compass with *east*, *west*, *suþ* and *norþ*.

The insertion of intermediate directions was a more complicated matter. The simplest procedure was for the observer to select natural features visible from his point of view (hill-tops, trees etc.), but in this case the indications and the 'names' were not transferable. The alternative, viz. to divide the 90° sectors between the cardinals into two, three or more equal angles, took a long time to impose itself. In the meantime Greeks and Romans used the names of winds to indicate intermediate directions, with as a result a good deal of arbitrariness and vagueness: the directions from which characteristic winds blew varied from one region to another, and so did their names; nor would these directions fit into a mathematically satisfactory and uniform system of subdivisions. The *Vulturnus*, for example, blew from the general direction of *Mons Vultur* in Apulia, which, from the point of view of Rome, practically meant ESE. In theory at least the *Vulturnus* would have fitted perfectly into an orientation system with sixteen points. In practice the word came to be used to indicate a 'south-east-by-one-third-south wind', and similarly *Aquilo*, though mostly used for 'north', would indicate a 'north-by-one-third-east wind' as a nautical term. Even the nomenclature of the four cardinal points was invaded by names of winds (*meridies* = *Auster* or *Notus*, *occidens* = *Zephyrus* or *Favonius* etc.; cf. *Aquilo* = north).[1] This profusion of terms was reduced to fit a twelve-point system by Isidore of Seville (*De Natura Rerum* xxxvii: *De Nominibus Ventorum*), but not without some arbitrary reshuffling: the

[1] See, e.g., Charlton T. Lewis and Charles Short, *A Latin Dictionary* (Oxford, 1958), *s.v.* J. F. Masselink, *De Grieks-Roeminse Windroos* (Utrecht and Nijmegen, 1956) gives a good idea of the plethora of names.

*Vulturnus* was shifted north of east to mark an east-one-third-north wind, *Aquilo* and *Eurus* were no longer north and east winds, but became a north-one-third-east and an east-one-third-south wind respectively.[1]

Isidore's work came to be widely circulated in the Germanic-speaking countries, but the exact impact of his system of orientation is not easy to assess.[2] On the one hand we have Bede's adoption of the system in *De Natura Rerum* xxvii[3] and Charlemagne's German adaptation of the terminology as reported by Einhard in the *Vita Caroli* xxix.[4] But Charlemagne's terms with their perfect morphological parallelism seem hardly to have won acceptance even in his own empire, nor did Bede attempt to use the system described in *De Natura Rerum* in his *Historia Ecclesiastica*.[5]

Orosius's terminology of orientation points in the main to a system with eight bearings, but his usage tends to vary according to the regions which he is describing. For Africa and Asia a four-point system (usually in the order *oriens, meridies, occasus/occidens, septentrio*) was all he needed; *Aquilo* occurs only three times, *Africus* once. In the description of Europe, *Aquilo* does not occur more often, but its place is frequently taken by *Boreas*. When used here, *Aquilo* is clearly distinguished from *septentrio* and hence must mean north-east. The description of Europe is further refined by the addition of *Circius* and *Africus* (each eleven times), *Eurus* (six times) and *Favonius* (once). This last term occurs in a sequence together with *occasus* (OH I. ii. 57) and hence cannot have its usual meaning 'west(wind)', whilst 'south-west' seems to be precluded by the frequent use of *Africus*. But since the single *Subsolanus* is also found together with *oriens* (OH I. ii. 100), it may be safer not to press this point. The only term which seems to require a sixteen-point compass is *Euronotus* (OH I. ii. 99), which should fit in between *Eurus* (SE) and *Notus* (S). But it is only these three – *Favonius*, *Subsolanus* and *Euronotus* – which do not seem to fit into the basic eight-point system.

At first sight the task of translating Orosius's orientation system into Old English looks like having been fairly simple and straightforward, but there is some evidence to the contrary. To begin with, the native vocabu-

---

[1] Jacques Fontaine, *Isidore de Séville, Traité de la Nature* (Bordeaux, 1960), pp. 295–8.
[2] *Ibid.* pp. 73–83.
[3] Migne, *PL* xc, cols. 247 ff.
[4] 'Ventis vero hoc modo nomina imposuit, ut subsolanum vocaret ostroniwint, eurum ostsundroni, euroaustrum sundsostroni, austrum sundroni, austro-africum sundwestroni, africum westsundroni, zefyrum westroni, chorum westnordroni, circium norðwestroni, septentrionem nordroni, aquilonem norðostroni, vulturnum ostnorðroni' (Hannover and Leipzig, 1940, ex *MGH, Script. Rer. Germ.*, p. 34).
[5] Bede uses *Aquilo, Aquilonaris* consistently for 'north' (*septentrio* occurs only once, though *septentrionalis* is fairly frequently used), and similarly *Boreas, Borealis*, e.g. *HE* I. 1 (Plummer, *Bede* I, 9/3 and 11/31), 3 (15/25) and 15 (31/27), II. 5 (89/12 and 20) and 9 (97/7) and III. 24 (180/13). Other 'winds', such as *Circius, Eurus* and *Vulturnus*, occur mainly or only in quotations from other authors, e.g. I. 12 (25/24), *duabus gentibus...Scottorum a circio, Pictorum ab aquilone* from Gildas; cf. the extracts from Adamnán, *De Locis Sanctis, HE* v. 16 (318/4 ff.).

lary only distinguished the four cardinals *norþ, east, suþ* and *west*. In *De Temporibus Anni* Ælfric mentions the difficulties which an Anglo-Saxon experienced when writing in his own language about Isidore's or Bede's twelve 'winds': 'Þas feower heafodwindas habbað betwux him on ymbhwyrfte oðre eahta windas, æfre betwux þam heafodwindum twegen windas; þæra naman 7 blawunge we mihton secgan, gif hit ne ðuhte æðryt to awritenne.' He describes only one of the eight intermediate winds, and in a way which may lead to confusion: 'Is swa ðeah hwæðere an ðæra eahta winda, Aquilo gehaten, se blæwð norðan 7 eastan, healic 7 ceald 7 swiðe drie; se is gehaten oðrum naman Boreas, 7 ealne ðone cwyld þe se suðerna wind Auster acenð, ealne he todræfð 7 afligð.'[1] Long before Ælfric, Anglo-Saxon glossators had run into trouble when trying to translate the names of the winds into Old English – not only, it seems, because their language lacked the necessary terms, but also because the meaning of some of these Latin terms was vague and the evidence contradictory. The *Corpus Glossary* has the following relevant entries, for all of which Orosius has been suggested as the most likely source: 'A 46 Ab Euro, eastansudan; A 47 Ad Euronothum, eastsuth; A 89 Ab Affrico, suðanwestan; A 92 Ab Borea, eastannorþan; A 113 A Circio, norðanwestan; A 360 A Fafonio, suþanwestan.' To these entries we may add the following items from the same glossary (though from different sources): 'A 364 Affricus, westsuðwind; A 951 Auster, suðuuind; B 152 Boreus, eastnorðwind; C 375 Chorus, eostnorðwind; C 419 Circius, westnorðwind; F 49 Faonius, westsuðwind.'[2] This is a far cry from Charlemagne's perfect alternation of the names of the cardinals in the composition of the terms for the twelve winds (and hence from a twelve-point system). All we can read into the *Corpus* items is a certain tendency to put east or west before north or south, which at the same time implies a certain grasp of an eight-point system. The two instances of 'south-west' (A 89 and A 360) and the one instance of 'north-west' (A 113) are compensated by two instances of 'west-south' (A 364 and F 49) and one of 'west-north' (C 419). It is not clear whether any importance should be attached to the fact that no such alternations occur with east. Later material from *Ælfric's Glossary* also suggests an eight-point system, though now the tendency is to place north or south first: 'WW 143,36 Subsolanus, eastenwind; 143,37 Auster uel nothus, suðenwind; 144,1 Fauonius uel zephirus, westenwind; 144,2 Septentrio, norðanwind; 144,3 Vulturnus, eastansuðanwind; 144,4 Eurus, euroauster, norðaneastanwind; 144,6 Euroafricus, suðaneasten-

---

[1] *Aelfric's De Temporibus Anni*, ed. H. Henel, EETS o.s. 213 (London, 1942), 76 (*De Duodecim Ventis* x. 21–3; cf. 24, *Us ðincð to menigfeald þæt we swiðor embe ðis sprecon*).

[2] J. H. Hessels, *An Eighth-Century Latin-Anglo-Saxon Glossary* (Cambridge, 1890), *s.v.*; W. M. Lindsay, *The Corpus Glossary* (Cambridge, 1921), *s.v.*; and *idem*, *The Corpus, Épinal, Erfurt and Leyden Glossaries*, Publications of the Philological Society 8 (London, n.d.), 106 ff.

wind; 144,7 Africus, suðanwestanwind; 144,8 Corus, norðanwestanwind; 144,9 Circius, norðaneastenwind; 144,10 Aquilo vel boreus, norðanwestanwind.'

Again, there is nothing here to point to the existence of a native nomenclature beyond the four cardinals. Yet both the tendency to restrict the order of the elements in the compound terms and the continuing signs of instability[1] clearly reflect attempts to create an integrated system of names for a compass with eight points. This situation of course did not preclude precise orientation both in everyday life and in those contexts where greater precision was required. Among the glosses to Bede there are these two items: *HE* v. 12 (Plummer, *Bede* I, 304/31), *contra ortum solis solstitialem:* [o]*ngean norðęstroder swa sunnan upgang bið to middan sumere*; and (307/6) *contra ortum solis brumalem: suðeast swa sunne on wintra upgæð.*[2] The corresponding passages in most manuscripts of the Old English Bede are almost identical, *ongen norðeastrodor, swa sunnan uppgong bið æt middum sumere* and *suðeast on ðon roðor, swa swa on wintre sunne upp gongeð,*[3] but in MSS O and Ca we find *norð 7 east* for *norðeast* (but not *suð 7 east* for *suðeast*). This brings us to the problem of the 'and' phrases. Whilst a meaning 'north-east' is clearly called for in the context just quoted, Ekblom was no doubt right when he would not impose a uniform interpretation on all phrases consisting of two cardinals linked by 'and'. The 'and' phrases in the description of the Isle of Wight will make this clear. The measurements which in Bede's Latin are given as *ab oriente in occasum XXX circiter milia passuum, ab austro in boream XII* are rendered by *þæt is þrittiges mila lang east 7 west, 7 twelf mila brad suð 7 norð:* 'from east to west...from south to north.'[4] A different meaning still may be suggested by instances where the two cardinals are separated by other words besides 'and', e.g. *be suþan him 7 be eastan* (Or. 16, 2), *be eastan him 7 be norþan* (16, 24), *be westan him 7 norþan* (22, 31), *be norðan hyre 7 eastan* (22, 34) etc., some of which at least must mean 'both to the...and to the...'. But in view of the instability of the compounds and the freedom with which the separate elements could be combined – the most striking example being Ohthere's *westanwindes 7 hwon norþan* (Or. 17, 15 f.) – the interpretation of the intermediate points will remain a tricky undertaking; and for all directions we shall be safe if we keep in mind what Ekblom had to say about their standing for sectors.

[1] E.g. A. S. Napier, *Old English Glosses, Chiefly Unpublished* (Oxford, 1900; repr. Hildesheim, 1969), 1. 4561 *a circio, norþanwestan*, but 2. 347 *a circio, westannorðan* and 8. 253 *a circio, westannorþan*. Cf. also 23. 17 *zepheri, westernes windes* and 26. 67 *zephiri, suðernes windes. Africum*, ps. LXXVII. 26, is glossed *westansuðanwind* in the Vespasian Psalter and the Cambridge Psalter, but *suðanwestanwind* in the Vitellius Psalter (and *syþerne wind* in the Salisbury Psalter).

[2] Herbert Dean Meritt, *Old English Glosses* (New York and London, 1945), 5. 1 and 2.

[3] *The Old English Version of Bede's Ecclesiastical History of the English People*, ed. T. Miller, EETS o.s. 95, 96, 110 and 111 (London, 1890–8), 424, line 20f. and 428, line 24.

[4] *HE* I. 3 (Plummer, *Bede* I, 15/25 f.); Miller, *OE Version*, p. 30, line 26.

For obvious reasons, the uncertainty increases when we examine other than purely geographical contexts.[1]

After this very cursory and incomplete survey, it comes rather as a surprise to find the orientation data of the Old English Orosius by and large correct and accurate. Instead of setting out to prove this for the dozens of indications discussed by Malone and Ekblom, and for the many more which they did not examine, I shall hasten to admit that there are a number of instances of a 'clockwise shift', although I doubt very much whether any sort of calculation will prove them to be a uniform 45° or 60°. I feel even less inclined to accept the suggestion that the clockwise shift reflects the presence in the background of an Old Scandinavian system of orientation. I also doubt whether Ohthere and Wulfstan themselves had such a system in mind when they told King Alfred about their voyages. I would rather suggest that the source of the deviations lay elsewhere, viz. in the use of a map.

The idea that the author of the Old English Orosius relied on a map at least for some parts of his geographical introduction is not new. A few years ago Linderski, following a suggestion of G. Labuda, took it up again. He reports Labuda as claiming that 'many inconsistencies and inaccuracies in Alfred's description may be explained on the theory that he had at his disposition a map by the help of which he determined the position of countries and tribes mentioned by him, but at the same time he reproduced geographical errors and misconceptions contained in the map'.[2] But whereas Labuda and Linderski, and others before them, have been concerned with limited areas such as central Europe or the Vistula country, I would suggest that the use of a map such as the eighth-century Isidore map described by Uhden,[3] or the map reconstructed by Miller[4] on the basis

---

[1] Alfred's *Boethius* provides a few interesting examples. In the translation of I met. v. 8 ff., 'Tua uis uarium temperat annum, / ut quas Boreae spiritus aufert / reuehat mites Zephyrus frondes' (*CC* xciv, 12), *Boreas* is correctly rendered by *wind norþan 7 eastan* (*King Alfred's Old English Version of Boethius De Consolatione Philosophiae*, ed. W. J. Sedgefield [Oxford, 1899], p. 10, line 11 f.) while by contrast *Zephyrus* becomes *suðanwesternan wind* in the prose version and *suðan 7 westan . . . wind* in the poetic version (Sedgefield, p. 10, line 13 and met. iv. 22). In the rendering of II met. iii. 5 ff. *Zephyrus* is again translated by *supanwestan wind*, but *Auster* becomes rather more unexpectedly *se stearca wind cymð norðaneastan*, whilst *Aquilo* appears as *þæs norðanwindes yst* (Sedgefield, p. 21, line 4 ff.). Similarly *Notus* in III met. i. 7 becomes *se stearca wind norðan and eastan* in the poetic version; in the prose version it is simply *norðanwindas* (Sedgefield, met. xii. 14 f. and p. 52, line 5). The climatic differences between Boethius's Italy and Alfred's England are no doubt responsible for these changes: in England a *nebulosus Auster* and a *Notus* which gave *imbriferos sonos* (rendered by *micle renas 7 snawas*) must necessarily blow from a northern region.

[2] Jerzy Linderski, 'Alfred the Great and the Tradition of Ancient Geography', *Speculum* xxxix (1964), 434–9 (quotation p. 436).

[3] Richard Uhden, 'Die Weltkarte des Isidorus von Sevilla', *Mnemosyne. Bibliotheca Classica Batava* 3rd ser. iii (1935–6), 1–28.

[4] Konrad Miller, *Mappaemundi, Die ältesten Weltkarten* (Stuttgart, 1895–8) vi: Rekonstruierte Karten, 61–8 and pl. 3.

of Orosius's geographical chapter, or finally, the Anglo-Saxon map in BM Cotton Tiberius B. v,[1] may have influenced the Old English Orosius on any point. To make this clear, a few words must be said about contemporary maps.

Generally speaking, maps representing the whole *orbis terrarum* would be circular and would either divide the world roughly into two halves – assigning the eastern half to Asia and dividing the western half between Europe and Africa ('T-O type') – or would represent the continents without any rigorous theoretical division of the circle but with some respect for the known outlines.[2] In either case the surfaces of the continents were adapted to the general shape of the world and a belt of ocean would separate the roughly circular land masses from the border of the map. Needless to say, these maps showed little respect for distances and proportions: the known subdivisions and geographical features were fitted in as space permitted. No meridians or parallels being drawn in, there was little danger that discrepancies and errors would be discovered. Although the points *septentrio, oriens, meridies* and *occidens* were marked on the circular border, these maps were utterly useless for purposes of orientation, though they were useful as a schematic representation of the relative positions of countries and peoples. However, as soon as they were confronted with 'live' information provided by travellers, difficulties would begin to accumulate. A traveller on the earth's surface found himself in a situation fundamentally different from that of the 'literary' geographer with his descriptions and his maps, at any rate as soon as the latter relied more on traditional lore and ancient authors than on sailors' reports and similar sources of information.[3] The traveller found his way by the sun and the stars, and so his system of orientation was bound to be the more reliable; nor could he be bothered to inscribe his world in a circle and to adapt the shapes of lands and seas accordingly. It is not difficult to imagine what must have happened when an early medieval geographer was instructed to insert the data from a traveller's report into an existing mappamundi. If he transferred the traveller's mainly astronomical system of orientation on to his map, turning each 'north' towards his *septentrio*, a good measure of distortion in the shapes and of errors in the distances was the result. If on the other hand he tried to preserve the shapes and distances as reported by the traveller, the orientation of the additions was bound to differ in varying degrees from that of the basic map. In either case the confrontation would lead to errors of varying importance, but there would be some 'system' in them, due precisely to this being a confrontation of two

---

[1] *Ibid.* II: Atlas, pl. 10, and III: Die kleineren Weltkarten, 29–37.
[2] Marcel Destombes, *Mappemondes A.D. 1200–1500*, Monumenta Cartographica Vetustioris Aevi I (Amsterdam, 1964), 10 ff.
[3] Masselink, *Windroos*, pp. 146 ff.

systems. A diagram may serve to make this clear. The informant who reported that he travelled 'due north' from one of the points A, B, C or D, all situated in the 'European quarter' of the map, would have in mind the astronomic north, which would be in the direction N of the same infinitely distant point. The mapmaker who made additions to his map on the basis of this report will have felt tempted to turn the four bearings in the direction of his north, viz. the *septentrio* of his map (S). As he did so, there would

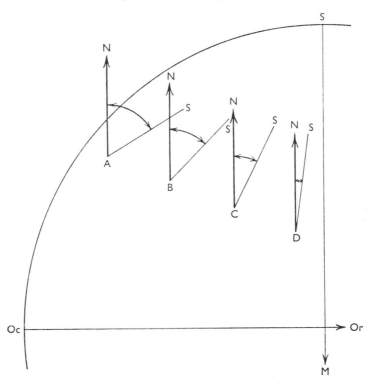

FIG. 8 Examples of the difference between astronomic north and map north in the 'European quarter'

be a deviation of varying importance, depending on the position of the starting point: for A it would be as much as 60°, for D less than 10°. All points on the line connecting S and Oc (*occidens*) would show a 45° shift, whilst it would be zero for all points between S and M (*meridies*). In the whole European quarter of the map the 'shift' from an astronomical orientation to one determined by the map would be clockwise. Of course the overall shift would pass unnoticed until either someone using the map forgot to take its peculiar system of orientation into account and began to read it in terms of an astronomic north, or else insisted on having correct distances and proportions (based on an astronomic orientation), without changing the orientation of the map. In the latter case a sailor on a NE course along the west coast of Norway would be sailing straight to the north of the map.[1]

One might suspect that the mechanism described here has mainly a theoretical value, and that contemporary maps had either more or less correct outlines and an astronomic north or distorted outlines and a *septentrio* on the enclosing circle. However, we have some evidence that the conditions for the confrontation mechanism to work did exist in Anglo-Saxon England. The evidence is not strictly contemporary, but it is sufficiently close in time to the Old English Orosius to deserve closer examination in this context. The map in question is preserved in BM Cotton Tiberius B. v, 1, 56ᵛ, where it accompanies Priscian's *Periegesis*.[2] The manuscript is dated xi[1] by Ker, and there is ample evidence to connect its compilation with the closing years of the tenth century.[3] At first sight the links with the Old English Orosius, or with the Orosius tradition in general, may seem rather tenuous. The map is not inscribed in a circle, as required by the Orosius text, but in an almost equilateral rectangle (21·2 × 17·6 cm.). The general outlines of the continents have been drawn accordingly, and in the process Europe has been drawn too large at the expense of Africa. In its general lay-out the map presents a striking resemblance to that of Pomponius Mela (A.D. 4) as reconstructed by Miller;[4] but the text is mainly derived from Orosius, to whom Miller could trace seventy-five of the 146 entries. These entries are unevenly spread, Britain and Italy being the only European countries favoured with more than one city (most countries have none). If there are numerous mistakes, such as the Danube reaching the sea south of Constantinople, Istria lying north of the Alps and Macedonia in the Peloponnesus, they are compensated by some strikingly English features, which lend special importance to this map. On *Island* (i.e. Scandinavia) we find the entry *Scridefinnas*, and in Gaul the only inscription is *Suðbryttas* (with *ð*, not *d* as read by Miller, and insular *r*). The scribe used *wynn* in the name *Sleswic* and insular *g* even in some purely Latin contexts such as *Carthago magna* (twice) and *Hunorum gens*. Though its shape is entirely different, there would be some justification, it seems, for examining this map in the light of our discussion of the

---

[1] I would not dare suggest at this point that this is how Ohthere's *norþryhte* arose – but can we be quite certain that his report was not 'interpreted' in terms of contemporary geography? His voyage after all is only a small portion of a fairly long geographical introduction, which we, perhaps wrongly, do not usually read in its entirety.

[2] Miller, *Mappaemundi* ii, pl. 10 and iii, 31–7.

[3] Ker, *Catalogue*, no. 193.

[4] *Op. cit.* vi, 102–7 and map 7. It will be noted that Pomponius's Ireland (*Iuverna*) is situated north of *Britannia* and hence would be 'first on starboard' of the man sailing from Norway to the Baltic. Both Ireland and Iceland have been given more correct positions on the Cottonian map (Pomponius puts the latter very close to his *septentrio*).

orientation of the Old English Orosius. Even at a first glance one may discover analogies with the Old English text. Thus Dalmatia (the name is written in the wrong place, but the outline of the country is easy to recognize) lies practically west of Athens and north of the Adriatic: cf. *be westan Achie...is Dalmatia þæt land, on norðhealfe þæs sæs* (Or. 22, 12); and the (unnamed) Alps extend all the way south of Gaul; cf. *Gallia Bellica... be suðan þa beorgas þe man hæt Alpis* (Or. 22, 23). It might be tempting to pursue this search, but I think it is more important at this stage to note that the orientation terms are missing (there ought to have been a point *septentrio* in the middle of one of the sides, as there still is in Higden's map).[1] Hence the burden of deciding by which orientation system to read the map has been shifted on to the reader.

Finally, I should like to point out one feature which links this map with another contemporary work, Alfred's *Boethius*. In one passage Alfred feels obliged to specify the philosopher's rather vague geography. *Indica tellus* and *ultima Thyle*, which in III met. v simply stand for 'from one end of the earth to the other', have prompted the following explicit statement: 'from Indeum, þæt is se suðeastende þisses middaneardes, oð ðæt iland þe we hataðTyle, þæt is on þam norþwestende þisses middaneardes, þær ne bið nawþerne on sumera niht, ne on wintra dæg' (Sedgefield, p. 67, lines 31 ff.). I leave it to the reader to decide whether India's south-eastern position is a case of a clockwise or counter-clockwise shift; but he will no doubt be pleased to find *Tylen* fitting nicely into the north-west corner of the earth on the Cottonian map. This of course is not the map used in compiling the geographical introduction to the Old English Orosius; but it will no doubt help us to visualize some of the problems which this compilation entailed.

[1] Such a position would not affect the principle of a 'map-bound' orientation; it would only mean that more places were in danger of getting a deviation larger than 45°. For Higden's map see *ibid.* II, pl. 15 and III, 94 ff.

# The ethic of war in Old English

## J. E. CROSS

> Abraham sealde
> wig to wedde,      nalles wunden gold,
> for his suhtrigan,      sloh and fylde
> feond on fitte.[1]

In recent years, fear of annihilation in total war and abhorrence of the waste in limited war have forced every civilized man to think deeply about the justifications for war of any kind. Such a man may be startled at this extension here of bare scriptural statement in Genesis XIV. 15 about Abraham's rescue of Lot, since the comment implies that war is not only an unquestioned necessity to this Christian poet, but, in this case, a praise-worthy alternative to ransom. Other Anglo-Saxon Christians agree. The compilers of *The Anglo-Saxon Chronicle*, who recorded memorable events to demarcate the years, note occasions[2] when the English paid money to avoid war. But open condemnation of the practice is voiced in Archbishop Wulfstan's words *scandlice nydgyld*, 'shameful extortion',[3] and in Byrht-noth's pointed naming and rejection of the *gafol*, 'tribute', *sceatt*, 'tax', demanded by the Viking in *The Battle of Maldon* in order to *leoda lysan*, 'ransom his people'.[4] While Bede, although in milder manner, needs to excuse Oswy of Northumbria's attempt to buy peace from Penda of Mercia with the phrase *necessitate cogente*, 'necessity compelling him'.[5]

Earlier scholars, writing before even the desolation of the first World War, saw nothing to surprise in the prose statements of fact, and, if called to comment on *Genesis A* or *The Battle of Maldon* would have assumed an Anglo-Saxon poetic attitude deriving from a reality among our Germanic pagan ancestors who thought fighting as natural as living.[6] Yet the most appropriate gloss to the statement in *Genesis A* is a rhetorical question of St Ambrose in apt context: 'Quanto illustrius Abraham captum armis

---

[1] 'Abraham gave battle as ransom (Grein-Köhler, *s.v. wed*), no twisted gold at all, for his nephew, struck and felled the enemy in war' (*Genesis A*, 2069–72). Quotations of Old English poetry are from *ASPR*.

[2] The earliest occasion appears to be 865 (866 C) when the people of Kent 'promised money for peace'. But Æthelweard's *Chronicle* adds that the Mercians paid in 872, and even King Alfred in 876; see Earle and Plummer, *Chronicles* II, 89 and 90. The most famous occasion for students of literature is the entry for 991 (C, D and E), the year of the Battle of Maldon.

[3] Whitelock, *Sermo Lupi*, p. 45, line 109.

[4] *The Battle of Maldon*, lines 32, 40 and 37.

[5] *HE* III. 24.      [6] Tacitus, *Germania*, ch. XIV.

victricibus recepit nepotem, quam si redemisset?'[1] Ambrose is here distinguishing two kinds of liberality, one that gives help in money and 'altera quae operum collatione impenditur, multo frequenter splendidior multoque clarior',[2] Abraham's action being the lauded example. The parallel between the Old English and the Latin statements is strengthened by the use of *wunden gold* in cliché phrase[3] as a metonomy for the liberality in goods of a secular lord.

No one may demonstrate that Ambrose is the direct source for the Old English poetic statement, but his name is relevantly remembered here since his century saw the alliance of church and state through the conversion of Constantine which eventually forced Christians to play their part in this area of secular affairs, and Ambrose himself (333–97) was the first Christian to justify physical war for other contemporary Christians.[4] The story of the emperor's conversion remained well known to the medieval church-goer from its use as introduction to the legend of the finding of the cross by Helena, mother of Constantine, which was read for the feast *Inventio Crucis* on 3 May. In this legend the account is given of Constantine's vision before battle with the barbarians as in Cynewulf's *Elene*,[5] or, as in earlier authorities and Ælfric,[6] against Maxentius, rival for the imperial throne, where an angel reveals the sign of the cross in the sky as token of God's aid for victory. In Cynewulf's poem Constantine had a standard made like the cross he had seen,[7] but from Eusebius's account,[8] it is realized that he adapted the ordinary cavalry-standard (*vexillum*) by replacing the Roman eagle with the sacred monogram ✶ at the top of the shaft. This substitution gives meaning to Ambrose's prayer for the success of Gratian's army against the Goths: 'Convertere, Domine, fideique tuae adtolle vexilla. Non hic aquilae militares, neque volatus avium exercitum ducunt, sed tuum, Domine Jesu, nomen et cultus.'[9] By the precise wording and the sentiments of this prayer for success in battle we may realize that the

---

[1] 'How much nobler was it that Abraham recovered his captured nephew by victorious arms than if he had ransomed him' (*De Officiis Ministrorum* II. xv. 74).

[2] 'The other which is expended in the contribution of deeds, [is] often much grander and much nobler' (*ibid.* 73). Note the word-play in *impendo* and *collatio*.

[3] Cf. *nales wunden gold* (*The Wanderer*, 32).

[4] For general accounts of the Christian attitude to war and its early history see Adolf Harnack, *Militia Christi* (Tübingen, 1905), C. J. Cadoux, *The Early Church and the World* (Edinburgh, 1925), R. H. Bainton, *Christian Attitudes toward War and Peace* (London, 1961) and Joan D. Tooke, *The Just War in Aquinas and Grotius* (London, 1965). Miss Tooke has an excellent summary of the early arguments in her ch. 1.

[5] Lines 19–21 etc.

[6] Lactantius, *De Mortibus Persecutorum* XLIV; Eusebius, *Vita Constantini* I, 27–32; and *The Homilies of the Anglo-Saxon Church,* ... *the Sermones Catholici, or Homilies of Ælfric,* ed. B. Thorpe (London, 1844–6) II, 304.

[7] Lines 99–104.     [8] Eusebius, *op. cit.* I, 31.

[9] 'Turn, O Lord, and raise the standards of your faith. No military eagles, nor flight of birds here lead the army but your name Lord Jesus, and your worship' (*De Fide* II. xvi. 141–2).

church had come to terms with the state on the necessity of war for lay Christians. It had now become easy for Christian leaders to define the conditions for war in clear language, and for help they turned to pre-Christian Latin writers who had been concerned with the ethic of acceptable war, notably to Cicero, who had made explicit relationship between the doctrine of natural law and that of *justum bellum* in *De Officiis*. The law of reason, he had argued, which is so universal that it is an international bond between men, contains rules of justice which should regulate the affairs of nations, including that of war. Ambrose first adapted the ethic of war from Cicero and his *De Officiis Ministrorum* is clearly based on Cicero's *De Officiis*,[1] but, as might be expected, Augustine firmly established the orthodox attitude by his reputation and influence, and many later Christians quoted Augustine's statements on individual cases, often word for word without acknowledgment.[2] Augustine wrote little on defensive war, obviously because he took it for granted that such war was justified, as in the case of some wars of the Romans: 'Sed plane pro tantis bellis susceptis et gestis iusta defensio Romanorum est, quod inruentibus sibi inportune inimicis resistere cogebat non aviditas adipiscendae laudis humanae, sed necessitas tuendae salutis et libertatis.'[3]

A just war of aggression however must be carried out with the authority of a prince and must have both a just cause and a right intention. A just cause could be to right the wrong done by an enemy: *Justa autem bella definiri solent, quae ulciscuntur injurias;*[4] or it could be to put down evils: 'Nocendi cupiditas, ulciscendi crudelitas, impacatus atque implacabilis animus, feritas rebellandi, libido dominandi, et si qua similia, haec sunt quae in bellis jure culpantur; quae plerumque ut etiam jure puniantur, adversus violentiam resistentium, sive Deo, sive aliquo legitimo imperio jubente, gerenda ipsa bella suscipiuntur a bonis',[5] and 'Bellum autem quod gerendum Deo auctore suscipitur, recte suscipi, dubitare fas non est, vel ad terrendam, vel ad obterendam, vel ad subjugandam mortalium superbiam.'[6] But the right intention was to obtain peace by restoring order: 'Pacem habere debet voluntas, bellum necessitas, ut liberet Deus

---

[1] Bainton, *op. cit.* p. 90. For a demonstration of some verbal indebtedness see H. Hagendahl, *Latin Fathers and the Classics*, Göteborgs Universitets Årsskrift 64 (1958), 348–72.

[2] Tooke, *op. cit.* p. 11.

[3] 'But clearly the Romans have a just defence for undertaking and waging such great wars since it was not eagerness to acquire human praise that drove them to resist their enemies' violent onsets but the necessity of guarding their safety and freedom' (*De Civitate Dei* III. x).

[4] 'Those wars may be defined as just which avenge injuries' (*Quaestiones in Heptateuchum* VI. x).

[5] 'A desire to injure, cruelty in revenge, a warlike and implacable spirit, savagery in revolt, lust for mastery, and such like are what are rightly condemned in war; and generally it is in order that they also be rightly punished that wars to be waged against the violence of those who resist are undertaken by good men at the bidding of God, or some other lawful power' (*Contra Faustum Manichaeum* XXII. lxxiv).

[6] 'But it is not right to doubt that war is justly undertaken when it is carried on under the authority of God to deter, humble or crush the pride of men' (*ibid.* lxxv).

271

a necessitate, et conservet in pace. Non enim pax quaeritur ut bellum excitetur, sed bellum geritur ut pax acquiratur.'[1] Although some interesting individual cases are decided in the course of Augustine's arguments elsewhere, these selections nevertheless make Augustine's position apparent, and this general attitude became the orthodox view which was not modified until after the Anglo-Saxon period.

Yet the encyclopaedia of Isidore of Seville may also be quoted because this was obviously a handy summary which lodged in Ælfric's mind, and Isidore also reaffirms the influence of Cicero's comments. 'Quattuor autem sunt genera bellorum, id est justum, injustum, civile et plusquam civile', says Isidore; and Ælfric accepts and glosses: 'Secgað swaþeah lareowas þæt synd feower cynna gefeoht, *iustum*, þæt is rihtlic, *iniustum*, unrihtlic, *ciuile*, betwux ceaster-gewarum, *plusquam ciuile*, betwux siblingum', but exemplifies from the contemporary Scandinavian invasions: '*Iustum bellum* is rihtlic gefeoht wið ða reðan flotmenn oþþe wið oðre þeoda þe eard willað fordon', whereas Isidore had defined *justum bellum* in general terms: 'Justum bellum est, quod ex praedicto geritur de rebus repetitis aut propulsandorum hostium causa.' Ælfric however, who is writing generally for the laity on this occasion,[2] is obviously not so concerned with foreign authorities and with specific rules for conduct in war which Isidore handily presents, and he merely abstracts general causes from, and adds results to, the Latin statement: 'Unrihtlic gefeoht is þe of yrre cymð (*injustum bellum est quod de furore...initur*). Þæt þridde gefeoht þe of geflite cymð betwux ceastergewarum (*civile bellum est inter cives orta seditio...*) is swyðe pleolic, and þæt feorðe gefeoht þe betwux freondum bið (*plusquam civile bellum est, ubi non solum cives certant sed et cognati*) is swiðe earmlic and endeleas sorh.'[3]

[1] 'You ought to have peace as your desire, war as a necessity, so that God may deliver you from the necessity and preserve you in peace. For peace is not sought for war to be aroused, but war is waged for peace to be obtained' (*Epistola* CLXXXIX, 6).

[2] See Ælfric's Preface to the *Lives of Saints*, *Ælfric's Lives of Saints*, ed. W. W. Skeat, EETS o.s. 76, 82, 94 and 114 (London, 1881–1900), I, 2 and 4.

[3] I translate the whole passages from Isidore, *Etymologiarum Libri XX*, XVIII. 2, 3 and 4, and from *Ælfric's Lives of Saints* II, 112–14. The source was first noted by C. G. Loomis, 'Further Sources of Ælfric's Saints' Lives', *Harvard Studies and Notes in Philology and Literature* XIII (1931), 3, n. 1.
Isidore, 2: 'There are four kinds of war, that is just, unjust, civil and more than civil [*plusquam civile*]. It is just war when it is waged about demanding satisfaction from an agreement or for the reason of repelling enemies. It is unjust war when it is begun from anger not from a lawful reason. Cicero says about this in *Republica*: "Those wars are unjust which are undertaken without cause."'
3: 'For, no just war can be waged except for punishment or repelling enemies. And the same Tully added a few extra words on this: "No just war exists, unless declared or proclaimed or for demanding satisfaction."'
Civil discord [*seditio*] gives rise to civil war among citizens...
4: 'It is more than civil war, where not only citizens fight, but also relatives...'
Ælfric: 'Nevertheless teachers say that there are four kinds of war, *justum* that is just, *injustum*, unjust, *ciuile*, between citizens, *plusquam ciuile* between relatives. *Iustum bellum* is just war against the cruel seamen or against other nations who desire to destroy our homeland.

There is no other categorized definition of the kinds of war in Old English literature but, both in comment on individual situations and in the manner of the comment, it is clear that influential Christians held an orthodox view about the necessity of war, yet the right kind of war. In his *Epistola ad Ecgbertum Episcopum* Bede denounces uncontrolled monasteries which 'neque Deo neque hominibus utilia sunt, quia videlicet neque regularis secundum Deum ibidem vita servatur, neque illa milites sive comites secularium potestatum, qui gentem nostram a barbaris defendant, possident', together with dissolute young men who 'patriam suam pro qua militare debuerant, trans mare abeuntes relinquant', and he urges the bishop to join with the king and help the province, whether in matters of church or state, lest (among other difficulties) 'rarescente copia militiae secularis, absint qui fines nostros a barbarica incursione tueantur'.[1] Here is a positive commitment of church, also expressed by the decrees of a synod at which Boniface was present: 'Statuimus quoque, cum consilio servorum Dei, et populi Christiani, propter imminentia bella, et persecutiones cæterarum gentium, quae in circuitu nostro sunt, ut sub precario et censu aliquam partem ecclesialis pecuniae in adjutorium exercitus nostri, cum indulgentia Dei, aliquanto tempore retineamus...',[2] and commonly presented by the recognition of the threefold division of society which included '*bellatores* synd þa ðe ure burga healdað and urne eard beweriað wid onwinnendne here', and which is expressed here in one quotation from Ælfric,[3] but is also formulated by Ælfric on other occasions, once to Wulfstan who echoes the sentiments in his *Institutes of Polity*. The formula was used also by anonymous homilists, and had been used in King Alfred's prose paraphrase of Boethius's *De Consolatione Philosophiae* as extension on the Latin text, as well as being used later in the medieval period.[4] In all these examples the extending definitions present the most

Unjust war is that which comes from anger. The third war, which comes from contention between citizens is very dangerous and the fourth war which is between kinsmen is very wretched and endless sorrow.'

[1] The text is from Plummer, *Bede* I, 414–15, the translation from Whitelock, *EHD*, pp. 740–1. '...are useful to neither God nor man, in that neither is there kept there a regular life according to God's will, nor are they owned by thegns or *gesiths* of the secular power who defend our people from the barbarians'; '...leave the country for which they ought to fight and go across the sea'; '...by the dwindling of the supply of secular troops, there arises a lack of men to defend our territories from barbarian invasion.'

[2] The text is from Migne, *PL* LXXXIX, col. 809, the translation from *The Letters of Boniface*, trans. E. Emerton, Columbia Records of Civilization 31 (1940), 93. 'We order also, by the advice of the servants of God and of the Christian people and in view of imminent wars and attacks by the foreign populations which surround us, that a portion of the properties of the church shall be used for some time longer, with God's indulgence, for the benefit of our army, as a *precarium* and paying a *census*...'          [3] *Ælfric's Lives of Saints* II, 122.

[4] Ælfric's Letter to Sigeweard in *The Old English Version of the Heptateuch* etc., ed. S. J. Crawford, EETS o.s. 160 (London, 1922), 71–2; Ælfric's Latin letter to Wulfstan in *Die Hirtenbriefe Ælfrics*, ed. B. Fehr, *BdaProsa* IX, 225; Jost, *Polity*, pp. 55–6; pseudo-Wulfstan homily L in Napier, *Wulfstan*, p. 267; *King Alfred's Old English Version of Boethius De Consolatione*

easily justifiable war, defensive war; and it is relevant to add some of the other occasions when war is identified in this way. At times the identification seems to have little immediate artistic point as in the frenetic exaltation at English victory in *The Battle of Brunanburh*:

> swa him geæþele wæs
> from cneomægum,   þæt hi æt campe oft
> wið laþra gehwæne   land ealgodon,
> hord and hamas,[1]

a statement which may be linked with the comment in *The Exeter Gnomes* (*Maxims I*):

> garniþ werum,
> wig towiþre   wicfreoþa healdan.[2]

But when Waldere is urged to have no fear about the outcome of his fight and the strength of his sword since Guthhere

> ... ðas beaduwe ongan
> [mi]d unryhte   ærest secan,[3]

this could well be the same motivation for Byrhtnoth's firmness in reply to the Viking, when he says

> ... her stynt unforcuð   eorl mid his werode,
> þe wile gealgean   eþel þysne,
> Æþelredes eard,   ealdres mines,
> folc and foldan,[4]

especially since these lines are immediately followed by that pointed variation on cliché formula

> hæþene æt hilde.[5]   Feallan sceolon

A Christian poet would certainly be conscious that the Englishmen were fighting a 'just war'.

In *Judith* also there seem to be hints that the poet knew and used one of the morals to be drawn from the scriptural heroine's example. Ælfric

---

*Philosophiae*, ed. W. J. Sedgefield (Oxford, 1899), p. 40. For some later medieval references see *Ælfric's Lives of Saints* II 449–50, and *Religious Lyrics of the Fifteenth Century*, ed. Carleton Brown (Oxford, repr. 1952), p. 271.

[1] '...for it was natural to men of their lineage to defend their land, their treasure, and their homes in frequent battle against every foe' (7–10). The translation is from Whitelock, *ASC*, p. 69.

[2] 'The strife of spears [is fitting] for men to hold the settlement in peace, against war' (127–8).

[3] '...sought battle first, wrongly' (26–7). Dr Arne Zettersten has considered the manuscript under ultra-violet light and informs me: 'Only the first two minims of *m* are visible. Traces of the upper part of a third minim and of *i* can be seen.' This confirms the expected emendation *mid* in *Waldere*, ed. F. Norman (London, 1933), p. 38.

[4] 'Here stands a dauntless nobleman with his troop, who will defend this homeland, the land of Æthelred my lord, people and earth' (*The Battle of Maldon*, 51–4).

[5] 'The heathens will fall at battle' (*ibid.* 54–5). This variation on the usual formula, *hysas* (*hæleð, hergum*) *to* (*æt*) *hilde*, is an indication of Byrhtnoth's confidence in himself; see further J. E. Cross, 'Oswald and Byrhtnoth, a Christian Saint and a Hero who is Christian', *ESts* XLVI (1965), 108–9.

stated this clearly in regarding Judith 'to bysne þæt ge eowerne eard mid
wæpnum bewerian wið onwinnendne here'.¹ In the poem, when Judith,
having killed Holofernes and returned to her people, now commands
them to go out and attack, the poet describes the men marching to battle,
now full of courage,

>  þa ðe hwile ær
> elþeodigra      edwit þoledon,
> hæðenra hosp.²

This comment was probably inspired by Judith's exhortation in scripture:
'and rush ye out, not as going down beneath [which implies a sense of
inferiority and a defeatist attitude], but as making an assault' (XIV. 2), yet
the Old English poet so pointedly clarifies this that the statement could be
intended for contemporary stiffening, and the later naming of the Bethu-
lians as *eðelweardas* (320) is most appropriate in the statement which ends
the description of the battle:

>  Hæfdon domlice
> on ðam folcstede      fynd oferwunnen
> eðelweardas,      ealdhettende
> swyrdum aswefede,³

since Judith's people have now really shown themselves to be 'guardians
of their homeland'.

Even in *Genesis A* slight extensions on the scriptural text indicate both
a bias towards the patriarchs' side and a consciousness of the right kind
of war. In the description of the battle of the five kings against the lord of
Elam the Old English poet inserts a reason for the battle from Abraham's
side:

>  woldon Sodome burh
> wraðum werian,⁴

immediately adapts the words of Genesis XIV. 4 by identifying the 'service'
to Elam as the paying of tribute:

>  þa wintra XII
> norðmonnum ær      niede sceoldon
> gombon gieldan      and gafol sellan
> oðþæt þa leode      leng ne woldon
> Elamitarna      aldor swiðan
> folcgestreonum,      ac him from swicon⁵

and clearly indicates that this insurrection was rightly motivated.

---

¹ '...as an example for you to defend your homeland with weapons against an attacking army'
(*The Old English Version of the Heptateuch* etc., p. 48).
² '...who before had endured the insolence of foreigners, the insult of the heathens' (214–16).
³ 'The guardians of the homeland had gloriously conquered the enemy on the battlefield, put
their old enemies to sleep with swords' (318–21).
⁴ 'They wished to defend Sodom against the enemy' (1975–6).
⁵ 'Twelve years they had by necessity to pay tribute and give tax to the men from the north
until the people would no longer support the lord of the Elamites with the nation's treasures
but renounced their allegiance to him' (1976–81).

Both in *Judith* and *Genesis A* the hints are slight, but should not be unnoticed, since it was common practice for Christians to regard the right wars of the Old Testament as just and also as examples. Indeed these scriptural wars were an important factor in creating an attitude of mind which eventually led to an acceptance of war for Christians, especially since both St Paul and St Stephen in the New Testament had praised these historical wars and had recalled with enthusiasm how God had subdued and destroyed the Canaanites through Joshua (Acts vII. 45 and xIII. 19). In Hebrews xI. 33–4 St Paul recalls heroes 'who by faith conquered kingdoms...became valiant in battle, put to flight the armies of foreigners'. Early heresies about these wars had also forced support from the orthodox. Marcion (mid-second-century) had postulated that the wars of the Old Testament were the work, not of the Supreme Being, but of an inferior deity, the just God of the Jews.[1] Such dualism could not be tolerated and was opposed by Tertullian (among others), who revealed in the course of his argument that the Old Testament was being used by Christians as a justification for bearing arms.[2] By rejecting a literal meaning for certain situations in the Old Testament Origen also hardened the orthodox in their defence of the scripture as a record of historical acts and caused these to look for good example there.[3] Ambrose warmly remembers the physical courage of the old warriors even in his *De Officiis Ministrorum*, and praise of soldiers by reference to Old Testament heroes became a literary mode. In the Old English period Eddius Stephanus says of King Ecgfrith in his *Vita Wilfridi* 'sicut Iudas Machabeus in Deum confidens, parva manu populi Dei contra inormem...hostem...invasit' and describes him as 'validus sicut David in contritione hostium',[4] and is generally attracted to this literary trait, while Bede even remembers Æthelfrith the *pagan* father of St Oswald as a warrior against the Britons 'ita ut Sauli, quondam regi Israeliticae gentis conparandus videretur', but with the saving clause: 'excepto dumtaxat hoc, quod divinae erat religionis ignarus'.[5] These wars of Æthelfrith appear to be both defensive in the expulsion of the Britons, and justly offensive in carrying the war across the frontier against the same enemy; but there are occasions in the *Historia Ecclesiastica* when Bede condemns unjust offensive wars, notably in the story of the invasion of Christian Ireland by Ecgfrith of Northumbria in 684 which

[1] Cadoux, *op. cit.* pp. 271 and 567.
[2] Tertullian, *De Idololatria* xix; see Bainton, *op. cit.* p. 82, and Cadoux, *op. cit.* p. 407 and n. 2 and p. 420.
[3] See *ibid.* p. 407.
[4] 'Trusting in God like Judas Maccabeus he attacked with his little band of God's people a vast enemy host'; 'strong like David in crushing his enemies'. Text and translation are from Eddius, pp. 40–3.
[5] '...in such a way that he might appear fit to be compared with Saul, once king of the people of the Israelites, excepting only this that he was ignorant of the divine religion' (*HE* I. 34).

was undertaken against the advice of the priest Egbert who told the king that the Irish had done him no harm. Ecgfrith's commander Berht however 'vastavit misere gentem innoxiam, et nationi Anglorum semper amicissimam...At insulani et, quantum valuere, armis arma repellebant, et invocantes divinae auxilium pietatis, cælitus se vindicari continuis diu imprecationibus postulabant' (like Byrhtnoth's followers at Maldon).[1] Bede believed that those who were justly cursed soon suffered the penalty, which was the death of Ecgfrith at the hands of the Picts in the next year, a war against which St Cuthbert gave warning.

Here Bede's patriotism and his religion are at variance, but more pointedly when, with a neat piece of sophistry, he comments on Cadwallon's killing of the two apostate kings who succeeded Edwin of Northumbria. The punishment of backsliders from Christianity was obviously a just reason for war, but the agent of God's vengeance was a pagan; thus Bede has to reconcile his joy at the punishment with displeasure at the unworthiness of the agent, and comments that Cadwallon was successful: 'Nec mora, utrumque rex Brettonum Ceadualla impia manu, sed iusta ultione peremit.'[2]

Two examples of just offensive war are recorded in Old English poetry, the rescue of Lot by Abraham with which we began the essay and which was a classical scriptural example of the right to save a friend from the enemy in the opinion of the later medieval commentator Nicholas of Lyra,[3] and King Edmund's *Capture of the Five Boroughs*, which was a case of righting wrongs. This act of liberation in Edmund's victory over the Norsemen of York in 942 is clearly named in a statement which extends for half the fourteen-line poem:

> Dæne wæran æror
> under Norðmannum  nyde gebegde
> on hæþenra  hæfteclommum
> lange þrage,  oþ hie alysde eft
> for his weorþscipe  wiggendra hleo,
> afera Eadweardes,  Eadmund cyning.[4]

These varied examples indicate that part of the Christian conscience is concerned with the ethic of war in Anglo-Saxon England; so now the

---

[1] '...miserably devastated that harmless nation, which had always been most friendly to the English nation...But the islanders, to the utmost of their power, repelled force with force, and invoking the aid of the divine mercy prayed long and incessantly to be avenged from heaven' (*ibid.* IV. 24 [26]).

[2] 'Without delay Cadwallon, king of the Britons, killed them both with impious hand but with rightful vengeance' (*ibid.* III. 1).

[3] Among twelve reasons for 'just war' cited in Cornelius a Lapide, *Commentaria in Scripturam Sacram* (Paris, 1874) II, 365, col. 2.

[4] 'Previously the Danes had long been subjected by force to heathen bondage under the Norsemen, until the defender of warriors, King Edmund, son of Edward, liberated them again to his glory' (8–14).

more complicated problem of *Beowulf* may be considered, where national wars form a background against which the hero's last decision to fight the dragon and his death become momentous for his people. While Beowulf lived, as he himself and the messenger say,[1] he defended his kingdom well; when he lies dead, as the messenger foretells,[2] old enemies will now move against the Geatish nation.

The Christian poet is crystal clear on Hygelac's battle with the Frisians, even when his main concern is with the history of the necklace of the Brisings worn by Hygelac:

> syþðan he for wlenco      wean ahsode
> fæhðe to Frysum,[3]

for whether under natural law, from which the later Christian formulization derived through Cicero, or in Christian statement this is an unjust war to the poet. We may recall the statement of Augustine quoted above and match *wlencu* with *superbia*, yet even if *wlencu* is not Christian sin but heroic fault ('presumption', 'reckless daring', as some translate) repercussions must rightly be expected by the Geats, as the poet emphasizes in the whole statement. These the messenger later foretells, when recalling the disastrous raid, by adding

>                 Us wæs a syððan
> Merewioingas     milts ungyfeðe,[4]

and even Beowulf, if not deluded by loyalty to his lord, could have recognized the wrong in Hygelac's act since he had promised help to the Danes if hostile neighbours were ever to threaten Hrothgar.[5] But, though the Geatish leader, Hygelac, and thus the nation are at fault, paradoxically Beowulf as retainer to Hygelac in this battle has no individual guilt in Christian eyes. He is merely a warrior owing allegiance to his leader, right or wrong, or, as Augustine puts it by citing the example of Julian the Apostate, pious or impious: *Julianus exstitit infidelis imperator...milites christiani servierunt imperatori infideli.* If such an emperor called on his men to worship idols they should prefer God's to his command, 'quando autem dicebat, producite aciem, ite contra illam gentem, statim obtemperabant.'[6] In this alternative disobedience and obedience, Augustine continues, they distinguished their eternal from their temporal master, yet for the sake of

---

[1] Lines 2732–6 and 3003–7.           [2] Lines 2910ff. and 3000ff.

[3] '...when, for pride (presumption), he sought trouble, feud with the Frisians' (1206–7).

[4] 'Ever since the favour of the Merovingian king has been denied to us' (2920–1).

[5] Lines 1826ff.

[6] 'Julian was an infidel emperor...Christian soldiers served an infidel emperor...But when he said, deploy into line, march against this nation, they obeyed at once' (*Enarratio in Psalmum CXXIV* 7). See also *Contra Faustum Manichaeum* XXII. 75, where Augustine emphasizes the innocence of a soldier obeying the unrighteous command of his king 'because his position makes obedience a duty'.

their eternal lord they were submissive to the temporal lord, obviously in matters which did not compromise their religion. Augustine could have valued Beowulf as a true retainer obeying the legally constituted authority and have seen no fault in him for his part in Hygelac's raid. But the poet, it seems, takes no sides on the imputation of guilt for the wars between the Geats and the Swedes. On the one hand the messenger, prophet of disaster for the Geatish nation, regards these wars as punishment justly deserved. For him the beginning of the struggle was when Hæthcyn and the Geats *for onmedlan ærest gesohton*[1] the Swedes, and their king, Ongentheow, appears rightly incited both to give *ondslyht*, 'a blow in return' (2929), and to rescue his wife who had been taken off. Ambrose would have accepted these as just motives for Swedish action. Even after this Ongentheow retires to his stronghold, admittedly because he recognizes Hygelac's power, and Hygelac's men advance into Swedish territory to avenge the death of Hæthcyn. But Beowulf, for his part, clearly refers to an earlier stage of the struggle when he speaks of the sons of Ongentheow making war across the lakes around Hreosnabeorh, which was avenged by the hero's kinsmen, Hygelac and Hæthcyn, although Hæthcyn died.[2] At the close of the messenger's speech the poet comments:

> Swa se secg hwata       secggende wæs
> laðra spella;       he ne leag fela
> wyrda ne worda,[3]

but the 'grievous tales' refer to the coming desolation, not to the truth of the events and comment on the Swedish–Geatish war. As Professor Greenfield has said in a sensitive analysis of the two speeches in which the main poetic purpose of these has been discerned, these are 'refractions of historical truth seen through the prisms of the speakers' perspectives and states of mind',[4] and the poet is concerned with the speakers and the whole poem rather than with history and blame. His own commentary[5] does not refer to the beginning of the war, and it would be imprudent to strain his words on Beowulf's part in the war as king. Although Heardred's action in sheltering the sons of Ohthere was foolish and provocative and led to his death, Beowulf can do no other as king than avenge his predecessor by carrying the war to Onela, even though Onela has allowed him to take the Geatish throne. This is obviously a part of the ensnarement in the responsibilities of leader. On this one issue of national war it appears that the poet makes no direct criticism of Beowulf as retainer or leader, but

---

[1] Line 2926.   [2] Lines 2473 ff.

[3] 'So the bold man was telling grievous tales; he did not lie much in words or events' (3028–30).

[4] S. B. Greenfield, 'Geatish History: Poetic Art and Epic Quality in *Beowulf*', *Neophilologus* XLVII (1963), 216.

[5] Lines 2349 b–99 a.

as leader of the nation Beowulf is forced to take on its guilt which is clearly demonstrated at least in the comment on Hygelac's raid.

So far we have considered the dominant and orthodox Christian ethic of war for laymen in the Old English period. The interesting case of St Martin both recalls a strong belief that physical war was wrong for Christians and emphasizes the power of the orthodox view. On the eve of the battle of Worms he had disobeyed the command of the emperor Julian with the bold words *Christi miles sum; pugnare mihi non licet*.[1] When he said this he was a lay conscientious objector, but when Ælfric wrote a pastoral letter in answer to priests who said that they 'must wear a weapon when needed' the homilist cited excerpts of Pseudo-Ecgbert from canon law, quoted Christ's command to Peter, 'Put up thy sword' (Matthew xxvi. 52 and John xviii. 11), and added the story and the words of Martin.[2] By now, and well before, Martin was joined to the ranks of the *oratores* in the threefold division of society.

Yet even in the Old English period there were some who suffered an agony of conscience about the shedding of blood even in necessary public war. Private penitentials in the earlier Old English period offer some evidence of this. In these, killing even in authorized war is logically considered under homicide, and penance is demanded. As Theodore of Canterbury (602–90) says in answer to the priest Eoda: 'Qui per jussionem domini sui occiderit hominem, XL diebus abstineat se ab ecclesia, et qui occiderit hominem in puplico bello XL dies peniteat.'[3] The length of penance, which is the same in other and anonymous penitentials of the period,[4] is very little when compared with penances for other kinds of manslaughter, or other sins.[5] But a fault is acknowledged, a demand for atonement made, and a clear reason is given elsewhere in sections of a penitential now regarded as unauthentic parts of Theodore's work. While there were prayers *super militantes* in the missal,[6] yet:

---

[1] 'I am a soldier of Christ; I am not permitted to fight' (Sulpicius Severus, *Vita S. Martini* ch. iv). See also *Ælfric's Lives of Saints* ii, 226.

[2] *Die Hirtenbriefe Ælfrics*, pp. 55–6.

[3] 'Let one who slays a man by command of his lord keep away from church for forty days; and let one who slays a man in public war do penance for forty days' (*Councils* iii, 180).

[4] See G. I. A. Draper, 'Penitential Discipline and Public Wars in the Middle Ages', *The International Review of the Red Cross* i (1961), 11: 'Recurring with unfailing regularity in the main groupings of penitential literature, whether the paternity be Celtic, Anglo-Saxon or Visigoth, is the clear penitential rule that he who kills a man in a public war must undertake a penance of forty days duration.' For some cited examples see *Medieval Handbooks of Penance*, trans. J. T. McNeill and H. M. Gamer, Columbia Records of Civilization 29 (1938), 187, 225 and 317.   [5] Draper, *loc. cit.*

[6] *The Leofric Missal*, ed. F. E. Warren (Oxford, 1883), p. 230. See also pseudo-Wulfstan homily xxxix in Napier, *Wulfstan*: 'Ðis man gerædde, ða se micela here com to lande' (p. 180), containing advice on fasting, almsgiving and other virtuous acts 'wið þam þe us god ælmihtig gemiltsige and us geunne, þæt we ure fynd ofercuman motan' (p. 181). Prayers for kings and soldiers were introduced into the liturgy at a very early date.

Si autem rex infra regnum exercitum duxerit adversus insurgentes seu rebelles, et permotus bellum egerit, pro regno vel aecclesiastica justitia decertando, quicunque illi opem ferendo homicidium incurrerit, absque gravi culpa erit; tantummodo, propter sanguinis effusionem, se, ut mos est, ab aecclesia XL diebus abstineat, et aliqua ferialia jejunia, pro humilitatis causa, ab aepiscopo suscipiat, et post XL dies reconciliatus, communionem habeat.

Quod si incursio paganorum terram occupaverit, aecclesias devastaverit, terram depopulaverit, et populum Christianum ad bellum concitaverit, quisquis aliquem dejecerit, absque gravi culpa erit, sed tantum per VII, vel XIIII, vel XL dies, ab aecclesiae ingressu se abstineat, et sic purificatus aecclesiam petat.[1]

On two occasions within the period, after the battles of Soissons (923) and Hastings, the church demanded penance for public war on a grand scale. At Soissons Charles the Simple, with an army which included a body of Norsemen from Normandy, attempted to crush the revolt of Robert, Count of Paris, by a surprise attack on Sunday, 15 June 923, when Robert's army was encamped and eating a meal. Robert's larger force eventually carried the day, but the battle 'stands out as a terrible instance of human butchery' and 'for a time the normal machinery of law and government was completely disrupted in the general confusion that prevailed after the battle'.[2] The church was forced to act, penalizing men of both sides equally in the decree of the Synod of Soissons (924). Dr Draper's speculations on the reasons for this public enactment reveal the continual problem for a church which had to concern itself with secular affairs. Charles as lawful king of France had the right to put down a revolt, but, as Draper says,[3] his Norsemen, who were very recent converts, may have needed a reminder not to delight in the butchery of war. Or the synod may have judged this to be a civil war, and a particularly horrifying battle between Christians. We have seen above how Ælfric felt about the third kind of war, and may now add that the Britons' activity in civil war was listed among their many vicious acts by Gildas: *belligerantes, sed civilia et iniusta bella agentes*.[4] But whatever were the synod's reasons in unrevealed

---

[1] 'If the king within the kingdom leads the army against insurgents or rebels, and being roused, wages war for royal authority or ecclesiastical justice, whoever commits homicide in carrying out the task for him shall be without grave fault, but, because of the shedding of blood, let him keep away from church for forty days as is the custom and let him receive some daily fasts from the bishop for the sake of humility and when reconciled after forty days let him take communion. Wherefore if an invasion of pagans overruns the country, lays churches waste, ravages the land and arouses Christian people to war, whoever slays someone shall be without grave fault but let him merely keep away from entering the church for seven or fourteen or forty days and when purified in this way let him come to church' (*Ancient Laws and Institutes of England*, ed. B. Thorpe [London, 1840] II, 5-6).

[2] G. I. A. Draper, 'Penitential Discipline, Part II', *The International Review of the Red Cross* II (1961), 65.       [3] *Ibid.* pp. 66-8.

[4] 'They make wars but the wars they undertake are civil and unjust ones.' Text and translation are from *Gildae de Excidio Britanniae*, ed. and trans. H. Williams, Cymmrodorion Record Series 3 (London, 1899), 66 and 67.

discussion, it appears that the church could be shocked into action, so that even presence on the battlefield called for penance.

The penitential decree which imposed penalties on William of Normandy's men alone and seemingly four years after the Battle of Hastings seems even more tantalizing in its motives. Sir Frank Stenton names this enactment of a council of Norman bishops under Ermenfrid, the papal legate, as a 'remarkable episode'[1] and prudently details its decisions without further comment. David Douglas also makes brief reference to the document but notes that 'it presents some perplexing features'.[2] For, although he was the invader, William had fought under a banner specially blessed by the pope[3] and, on the evidence of the Bayeux tapestry and Norman writers,[4] Harold appears to have sworn to help William some time before the battle and thus become a perjured and disloyal vassal when he claimed the crown of England. The motivation for the tardy and one-sided decree, as Draper suggests, may have been the magnitude of the Norman devastation of England which was the aftermath of Hastings, but by it the church appears to have been inconsistent with regard to the Conqueror's army in the actual battle.

Yet, in these two general decrees as well as in private penitentials, some members of the church seemed to preserve, at least ambivalently, the attitude of some named Christians before the time of Ambrose and Augustine when church and state were not in consort. Obviously within the Anglo-Saxon period there was no argument, as there had been in the early days of the church, about the necessity for lay Christians to do their secular duty in just and public war, but the penitentials reveal that, to some, a light sin was committed even in this lawful act.

[1] *A-S England*, p. 653.
[2] D. C. Douglas, *William the Conqueror* (London, 1964), p. 192, n. 1.
[3] Draper, 'Part II', p. 71.　　　　[4] Stenton, *op. cit.* pp. 567–8.

# The use in *Beowulf* of earlier heroic verse

## ALISTAIR CAMPBELL

Scholars have not failed to notice the similarity of *Beowulf* to the *Æneid* in one major matter of structure: in both epics the poet plunges midway into the story and leaves his hero to supply later in his own words, not indeed his whole early history, but enough of it to give quite a good idea of his character and background.[1] The poet of *Beowulf* introduces his hero's narrative with considerable skill, making Beowulf's personally narrated *enfances* a part of the Unferth episode,[2] while Virgil merely reproduces the Homeric narrative at a feast, but it is to be doubted if the later poet would have lighted upon the device at all without a hint from the older one.[3] Firstly, it can hardly be doubted that the poet of *Beowulf* knew Virgil's poem. He can hardly have worked anywhere but in a monastery, where the materials for recording a long poem and the leisure necessary for their effective use were alike available. Now the considerable body of Latin verse by Anglo-Saxon writers which survives shows that Virgil was the best known of all poets in the Anglo-Saxon monasteries. Secondly, the device of a narrative by the hero is not an inevitable or even a natural element in the structure of an epic. It was devised by the constructor of the present form of the *Odyssey*, who felt no doubt that the *Iliad* had left too much of the earlier adventures of Achilles untold. Indeed mythographers and minor poets have been trying to fill this want ever since. But only under the direct influence of the *Odyssey* or under its indirect influence through Virgil is the device repeated. Some types of epic remain free from it. It does not appear in the Argonautic epic, or in the historical epics of Lucan and Silius Italicus.[4] Furthermore, when long narratives are introduced into epics in imitation of Homer and Virgil, poets frequently fail to realize that the function of the narrative in those writers is not only to recall an earlier part of their main story, but also to illuminate the character and background of their heroes. Statius has a considerable narrative, but it concerns a minor character into whose mouth it is put.[5] Milton has

---

[1] This similarity is, for example, noticed by T. B. Haber, *A Comparative Study of the Beowulf and the Æneid* (Princeton, 1931), p. 49.

[2] Lines 499–581.

[3] The *Beowulf* poet was, of course, wise to make his narrative far shorter proportionally than that of Virgil, for an episode of about 500 lines would be intolerable in a poem of not much more than 3000 lines.

[4] Naevius may have made use of it.   [5] *Thebaid* v. 17–498.

a narrative of great length, but its sole object is to provide a summary of previous history.[1] Such historical summarizing is not at all usual in epic. Statius indeed opens by abjuring it,[2] while Tasso reduces it to a stanza. No Argonautic epic tells the intricate story of how the golden fleece reached Colchis, though it would be highly relevant to the history of Jason's quest. The *Beowulf* poet stands practically alone in using the Homeric-Virgilian device of an inserted narrative in its original structural function.

The value of the insertion in enlarging our view of Beowulf is easy to see. He has not only been a bold youth, he is a master swimmer who can bear arms in water. This prepares us for his invasion of the retreat of Grendel's mother and for his astonishing escape from the Geatish military disaster in the land of the Franks. The episode also gives a hint that Beowulf, like the Sophoclean Herakles, is to be a hero who purifies the earth from monsters hostile to men.[3] It is less easy to determine what pre-existing material the poet has used in the episode. There would seem to be an underlying heroic lay, firstly because these few lines contain quite a number of examples of a strained use of words, which is quite foreign to the usual style of the *Beowulf* poet. The swimmers 'row' out to sea (512 and 539),[4] they 'cover' the sea with their arms (513), the high seas, the path of seafarers, are termed a 'ford' (568).[5] Secondly, Breca of the Brondings is known from another source. The poet of *Widsith*[6] includes him in a list of rulers, who are all, so far as they are known to us, celebrated in heroic poetry. The list includes major figures of Germanic heroic legend, Atli, Eormenric, Theodric the Frank (Wolfdietrich) and Offa of Angel, and lesser ones, Hagene, Sæferth, Finn, Hnæf and Ongentheow. There can be little doubt that Breca, appearing in such company, was also a hero of epic. It is less easy to form an idea of the contents of the presumed poem on Breca used in *Beowulf*. One can be reasonably sure that Beowulf did not appear in it, for he is not a figure of Germanic epic. It is the peculiar art of his poet to make him move in worlds to which he does not belong. He is even introduced into the theme of what must have been an historical lay, when he takes part in the ill-fated Frankish expedition of Hygelac, and takes his superhuman powers of swimming with him into the world of King Theodric and his generals.[7] If then we assume that Breca's opponent

---

1 *Paradise Lost* v–vii.
2 *Thebaid* i. 7, the reader is told that he will not be given *longa retro series*.
3 Lines 567–9; cf. Sophocles, *Trachiniae*, lines 1060–1.
4 The scribe of our manuscript probably did not recognize *reon* in so strange a sense, or he would have modernized to *reowon*.
5 Elsewhere *ford* means only 'ford' in Old English. It is surprising that it has not been proposed to read *flod*.    6 Line 25.
7 On the unheroic nature of Beowulf's reliance on the handgrip, see M. Puhvel in *Folklore* LXXVII (1967), 282. That there were different grades of story there can be no doubt. J. de

in the lay was not Beowulf, we are left with two possibilities: firstly, Beowulf may have replaced another rival of Breca in the story as we have it; secondly, Breca may not have originally had a rival, but may have pitted himself against the dangers of the sea alone for a wager, to fulfil a boast, or when stung by a taunt. Yet the latter possibility is probably to be rejected, for Germanic epic is generally concerned with human collisions, apart from tales of *wreccan* or wandering heroes. It is more likely that Beowulf has replaced another rival of Breca. The story as we have it is that Breca was borne up near his home among the Brondings, while Beowulf landed among the Finns. There seems no good reason why Beowulf should be carried to Finland, while his rival is carried home. Beowulf has perhaps replaced a Finnish hero of the original story. Then the lay would have concluded with two verses describing the arrival of the heroes in their respective homes. The mention of a king of the Finns in *Widsith* (20) assures us that Finns (like Huns) might move in the Germanic heroic world.

The form of the original lay of Breca would probably be, in part, of a repetitive nature. The preparations, deeds, and eventual landing of each hero would be described in similar words, and these repetitions have left their mark on the *Beowulf* poet's adaptation, where the words of Unferth seem based on the account of Breca's swim in the lay, the words of Beowulf on the account of that of his rival, and the two speeches have considerable common elements.

In two perceptive articles,[1] Professor F. P. Magoun has argued that *Beowulf* is the work of three authors, whose work he distinguishes as A, A' and B. B is lines 2200 to the end, but while A is lines 1–2199, Professor Magoun argues that an insertion has been made into it, which he terms A', an originally independent version of Beowulf's adventures in Denmark, approximately lines 2009b–176. This insertion recalls that of *Genesis B* into *Genesis A*, but it has to be assumed that it has been far more skilfully done, and that suitable connecting verses have been added. Much of the alleged insertion is neatly worked into Beowulf's speech to Hygelac. Professor Magoun's main argument for the assumption of separate authors for A and A' lies in inconsistencies between the main account of Beowulf's adventures in Denmark (A) and the shorter account in Beowulf's speech to Hygelac (A'). Similarly, Professor Magoun finds inconsistencies between A and B, which point (he argues) to separate authorship. A detailed

Vries's study, *Betrachtungen zum Märchen* (Ff Communications 150 [1968], 2nd ed.) necessitates no change of attitude to this, but greater care in terminology, and more hesitancy in calling anything 'folktale' which is not epic.

[1] '*Beowulf A*': a Folk-Variant', *Arv* xiv (1958), 95–101, and '*Beowulf B*: a Folk-Poem on Beowulf's Death', *Early English and Norse Studies*, ed. A. Brown and P. Foote (London, 1963), pp. 127–40.

examination of these arguments does not lie in the plan of this paper, but the present writer doubts whether they will in the long run command general conviction.[1] Professor Magoun, however, adds to them an important stylistic point. Half-lines consisting of a masculine compound in the accusative followed by *þone* are not found in the early part of *Beowulf*. The type appears first in 2007b (*uhthlem þone*), which Professor Magoun now places in A' without comment.[2] The other instances are all in B.[3] The type seems not to be found outside *Beowulf*. Professor Magoun's point is remarkable, and it will be necessary for those who do not feel convinced by his theory of separate authors for *Beowulf* to advance another explanation. Such an explanation is, however, readily available. We need not doubt that *Beowulf*, like another and a greater epic, was *multum uigilata per annos*. The poet shows no knowledge of Swedish affairs in the earlier parts of his work, but later he gives evidence that he knew an heroic lay, summarized and probably in part reproduced in lines 2922–98,[4] which dealt with the death of Ongentheow,[5] and at least one other lay on Swedish affairs, that on the story of Eanmund and Eadgils and the death of Onela.[6] It would seem that the poet came to know of these lays after his poem was far advanced. The one on Ongentheow's death has in the *Beowulf* poet's summary the half-line *freoðowong þone* (2959a). This may have stood in the original lay, and this may be the source from which the *Beowulf* poet learned this line-type in time to use it in the second part of his poem and at the very end of the first.

The light which we get on the *Beowulf* poet's use of older vernacular poetry from the episode of Finn is disappointingly small. It is true that we have an ancient lay about Finn, but its content is not reproduced by the *Beowulf* poet, and indeed he may not have known it. However, it may be that he is referring to the night-attack described in the lay in the line *Finnes eaferum ða hie se fær begeat* (1068). Yet the part of the story upon which the poet enlarges begins with the death of Hnæf, and of many of his

---

[1] A number of Professor Magoun's points are answered by K. Sisam, *The Structure of Beowulf* (Oxford, 1965), pp. 44 ff., though he does not specifically mention Professor Magoun's article.

[2] Professor Magoun is not entirely consistent in his statements about the limits of his postulated A' passage. At the beginning of the first of the articles mentioned above, he speaks of 'that section...which includes 2009 b–176', but at the beginning of the second article he gives the same figures as definite limits. Then on p. 135 he definitely places 2007 b in A'. Of course, this is necessary for his point.

[3] They are in the first half-line in lines 2588 and 2959; in the second in lines 2334, 2969 and 3081.

[4] Some additional points are given in lines 2472–84.

[5] There is a discussion of this lay by H. Weyhe in *ES* xxxiv (1908), 14–39. The use in *Beowulf* of lays (probably Geatish) on the wars of the Swedes and Geats was first pointed out by Ten Brink, *Beowulf: Untersuchungen*, QF 62 (1888), 189–90.

[6] This lay is used chiefly in lines 2379–96. Cf. lines 2201–8 and 2611–18.

men. He describes the funerals and the uneasy peace and its sequel. The linguistic atmosphere of the passage is archaic, like others in *Beowulf* dealing with ancient legend.[1] It is extremely difficult to decide how many lays on the story of Finn the *Beowulf* poet used. It is possible that one long lay covered the story from the death of Hnæf to that of Finn. Yet a conclusion may be indicated at line 1124, *wæs hira blæd scacen*, and another lay may have been devoted to Hengest's winter sojourn with Finn and the breaking of the truce in the spring. Even if this is doubted, it is hardly to be denied that there existed at least two lays about Finn, one about the night attack and its temporary repulse (i.e. the extant lay) and another about the death of Hnæf and subsequent events. Two lays have been mentioned above which must also have been complementary to each other, those on Ongentheow's death and on the story of Eanmund and Eadgils. Similarly, the lay on the marriage of Ingeld probably reached a climax with the breaking of the peace by the young Heathobeard warrior and had a sequel in another lay describing the burning of Heorot.[2] The lay of Offa used in *Beowulf* would also seem to have been one of a cycle, another poem from which was used by the poet of *Widsith*.[3] There is thus sufficient evidence that the lays used by the *Beowulf* poet belonged to cycles. Yet in the article quoted above, in which he attacks the unity of authorship of *Beowulf*,[4] Professor Magoun argues that formulaic poetry is never cyclic. It may be well to quote his exact words: 'Seldom if ever does a folk-singer, composing extemporaneously without benefit of writing materials, compose a cyclic poem, that is, sing in a single session or series of sessions, a story which he or she feels is a unit dealing with several consecutive events in a character's life.'[5] It is not very clear how Professor Magoun can prove this. He cites Lönnrot's admission that the songs of the Kalevala turn up singly, and the testimony of Professor Lord that Serbian reciters sometimes know the lay of a feud but do not know its sequel in a lay of vengeance.[6] It is doubtful if any of this throws light on *Beowulf*, for it is

---

[1] See A. Campbell, 'The Old English Epic Style', *English and Medieval Studies*, ed. N. Davis and C. L. Wrenn (London, 1962), p. 18. Another archaism in this passage is *bearnum ond broðrum* '[deprived of] her child and her brother' (1074), an ancient manner of expressing the dual; cf. Catullus's *Veneres Cupidinesque*, 'Venus and Cupid', and A. J. Bell, *The Latin Dual and Poetic Diction* (London, 1923), p. 66.

[2] Cf. *English and Medieval Studies*, p. 20.      [3] Lines 37–42.

[4] *Early English and Norse Studies*, pp. 127–40.      [5] *Ibid.* p. 128.

[6] In *Tennessee Studies in Literature* XI (1966), 131–43, R. P. Creed adduces as additional support for Professor Magoun's view the three poems sung by Demodocus in *Odyssey* VIII. He regards these as being treatments of single episodes and not cyclic. This may be true of the second one (a comic lay about gods, not heroes, and hence not relevant to the present subject), but it is incorrect of the other two. The first (73–82) describes a quarrel of Achilles and Odysseus at a festival. This story had point only in the background of the whole Trojan war: the quarrel was a sign that the fall of Troy was near. The lay about it would therefore be a preparatory lay to one about the fall of Troy. The third lay of Demodocus (499–520) dealt with the fall of Troy, and is marked as dealing with a series of incidents by the introductory words, where the bard is said to have sung ἔνθεν ἑλὼν ὡς..., 'starting from where...'.

more than doubtful if that work was composed 'without benefit of writing materials'. The Finnish and Serbian parallels are doubtfully applicable even to Germanic poetry older than *Beowulf*, and admittedly pre-literary. How can it be proved that a real scop might not have known several lays about Finn, like the imaginary scop in *Beowulf*? Why should not the original forms of one or more of these lays have been due to one poet? It would seem, furthermore, that the ancient Germanic lays were particularly suitable to be grouped into cycles. The form of Germanic lay, as we are able to reconstruct it from the two extant specimens (*Finnesburg* and *Hildebrand*), included a summary at the end, which indicated precisely the point reached, and this would inevitably create expectation of another lay to tell what followed: 'they fought for five days without any one of them, the retainers falling;' 'they fought...until their shields were [hewn] small.' This tendency towards cyclic lays corresponded to a strong cyclic tendency in the development of Germanic heroic legend, which tended to draw all the stories around one or two figures. In this matter, two lines of development can be distinguished. In the West Germanic development, all the main stories are grouped round Dietrich von Bern, whose contemporary and rival Eormenric becomes. Wolfdietrich is his ancestor, Wayland the father of one of his champions. The vast cycle of Sigurd and the Burgundians is joined to that of Dietrich by the presence of the latter at the slaughter in Atli's hall. In the Scandinavian development, the stories are differently welded together, because Dietrich is scarcely known.[1] The figure of Guthrun is the strongest link used to join the stories. As the wife first of Sigurd and then of Atli, and as the mother (by a third husband) of Hamthir and Sörli, she joins the three cycles of Sigurd, the Burgundians and Eormenric strongly together. In this process of rendering stories and lays more and more cyclic, stories would no doubt be modified, if need arose, in expectation of what was to follow. Once the adversaries of Walther had been identified with Gunnar and Hagen of the Niblung story, obviously they could be only wounded and not killed.[2] Their deaths were reserved for a more famous hour. So a Norse poem implies that Hildebrand killed his son in their famous duel, but to judge from *Thithreks saga* and a late variant of the lay, the West Germanic tradition modified the story to end happily.[3] This chariness to kill is found elsewhere

[1] *Thithreks saga*, of course, is based on a West Germanic, not a Scandinavian, development of Germanic legend.

[2] The view of the original form of the story of Walter taken above most resembles that of Boer, *Zeitschrift für deutsche Philologie* XL (1908), 43 ff. The latest discussion of the story is by H. Kuhn, *Festgabe für Ulrich Pretzel* (Berlin, 1963), pp. 5–12. While not in entire agreement with what is said above, Kuhn strongly refutes the view of some scholars that the original version is the Latin *Waltarius*, which they assume to be built not from heroic legend, but from scraps of Latin poetry. Kuhn also stresses that the original story had a tragic ending.

[3] The Norse poem is edited in A. Heusler and W. Ranisch, *Eddica Minora* (Dortmund, 1903), pp. 53–4. On *Thithreks saga* and the late lay see W. Kienast in *Archiv* CXLIV (1922), 155–69.

in heroic verse: the poets of the *Iliad* seem to kill only heroes whom they themselves had invented, and never heroes of saga, who would appear in sequels.[1]

From what has been said, it would seem that the evidence for cycles of complementary lays in Germanic is sound. It is natural to ask if the passage in *Beowulf* on Sigmund and Sinfjötli[2] affords evidence for the existence of a cycle of Völsung lays, as there are extensive remains of such a cycle in Old Norse. The *Beowulf* passage is unfortunately vague. We are told of wide journeys by Sigmund, which he described to Sinfjötli, in whose company he had killed many monsters. But Sinfjötli was not with Sigmund at the dragon fight which brought him fame after death. Unlike the passages on Breca, Finn, Hygelac, Ongentheow, Onela, Ingeld and Offa, where the poet is clearly using lays, the one on Sigmund has little concrete information to offer, indeed none except about the dragon fight. This fight is the point of the episode. There is a tacit comparison of Beowulf the dragon-slayer with a dragon-slayer of legend. Now in some story unknown to us, Sigmund may have killed a dragon, but the intention clearly is, not to compare Beowulf's dragon fight with some unnotable one, but with the greatest dragon-slaying of which the Germanic world had ever heard, and that could only be that of Sigurd. The *Beowulf* poet (or his source) has totally confused Sigmund and Sigurd, giving to the father the dragon fight of the son.[3] He had no clear knowledge of Sigmund's career before the fight, or of the adventures of Sinfjötli, and he has, therefore, to be vague about these matters. The dragon fight is described with some exactitude, and here a lay is probably being used.[4] To this lay may belong the confusion of father and son. A bad tradition is indicated also by the extraction of a name Wæls from Wælsing, as if the latter were a patronymic.

The case for the existence of a lay on Sigmund, which the *Beowulf* poet uses, is further strengthened by the manner in which a passage on Heremod follows that on Sigmund. That these two heroes were linked in poetry is well known.[5] The passages about them are linked not only by their position in *Beowulf*, but by their use of a line-type in which a pronoun in dip and a preposition governing that pronoun in final lift are separated by a noun.[6] All things considered, the case is fairly good for the use of a lay

---

[1] See W. Kullmann, *Die Quellen der Ilias*, Hermes, Einzelschriften 14 (Wiesbaden, 1960), *passim*.

[2] Lines 875–97.

[3] Unless we accept the view of Heusler (following early authorities) that *wiges heard* (886) is a kenning for Sigurd; see J. Hoops, *Reallexikon der germanischen Altertumskunde, s.v. Sigfrid*, § 3.

[4] From this lay may come the curious use of *aglæca* to mean 'warrior' (893). The only near parallel is *aglæcean* as a virtual dual, 'the monster and his adversary' (2592).

[5] They are mentioned together in *Hyndluljóð*, strophe 2.

[6] *ne wæs him Fitela mid* (889 b) and *se þe him bealwa to* (909 a); cf. *siþþan hine Niðhad on* (*Deor*, 5 a). The type appears only in these passages, of which all refer to ancient Germanic legends.

in the Sigmund-Heremod passage, but there is no evidence that a cycle of Völsung lays was known to the *Beowulf* poet.

Two lays known to the *Beowulf* poet, that on the death of Hygelac, and that on the death of Onela, have been mentioned already, but they must now be considered briefly together, because the material derived from them is clearly integrated with the main plot of the poem. Beowulf's succession to the Geatish throne took place only because of the successive deaths of Hygelac and Heardred (who was killed in Onela's invasion of the land of the Geats). Beowulf is himself introduced into the action of both these lays as they are summarized by the *Beowulf* poet. He accompanies Hygelac on his fatal expedition, and after the death of Heardred and his own succession, he supports Eadgils in a successful attack on Sweden, in which Onela is killed. The addition of Beowulf as a follower of Hygelac would not enforce any modification of the story of the lay of Hygelac, but in the *Beowulf* poet's summary of the lay of Onela, Beowulf no doubt replaced some other person as the supporter who helped Eadgils to defeat Onela. In our complete ignorance of Geatish legendary history after the death of Heardred, we can form no idea who this can have been.

The chief passages have now been reviewed in which the *Beowulf* poet appears to be drawing upon heroic lays. There are others of less importance where stories are mentioned which may well have been the subjects of lays. An example is the story of Herebeald and his unlucky death by a shot of a *hornboga*. Another is the story of Heorogar, the elder brother of Hrothgar, who seems to have had some quarrel with his son Heoroweard, and to have died young. It is, however, advisable to be cautious in postulating the existence of lays, when a story may be based on no more than an annotation to a genealogy. Such annotation is clearly the source of the story of Scyld Scefing, for we can see a version of it (though with Sceaf instead of Scyld for hero) in the genealogy of Æthelwulf of Wessex in Æthelweard.[1] The beginning of *Beowulf* indeed shows affinity with the genealogical literature which was so popular in the early Old English period.[2] The *Beowulf* poet made his epic spring from a genealogy; the Alfredian chroniclers made their chronicle do the same.

The lays known to the *Beowulf* poet were mostly about Scandinavia and the coast of the North Sea. Of the great heroes known to the whole Germanic

---

[1] See *The Chronicle of Æthelweard*, ed. A. Campbell (London, 1962), p. 33.

[2] Professor Magoun, *Early English and Norse Studies*, pp. 132–3, contrasts the clarity of the Danish genealogical matter at the beginning of *Beowulf* with the interrupted and obscure manner in which similar Swedish and Geatish material is given in the second part of the poem, and regards this contrast as support for his theory of separate authors. The difference arises from the difference in the nature of the sources. The Danish material is purely genealogical, the Swedish and Geatish is derived from a variety of heroic lays.

world he has little to say. He knew the story of Sigurd in a confused form, and also a story about a feat of Hama unknown to us.[1] But as he clearly regards Hama as opposed to Eormenric it may be that the *Beowulf* poet knew a development of Germanic legend in which Eormenric had already displaced Odoacer as the chief enemy of Dietrich von Bern and his peers. Nevertheless, the amount of Germanic heroic legend that the *Beowulf* poet summarizes, or to which he at least alludes, is considerable. This has long been recognized, and able critics have discussed the relevance of the heroic interludes, or 'episodes' as they are usually called, to the main plot, and others, no less able, have applauded or deplored the decision of the poet to take his main plot from another world of story. It cannot be said that the question why the *Beowulf* poet did not take his main plot from the heroic legends in which he was clearly so interested has been answered, especially as the *Waldere* fragments show that the heroic epic was a form used in Old English. It is possible that the poet himself was not entirely confident that he had chosen his subject wisely. Virgil may again have come to his aid. That poet had refrained from writing directly on the history of Rome, and had chosen a legendary subject. Yet he still poured into his epic the history of Rome, especially in the scenes in the lower world, and the events depicted on the shield of Aeneas, and perpetually by allusion and hint. The *Beowulf* poet, a lesser constructor, but not a poor one, gave the Germanic heroic legend, which he had rejected as a source for his main plot, a considerable part in his poem by means of background and episode. Whether he could have achieved this without consciously noting the Virgilian example is uncertain. What is certain is that the composition of such a poem as *Beowulf*, working in two worlds of story, and blending them just as much as is necessary, but no more, is a work of plan and sophistication.

It is generally emphasized today that *Beowulf* is a formulaic epic. This is, of course, not open to dispute. What can be disputed is the common view that a formulaic poem will always be the work of an illiterate singer. This view has been strongly put by Professor A. B. Lord,[2] and has much weighty support, including that of Professor Magoun.[3] If it be accepted, then obviously the view of *Beowulf* just advanced as a carefully constructed literary work is untenable. It has, however, been attacked from various points of view. It may be sufficient to mention here that the Old English verse psalms, surely the fruit of hard work in the study, are highly formulaic.[4] It is, in any event, a mistake to regard Old English verse as formulaic

---

[1] Lines 1198–201.
[2] Especially in *The Singer of Tales* (Cambridge, Mass., 1960).
[3] See especially *Speculum* xxviii (1953), 446–67.
[4] See R. E. Diamond, *The Diction of the Anglo-Saxon Metrical Psalms* (The Hague, 1963).

in the sense that the Serbian and Russian heroic lays are formulaic. Professor Randolph Quirk has shown that in Old English the formula has had a development which has given to it a fine emotional sensitivity.[1] Furthermore, Old English verse has been developed as a more sophisticated instrument of expression than any verse known to be of oral origin, or even than any verse closely related to verse of oral origin. It has got entirely rid of the regular practice of oral poets of repeating not only formulae, but whole passages in the same words. This practice, of extreme frequency in Russian and Serbian heroic lays, and still frequent in Homer,[2] is hardly to be traced in *Beowulf* at all.[3] The style of *Beowulf*, with its artistic control of the formula, its avoidance of long repetitions and its careful building of long paragraphs,[4] recalls, not so much oral epic verse, as the sophisticated development of the Homeric style found in late Greek epic. Milman Parry, in one of the series of studies which opened modern work in the epic formula, discussed Apollonius Rhodius briefly.[5] He pointed out Apollonius's un-Homeric enjambement, and the way in which his thought looks beyond the line-end, even if this be capable of carrying heavy punctuation. He also pointed out Apollonius's moderation in the repetition of Homeric formulae. To these two points might be added the avoidance of the repetition of whole passages. These three features we have already found in *Beowulf*. Of course, comparison of *Beowulf* with Apollonius might be pressed too far. Apollonius is a poet of exceptional learning, coming at the end of a great literature, and many strands are to be found in his language, reminding us that the Greek tragedians and philosophers had passed before him. Yet in Apollonius, and some of his successors, especially Nonnus, and in *Beowulf* we have developments of oral formulaic verse, such as might be expected when poets wrote in the study and, even though verse was still meant to be recited, not to be read, there could be confidence that it would be preserved as written, and when the rôles of poet and reciter were no longer confused.

[1] *Early English and Norse Studies*, pp. 150–71.

[2] These repeated passages seem to have been more numerous when the text was in an earlier stage of transmission than they are in the received text, see, e.g., notes in the Oxford Homer on *Iliad* III. 302 and VIII. 53; and on the subject of Homeric repetitions see G. Jachmann, *Vom frühalexandrinischen Homertext*, Nachrichten von der Akademie der Wissenschaften in Göttingen (1949), pp. 167–232. These repetitions do not, of course, prove the extant Homeric poetry to be of oral origin. On flaws in current arguments concerning oral verse, with especial reference to Homer, see D. Young in *Arion* VI (1967), 279–324. Of course, if the view of Lord, that an oral poet hardly ever alludes to stories other than the one he tells (*op. cit.* p. 159), were taken seriously, the Homeric poems and *Beowulf* would have to be regarded alike as non-oral.

[3] In the Breca passage, Beowulf to some degree echoes the words of Unferth, and this may indicate that the underlying lay was repetitive, the deeds of the rival swimmers being described in the same words.

[4] See *English and Medieval Studies*, pp. 19–20.

[5] *Transactions of the American Philological Association* LX (1929), 213–14; see also *Harvard Studies in Classical Philology* XLI (1930), 115.

# Cynewulf's image of the Ascension

## PETER CLEMOES

As has been realized since 1853[1] Cynewulf derived the underlying train of thought for his poem on the Ascension[2] from that part of Gregory the Great's Ascension Day homily in which Gregory makes a series of points *de ipsa tantæ solemnitatis consideratione*.[3] The origin of the first part of the poem (440–599) lies in this passage:

Hoc autem nobis primum quærendum est, quidnam sit quod nato Domino apparuerunt angeli, et tamen non leguntur in albis vestibus apparuisse, ascendente autem Domino, missi angeli in albis leguntur vestibus apparuisse. Sic etenim scriptum est: 'Videntibus illis elevatus est, et nubes suscepit eum ab oculis eorum. Cumque intuerentur in cœlum euntem illum, ecce duo viri steterunt juxta illos in vestibus albis' (Acts I. 9–10). In albis autem vestibus gaudium et solemnitas mentis ostenditur. Quid est ergo quod nato Domino, non in albis vestibus, ascendente autem Domino, in albis vestibus angeli apparent, nisi quod tunc magna solemnitas angelis facta est, cum cœlum Deus homo penetravit? Quia nascente Domino videbatur divinitas humiliata; ascendente vero Domino, est humanitas exaltata. Albæ etenim vestes exaltationi magis congruunt quam humiliationi. In assumptione ergo ejus angeli in albis vestibus videri debuerunt, quia qui in nativitate sua apparuit Deus humilis, in Ascensione sua ostensus est homo sublimis.[4]

Cynewulf paraphrases Gregory's question,[5] greatly amplifying the refer-

[1] See F. Dietrich, 'Cynevulfs Crist', *Zeitschrift für deutsches Alterthum* IX (1853), 204.

[2] The most copious edition is A. S. Cook's *The Christ of Cynewulf*, 2nd rev. impression (Boston, 1909, repr. with a preface by J. C. Pope 1964), Part II – The Ascension (i.e. lines 440–866). My references are to the line numbers of this edition.

[3] Migne, *PL* LXXVI, cols. 1218–19.

[4] 'Now we must ask this first, why it is that angels appeared when the Lord was born and yet we do not read that they appeared in white garments, whereas when the Lord ascended we read that the angels which were sent appeared in white garments. For thus it is written: 'While they beheld he was taken up, and a cloud received him out of their sight. And while they looked steadfastly towards heaven as he went up, behold, two men stood by them in white apparel' (Acts I. 9–10). Now white garments are a sign of joy and celebration. Why therefore do angels not appear in white garments when the Lord is born but appear in white garments when the Lord ascends, unless it is because it was a cause of great celebration for angels when God as man entered into heaven? For when the Lord was born divinity seemed humbled; when the Lord ascended humanity was exalted. White clothes suit exaltation more than humiliation. And so in his assumption it was right for angels to be seen in white garments, since he who at his nativity appeared as God made humble, at his ascension was revealed as man exalted' (*ibid.* col. 1218). It should be noticed that Gregory assumes that the *duo viri in vestibus albis* were angels.

[5] I should prefer to regard lines 448b–9a as belonging to the sentence which Cook begins with 449b.

ence to Acts with a narrative based mainly on Acts I. 1–14 but also drawing on the accounts in Matthew XXVIII. 16–20, Mark XVI. 14–20 and Luke XXIV. 36–53.[1] What survives of Cynewulf's version of Gregory's answer[2] is to the effect that the radiant garments of the angels were appropriate to the great feast which was held in heaven to greet Christ's arrival. Amplification of this answer is in the form of a speech which is addressed to those within heaven by one of the angelic throng escorting the ascending Christ and which depicts Christ as arriving in triumph accompanied (as in *The Dream of the Rood*, 150–6) by the host of those whom he has redeemed in the Harrowing of Hell.[3] Finally (586–99) Cynewulf relates this first part of his poem to the absolute choice between hell and heaven which the Incarnation has given to every man. Thus in his expansion of Gregory's question the Ascension is viewed as a departure from earth and in his expansion of Gregory's answer it is seen as an arrival in heaven. The former (456–545a) is my subject here.

The metaphorical connection which Cynewulf establishes between the narrative of the Ascension and the elements of heroic society stresses primarily the relationship between Christ the *brega* (456a), *þeoden* (457a), *hlaford* (461a), and the apostles, *his þegna gedryht* (457b), *hæleð* (461a), *gesiþas* (473a). Several secondary motifs enter into this relationship: Christ summons his band of followers (*gelaðade*, 458a); he is their distributor of

[1] Mark's gospel supplies the gospel reading for the day and Acts the epistolary reading. Homilists commenting on the biblical text confine themselves to these two versions and do not conflate them. (A composite account, drawing on Acts and the three gospels, is, however, found in a homily of a different type, the unpublished one for Ascension Day on pp. 431–41 of CCCC 162, a manuscript of the beginning of the eleventh century.) The liturgy of Ascension-tide did not furnish Cynewulf with his particular selection. He may have used a harmony of the gospels in conjunction with Acts, though he certainly could have made his own. All the elements which derive from the gospels (except that of the fulfilment of prophecies through Christ's Passion [lines 468–70a; cf. Luke XXIV. 44–6]) are included in the Latin version of Tatian's *Diatesseron* which is in Fulda, Landesbibliothek, Bonifatianus 1, and which has been published from this manuscript (*Codex Fuldensis...*, ed. E. Ranke [Marburg and Leipzig, 1868]). This manuscript, written in the sixth century in southern Italy, was known to Englishmen in the eighth century, for it contains some corrections in eighth-century insular uncial and, on certain folios, numerous glosses which may be in the hand of Boniface; see E. A. Lowe, *CLA* VIII, no. 1196 and accompanying plate. As is well known, in the first half of the ninth century the Latin Tatian was used as the source for the Old Saxon poem *Heliand*, written in the tradition of vernacular religious epic which had come to the continent from England. If the Tatian was known in Northumbria in Cædmon's time it would certainly have been useful for his versification of gospel narrative.

[2] Owing to the loss of a leaf from the Exeter Book after fol. 15 some sixty-five to seventy lines of the poem are missing between *frætwum* and *ealles waldend* in line 556b; see J. C. Pope, 'The Lacuna in the Text of Cynewulf's *Ascension* (*Christ II*, 556b)', *Studies in Language, Literature, and Culture of the Middle Ages and Later* (in honour of Rudolph Willard), ed. E. B. Atwood and A. A. Hill (Austin, Texas, 1969), pp. 210–19.

[3] Cynewulf owed this speech to the dramatic dialogue which, modelled on ps. XXIV. 7–10, was included in an Ascension hymn by Bede (*CC* CXXII, 419–23). A. S. Cook (*op. cit.* pp. 116–18) was the first to point out the use of this hymn as a source. Concerning this hymn, see H. Gneuss, *Hymnar und Hymnen im englischen Mittelalter* (Tübingen, 1968), p. 53.

treasure (*sincgiefa*, 460a and *tires brytta*, 462b); their place of assembly is a *burh* (461b), a *þingstede* (497a); he rewards them (*lean æfter geaf*, 473b); he exhorts them to destroy enemy idols (*hergas breotaþ, fyllað ond feogað, feond-scype dwæscað*, 485b–6b[1]); they protect him (*last weardedun*, 496b); they depart grieving from the place where they had watched him ascend (533–40a).[2] The plentiful terms used of Christ[3] vary according to the movement of the narrative: when he teaches the apostles, he is *sincgiefa* (460a) and *tires brytta* (462b); when the apostles glorify him, he is *lifes agend* (471b) and *fæder frumsceafta* (472a); when he lays his commission on them to evangelize the world, he is *waldend engla* (474b) and *frea mihtig* (475a); in his ascension he is *cyning* (494b), *cyninga wuldor* (508a), *sigores agend* (513b) and *ealles waldend* (544b). This descriptive, celebratory terminology is in itself enough to show that Cynewulf's aim is not merely to tell the story of the Ascension but to create out of it an image of devotion to Christ the king.[4] The cult of Christ as king had been a dominant one in the church since the

---

[1] A comma after *feogað* seems preferable to Cook's semi-colon.

[2] Cf. *The Dream of the Rood*, 68b–9a. Their sadness contradicts Luke xxiv. 52. Bede's commentary on Acts I. 11 (Migne, *PL* xcii, col. 942) implies sadness.

[3] There are thirty-one different ones in 74½ lines of verse (i.e. lines 456–545a minus Christ's speech to the apostles in which, naturally, they do not occur, lines 476–90); the only ones repeated are *þeoden* (two occurrences) and *hlaford* (three).

[4] Cynewulf uses the ideas he derives from Gregory as starting-points for imagistic writing throughout the poem. For instance, the thought *Forþon we a sculon idle lustas... forseon* (756–7a) (Gregory, *Desideria terrena fugiamus*), through a simple correlation of *idle lustas* (756b) and *synwunde* (757a), introduces a lively and dramatic treatment of the ecclesiastical image of the devils' arrows and the protection which God affords us against them through his angels (758–82a), in substitution for Gregory's further statement *nihil nos jam delectet in infimis, qui patrem habemus in cælis*. By contrast, the same image is strictly subordinated to the line of thought in Cynewulf's *Juliana* (lines 397b–409a) and is part of the homiletic argument in Hrothgar's 'sermon' in *Beowulf* (lines 1741b–7). In the Ascension poem Cynewulf attaches his images to general, commonplace thought. For instance, Gregory makes the specific, doctrinal point that the sentence of damnation which God had passed on humanity, *Terra es et in terram ibis*, was annulled when human nature ascended to heaven in the person of Christ. From this Cynewulf takes the image of the cancelled sentence of damnation and uses it as a special illustration of the bounty of God which gives us food, possessions and the blessings of nature. By an opposite process both the author of Blickling homily xi and Ælfric in his Ascension Day homily in the First Series of *Catholic Homilies* take over Gregory's thought entire and incorporate it, without any of Cynewulf's vivifying, actualizing treatment, in a commentary on Acts I. 10. So with Gregory's point about the angels' garments. Whereas the Blickling homilist and Ælfric each make it part of their commentary on Acts I. 10, it demonstrates for Cynewulf the salvation which has been brought to us by the Incarnation and which gives every man the choice between hell and heaven. As to why the angels did not rejoice at the Nativity but did at the Ascension, perhaps in the missing lines (see above, p. 294, n. 2 and the reference there to Pope's article) Cynewulf explained this, not in Gregory's precise theological terms, but with reference to the Nativity as the beginning and to the Ascension as the end of the process of man's redemption: at the former the angels were Christ's messengers readily helping their leader when he set out on his noble expedition (448b–53a); at the latter they were welcoming back their victorious king. Perhaps too, in these missing lines, Cynewulf touched on the provisional nature of the redemption gained for men on earth, an implication which was seen in the angels' reference to the Second Coming and which is brought out in a later passage of Gregory's homily, in Bede's hymn and in the liturgy of Ascensiontide generally.

fourth century,[1] and the Ascension, sequel to the Resurrection, was seen as a supreme manifestation of that sovereignty.[2] Cynewulf is bringing into the service of this cult the elements of heroic literary tradition as linguistic resources for image-making just as, centuries before, in the service of the same cult, early Christian artists had adapted formulae in Roman imperial iconography to depict the Ascension visually.[3]

To compare Cynewulf's image in words with representations in contemporary Anglo-Saxon art is, indeed, to find that they have much in common, both in general conception and in specific motifs.[4] If, with Dr Sisam,[5] we think of Cynewulf as a ninth-century Anglian, either Mercian or Northumbrian, two surviving carvings exemplify the sort of visual representations which we may reasonably suppose him to have seen. One is on a fragment of the upright of a ninth-century[6] cross now serving as the stem of the font in Rothbury church, Northumberland (see pl. I).[7] The other is one of several scenes carved in two bands across an eighth-century[8] stone slab which, imperfect at both ends and of uncertain original use, is preserved in Wirksworth church, Derbyshire (see pl. II).[9] As in Cynewulf's poem, in both these carvings the Ascension is conceived of as a representational, narrative image, quite different from the static, schematic treatment of it in Irish art as instanced by the ninth-century Bobbio gospel book.[10] All three – Cynewulf's poem and the Rothbury and Wirks-

---

[1] On its origins see P. Beskow, *Rex Gloriae: the Kingship of Christ in the Early Church* (Stockholm, 1962).

[2] For instance, in Bede's hymn Christ is celebrated as *rex gloriae, rex saeculi, rex altithronus, rex regum* and *rex gloriae, virtutis atque gratiae.*

Of the distinctive terms that Cynewulf uses of the ascending Christ *cyninga wuldor* (508a) occurs three times in Cynewulf's other extant signed poems (*Elene*, 5b and 178b and *Juliana*, 279b) while *æþelinga ord* (515a) occurs once (*Elene*, 393a). In all three cases in *Elene* (5b, 178b and 393a) the reference is to Christ in the Nativity. *Æþelinga ord* also occurs twice elsewhere in the Ascension poem, once (741a) with reference to Christ in the Ascension and once (845a) with reference to him as Judge. Several of these terms (*frumbearn*, 507a; *sigores agend*, 513b; *ealra folca fruma*, 516a; *heahengla cyning*, 528a; *haligra helm*, 529a; and *eadfruma*, 532a) do not occur elsewhere in Cynewulf's signed poems (although similar ones do), while *liffruma* (504a) occurs only at 656b – again with reference to the Ascension.

[3] See, e.g., A. Grabar, *Christian Iconography: a Study of its Origins* (London, 1969), p. 35.

[4] K. Mildenberger's comparison ('Unity of Cynewulf's *Christ* in the Light of Iconography' *Speculum* XXIII [1948], 426–32, a reference of which I first learned from Mr D. Kent of the University of Liverpool) is quite differently based, as its title shows.

[5] *Studies*, p. 7.

[6] Rosemary Cramp refers to the cross as 'obviously late in the Anglian tradition' and suggests a late-ninth-century dating (*Early Northumbrian Sculpture*, Jarrow Lecture 1965, p. 11).

[7] The bottom $25\frac{1}{2}$ in. of the carving (measured at the centre) survive in a damaged state; probably about 7 in. have been lost at the top. At the level of the lower row of apostles' heads the width is $14\frac{1}{2}$ in. The measurements are approximate.

[8] See T. D. Kendrick, *Anglo-Saxon Art to A.D. 900* (London, 1938), p. 165: 'It is hardly likely to be later than 800, and may indeed be a carving of Offa's reign.' For a reproduction of the whole slab see Kendrick's pl. LXVII. 2, and for a discussion of its various scenes see B. Kurth, 'The Iconography of the Wirksworth Slab', *Burlington Magazine* LXXXVI (1945), 114–21.

[9] The Ascension has a height of approx 18 in. and a maximum width of approx. 32 in.

[10] F. Henry, *Irish Art during the Viking Invasions (800–1020 A.D.)* (London, 1967), pl. 37.

worth carvings – present a symbol which is intended to be universal, inclusive for all mankind. This is the symbolism of the *comitatus* in the poem, responding to Christ as a single, undifferentiated body, obeying him, praising him, taught by him, watching over him, grieving for him in unison:

> Þær wæs wopes hring;
> torne bitolden    wæs seo treowlufu,
> hat æt heortan;    hreðer innan weoll,
> beorn breostsefa (537 b-40 a).

Likewise the rows of upturned faces in the Rothbury carving represent variations of a single, generalized participation. In both carvings the distinct yet unparticularized human figures, neither old nor young, are, like the *comitatus*, outside time. In neither carving is it shown where the humans are standing. On the Wirksworth slab no limiting boundary divides the Ascension from the adjacent subjects. The result, in the poem and carvings alike, is abstraction from time and place. In all three the angels play an important part in the universals thus created. On the Rothbury cross they were much more prominent when the carving was complete than they appear to be now from the damaged remains.[1] In the Wirksworth carving they dominate. In the poem they come in a radiant throng[2] when Christ is about to ascend (491–4 a), praise him as he ascends in radiance (502 b-5) and accompany him joyfully above the vault of the

---

[1] Originally there may well have been four angels, two on each side of Christ.

[2] Later in the poem, when introducing his version of Gregory's answer, Cynewulf says:

> Ðæt is wel cweden,    swa gewritu secgað,
> þæt him ælbeorhte    englas togeanes
> in þa halgan tid    heapum cwoman,
> sigan of swegle (547–50 a).

The *gewritu* are not the bible for which Cynewulf's word is regularly *bec*, as in line 453 b. The angels' radiance is the equivalent of the white garments mentioned by Gregory (545 b-50 a), but Gregory does not refer to their large numbers. In Bede's hymn throngs of angels escort the ascending Christ. In *Christ and Satan* their great number is explicit (see below, p. 299). In one of his homilies, Wulfstan, like Cynewulf, refers to the great throng coming to meet Christ: 'Hit gewearð ymbe .xl. daga þæs þe he of deaðe aras þæt him com of heofonum ongean mycel engla werod, ⁊ he mid þam werede to heofonum ferde' (Bethurum, *Wulfstan*, homily VI. 188–90). Presumably in origin the large numbers of angels were transferred to the Ascension from the Day of Judgment by a reverse application of the 'in like manner' of Acts I. 11. How easy this would be is illustrated by Blickling homily XI where it is explained that Christ's disappearance into a cloud (Acts I. 9) was a sign that he will come again on the Day of Judgment in the same way, *in wolcne ⁊ mid engla þrymme*. The angels that support Christ's mandorla in visual representations presumably are iconographically descended from the winds that bore aloft the emperor in some portrayals of imperial apotheosis, as on a fifth-century ivory in the British Museum; see A. Grabar, *Byzantium from the Death of Theodosius to the Rise of Islam* (London, 1966), pls. 327–8. Cf. *hlaford fergan* in Cynewulf's poem (518 b). Some Christian commentators found it necessary to point out that Christ as creator of all was quite capable of elevating himself; for instance Gregory writes in his homily: 'Redemptor autem noster non curru, non angelis sublevatus legitur, quia is qui fecerat omnia nimirum super omnia sua virtute ferebatur' (Migne, *PL* LXXVI, col. 1216). (Concerning the chariot see Grabar, *Christian Iconography, loc. cit.*)

heavens[1] to the celestial city (517–19). In all three, poem and carvings, they combine with man to form a single Christo-centric order: in the poem apostles and angels are correspondingly Christ's *gedryht* (457b and 515b), his *weorud* (458a and 493a), and correspondingly praise him as the source of life (470b–2a and 503b–4a);[2] in the carvings angels and men share conventions of facial expression and clothing. In both carvings there is little or no attempt to give the scene an illusion of depth; especially in the Wirksworth one all the figures are brought forward equally on to a brilliant artificial surface. In the poem there is a similar effect.[3] In more particular ways too the poem and carvings agree. Cynewulf emphasizes the teaching which Christ transmits to the apostles before ascending: there is a specific correlation between *lareowes* (458b) and *sincgiefan* (460a) and this association is restated in

> þær him tacna fela      tires brytta
> onwrah, wuldres helm,      wordgerynum (462–3).

In the Rothbury carving the same transmission of teaching is expressed by the scroll which Christ carries in his left hand and the scrolls and books held by the apostles.[4] The Rothbury frontally seated Christ, probably supporting an orb in his right hand,[5] is the universal sovereign referred to as *cyning ure* in the poem (494b). Likewise the resurrection cross carried by the Wirksworth Christ signifies the victory which is celebrated in the poem when Christ is called *sigores agend* (513b) and *ealra sigebearna þæt seleste ond æþeleste* (520–1a). This last phrase is set within the descriptive reference to Christ's angel-escorted journey which Cynewulf introduces into the speech of the two angels to the apostles:

> We mid þyslice      þreate willað
> ofer heofona gehlidu      hlaford fergan
> to þære beorhtan byrg      mid þas bliðan gedryht –
> ealra sigebearna      þæt seleste
> ond æþeleste –      þe ge her on stariað
> ond in frofre geseoð      frætwum blican (517–22).

---

[1] *Ofer heofona gehlidu* (518a). Presumably Cynewulf means that Christ passed above the *cælum aereum*. The distinction between this and the upper *cælum aethereum* into which Christ ascended is explained by Gregory earlier in the homily in his commentary on Mark XVI. 19.

[2] Cf. at the conclusion of the speech addressed by an escorting angel to the inhabitants of heaven (see above, p. 294 and n. 3):

> Sib sceal gemæne
> englum ond ældum      a forð heonan
> wesan wideferh (581b–3a).

[3] For some comments on the outward pattern-making propensities of Cynewulf's use of language in this poem, see my inaugural lecture, *Rhythm and Cosmic Order in Old English Christian Literature* (Cambridge, 1970), pp. 11–15, especially – concerning lines 527–32 – pp. 13–15.

[4] In the lower row the first, third and fifth apostles (from left to right) hold scrolls, while the second, fourth and sixth hold books. Concerning the scroll as a symbol of the philosopher, author, teacher, see Grabar, *Christian Iconography*, p. 33.          [5] Or perhaps blessing.

The speaking angels, the watching apostles, Christ ascending victoriously with the happy, radiant throng are thus united in a lively composition. By interjecting the reference to the victorious Christ (520–1a) within the one to the angelic throng (519b and 521b–2) Cynewulf suggests an arrangement in space at an instant, as it would be seen. Yet this moment, since it interrupts the regular narrative sequence and hence is outside it, is a point of non-natural, symbolic time.[1] Similarly in the Wirksworth carving the representation of the same narrative elements is both visual and symbolic: here they are projected on to the surface-plane of non-natural, symbolic space.

Should we infer, then, from these affinities that Cynewulf's imagination was influenced by visual representations which he had seen? Certainly he shows an awareness of the dramatic directness of visualization in *þe ge her on stariað* (521b). And, I believe, at least one detail in his image has been visually derived. The radiance of the ascending Christ which the angels adore comes specifically from his head:

> leohte gefegun
> þe of þæs hælendes     heafelan lixte (504b–5).

These lines seem to me clearly to reproduce a visual impression of a nimbed, haloed Christ.[2] A luminous aureole was traditionally the essential visual symbol of a theophany. A mosaic in the apse of the St John Lateran basilica in Rome provides an example: a full-faced head of Christ is encircled by a large golden halo which is uncrossed and vividly lustrous against a deep blue sky; above and to each side of the head are adoring angels.[3] But if impressions from the visual arts contributed to the image he created, Cynewulf did not put a picture into words as simply as the author of *Christ and Satan* did:

> Astah up on heofonum     engla scyppend,
> weoroda waldend.     Þa com wolcna sweg,
> halig of heofonum.     Mid wæs hond godes,
> onfeng freodrihten,     and hine forð lædde
> to þam halgan ham     heofna ealdor.
> Him ymbflugon     engla þreatas
> þusendmælum.[4]

---

[1] Cynewulf uses the same device of departing from the normal order of syntactic parts elsewhere – for example in lines 466–70a, where, in referring to the temporal link between the Ascension and the Resurrection and to the fulfilment of prophecies which the Passion had represented, he interweaves syntactic units so that the reference becomes non-consecutive and thus related to non-finite time.

[2] I do not know of any text which could have supplied this motif. For example, Bede's hymn does not locate Christ's radiance in his head.

[3] For a reproduction in colour see W. Oakeshott, *The Mosaics of Rome* (London, 1967), pl. VIII. As we see it today the mosaic is a nineteenth-century replacement of a thirteenth-century reconstruction of a late classical original; see the discussion and references, *ibid.* pp. 70–3.

[4] Lines 562–8a: *ASPR* I, 153.

If we allow for a multiplying factor in *þusendmælum*[1] the visual elements of this description come straight out of a picture of the type represented in the Benedictional of St Æthelwold.[2] In Cynewulf's image on the other hand the visual elements are part of a much more complex synthesis.

There are several ingredients in this synthesis which are absent from the carvings. One is a strain of psychological realism. Christ's disappearance *wolcnum bifongen* (527b), the critical moment psychologically for the terrestrial observer, is related to the point of view of that observer by the phrase *ofer hrofas upp* (528b).[3] Earlier in the narrative the viewpoint of the watching apostles is identified with that of the contemporary pilgrim when it is said that Christ departed *þurh þæs temples hrof, þær hy to segun* (495).[4] Another ingredient is a dramatic strain. The chief dramatic moments of Christ's departure from the earth and of his disappearance in the clouds are made prominent. Direct speech is effectively used. The sound which heralds the presence of the angelic host as the Ascension is about to take place is sudden and loud:

> Ða wearð semninga        sweg on lyfte
> hlud gehyred (491–2a).

The sound is not merely reported, it is *heard*; just as the angelic host is *seen* by the apostles (*þe ge her on stariað*, 521b). Closely associated is an emotional devotional strain. The apostles obey Christ joyfully (458b–60a); they actively sorrow when he leaves them on earth (499b–502a) and when they return to Jerusalem without him (533–40a); angels and apostles praise and glorify him.

This emotional participation is transferred to us. The terms used of Christ as the centre of the apostles' and angels' devotion elicit a response from us too. The Christ whom the apostles watch ascending is *cyning ure*

---

[1] See above, p. 297, n. 2.

[2] See D. Talbot Rice, *English Art 871–1100* (Oxford, 1952), pl. 50b. The iconography in which the ascending Christ is depicted in profile, or semi-profile, climbing a slope, his right hand grasping, or extended towards, the right hand of God which issues from the clouds, is of ancient tradition; see, for example, the fifth-century ivory in Munich which is often reproduced (e.g. Grabar, *Byzantium from the Death of Theodosius to the Rise of Islam*, pl. 332). Dr H. M. Taylor and I, independently of one another, have noticed that an Ascension of this type survives in fragmentary form on one of the stone pieces which are now preserved in the crypt of Canterbury cathedral and which almost certainly were originally parts of the cross that stood in front of the chancel-arch in Reculver church; see H. M. Taylor, 'Reculver Reconsidered', *AJ* cxxv (1968), 292–3 and n. 10.

[3] For comments on this and on its anticipation of the portrayal of the disappearing Christ in English art from the tenth century, see my inaugural lecture, *op. cit.* p. 14 and n. 13.

[4] Cynewulf has in mind the round church which was built on the top of the Mount of Olives to mark the place of the Ascension and from which, at its unroofed centre, pilgrims looked up to the sky. Adamnán's *De Locis Sanctis* (as first pointed out by J. W. Bright, 'Cynewulf's *Christ* 495 and 528', *Modern Language Notes* xiii [1898], 14), could have been Cynewulf's source. But equally he may have owed his knowledge to an intermediate source, or to direct experience if he had been a pilgrim himself, or to what a returned pilgrim had told him, or to an illustration he had seen.

(494 b). The praise which they and the angels offer is the praise we offer: the words used of the apostles

> lufedun leofwendum     lifes agend (471)

are used also in an exhortation to all Christians in verses in the mid-tenth-century BM Cotton Vespasian D. vi:

> Wuton wuldrian     weorada dryhten
> halgan hlioðorcwidum,     hiofenrices weard,
> lufian liofwendum     lifes agend.[1]

Cynewulf's devotional appellations are very close indeed to liturgical invocations.[2] His poem and the liturgy are alike in combining biblical text with devotional elements.[3] Although not to the same degree, his image acts upon us as liturgical worship does. Especially we feel this to be so because in the poem, as in the liturgy, Christ is not outwardly described, but instead is an all-absorbing, felt presence. In contrast to the visual explicitness of the carvings, all that is overt in the poem is that Christ speaks and that his head is a source of light. Much of the material in Gregory's homily had a liturgical background[4] and the homily itself was used for readings in the Ascensiontide Offices.[5] There are signs that Cynewulf is thinking of his image within the framework of the great liturgical sequence of Resurrection–Ascension–Pentecost, for he explicitly places the Ascension forty days after the Resurrection – when Christ had fulfilled the universal prophecies of the Old Testament through his Passion (466–70a) – and ten days before Pentecost (542b). Throughout, Cynewulf shows a keen awareness of the impact of sound. Music, heard loud and sudden, at the end of Christ's words to the apostles, heralds the act of ascension (491–4); the joyful song of the angels hymning the ascending Christ (502b–5) interrupts a sequence of references to the apostles (*hi*, 498a; *him*, 499b; *hi*, 501a; and *hy*, 506a) and contrasts sharply with the sadness that they are feeling (499b–502a). And at one point, I believe, Cynewulf has carried over into his poem a direct impression of liturgical practice. When the two angels speak to the apostles their voices ring out:

> Cleopedon of heahþu
> wordum wrætlicum     ofer wera mengu
> beorhtan reorde (508b–10a).

---

[1] *The Kentish Hymn*, 1–3: *ASPR* vi, 87.

[2] *Sigores agend* (513b) is an exact equivalent of *triumphator* in the antiphon referred to below, p. 302, n. 7.

[3] The liturgical source on which Cynewulf drew to expand his answer to Gregory's question (see above, p. 294, n. 3), the hymn by Bede, has this character.

[4] For instance, in § 10 the texts quoted from the psalms and from Ephesians iv. 8 are parts of the liturgy of Ascensiontide. Bede's hymn exemplifies the liturgical celebration of the theme of angelic rejoicing.

[5] As pointed out by Cook, *op. cit.* pp. 115 and 119.

The words of the two men in white quoted in Acts I. 11, *Viri Galilaei...*, furnished the text for several of the sung parts of the Mass and Offices at Ascensiontide. We do not know how these were sung in ninth-century England, but, as a consequence of the assumption (as in Gregory's homily) that the speakers were angels, they were sung from a height, as we know,[1] at Essen somewhat later. The buildings surviving at Brixworth in Northamptonshire[2] and Deerhurst in Gloucestershire[3] and Eddius's description of the church built by Wilfrid at Hexham[4] show that churches in which internal space was used at more than one level existed in seventh-, eighth- and ninth-century England. The substantial seventh-century remains at Brixworth today give an indelible impression of a spacious interior designed for sophisticated liturgical use in three dimensions. We can say that architecturally conditions existed in Cynewulf's England for giving symbolic height to the liturgical singers of the angels' words.[5] It is at least feasible that it was this practice that prompted him to portray his speakers calling *of heahþu*, whereas in Acts (and hence Gregory's homily) and the Wirksworth and Rothbury[6] carvings they are on the ground, and in the hymn attributed to Bede they are unplaced. This is a practice that would have prompted him to use the adjective *beorht* of their voice; and the phrase *ofer wera mengu* is certainly more applicable to liturgical listeners in a large church or cathedral than to the assembled apostles of the narrative.[7]

Cynewulf's image of the Ascension was, I believe, moulded by liturgical worship as well as by the visual arts. If I am right, these are the sources from which he drew the ecclesiastical experience which he blended with biblical narrative and the traditions of heroic literature. Freed from the limitations of real time and place his image keeps within the bounds of representational conventions. Its conceptual framework seems clearly to have been that of the two Jerusalems. The cities in which there was joy at Christ's arrival in heaven – *blis in burgum* (530a) – are surely the heavenly one to which he went – *to þære beorhtan byrg* (519a)[8] – and the earthly one

---

[1] From the Essen *Liber Ordinarius* as reported by C. Heitz, *Recherches sur les Rapports entre Architecture et Liturgie à l'Époque Carolingienne* (Paris, 1963), pp. 197–8. The *Liber* is extant only in fourteenth- and fifteenth-century copies but is of much older origin.

[2] See H. M. and J. Taylor, *Anglo-Saxon Architecture* (Cambridge, 1965), pp. 108–14.

[3] See *ibid.* pp. 193–209.  [4] See *ibid.* pp. 297–312.

[5] The dialogue in Bede's hymn (see above, p. 294, n. 3) affords a good example of the dramatic elements present in liturgical celebration.

[6] In the Rothbury carving there are two pointing hands above the top row of apostles, one at each end of the row.

[7] The liturgy is amalgamated with biblical narrative in a more obvious way in the homily in CCCC 162 (see above, p. 294, n. 1). In this homily (p. 440) the apostles praise the ascending Christ. The words attributed to them are an Old English equivalent of the antiphon *in evangelio* and of part of the collect for second vespers on Ascension Day as in the Leofric and Wulfstan Collectars (HBS XLV [1913], col. 175, and LXXIX [1956], 64). The verb *clypian* is used of the apostles here as it is of the angels by Cynewulf: *hi þa clypedon anre stefne*.

[8] It is to be noticed that Cynewulf uses the singular of *burh* when referring to heaven here and in line 553a, the only other instance.

which he had hallowed by his presence – *in ða halgan burg* (534b) – and in which the apostles awaited Pentecost after the Ascension – *in þære torhtan byrig* (542a).[1] In his portrayal of the heavenly city Cynewulf does not go beyond what Bede's hymn contains: Bede's city has a high throne, seats for the blessed, gates and walls; in Cynewulf's poem – in the narrative of the Ascension as a departure from earth, in what remains to us of the narrative of it as an arrival in heaven, and in a further brief but graphic reference to the joy of the angelic citizens when they saw Christ approaching (740b–2a) – heaven is a *burh* or *ceaster* (578a) with a throne (516b and 555a) from which gifts are dispensed (572a) and with gates (576b) and shining buildings (742a). To complement this, the picture which Cynewulf had in mind of the Ascension taking place above the earthly city, has, it seems to me, these elements: the apostles standing in the round church of the Ascension (therefore *on hwearfte*, 511b), looking upwards; other buildings in the background; above (*ofer hrofas upp*,[2] 528b), Christ ascending in an area of clouds,[3] his head luminous, an emblem of victory in his hand and radiant angels escorting him. In composition this is a picture not unlike the mosaic of the apse in the church of St Pudentiana, Rome (*c.* 400), portraying Christ teaching the apostles:[4] this mosaic has a similar architectural background of a building, circular in appearance and open to the sky (an exedra) in front of the roofs of further buildings (the churches of Jerusalem), and, against the sky, where Christ would be flanked by angels in the Ascension, a great gold and bejewelled cross (on Golgotha) flanked by the symbols of the evangelists. The mosaic differs from an Ascension mainly, of course, in showing Christ seated among the apostles (who are accompanied by female personifications of the church of the Jews and that of the Gentiles); it is a symbolic version of the scene which in Cynewulf's poem immediately precedes the Ascension. In essence what his picture

---

[1] The concept of the earthly city rejoicing is separate from, but not incompatible with, the sadness which the apostles felt that Christ was no longer with them.

[2] The distinction between the plural *hrofas* here and the singular in *þurh þæs temples hrof* (495a) is to be noted.

[3] The word *gehlidu* (518a), 'lids' ('above the lids of the heavens') may have been occasioned by the thin clouds representing the *cælum aereum* (see above, p. 298, n. 1) in, for example, the seventh-century mosaic of the apse in the chapel of St Venantius in the baptistry of St John Lateran, Rome (see Oakeshott, *op. cit.* pl. 99; I am grateful to Professor C. R. Dodwell for suggesting this example and for kindly answering other questions which I have put to him). *Gehlidu* occurs also in the same sense and same plural form at *Christ III*, 904 and *Genesis B*, 583. The usual Latin words for the *cælum aereum* in its full height are *arx* and *culmen*, both sometimes plural (e.g. Bede's Ascension hymn has *cuncta transiens caeli micantis culmina*), and the usual OE word is *hrof* (see, e.g., *til hrofe*, *Cædmon's Hymn*, 6a, and Bede's paraphrase of it, *pro culmine tecti*; *of heum heofnes hrofe* [*ex summa cæli arce*], *Durham Ritual*, EEMF 16 [1969], 48v 3; Cynewulf, Ascension poem, 749b and *Elene*, 89b; and other references BT and *Suppl*, s.v. *hróf*). I do not know of any patristic comment which would account for *gehlidu*. Nor does the alliteration depend on it in any of its three occurrences.

[4] For a reproduction in colour, see W. F. Volbach, *Early Christian Art* (London, 1961), pl. 130.

involves is the combination of the normal iconography of the Ascension[1] with an architectural setting of this type.[2] This was certainly within the contemporary resources of the visual arts: Carolingian art provides a number of instances of human figures encircled by a building represented so as to display both its interior and its surroundings.[3] All that is required is that this building should resemble the church of the Ascension. One can well imagine a visual artist effecting this.[4] But after all we cannot be sure how closely Cynewulf kept to a visual representation that he had seen: the large number of angels is one feature for which *gewritu* were responsible, and I have suggested that he owed at least one other, the positioning of the speaking angels, to liturgical influence. What we can be sure, I believe, is that his image had some main source of visual stimulus. This could have been a picture in a church in which he worshipped.[5] It could have formed the background against which he took part in liturgical celebration of the Ascension[6] that included the singing of the angels' words from an upper level. If it did, all his ecclesiastical impressions came to him as a single liturgico-visual whole. To respond to this conception and to see in it an extension of Gregory's question about the garments of angels would have accorded with the nature of his imagination. A poetic art which has its source of inspiration in a question of this kind is one that is keenly alive to externals.

[1] Though in the poem the Virgin is not present among the apostles, as she is (without, of course, any biblical authority) in many visual representations.

[2] This association can occur when the Ascension and Pentecost are depicted together, the former above and the latter below, as in the late-ninth-century Carolingian bible of San Callisto, now in the possession of the basilica of San Paolo fuori le Mura, Rome (see O. Pächt, C. R. Dodwell and F. Wormald, *The St Albans Psalter* [London, 1960], pl. 119d). Here the arrangement of the apostles at Pentecost, in a circle within an open building and seen from somewhat above by the beholder, is very like that which I have postulated for Cynewulf's image of the Ascension. I am much indebted to Miss Barbara Raw for drawing my attention to this portrayal. One possibility that it suggests is that Cynewulf had seen a representation of the Ascension above one of Christ teaching the apostles in an architectural setting. In that case, for the purposes of his poem, he imagined that the setting of the teaching was extended to the Ascension and was identified with the church of the Ascension. This would have been a less simple process for him than merely to generalize to the teaching a setting which he had seen already applied to the Ascension (see below, n. 4).

[3] See, e.g., J. Hubert, J. Porcher and W. F. Volbach, *Carolingian Art* (London, 1970), pls. 107 (Christ in the Temple) and 131.

[4] The result would have been a structure suited to be the setting of both the teaching and the Ascension, one for which Cynewulf's terms *burh* (461 b), *tempel* (495 a) and *þingstede* (497 a) would all have been apt.

[5] One thinks of the representation of the Ascension which we know was on the south side of the nave of Angilbert's church (dedicated 799) at Centula (now Saint-Riquier in northern France) and which was one of the principal stations for prayer by the daily processions of the monks.

[6] Doubtless it was the splendour of the liturgical festival that gave the Ascension its initial attraction as a subject for a poem, for since the fourth century Ascension Day had become increasingly prominent in the Easter season that formed the climax to the annual cycle of the cult of Christ the Saviour. And doubtless it was this too that gave Cynewulf his sense of the relationship between his image and the general theme of man's salvation (see above, p. 295, n. 4).

I   Part of the Rothbury cross: the Ascension

II   Part of the Wirksworth stone: the Ascension

III*a*  Oxford, Bodleian Library,
Junius 27, 118r, initial

III*b*  Oxford, Bodleian Library,
Junius 27, 121v, initial

III*c*  Oxford,
Bodleian Library,
Tanner 10, 93r,
initial

III*d*  Paris, Bibl. Nat., lat. 6401, 5v, miniature

IV*a*  Fragment of wall-painting from the foundations of the New Minster, Winchester

IV*c*  Oxford, Bodleian Library, Junius 27, 115v, initial

IV*b*  Oxford, Bodleian Library, Junius 27, 55v, initial

V*a*  BM Add. 40618, 22v

V*c*  Paris, Bibl.
Nat., lat. 6401, 159r,
miniature

V*b*  BM Add. 40618, 49v

VI   Paris, Bibl. Nat., lat. 6401, 158v

tua increpet & uide quam malum & amarum ʒ

reliquisse dnm dm tuum & non esse timore ei'

apud te. Conuertimini filii reuertentes dicit

dns. State super uias & uidete. & interrogate

de semitis antiquis quae sit uia bona. & ambulate

in ea & inuenietis refrigerium animab; uestris;

Hec dicit dns ds exercituum. conuertimini ad me.

& saluus eris amen

Se þe hys feþ lyfdan nele aræded niman. nec cupiet ic ær
magan. Þ he pille zyman spasa hefcode hif azenre
þeap ʒe. Ne do spa te leξe lupa god geo; ne · þe
feol on þinξe heoþtan gelome coh̄ hif lupa. Þon sceal
þe fpolan ⁊ þebec limpan · for zode ⁊ for for ulde ·
ʒe lupe ʒeffu pille · Ælc man behofaþ ʒafclicef foðþef ·
Se þebið ofeayde ⁊ for of hif cydde · hu mæh̄ heþa cuman ʒþe nele
leorman hu fe þeþ luξe feld coh̄ hif cydde ·
Hu mæʒe coheþeran yfhtne þeξ apedian · buton þeʒe þuman ·
ffe ofefpyþan · ⁊ þeoþnlicef fmeaʒean hupe mazan dydeþ cuman ·
· · · þ fie fecξ · ʒelupe feheþille · seξeʒaþ ʒefelfce þeʒodcunde
· · opcofe þehyþeð ⁊ þeoþnlicofe ʒymeð · xiiii ·
Qui ʒ ex deo · uerba dei audit · Non in solo pane
uiuit homo · sed in omni uerbo quod pcedit
de ore dei · Beati qui audiunt uerbum dei ·
⁊ custodiunt illud ·

VIII *a*    The Sulgrave brooch

VIII *b*    The Hereford *Agnus Dei*
penny (enlarged)

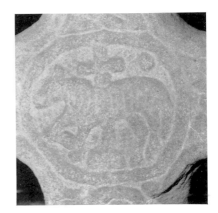

VIII *c* and *d*    The Durham cross-heads, details (reduced)

# The 'Winchester School' before
# St Æthelwold

## FRANCIS WORMALD

The discovery by Mr Martin Biddle in 1966 of a fragment of late-ninth-century wall-painting in the foundations of the New Minster at Winchester has rendered it necessary to look again at what is known of English illuminated manuscripts in the period between the reign of Alfred and the monastic revival of the middle of the tenth century.[1] Before this discovery all that was known was a group of manuscripts, which, although much studied, have tended to be regarded as separate entities without much connection with one another or with the splendid books which were to appear in the second half of the century. What will be attempted here will be to have a second look at these scattered examples and to indicate something of what had passed and what was to come.

Although, as will become clear, a fair proportion of the figure style differs from that found in English manuscripts of the ninth century and seems to be caused by continental influences, the style of the initial ornament is clearly derived from insular sources, though transformed and enriched. Many of these insular characteristics are already to be found in the early-ninth-century manuscripts such as the Barberini Gospels in the Vatican and the Book of Cerne. The chief elements in the ornament are small animal heads, which grip on to the various parts of the letters, and bunches of foliage forming the finials. In the early tenth century gripping heads grow much more robust and turn into winged dragons and birds which interlace with one another, thereby forming the letter.

This transformation is clearly seen in three manuscripts dating from the first half of the tenth century. They are the psalter in the Bodleian, Junius 27; the Old English Bede, also in the Bodleian, Tanner 10; and the Tollemache Orosius, now BM Add. 47967. Both the psalter and the Orosius have been associated palaeographically with Winchester. In the case of the Junius Psalter this ascription is reinforced by the liturgical relationships between the metrical portions of the calendar and the calendar of BM Cotton Galba A. xviii whose English additions, of which the calendar is one, are clearly of Winchester origin.[2] In Tanner 10 there is a significant introduc-

---

[1] For this painting see M. Biddle, *AntJ* XLVII (1967), 277–9; also F. Wormald, *ibid.* pp. 162–5.
[2] See E. Bishop, *Liturgica Historica* (Oxford, 1918), pp. 254–5.

tion into the vocabulary of English ornament by the use of human figures to form part of the construction of the letters. Such figures do not appear in the earlier English manuscripts and do not appear again until the second quarter of the eleventh century in the psalter in the University Library at Cambridge.[1] The construction of these figure initials recalls the later Romanesque initials. If one examines a 'thorn' from Tanner 10 it will be seen that it is composed out of a dragon biting the tail of another. Clinging on to this dragon with his legs enmeshed in the creature's crest is a man wearing a kilted dress (see pl. III*c*). Such a gymnastic display becomes a common feature of Romanesque initial ornament, but was virtually unknown in Carolingian manuscripts.[2] The figure in the Tanner Bede has all the verve of the later initials. Where the artist got the idea of using the human figure in this manner it is impossible to say, though figure initials were known in Byzantine centres. Although they bear no direct resemblance to them, the initials in Merovingian manuscripts may have had some influence on the scale of these tenth-century initials.

Most of the letters in the Tanner Bede are, however, composed of biting dragons and birds. Both have large and savage claws. Some of the dragons' heads are rendered in three-quarter view with a peculiarly protruding left eye. This seems to be derived from earlier English manuscripts, as it is characteristic of the initials in a manuscript containing grammatical treatises from Fleury, now in Bern, which, although of French origin, is full of insular ornamental details and is written partly in insular script.[3] The bodies of the creatures are well formed with wings which have a rudimentary representation of feathers. The lower jaws of both dragons and birds are very shallow and the tails of the former are composed of bunches of foliage. While such tails are to be found in earlier initials in books like the Barberini Gospels they now seem to be borrowed from Carolingian ornament, particularly from manuscripts connected with Metz, such as the Drogo Sacramentary, though the treatment is a good deal more stylized.[4]

This sumptuous Carolingian leaf-work which was now combined with the native tradition of gripping heads and monsters is also found in a purer form in another great work of art from Winchester: the embroidered

[1] Ff. 1. 23; see Ker, *Catalogue*, no. 13.

[2] The most significant exception is the early-ninth-century psalter from Corbie, Amiens MS 18. These proto-Romanesque tendencies have been discussed by O. Pächt, 'The Pre-Carolingian Roots of Early Romanesque Art', *Studies in Western Art*, Acts of the Twentieth International Congress of the History of Art (Princeton, 1963) I, 67–75.

[3] Bern, Burgerbibliothek, Cod. 207; see O. Homburger, *Die illustrierten Handschriften der Bibliothek Bern, Die vorkarolingischen und karolingischen Handschriften* (Bern, 1962), pp. 32–9 and figs. 19 and 22; also G. L. Micheli, *L'Enluminure de Haut Moyen Âge et les Influences Irlandaises* (Brussels, 1939), fig. 81.

[4] For the Drogo Sacramentary see, particularly fol. 9, W. Köhler, *Die karolingischen Miniaturen* III (Berlin, 1960), pl. 68 b.

vestments from the tomb of St Cuthbert at Durham.[1] These are datable by an inscription to the years 909 and 916 and associated with Frithestan, bishop of Winchester. A comparison between the scroll which forms the initial on 121v of the Junius Psalter and the leaf-work on the stole of St Cuthbert shows the same type of ornament (see pl. III*b*). A very noticeable characteristic is the way the scrolls grow out of cup-like leaves. The existence of this type of ornament suggests that already by the reign of Edward the Elder Carolingian leaf ornament was both known to and adopted by Winchester artists.

The initials in the Junius Psalter show thus a splendid variety of ornamental motives which have been shown to be a combination of the insular biting monsters and more sophisticated Carolingian leaf-work. The artist of the Junius Psalter also introduced into his repertoire a series of human heads. Like the gymnasts in Tanner 10 these have a solely decorative function. The practice of using the human head in this way was not something new, but was probably a survival of an older practice which can be seen in the Barberini Gospels in the Vatican and other manuscripts.[2] Admittedly the heads in the Junius Psalter are treated in a less conventional manner, yet their general pose and arrangement should be compared with the roundels surmounting the evangelists in the Book of Cerne of the middle of the ninth century. Thus in these initials we see transformations of survivals of earlier insular work just as significant as, perhaps even more significant than, the introduction of continental motives, in these early Winchester works (see pls. IV*b* and *c*).

It is unfortunate that all but one of the large initials in the Junius Psalter have been removed. Only the initial before ps. CIX (118r) remains. It shows David killing the lion. Originally there were probably seven others, for a large initial before ps. CIX suggests the use of the eightfold liturgical division of the psalter. They may have constituted a David cycle (see pl. III*a*).

The style of the heads used in the smaller initials can usefully be compared with the head on the fragment of wall-painting found in the foundations of the New Minster (see pl. IV*a*).[3] All have the same characteristic narrow shoulders, staring eyes and long faces with a wig-like hair arrangement. The fact that the wall-painting can be related to these heads suggests that this style was already established by the end of the ninth century and

---

[1] For good reproductions of St Cuthbert's vestments see *The Relics of St Cuthbert*, ed. C. F. Battiscombe (Oxford, 1956), pp. 375–432.

[2] See H. Zimmermann, *Vorkarolingische Miniaturen* (Berlin, 1911), pl. 316. Perhaps even closer, though not initials, are the roundels with heads in the Codex Aureus in Stockholm (*ibid.* pl. 280) and the gospels in the treasury at Trier cathedral (*ibid.* pls. 270–3).

[3] The initials with heads in the Junius Psalter are to be found on 43r, 50r, 52v, 55v, 56r, 61r, 62v, 72v, 86r, 112v, 114v, 115v and 135v. For the wall-painting see refs. cited above, p. 305, n. 1.

this is supported by the vestments from Durham where the figures have the same narrow shoulders and staring eyes. While it is possible to describe the characteristics of this early Winchester style, it is much more difficult to suggest any satisfactory origin for it. Freyhan in his important discussion of the St Cuthbert vestments postulated some influence from eastern Europe or at any rate the Byzantine Empire.[1] This may be true in essence, but it is equally possible, and indeed more probable, that what we really have here is a survival of an earlier English style going back to the early years of the ninth century. In manuscript-painting the most nearly comparable is to be found in the Barberini Gospels in the Vatican, though the style of the early-tenth-century initials is somewhat more sophisticated.

The miniatures introduced at Winchester into the ninth-century psalter of continental origin, now Cotton Galba A. xviii, present a similar problem. Their style is quite unlike anything to be found in Carolingian art. There are three miniatures. The first and second show Christ enthroned surrounded by the various choirs of heaven: angels, prophets and apostles in one and martyrs, confessors and virgins in the second.[2] The third is a miniature of the Ascension of Christ.[3] A fourth miniature, of the Nativity, now in Oxford, almost certainly comes from the same manuscript.[4] In general arrangement and to a certain extent in colour these miniatures recall much earlier manuscripts and iconographically both the Ascension and Nativity belong to early types; the Ascension recalling such objects as the ampullae from Monza which belong to the end of the sixth century.[5] It is not suggested that these miniatures are necessarily copied directly from early originals, but that they may be derived from earlier English illuminations themselves going back to early and exotic sources. In this connection there is a small detail which may give some light on the nature of these sources. On either side of the Virgin in the miniature of the Ascension are growing long spindly plants. A very similar plant-form appears flanking the figure of St Matthew in the Barberini Gospels.[6] These plants also appear in a miniature of the Crucifixion in a later Winchester manuscript: the prayer-book of the New Minster made between 1023 and 1035.[7] Another feature which brings this later miniature into connection with those in the psalter is the rather lavish use of inscriptions. They appear in both the Nativity and the Ascension miniatures in the psalter and again

[1] R. Freyhan, *The Relics of St Cuthbert*, pp. 409–32.
[2] 2 v and 21 r; see E. G. Millar, *English Illuminated Manuscripts from the Xth to the XIIIth Century* (Paris and Brussels, 1926), pl. 2 a and b.
[3] 120 v; see *ibid.* pl. 2 c.
[4] Oxford, Bodleian Library, Rawlinson B. 484, 85 r; see *ibid.* pl. 2 d.
[5] See André Grabar, *Les Ampoules de Terre Sainte* (Paris, 1958).
[6] Vatican Barb. lat 570, 11 v; see T. D. Kendrick, *Anglo-Saxon Art to A.D. 900* (London, 1938), pl. LVI.
[7] See Millar, *op. cit.* pl. 24 a.

suggest a derivation from an early set of miniatures, labels of this kind being found in such books as the Ashburnham Pentateuch and the Gospels of St Augustine in Corpus Christi College, Cambridge.[1] It seems, therefore, that we may have in these miniatures the remains, though very fragmentary, of a cycle of early miniatures which survived at Winchester to serve artists in later periods.

When this has been said it must not be thought that in the half-century preceding the monastic revival this native strain was the sole source of inspiration. As in the ornament so in the miniatures the Carolingian styles were beginning to exercise influence. The clearest case of this is to be seen in the copy made in England of the *De Laude Crucis* of Rabanus Maurus in Trinity College, Cambridge.[2] This manuscript with its curious mixture of illustrations and diagrams is a close copy of a Carolingian original made at Fulda.[3] Among other English miniatures the closest in style to it is the frontispiece to Bede's Life of St Cuthbert, now CCCC 183, which may without much doubt be identified with a Life of St Cuthbert given by King Athelstan to the congregation of St Cuthbert at Chester-le-Street in 937.[4] This frontispiece, which shows the king presenting the book to St Cuthbert, has been compared by Peter Bloch with other dedication pictures in the poem of Rabanus.

A pair of little-known miniatures of the first half of the tenth century stand at the cross-ways between such miniatures as those found in the Athelstan Psalter and the manuscripts of what is known as the Winchester School of the second half of the century. These are found added to an Irish pocket gospel book, now BM Add. 40618.[5] Besides the miniatures a scribe, *Eduardus diaconus*, made some textual additions and two illuminated capital letters were added in the tenth century over earlier ones probably by the same artist as the one who added the miniatures (see pls. V*a* and *b*). The miniatures are evangelist pictures of St Luke and St John. They are shown busy writing their gospels into codices which they hold in their left hands. Below St Luke's book there is some hanging drapery. It is not clear whether this is intended for the chemise of the volume or whether it is really the vestige of a cloth placed over a book-rest in the manner of other English evangelist pictures.[6] A very similar arrangement may be seen in the miniature for the feast of St John the Baptist in the Benedictional of St Æthelwold.[7] Above the writing evangelist is

[1] For the Ashburnham Pentateuch (Paris, Bibl. Nat., Nouv. Acq. lat. 2334) see A. Grabar and C. Nordenfalk, *Early Medieval Painting* (Lausanne, 1957), p. 103; for the Gospels of St Augustine (CCCC 286) see F. Wormald, *The Miniatures in the Gospels of St Augustine* (Cambridge, 1954), pl. v.     [2] B. 16. 3 (379).

[3] See P. Bloch, 'Zum Dedikationsbild in Lob des Kreuzes des Hrabanus Maurus', *Das erste Jahrtausend* I, 471–94.     [4] Ker, *Catalogue*, no. 42.

[5] 22 v and 29 v; see New Palaeographical Society Ser. II, nos. 140 and 141.

[6] E.g. York Gospels, 60 v.     [7] BM Add. 49598, 92 v.

a tumble of twisted drapery from which emerges upwards his symbol in anthropomorphic form holding a book. The border of the St Luke miniature is formed from two ellipses joined in the middle by a pair of gripping heads similar to those found in the initials in the Junius Psalter. Even the curious convention of one of the eyes is found. It is clear, however, that they are not by the same hand as the Junius Psalter which is probably earlier. Within the border is a delicately drawn leaf-scroll, which, though less elaborate, recalls the border to the miniature of Athelstan and St Cuthbert in CCCC 183 and an initial *P* in the same book. A later example of such a scroll is to be found in a late-tenth-century manuscript of Boethius's *De Consolatione Philosophiae* in Paris.[1] At the apices of the miniature are bosses of leaf-work which are comparable with the leaves decorating the border of the miniature on fol. 21 of Galba A. xviii.

St John's miniature is less elaborate than St Luke's, though in the general composition it resembles it. There is the seated evangelist with his book and above him the symbol of the eagle emerges from a similar tangle of drapery. On the other hand the border is quite different. Unfortunately its ornament has almost perished, but from what can be seen it seems to have been more restrained and classical, resembling somewhat the borders to the evangelist miniatures in the York Gospels. There is no sign of the typical leaf-work of the 'Winchester School' of the later period.

In both these miniatures there are signs of new stylistic influence, which separates them from such manuscripts as the miniatures in Galba A. xviii and the initials in the Junius Psalter. The most remarkable feature is the tangle of drapery which divides the evangelist from his symbol. Such a device is not to be found in either Carolingian or earlier gospel books. Perhaps the best parallel, and it is not a very close one, is to be seen in the famous miniature of the Adoration of the Lamb in the early-ninth-century gospels from Saint Médard de Soissons, now in Paris.[2] This manuscript belongs to the Court School of Charles the Great and it is with this school that long ago Otto Homburger associated some of the features of the 'Winchester School'. Besides this drapery the treatment of the folds of the evangelists' robes may also be compared with these Carolingian manuscripts and even more clearly with some of their later derivatives of the school of Fulda. Unfortunately no gospel book either from the Court School or from Fulda is known to have been in England at this period. There is, however, evidence that there was an example of the Court School in England by the sixteenth century. BM Cotton Claudius B. v is a ninth-century continental copy of the Acts of the Council of

---

[1] Bibl. Nat., lat. 17814, 46r. I owe my knowledge of this beautiful manuscript to Miss Diane Bolton of the Victoria County History.

[2] Bibl. Nat., lat. 8850, 1v; see Köhler, *op. cit.* II, pl. 67.

Constantinople in 680 which has in it a tenth-century inscription recording its gift by King Athelstan to the abbey of St Peter at Bath.[1] On the margin at the foot of the last page there is pasted a small miniature of Zacharias and the Angel which has been shown by Wilhelm Köhler to have come from a manuscript illuminated in the Court School.[2] It is probable that it was inserted by Sir Robert Cotton who was given to decorating his manuscripts with fragments of others. Nevertheless it is possible that the book from which this scrap was taken may have been one of the models for the new style.

A later and very curious survival of this stage of English illumination, in which we see the transition from an early style to the more developed style of the second half of the century, is to be found in a manuscript which, while written at Fleury, has three miniatures which are clearly by an English illuminator working in an early style. Indeed if it were not for an initial in the manuscript one would be very tempted to regard them as dating from the middle of the tenth century. The script of the text, however, seems to indicate that the last quarter of the century is more acceptable.

The manuscript in which these interesting miniatures are found is Paris, Bibl. Nat. lat. 6401, and its most important contents, written in the original hand, are two works of Boethius: the *De Consolatione Philosophiae* and the *Institutio Arithmetica*. There are a number of later additions including the epitaph of Gauzlin, abbot of Fleury 1004–13, and a famous group of mathematical problems in the form of letters.[3] The three miniatures which are relevant to our problem are found on 5v, 158v and 159r. A fourth, on 13v, is by an entirely different hand from the others and is clearly continental. The first (5v) illustrates the vision of Boethius of Philosophia as described in the opening chapter of the *De Consolatione Philosophiae* (see pl. III *d*). Philosophia is represented as a tall and commanding female figure. Boethius lies on a bed nearby. His prison is shown as a gabled building. The drawing is unfinished and the three females on the right are not completed. Moreover the rectangular border below the drawing is devoid of ornament. It is important to note that the text has nothing to do with the miniature.

The second miniature, which is on 158v, comes after the *Institutio Arithmetica* (see pl. VI). It shows a nimbed figure seated under an elaborate arched canopy in the half-circle of which is a figure of Christ the Judge flanked by two winged seraphs, each with six wings, as described in the

---

[1] See *Catalogue of Ancient Manuscripts in the British Museum*, Part II, Latin (London, 1884), p. 88.
[2] 'An Illustrated Evangelistary of the Ada School and its Model', *Journal of the Warburg and Courtauld Institutes* xv (1952), 48–66.
[3] 1v–11r; see P. Tanney, 'Une Correspondance d'Écolâtres du XIe Siècle', *Notes et Extraits des Manuscrits* xxxv. 2 (1901), 487–543.

vision of the prophet Isaiah. It is not clear whom this figure is intended to represent, though it is obvious that he is derived from an evangelist figure. He sits between two looped-up curtains and with his left hand touches an open book and with his right an inkhorn. Iconographically the composition is close to some of the manuscripts of the Court School of Charlemagne and particularly the figures of St Mark in the Ada Gospels at Trier and the St John in that part of the Lorsch Gospels which is now in the Vatican.[1] Nevertheless the direct inspiration may have come from one of the later derivatives of the Court School, possibly again one of the Fulda books. In the colour the miniature is wholly English and recalls Tanner 10 in the Bodleian and the psalter in the Cathedral Library at Salisbury, MS 150.

On the following leaf, 159r, is the third miniature (see pl. V c). It is a long narrow rectangular panel divided into four compartments. In the upper compartment is a seated figure of the Almighty holding a scroll rather in the manner of the figure seated in the arch of the preceding miniature. Below is the Agnus Dei in a circle and below that the Holy Spirit in the form of a dove. In the lowest compartment is a figure of a saint with hands outstretched in prayer. The whole composition shows the Holy Trinity adored by a saint. What is both important and interesting about this miniature is that it is a very early representation of the Trinity, preceding by about a century the rather similar pictures of the same subject in the psalter of Bury St Edmunds in the Vatican.[2] It should not be forgotten that pictures of the Holy Trinity, while not very common on the continent, assumed a variety of forms in England in the tenth and eleventh centuries.

What is remarkable about these three miniatures is their irrelevance to the texts with which they keep company. As has been already noticed, the miniature of the vision of Boethius is unfinished and the other two, though in full colour, are found on blank leaves. This at once poses the question as to what they are doing here and prompts us to ask whether we have here spare leaves of a pattern-book used at Fleury to receive later writing. Though the drawings and miniatures are by an Englishman, yet because of the initial mentioned above, it is unlikely that the illuminations were done in England. We must therefore assume that they are the work of an Englishman at Fleury. This is not a unique occurrence, since rather later, about the year 1000, there was a miniaturist at work there who produced the magnificent drawings of the constellations in an Aratea now

---

[1] See W. Braunfels, *Lorsch Gospels* (New York, 1966), Intro., figs. 8 and 9; also Köhler, *Die karolingischen Miniaturen* II (Berlin, 1958), pls. 95 and 110.

[2] Cod. Regin. lat. 12, 158 v and 159 r. For other English representations of this period see F. Wormald, 'Late Anglo-Saxon Art: Some Questions and Suggestions', *Studies in Western Art* I, 19–22.

BM Harley 2506 and the drawing of Christ and saints in the copy of St Gregory on Ezekiel now in the Bibliothèque Municipale at Orléans.[1]

As has been already suggested, these miniatures from Fleury manuscripts are so English in style that they cannot be regarded as continental copies of English originals, and in any case both in colour and ornament they cannot be compared with any continental illuminations. In colour the miniatures in Paris 6401 are nearest to the initials in Salisbury 150, a psalter made early in the last quarter of the tenth century, but rather retarded in style. It is possible that this artist of the Paris miniatures had also been trained in a somewhat old-fashioned style which really represents an earlier stage of the Benedictine reform.

From what has been said in the brief sketch given above it would seem that from the reign of Alfred onwards there was a steady stylistic development in the production of illuminated books in southern England and that the basis of the style rested upon earlier illumination which was not wholly Carolingian. At the same time, from quite early in the tenth century Carolingian manuscripts were modifying the style and preparing the way for the introduction of the much more spectacular changes in the second half of the tenth century which are rightly associated with the reforms of St Dunstan and St Æthelwold.

[1] See F. Wormald, *English Drawings of the Tenth and Eleventh Centuries* (London, 1952), nos. 35 and 45 and pls. 13 and 14.

# The handwriting of Archbishop Wulfstan

## NEIL KER

Writing about Hemming's Cartulary in 1948 I suggested that annotations in the cartulary and in other manuscripts were likely to be in the hand of Wulfstan, the homilist, bishop of Worcester and archbishop of York, d. 28 May 1023: 'if they are not actually the archbishop's, they must at least proceed from his immediate circle and time.'[1] In the *Catalogue of Manuscripts containing Anglo-Saxon* I gave a list of ten manuscripts containing writing in a hand that was, I thought, 'very probably' Wulfstan's.[2] More recently Professor Whitelock wrote of the hand of marginalia in Hatton 42 that 'It seems almost certain that it can belong to no one but Wulfstan himself'[3] and Professor Clemoes said that BM Cotton Nero A. i contains 'many entries in his hand'.[4] In a matter of this kind it is hard to drop the word 'probably', but it should be dropped. In what follows I call the hand Wulfstan's, first describing it and then giving as faithful an account as I can of what is written by it in the margins, between the lines, in blank spaces and occasionally as part of the text of the ten manuscripts in question. A good deal of what I say has been said before, but a *mise ensemble* will be useful to show how difficult it is to suppose that anyone but Wulfstan himself was the scribe and to aid the imagination. In these manuscripts we are looking at a small part of the work of an experienced interpolator. What Wulfstan did in Nero A. i he will have done much more densely in the manuscript of Ælfric's *De Septiformi Spiritu* when he converted it into rhythmic prose of his own kind.[5] And what he did in Nero was probably what he did in the lost exemplars of Nero's texts and will account for some of Nero's errors.[6] Wulfstan was not well served by his scribes, or not by some of them, but the exemplars they followed were probably not easy.

[1] 'Hemming's Cartulary', *Studies in Medieval History presented to Frederick Maurice Powicke* (Oxford, 1948), p. 71.
[2] P. 211. In addition to the manuscripts listed in Ker, *Catalogue*, about a score still exist which may have been at Worcester as early as Wulfstan's time. Two of them are the sort of books in which he was particularly interested: his hand is in one of them, Oxford, Bodleian Library, Hatton 42, but not in the other, CCCC 279.
[3] *Sermo Lupi*, p. 30.
[4] In *Die Hirtenbriefe Aelfrics*, ed. B. Fehr, repr. (Darmstadt, 1966), p. cxxviii.
[5] A. McIntosh, *Wulfstan's Prose*, Sir Israel Gollancz Memorial Lecture 1948, *Proceedings of the British Academy* (1949), p. 138.
[6] See, e.g., Whitelock, *Sermo Lupi*, p. 57, note on lines 86–93, and below, p. 319.

The ten manuscripts were used by Wulfstan either at Worcester or at York, and perhaps, especially if they were his own books, at both Worcester and York. About Hatton 20 and Hatton 42 there is no question. They were Worcester books before his time, 20 given by King Alfred and 42 traditionally a *Liber Sancti Dunstani*. Cop., Claud., Nero, Tib., Vesp. and the York Gospels, on the other hand, were new books when Wulfstan used them. Harl., a bit of a book only, is also contemporary with him. Tib. is from Worcester. Harl., though its connections are with York, was at Worcester by the early thirteenth century. There is palaeographical evidence that the York Gospels were at York in Wulfstan's lifetime.[1] Cop., Nero and Vesp. are likely to be books which owed their existence to Wulfstan and they may have been in his possession until he died. Claud. and Vesp. are probably from the north of England and Nero is more suitably placed at York than at Worcester, as Professor Whitelock has shown.[2]

### THE HAND[3]

#### Minuscule letters

The most obvious point about Wulfstan as a scribe is his disregard for the conventional distinctions of letter-form according to whether the language used is Latin or Old English.[4] In his alphabet only four letters and one combination of letters are distinguished, *f*, *r* and *st* invariably, *d* usually and *g* occasionally. There is only one form of *a*, *e*, *h* and *s*, and the distinction in *r* is only rarely the usual one. The hand has a forward slope and if a ruled line is not being followed it tends to drift slightly upwards. Ascenders are long, plain at the top, or in more careful writing wedge-shaped or split and somewhat tagged to the left (Cop. 66 v 4 and 6 and Vesp. 148 v).

    *a* Except in the ligature *æ* (*q.v.*), *a* is usually triangular, the left side and the right side rising at an almost equal angle to a point. Caroline *a* is used in careful writing on Vesp. 171 v.

    *d* Rounded *d*, used invariably in Old English and occasionally in Latin, has a rather long curving upstroke. Upright *d*, used generally in Latin, is

---

[1] As I failed to notice in *Catalogue*, the script of art. *a* is very like the script of arts. *b* and *c*.

[2] *Sermo Lupi*, pp. 1 and 31, and 'Wulfstan at York', *Franciplegius: Medieval and Linguistic Studies in Honor of Francis Peabody Magoun* (New York, 1965), pp. 217–30. York is a library of which we know very little. Librarians there seem to have written a title at the head of the first leaf in some of their books, not an uncommon nor yet a very common position for a title. Harley 208, and Lincoln, Cathedral Library, 101 and 102 have it here, and so does York Minster Library, xvi. A. 8 (as Mr Bernard Barr kindly reminded me), a book of unknown provenance which may have been always where it is now. It seems therefore just worth drawing attention to *Alquinus* at the head of 114 r of Vesp. and to *Apollogus de ordine romano* at the head of 1 r of Cop.

Cop. 66 v (pl. VII) has the whole range of Wulfstan's writing from its most careful in lines 7–12 to its most current in lines 14–16. It does not include *x*, tailed *e* and caroline *f* and *g*. These letters and Wulfstan's majuscule are to be seen in the plates of EEMF 17, in preparation at the time of writing.     [4] For the distinctions see Ker, *Catalogue*, p. xxvi.

a three-stroke letter: a curve, nearly as for *c*, and a vertical ascender are joined by a short horizontal stroke.

*e* It is round backed. The tongue of final *e* projects some way to the right.

*f* Caroline *f* is a descender. On Vesp. 148 v Wulfstan's name is written six times, twice with caroline *f* and four times with insular *f*.

*h* It always has its second limb turned up at the end, a form which most scribes use only when they are writing Old English.

*m* and *n* In hasty writing they are made without raising the pen: cf. Cop. 66 v 1–6 and 11–16 with 7–10.

*r* With its sloping shoulder it is distinctive.[1] The form used in Latin differs from the form used in Old English only in the length of the descender. It is only just a descender in the careful writing of Vesp. 148 v. There are a few examples of normal insular *r* (Cop. 66 v 10, *ðyder*).

*s* It is tall and descends below the line, but less far than most other descenders (Cop. 66 v 2 and 5). The shaft tends to slope forwards.

*u* It is normally in two strokes, even in current writing. But a currently made *u*, carefully distinguished from *n*, is at Cop. 66 v 16. The pointed *v* form of *u*, which takes up less space, is used in marginalia (Vesp. fols. 116–18).

*x* It has a long descending stroke from right to left (Nero 71 v).

*y* The second stroke has a hook at the top and a long tail. There is no dot.

*ð* The back is longer than in *d* and turns over to the right at the top.

### Combined letters

*æ* is like printed roman '*æ*'.

The tailed *e* is used in Latin (e.g. Nero 125 v, *ętatibus*). The tail is open and angular.

The form of the *et* ligature is distinctive (Cop. 66 v 16).

The *st* ligature is used in Latin (Cop. 66 v 16), but not in Old English. On Vesp. 148 v *st* in *Wulfstan* is twice a ligature and four times uncombined.

### Abbreviations

-*q*. and -*b*. for -*que* and -*bus* (Nero 80 v and 125 v).   ÷ for *est*.[2]

### Majuscule letters

Wulfstan's majuscules – he wrote a good many headings – are distinguished from the majuscules of other scribes in these manuscripts by the use of uncial instead of rustic capital *E* and, except sometimes at the

---

[1] But it is not unlike the *r* used in Latin by another corrector of Nero; see below, p. 322, n. 1.
[2] Cf. Clemoes, *op. cit.* p. cxxxvi.

beginning of a word, of uncial instead of rustic capital *D*. The long vertical head of *A* is curious. To judge from *A* in *AD*, Cop. 74r, it is a narrow ink-filled loop. Too often a smother of red paint half obscures the headings.[1] Where it is absent the formation of the letters can be seen (Vesp. 173 v).

At the beginning of a new paragraph or where the beginning of a sentence coincides with the beginning of a new line Wulfstan's initial letter is in the space between the pair of vertical ruled lines (Cop. 66 v).[2]

## Punctuation

Sentences written by Wulfstan are amply punctuated by means of the punctus versus (;) at the end of a sentence and either a simple point (.) or the punctus elevatus (⸵) within the sentence. The punctus elevatus is used more in Latin than in Old English. Texts written in these manuscripts by scribes contemporary with Wulfstan have similar punctuation, either original or added.[3] The added punctuation may be by Wulfstan himself: one can hardly tell.[4] In manuscripts written before his time the kind of punctuation he used tends to be added in places where his hand occurs: for example in Hatton 42 in the chapter *De Sorte* and throughout fols. 189–204. In other parts of Hatton 42 the original sparse punctuation has not been added to.

A heading is often followed by a colon and a mark something like a large very open *r* (Cop. 65 v and 80 r, Claud. 32 r and Nero 102 r).

The *hyphen* is not used.

The *signe de renvoi*, a curving diagonal with a point beneath it (Nero 80 v), may be combined in a single stroke (Cop. 48 r and 66 v 6 and 13).

A *jagged line* is used to separate one passage from another and to mark runovers (Cop. 66 v 16, Nero 80 v and 119 v and Vesp. 148 v and 173 v). On Vesp. 116 v a line like this surrounds the words *Semper...ei deus*, a parenthesis which had become nonsensical through the substitution of *Semper* for *Secundum*.[5] A more level line surrounds the redundant *Eac we witan...gewearð* on Nero 112 r.[6] These examples suggest that the jagged line round *7 se ðe to gelome...þe seo dæd sy* in the York Gospels, 159 r, is intended to cancel a passage which did not have Wulfstan's final

---

[1] Wulfstan annotated Nero before the decorator put his red fillings into the manuscript: see esp. 115 v.

[2] Cf. Clemoes, *op. cit.* p. cxxxvi.

[3] For the punctuation of *Sermo Lupi*, lines 55–68, in Nero and the other copies, see McIntosh, *loc. cit.* pp. 131–2.

[4] In *English Manuscripts in the Century after the Norman Conquest* (Oxford, 1960), p. 49, I noticed that Cop. has the interrogation mark above the first word of a question as well as after the last word. The same is true of Hatton 42 and Vesp., e.g. Hat. 192 v, *Quid est...*, and Vesp. 115 v, *Cur in alium...* Was Wulfstan responsible for the question marks in these manuscripts and in Worcester, Cathedral Library, F. 91?

[5] *MGH, Epistolae* IV, 51, lines 20–1.          [6] *Sermo Lupi*, line 86.

approval, perhaps because he did not wish to introduce a specific penalty, more suitable to a law-code, into his general exhortation.[1]

## Spellings

On spellings in Old English see Whitelock, *Sermo Lupi*, pp. 37–40. In Latin *eclesia* or *eclesia* is written, not *ecclesia* or *ecclesia*; *-mn-* not *-mpn-* in a word like *damnatio*;[2] *inp-* not *imp-* (*inpressit, inportune*); and *pulchritudo*, not *pulcritudo*.

### THE ENTRIES IN THE MANUSCRIPTS

Wulfstan's additions to the manuscripts are of two kinds. Some are the changes made by a man of letters who wishes to improve on what he himself has written or on what others have written and occasionally even to take the pen from an amanuensis and write a few lines of the text himself. Others are the changes made by a corrector looking over what a scribe has written and mending the errors he finds. As reviser, Wulfstan adds two-stress phrases like *swa swa god wolde, wrece god swa he wille* or *gyme se þe wille* which were not in the scribe's text because they were not in his exemplar. As corrector, he inserts *we* to change a nonsensical *lædum* into *læwedum*. Additions of this second kind are not of much interest and I have included only a few of them in my account of the manuscripts.[3] Some examples of errors repaired in Wulfstan's hand in Nero and Vesp. are: Nero 104r *'þincan' mæg*, 104r *dyrn'lican' galscipe*, 114r *ma'ne'ge*, 116r *'for gode'* 7, 150r *docto'r'*, 163v *po'tu'issent* and 164r *peniten'tibus'*; and Vesp. 116r *et* replacing *ad*, 116v *sed 'et' omnes*, 117r *exercituum* instead of *exercitus*, 117r *equitas* replacing *equalis* and 171v *in 're'gionibus*.[4]

### Copenhagen, Kongelige Bibliotek, Gamle Kongelige Sammlung 1595 4°

E. Jørgensen, *Catalogus Codicum Latinorum Medii Aevi Bibliothecae Regii Hafniensis*, pp. 43–6.[5] Ker, *Catalogue*, no. 99. P. Clemoes in *Die Hirtenbriefe Aelfrics*, ed. B. Fehr, repr. (Darmstadt, 1966), pp. cxxxi–ii and cxxxv–ix. A microfilm is in the Bodleian, MS Film 513. Pl. VII, above, shows 66v.

Wulfstan wrote on 48r, 65v–6v and 81r and headings elsewhere.

---

[1] Napier, *Wulfstan*, p. 309, lines 18–20. Cf. Jost, *Wulfstanstudien*, p. 267.

[2] Cf. Clemoes, *op. cit.* p. cxxxvi.

[3] Cf. below, e.g. Claud. 37r, *riht* and 37v, *sylf on*.

[4] Nero, 104r, Jost, *Polity*, p. 125; 114r, Whitelock, *Sermo Lupi*, line 176; 116r, Napier, *Wulfstan*, p. 168, line 18. Vesp. fols. 116–17, *MGH, Epistolae* IV, 51, lines 7, 14, 30 and 37.

[5] The thirty-three items, listed, but not numbered, by Jørgensen, are distributed as follows: 1 and 2 on quires 1 and 2; 3 and 4 on quire 3; 5–12 on quires 4 and 5; 13 on quire 6; 14–17 on quire 7; 18–22 on quire 8; 23–8 on quire 9; and 29–33 on quires 10 and 11. The collation is: 1⁸, 2 nine (fols. 9–17), 3–4⁸, 5⁸ wants 8, probably blank, after fol. 40, 6 two (singletons, fols. 41–2) and 7–11⁸ (fols. 43–82).

26 r    *The words* uel de reconciliatione post penitentiam, *an addition to the heading* Sermo de caena domini.

A sermon of Abbo of St Germain, ptd Bethurum, *Wulfstan*, pp. 367–73, from CCCC 190.

48 r    si gula. si iurgatrix si maledica *marked for insertion into the text after* si fatua.

65 v–6 r    *Heading* De uisione *and last words* Hec dicit dominus et reliqua *of a series of extracts from Isaiah; also in this piece, 65v, the words* scilicet propterea *above* deserta *and – over erasure –* In auribus meis sunt hec dicit dominus. Item.

The extracts are ptd Bethurum, *Wulfstan* no. XI: see there the footnotes to lines 9 and 29. Cop. reads with the Vulgate *Terra...deserta* (Isaiah 1. 7). The two later manuscripts, CCCC 201 and Hatton 113, introduce the un-biblical *ideo* before *terra*.

66 v    Se þe þyses lytlan nele andgyt niman. ne truwie ic æt maran þæt he wille gyman swa swa he scolde his agenre þearfe. Ac do swa ic lære lufa god georne. 7 beseoh on þinre heortan gelome to his laran. þonne sceal þe spowan 7 þe bet limpan. for gode 7 for worolde. gelyf gif þu wille;
    Se þe bið of earde 7 feor of his cyððe. hu mæg he ham cuman gif he nele leornian. hu se weg licge þe lið to his cyððe;
    Hu mage we to hefenan rihtne weg aredian. buton we gewunian. þæt we oft spyrian. 7 geornlice smeagean hu we magan ðyder cuman;
    Soð is þæt ic secge. gelyfe se þe wille. Se gefærð gesællice þe godcunde lare. oftost gehyreð 7 geornlicost gymeð. AMEN;
    Qui est ex deoꞌ uerba dei audit;
Ælc man behofað gastlices fostres. Non in sola pane. uiuit homo. sed in omni uerbo quod procedit de ore dei; Beati qui audiunt uerbum dei et custodiunt illud;

Sixteen lines filling and overflowing the space left blank on the verso of the last leaf of quire 9. They follow the extracts from Jeremiah ptd Bethurum, *Wulfstan*, no. XI. *þyses lytlan* in the first line refers, no doubt, both to the extracts from Isaiah on 65 v–6 r and to the extracts from Jeremiah on 66 v. The writing and spacing suggest that the original passage, *Se þe þyses lytlan ...wille* (lines 1–6), was added to on three or four occasions; cf. Ker, *Catalogue*, p. 140.

67 r and 74 r    *Headings* Sermo episcopi ad cler' *and* Item sermo ad sacerdotes *before Ælfric's first and second Latin letters for Wulfstan* (*Briefe 2 and 3*).

78r   *Heading* Incipit de baptism' *before the Latin text printed from other copies by Napier* Wulfstan, *no.* IV.

79v   *Heading* De officio missae

*Headings* De sacerdotibus (*80r*), Item de sacerdotibus (*80v*), De hostiariis (*82v*), De lectoribus (*82v*) *and the marginal note* Ordo misse prim[o] a sancto petro est insti[tuta] (*81r*) *in extract from Amalarius.*

### BM Add. 38651, fols. 57–8

Ker, *Catalogue*, no. 130. 57v and 58r reprod. in EEMF 17.

I have little to add to what is said in the *Catalogue* about these hardly legible jottings, written apparently by Wulfstan in smaller script than he used elsewhere. The writing is dense in places and there is much more of it than can be read, but it is not continuous nor all at the same angle. The leaves look like endleaves or covers and come, no doubt, from the medieval binding of some rebound manuscript in the Cotton, Harley or Royal collections in the British Museum. One thinks, in the first place, of Nero or Vesp., the two manuscripts with the closest links to Wulfstan. Vesp. seems too big and Nero too small. Nero has been cut down a good deal, however, and is not quite out of the question.[1]

### BM Cotton Claudius A. iii, fols. 31–86 and 106–50

Ker, *Catalogue*, no. 141. Whitelock, *Sermo Lupi*, pp. 23–4. Whitelock, 'Wulfstan at York', *op. cit.* pp. 217–18. 37v reprod. in EEMF 17.

The Latin and English versions of VI Atr. (Liebermann, *Gesetze*, pp. 246–59), written on a quire in front of a benedictional of *s.* x/xi, have been given a heading and added to in a few places in Wulfstan's hand.

32r   *Heading* Incipiunt sinodalia decreta:-

35r   æþelredo *above* N̄.

35r   wulfstanus *above* N̄.

36v   heah

37r   riht

37v   sylf on, eac, gyt, georne.

> Liebermann, *Gesetze*, p. 247, sec. 40. 2 (Latin) and secs. 25, 25. 1, 35, 41 and 42 (OE).

### BM Cotton Nero A. i, fols. 70–177

Ker, *Catalogue*, no. 164. Whitelock, *Sermo Lupi*, p. 1. *Die Hirtenbriefe Aelfrics*, ed. B. Fehr, pp. 250–5. The whole MS reprod. in facsimile in EEMF 17.

Wulfstan's additions and corrections occur throughout and in five places he wrote some words or lines of the text (100v, 102r, 109v, 120r and

---

[1] See below, Nero 105r, 109v, 112r, 119v and 155r, for notes by Wulfstan which have been partly cut off by the binder.

125 v). Two-stress phrases have been added on 71 v, 79 v, 80 v, 105 r, 112 r, 115 v and 119 r.[1]

71 v   on cristenre þeode. Jost, *Polity*, p. 56.

79 v   Scylde man wið [ga]lnesse 7 wið æw[b]ryce georne;

> Napier, *Wulfstan*, p. 70, footnote to lines 1 and 2. Bethurum, *Wulfstan*, p. 204, footnote to lines 86–7.[2]

80 v   7 mid dædbote clænsie hine sylfne.

> Napier, *Wulfstan*, p. 71, footnote to lines 10 and 11. Bethurum, *Wulfstan*, pp. 205–6, footnote to lines 112–13.

80 v   Multum enim utile ac necessarium est ut peccatorum reatus episcopali supplicatione soluatur. Mediator enim dei et hominum iesus cristus prepositis ęclesię potestatem tradidit. ligandi uidelicet atque soluendi; Conuertimini igitur ad dominum in toto corde uestro et ne differatis de die in diem. In euangelio enim scriptum est. penitentiam agite. et reliqua.[3]

> Napier, *Wulfstan*, p. 71, footnote to line 13 (omitting *Conuertimini...*). Bethurum, *Wulfstan*, p. 206, footnote to line 115.

99 v   na Jost, *Polity*, p. 214.

100 v and 102 r   *The first sixteen words of the text,* Biscpas scoldan symle. godes riht bodian. 7 unriht forbeodan. 7 witodlice sona swa biscpas rihtes adumbiað., *and the last six,* on dollican dædan. oþþon on gebæran; *Ibid.* pp. 262 and 267.

102 r   *Heading* Be sacerdan:- *Ibid.* p. 84.

104 v   Ðæt is *and* hit   *Ibid.* p. 127.

105 r   swa swa god w[olde] *and* ryperas, *the latter over erasure. Ibid.* p. 81.

109 v   [He] cwæð. Se ðe eow [hy]reð: me he gehyreð; [Se] þe forhogað eow: [m]e he forhicgeð;   *Ibid.* p. 64.

109 v   *The last six words of the text,* þera þinga. þe dereð þisse þeode; *Ibid.* p. 66.

112 r   to eacan [oðran ealles t]o manega[n þe man] unscyld[ige] forfor [ealles to wide;]

> Whitelock, *Sermo Lupi,* p. 57, textual note to line 81.

115 v   *The first four words,* Her is 'gyt' rihtlic, *and the last four words,* Gyme se þe wille; *of the heading, the former over erasure.*

> Napier, *Wulfstan*, p. 167, footnote to line 11. Bethurum, *Wulfstan*, p. 276.

---

[1] Wulfstan was not the only corrector of Nero in the early eleventh century. Marginalia of some length not in his hand are on 98 r, 141 v, 144 r, 147 r, 152 v and 166 r. I wrongly attributed the last of these to Wulfstan in *Catalogue,* p. 212, line 1.

[2] As *S* in *Scylde* is a capital it is unlikely that a preceding 7 has been cut off.

[3] See Bethurum, *Wulfstan,* pp. 18–19 and 331, on this addition and the significance of the erasure of the words *ealswa þæt godspel cwæð* in the text opposite it.

119r   gif man þæt geræde:⁄

Liebermann, *Gesetze*, p. 242, V Atr., sec. 27.

119v   7 eal swa [. . .] swica beon wille. [l]a[di]g[e. . .]

Liebermann, *Gesetze*, p. 244, V Atr., sec. 30, n.

120r   *The heading and first two words,* Cristenum cyninge, *of this text* (Ker, Catalogue, *art. 24*) *are not in Wulfstan's hand, but he wrote the next fifty-one words:* gebyreð swyðe rihte. þæt he cristen folc rihtlice healde. 7 þæt he sy swa hit riht is. folces frofer. 7 rihtwis hyrde. cristenre heorde. 7 him gebyreð þæt he eallum mægene cristendom rære. 7 godes cyrcan æghwar georne. fyrðrige 7 friðige. 7 eal cristen folc sibbige 7 sehte. mid rihtre lage. Jost, *Polity,* pp. 41–3.

124v   (*1*) igitur (*2*) itaque (*3*) pro illorum neglegentia.

These interlineations are near the end of the piece beginning *Bonus itaque pastor* (Ker, *Catalogue,* art. 26).

125v   *Wulfstan completed the text beginning* Dominus igitur per ezechielem (ibid. *art. 27*), *writing the last thirty-nine words:* supra gregem cristi; Predicantes maiori ac minori. diuiti et pauperi omne consilium dei omnibus gradibus uel ętatibus. in quantum deus donauerit posse; Gregorius itaque dicit; Cum enim malorum peruersitas crescit. non solum frangi predicatio non debet:⁄ sed etiam augeri;

Bethurum, *Wulfstan,* p. 239, end of no. xviA.

138r   *Reference to source,* Can' Hib'

In the margin against the section *Si quis alicui. . .ęclesia catholica* of the text called by Thorpe *Excerptiones Ecgberti* (*Ancient Laws and Institutes of England,* ed. B. Thorpe [London, 1840] II, 332). I have not found this passage in Wasserschleben's edition of *Collectio Canonum Hibernensis, Die irische Kanonensammlung,* 2nd ed. (Leipzig, 1885).

155r   *The extract in the text from the penitential of pseudo-Theodore ends with the words* uulnera animarum medicamento uere penitentię curanda sunt; *Wulfstan added the next sentence of pseudo-Theodore:* Medicus enim [debet] sanare egrotum [secundum] austeritatem a[rtis sue] et non palpare [molliter] secundum uolunta[tem] infirmi;

Ed. F. W. H. Wasserschleben, *Die Bussordnungen der abendländischen Kirche* (Halle, 1851), p. 569, lines 3–5; my readings in square brackets are from the edition.

158r   et maior excommunicationis damnati[o] est:⁄ et eam diutius su[stinet]

Fehr, *op. cit.* p. 246, lines 16–17.

160r and 162r  *Two additions supplying omissions in this copy of the* Sermo de Reconciliatione post Penitentiam *of Abbo of St Germain are in Wulfstan's hand*. (*1*) per suam passionem⸴ et liberauit e[um] (*2*) uite eternę; Fratres iam modo est adam [receptus] in celesti para[diso] propter multum l[aborem et] *above cancellation of* laboriosam.

Bethurum, *Wulfstan*, app. 1, lines 33 and 95–6.

164r and v  *Additions to the section* De medicamento animarum. (*1*) de cura ęclesiarum. et (*2*) inportune

Fehr, *op. cit.* p. 251, line 15 and p. 252, line 9.

166v  *Wulfstan added the words, here printed within carets, of the sentence of* De Cotidianis Operibus Episcoporum *ending* exaltata: ...aliquando expedit ut clerici inter epulas ˋuel legant⸴´ uel´ lectiones recitent ˋuel uersificent´ ymnizentque post mensam canent organizent in uoce moderata non ˋadeo´ exaltata.

*Ibid.* p. 253, lines 30–2. *uel uersificent* is written in as an alternative to *ymnizent*, as its position shows.

### BM Cotton Tiberius A. xiii, fols. 1–118

*Hemingi Chartularium Ecclesiae Wigorniensis*, ed. T. Hearne (Oxford, 1723). Ker, 'Hemming's Cartulary', *Studies in Medieval History presented to Frederick Maurice Powicke* (Oxford, 1946), pp. 49–75. Ker, *Catalogue*, no. 190. 48r and 116r reprod. in EEMF 17.

1. Wulfstan's hand occurs on almost every leaf from 1 to 57 and from 97 to 108, writing usually no more than a single word in the margin against each charter, the name of the estate to which it refers.[1] The script is often majuscule or a mixture of majuscule and minuscule. The margins have been damaged, especially at the beginning, and a certain amount of writing has been lost or cannot be read. Most of the names are printed by Hearne, and Birch adopted many of them as headings in his *Cartularium Saxonicum*. I give the Birch numbers in brackets and follow the arrangement in 'Hemming's Cartulary', pp. 52–5.
Group A:  1v [.]to weora[...] (*579*); 3r we[....] 7 wre[....] (*455.1*); 4r Ælfgyðecyrc[e] (*455.2*); 4v [Ælfg]yþecyrce (*701*); 6r Ælfgyðecy[rce] (*847*); 6v Lænhaga 7 landlæn æþerede 7 æþelflæde (*608*);[2] 9r Brem[...] (*308*); 9r Fled[...] (*76*); 10r Fledanbyrg (*76*); 11r *lost* (*368*); 11r Breodun (*236*); 12r Wassanburna (*430*); 13r Breodun (*434*); 14r Uptun (*575*); 14v Bloccanleah (*489*); 15v [Bæ]ccesoran (*163*); 15v

[1] Wulfstan usually wrote a point after each name and at the end of each entry. I omit the latter.
[2] Printed by Hearne, but not by Birch. The dictionaries record *lænland*, but not *lænhaga* or *landlæn*.

Eulangelad (*210*); 16r Tredinctun (*183*); 17v Benningweorð (*616*); 18r Lunden (*561*); 19r *lost* (*492*); 20r Lunden (*171*).

Group Ai:    20v rippel (*51*); 21r Heanbyri (*416*).[1]

Group B:    22v [ . . . . . ]a (*309*); 23r Clife (*246*); 24v Onnanford (*187*); 25r Wudiandun (*156*); 25v Wudiandun (*217*); 26r dogedeswyllan. 7 [æt] tireltune 7 æt on[nan]dune (*283*); 26v [E]astun 7 Na[t]angraf (*165*); 27r dæglesford (*540*).

Group C:    28r Pyrigtun (*221*); 28v Byrhtanwyllan. 7 wæclingtun (*547*); 29v Eatun (*509*); 30v Eatun (*607*); 31r Eatun (*666*); 31v [dæ]glesford (*139*); 32r dæglesford (*436*); 32v Hwiccewudu (*432*).

Group D:    39r Beaganbyrig (*166*); 39r Eadboldingtun Pultun. Ber[ . . . ]-deslea. Eseg (*487*); 40v Eadboldingtun (*580*); 41r Bearmodeslea. 7 Colesburna (*304*); 42r Ductun. 7 Eseg (*226*); 42v Wuduceaster; 43r Wuduceaster.

Group E:    103r Wudutun (*157*); 103v Hamtun. 7 fehhaleah (*239*); 104v Strætford (*450*); 106r Offan freols (*241*); 107r Scottarið (*123a*); 107v Scottarið (*123b*); 108r Hnuthyrst (*534*).

Group F:    47r Westburh (*379*); 48r Westburh. 7 heanburh (*273*); 49r Westburh. 7 Stoc (*313*); 50r Stoc (*551*); 51v Huntenatun (*218*); 52r Huntenatun (*278*); 52r Westburh (*274*); 52v Heanburh (*220*); 53r Austan (*665*); 54r Austan (*269*); 54v Geat (*231*); 55r Wuduceaster (*164*); 55v [A]lhmundingtun (*559*); 56r Soppanbyrig (*582*).

Group G:    57r Geanbec into glewe[ . . . ] *From here to 96v the names of places and persons in the margins against the leases are not by Wulfstan, except, I think, the last two of the ten words in the margin of 70r:* æt grimanlege 7 æt moselege osulfe 7 æþelstane 7 ufede (*1139*). *He begins again at 97v, writing place-names, but, save once, not personal names:* 97v Byrhtanwylle (*1293*); 98r Langandun (*1243*); 98v Bynningweorð (*Kemble, 625*); 99r dæglesford (*Kemble, 623*); 100r Eowlangelad. Ealhstan. æþelstan (*1238*); 101r Cungle (*1091*); 101r Tedecesleage. 7 leage (*sic*) (*1111*).

2. Alterations to the homily beginning *Adam se æresta man*. Apart from two words on 115r all Wulfstan's writing is in the part of the homily beginning at Napier, *Wulfstan*, p. 3, line 19: cf. Bethurum, *Wulfstan*, p. 42, and Jost, *Wulfstanstudien*, pp. 185–7.

115r    þing *and* na

Napier, *Wulfstan*, p. 2, footnotes to lines 5 and 11.

116r    ealles

*Ibid.* p. 3, line 19.

---

[1] Another hand added wið þære wic.

116r  *In the passage* 7 swutule...manna banan, *the words printed here within caret-marks were added by Wulfstan:* 7 swutule 'eac' mæg gecnawan be mistlican tacnan se þe wile soð witan. þæt þa habbað god lean 'æfter heora liffæce'. þa ðe wisdomes gymað. 'þa hwile þe hy libbað.' 7 þa ðe gode hyrað. 7 godes lage healdað. 7 soþes gelyfað 7 georne þæt smeageað; '7' Sylfe we gesawon 'þæs' swutele bysene; We gesawan 'foroft' æt sumra þæra byrgenan þe gode wel gecwemdan;' manege 'men' gefectan lichamlice hæle. '7 þær wurdan hale.' þe ær wæran limmlaman;' þæs þe we sylfe. wistan ful georne; Blinde gefettan þæt hy locedan brade;' 7 halte wurdan hale 7 mistlice gebrocade hæle geforan 'þurh godes mihta.' æt halgra manna banan;

*Ibid.* p. 4, line 3 – p. 5, line 3.

## BM Cotton Vespasian A. xiv, fols. 114–79

*MGH, Epistolae* IV, 9. Ker, *Catalogue*, no. 204. Whitelock, *Sermo Lupi*, pp. 32–3. Whitelock, 'Wulfstan at York', *op. cit.* pp. 218–19. 148v, 171v and 173v reprod. in EEMF 17.

This collection of Alcuin's letters, collated by Dümmler in *MGH, Epistolae* IV as A 2, was almost certainly made for Wulfstan. He wrote on 116r–18v, 148v, 171v and 177v and made minor corrections – not included here – on other pages.

1. Changes to the first letter in the manuscript, Alcuin to King Æthelred, beginning *Suavitas sancti amoris* (*MGH, Epistolae* IV, Ep. 18).

115r  mendacia *alt. to* mendacium *and* periurium *interlined.*
116v  enim *added before* rapinas
118r  ipsum *added after* se *and* non stabit *alt. to* desolabitur
118r  sue *alt. to* sua

> *Ibid.* p. 50, line 12; 51, line 27; and 52, lines 22 and 29. *sue* to *sua* was a necessary change to make sense, since the text has not got the word *patria.*

118v  et *alt. to* Sacerdotum est

> *Ibid.* p. 52, line 31. According to the text here and in the four other manuscripts of this letter collated by Dümmler it is the duty of the bishop *monasteria corrigere. seruorum dei uitam disponere. populo dei uerbum predicare* and the duty of laymen *oboedire predicationi et diligenter plebem erudire subiectam.* Wulfstan's change brings Vesp. nearer to the *textus receptus* which transfers *et diligenter...subiectam* to the bishop's duty after *predicare*, but apparently without manuscript authority.

2. 148v  Qui legis hunc titulum domino da uota tonanti.
        Archipontifice pro uulfstano uenerando;

Floret in hoc opere pia mentio presulis archi.
Wlfstani cui det dominus pia regna polorum.
'Et sibi commissos tueatur ab hosti maligno;'
Pontificis bonitas manet hic memoranda ierarchi.
Wlfstani supero qui sit conscriptus in albo;

Est laus uulfstano mea pulchritudo benigno.
Pontifici cui sit dominus sine fine screnus;
Comere me comiter iussit ita presulis archi
Wlfstani pietas data sit cui arce corona.
Presule uulfstano hoc opus est censente paratum.
Pollice quod docto inpressit subtilis aliptes.

These five couplets and a triplet written on a blank page have been printed three times already: by W. Stubbs, *Memorials of St Dunstan*, Rolls Series 63 (1874), liv; by Birch, no. 896; and by Bethurum, *Wulfstan*, pp. 377–8. They are in Wulfstan's best hand, resembling Cop. 66 v 7–12. The margin has been cut. Wulfstan wrote in it [. . .]*uolueris* against the first line. Perhaps we should read *Si uolueris*, the intention being to tone down the imperative *da*. He wrote also *Item* against each new couplet, but only traces of the word remain. The fifth line is an addition (of Wulfstan's own composing?), squeezed in and partly in the margin.

I take *hoc opus* to be something else than Vesp. itself.

3. 171 v   The short letter of Alcuin to Paulinus (*MGH, Epistolae* iv, Ep. 96) fitted into the blank space at the end of a quire.

4. 173 v   (*1*) *Heading* De rapinis eclesiasticarum rerum: (*2*) *below the brief text so headed* Agustinus; Si quis retraxerit quod deo dedit:´ a suo gradu mouendus. et ab eclesia dei damnandus est; Quantomagis qui donum alterius. per uim ab eclesia dei diripit; Pecunia eclesiastica. rapta uel furata reddatur quadruplum:´ popularia dupliciter.

Cf. Bethurum, *Wulfstan*, p. 100.

5. 177 v   *Heading and first three words of a text:* De actiua uita et contempla-tiua :- Actiua uita est

### BM Harley 55, fols. 1–4

Ker, *Catalogue*, no. 225. 3 v and 4 r and v reprod. in EEMF 17.

Wulfstan corrected a scribal error in art. 2, the Laws of Edgar, and wrote the heading, the last five words and three additions to the text of art. 4. The words he wrote are listed in Ker, *Catalogue*.

### Oxford, Bodleian Library, Hatton 20 (SC 4113)

The whole MS reprod. in facsimile in *The Pastoral Care*, ed. N. R. Ker, EEMF 6 (Copenhagen, 1956). Ker, *Catalogue*, no. 324.

Wulfstan's additions and alterations to the text of Alfred's preface, 1r–2v, are listed in the introduction to the facsimile edition, pp. 24–5.

*Oxford, Bodleian Library, Hatton 42 (SC 4117)*[1]

47r and 194v reprod. in EEMF 17.

Wulfstan's hand occurs (1) in the chapter *De Sorte* of the *Collectio Canonum Hibernensis* and (2) in bk 1 of the capitulary of Ansegisus (188v–204r).

1. Nearly all Wulfstan's additions are in the paragraph of *De Sorte* beginning *De quatuor causis* (47r).[2] The changes he made are minor 'improvements', aimed at making the text clearer. They are shown here within caret-marks. The punctuation with ; and ꞉ is added, no doubt by Wulfstan.

. . . 'Et' in nouo 'testamento' statuerunt ıı id est bar'n'aban et mathian et sequentia usque dicit. et cecidit sors super madian (*alt. to* ma't'h'i'an) et 'con'numeratus est cum xi apostolis; De ac sorte statuunt duos apostolos pares merito scilicet preferre alterum alteri dei erat. 'Tertio' (*over eras.*) super causam incerti peccati mittitur 'sors'. ut de achan 'filio charmi' legulam furante legitur; et 'ut de' iona profeta unde dicitur; uenite mittamus sortes ut cognoscamus cuius causa malitiæ hec est super nos tempestas magna; 'Quarto' (*over eras.*) super diuissiones regionum. ut ad iesum dicitur; In sorte diuides terram populo huic; De hac sorte dicitur 'in psalmo;' funes ceciderunt mihi in preclaris 'et reliqua; Et' (*over eras. of* Inde) hereditas aliquando sors dicitur꞉ ut petr: ad simonem dicit; non est tibi sors in hac uita; In salmo 'quoque scriptum est; 'non derelinquet dominus uirgam. . .

2. Bk 1 of the capitulary of Ansegisus, headed here *Incipiunt excerpta quę congregauit karolus rex de senodis* (alt. to *sinodis*) *gallicis* was read by Wulfstan with close attention. His additions to it – my list does not aim at completeness – are printed here within caret-marks. Some of them, marked here with an asterisk, are, or may be, derived from another copy. The rest are probably improvements out of his own head. I refer to the edition by A. Boretius, *Capitularia Regum Francorum, MGH, Legum*, sec. ıı, 1, 394–413.

189r (ch. 5)   interdictum est 'omnibus' Ed. p. 398, line 15.

190r (ch. 19)   Item in eodem concilio ut 'non nisi' canonici libri tantum legantur in ecclesia.   Ed. p. 399, lines 17–18.

191r (ch. 44)   non habeant potestatem 'quicquam' dicendi Ed. p. 400, line 43.

*191r (ch. 46)   'oblata' Ed. p. 401, line 3.

---

[1] The first quire of Hatton 42 is of *s.* x/xi. It looks like the beginning of an attempt to replace the old and bad text.

[2] Ed. F. W. H. Wasserschleben, *Die irische Kanonensammlung*, 2nd ed. (Leipzig, 1885), pp. 83–4.

192 r (ch. 59)   ad altare 'offerendum est'   Ed. p. 401, line 41.

192 r (ch. 59)   'quia et' *over erasure.*   Ed. p. 401, line 41 (*et ut est*).

192 v (ch 60)   'nobis' uidetur   Ed. p. 402, line 10.

192 v (ch. 61)   un'i'us'cuiusque iuramenti' *over erasure.*   Ed. p. 402, line 22 (*unusquisque uestrum*).

*192 v (ch. 62)   'Et ubicumque sunt:' emendentur. uel damnentur;'   Ed. p. 402, line 30.

193 r (ch. 64)   cauenda 'est'   Ed. p. 402, line 40.

*193 r (after ch. 65)   'Hic deest de homicidio. et de furto. uel falso testimonio.'

>   Cf. ed. p. 402, n. *b*: the chapters in question, 67–8 of the capitulary of 787 (ed. Boretius, p. 59), are found in some manuscripts of Ansegisus.

193 r (ch. 66)   fidem. 'et'   Ed. p. 403, line 2.

*193 r (ch. 66)   'bene'   Ed. p. 403, line 4.

193 r (ch. 66)   'ut' intelligant   Ed. p. 403, line 5.

193 r (ch. 67)   'cum' magna   Ed. p. 403, line 13.

193 v (ch. 68)   uel *alt. to* 'Et'   Ed. p. 403, line 21.

193 v (ch. 68)   'ut obseruent' obsecramus 'et'   Ed. p. 403, line 21.

193 v (ch. 68)   'discentes' psalmos   Ed. p. 403, line 26.

193 v (ch. 68)   'scilicet indocti' *above* cupiunt   Ed. p. 403, line 28.

193 v (ch. 69)   'ut' *over erasure of* secundum quod   Ed. p. 403, line 34.

194 r (ch. 69)   'uel suscipiantur' *above* accipiantur   Ed. p. 403, line 37.

*194 r (after ch. 69)   'deest de mensuris et ponderibus.'

>   Cf. ed. p. 403, n. *c*: the chapter in question, 74 of the capitulary of 787 (ed. Boretius, p. 60), is found, like chs. 67–8, above, in some manuscripts of Ansegisus.

194 v (ch. 75)   'id est' quod   Ed. p. 404, line 24.

194 v (ch. 75)   'scilicet opera' *above* exerceant   Ed. p. 404, line 24.

*194 v (ch. 75)   'uel' in petris   Ed. p. 404, line 26.

194 v (ch. 75)   'con'struere   Ed. p. 404, line 26.

*194 v (ch. 75)   o *in* copulent *expuncted*: 'a' *above*.   Ed. p. 404, line 29.

194 v (ch. 75)   'aliqua pictilia' *over erasure of, probably,* acupicule   Ed. p. 404, line 30.

194 v (ch. 75)   Ut omnimodis 'honoribus' requies die'i' dominic'i' 'seruetur' (*the first, third and fourth alterations over erasure*)

>   Ed. p. 404, lines 31–2 reads *omnimodis bonorum requies die dominico persoluatur.*

194 v (ch. 75)   'uel facit;' *after* fecit   Ed. p. 404, line 33.

194 v (ch. 76)   'pre' *over cancellation of* uestrum   Ed. p. 404, line 34.

*195 r (ch. 76)   'et terram'   Ed. p. 404, line 43.

*195 r (ch. 76)   se resurrectionem *in* Item diligenter predicandum est se resurrectionem mortuorum accepturos *altered to* 'de' resurrectione *and* 'ut sciant et credant in eisdem corporibus premia meritorum' *added after* mortuorum

Ed. p. 405, line 3. A footnote to the older edition by Pertz, *MGH, Leges* I (1835), p. 281, line 40, shows that *ut...meritorum* is in the capitulary of 787 (ed. Boretius, p. 61, ch. 82) and in some copies of Ansegisus.

*196r (ch. 79)   'uel uernantes' *above* uenerantes   Ed. p. 405, line 40.

196v (ch. 82)   'alicuius' *over erasure of* quilibet   Ed. p. 406, line 21.

198r (ch. 95)   ton'de'rentur *instead of* tonsorentur   Ed. p. 407, line 47.

199v (ch. 102)   glorificatio 'nostra' cuiuslibet 'uel alicuius'   Ed. p. 409, line 8.

*200r (ch. 103)   missa'le' *instead of* missarium   Ed. p. 409, line 14.

200r (ch. 103)   'uel possumus' *above* possederit   Ed. p. 409, line 21 (*posse dederit*).

201v (ch. 118)   'qui' sibi   Ed. p. 410, line 34.

201v (ch. 118)   labor'are' (*over erasure*) 'et uictum adquirere possunt:'' Ed. p. 410, line 34.

202r (ch. 126)   'uel purgato' *above* parato   Ed. p. 411, line 15.

203v (ch. 147)   uel 'ubi' placitum ibi (*erased*) habuerit:' 'uel fuerit.'   Ed. p. 412, line 25.

204r (ch. 157)   'consuetudo' 'prouidentia' 'qui'

These additions are in a part of ch. 157 which follows after the last word printed in ed. (p. 413, line 6, *donent*): 'et qui tale beneficium habent ad medietatem laborent. et de eorum portione proprio presbitero decimas donent:' et de omni conlaborato et de uino et de feno fideliter et pleniter ab omnibus nona et decima persoluatur. de nutrimine uero pro decima sicut a'c'tenus (c *over erasure*) constitudo (*altered to* 'consuetudo') fuit:' ab omnibus obseruetur; si quis tamen episcoporum fuerit qui argentum pro hoc accipere uelit:' in sua maneat 'prouidentia' iuxta quod ei et illi [...] (*altered to* qui) hoc persoluere debet conuenerit.'

## York, Minster Library, Add. 1

Ker, *Catalogue*, no. 402. Whitelock, 'Wulfstan at York', *op. cit.* pp. 216–17. Whitelock, 'Wulfstan and the Laws of Cnut', *EHR* LXIII (1948), 452. Jost, *Wulfstanstudien*, pp. 86–94 and 266–8. 159v reprod. in EEMF 17.

In virtue of its position in a gospel book, the *Sermo Lupi* here, with its appendices *Be hæðendome* and *Be cristendome* (Napier, *Wulfstan*, nos. LIX–LXI), is likely to be a considered statement of what Wulfstan thought was vitally important for the spiritual welfare of his clergy and people. The copy here is closely datable: it cannot be earlier than 1020 nor later than May 1023, since Wulfstan himself altered what the scribe had written in four places.

Probably he was working at this statement at the same time as or immediately before he was working at I and II Cn., since he used the same matter in both places.[1] His additions are:

158r   we *and* mid
159r   uel nullus cristianus *above* Nemo cristianorum
159v   uel sende *above* bringe

> Napier, *Wulfstan*, p. 307, lines 8 and 23, p. 309, line 11, and p. 311, line 3. On 159r Wulfstan was smoothing out the clumsy construction derived from his source, *Excerptiones Ps. Ecgberti*, cxlviii (ed. B. Thorpe, *Ancient Laws and Institutes of England* [London, 1840] II, 123).

> [1] For the probable relationship see Whitelock, 'Wulfstan and the Laws of Cnut'.

# The nummular brooch from Sulgrave

## MICHAEL DOLLEY

Recent excavations for the Royal Archaeological Institute by Mr Brian K. Davison of the Ministry of Public Buildings and Works at Sulgrave, Northamptonshire,[1] have brought to light significant remains of what was clearly a substantial stone and timber tower-building attached to the late Saxon manor. A little above subsoil, itself securely dated *c.* 1000 by the occurrence of a truly *fleur-de-coin* London penny of Æthelred II's *Long Cross* issue,[2] in a context that must suggest loss before rather than after the end of the first third of the eleventh century, there was found in September 1968 a nummular bronze brooch of quite unusual type and fabric (see pl. VIII*a*). It is through the generosity of the excavator that it is possible for there to be given here a description and provisional discussion of the brooch in the hope that some account of an unpublished object of the period of Archbishop Wulfstan, and conceivably reflecting his influence, may be thought not entirely out of place in a volume of essays offered to a scholar whose contribution to Wulfstan studies has been as distinguished as it is certain to be enduring.

The brooch is of a yellowish bronze that could have given an impression of gold, and the present uneven patination affords a very distorted idea of the ornament's original appearance. The maximum diameter is approximately 45 mm., the very nature of its manufacture precluding an exactly circular form, and the fabric is one that is highly unusual if not unparalleled in Anglo-Saxon metalwork of this date.[3] The design in relief was impressed from the back on a paper-thin disc of bronze, the diameter

---

[1] Pending the appearance of Mr Davison's definitive report on the excavations there may be consulted with advantage his admirable preliminary account, *Current Archaeology* II. 1 (January 1969), 19–22.

[2] For the provisional dating of the currency of this issue between Michaelmas 997 and Michaelmas 1003 see R. H. M. Dolley, 'The Sack of Wilton in 1003 and the Chronology of the "Long Cross" and "Helmet" Types of Aethelraed II', *NNUM*, 1954, pp. 152–6. In a recent doctoral dissertation, however, it has been suggested that the type-cycle under Æthelred II may have been septennial rather than sexennial, and *Long Cross* is there dated 995–1002 which if right – and this must seem very doubtful – scarcely affects the position as regards the stratigraphy at Sulgrave; cf. H. B. A. Petersson, *Anglo-Saxon Currency* (Lund, 1969), *passim*.

[3] Mr L. N. W. Flanagan, F.S.A., kindly draws my attention to earlier use of the technique in the Frankish lands, and Mr Richard Warner, also of the Ulster Museum, informs me that the technique is one occasional in Ireland throughout the Early Christian, Viking and Anglo-Norman periods. For a full discussion of some early examples see M. J. O'Kelly, 'The Belt-Shrine from Moylough, Sligo', *JRSAI* xcv (1965), 149–88.

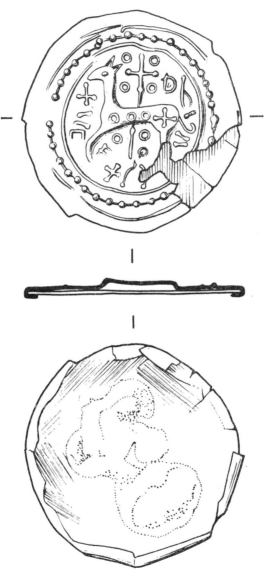

FIG. 9 The Sulgrave brooch

of this disc being in the neighbourhood of 49 mm. Behind this was placed a second and more substantial bronze plate of slightly smaller diameter, and the excess of the *cliché* was then turned over all around the circumference. There is no evidence that the *cliché* was first backed with lead or solder or even with wax, and the greatest care must have been taken at every stage of the manufacture to avoid crushing the *repoussé* design. Significantly the diameter of the outermost embossed circle of the obverse type is 8 mm. less than that of the brooch, and this would have allowed the maker to apply a considerable degree of force when lapping the edge, presumably with repeated taps of a light hammer on the very lip of a last or small anvil. Of the fastenings of the brooch nothing remains, but two areas of solder are entirely consistent with the theory of a conventional loop-and-pin and catch-plate.[1] Otherwise the back of the brooch seems to have been entirely plain, and minimal corrosion has not effaced a series of tangential abrasions which suggest an attempt to bring the backing-plate to something approaching the high finish of the *cliché*. Generally the front of the brooch is well preserved, but there is one segment where the foil has been torn away and lost. The differential patination, which it has been thought prudent not to attempt to remove, is undoubtedly disturbing, but affords valuable evidence of the high copper content of the bronze. Broadly speaking the reddish browns represent copper oxide and the greens copper carbonate, and treatment in the laboratory means that one can hope that the corrosion is now completely stabilized.

A description of the front of the brooch follows. The border consists of two embossed circles, with diameters of 37 and 29 mm. respectively, and between them a third embossed circle, on which are superimposed beads or pellets at more or less regular intervals. Originally these beads may have numbered forty, but no more than thirty-three survive. The analogy with the outer border found on late Anglo-Saxon pence need not be laboured. Virtually the whole of the field is taken up by a representation of the *Agnus Dei* or Lamb of God. The animal, of remarkable slightness and even agility, is shown from the flank, and the position of the legs suggests movement across the field from right to left. The eye is put in with a simple pellet, and the side of the animal is adorned with three annulets, and the haunch with a cross *boutonnée*. The ears are pricked, and the tail takes the form of a question mark. There is no nimbus. The whole is superimposed upon a more or less vertical cross of unusually slender form. The cross proper is equal-armed and *boutonnée*, and the long shaft that passes behind

---

[1] For the general type of this fastening on English bronze and/or copper brooches in the British Museum, see D. M. Wilson, *Anglo-Saxon Ornamental Metalwork 700–1100* (London, 1964) – henceforth cited as Wilson (1964) – p. 122, no. 8; p. 130, no. 15; p. 153, no. 47 (in its positioning perhaps the closest parallel); p. 160, no. 60; p. 177, no. 84; and (?) p. 208, no. 151. All are dated by Mr Wilson to the ninth, tenth and eleventh centuries.

the Lamb is ornamented with a pellet about half-way between the cross and the splayed foot. In the angles of the cross are four annulets, and three more are disposed one and two on either side of the lower portion of the staff or shaft. Below the nose of the Lamb is a smaller cross *boutonnée* which seems to begin a legend which one is tempted to read backwards and outwards *A* (unbarred) *G* (square). The legend is then clearly broken by the foreleg of the Lamb, and between it and the splayed foot of the cross there seems to be an even smaller cross *boutonnée*, with a retrograde *E* out of alignment and nearer the centre of the field. What followed on the other side of the foot of the cross can only be guessed at owing to damage, but between the Lamb's hindleg and tail two converging strokes suggest *A* (unbarred) or *V* or *U*. To the right of the lower half of the cross proper are disposed horizontally the letters *D I*, the latter tailing away into a quite obscure pattern of lines which seem to terminate the concentric legend already described but which may not all be entirely intentional. It is the opinion of the writer that it cannot well be a coincidence that those pairs of letters which do seem incontrovertible are *AG* and *DI*. The former begin the Latin word *Agnus*, while the latter are a perfectly acceptable contraction of the Latin *Dei*.[1]

As we have seen, the archaeological context in which the brooch from Sulgrave was discovered demands for its loss, if not manufacture, a date somewhere in the first third of the eleventh century. It is the suggestion of this note that we would have had to give it a date in roughly the same bracket even if it had occurred as a single find without stratification or even without an Anglo-Saxon provenance. One of the iconographies that has still to be worked out is that of the *Agnus Dei*, and where the continent is concerned the task is rendered formidable by the sheer volume of the available material.[2] As it happens, though, the insular evidence is not so extensive that it is not perfectly feasible for there to be established a broad evolution of the iconography over the period *c.* 800–*c.* 1200, using only the better known examples which are capable of being dated with a reasonable degree of precision. The earliest concept is known from a ninth-century gold finger-ring, from an early-tenth-century piece of embroidery, and from three stone crosses, one Northumbrian and two Irish, dating from the ninth and early tenth centuries. The ring[3] was found in Yorkshire between Aberford and Sherburn a century ago, and is dated by its

---

[1] $\overline{DI}$ for *Dei* occurs, for example, on the Driffield finger-ring, the Cuthbert stole and the Brussels reliquary-cross; see below, p. 342.

[2] Professor P. E. Lasko of the University of East Anglia has been kind enough to encourage me in my belief that there exists as yet no systematic analysis of the iconography of the *Agnus Dei*. For the Early Christian period a useful body of material is brought together by Cabrol, *Dictionnaire d'Archéologie Chrétienne et de Liturgie* III. 2 (Paris, 1914), *s.v.*

[3] The ring is Wilson (1964), p. 117, no. 1 and no. 107 in Dr Elisabeth Okasha's *Hand-List of Anglo-Saxon Non-Runic Inscriptions* (Cambridge, 1971) – henceforth cited as Okasha (1971).

inscription with the name of Queen Æthelswith, Alfred the Great's sister, between 853 and 889, and probably before 875.[1] The embroidery is the celebrated stole from the coffin of St Cuthbert which is dated after 909 and before 916 by the names of historical personages woven into it.[2] In each case the Lamb is shown nimbate and standing motionless, the captions being respectively $A \bar{D}$ and $AGNV(S)$ $\overline{DI}$. On the stole, but not on the Æthelswith ring,[3] the head of the Lamb is to the viewer's left. The same holds good for all three of the stone crosses where the Lamb likewise stands motionless, the only essential difference being the omission, natural for the medium, of the nimbus and of the captions. The crosses are one of those at Hoddam in Dumfriesshire, which is dated by W. G. Collingwood 'somewhat later' than 'shortly after 800';[4] the 'cross of the tower' (*alias* of SS Patrick and Columba) at Kells in Co. Meath, of which Miss Henry has written that 'there is a probability, but no more, that it belongs to a time very near the foundation of the monastery in the first decade of the ninth century';[5] and the cross at Durrow in Co. Offaly, which appears to be inscribed at the base *DUBTACH* and which is plausibly identified with an abbot of that name whose dates are usually given as 927–38.[6]

The second of our groupings consists of the Sulgrave brooch, two stone crosses from Durham dated about the millennium, an elaborate reliquary-cross of wood clad with silver in the church of SS Michael and Gudule at Brussels which most authorities have ascribed to the late tenth century or the early eleventh, and last but not least a handful of Anglo-Saxon silver pennies of Æthelred II which are now dated with fair plausibility as well as precision to the summer and early autumn of 1009 (see pl. VIII*b*). As we have seen,[7] the excavator of the Sulgrave brooch is satisfied from the archaeological context that it was lost not much later than the end of the first third of the eleventh century. The Durham cross-heads (see pls. VIII*c* and *d*) were associated by W. G. Collingwood[8] with 'the founders of Durham abbey in 995', a dating only slightly modified in effect by Ken-

---

[1] Cf. R. I. Page in Wilson (1964), pp. 82–3.

[2] *The Relics of Saint Cuthbert*, ed. C. F. Battiscombe (Oxford, 1956), p. 375 and pls. xxxiii and xxxiv.

[3] The ring is not a signet and so the mirror-image of the seal engraver cannot well be invoked to explain the exceptional right-facing type.

[4] *Northumbrian Crosses of the pre-Norman Age* (London, 1927), p. 40 and fig. 51; and *Seventh Report of the Royal Commission for the Antiquities and Historical Monuments of Scotland: Dumfries* (Edinburgh, 1920), p. 103, but care should be taken to distinguish no. 9 on fig. 77 from no. 7 which is post-Norman.

[5] F. Henry, *Irish High Crosses* (Dublin, 1964), p. 60; cf. *idem*, *Irish Art during the Viking Invasions* (London, 1967), where a dating 'from the first decade of the ninth century' is described as 'contradicted neither by its iconography nor by its style'.

[6] Henry, *High Crosses*, p. 31, and *Irish Art*, pp. 139–40.

[7] Above, p. 333.

[8] *Northumbrian Crosses*, p. 80 and fig. 98.

drick[1] who seems to give absolute limits of 995 and 1083, and by Talbot Rice[2] who justly observes that 1050 is a more realistic *terminus ante quem*. In its country of origin the Brussels reliquary may be said to have received only less inadequate attention from students of literature and epigraphy than from archaeologists and art historians,[3] but there seems nothing in what has been written that would preclude manufacture in the first quarter of the eleventh century, and it may be observed, not for the first time, that the protothemes of the names of the donors and the very nature of the lost relic could be thought to suggest an association with a cadet branch of the West Saxon royal house.[4] Could, too, this nexus once be established with certainty, it might be argued that a date before rather than after the Danish usurpation of 1016 would present fewest difficulties.

The so-called *Agnus Dei* issue of Æthelred II is known from coins from eight mints and from nine obverse dies.[5] The number of recorded specimens is eleven with one 'mule'. The first point to be noted is that three different engravers were employed to cut the dies. Hand A is responsible for the coins of Derby,[6] Malmesbury,[7] Northampton[8] and Stafford,[9] the most obvious criterion being the tablet beneath the Lamb which is in the shape of a parallelogram inscribed $A:G:$, $AG:N:$ or $A'W$. Hand B can best be identified by its trapezoidal form of tablet which is either blank or inscribed $AGN$ or $AGNV$ without punctuation. The mints are Leicester,[10] Nottingham[11] and Stamford.[12] Hand C at present is known from

[1] T. D. Kendrick, *Late Saxon and Viking Art* (London, 1949), p. 61 and pl. XLIII. 1.

[2] D. Talbot Rice, *English Art 871–1100* (Oxford, 1952), p. 137.

[3] Okasha (1971), no. 17. Unbelievably there would seem to be no illustration of the faces of the cross more recent than the not very sharp photographs at the end of H. Logeman, 'L'Inscription Anglo-Saxonne du Réliquaire de la Vraie Croix au Trésor de l'Église des SS. Michel et Gudule à Bruxelles', *Mémoires de l'Academie Royale de Belgique* XLV. 8 (1891), 1–31, and accompanying H. Velge, *La Collégiale des Saints Michel et Gudule à Bruxelles* (Brussels, 1925).

[4] We may contrast this neglect with the generally excellent discussion of the cross by S. T. R. O. d'Ardenne, 'The Old English Inscription on the Brussels Cross', *ESts* XXI (1939), 145–64.

[5] The analysis of the coins is based on personal inspection of all the coins listed with the exception of the Stamford penny missing since the nineteenth century.

[6] Die-duplicate coins in the British Museum (cf. M. Dolley, *Anglo-Saxon Pennies* [London, 1964], pl. XV, no. 43) and the University Museum at Bergen (*ex* Nesbø Find).

[7] Die-duplicate coins in the British Museum (accession since 1893 catalogue but cf. J. Lindsay, *A View of the Coinage of the Heptarchy* [Cork, 1842], pl. 6, no. 155) and in the Royal Coin Cabinet at Stockholm (cf. Hildebrand, Æthelred 3086).

[8] Coin in Royal Coin Cabinet, Stockholm – Hildebrand, Æthelred 1224 and there wrongly attributed to Southampton (cf. [R. H.] M. Dolley, 'Further Southampton/Winchester Die-Links in the Reign of Æthelred II', *BNJ* XXXV [1966], 25–33).

[9] Coin in Royal Coin Cabinet, Stockholm – Hildebrand, Æthelred 3423.

[10] Coin in Royal Coin Cabinet, Copenhagen (cf. *SCBI Copenhagen* II, no. 507).

[11] Die-duplicate penny in Royal Coin Cabinet, Copenhagen – *SCBI Copenhagen* II, no. 1107 – and cut farthing in Royal Coin Cabinet, Stockholm – Hildebrand, Æthelred 1293 and there wrongly attributed to Southampton.

[12] Lost coin recorded in the nineteenth century by Erbstein (cf. W. C. Wells, who reproduces drawing, *BNJ* XXIV [1941–4], 95–7) and cut halfpenny 'mule' in Royal Coin Cabinet, Stockholm – Hildebrand, Æthelred 3445.

a single coin which is of Hereford[1] and of very distinctive style as regards both the obverse and the reverse. Here the tablet is a rhomboid, and the inscription on it the Greek letters *alpha* and *omega* without punctuation.[2] Historians, unfortunately, appear to have been hypnotized by a passage in Domesday Book which admittedly seems to imply that all dies were being cut in London by 1065, but already in 1954 Sir Frank Stenton was recommending caution for earlier periods pending further research, and the relatively few numismatists who have handled the late coins of Æthelred II by the thousand are well aware that they present a pattern very different from that which undoubtedly did obtain at the very end of the reign of Edward the Confessor.[3] Patently three different craftsmen were responsible for the dies of the extant dozen coins of the *Agnus Dei* issue, and their highly individual work can be followed through, as it happens, into the prolific coinage of Æthelred's last years where a regional pattern cannot well be disputed.[4] Not only the present writer is reluctant to swallow what can be no more than a whispered hypothesis that the engravers all resided in London and divided up their *clientèle* on a geographical basis. Much more plausible surely is the theory of their provincial residence, and on the analogy of the pattern that emerges in the succeeding issue it could be that we are to associate hand A with London, hand B with Winchester and hand C with Chester.

Uncontroversial among specialists at the present time is the date of the issue which was an abortive one. It is surprising, though, how in more popular writing the older association of the type with the millennium persists, and this must be due in part to its uncharacteristically uncritical endorsement by Brooke.[5] To be noted is the fact that the copulative in the reverse legends is in each and every case the preposition *on* ('at'). This is a convention not found on Anglo-Saxon coins of Æthelred II earlier than those of his last substantive type, when it is general at all mints outside the Danelaw. Recently, too, it has been shown that this *Last Small Cross* type began shortly before the sack of Oxford at Christmas 1009, and Michaelmas 1009 remains a date for the recoinage that it is not easy to overturn.[6]

---

[1] Coin in Royal Coin Cabinet, Stockholm – Hildebrand, Æthelred 1332. See above, pl. VIII*b*.

[2] Omitted from the above survey is a thirteenth coin of not quite certain attribution, formerly in an Esthonian private cabinet but missing since the Second World War. It was illustrated in the 1935 *Acta et Commentationes Universitatis Tarnensis (Dorpatensis)* and appears to be a duplicate of *SCBI Copenhagen* 11, no. 507. Scandinavian imitations exist in surprising quantity, e.g. *SCBI Copenhagen* 11, nos. 1687–9, presumably because of the consistently high weights of the prototype. Mention should also be made of an alleged coin of the Wareham mint shown to be mythical by (R. H.) M. Dolley, *BNJ* xxviii. 2 (1956), 412–14.

[3] Stenton, *Charters*, p. 24.

[4] (R. H.) M. Dolley, 'Some Reflections on Hildebrand Type A of Æthelred II', *Antikvariskt Arkiv* ix (Stockholm, 1958), *passim*.

[5] G. C. Brooke, *English Coins* (London, 1950), p. 65.

[6] C. S. S. Lyon, 'The Significance of the Sack of Oxford in 1009/1010 for the Chronology of the Coinage of Æthelred II', *BNJ* xxxv (1966), 34–7.

There seems general agreement, too, that the sequence of the last three substantive types of Æthelred II is *Long Cross*, *Helmet* and *Last Small Cross*, and that of the first two of Cnut, *Quatrefoil* and *Pointed Helmet*.[1] In the following table are set out the types for which each of the moneyers of the *Agnus Dei* type is known:[2]

|  | LC | H | LSC | Q | PH |
|---|---|---|---|---|---|
| *Derby*, Blacaman | − | + | − | − | − |
| *Hereford*, Æthelwi(g), Elewig etc. | + | + | + | + | + |
| *Leicester*, Ælfric | + | + | + | − | − |
| *Malmesbury*, Ealdred | + | − | + | − | − |
| *Northampton*, Wulfnoth | − | + | + | − | − |
| *Nottingham*, Oswold | − | + | + | + | − |
| *Stafford*, Alfwold | − | − | + | − | − |
| *Stamford*, Æthelwine | − | − | + | − | − |

On this evidence alone, the millennium theory must fall to the ground: whatever precise dates may be given for the duration of the *Long Cross* type, there cannot be many students who would dispute that *Long Cross* was the issue current in 1000. It is clear from this table, too, that the one natural position for the *Agnus Dei* coins is between *Helmet* and *Last Small Cross*, and support for this line of argument is afforded alike by metrology and by the evidence of the cut halfpenny 'mule'. A feature of the *Agnus Dei* coins is their relatively heavy weight,[3] and the presumptive weight-standard of 27 grains is precisely that of the earliest of the *Last Small Cross* coins.[4] It is a truism, too, where 'mules' in the late Anglo-Saxon series are concerned, that the obverse type is the earlier, and significantly the unique 'mule' links an *Agnus Dei* obverse with a *Last Small Cross* reverse.[5]

On such evidence the numismatist has little hesitation in dating the *Agnus Dei* coins to the late summer and early autumn of 1009, and it will have been noted that they fall in consequence well within the necessarily wider bracket that others have proposed for the Sulgrave brooch, the Durham cross-heads and the Brussels reliquary. Indeed, it may be observed at this point that there would seem to be no argument that of itself would preclude an association of all the material, coins and other objects alike, with the close of the first decade of the eleventh century, though for obvious reasons so close a dating would seem as improbable as incapable

[1] Cf. Petersson, *op. cit.* p. 80, where *Helmet* is given the alternative name *Ornamental Cross*.

[2] The table is based essentially on Hildebrand, on C. F. Keary and H. A. Grueber, *BMC* II and on all the relevant fascicles of *SCBI* to have appeared so far.

[3] Petersson, *op. cit.* p. 88, n.

[4] *Ibid.* pp. 115–19.

[5] For the chronological primacy of the reverse die in the case of 'mules' in the later Anglo-Saxon series, see (R. H.) M. Dolley, 'An Unpublished Link between the *First* and *Second Hand* Types of Æthelred II', *BNJ* xxxv (1966), 22–4.

of proof. To be stressed, on the other hand, is the quite remarkable homogeneity that is exhibited by the whole grouping as regards the treatment of the Lamb. In each case a lithe and even agile animal moves across the field and is superimposed upon, but is unconnected with and still less supports, a slender cross with a long shaft that extends to the ground.[1] Especially to be remarked is the exceptional congruity of the treatment of the foot of this shaft in the case of the Sulgrave brooch and of both the Durham cross-heads,[2] and in all these cases the Lamb moves to the viewer's left, not altogether surprisingly when it is recalled that coin-dies are engraved in reverse. At this point, too, there may properly be emphasized one detail that must more than suggest that the Sulgrave brooch is modelled on the coins and so belongs no earlier than the summer of 1009. Below the head of the Lamb there is a small cross beginning the circular legend, and it is probably not a coincidence that this feature in this position is one proper to the coins and even to the less crude Scandinavian imitations thereof.[3] Thus the Sulgrave brooch would seem to belong not earlier than 1009 nor later than *c.* 1035, with the balance of probability favouring a date early rather than late within this already close bracket.

For the third and last grouping of insular representations of the *Agnus Dei* it is not necessary to go beyond the illustrations in Romilly Allen's still serviceable manual of eighty years ago.[4] Five tympana are involved, those from Elkstone,[5] Hognaston,[6] Hoveringham,[7] Parwich[8] and Stoke-sub-Hamdon,[9] and two fonts, those from Helpringham[10] and Hutton Cranswick.[11] The workmanship is very diverse, and it is clear that the series extends over a considerable period. Various attributes, too, appear

---

[1] An essential feature is that the cross is in nowise held by the Lamb, something that would have precluded all but the most halting motion.

[2] In each case the heel of the cross-staff gives the impression of being splayed or forked. The different media probably explain why at Durham this foot appears to be a solid hemisphere while in the case of the Sulgrave brooch the impression given is much more that of a fork. In the case of the Brussels reliquary-cross the foot of the staff is again forked and flared but this time in stages that approximate to the steps of the later heraldic cross calvary.

[3] To the near-contemporary copies already cited – *SCBI Copenhagen* II, nos. 1687–9 – there may be added later pieces such as P. Hauberg, *Myntforhold og Udmyntninger i Danmark indtil 1146* (Copenhagen, 1900), pl. II. 6 (mirror-image and legend beginning *ANGNVS DEI*), pl. IV. 4–6 (all with the name of Harthacnut), pl. VII. 15 (attributed to Magnus), pl. VIII. 17 and pl. X. 60 and 61 (attributed to Sven). It is only with the latest and virtually anepigraphic pieces that an initial cross is not to be found at the Lamb's chin.

[4] J. Romilly Allen, *Early Christian Symbolism in Great Britain and Ireland before the Thirteenth Century* (London, 1887) – henceforth cited as Romilly Allen (1887).

[5] Romilly Allen (1887), p. 162, fig. 42; the cross is nimbate, a Norman and post-Norman feature.  [6] *Ibid.* p. 254, fig. 86; again the cross is nimbate.

[7] *Ibid.* p. 163, fig. 43; on p. 261 there is confusion with the font from Helpringham. The retrospective Lamb is the earliest known to me in the insular series.

[8] *Ibid.* p. 254, fig. 85; the cross is once more nimbate.

[9] *Ibid.* p. 255, fig. 87.

[10] *Ibid.* p. 260, fig. 89; the cross is with pennon, an indication of late date within the Norman series.  [11] *Ibid.* p. 256, fig. 88.

to accompany the Lamb which may face to right or left indifferently,[1] but a common feature is that it now supports with the upturned hoof of either of its forelegs a much thicker cross which passes behind the body. No longer is there any sense of the Lamb moving across the field, and it is unlikely that there will be many to quarrel with Romilly Allen's individual datings which characterize the whole corpus of material as Norman.[2] What is very clear, though, is that there has been another major step forward in the evolution of the insular iconography of the *Agnus Dei*, and it may be profitable at this stage to give some thought to the problem of what was in the mind of early medieval artists in England when attempting a plastic representation of one of the very oldest of Christian symbols.

In his invaluable discussion of the Cuthbert stole, Höhler[3] has suggested that the inspiration should be sought in the liturgical (*Ecce*) *agnus Dei qui tollit* (*tollis*) *peccata mundi* taken almost word for word from the Gospel according to St John.[4] That he is right can scarcely be doubted, and especially when there is taken into consideration the ninth-century Driffield finger-ring which is actually inscribed + *ECCE AGNUS DĪ*.[5] Significantly, too, the Cuthbert stole Lamb is labelled *AGNV DĪ*, which may be compared with the *AGNVS DĪ* of the Brussels reliquary; it is to be observed in this connection that the Lamb of the Apocalypse[6] is invariably 'the Lamb' (*agnus*) and never once 'the Lamb of God' (*agnus Dei*). Curiously, extant Old English literature, translations of the gospels apart, affords few instances of *lamb* and/or *Godes lamb* being used as an image of the Redeemer.[7] The invocation in a poem of praise in the mid-tenth-century BM Cotton Vespasian D. vi includes an interesting example:

> Đu eart heofenlic lioht     and ðæt halige lamb,
> ðe ðu manscilde     middangeardes
> for þinre arfęstnesse     ealle towurpe...[8]

---

[1] Left-facing (viewer's left) are the tympana from Hoveringham and Stoke-sub-Hamdon and the fonts from Helpringham and Hutton Cranswick; right-facing the tympana from Elkstone, Hognaston and Parwich.

[2] To be stressed is the fact that the discussion of the Norman material is confined to the selection conveniently assembled in Romilly Allen (1887). The corpus is obviously much wider – quite by chance I have noted a sixth tympanum from Tarrant Rushton in Dorset (brought to my notice by my former student Miss Marion Meek) and the small post-Conquest panel from Hoddam mentioned above, p. 337, n. 4, no. 7.       [3] Battiscombe, *op. cit.* pp. 400 and 401.

[4] *RSV*, John I. 29; the liturgy generally substitutes *peccata* for the Vulgate's *peccatum*.

[5] Okasha (1971), no. 33. This lost ring is known from the by no means unconvincing engraving that accompanies J. T. Fowler's workmanlike description in the *Fifth Report of the Geological and Polytechnical Society of the West Riding of Yorkshire* (Leeds, 1870), pp. 157–61.

[6] *RSV*, Revelation v. 6, 12, 13 etc.

[7] Professor P. A. M. Clemoes has been kind enough to draw my attention to what seems to be the only mention of the Lamb of God in the writings of Abbot Ælfric (*Catholic Homilies*, ed. B. Thorpe [London, 1844–6] I, 358). Significantly it occurs in the course of a commentary on John I. 29. There does seem reason to think that the Apocalyptic concept of the Lamb had little appeal where the late Anglo-Saxon church was concerned.

[8] *The Kentish Hymn*, 22–4: *ASPR* VI, 87. I owe this reference also to Professor Clemoes. For the dating see Ker, *Catalogue*, p. 268.

The cross and a petition for mercy are among the associated themes. It is to be noted too that Searle[1] records a personal name *Godlamb* only on the basis of an extremely rare coin of Cambridge in the British Museum.[2] The coin can be dated to the early 1060s, and it is an intriguing possibility that its moneyer could very well have received his name in baptism as a result of the recrudescence of the cult of the *Agnus Dei* which does appear to have occurred in the latter part of the reign of Æthelred II.[3]

The key to the problem of this revival may well be the clause *qui tollit peccata mundi*. Is it being too fanciful to suggest that the Lamb in motion on the coins and on the related objects is to be thought of as a 'scape-lamb', a Christian analogue of the Old Testament scapegoat, and that we should stress the 'taking away' sense of the verb *tollere* implicit in the *RSV* rendering of John 1. 29? In the same way we might see an extension of the idea in the Norman concept of the motif, the upturned foreleg literally 'carrying' the cross, with the parallel between Christ taking up the cross and taking on himself the sin of the world. What does seem clear is that we are dealing beyond all reasonable doubt with the imagery of John 1. 29 and not with that of Revelation v. 6, 12, 13 etc. which seems to underlie the later medieval concept of the Lamb seen at its noblest in Van Eyck's masterpiece at Bruges and in a more degraded form in the Lamb and Flag of English inn-signs and of British regimental cap-badges.[4] However this may be, the clause *qui tollit peccata mundi* does appear potentially critical, though it remains to consider why there should have developed early in the eleventh century what would seem to be new insights into a scriptural passage which one might have thought already hackneyed by liturgical use.

The first point to be taken is that the triple invocation beginning *Agnus Dei*... occurs in the Canon of the Mass where it is essentially the chant of the *confractorium*.[5] As such it is of considerable antiquity, and it has been

[1] Searle, p. 262.

[2] *BMC* II, Edward the Confessor 479. The issue is one that I would seek to date between Michaelmas 1062 and Michaelmas 1065, and the coin would seem to fall late rather than early within this bracket.

[3] The Cambridge collector Mr K. A. Jacob, who is making a special study of the coins of the Cambridge mint, kindly informs me that he knows of no more than three coins of the moneyer *Godlam(b)*. They are the British Museum coin already cited, *SCBI Cambridge*, no. 960, and an unpublished accession to the British Museum. Both the coins unknown to Searle prove to be of Edward the Confessor's last substantive type, and so can be dated with fair probability between Michaelmas 1065 and January 1066. For the chronology of the English coinage at this period see (R.H.) M. Dolley, 'The Unpublished 1895 Find of Coins of Edward the Confessor from Harewood', *Yearbook of the British Association of Numismatic Societies (1961)*, pp. 17–25.

[4] What may be termed 'late' features include the representation of the Lamb as standing or reclining on an altar, and the addition to the cross borne by the Lamb of a flag or banner. Generally, too, there is a tendency for the Lamb to be 'thick-set' and very unlike the lithe beast characteristic of the Anglo-Saxon material.

[5] J.-A. Jungmann, *Missarum Sollemnia* (French trans. of 3rd German ed., Paris, 1956), III, 261.

shown quite convincingly that it was introduced into the Latin Mass from the East already in the second half of the seventh century.[1] Late in the tenth century, for example in the Winchester *troparium*,[2] we begin to find an innovation in the actual formula, the third *miserere nobis* being replaced by the petition *dona nobis pacem*, and in the eleventh century the change became general. In other words, there would seem to have been liturgical innovation affecting the *Agnus Dei* chant at precisely the period with which our second grouping of coins and objects is associated, though there is no need for us to accept the theory held by some that the innovation was inspired by a recurrence late in the tenth century of the great Viking attacks on western Europe. What is worth stressing, on the other hand, is that the *Agnus Dei* was very much a chant of the congregation as opposed to the celebrant, so that the innovation is one that could not fail to have been remarked by the people as a whole.[3] The other liturgical use of the *Agnus Dei...* formula is as constituent element in the so-called Litany of the Saints, and it is interesting that there is documentary evidence for a marked increase in the number of liturgical processions, obvious occasions for the Litany's public recitation, at precisely the period of the *Agnus Dei* coins and of the Sulgrave brooch. The evidence will be found in the Bath edict of 1009–11[4] (VII Æthelred 2) with its *7 gan ealle ut mid haligdome* rendered with less vividness in the *Quadripartitus* as *et eat omnis presbiter cum populo suo ad processionem*.[5] This particular edict is one of those where we can surely detect the hand of Archbishop Wulfstan of York,[6] and to be given very serious consideration is the possibility that this early-eleventh-century vogue of the *Agnus Dei* could owe more than a little to the influence and spirituality of one of the greatest figures of the Anglo-Saxon church.[7]

Wulfstan (d. 1023) was a prelate very conscious of his pastoral responsibilities, and the title of his most famous work, the *Sermo Lupi ad Anglos*, evidences his awareness of the significance of his name's prototheme. There is, it may be thought, an association of ideas between the concepts 'shepherd', 'lamb' and 'wolf' that it would be as foolish to ignore as to over-emphasize. From 996 when he became bishop of London he was at the centre of English affairs,[8] and it has well been said that 'in the crucial

[1] *Ibid.* III, 262.　　　　[2] *Ibid.* III, 267.　　　[3] *Ibid.* III, 264–6.

[4] Whitelock, *EHD*, p. 409. Professor Whitelock's preference for the autumn of 1009 seems as convincing as her argumentation is authoritative.

[5] The Old English and Latin texts are probably most accessible in Robertson, *Laws*, pp. 108 and 114.

[6] Whitelock, *EHD*, *loc. cit.*, conveniently summarizing earlier and fundamental work there cited.

[7] D. Whitelock, 'Archbishop Wulfstan, Homilist and Statesman', *TRHS* 4th ser. XXIV (1942), 25–45.

[8] D. Whitelock, 'A Note on the Career of Wulfstan the Homilist', *EHR* LII (1937), 460–5.

years 1008 to 1012 he served Æthelred as adviser and lawmaker, striving to cure the ills of the English nation by moral regeneration.'[1] A theme that runs through much of his writing is that the calamities besetting the English nation are God's retribution for the sins of the English people. Although, then, there has not survived any work of his which treats specifically of the Lamb of God as the taker away of the world's sin, it cannot well be a coincidence that the *Agnus Dei* coins fall within the period of his greatest influence at the English court. The Sulgrave brooch we have seen to be based upon them and unlikely to have been made more than a few years later; the Brussels reliquary fits most naturally into the first half of his archiepiscopate; and the Durham cross-heads cannot antedate by more than a year his consecration to the see of London and could well be dated after his translation to York. Albeit, then, association of Wulfstan with a revival of emphasis on the theology of John 1. 29–35 must be regarded as 'not proven', the possibility is one that cannot well be disregarded. Even if, too, it could be demonstrated that Wulfstan preached the theme of the 'scape-lamb', it would still be necessary to seek to establish whether the development was spontaneous or part of a broader European pattern, and certainly a review of the continental material would seem long overdue. In particular one would like to see a new study of the waxen *Agnus Dei* emanating from Rome,[2] for this could have been a potent influence on other media. A survey of this kind, however, lies well outside the scope of this paper, and it is hoped that it may be thought sufficient to have established an insular sequence in the iconography of the motif that should at least permit of further examples of insular provenance being dated before *c.* 950, between *c.* 950 and *c.* 1050, or after *c.* 1050.

Mr Davison's brooch from Sulgrave, then, represents a significant addition to the corpus of late Anglo-Saxon ornamental metalwork, and it has a particular value insofar as it would seem to be the latest in the series of nummular brooches as such. This series has not received the attention it deserves, and a definition may not be out of place. A nummular brooch is one that gives the impression of a mounted coin, and the tradition is one that went back to the fourth century when we find the Roman emperors rewarding their Germanic allies with uniface gold medalets that appear to have been struck from coinage-dies and to have been furnished before

---

[1] Bethurum, *Wulfstan*, p. 62.

[2] On which see a very full article in Cabrol, *Dictionnaire* III. The more recent if more limited geographically *Kulthistoriskt Lexikon för Nordisk Medeltid* (Malmö, 1956–) agrees (I, 58) that the practice is one that goes back at least to the ninth century – though we should not attach too much significance to what may be no more than a fortuitous coincidence of date with the earliest of the insular representations in more enduring media – but confirms that the earliest of the surviving waxen medallions is of much later date than the objects discussed in this paper.

distribution with loops for suspension.[1] The next stage in development is the gold bracteate of the Scandinavian coin-hoards,[2] but the later insular series is probably of independent origin though not lacking in contemporary western European parallels.[3] Examples of English work known to me are as follows:

(a) From Cloak Lane, London; uniface and imitating Kufic *dirham*; pewter, tenth-century?[4]

(b) Uncertain provenance; uniface and imitating Roman coin of house of Constantine; pewter, tenth-century?[5]

(c) From York; imitating obverse of Roman coin of Valentinian; silver, tenth-century?[6]

(d) From Rome; imitating obverse and reverse of late portrait-type penny of Edward the Elder; silver, c. 920?[7]

(e) From Compton, Hampshire; imitating reverse of Derby(?) penny of Edward the Elder; bronze, c. 920?[8]

(f) From Winchester; imitating (?) reverse of two-line penny of Edward the Elder; bronze, c. 920?[9]

(g) From Canterbury; imitating obverse of portrait penny of (?) Edgar; silver, c. 970?[10]

(h) Uncertain provenance; imitating obverse of portrait penny of (?) Edward the Martyr; silver, c. 975?[11]

(i) From Sulgrave, Northamptonshire; imitating obverse of *Agnus Dei* penny of Æthelred II; bronze, c. 1010?[12]

It will be noticed that a very high proportion of these brooches are base, and this could be thought an additional argument that all post-date the Viking attacks of the ninth century. None is of gold, and only three are of silver. To be entertained seriously in my view is the proposition that gold had ceased to be used for personal ornaments by the tenth century, and that silver suffered virtually the same fate in the generation following Edgar's great reform of the coinage which cannot well be dated before 973.

[1] On which much neglected series see R. Münsterberg, 'Einseitige Goldmünzen Constantins und seiner Söhne', *Numismatische Zeitschrift* xxxvi (1923), 25–8.

[2] On which see M. B. Mackeprang, *De Nordiske Guldbrakteater* (Århus, 1952).

[3] A group of silver exemplars of very fine workmanship and apparently from the Lower Rhine area are the subject of current study by Professor Peter Berghaus of Münster University.

[4] Wilson (1964), p. 147, no. 39.

[5] *Ibid.* p. 204, no. 142.

[6] G. Baldwin Brown, *The Arts in Early England* (London, 1903–37) iii, pl. xlvi. 6 – in the Yorkshire Museum. For the date see Wilson (1964), pp. 35–6.

[7] Okasha (1971), no. 104; Wilson (1964), p. 163, no. 64.

[8] Okasha (1971), no. 141 – in the Library of Winchester Cathedral.

[9] *Ibid.* no. 139 – unpublished brooch from Mr Martin Biddle's current excavations at Winchester.

[10] *Ibid.* no. 19 – in the Ashmolean Museum, Oxford.

[11] *Ibid.* no. 153 – again in the Ashmolean Museum, Oxford.

[12] The subject of this note. Concerning the ultimate repository a final decision has still to be taken.

The 155 objects listed in D. M. Wilson's catalogue of the British Museum collection may be considered to afford a representative sample of English ornamental metalwork of the eighth, ninth, tenth and eleventh centuries,[1] and an analysis by metal of the datings there suggested for the different objects is not without relevance. No object in gold is dated later than the ninth century – there are a dozen of them – and of forty-four objects that are essentially silver only two are given a date after the millennium, the Pevensey spoon[2] and the Sutton brooch.[3] The former's date may be thought quite uncertain – Mr Wilson rightly stresses the too often forgotten truism that use and loss at one period are not necessarily incompatible with much earlier manufacture[4] – and one begins to wonder whether in fact there is any individual argument that would preclude absolutely the Sutton brooch being two generations old at the time of its concealment soon after the Norman Conquest. One may wonder, too, whether Dr Page would wish to insist on the utter validity of the philological evidence – leaving aside the engaging possibility that the inscription could be a secondary addition – and Mr Wilson's stylistic verdict is a properly cautious 'late tenth or early eleventh century'.[5] At this point, too, one may perhaps refer back to the Brussels reliquary, where incidentally very comparable inscription-verses likewise occur, and question whether the silver cladding of the poverty-stricken wooden setting for the lost relic of the *lignum crucis* is not in itself an argument that the precious metal was already in short supply.

This is not to claim that after *c.* 973 there was any formal ban on the use of silver for personal ornaments. The argument here put forward is merely that a rise in the price of silver, consequent on embarkation on a deliberate and nicely calculated policy of fluctuating overvaluation of silver coin even more than on the renewed Viking depredations, meant that fewer and fewer private individuals could afford to patronize a silversmith as opposed to a jeweller turning out ornaments in bronze and pewter, the latter an alloy that does not appear to have been in general use before the tenth century.[6] Such overvaluation must have brought to the crucible all but the most treasured heirlooms, and one would like to stress how relatively few silver objects of English manufacture seem to have been found in the great Scandinavian hoards of the late tenth and early eleventh centuries.[7] What

---

[1] Wilson (1964), p. 3.   [2] *Ibid.* p. 159, no. 59.   [3] *Ibid.* p. 174, no. 83.
[4] D. M. Wilson, 'Almagren and Chronology', *MA* III (1959), 112–19.
[5] Wilson (1964), p. 50.
[6] The pewter objects catalogued in Wilson (1964) all are dated by the author to the tenth and eleventh centuries.
[7] A Scandinavian provenance attaches to fewer than 10% of some 350 objects in all metals listed on pp. 99–116 of Wilson (1964). Unfortunately the precise metal of the individual objects is not normally specified, but it seems doubtful if as many as twenty of the objects from Scandinavia are of silver and of Anglo-Saxon workmanship.

one is saying in fact is that a generation after Edgar's great reform the production of ornaments in silver, church-plate apart, may virtually have ceased, and the final contention of this paper is that it is now for the archaeologists to disprove the accuracy of this claim by adducing even one secular object in silver that can be securely dated after the accession of Cnut and shown to have been produced within the boundaries of the Old English kingdom. This is not an empty controversy where the numismatist is concerned, for certain knowledge that silver was being 'cornered' for coinage purposes must affect materially any view he takes of royal control of the sources of precious metal both before and after the Norman Conquest.[1]

Executed as it is in bronze, the Sulgrave brooch fits perfectly into place as a product of the second decade of the eleventh century, and as such it brings to a close the whole series of English pre-Conquest nummular brooches. Admittedly crude in some of its techniques, it is not altogether lacking in artistic merit, and it is hoped that this note will have suggested that it is of interest to a wider audience than would normally be the case with an object of patently provincial manufacture and aimed at a relatively humble class of purchaser. For permission to publish it here I am indebted in the first place to the kindness of Mr Davison, but others have been as generous with their advice and criticisms. In particular I would mention my colleague Mr Colin G. Slack, Dip.Cons., of the Conservation Laboratory of the Queen's University of Belfast, who was principally responsible for the final stages of the brooch's cleaning and for the production of the electrotype copy which has revealed much that the original's present uneven patination still conceals; Dr Elisabeth Okasha, now of Norwich, who placed at my disposal both the typescript of her *Hand-List of Anglo-Saxon Non-Runic Inscriptions* and her unrivalled knowledge of that material; Dr Nils Ludvig Rasmusson, the Keeper of the Royal Coin Cabinet at Stockholm, who has interested himself in and encouraged my study of the *Agnus Dei* coins over the last decade and more; Professor Peter E. Lasko, of the University of East Anglia, and Mr D. M. Wilson, of University College, London, former colleagues at the British Museum, whose encouragement and advice at more than one juncture were as critical as welcome; Mrs Veronica Smart, now of St Andrews, who coined the term 'nummular' when we first discussed the Sulgrave brooch; Miss Rosemary Cramp, of the University of Durham, who obtained for me the photographs of the Durham cross-heads with permission for their reproduction;

---

[1] It seems worth noting in this context post-Conquest practice. The author of the *Dialogus de Scaccario*, writing a century later, appears to envisage a proportion of the king's silver bullion being used for plate for the church and for the royal household, *Dialog über das Schatzamt*, ed. M. Siegrist (Zurich and Stuttgart, 1963), pp. 24–5; C. Johnson, *The Course of the Exchequer by Richard, Son of Nigel* (London, 1950), p. 11.

Miss M. A. O'Donovan, of Exeter University, who organized for me in Cambridge simultaneous access to a range of literature not easily available to me in Ulster; and last but certainly not least the editors of the present volume. That all the above-named would agree with every word I have written would be asking too much, but it is at least certain that without their friendly criticism this paper would have been even more unworthy of its dedication.

# Repton reconsidered:
# a study in structural criticism

## H. M. TAYLOR

During the course of the last century it has been established that certain features can be reliably used to distinguish Anglo-Saxon buildings from those of Norman and later date; but we are still far from having any adequate list of features that would by themselves serve with equal reliability to assign an Anglo-Saxon building to any particular century within the era. There is, indeed, wide disagreement at present in the dates that are assigned by different writers to one and the same building; and until these discrepancies can be reduced it is almost impossible to construct a reliable architectural history of Anglo-Saxon England.

A few Anglo-Saxon buildings can be securely dated from contemporary written evidence; but the number is far too small to serve as a secure base for a general architectural history; and therefore it becomes necessary to try to secure help from buildings which, although not themselves securely dated from written records, yet contain within themselves structural evidence that shows that their erection and subsequent modification extended over many years. If an adequate number of these buildings were to be examined in detail it would almost certainly be found that some features regularly appeared in the original fabric while others appeared only in later modifications. Thus the buildings would themselves provide lists of features that would distinguish between early and later workmanship; and these lists would become correspondingly more reliable as the detailed examination was extended to more and more buildings.

In order to be of use in this search for early and late features, a building must of necessity have been built and modified over an extended period; only then will it contain early and late features and only then will there be some hope that later features will prove their lateness, for example by partially destroying some of the earlier ones. Buildings of this sort are necessarily somewhat complicated; and their secrets will not be disclosed by cursory examination. Detailed study and measurement are needed, as well as carefully drawn plans, sections and elevations. Every feature needs study, for example to see whether it shows signs of modification, or whether, by resting on or cutting away another feature, it proves that the other is earlier.

For this detailed examination of the way a building is put together

I propose the name *structural criticism*. As an example of its methods I apply them in the remainder of this essay to the important Anglo-Saxon fabric in St Wystan's church at Repton. This is, of course, primarily an example of the use of these methods, and no very striking results should be expected from such a study of only one building.

By stressing the importance of detailed study of the structure of a building I do not wish to imply any neglect of the importance of any written records that may relate to it. Indeed the position is quite the reverse: written records are almost always the most important single group of sources for architectural history, for usually they alone can provide precise dates. But, as a rule, the early contemporary records are too lacking in architectural detail to enable us to associate them reliably with any particular phase of a surviving building, and it is here that structural criticism can often help by enabling us to construct from the building itself a picture of the sequence in which it must have been built. If that picture contains some episodes that tally with those of the written records then we will have made a first step towards associating the two groups of evidence reliably together.

It is important to make the clearest possible distinction between those parts of an essay which purport to be evidence and those which contain the writer's personal comments or inferences. To this end, and also for ease of cross-reference, I have set out the evidence in separate short paragraphs that are distinctively numbered from E 1 to E 78. By contrast, my personal comments and inferences are given separately in paragraphs without numbers; save that in the section in which I put forward a tentative time-sequence for the development of St Wystan's church the several steps in that sequence are set out in paragraphs that are numbered from S 1 to S 20.

The evidence contained in paragraphs E 1–78 goes far beyond what is required for the deductions in paragraphs S 1–20. I have tried to set out all the evidence about the building, whether from records or from the building itself, so that it shall be available for further study.

In addition to the evidence which is given in words in the text, important evidence from the building itself is given in the figures. With the exception of figs. 22, 23 and 24, which are attempted reconstructions, all the figures are the result of observation and measurement of the surviving fabric. In order to show visually the sizes and jointing of the stones in the building, all the figures include the outlines of individual stones, measured *in situ*. All the profiles of mouldings have also been checked by measurement, even when this required access by tall ladders.

# Repton reconsidered

## Medieval

Repton does not appear to have had any medieval chroniclers, and therefore the references to it in Anglo-Saxon and later medieval sources are
comparatively few in number and scanty in detail. In particular, no mention is made of structural details of the church until the eighteenth-century
records, and even then the details are sometimes ambiguous.

## Pre-Conquest

E1. The existence of a religious house for men and women at Repton
about the close of the seventh century is shown by the statement in the
eighth-century *Life of St Guthlac* that he received the tonsure there from
Abbess Ælfthryth.[1]

E2. That Repton was considered an appropriate place for royal burials
is first shown by the record in *The Anglo-Saxon Chronicle* that Æthelbald
(king of Mercia, 716–57) was buried there in 757 after his murder at
Seckington.[2]

E3. That Æthelbald's place of burial was 'in the monastery of Repton'
is recorded in Æthelweard's Chronicle.[3]

E4. *ASC* records Wiglaf's accession to the kingdom of Mercia in 827;
it also records the conquest of that kingdom in 829 by Egbert, king of
Wessex, and Wiglaf's subsequent restoration to the kingdom of Mercia
in 830.[4]

E5. *ASC* records that the Danish host took up winter quarters in
Repton in 874 and left in 875.[5]

## Norman

E6. Florence of Worcester (d. 1118) records that Wiglaf (king of Mercia,
827–40) was buried at Repton.[6]

E7. Florence of Worcester tells the story of the murder of St Wystan

---

[1] *Felix's Life of St Guthlac*, ed. and trans. B. Colgrave (Cambridge, 1956), pp. 83 and 85.

[2] Whitelock, *ASC*, p. 31. Seckington is about twelve miles south-west of Repton and is much
nearer to both Lichfield and Tamworth.

[3] *The Chronicle of Æthelweard*, ed. and trans. A. Campbell (London, 1962), p. 24.

[4] Whitelock, *ASC*, pp. 40–1.

[5] *Ibid.* p. 48. *ASC* gives no record of the extent to which the Danes damaged the town or the
abbey; nor do I know of any reliable record. The late medieval spurious chronicle of Ingulf
records that 'the pagans in the year of Our Lord 874 returned to Mercia and wintered in
Repton where they levelled to the ground that famous monastery the sacred mausoleum of all
the kings of the Mercians'; see *Ingulf's Chronicle of Croyland Abbey*, trans. H. T. Riley (London,
1854), p. 53.

[6] *Florence of Worcester, Chronicon ex Chronicis*, ed. B. Thorpe (London, 1848), p. 266. The main
body of the history (*ibid.* p. 69) simply records his death under the year 838; but the supplementary tables (*ibid.* p. 266) record his burial at Repton.

and of his subsequent burial 'in the famous monastery called Repton in the mausoleum of his grandfather Wiglaf'.[1]

E8. The chronicles of the abbey of Evesham contain a Life of St Wystan, dating in part from the first half of the twelfth century, with later continuations. This Life records the murder and burial of Wystan in much the same words as Florence of Worcester, but it has additional information about how King Cnut (1016–35), on learning that Wystan was of the family of the patron of Evesham abbey, 'had that glorious martyr transferred from Repton to Evesham to be protector of that church.'[2]

E9. Domesday Book records that the church at Repton was served by two priests. It does not record any abbey there.[3]

The Domesday record seems to justify the tradition that the abbey did not survive the Danish occupation of Repton and that its church was subsequently used as the parish church.

I do not know of any other Anglo-Saxon or Norman references to Repton except the claim made by Rhygyfarch (d. 1099) in his Life of St David that the saint founded twelve monasteries, including one at Repton.[4]

### Eighteenth-century and later

Records about the church from the eighteenth century and later are of importance principally for the evidence they give about alterations and repairs. Some of these records are difficult to interpret in spite of their recent date, and from the original papers it is difficult to build up the whole story about any one feature of the church. I have accordingly taken each important part of the building in turn, grouping together all the references that relate to it, albeit from a variety of different sources. Immediately after my summary of the evidence contained in each such group of references I give, where necessary, my own view about the implications of the evidence.

[1] 'Corpus autem illius ad monasterium tunc temporis famosum, quod Reopedun nominatur, delatum in mausoleo avi sui regis Wiglaui est tumulatum' (*ibid.* p. 72). I am indebted to Mr R. D. Gem of Peterhouse for drawing my attention to a pre-Conquest source which confirms this twelfth-century record that St Wystan was buried in the monastery at Repton. See F. Liebermann, *Die Heiligen Englands* (Hannover, 1889), where reasons are given for believing that the Anglo-Saxon version was written in Wessex between 995 and 1013–30 and that the Latin translation was a Canterbury work of 1038–85.

[2] *Chronicon Abbatiae de Evesham*, ed. W. D. Macray, Rolls Series (1863), pp. 331 and 325–6. See also p. 326 for a note about the return of small parts of the relics in the thirteenth century, when they were apparently placed in the Norman priory rather than in the church of St Wystan.

[3] F. M. Stenton, 'The Derbyshire Domesday', *VCH, Derby* 1 (London, 1905), 332.

[4] *Rhygyfarch's Life of St David*, ed. and trans. J. W. James (Cardiff, 1967), p. 33. It has recently been suggested that there is no reason except English prejudice for doubting the sixth-century foundation of the abbey at Repton by St David; see E. Gilbert, 'St Wystan's, Repton', *Cahiers Archéologiques* XVII (1967), 84. A more cautious view is suggested by James, *op. cit.* p. vii.

# Repton reconsidered

## The eastern arches of the nave arcades

The present nave is separated from its aisles by walls each of which is carried on an arcade of six arches resting on hexagonal piers. The four western arches of each arcade were built at varying dates between the thirteenth century and the fifteenth. By contrast, the two eastern arches of each arcade were inserted in 1854, in imitation of the others, while the wall above them shows every sign of being Anglo-Saxon, as will appear in E 20. But prior to 1854 this area of walling had been supported by two round-headed arches on each side of the nave, for which we have not only the written evidence cited below in E 14–16 but also two independent drawings to which reference is there given. But even these round-headed arches had been the subject of controversial alterations in 1792, when the transeptal areas then known as the 'sleepy quire' and 'Thacker's quire' at the east ends of the south and north aisles were opened out to the church.

E 10. *The demolitions of 1792*. Walling which divided the 'sleepy quire' and 'Thacker's quire' from the body of the church was removed in 1792 when the arrangement of pews was changed.[1] The walls were replaced by arches of semi-circular form.

The references quoted for E 10 show clearly that certain walls were removed and replaced by round arches, but they leave some ambiguity about the precise extent of the work that was carried out. The Faculty dated 26 July 1791 gives no authority for any alterations to the building itself, but relates only to taking down old pews and replacing them by new ones.[2]

Arguments will be advanced after E 15 for believing that before 1792 each of the side-chapels or 'quires' opened to the central area of the nave through a single round-headed arch, and that on each side of the church the wall that was removed lay between that single arch and the four pointed, Gothic arches of the main arcade of the nave.

E 11. *The eastern arches (1792–1854)*. After the alterations of 1792 there were two round-headed arches on each side of the nave, opening from it to the 'quires' on either side.[3]

E 12. The eastern responds had capitals (abaci) of the same character as those in the crypt; the eastern arch on each side was semi-circular, with a plain square soffit; and the next arch westward was higher and of wider span than the first.[4]

[1] R. Bigsby, *Description of Repton* (London, 1854), pp. 122 and 392–3; F. C. Hipkins, *Repton* (Derby, 1894), p. 16; and J. C. Cox, *Churches of Derbyshire* III (Chesterfield, 1877), 437.
[2] I am indebted to the Vicar of Repton and to the Derbyshire Record Office for access to the Faculties from 1791 to 1962. See also below, p. 356, n. 5.
[3] Bigsby, *op. cit.* p. 122.
[4] D. H. Haigh, 'The Ancient Saxon Monastery at Repton', *Transactions of the British Archaeological Association, Winchester, 1845* (London, 1846), pp. 448–51.

E 13. Not only the eastern responds but also the round pillars between the arches had square-cut capitals of the same style as those in the crypt.[1]

E 14. The 'piers next to the arches' were cased in wood.[2]

E 15. A string-course (cornice-moulding) ran along each wall high above the pair of arches and ended where the Early English work of the nave began.[3]

It is not certain whether Cox saw the arches of 1792 before their demolition in 1854, but both Bigsby and Haigh described them from personal observation. Moreover their descriptions in words can be compared with two drawings, one by Gorham and one by Bigsby, both of which show the arches and capitals.[4] Gorham's drawing shows square-cut capitals on the eastern responds and also on the central pillars as noted in E 13, whereas Bigsby's shows square capitals on the responds and hexagonal ones on the central pillars. On the whole, Gorham's drawing has much more appearance than Bigsby's of being a faithful representation. Neither drawing would of itself prove the wider and taller nature of the western arch in each pair as noted in E 12; but neither drawing is inconsistent with the accuracy of that statement, provided the difference between the two arches was not very great.

On balance it seems to me that the evidence of E 11–14 is strongly in favour of the interpretation that the eastern and smaller arch of each pair was already present in each wall before 1792, with each of its sides resting on a square capital supported by a round column. The operation of 1792 would therefore have consisted of inserting a wider and taller arch into the formerly solid wall to the west, and possibly also of widening the original arches themselves (see fig. 22). This operation of cutting an arch through a standing wall is well attested in many buildings; and here at Repton it was repeated once again in 1854 when the two pointed arches were cut through each of these side walls, still leaving the Anglo-Saxon walling and string-course of E 15 in place above.

E 16. *The destruction of columns and arches in 1854.* 'By a gross and ignorant piece of vandalism, these ancient responds and pillars were taken down at as late a date as 1854, in order to secure uniformity in the arches. Fortunately, owing to a vigorous remonstrance made to the bishop, the pillars and capitals were not macadamised.'[5]

---

[1] Cox, *op. cit.* p. 435.  [2] Haigh, *op. cit.* p. 450; also Bigsby, *op. cit.* pp. 122 and 125.

[3] Haigh, *loc. cit.*

[4] One of these drawings was made in 1847 by Mr G. M. Gorham while he was a pupil at Repton School. It was first published by F. C. Hipkins, in *Repton and its Neighbourhood* (Repton, 1899) and it is reprinted as fig. 555 in H. M. Taylor and Joan Taylor, *Anglo-Saxon Architecture* (Cambridge, 1965). The other drawing was made by Bigsby and was published facing p. 121 of his *Description of Repton*. Gorham's drawing shows the capitals of the round arches at the same level as those of the pointed arches of the nave; but the evidence is scarcely adequate to justify a positive assertion that the levels were identical.

[5] Cox, *op. cit.* p. 435. Repton was in the Diocese of Lichfield until the formation of the Diocese of Southwell in 1884. Searches instituted on my behalf at the two diocesan registries have

E17. 'The bases of the Saxon responds...that were hacked away in 1854 are now exposed, about 2 ft of them remaining. The raised flooring of 1792 fortunately prevented the barbarians of the later date from sweeping away all trace of them.'[1]

I have not been able to trace a Faculty for this destruction of 1854 and therefore I have given the evidence in the form of direct quotations from Cox's observations which were made within thirty years of the alterations to the church. Two pillars and capitals now stand in the south porch of the church, and the lower parts of both eastern responds may be seen *in situ* on either side of the raised area leading up to the sanctuary. These seem to me to determine beyond all doubt the original position of the columns that stood upon them, in spite of a contrary view which has recently been published.[2]

### The alterations to the level of the floor

E18. After a visit to the church during the extensive restorations then in progress, Cox recorded in 1886 that 'the floor, which was so disastrously raised in 1792, is now being restored to its former level, exposing the bases of the piers which in several cases have been much mutilated'.[3]

E19. Independent evidence of changes in the levels of the floor is given in a plan and sections that were prepared by Mr R. Garwood, clerk to the builders, during the restorations of 1886–7 (see fig. 10).[4] The longitudinal section in Garwood's plan clearly shows three separate floor levels: the earliest one (ancient floor) coinciding with the Anglo-Saxon respond (U) that is still *in situ*; the medieval floor (early floor) about 1 ft higher, with the bases of the medieval piers resting upon it; and the raised floor of 1792–1866 a further 1 ft 6 in. higher, completely hiding the bases of the medieval piers.

### The former central tower

E20. Clear indication of the former existence of a square central tower is given in Garwood's plan (fig. 10) where its foundation walls are marked ZYXW. The external walls and angles at Z and Y are visible to this day, while internally the continuous walls ZW and YX are to be seen above the

confirmed the issue of the Faculty dated 26 July 1791 from Lichfield (see above, p. 355, n. 2) and the issue of a Faculty dated 31 August 1885 from Southwell for the alterations of 1886 (see below, p. 357, n. 3). By contrast, there is no record of the issue of any Faculty for the alterations carried out in 1854.
[1] Cox, 'A Note on the Restoration of Repton Church', *JDANHS* VIII (1886), 233–4. Cox gives a drawing of the northern respond which agrees with the remains that are still visible *in situ*.
[2] Gilbert, *loc. cit.* p. 98.
[3] Cox (1886), p. 232. These alterations were authorized by the Faculty of 31 August 1885.
[4] Garwood's plan was published after his death by J. T. Irvine, 'Plans of Discoveries Lately Made in Repton Church', *JBAA* L (1894), 248–50. My copy in fig. 10 omits the tints added by Irvine, and adds letters for ease of reference.

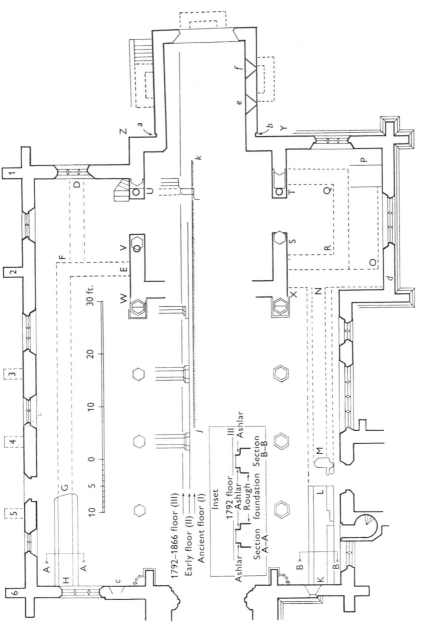

FIG. 10 *Garwood's record of the church in 1886.* This plan was published by Irvine in 1894 (see p. 357, n. 4). My copy omits the date-tints added by Irvine, and it incorporates key-letters for ease of reference in the text; these letters are fully explained in E 19–21 and 32, with the following exceptions. The recesses *a* and *b* do not now exist, but signs of patching are to be seen, as at *b* in fig. 19. Traces of an Early English window not shown in Garwood's plan are to be seen at *c*. A doorway exists at *d*, but is not shown on Garwood's plan. The windows shown at *e* and *f* are very problematic.

pairs of pointed arches that were cut through them in 1854. The early string-course noted by Haigh in E15 is still present along the whole length of both these internal walls.

E21. The existence of the west wall of the tower is clearly indicated on the plan by the walls running south from W and north from X. These are shown in continuous lines, by contrast to the broken lines which elsewhere seem to indicate walls that were inferred rather than actually seen.

E22. Moreover after his visit to the church in 1886 Cox reported that he had seen these walls returning north and south about 2 ft below the level of the floor of 1792.[1]

## *The rediscovery of the crypt*

In the eighteenth century the existence of a crypt below the chancel at Repton had become forgotten and all its entrances were covered by accumulations of rubbish.

E23. The crypt was rediscovered by chance in 1779 when a workman, digging in the chancel to prepare a grave for the deceased headmaster of the school, was surprised by the collapse of part of the floor under his feet.[2]

E24. In 1802 or 1803 workmen clearing out a shed attached to the north wall of the chancel discovered the north flight of steps, not previously known to exist.[3]

E25. The western stairways leading up from the crypt to the north and south aisles were opened out during the restorations of 1886–7.[4]

## *Other features of the crypt*

The difficulties of interpreting the building after the first rediscovery of the crypt were increased by the way the ground had risen so as to obscure many of its features. Some excavations were therefore undertaken, and trenches were also made beside the church to protect it against damp.

E26. *Exterior features.* Evidence of a building formerly projecting south from the chancel was found in 1901 by excavation. Two blocks of stone were discovered, supported on a third block of stone, the whole extending 6 ft 2 in. parallel to the south wall of the chancel.[5]

E27. Excavations at the east revealed a set of six stone steps, of roughly hewn blocks of varying length, resting on the earth, without mortar.[6]

These blocks and five of the steps are still visible in and beside the trenches which are kept open beside the church. They are shown in fig. 18, where the blocks are marked with the numbers 1 and 2 used by Hipkins and the steps now visible are numbered from 2 to 6 as an indication that

[1] Cox (1886), p. 232.  [2] Bigsby, *op. cit.* p. 240.
[3] *Ibid.* p. 240.  [4] Cox (1886), p. 233.
[5] Hipkins, 'A Note on the Most Recent Discoveries in Repton Church Crypt', *JDANHS* XXIII (1901), 106.  [6] *Ibid.* p. 107.

the top step is probably concealed beneath the turf. The blocks 1 and 2 are also shown in elevation and plan in fig. 19.

*The recesses of the crypt.* The main body of the crypt is today of square plan, with a shallow rectangular recess projecting from each of the four sides. Only the western recess is in anything like its original condition. Unlike the others, its floor is raised one step above the main floor, and in its west wall is a small cavity of roughly triangular shape.

The recesses on the north, east and south have been considerably modified through the years. That at the east must at one time have served as an entrance for which there must have been six or seven steps inside the body of the crypt in addition to the six which have survived outside. The former shape of the south recess is, I believe, defined by the blocks of stone mentioned in E 26, which indicate a building about 6 ft wide, projecting about 2½ ft from the main wall of the chancel. No doubt there was originally a similar recess on the north, which was finally swept away in the fourteenth century to make way for the stairs that now lead out through its former position.

A small cavity of roughly triangular shape in the west wall of the western recess has been variously interpreted as a window leading into the open,[1] a window leading into the church through the chancel steps,[2] and a recess for a lamp.[3] This small cavity has in recent years been filled in, so that it extends only an inch or so into the thickness of the wall; but in Irvine's drawings of 1883 its depth was shown as 1 ft 6 in.[4]

E 28. The inner face of the cavity was inspected by both Irvine and Cox; but their observations are inconclusive, save perhaps to suggest that the original work has been disturbed: Irvine recorded that the back of the cavity was made of brick, probably the end of a vault or grave;[5] and Cox recorded that the western faces of the stones composing the opening were altogether rough and unworked.[6]

*Modern repairs.* After a visit to the church in 1914, Cox reported the following works that had recently been carried out:

E 29. The damaged north-east column had been mended with tiles set in cement; an oak door with a ventilating grille had been placed in the north doorway; and movable glazed window frames had been placed in the south and east windows.[7]

### The windows

No pre-Conquest window has survived *in situ*, either wholly or in part. But the Early English windows can be used in elucidating the history

[1] Gilbert, *loc. cit.* p. 88.     [2] Cox (1877), p. 434.
[3] Irvine, 'On the Crypt Beneath the Chancel of Repton Church', *JDANHS* v (1883), 171.
[4] *Ibid.* pl. xii.     [5] *Ibid.* p. 171.
[6] Cox (1886), p. 234.     [7] Cox, 'A Budget from Repton', *JDANHS* xxxvi (1914), 102.

of the building and for this purpose it is useful to have records of recent works on them.

E 30. On a visit to the church in 1914 Cox noted that a blocked Early English lancet in the north side of the chancel had been opened out and glazed; a slightly larger one in the north-east angle of the nave (i.e. the former central tower) had also been opened and glazed; and so also had a similar one at the west of the south aisle.[1]

E 31. The plaster was removed from the interior of the chancel in 1940 and this exposed a large patch of brickwork on the south side. Behind this was a three-light oak window of the sixteenth century and above it the head of an Early English lancet. The wooden window was removed and the lancet restored to match that on the north.[2]

### The excavations within the church

Reference has already been made in E 19 and 20 to parts of the evidence contained in the plan and sections prepared by Garwood while the interior of the church was being excavated to restore the floor to its medieval level. Although certain features of the plan lack adequate explanation, nevertheless the plan as a whole must be accepted as the best evidence that is at present available for the area beneath the floor.

E 32. Attention should therefore be directed to the following further pieces of evidence implicit in the plan:

(a) The early walling seen beneath the floor is shown in full lines in the regions of U, V, W, X, S and T, where parts of it can still be seen at U and T, and where independent evidence for its existence has been cited in E 22 for the parts shown between W and X.

(b) The early walling shown in full lines at GH and KL is also separately confirmed by the inset cross-sections AA and BB which give details of the rough foundations and ashlar walls in a way which clearly shows that the author had observed them in detail.

(c) No explanation is given for the reliability of the walls shown in broken lines; normally this marking would imply walls that had not been seen but could reliably be inferred from other evidence. This is easily understandable for the walls GF and MN; but it is hard to understand for EFD and TQRS. Modern excavation within the church has provided evidence for a wall in a position close to, but not identical with, TQ. As will be seen in E 78, this wall has been left open for inspection.

(d) No walling, either in broken or full lines, is shown under the western four arches of the arcades of the nave.

---

[1] *Ibid.* pp. 102–3.
[2] Anonymous, *The Story of St Wystan's Church, Repton* (Derby, 1950), p. 26. The work was authorized by a Faculty dated 30 December 1939.

(e) The lower parts of the Anglo-Saxon columns T and U, which can still be seen *in situ*, are shown in full outlines on the plan, and the longitudinal section correspondingly shows a profile of U. A further column is shown at V on the plan, but its reliability is rendered problematic by its omission from the longitudinal section. No corresponding column is shown on the south side of the plan in the region of S; but the building itself provides reliable evidence on this matter, as will be seen in E 77.

(f) The Anglo-Saxon flooring (ancient floor) was observed beside the column U where its level *k* agreed with what was then the uppermost step of the stairs leading up from the crypt.[1]

(g) This early flooring was observed as far west as *j*.

### EVIDENCE FROM THE BUILDING

In our *Anglo-Saxon Architecture* we gave a brief description of the church and of the reasons for asserting that the following major parts of its fabric are Anglo-Saxon: the crypt; the chancel; the eastern parts of the nave; and parts of the eastern area of the present north aisle.[2] The purpose of this part of my essay is to amplify that brief account with detailed evidence which clearly could not be given in a book concerned with the whole of England but which is necessary for a full understanding of this important building. The detailed evidence is displayed in figs. 11–22 and is amplified by descriptions on pp. 363–79, where again the basic evidence is clearly distinguished from my personal comments.

### The crypt

A plan and a series of sections of the crypt were published by Irvine in 1883; but the lower parts of the external walling were then still covered with earth, and his drawings therefore do not show the interesting and important plinths.[3] Moreover his sections showed the jointing of the stones only on some of the interior walls. My figs. 11–15 are therefore intended to replace his of 1883 and to serve as detailed source material for future study: they give full information about the relation of the crypt to the exterior plinths and to the upper walls of the chancel; they also show in detail the jointing of the stonework on all the walls. Moreover figs. 14 and 15 show the relation of the crypt to the columns that in part remain *in situ* in the church above.

### The date of the recesses

It has sometimes been claimed that the crypt was first built as a square room with a single recess at the west, and that the three recesses in the

---

[1] Irvine, 'Discoveries Made in the Nave and Aisles of Repton Church', *JDANHS* xiv (1892), 160.
[2] Taylor and Taylor, *op. cit.* pp. 510–16 and figs. 249 and 554–8.
[3] Irvine (1883), pl. xii.

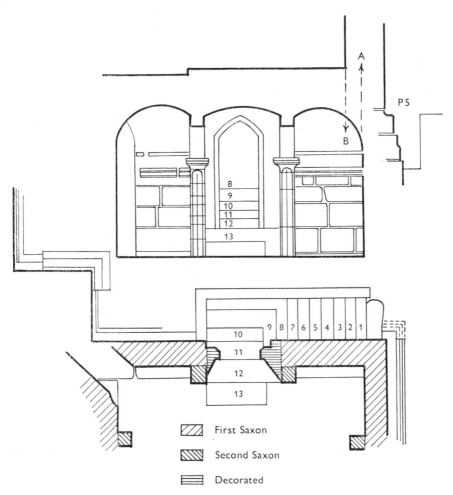

FIG. 11 *Elevation and plan of the north wall of the crypt.* This figure represents a section along the axis of the north 'aisle' of the crypt. The vertical alignments A and B show how the inner part of the walling of the chancel overhangs the inner face of the wall of the crypt and thus rests on the vaulting.

north, east and south sides were only later constructed, by cutting openings through the walls and by building side walls and outer walls and gabled roofs.[1] The present outer walls of the east and south recesses as seen within the crypt are manifestly of quite different workmanship from the main walls of the crypt, but the side walls of those two recesses tell a different story.

E33. No part of the side walls of the north recess remains visible; if any

[1] See, e.g., A. Macdonald, *A Short History of Repton* (London, 1929), pp. 11–12, or Gilbert, *loc. cit.* pp. 86–9 and fig. 2.

parts remain, they are hidden from view by the chamfered jambs of the fourteenth-century doorway built within the earlier recess.

E 34. By contrast, the lower and inner parts of the original side walls of the east and south recesses remain visible and the latter are illustrated in the insets in fig. 14. These side walls are uniform in fabric with the main walls of the crypt and with the side walls of the western recess. There is a complete absence of broken stonework or patching such as would almost necessarily result from any attempt to cut such recesses through existing walls.

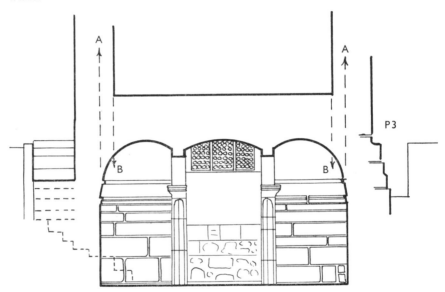

FIG. 12 *The east wall of the crypt*. This figure represents a section along the axis of the east 'aisle' of the crypt. Larger scale sections of the external plinth are shown in fig. 16 and the positions of the various sections are specified in fig. 18.

I accordingly believe that all four recesses were parts of the original design, but that three have been shortened by removal of the walls that projected beyond the main walls of the church.

### The string-courses or cornices in the crypt

E 35. The main walls of the crypt on the north, east and south (but not the recesses opening from these walls) each carry two horizontal string-courses or cornices: the upper one is of plain rectangular profile while the lower is of double-stepped profile with two vertical faces separated from each other and from the wall below by *oblique* steps (see measured details in fig. 15).

E 36. There is no cornice on the two short stretches of the main west

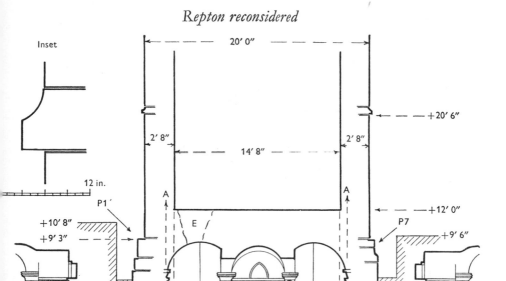

FIG. 13 *The west wall of the crypt.* This figure represents a section of the chancel and crypt along
the axis of the west 'aisle' of the crypt. The inset shows an enlarged section of the
string-course which runs round the exterior walls of the chancel 20 ft 6 in. above the
floor of the crypt. The small drawings at either side show the lateral faces of the west
recess. The western stairs to the church lead up from C and D; E represents the break
in the vaulting made in 1779; F is the western recess.

wall; and all three walls of the west recess carry only the lower, double-
stepped cornice (see fig. 13).

These string-courses or cornices form one of the most difficult problems
of the crypt. Their total absence from the east, north and south recesses
has been one of the principal arguments for regarding these three
recesses as later modifications. If my argument from E 34 be regarded as
proving that the recesses were contemporary with the main chamber then
it follows that the absence of the cornices must have had a different reason,
perhaps associated with the functional use of the recesses. I return to this
and other associated problems in S 4, S 7 and S 14.

### The external plinths

The plinths which surround the outer walls of the crypt are one of the
most remarkable features of the building; and they have been given singu-

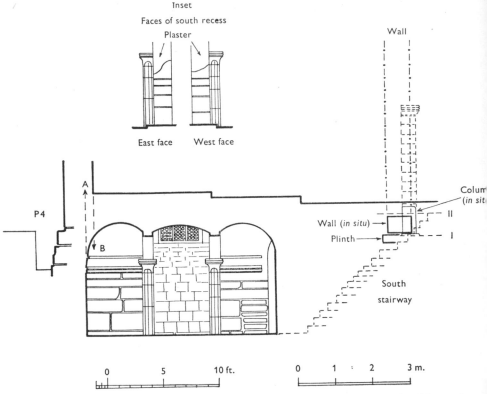

FIG. 14 *The south wall of the crypt.* This figure represents a section along the axis of the south 'aisle' of the crypt. It also shows in full lines the part of the Anglo-Saxon column and wall still *in situ* in the south chapel. In broken lines there is represented the result of placing on top of the short lower part of the column the larger part that at present stands in the south porch.

larly little attention in published accounts of the church, no doubt because they are rather difficult to examine closely in the trenches beside the building.

E 37. Fig. 16 shows sections of the plinths which are to be found on thirteen separate units of the eastern part of the church. Of these, the sections P 2 to P 7 relate to the building containing the crypt; and it will be seen that the stones are laid in courses of considerable height, comparable with those of the inner walling of the crypt.

E 38. The external plinths of the crypt are also remarkable for the massive length of the stones of which they are built, as will be seen from fig. 17, which shows the south-east angle of the building, from the present south window to the present east window of the crypt.

E 39. These plinths are also remarkable for the way in which certain important off-sets are cut in the stones themselves (e.g. in fig. 17 the

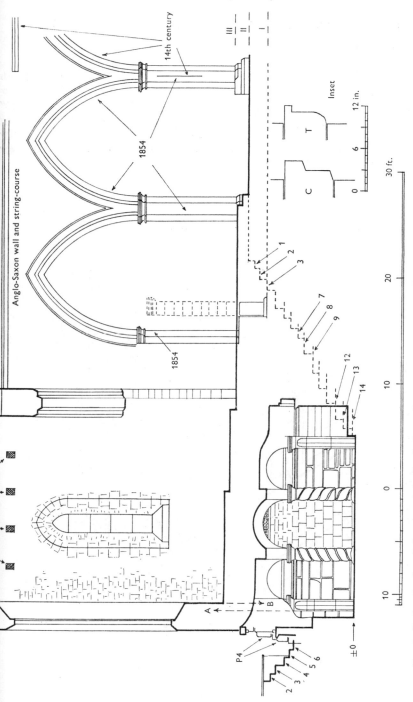

FIG. 15 *Longitudinal section through the centre of the church.* As in fig. 14, the Anglo-Saxon column is represented as if the part now standing at the entry to the church had been placed on top of the small part which remains *in situ*. This should not be taken as giving conclusive evidence that the original position of the capital was lower than those of the pointed arches, as shown here, because some of the stones of the Anglo-Saxon column may have been lost. N. 4 on p. 356 indicates that the capitals were at the same level as those of 1854, and in fig. 22 this has been assumed to have been the case. The stairs shown in broken lines are those of the north-west entry. The inset C gives the profile of the double-stepped string-course of the crypt and the inset T gives the profile of the string-course in the former central tower above the arches of 1854.

Anglo-Saxon wall and string-course

14th century

1854

1854

Inset

C

T

0    6    12 in.

30 ft.

20

10

0

10

±0

P4

2  3  4  5  6

1
2
3

7
8
9

12
13
14

A
B

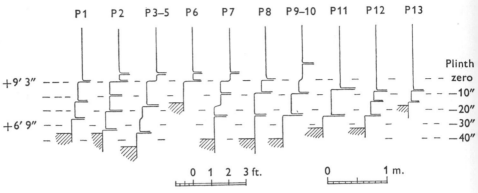

FIG. 16 *Cross-section of the plinths.* The positions of these thirteen sections are shown in fig. 18. The levels +6′ 9″ and +9′ 3″ denote heights above the floor of the crypt.

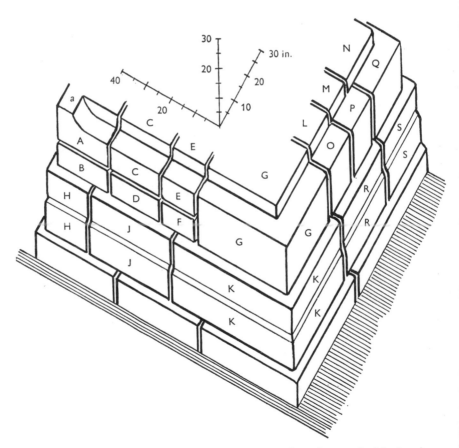

FIG. 17 *Isometric drawing of the plinths, P3 and P4, at the south-east angle of the chancel*

upper off-set cut on stones A, C, E and G and the lower off-set cut on stones H, J, K, R and S). It should also be noted that this lower off-set is oblique, like the off-sets in the lower, double string-course inside the crypt.

E 40. Not much remains of the plinths of the north of the crypt, but, on the south, the part (P 2) to the west of the south window is different in cross-section from the part (P 3) to the east (see fig. 16).

The external plinths are, therefore, similar to the interior walling of the crypt in three important ways: in the use of courses as tall as 20 in.; in the use of long stones, between 30 and 50 in.; and in the use of oblique off-sets cut into the stones themselves. I therefore deduce that the plinths are contemporary with the interior walling. This is in sharp contrast to Gilbert's recent claim that a building with very thin walls was subsequently modified by adding the plinths externally.[1]

## The date of the vaulting

It has commonly been accepted (and I believe correctly) that the vaulting was not built at the same time as the main side walls of the crypt, but that it was a later addition.[2] This belief rests on the following evidence.

E 41. The elaborate pilasters which support the outer ends of the transverse arches of the vault are not bonded into the main walls but are simply set against them, with the joints of their courses at different heights from those of the walls (see figs. 11–15).

E 42. The capitals of the pilasters are nowhere aligned with either the upper or the lower of the string-courses (see figs. 11–15).

## The nature of the vaulting

E 43. The square area of the main crypt is divided into nine bays by transverse arches which spring from two pilasters at each wall and which rest on four free-standing central columns.

E 44. The bays are not square because the four central columns are not aligned between the pilasters (see fig. 18).

E 45. The transverse arches are semi-circular in elevation and of plain rectangular section (see figs. 14 and 15).

E 46. The nine bays are covered by roughly domical vaults (not groined) which do not seem to have been constructed of large separate stones like a Gothic vault but rather to have been laid as a mass of concrete. The

---

[1] *Loc. cit.* pp. 86–8. The walls of this building are stated on p. 86 as having been 2 ft 2 in. thick before the plinths were added; but no indication is given to show how this could be ascertained.

[2] See, e.g., G. Baldwin Brown, *Anglo-Saxon Architecture, The Arts in Early England* II, 2nd ed. (London, 1925), 319; A. W. Clapham, *English Romanesque Architecture before the Conquest* (Oxford, 1930), p. 157; and Gilbert, *loc. cit.* p. 97.

patching of the hole broken by the workman in 1779 can still be seen in the south-west bay (see fig. 13).

E47. The western recess is covered by a simple barrel vault whose crown is about a foot lower than that of the adjoining bay (see figs. 13 and 15).

E48. In the three bays that contain the north, east and south recesses, the vaults are swept up into the recesses in a form which can best be described as a shallow barrel vault whose crown is curved upward as it approaches the outer wall (see figs. 12 and 15).

### The pilasters and columns

E49. *Pilasters*. All eight pilasters are roughly square in plan, and they stand beside the recesses, with one face set against the main wall (figs. 13–15). The three exposed faces of each pilaster are each enriched by a single tall recessed blind arch.

E50. *Columns*. All four columns are circular in plan and each is decorated by two narrow fillets which run spirally upward like ropes binding and supporting a sheaf of corn. The fillets run like a right-handed screw on the north-west and south-east columns and left-handed on the two others (fig. 15).

E51. *Capitals*. Both on the columns and on the pilasters the capitals project boldly and are square in plan, with vertical faces enriched by two horizontal grooves. Below these vertical faces the capitals are swept back by hollow chamfers to the size of the column or pilaster; but only the slightest effort is made to adapt the square plan of the capital into the circular plan of the column. There is clear evidence on several capitals of surviving paint, mainly red in colour.

E52. *The eastern recess*. The capitals of the pilasters on either side of the eastern recess differ from all the others in one important respect, namely that their faces toward the recess are not set forward, but rise vertically from the pilaster. This might be thought to be due to subsequent cutting back; but it seems to be an original feature, because the decorative horizontal grooves are carried round, unchanged, from the adjoining face (fig. 12).

### The relation of the crypt to the chancel above

E53. The interior width of the chancel (14 ft 8 in.) is appreciably less than that of the crypt (about 16 ft) at the springing of the vault (fig. 13).

This has caused confusion in the past as a result of inaccurate drawing of the walls of the chancel and crypt. The walls of the crypt have often been said to be thinner than those of the chancel; but this is not so, because the outward projection of the plinths more than compensates for the greater internal width of the crypt (see fig. 18).

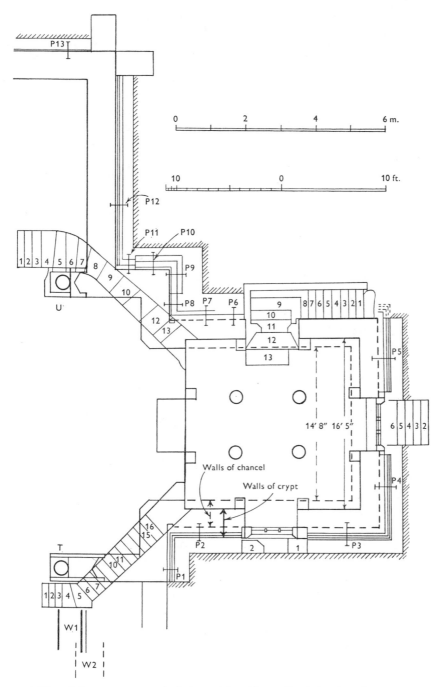

FIG. 18 *Plan of the main surviving Anglo-Saxon fabric.* The walls of the chancel are shown in broken lines to distinguish them from the walls of the crypt which are shown in continuous lines. Beside the northern stairway the Anglo-Saxon plinth has been cut back, so that the outer wall of the crypt coincides with the wall of the chancel above; thus in this region the continuous line represents both walls. The plan shows the three complete stairways, and it also shows the surviving steps 2 to 6 of the partially destroyed east stairway.

E 54. The vertical alignment of the inner faces of the walls of the chancel lies about 9 in. inside the interior space of the crypt. This relationship is clearly indicated in all of figs. 11–15 by the vertical alignments A and B, which show how the inner parts of the walls of the chancel rest on the vaulting.

This fact seems necessarily to imply that the vaulting of the crypt was completed before the main walls of the chancel were built above it.

### The windows and doorways

The rectangular wooden window frames in each of the east and south recesses are set in stone surrounds. The wooden frames date from about 1914;[1] but the stone surrounds are probably of much the same fourteenth-century date as the north doorway and steps.

E 55. Above these windows, and above the pointed medieval doorway in the north wall, triangular areas of whitish stone patching indicate that the main walls of rather browner stone were formerly pierced by tall gabled openings (fig. 19).

E 56. Above the flat heads of the east and south windows this white stone patching shows no sign of disturbance such as would almost necessarily have been caused by later insertion of these windows in a previously existing wall.

From these observations it seems to follow that the crypt originally had north, east and south annexes with gabled roofs; that these were later torn down; and that about the fourteenth century the north door and the two windows were inserted in the gaps and the walling made good above them with the whiter stone.[2]

It then seems naturally to follow that the large stones found by Hipkins, as recorded in E 26, marked the corners of the walls of the original south recess and gable, which were no doubt matched by similar walls and gable on the north. We may also assume that the steps recorded in E 27 led out eastward from the crypt through a gabled doorway in the east wall (see a suggested reconstruction in fig. 24). It should be noted that the vaulting of the crypt in each of these three recesses is swept up to heights that would just allow of access through such an eastern stairway and would provide ample space for light through splayed windows in the side recesses.

### The western passages to the crypt

The present entry to the crypt is by a stair which leads down from the east end of the north aisle into the north-west corner of the crypt, and

---

[1] See E 29.

[2] By contrast it has recently been suggested that the triangular in-filling of whitish stone should be assigned to a pre-Conquest date, probably about 840 (see Gilbert, *loc. cit.* pp. 97 and 101). The evidence of the stones immediately above the windows seems to me conclusively to refute this suggestion.

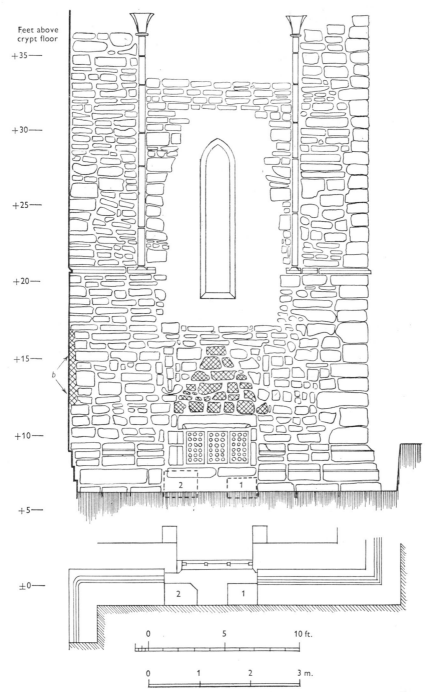

Feet above
crypt floor

+35—

+30—

+25—

+20—

+15—

*b*

+10—

+5—

±0—

2

1

2

1

| 0 | | 5 | | 10 ft. |

| 0 | 1 | 2 | 3 m. |

FIG. 19 *Plan and elevation of the south wall of the chancel.* The cross-hatched gabled area is described in E 55 and 56. The stones 1 and 2, first discovered in 1901, are described in E 26. The cross-hatched area *b* at the west of the chancel probably represents later patching of the recess *b* shown in Garwood's plan (fig. 10).

a second similar stairway can be seen leading up from the south-west corner to the south aisle.

E 57. The irregular and broken stonework in the sides of these passages gives clear evidence that they were cut after the walls of the crypt had been completed.

E 58. The treads of the northern passage are well worn, notwithstanding that the stairs had long been forgotten until they were re-opened in 1886–7.

### The exterior of the church

It has commonly been asserted that the upper walls of the chancel show clear evidence of a change of fabric about the level of the sill of the medieval four-light east window: below this level the stone is browner in colour and in large, almost square, blocks; while above, the stone is white or grey in colour, and in smaller, flatter blocks.[1] Moreover the lower part is quite devoid of ornament, while in the upper part there is a horizontal string-course from which two pilaster-strips run up each of the three faces of the chancel.

E 59. The string-course and pilaster-strips of the upper walling and the plain faces of the lower walling are in marked contrast (fig. 19).

E 60. The change in size and colour of the stones is less marked, but nevertheless fairly clear, particularly on the south face.

E 61. The type of quoining, unique to Repton, continues unchanged from the lower walling through the full height of the surviving upper walls, all being of large stones laid on their faces and extending much the same distance along both adjoining faces of the angles.

### The pilaster-strips

E 62. On the north and south walls of the chancel the pilaster-strips are complete for a total length of about 15 ft, from the string-course to strange splayed capitals immediately below the present eaves. They are about 6 in. in width, projecting about 3 in., and in lengths which average about 2 ft, with no alternation of short stones between the long ones. The lower stones in each pilaster are markedly taller than 2 ft, while the upper ones are as short as 1 ft.

E 63. On the east face of the chancel the pilaster-strips have largely been destroyed by the insertion of the four-light east window, but two or three parts of each strip, totalling about 6 ft in length, survive directly above the jambs of the window.

The splayed capitals above the pilasters on the side walls of the chancel strongly suggest that the walls originally rose higher and that the pilasters

[1] Baldwin Brown, *op. cit.* p. 318; Taylor and Taylor, *op. cit.* p. 512; and Gilbert, *loc. cit.* pp. 86 and 95–7.

were joined by strip-work arches such as exist at Wing and Deerhurst, and in fragmentary form at Brixworth.

E64. There are no pilasters on other parts of the building, but a very marked straight vertical joint on the east wall of the north aisle strongly suggests that a pilaster originally ran up the wall at this point and served to protect the southern part of the wall when the wall to the north was torn away. This suggestion is strengthened by the way the straight joint runs down from the eaves to a level which matches that of the string-course on the chancel. Below this level, where there would have been no pilaster, the walling shows a ragged joint.

### The Anglo-Saxon windows

E65. No Anglo-Saxon window has survived *in situ*, but a monolithic window-head with a single-splayed aperture 7 in. wide externally is preserved in the porch, and two larger and rather rougher specimens lie in the churchyard about 15 yd south-west of the porch.

I believe that the original windows of the chancel were in the places now occupied by the upper parts of the Early English lancets which were no doubt inserted in the thirteenth century to make the chancel lighter. Clear evidence of a similar operation at Wing is given by the survival of the Anglo-Saxon window-heads above the later windows.[1]

### The string-course round the chancel and tower

E66. A horizontal string-course runs continuously round the chancel except where it has been cut away by the three later windows (fig. 19). It is also visible at the same level on the adjoining walls of the former central tower, but with many gaps cut in it on the northern part of the tower.

### The imposts on the eastern faces of the tower

E67. About 12 ft above the string-course the eastern faces of the tower are ornamented by two imposts, one placed beside the north quoin and one beside the quoin to the south (fig. 24).

It has recently been suggested that these are survivals of a continuous string-course.[2] But their north and south faces are flush with the wall, and yet seem to be original; therefore I believe that they never continued further than at present.[3]

---

[1] Taylor and Taylor, *op. cit.* p. 666 and fig. 343.

[2] Gilbert, *loc. cit.* p. 98.

[3] There is a similar isolated impost at the north-east angle of St Sampson's church at Cricklade, Wiltshire.

### The interior of the church

#### The chancel

E 68. Until 1940 the interior of the chancel was plastered, but the fabric is now exposed. It is of roughly coursed stones of much the same size as those of the outer face.

#### The present north aisle

E 69. In the south part of the east wall of the north aisle where early walling survives outside, there is also early walling inside, of much the same character as that in the chancel.

#### The former central tower

E 70. Above the pointed arches that were inserted in 1854 the early walling is of squared and coursed stones which are nevertheless clearly distinguishable from the much more finely dressed stonework of the medieval nave.

E 71. In this early walling the Anglo-Saxon string-course has survived in both the north and south walls at a height of 23 ft above the present floor (fig. 15). No trace of a similar string-course can be seen in the east wall.

E 72. The lower part of the east wall has been largely cut away by the insertion of a wide medieval chancel-arch; but enough remains to show that it was of different fabric from the upper part of the same wall and also from the north and south walls. Here therefore there seems to be some evidence of an even earlier Anglo-Saxon building.

E 73. The upper part of the east wall has been greatly disturbed, but there is little difficulty in seeing how only a central gabled area has survived, while the areas above and on each side represent a rebuilding at the time when the clearstorey was added to the nave. Within the central area two jambs in upright-and-flat construction define the former presence of a window or doorway about 10 ft wide and about 10 ft tall with its sill about 25 ft above the floor.

#### The lateral arches of the tower

E 74. The base and about 2 ft of the shaft survive *in situ* from each of the eastern columns or responds of the arches that led north and south from the central tower. The bases define a floor level about 1 ft 10 in. below that of the present nave.

E 75. This level corresponds roughly with the third of the present steps leading to the crypt. The uppermost three treads and four risers appear to be of modern workmanship, in agreement with the evidence of the levels.

These levels indicate that four or five steps would have been needed to lead from the Anglo-Saxon nave to the chancel at the level of the main western floor of the present chancel.

At first sight there appears to be no possibility of determining the original width of the Anglo-Saxon arches from the central tower to the lateral *porticus*; but it will be seen below that the bases and plinths of the piers of 1854 contain evidence bearing upon this matter.

### The walls to the west of these arches

Information about partial survival of the side walls of the Anglo-Saxon nave and tower can be secured by detailed study of the bases and plinths of the piers built in 1854. Those at S and V in fig. 10 are wholly of 1854, while of those at W and X the western parts are the responds of the medieval nave arcades and only the eastern parts date from 1854. When the new pointed arches were inserted in 1854, the whole floor of the church was at the uniform level introduced in 1792, about 18 in. above the present floor of the nave and thus covering the plinths and bases of the medieval piers. Therefore the new piers were themselves given no bases, but had straight sides rising directly from the floor. The piers were placed directly on the flagstones of the floor, which at these points rested directly on the Anglo-Saxon walls that had been cut down just to that level in 1792 when the additional round arch had been cut through each of the side walls. What has been said so far may sound little more than conjecture; but its reality can be seen in the fabric itself.

E 76. The pier S on the south side now has a chamfered base (see fig. 20); but it is patently of different workmanship, and that this base was not any part of the work of 1854 is confirmed by its absence from Garwood's plan of 1886. Part of the eastern edge of the pier itself projects into space, as was shown in Garwood's drawing, and there is no support at all for the eastern angle of the base.

E 77. The structure of the pier X, next to the west, is even more striking (see fig. 21). The western part, which is the medieval respond, has a properly shaped, half-hexagonal, chamfered base, which in its turn rests on a square base, also of chamfered profile. By contrast, the eastern part of the pier dates from 1854 and rests, without any base, on a rude block of masonry.

But there seems little doubt that the strange structure of this block is to be explained on the following lines as arising from the several changes which have taken place in this area: first, the thin flat slab *a* seems to represent part of the flagstones of the raised floor of 1792, while the tall dark stone *b* running down from the flagstone into the present floor represents the core of the original Anglo-Saxon south wall, which re-

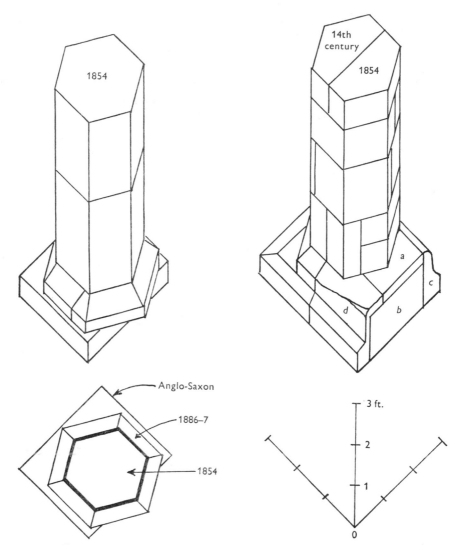

FIG. 20 *Isometric drawing and plan of pier S*   FIG. 21 *Isometric drawing of pier X*

mained *in situ* immediately beneath the floor of 1792; and finally the white stones *c* and *d* were added in 1886 when the floor was lowered to its present level and the Anglo-Saxon wall was consequently cut away between piers X and S. The corresponding northern pier W tells a similar story which need not be developed further.

The importance of these details is twofold. First, the detail of the bases at X and W shows that the side walls of the Anglo-Saxon nave continued westward in the same alignment as those of the tower. Secondly, the strange position of the 1854 pier at S, not quite over the wall on which it rests, serves to define with precision the former size of the destroyed Anglo-Saxon arch that opened between S and T into the south *porticus* (see fig. 22). The wall *e* supporting the pier S and rising a little above the medieval floor is part of the south wall of the Anglo-Saxon tower. It was not cut down in 1792 any lower than was needed to allow the raised floor of that date to pass over it. The point *f* where it suddenly stops at the east, short of the eastern edge of the 1854 pier, is the original jamb of the Anglo-Saxon opening, against which a column *g* no doubt stood, by analogy with the surviving column *h* against the eastern jamb *j*. The strange poising of the pier of 1854 partially in space is to be explained in terms of the original size of the Anglo-Saxon opening and the desire of the builders of 1854 to make their new piers and arches have the same spacing as that of the medieval arches to the west.

From all these observations I deduce that the Anglo-Saxon openings from the tower to the lateral *porticus* were as shown in fig. 22, diagram A, and that the round column shown at V in Garwood's plan did not belong to the original arrangement but to the work of 1792.

## The east wall of the south porticus

E 78. Under authority of Faculties dated 20 January 1949 and 17 August 1950 extensive works were carried out to clear the south transept of a large organ and to open the southern flight of stairs from the west of the crypt. As a result of these works two further important early features were made permanently accessible. First, the column and base that remained *in situ* at the east of the south arch from the tower to the *porticus* were cleared and left open to view (*h* in fig. 22). Secondly, beside the south wall of the stairs, immediately opposite this column, there came into view a cross-section of the east wall of the *porticus* and its plain flat plinth. The piece of wall that survives consists of a single block of stone 27 in. thick and 17 in. tall, resting on a plinth which projects 5 in. towards the east. Its eastern face lies 68 in. west of the inner face of the east wall of the transept. This wall is shown as $W_1$ in fig. 18; for comparison $W_2$ shows the position of the wall shown as TQ in broken lines in Garwood's plan (fig. 10).

### TENTATIVE ARCHITECTURAL HISTORY

From all the evidence so far advanced it now remains to try to construct a picture of the abbey church at the height of its importance and to draw up a self-consistent architectural history that will explain the development of the building as we see it today. First a tentative time-sequence is set out for the development of the building, with a minimum of argument but

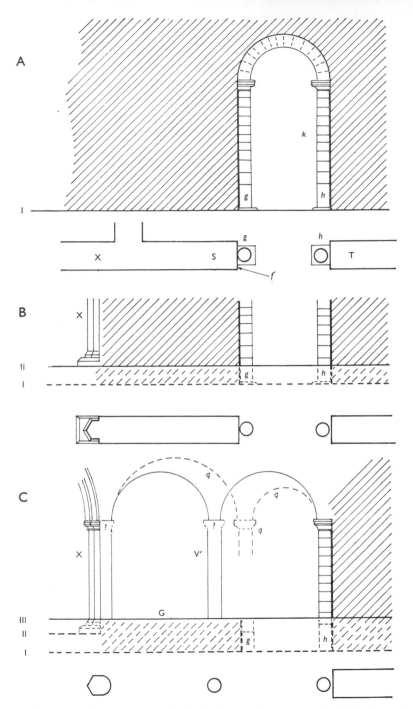

FIG. 22 *The history of the openings to the side-chapels* The five diagrams A to E of this figure show how from the evidence cited below it is possible to reconstruct, step by step, the changes which the side walls of the nave underwent in order finally to reach their present form. The diagrams show the south elevation of the south wall X S T (cf. fig. 10) at the following periods:

A. From its erection until the fourteenth century

B. From the fourteenth century until 1792

C. From 1792 until 1854

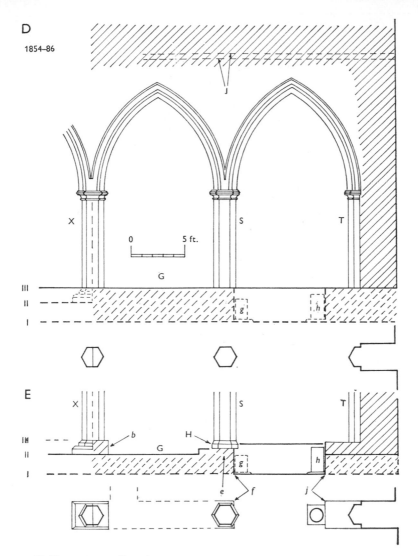

D. From 1854 until 1886

E. From 1886 up to the present.

In order to save space, diagrams B and E show only the lower part of the wall where alterations were made, the upper parts being left as in diagrams A and D. The diagonally hatched areas in each diagram represent original Anglo-Saxon walling, features below the current level of the floor being shown in broken lines.

The evidence for the features as shown can be summarized thus. In diagram A the lowest drum *h* of the east column, and its base have remained *in situ*; the west column *g* has vanished but the jamb *f* is still *in situ*; the upper parts of the columns and their capitals are copied from the pieces preserved in the south porch, and the height of the capitals is based on the drawings by Gorham and Bigsby, both of whom saw them at the same level as the medieval ones (cf. diagram C); finally the Anglo-Saxon floor-level I is fixed by the base *h* which is *in situ*. Diagram B shows how the floor was raised in the Middle Ages to the level II; this is fixed by the medieval respond X and its base, which have remained *in situ*; and Garwood traced this level further eastward (cf. fig. 10). Thus from the Middle Ages the base *h* and the jamb *f* were buried, until they were finally brought to light again in 1950. In diagram C the raised floor level is based not only on Garwood's plan and Cox's description (E 18), but also on the masonry beside the eastern respond T in diagram E. The position of the column V′ must be regarded

[*continued at foot of following page*

with full reference back to the supporting sources of E 1–78. Then an attempt is made to assign dates to certain key stages in the architectural time-sequence by linking them to the written history contained in E 1–32.

### The architectural time-sequence

#### The earliest surviving building

S 1. The earliest surviving fabric, underlying all other parts of the building, is a former burial chamber which forms the core of the present crypt. Always partly below ground, it consisted of the main square chamber with three rectangular recesses opening off it to the north, west and south; that at the west was probably from the first covered by the low stone barrel vault which still survives; those to the north and south were formerly of much the same depth as their western counterpart but were covered by sloping gabled roofs which were built against the main side walls and which have vanished. The main chamber itself was probably covered by a timber-framed roof, and access was from the east through a door covered by a gabled roof like those at the north and south (fig. 23).

S 2. The original level of the ground beside this burial chamber is indicated by the lowest course of the triple plinth, about 6 ft above the interior floor level.

S 3. The ground level rose during the time the eastern access was in use, and in consequence five or six additional steps had to be added outside the building. This indicates either a very considerable lapse of time or else an unusually rapid rising, or deliberate raising, of the ground.

S 4. Within the present crypt the main walls of the original burial chamber are visible up to and including the lower, double-stepped string-course. The upper string-course, of plain square section, was probably

---

as tentative; it yields two arches of roughly equal span as shown in Gorham's and Bigsby's drawings, and it corresponds to the column V shown by Garwood on the north side. By contrast the capital and arches shown by broken lines q show what would have resulted if the Anglo-Saxon arch and columns g and h had been left *in situ* in 1792 and a new wider arch had been pierced at the west. Although Haigh's description (E 12) refers to the western arch as wider and taller than its companion, so great a discrepancy seems quite at variance with the two contemporary drawings. It therefore seems most likely that the Anglo-Saxon arch and its west column g were removed and destroyed in 1792. In diagram D the hexagonal piers and pointed arches of 1854 are as they were built, resting on the raised floor III of 1792. These all survive unchanged to the present day, with Anglo-Saxon walling *in situ* above them; the broken lines J show the position of the distinctive string-course on the north face of this upper wall. Finally, diagram E shows the changes that have been made in the lower part of the wall in 1886 and thereafter: the floor was lowered to its medieval level II and a considerable part of the Anglo-Saxon walling G was therefore cut away in 1886, but a small piece was left enclosed in the base b of the pier X; the pier S was given a chamfered base H enclosing the upper part of the Anglo-Saxon walling e; and finally the jambs f and j of the original Anglo-Saxon archway, as well as the shaft h and its base, were again exposed to view in 1950.

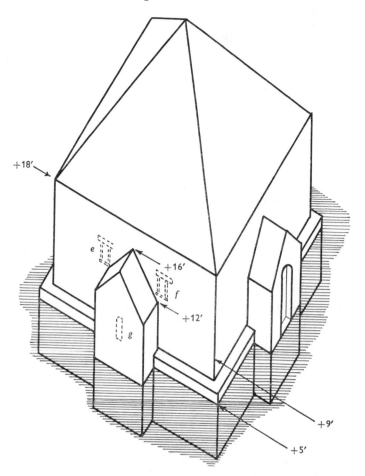

FIG. 23 *Suggested reconstruction of the original burial chamber.* The windows *e* and *f* must be regarded as very problematic; they were shown in Garwood's plan (fig. 10) and in Irvine's plan and sections of the crypt (p. 360, n. 3 and p. 362, n. 3) but the evidence for them in the surviving walling is very inconclusive. The window shown at *g* is suggested by the splayed side of stone 2 in fig. 19.

added later in connection with the vaulting of the main chamber (which explains its absence from the western recess). The lateral recesses intended for shrines of the kings were perhaps enriched by painting, panelling or tapestries, and for this reason probably never had any cornice.

S 5. The outer walling of this burial chamber survives in the lower walls of the present chancel, from its bold triple plinths, up its brown stone walls, to the tops of the whiter triangular in-fillings that close the gaps left by the tearing away of the gabled roofs on the south, east and north faces.

## The later sanctuary

S 6. Later the burial chamber was covered by a concrete vault of nine domed bays resting on transverse arches, and a tall building was erected above to form the sanctuary of a church.

S 7. The whole original fabric of the burial chamber was incorporated into the new building by a series of steps which may be summarized thus:

(a) The exterior walls were left unchanged on the north, east and south.

(b) Internally two pilasters were placed against each main wall, but otherwise the walls were left unchanged until above the height of the double-stepped string-course.

(c) Above this level it is probable that the plain square string-course was inserted into the walling to provide a secure springing for the new vault.

(d) The columns, arches and vault were built.

(e) Above the vault an additional 9 in. thickening was added inside each of the north, east and south walls, resting on the vault.

(f) It is probable that the original west wall was then demolished to the level of the floor of the sanctuary, so as to open the new sanctuary to a church that already existed or had meantime been built to the west (see S 11).

S 8. At the level of the eaves of the original burial chamber, or a little higher, the present external string-course was laid round all three walls of the new sanctuary; and above this level the new walls were continued upward as they stand today, but to a rather greater height.

S 9. In this new walling pilaster-strips were incorporated for decoration and to give additional strength. The prior existence of the walling below the string-course explains why these pilasters begin from the string-course and not from the plinth.

S 10. The original eastern stairway continued in use as the entry to the burial chamber beneath the new sanctuary, as is indicated by the provision of special capitals on the eastern pilasters, designed so as not to project into the space of the stairway.

## The church to the west of the new sanctuary

S 11. *The earlier church.* There are several English and continental instances of the extension of an existing church eastward so as to bring its sanctuary above the place of burial of some important person formerly buried near to but outside the church.[1] Moreover it is well known that burial close to the sanctuary of a church was a specially desired privilege. The sequence described above therefore suggests that the original burial chamber lay close to the east of an earlier church, and Garwood's plan does indeed indicate walls which might have belonged to such a church.

---

[1] E.g. Glastonbury in Anglo-Saxon England and Werden in Carolingian Germany.

But until greater certainty can be secured about the walls shown as Q R S T and D E F of that plan I prefer to make no suggestions about the possible shape of that church.

S 12. *The church contemporary with the new sanctuary.* The central tower and the *porticus* lying to the north and south of it must have been built about the same time as the new sanctuary. Their plinths are not bonded into or identical in fabric with those of the burial chamber, but are similar. Moreover the tower is bonded into the walls of the new sanctuary although not into the lower walling of the burial chamber. The nave was of the same width as the tower, and that it continued westward at least 20 ft from the tower is indicated by the 'ancient flooring' shown in Garwood's plan. I do not at present have any evidence to indicate whether or not there were any *porticus* flanking the nave to the west of the tower.

### The reliquary crypt

S 13. After some time western stairways were cut from the north and south *porticus* into the crypt (as the burial chamber had now become). That this must have been an immense labour is apparent from the exceptionally massive nature of the walling through which they were cut. The only adequate reason for undertaking so great a task would seem to be that the presence of a major relic in the crypt had given rise to so great a press of pilgrims that it had become necessary to provide a system of one-way circulation with entry and exit under proper control, inside the church. The top three steps of each of these stairways are modern, to provide for the raising of the floor of the church. Thus in their original state these stairways would not have obstructed the doorways to the lateral *porticus*.

S 14. The breaking of these passages into the western corners of the crypt left rough ends of the string-courses in the north and south walls, where they are still visible. No trace of anything similar is to be seen on the much shorter sections of wall at the west. It seems just possible that the west wall was always differently treated, just as the western recess seems to have had some special significance.

S 15. Although there is no proof, the eastern stair was probably abandoned at this stage and its steps removed from within the crypt so as to give extra space. Removal of this entry would also have given greater security for the important relics.

### The church at its zenith

S 16. The buildings so described (and illustrated in fig. 24) probably represent the abbey church at the height of its importance. The walls of the sanctuary probably rose about 6 ft higher than at present, to accommodate arches that might have connected the tops of the pilaster-strips,

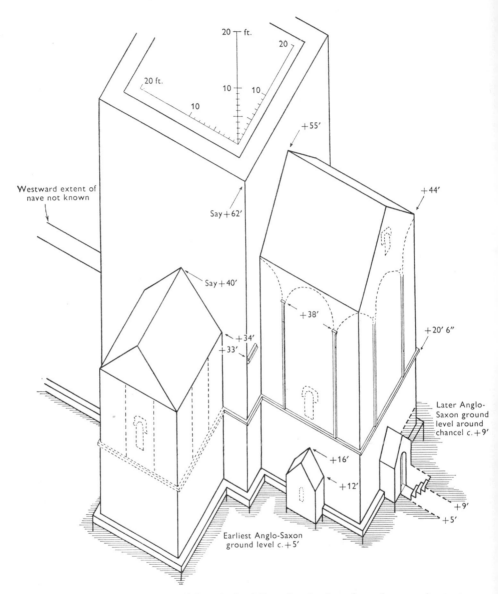

FIG. 24 *Suggested reconstruction of the main church.* Round arches have been shown, rather tentatively, springing from the splayed capitals which at present stand at the eaves of the chancel. Such a reconstruction recalls the similar work at Wing. It is, however, possible that there were no such arches and that the pilasters and their capitals supported an eaves-course, much as is to be seen at Corhampton; if so, the chancel would have been about 6 ft lower than is shown here.

and the stonework of the central tower probably rose a few feet higher still. Above that level it is probable that the tower would have had a wooden capping, in receding stages, of the type often represented in contemporary drawings.[1]

### *The decline of the church*

S17. At some stage this church was severely damaged and the east wall of the central tower clearly shows that after this calamity the nave and chancel were covered by a single gabled roof at about the height of the present roof of the chancel. Serious damage of this sort would be a natural consequence of complete burning of the woodwork, with consequential outward toppling of the upper parts of the tall stone walls as a result of lateral pressure of the rafters.

S18. We do not know when the church was again brought into use after the disaster, but the fallen masonry could well have hidden all the openings to the crypt and thus have led to its abandonment.

S19. Alterations to the church after the Norman Conquest can be summarized as follows:

(a) Early English windows were pierced in the side walls of the chancel and in the short side walls of the old central tower.

(b) A very narrow south aisle was added, perhaps even by the Normans.

(c) This was widened to its present size in the thirteenth century as is shown by its Early English west window.

(d) An aisle of the same width was added on the north, as shown by a steep roof-line and vestiges of an Early English west window.

(e) The western arch and wall of the tower were removed to make an open nave.

(f) The north aisle was widened in the fourteenth century, bringing its north wall into the alignment of the Anglo-Saxon north *porticus*.

(g) The Anglo-Saxon south *porticus* was engulfed in the large eastern chapel added to the end of that aisle.

(h) Works of the fourteenth century also included the north stairs to the crypt, the new chancel-arch which destroyed all trace of its Anglo-Saxon predecessor, and the large east windows of the chancel and north aisle.

(i) In the fifteenth century the south porch and west tower were built and rather later in the century the clearstorey was added to the nave.

S20. After the Dissolution the crypt again passed out of memory until it was rediscovered in 1779. In 1792 the single arches opening to the 'quires' were given taller and wider companions on their western sides;

---

[1] Clapham, *op. cit.* figs. 20 and 21. The existing roof of the tower at Breamore in Hampshire may represent a survival of the type although not the original fabric.

and in 1854 all these arches were replaced by pointed copies of the arches of the nave, but fortunately without destroying the Anglo-Saxon walling and string-course that survive above on both sides of the nave.

## An attempt to assign dates to the major periods of the architectural time-sequence

The task which now remains is to attempt to associate some of the events of the historical record in E 1–9 with some of the phases of the architectural time-sequence S 1–18. Such a task is always difficult unless some happy chance provides evidence that links a particular historical record unambiguously with some special feature of the building.

It has commonly been accepted on stylistic grounds that the vaulting of the crypt and the pilaster strip-work of the chancel are relatively late features of Anglo-Saxon architecture.[1] Recently, however, Gilbert has set forward in detail arguments for accepting the burial chamber as an early building, comparable to the well-known Hypogée des Dunes at Poitiers; and he has sketched an elaborate series of changes to show how it was incorporated into the body of churches built and adapted in the reigns of Kings Æthelbald and Wiglaf to become finally the resting place of St Wystan after his murder in 850.[2] I do not regard the evidence in Garwood's plan as being sufficient to serve as the basis for any secure reconstruction or dating of churches which may have preceded the present fabric; but I believe that the surviving crypt, with the access passages cut later into it from the west, gives very strong evidence that the relics of a saint were housed there for veneration. Moreover the recesses in the side walls are entirely appropriate for a royal burial chamber.[3] When therefore we note the record in E 7 that Wystan was buried 'in the mausoleum of his grandfather in the famous monastery called Repton' and when we note from E 3 and E 6 that Kings Æthelbald and Wiglaf were both buried in that monastery I believe there is very strong ground for associating the surviving crypt with 'the mausoleum of Wiglaf'.

## Summary

The conclusions of this essay may therefore be summarized by assigning dates to the surviving Anglo-Saxon fabric at Repton as follows:

[1] Baldwin Brown (*op. cit.* p. 312) suggested 'an advanced date in the Saxon period, impinging as some would think on the Norman domain, while some parts may carry us back to the tenth century or beyond'. Clapham (*op. cit.* p. 46) said that 'the early buildings of Repton have left no trace'; but by implication (on p. 96) he assigned the tower to the Carolingian period.

[2] *Loc. cit.* pp. 83–102; esp. pp. 99–101. Macdonald, *op. cit.* pp. 29 and 84–5, had proposed a somewhat similar theory, based on discussions in the 1920s with Mr T. L. Tudor; but he gave no supporting evidence.

[3] Compare the so-called mausoleum of Galla Placidia at Ravenna, *c.* 425. See R. Krautheimer, *Early Christian and Byzantine Architecture* (London, 1965), pp. 137–8.

*The burial chamber.* The main fabric including the recesses and the massive external plinths, but not the vaulting: *temp.* Æthelbald (716–57).

*The church above.* The chancel, central tower and lateral *porticus*, together with the vaulting of the crypt: *temp.* Wiglaf (827–40).

*The western stairways to the crypt.* Shortly after Wystan's burial in the crypt in 850.

*The gabled annexes to the crypt.* The eastern doorway was probably first blocked soon after the western stairs were built. All three annexes were probably covered with debris after the destruction of roofs and upper walls and then forgotten. In the fourteenth century the crypt was taken back into use, probably as an oratory attached to the nearby priory, and from this period I date the north stair and doorway, the east and south windows and the blocking of the triangular gables in all three walls.

# Archaeology and the beginnings of English society

## MARTIN BIDDLE

Anglo-Saxon history and Anglo-Saxon archaeology, interpenetrating views of a single society, can often stand in little discernible relation one to another. The historian faced with an increasing quantity of ever more complex archaeological discussion can fail to recognize therein the society whose documentary records he knows so well. Trained in the criticism of written sources, and acquainted with the technicalities of modern archaeology, he may well feel, even if he recognizes the potential importance of the archaeological evidence, that he is unable to criticize it and must therefore leave it to one side. The archaeologist can find himself in a similar situation. He is still normally trained in the recovery and interpretation of the material culture of pre-literate societies, and little in this training equips him to comprehend the complexities and techniques of documentary research, or to move with ease among the immense literature of modern historical enquiry. Accustomed to an independent structure of archaeological reasoning, he is apt to be too easily satisfied by the seeming self-sufficiency of his evidence, incomplete as it must be. In a period for which archaeology provides only a part of the evidence available, this apparent independence, coupled with the daunting apparatus of the historian's world, can lead to an inadequate appreciation of the broader issues involved, and thus to an unhistorical archaeology. For both historians and archaeologists the real crux lies not so much in their lack of knowledge of another field, as in their mutual difficulty in reaching a critical evaluation of each other's results.

Many of the major works of historical scholarship dealing with Anglo-Saxon England show that this situation has not been exaggerated. Except when dealing with the pagan period, there is usually little reference to archaeological work, apart from the recent great advances in the allied field of numismatics. This lack was particularly apparent in the latest series of books and articles on the Norman Conquest, most of which drew a picture of late Saxon England without reference to archaeological research.[1] To some extent this can be explained by the small amount of

[1] An exception was R. A. Brown, *The Normans and the Norman Conquest* (London, 1969).

relevant material as yet available, but it is also due to the two main attitudes outlined above: the historian's uncertainty about the value and relevance of archaeological evidence; and the archaeologist's inability to relate his results to the main issues of Anglo-Saxon history.

Among all the writing on Anglo-Saxon history, one book stands out for the clarity of its view of Anglo-Saxon society, and for the way in which it implies at every turn the need to study all the available evidence, whether from documents, place-names, or archaeology. In *The Beginnings of English Society*, Professor Dorothy Whitelock drew a picture of a people 'worthy of respect and study for their own sake'. It is in this belief firmly held that I shall try in these pages to suggest a few ways in which our knowledge of Anglo-Saxon society might be broadened and extended through a closer concentration by both documentary and archaeological historians on the historicity of archaeology.

The historical and physical accident of the growth of Anglo-Saxon archaeology out of the study of pagan cemeteries has influenced the archaeology of the Christian Saxon centuries with which this article is primarily concerned. Much of Anglo-Saxon archaeology has been until recently almost synonymous with art history, and most university courses dealing with the subject have tended to stop around 800, or if continuing to a later date, to be strongly biased towards the fine arts. It is probably this situation more than anything else which has led to the comparatively slight impact of archaeology on Anglo-Saxon history, and in historical writing to the restriction of archaeology to discussions of the cultural background. The implications of the current bias of university teaching in Anglo-Saxon archaeology will be considered at the end of this article. I shall attempt now, by surveying briefly the present position and future possibilities of Anglo-Saxon archaeology in a number of fields, to show that archaeology has a positive contribution to make to Anglo-Saxon history, not simply by providing a physical and cultural setting for recorded events, but by adding substantially to our knowledge of those events and by informing us of other events and processes of which little or no written record survives.

## TOWNS

The archaeological study of urban settlements provides one of the clearest examples of the actual and potential contribution of archaeology to Anglo-Saxon history. There can be no doubt of the importance of understanding the place of towns in the development of Anglo-Saxon England, and yet there has been little advance by historians since 1936 when Tait[1] disposed once and for all of the idea that towns were in the main a post-Conquest

[1] J. Tait, *The Medieval English Borough* (Manchester, 1936).

development.[1] Although Stephenson had himself attempted to use the physical evidence of the towns to support his views, and the late Professor H. M. Cam had given a striking demonstration of the potential contribution of archaeology in her own reply to Stephenson's thesis,[2] archaeology has so far made little impact on the historian's view of the Anglo-Saxon town.[3] It seems clear that the reason for the historian's comparative lack of concentration on Anglo-Saxon towns lies partly in what has been called the 'anti-urban bias' of English historical studies,[4] and partly in the relative paucity of the documentary evidence, but it is unfortunate that there is still no critical and comprehensive study of the very considerable charter evidence, and surprising that the Winton Domesday, originally published in 1816,[5] is only now receiving its first extended treatment.[6] There is thus still a need for Professor Loyn's recent firm statement rejecting 'any notion that the Anglo-Saxons had no towns'.[7]

Like medieval archaeology as a whole, the archaeological study of Anglo-Saxon towns is mainly a product of the post-war years.[8] Until now, with the notable exception of Thetford, attention has tended to concentrate on the burhs of Wessex and on some of the midland towns. The work is as yet comparatively limited and much of it is still in progress, with only preliminary reports in print, but the results have been encouraging. It will be best to begin, however, with the vexed question of the part played by urban places in the earliest days of the Anglo-Saxon settlement, for the results achieved in this borderland between Romano-British and Anglo-Saxon studies have great importance both for the history of the settlement and for the re-emergence of towns in the late Saxon period.

There has always been an unhappy relationship between the view derived from the literary sources that the English were awed by and therefore shunned the wrecked cities of Roman Britain, and the undoubted fact that it was upon these cities that the first organization of the Anglo-Saxon

---

[1] Carl Stephenson, *Borough and Town: a Study of Urban Origins in England* (Cambridge, Mass., 1933).

[2] H. M. Cam, 'The Origin of the Borough of Cambridge', *Proceedings of the Cambridge Antiquarian Society* xxxv (1933–4), 33–53; repr. H. M. Cam, *Liberties and Communities in Medieva England*, corr. ed. (London, 1963), pp. 1–18.

[3] See, e.g., H. R. Loyn, *Anglo-Saxon England and the Norman Conquest* (London, 1962), or the same author's *The Norman Conquest*, 2nd ed. (London, 1967), pp. 173–82.

[4] H. J. Dyos, 'Agenda for Urban Historians', *The Study of Urban History*, ed. H. J. Dyos (London, 1968), p. 46.

[5] *DB* iv, *Additamenta*, 531–62. There is a short essay on the Winton Domesday by J. H. Round in *VCH Hampshire* i (1900), 527–37, and it was of course used by Professor Whitelock, *The Beginnings of English Society* (London, 1952), ch. 6.

[6] Ed. F. Barlow, M. Biddle and D. J. Keene as Winchester Studies 1, to be published by the Clarendon Press, Oxford.

[7] *The Norman Conquest*, p. 173.

[8] I have given some of the relevant bibliography in 'Archaeology and the History of British Towns', *Antiquity* xlii (1968), 109–16.

church was built. With the possible exceptions of York and London, it is not sufficient to argue that there was some master plan to establish churches in the old towns of Roman Britain, memories or records of which were still preserved in Rome. The purpose of missionary life would require that missionary churches should be established in or close to frequented places, and Bede's account of Augustine's experiences in Canterbury shows that it was certainly a royal centre, if not an urban community in the full sense. The establishment of the first see of Wessex at Dorchester on Thames, a minor town of Roman Britain, seems also to reflect an existing situation rather than the fulfilment of a plan based on memories of the past – for why then at Dorchester and not at Winchester?

There are therefore some questions to be asked: what were these pre-Christian English communities in or around some erstwhile Roman towns; how had they come there; and why does there seem to be a recurring royal element in their make-up?

In recent years it has been possible to isolate some pottery and certain distinctive objects which can be attributed to the presence of alien, and probably Germanic, soldiers in late Roman Britain.[1] Several groups of material are involved, of somewhat differing date, but it is striking to note how many of these finds have come from Roman towns and their cemeteries, including Dorchester on Thames,[2] Canterbury[3] and Winchester.[4] Professor Sheppard Frere, whose excavations have made an outstanding contribution to our understanding of this difficult period, has shown how refortification of Roman towns in the middle or later fourth century, and their garrisoning by mercenary troops, could mean their continued existence well into the fifth century, safe from attack by raiders unequipped

---

[1] For Romano-Saxon pottery, the historical implications of which have not been universally accepted, see J. N. L. Myres, *Dark-Age Britain*, ed. D. B. Harden (London, 1956), pp. 16–39. For Anglo-Frisian pottery see J. N. L. Myres, 'Some English Parallels to the Anglo-Saxon Pottery of Holland and Belgium in the Migration Period', *L'Antiquité Classique* XVII (1948), 453–72, and *idem*, 'Anglo-Saxon Pottery of the Pagan Period' in 'Anglo-Saxon Pottery: a Symposium', *MA* III (1959), 7–13. The same author's 'Archaeology and History: Britons and Saxons in the post-Roman centuries', *Council for British Archaeology, Report XI for the year ended 30 June 1961*, pp. 35–45, is a thought-provoking essay, and his recent *Anglo-Saxon Pottery and the Settlement of England* (Oxford, 1969) is now the basic introduction to a field he has made particularly his own. For the military metalwork, see S. C. Hawkes and G. C. Dunning, 'Soldiers and Settlers in Britain, Fourth to Fifth Century', *MA* V (1961), 1–70. John Morris, 'Dark Age Dates', *Britain and Rome: Essays presented to Eric Birley*, ed. M. G. Jarrett and B. Dobson (Kendal, 1965), pp. 145–85, provides an important critique of much of the relevant evidence, both documentary and archaeological.

[2] Hawkes and Dunning, *loc. cit.* pp. 4–10, fig. 1; and S. S. Frere, 'Excavations at Dorchester on Thames, 1962', *AJ* CXIX (1962), 114–49.

[3] S. S. Frere, 'The End of Towns in Roman Britain', *The Civitas Capitals of Roman Britain*, ed. J. S. Wacher (Leicester, 1966), pp. 87–100, and 'The End of Roman Britain', ch. 17 in the same author's *Britannia* (London, 1967), pp. 360–83. See also S. C. Hawkes, 'Early Anglo-Saxon Kent', *AJ* CXXVI (1969), 186–92.

[4] M. Biddle, *AntJ* XLVIII (1968), 270; and *ibid.* L (1970), 292–8 and 311–14.

for siege-warfare.[1] In Canterbury the presence of Germanic elements is shown by the discovery of Anglo-Frisian pottery in sunken huts which seem to have respected, and therefore co-existed with, the Roman street network.

The process by which in Kent the Germanic mercenaries finally displaced their British employers is known in outline from *The Anglo-Saxon Chronicle* and other sources, although the chronology is very uncertain. The name of only one federate leader is given, and since Hengest appears to have arrived in Britain around the middle of the fifth century, our archaeological evidence now shows that he can have been only a comparative newcomer in a Germanic mercenary setting which began well before the end of the fourth century. For our present purpose the important point is that *Hengest* appears at the head of the genealogy of the Anglo-Saxon kings of Kent. If one can accept the identity of the two *Hengests*, it may thus be argued that the Kentish royal house emerged, or at least believed that it had emerged, out of a mercenary group whose very purpose had been the defence of late and sub-Roman Canterbury and its territory. These would not be people to whom a Roman town would be unusual; they might well be awed by the buildings which were there, but they would be unlikely seriously to believe that they were 'the work of giants', or to be frightened of the place in which as a group they may first have gained their coherence out of a succession of arrivals, among whom Hengest himself seems to have been a late-comer.

The Canterbury evidence may be used to construct a model for the transference of power from some of the late Roman *civitates* of Britain to the emergent English groups, themselves soon to be strengthened by further settlement – the *adventus Saxonum* – which must be seen as part of a continuing process reaching back into the fourth century. This model places great importance on the part played by late Roman towns in the emergence of Saxon England, but it does not imply that these places continued to be urban communities in the sense of relatively populous places, with a diversified economic base, in close economic and administrative relationship with their hinterland. The evidence points completely against this view, and we must think of such places in early Anglo-Saxon England as both post-urban and non-urban.

This model suggests that in southern and eastern England the control of the late Roman *civitates* passed into the hands of Germanic groups, who had been reinforced from time to time for the defence of individual towns. There is no reason to suppose the elimination of the British population, and it would seem likely that relationships between British and Saxon varied from place to place. As the economic base of Roman Britain col-

[1] *Civitas Capitals, loc. cit.*

lapsed, the towns ceased to be urban places, but retained some importance as the seat of the groups who had originally defended them, and particularly as the residence of their leaders, who perhaps retained some aura of the *romanitas* they had replaced. In the case of Canterbury the local royal house seems to have emerged from one of these leaders, and it may be imagined that this happened also in other places.

The establishment of the first see of Wessex at Dorchester on Thames in 635 could well be explained by the view that it was then a place of royal importance that had emerged from late Roman Britain by some such process as that described. This process may also help in understanding the complexities which surround the origin of Wessex, in which the fluctuating importance of north and south, of Dorchester and Winchester, appears crucial. Bede knew Winchester as the city of the *Gewisse*, and there is no doubt of its intimate connection with the royal house from an early date. The only reason for Cenwalh's foundation of a church in Winchester seems to be that it too was attached to a pre-existing royal establishment within the walls of the Roman town. Military metalwork, possibly indicating the presence of foreign, and perhaps Germanic, troops, has been found in some fourth-century graves in a Roman cemetery outside the north gate.[1] In the fifth century the Roman street plan was being obscured by the construction of timber buildings on top of the Roman streets, and in the centre of the town there is evidence for the presence of fifth-century Germanic elements.[2] By 500 there was an Anglo-Saxon settlement at King's Worthy, two miles north of the town.[3] The view that the former town remained of importance only for a ruling element, and that it was ringed with developing agricultural settlements, would be consonant with Frankish adaptation to Roman towns in the Rhineland, such as Cologne or Mainz and their hinterland.[4] It would also help to explain why Winchester seems to have been a royal and ecclesiastical centre from the seventh century onwards, but not an urban place in a full economic and social sense before the later ninth century.

Some of these erstwhile Roman towns may never quite have lost their urban character. London at any rate was known to Bede as a trading centre, and Canterbury and Rochester seem to be urban in physical terms by the

---

[1] *AntJ* L, *loc. cit.*

[2] *Ibid.* XLIV (1964), 206; XLVI (1966), 320; and XLVIII (1968), 270. In 1969 a decorated triangular bone comb of fifth-century date and of probable Frisian/Rhineland origin was found in a pit cut into late Roman levels south of the forum; see *ibid.* L, *loc. cit.*

[3] *MA* VI–VII (1962–3), 307; and *ibid.* VIII (1964), 233.

[4] The topographical approach to the study of early medieval towns, especially those occupying the sites of Roman settlements, is yielding important results in Germany, notably in the Rhineland. Much of this work is still unpublished and I am grateful to Professor Dr Kurt Böhner for introducing me to it. Some outline accounts can be found in the relevant volumes of the *Führer zu vor- und frühgeschichtlichen Denkmälern*, published by the Römisch-germanisches Zentralmuseum, Mainz I (1964) onwards. See further, below, p. 408, n. 1.

ninth century. Most of these places were, however, not to re-emerge as towns until the later ninth and tenth centuries, and meanwhile other and quite new settlements were growing to urban status. In the seventh to ninth centuries the contrast between Winchester and *Hamwih* (Southampton) is both striking and informative. During this period Winchester was an ecclesiastical and probably a royal centre, but there is no indication – certainly not in the archaeological evidence as yet – that it was an urban place or contained more than the service population required for the cathedral monastery and possible royal establishment. *Hamwih*, on the other hand, has produced an exceptional range of objects, and evidence for an extensive settlement, of this very period, and this should reflect the fact that it was from *Hamwih* and not Winchester that the shire was named.[1]

While recent work on the part played by towns in the earliest phases of the English settlement, and on the growth of early centres such as *Hamwih*, has already begun to yield important results, it is probably in the study of the physical character of the Wessex burhs that the most notable results have been achieved in the last ten years. These advances have been made possible by fresh examination of the well-known written sources, by topographical study of the sites, by excavation, but principally by the reasoned combination of all three lines of enquiry. Mr D. H. Hill's establishment of a satisfactory text of the Burghal Hidage, by a correlation of all the surviving manuscripts, is in the classic tradition of textual criticism,[2] and has led logically to his topographical study of many of the sites on the ground.[3] Excavations at Lydford, Wareham, Wallingford, Cricklade and Cadbury have defined with some precision the nature of the defences to be expected on such sites,[4] and the work at Winchester has shown that the regular street-pattern characteristic of all the larger and many of the smaller burhs can probably be associated with their initial foundation in the later ninth century.[5] The net result is a clear demonstration of the truly urban character of this group of Saxon settlements, some of which had achieved before the end of the tenth century a highly diversified, and in some respects specialized, economic base. While more evidence is required on every

---

[1] For *Hamwih*, see P. V. Addyman and D. H. Hill, 'Saxon Southampton: a Review of the Evidence', *Proceedings of the Hampshire Field Club* xxv (1968), 61–93, and xxvi (1969), 61–96. For the excavations of 1968–9 see P. V. Addyman, D. H. Hill and P. J. Lewis, 'Saxon Southampton: an Interim Report', forthcoming.

[2] David Hill, 'The Burghal Hidage: the Establishment of a Text', *MA* xiii (1969), 84–92. See also N. Brooks, 'The Unidentified Forts of the Burghal Hidage', *ibid.* viii (1964), 74–90.

[3] In progress, but see for example his work on Lyng: *Proceedings of the Somerset Archaeological and Natural History Society* iii (1967), 64–6.

[4] Lydford: *MA* viii (1964), 232; ix (1965), 170–1; x (1966), 168–9; xi (1967), 263; and xii (1968), 155. Wareham: *ibid.* iii (1959), 120–38. Wallingford: *ibid.* x (1966), 168; and xi (1969), 262–3. Cricklade: *Wiltshire Archaeological Magazine* lvi (1955–6), 162–6. Cadbury: *AntJ* xlvii (1967), 75; xlviii (1968), 15–16; and xlix (1969), 39–40.

[5] Originally *ibid.* xliv (1964), 215–16; but see now M. Biddle and D. H. Hill, 'Late Saxon Planned Towns', *ibid.* li (1971), forthcoming.

aspect of these burhs, the investigation of the conditions under which they were established demands particular attention. The Winchester evidence may suggest some deliberate encouragement of settlement, perhaps on lines not very different from those used in the plantation of post-Conquest towns, or in the establishment of Edwardian bastides. The recovery of the early pattern of plots, houses and churches within these burhs is well within the competence of archaeological technique and can be expected to yield a good deal of information on the conditions under which these places were established. It is for this reason that it is vital to excavate areas and not just single houses or even whole plots. Some success has been achieved in this direction at Lydford; and the Brooks site at Winchester, which might include the greater part of a whole 'urban manor', with its private church, can be expected to reveal the original late Saxon arrangement on this site by the end of the excavation in 1971.[1]

There is no space here to extend this treatment of the results and possibilities of urban archaeology to the problems of the Five Boroughs, or to other Scandinavian settlements such as York, or to the modification and expansion of the burghal system in the reigns of Edward the Elder and Athelstan, but the results obtained in the study of the original Wessex burhs suggest that in all these directions there is much to be gained by a combination of further documentary research, topographical study and excavation.[2] One group of towns must, however, be mentioned. Almost nothing is yet known in detail of the early development of the large towns of the eastern seaboard – Ipswich, Norwich and Lincoln, for example. It is clear that these towns are quite different in origin from the burhs of Wessex or most of the midland towns, and they may have commercial roots rather more akin to those which conditioned the growth of towns in the Low Countries and northern France. The detailed study of these eastern towns by the combined methods suggested is an urgent priority before their archaeology is for ever destroyed by modern development. Historians must never forget that much of the archaeological evidence of potential interest to them is under constant threat and is being daily destroyed throughout the country. At Thetford recent rescue excavations have shown how much material is potentially available for the study of these eastern towns.[3] Norwich is perhaps the most important town of this

[1] *Ibid.* XLIV (1964), 196–202; XLV (1965), 243–9; XLVI (1966), 313–19; XLVII (1967), 259–66; XLVIII (1968), 259–68; and XLIX (1969), 303–12.
[2] This point is underlined by *Historic Towns* I, ed. M. D. Lobel (London, 1969), the first volume of an atlas which will eventually cover most of the historic towns of the British Isles. Here it is possible for the first time to make direct comparisons between towns by means of plans, published to uniform scales, and accompanied by a written account of the salient features in the topographical development of each place. The maps and descriptions of Nottingham, Hereford and Gloucester are of great importance for the study of Anglo-Saxon towns, and include what are certainly the finest plans yet published of any early medieval town.
[3] B. K. Davidson, 'The Late Saxon Town of Thetford', *MA* XI (1967), 189–208.

type: previous work has shown the possibilities,[1] the written sources are as rich as for any other town in the country and most of the archaeological evidence will have been destroyed by 1980, much of it in the next five years. The archaeology of Norwich is a national responsibility which must be investigated before the opportunity is gone for ever.

## THE MONARCHY

The excavation of the Sutton Hoo ship-burial, the immediate publication of a preliminary account and discussion,[2] and the extensive literature that it has already evoked, even before the appearance of a full report, have left no doubt of the importance of this discovery for the study of the East Anglian royal house, and, by inference, for the early history of the Old English monarchy. It is thus entirely fitting that, in clearing the ground for the final publication, Mr R. L. S. Bruce-Mitford should have undertaken what seems to have been the first systematic attempt to estimate the character and locate the site of an Anglo-Saxon royal palace, the *vicus regius* of the East Anglian kings at Rendlesham.[3] It was hoped that the ship-burial and the royal *vicus* would shed light on each other and produce a comprehensive picture of the life and progress of an Anglo-Saxon dynasty. Although the general area which emerged from this investigation has not been further examined, much of what Mr Bruce-Mitford wrote in 1948 of the possible nature of an early Anglo-Saxon royal residence reads today as a remarkable anticipation of the discoveries made in 1953–7 at the *villa regalis* of the later-sixth- and seventh-century Bernician kings at Yeavering, Northumberland.[4] The success of the excavation at Yeavering, the work in the same years on the late Saxon and early Norman palace at Old Windsor, Berkshire,[5] and the subsequent excavation of the *palatio regis* at Cheddar in 1960–2[6] may give the impression that our knowledge of such

[1] E. M. Jope, 'Excavations in the City of Norwich, 1948', *Norfolk Archaeology* xxx. iv (1952), 287–323; J. G. Hurst and J. Golson, 'Excavations at St Benedict's Gates, Norwich, 1951 and 1953', *ibid.* xxxi. i (1955), 4–112; J. G. Hurst, 'Excavations at Barn Road, Norwich, 1954–5', *ibid.* xxxiii. ii (1963), 131–79; and Barbara Green and Rachel M. R. Young, *Norwich: the Growth of a City*, 2nd ed. (Norwich, 1968).

[2] O. G. S. Crawford devoted the whole of the March 1940 issue of *Antiquity* to the discovery: xiv (1940), 1–87. See also *AntJ* xx (1940), 149–202.

[3] R. L. S. Bruce-Mitford, 'Saxon Rendlesham', *Proceedings of the Suffolk Institute of Archaeology* xxiv. iii (1948), 228–51.

[4] The site was located by chance on air photographs taken by Dr J. K. S. St Joseph in 1948–9, when he also found what seems to be the site of *Mælmin*, the late-seventh-century successor to Yeavering (David Knowles and J. K. S. St Joseph, *Monastic Sites from the Air* [Cambridge, 1952], pp. 270–1). For brief accounts of Dr Brian Hope-Taylor's excavations of Yeavering see *MA* i (1957), 148–9, and cf. *ibid.* x (1966), 175–6; see also *The History of the King's Works*, ed. H. M. Colvin (London, 1963) i, 2–5, fig. 1.

[5] By Brian Hope-Taylor: *MA* ii (1958), 183–5.

[6] Philip Rahtz, 'The Saxon and Medieval Palaces of Cheddar, Somerset – an Interim Report of Excavations in 1960–2', *MA* vi–vii (1962–3), 33–66; and *The History of the King's Works* ii, 907–9, fig. 67.

sites is now considerable. In fact, despite the very real contribution made by these excavations, the general study of Anglo-Saxon royal palaces is in its infancy, and compares poorly in scope and achievement, if not in archaeological method, with the work now in progress on the continent. As with the investigation of towns, the crux lies in the need for combined studies, historical, archaeological and topographical. With the exception of Mr H. M. Colvin's outline account in *The History of the King's Works*,[1] English historians have shown little interest in the study of early palaces, although their importance for understanding the development of the Old English monarchy and the social and economic significance of royal estates in town and country would seem obvious. The documentary sources necessary for topographical investigation, either of the distribution of palaces, or of the individual sites, are particularly difficult and scattered. This has probably deterred local historians from making any significant contribution in this field, but the result is that, with the exception of the excavations already mentioned, we know very little about Anglo-Saxon palaces, or the part they played in society. It cannot be too strongly emphasized that this lack of knowledge is due to past and current trends in the study of Anglo-Saxon history, and not to lack of evidence, for the evidence is there, even if it must be gathered from several disciplines in combination. The work of German historians demonstrates the results that can be achieved from such combined studies, whether they relate to the social and economic importance of palaces in general[2] or to the investigation of an individual site:[3] *Pfalzenforschung* is an established and respected part of medieval history, and there is little in the German work that is not relevant to, or could not be achieved in, this country.

[1] 1, 1–6 and 42–8.

[2] Basic problems are discussed in *Deutsche Königspfalzen: Beiträge zu ihrer historischen und archäologischen Erforschung* i and ii, Veröffentlichungen des Max-Planck-Instituts für Geschichte ii. 1 (Göttingen, 1963 and 1965) and in *Geschichte in Wissenschaft und Unterricht*, Zeitschrift des Verbandes der Geschichtslehrer Deutschlands 16/8 (August 1965), the whole of which is devoted to *Pfalzenforschung*. For a wide-ranging discussion of royal residence and *civitates regiae* in the fifth to ninth centuries see E. Ewig, 'Résidence et Capitale pendant le Haut Moyen Age', *Revue Historique* ccxxx (1963), 25–72. For Carolingian palaces see W. Sage, 'Zur archäologischen Untersuchung karolingischer Pfalzen in Deutschland', *Karl der Grosse* iii, 323–35. An important discussion of the physical development of royal and near-royal palaces in France is P. Héliot, 'Sur Résidences Princières Bâties en France du $X^e$ au $XII^e$ Siècle', *Le Moyen Age* $4^e$ sér. x (1955), 27–61 and 291–317.

[3] A particularly interesting example of the results possible from combined research is *Ingelheim am Rhein*, Forschungen und Studien zur Geschichte Ingelheims (Stuttgart, 1964), which contains an account of the prehistoric, Roman and early medieval archaeology of the Ingelheim area, including an important study of field-names, by K. Böhner; an account of the archaeology and architectural development of the palace by W. Sage; and an historical discussion by P. Classen. A report on the excavations of 1963 and 1965 will be found in *Germania* xlvi (1968), 291–312. For an archaeological-architectural account of Charlemagne's palace at Aachen see L. Hugot, 'Die Pfalz Karls des Grossen in Aachen', *Karl de Grosse* iii, 534–72, and compare with the contrasting historical account by W. Kämmerer, *ibid.* i, 322–48.

One of the first requirements is a systematic list of possible sites, compiled from written sources, particularly *The Anglo-Saxon Chronicle*, and from the dating and boundary clauses of charters.[1] Each site would then need to be investigated in its local context, initially by study of the documentary evidence and then by observation on the ground. The documents cannot normally be expected to produce unequivocal evidence of the location, or even the existence, of a former royal palace, but the occurrence of royal demesne in Domesday Book, the presence of a royal free chapel or of isolated glebe land, and the survival of distinctive place-names, especially field-names, may each help to prove or disprove the initial identification and to indicate the actual site on the ground. The site of the Cheddar palace was first suspected from an Inquisition of 1381 set up to enquire into an alleged royal free chapel;[2] glebe land may indicate the site of the Rendlesham palace;[3] and there and at Brixworth field-names in maps of 1828 and 1686 respectively could conceivably preserve what might be remarkably long-lived local traditions of the existence of a former palace.[4] The important point is that records of almost any date may be relevant to this kind of enquiry.

Once a possible area has been delimited in this way, field archaeology can take over the actual task of finding the site, by air photography, as at Yeavering, or, as in the case of a possible Offan palace at Hatton Rock in the valley of the Warwickshire Avon,[5] by geo-physical prospection, by phosphate analysis, by consideration of previously recorded finds, or simply by visual observation of the detail of the ground.[6] When the possible site of a palace has been thus located, excavation is the final test and the sole means of acquiring detailed information about its character and historical development.

An outline report on the excavation of a lesser palace has recently appeared in English: P. Grimm, 'The Royal Palace at Tilleda, Kr. Sangerhausen, D.D.R: Excavations from 1935–1966', *MA* xii (1968), 83–100.

[1] For the location of some important place-names, and royal sites known from archaeological evidence, see *Map of Britain in the Dark Ages*, 2nd ed. (Ordnance Survey, 1966), with discussion on pp. 16–17. The evidence of boundary clauses is difficult to interpret, see for example *witan dic* in the bounds of King's Worthy, Hants. (Kemble, no. 743, of 1026).

[2] *MA* vi–vii (1962–3), 54–5.

[3] *Proc. Suffolk Inst. Arch.* xxi (1948), 228–51.

[4] Areas at Rendlesham are called 'Woodenhall', 'Great Woodenhalls', 'Little Woodenhall' etc., *ibid.* 251. For Brixworth, where there are fields called 'The Palace', 'Palace Meadow' and 'Palace End Rick', see R. H. C. Davis, 'Brixworth and Clofesho', *JBAA* 3rd ser. xxv (1962), 71. These names are curious and require more investigation before they can be accepted as valid evidence for the former existence of a palace. Could 'Palace' in the Brixworth names be a corruption of some form of 'pale' or 'palisade', implying simply a fenced enclosure?

[5] P. A. Rahtz, 'A Possible Saxon Palace near Stratford-on-Avon', *Antiquity* xliv (1970), 137–43.

[6] For a useful summary of 'field archaeology' as distinct from excavation, see Graham Webster, *Practical Archaeology* (London, 1963), pp. 22–57. M. J. Aitken, *Physics and Archaeology* (London, 1961) provides a full statement of the various methods of locating sites by scientific means.

Almost everything in this field of palace research remains to be done. If we know little of rural palaces, we know nothing of town palaces. In what kind of palace did King Edgar live, who 'showed by his impressive coronation ceremony at Bath in 973 that he grasped the political value of external magnificence'?[1] What were the halls and chambers of wood or stone which Asser attributed to Alfred? If the great series of royal churches in Winchester is anything to judge by, the Old English royal palace which completed that complex will have been of 'Carolingian' scale and magnificence, and everything in the art and architectural history of Alfred's time suggests the possibility that actual continental models, Aachen itself perhaps, may have influenced it. But we know nothing concrete. We need to be able to study palaces as a phenomenon in themselves, to compare them one to another, to contrast urban and rural examples, to examine their development and investigate their use and social function. At present we must simply beware of regarding as typical the palaces we already know: Yeavering of the sixth and seventh centuries in Northumbria; Cheddar of the ninth, tenth and eleventh centuries on the marches of Wessex; Old Windsor of the end of the Saxon period in the centre of the kingdom.

## THE CHURCH

More attention has been devoted to the architectural investigation of Anglo-Saxon churches than to any other aspect of the material culture of the period. A century of research has now culminated in the two great volumes by Dr H. M. Taylor and the late Mrs Joan Taylor,[2] and a third volume is eagerly awaited. The Taylors concentrated on structural · analysis, with proper reference to the historical evidence, and in this present volume Dr Taylor demonstrates again in his study of St Wystan's church at Repton the important new results that can be obtained by the detailed structural analysis of what might seem to be a well-known building.[3]

The other main line of enquiry, apart from excavation, has been the critical examination of the documentary evidence relating to the fabric of now vanished churches. The late Mr Roger Quirk's papers on the Old and New Minsters at Winchester are perhaps the most instructive examples of

[1] Whitelock, *op. cit.* p. 50.
[2] H. M. Taylor and J. Taylor, *Anglo-Saxon Architecture* I and II (Cambridge, 1965).
[3] The long series of papers by the late E. Dudley C. Jackson and Sir Eric Fletcher in *JBAA* 3rd ser. IX (1944) onwards, are important not only for their results, but also for their insistence on the *minutiae* of structural analysis. British architectural history has been strong in the detailed investigation and description of the structural sequence of medieval buildings and in the use of plans, but less attention has been paid to elevations and sections. Detailed presentation of the evidence, as, e.g., in F. Kreusch, *Beobachtungen an der Westanlage der Klosterkirche zu Corvey*, Beihefte der Bonner Jahrbücher 9 (Köln Graz, 1963), is not often found in the British literature.

what can be achieved in this way, and in the case of the Old Minster his deductions have been confirmed in all their essentials by the excavations of 1962–9.[1] Dr Taylor has himself recently reviewed the previous attempts to reconstruct the layout of the Anglo-Saxon cathedral of Canterbury, and his results are convincing, particularly in regard to the ring-crypt of the east end, which can now be understood more clearly than was possible fifty years ago, as a result of the excavations begun in 1939 under St Peter's at Rome.[2]

The last ten years have thus seen a great advance in our understanding of Anglo-Saxon church architecture on a wide front, but there are major problems of approach, method and objective to be solved. As in the other fields already discussed, the great need is for combined study, in this case by historians, of the church and of the liturgy, by architectural historians and by archaeologists. The problem was clearly put by Mgr M. Andrieu in the introduction to his edition of the *Ordines Romani*:

On a beaucoup écrit et savamment, sur l'architecture de nos cathédrales et de nos vieilles églises, mais l'on s'est rarement demandé ce qui avait pu se passer à l'intérieur de ces édifices et pourquoi nos ancêtres les avaient bâtis à si grands frais. On n'a considéré que le cadre de pierre, comme si, ayant lui-même sa raison d'être, il était toujours demeuré vide.[3]

I do not wish to imply that those who have written on Anglo-Saxon churches have not attempted to discuss their results in functional terms, for this would be demonstrably false. It is rather that these interpretations have tended to concentrate on individual features, such as the housing of relics or the position of altars.[4] They have not usually seen the entire church as the physical embodiment of the liturgy. If it is also recalled that there may be differing liturgical requirements according to the status and function of a particular church, that the staging of the great festivals of the year, notably Easter, was intimately related to the structure of the building,[5]

[1] R. N. Quirk, 'Winchester Cathedral in the Tenth Century', *AJ* cxiv (1957), 28–68; and *idem*, 'Winchester New Minster and its Tenth-Century Tower', *JBAA* 3rd ser. xxiv (1961), 16–54; see also M. Biddle and R. N. Quirk, *AJ* cxix (1962), 173–82. For the excavations of 1962–9 see *AntJ* xliv (1964), 202–11; xlv (1965), 249–58; xlvi (1966), 319–26; xlvii (1967), 266–72; xlviii (1968), 268–80; xlix (1969), 312–23; and l (1970), 311–21. A consideration of the varying archaeological *interpretations* in these reports will show how only total excavation can provide a firm architectural basis for even so perceptive and detailed an analysis of the documentary evidence as that undertaken in Quirk's papers.

[2] H. M. Taylor, *AJ* cxxvi (1969), 101–30.

[3] M. Andrieu, *Les Ordines Romani de Haut Moyen Âge* i, *Les Manuscripts* (Louvain, 1931), pref., quoted in C. Heitz, *Recherches sur les Rapports entre Architecture et Liturgie à l'Époque Carolingienne* (Paris, 1963), p. 15.

[4] E.g. C. A. Ralegh Radford, 'Two Scottish Shrines: Jedburgh and St Andrews', *AJ* cxii (1955), 43–60; and 'The Bishop's Throne in Norwich Cathedral', *ibid.* cxvi (1959), 115–31; and H. M. Taylor, 'Reculver Reconsidered', *ibid.* cxxv (1968), 291–6. A notable exception is R. N.Quirk's treatment of the postulated west-work at Winchester, *ibid.* cxiv (1957), 48–56.

[5] Heitz, *op. cit.* pp. 75–91.

and that the liturgy itself developed during the four and a half centuries from 597 to 1066, it is easy to see how complex may be the relationship between the fabric of a church and its use. These are deep waters for the non-specialist, but there is no doubt that much progress could be made by the archaeologist and architectural historian if he could be guided by a liturgicist's critical analysis of the architectural implications of the surviving evidence for pre-Conquest liturgical practice.

Liturgical interpretation is certainly the crucial problem now facing the architectural historian of the Anglo-Saxon church, but there are other difficulties scarcely less daunting. Most of the Anglo-Saxon churches surviving today are small churches, or, put another way, none of the greatest churches has survived even reasonably intact. 'We cannot judge Anglo-Saxon architecture,' as Professor Whitelock has said, 'from its minor monuments, which are all that are left.'[1] Unfortunately people still continue to do so, and the false interpretations that arise stem quite as much from the minor impact of archaeological excavation on this problem, as from the continued partisanship of the debate over the Anglo-Saxon contribution to the Norman kingdom.[2]

It is sometimes claimed that the great number of excavations under standing churches on the continent is the result of opportunities presented prior to reconstruction after war damage. This was true in the later 1940s and perhaps until about 1960, but it was not true before the war and it is no longer true today.[3] The varying arrangements made for the care and maintenance of church fabric on the continent, usually with some degree of state involvement, have ensured that opportunities for investigation and record are taken whenever possible. This is not the case in this country, where churches in current ecclesiastical use are specifically excluded from the control of the Ancient Monuments Acts. Only in the case of the most sympathetic attitude by the church authorities, as for example the Dean and Chapter of Winchester from 1962 onwards, or under conditions of the most dire emergency and then with the active encouragement of the architect, as now at York, has it been possible to excavate under standing churches, even when alterations such as the installation of heating systems have undoubtedly led to the destruction of important evidence.

The comparative lack of archaeological investigation has three important results: it tends to perpetuate the bias resulting from the survival of

[1] *Op. cit.* p. 240.

[2] See R. A. Brown's introduction, *op. cit.* pp. 1–7 and cf. p. 102.

[3] See, e.g., the *Berichten* of the Dutch State Service for Archaeological Investigation (Amersfoort, 1950 onwards); the reports of Danish work in the periodicals *Kuml* (Aarhus, 1951 onwards) and *Årbøger for Nordisk Oldkyndighed og Historie* (Copenhagen); and the German work scattered through innumerable publications, but now being brought together in *Vorromanische Kirchenbauten* I (A–J), II (K–Q) and III (R–Z) (Zentralinstitut für Kunstgeschichte, Munich, 1966–71).

smaller churches and the loss of the greater churches; it leaves comparatively unchallenged the often fairly simple structural development usually to be seen in the surviving fabric above ground;[1] and it means that the early internal arrangements, vital to a liturgical interpretation, remain unknown. Without excavation and the systematic recording of structural detail whenever it is exposed in repairs and alterations, our records and interpretation of even the smaller churches must remain inadequate, with the consequent acceptance of too simple a picture of what was often a long series of changes over more than four centuries. At this moment in time the situation is critical, for the impending demolition, or change in use, of redundant churches all over the country presents both an opportunity to carry out the necessary work and a threat to the survival of the evidence in any form. There is an urgent necessity here for national action, both scholarly and administrative.

One aspect of this problem is the question of the conversion of pagan temples into Christian churches. In spite of Pope Gregory's instructions to this effect, there is little evidence, as Professor Whitelock has said, that the missionaries went so far as to use a heathen building for a Christian church.[2] This does not of course mean that it never happened and there is now some evidence from Yeavering for apparently just such a conversion.[3] Other possible examples are at Lullingstone[4] and at Stone-by-Faversham in Kent.[5] The whole problem is one of great difficulty: Olaf Olsen's recent review of the Scandinavian evidence has shown that there is no clear case there for the conversion of pagan temples into Christian churches, that the whole concept of a pagan temple as a distinct building is itself suspect, and that even at Gamla Uppsala the evidence for the pagan temple is quite inadequate, while at Jelling it is probably unacceptable.[6] Olsen's review had the benefit of many church excavations on which to draw; in England this evidence is not yet available. Pope Gregory's letter may be based on ignorance of pagan practice, but the Yeavering example, if acceptable when fully published, may indicate the reverse. Here again we can only hope to advance our present knowledge by further research, drawing like Dr

---

[1] The standing fabric of Deerhurst church shows how complex this development can be, but the Anglo-Saxon structure is exceptionally well preserved, and there must be many cases in which the evidence survives only, if at all, below ground: E. D. C. Jackson and E. G. M. Fletcher, 'The Anglo-Saxon Priory Church at Deerhurst', *Studies in Building History*, ed. E. M. Jope (London, 1961), pp. 64–77; and Taylor and Taylor, *op. cit.* I, 193–209.

[2] *Op. cit.* p. 24.

[3] *MA* I (1957), 149.

[4] Taylor and Taylor, *op. cit.* I, 402. The date of the church is uncertain, but the superimposition is remarkable.

[5] *AntJ* XLIX (1969), 273–94; and Taylor and Taylor, *op. cit.* II, 474–7.

[6] Olaf Olsen, *Hørg, Hov og Kirke* (Copenhagen, 1966, as the 1965 volume of *Årbøger for Nordisk Oldkyndighed og Historie*); see also Knud Krogh, 'Kirken mellem højene', *Skalk*, 1966 (2), pp. 5–10, and P. V. Glob, 'Kong Haralds Kumler', *ibid.* 1969 (4), pp. 18–27.

Olsen on archaeology, topography, place-name evidence and literary sources in combination.

So far this discussion has dealt with the churches themselves, the fabric of the actual church building, and not with the whole complex of which, in the case of the monasteries and larger churches, the church itself was only a part. Comparatively little attention has been paid to pre-Conquest monastic sites in England, with the notable exceptions of Miss Rosemary Cramp's excavations now in progress at Monkwearmouth and Jarrow,[1] and the work at Glastonbury.[2] Quite apart from the intense interest of such sites in their own right, without more excavation and allied research it will be impossible to widen the architectural and art-historical study of Anglo-Saxon churches towards a comprehension of the part played by churches and monastic establishments in the social, economic and industrial development of Anglo-Saxon England. These aspects have so far been almost totally ignored by archaeologists, but Professor E. M. Jope's work on the building-stone industry of southern and midland England in the Saxon period provides an important indication of what might be achieved.[3]

The location of pre-Conquest monastic sites is clear enough when they are known to have been rebuilt in the Norman period, as at Abingdon.[4] Many early sites, however, particularly those where there has been a known or suspected migration from one place to another, or where the monastery did not survive the Danish attacks of the ninth century, can be located only by detailed topographical research, as in the case of palaces. These sites would be particularly rewarding to excavate, however, since they might not have been disturbed by subsequent rebuilding, unless lying today within areas of modern development.

Bishops' residences are another subject for further enquiry. Almost

---

[1] Monkwearmouth: *MA* IV (1960), 139–40; VI–VII (1962–3), 315; VIII (1964), 232; IX (1965), 171; XI (1967), 264; and XII (1968), 156. Jarrow: *ibid.* VIII (1964), 232; X (1966), 169–70; XI (1967), 263–4; and XII (1968), 155–6. For both, see now esp. *ibid.* XIII (1969), 21–66.

[2] Taylor and Taylor, *op. cit.* I, 250–7; *MA* II (1958), 188–9; IV (1960), 136–7; and VIII (1964), 243–4; and *Somerset and Dorset Notes and Queries* XXVII (1955–61), 21–7, 68–73, 165–9 and 251–5; and XXVIII (1962–8), 114–17. The excavations at St Augustine's Abbey, Canterbury, from 1913 onwards revealed the outline of what may be a tenth-century claustral arrangement, but fresh excavation is required before the plan or dating can be accepted: *Archaeologia Cantiana* XLVI (1934), 179–94, esp. 191 ff., and plan in pocket at back; see also Taylor and Taylor, *op. cit.* I, 142. The monastic buildings found at Whitby (*Archaeologia* LXXXIX [1943], 27–88; cf. Taylor and Taylor, *op. cit.* II, 654) are now the subject of critical comment, and must be regarded with caution (*MA* XII [1968], 65, n. 162). I am aware that such comments lead historians to wonder what, if any, archaeological evidence they can accept, but it must be recognized that excavation techniques in medieval archaeology were primitive until the years immediately before the Second World War, and that all excavation reports, like any other kind of historical writing, must be used critically and not accepted outright.

[3] *Ibid.* VIII (1964), 91–118.

[4] M. Biddle, the late Mrs H. T. Lambrick and J. N. L. Myres, 'The Early History of Abingdon, Berkshire, and its Abbey', *ibid.* XII (1968), 26–69.

nothing is known of such sites in the late Saxon period, despite their importance soon after the Conquest. There is some evidence for a tenth-century phase of the episcopal palace at Wolvesey in Winchester, but most of it seems to have been destroyed by a later moat.[1] It would be useful to gather together the written evidence for such places in the late Saxon period, to attempt to define the date at which the bishop's residence becomes distinct from the monastery, and to estimate its separate economic and social function. The investigation of the development of an entire cathedral or monastic precinct, such as has been in progress for some years now at Xanten,[2] might seem a difficult undertaking in this country, but it may in fact have already been partially achieved at North Elmham.[3] It is too early yet to reach any final interpretation of Mr Peter Wade-Martins's excavations, which are still in progress, but they underline the fact that extensive knowledge of these and similar sites may best be sought in places which have, for one reason or another, been abandoned at an early date, and not subjected to the massive disturbance caused by sub-sequent rebuilding.

I have chosen in this brief survey to examine three aspects of Anglo-Saxon society – the towns, the monarchy and the church – and to try and say something about the present and future contribution of archaeology to their understanding. It might have been useful, had space allowed, to discuss trade and industry and rural life, but I think the lessons to be drawn would have been the same: the necessity for combined studies; the need to examine the Anglo-Saxon experience in a European setting, not least in terms of archaeological approach and method; and the urgency of the problems posed by the speed and scale of destruction through modern development.

It is in relation to this last point that I want to end by taking up the question raised at the beginning of this article about the teaching of Anglo-Saxon archaeology in the universities. For the next few decades at least we are going to be faced with an enormous problem of recording the archaeological evidence for Anglo-Saxon England before much of it is lost for ever. To do this adequately requires both financial resources and trained manpower, and it is for the latter that the universities must be

[1] *AntJ* XLIV (1964), 212–14; XLV (1965), 258–60; XLVI (1966), 326–7; XLVII (1967), 273; and XLVIII (1968), 282–3.

[2] H. Borger, 'Die ehemalige Stiftskirche St Viktor und die Stifts-Immunität in Xanten', *Kirche und Burg*, Führer des Rheinischen Landesmuseums in Bonn 8 (Düsseldorf, 1962), 115–26; and *idem, Xanten, Entstehung und Geschichte eines niederrheinischen Stiftes* (Xanten, 1966). See now *idem, Beiträge zur Frühgeschichte des Xantener Viktorstiftes*, Rheinische Ausgrabungen 6 (1969).

[3] Peter Wade-Martins, 'Excavations at North Elmham, 1967–8: an Interim Report', *Norfolk Archæology* XXXIV. iv (1969), 352–97; and '1969' *ibid.* XXXV. i (1970), 25–78.

responsible. Contrary to the present comparatively small scale of state finance for archaeological research in Britain, as compared with some other European countries, and in spite of all that is said of the current condition of the national economy, experience since the war suggests that the money can be found if the case is pressed with authority and conviction. The controlling factor is the supply of people competent to undertake the work involved. The current bias towards the art-historical aspects of Anglo-Saxon archaeology and the tendency in some places to concentrate on the earlier periods up to about 800, the situation that in departments of archaeology the teaching is not sufficiently historical and that in departments of history too little attention is paid to archaeology, all combine to ensure that the training available does not normally produce scholars of the rounded professional competence that is urgently required. Most of us working in Anglo-Saxon archaeology have been trained in one field alone, whether history or archaeology, and have had to try to acquire knowledge of the other disciplines involved as we went along. For the Anglo-Saxon period, and for the medieval period as a whole, the time has come for the thorough integration of historical and archaeological teaching in the historical departments of our universities. The taking of optional subjects is not sufficient for the person who wishes to reach professional standards in the history and archaeology of the early Middle Ages. New teaching posts are required, and new courses leading to a first degree, probably after four years, to be followed by post-graduate work. The range of material to be covered is great, but to achieve this by lowering the standards required by both historians and archaeologists would be self-defeating. The historian cannot just pick up archaeology, any more than the archaeologist can casually become a documentary historian. Whatever his final personal bent, each needs a thorough training in both disciplines. Perhaps in this way we can ultimately discard what seems to be an unnecessary and inhibiting distinction between documentary and archaeological historians.[1]

[1] Since this article was written two important papers have appeared dealing with the late and post-Roman periods in Cologne and Mainz. They should be added to n. 4 on p. 396, above: O. Doppelfeld, 'Das Fortlebender Stadt Köln vom 5. bis 8. Jahrhundert nach Chr.', *Early Medieval Studies* I, *Antikvariskt Arkiv* xxxviii (Stockholm, 1970), 35–42; and K. Weidemann, 'Die Topographie von Mainz in der Römerzeit und dem frühen Mittelalter', *Jahrbuch des Römisch-germanischen Zentralmuseums, Mainz* xv (1968), 146–99.

# Index

# Index

St Patrick, Second Synod of, 61
Salisbury, 124
Sallust, used by translato rof Orosius, 245, 251
Samthann, St, 65
Sandwich, granted to Christ Church, Canterbury, 121
Saxons: English connection with, 35; Frankish campaigns against, 37, 39, 46
Scandinavian language, survival of, in England, 165–81
Scandinavian personal names: in Danelaw, 148–9; in Grimston-hybrid place-names, 149–52
Scotland, rune-stones in, 167
Sedulius Scotus, *De Rectoribus Christianis* by, 131, 132, 136
Servius, used by translator of Orosius, 239
Settle, rune-stone from cave near, 173–4
Sigebert III, Merovingian king, 37
silver, confined to coinage after Edgar's reform, 346–8
Skelton-in-Cleveland, runes on sundial at, 165, 174
Sléibíne, abbot of Iona, 55
Smaragdus, *Via Regia* by, 129, 131
Soissons, Synod of (924), enacts penalties for killing in war, 281
Southampton, 127, 397
Stafford, mint at, 338, 340
Stamford, 118; mint at, 338, 340
Stamford Bridge, *ASC* on battle of, 234
Stoke-sub-Hamdon, tympanum at, showing *Agnus Dei*, 341
Stone-by-Faversham, conversion of heathen building to church at?, 405
Strassburg, bishopric of, 39
Suetonius, missing opening of *Life of Caesar* by, used by translator of Orosius, 241
Sulgrave, 127; nummular brooch from, 333–49
Sutton, Isle of Ely, inscribed brooch from, 175, 176
Sutton Hoo, ship burial at, 399
Sweden: affairs of, in *Beowulf*, 286; rune-stones in, 166
Swithun, St, Ælfric's *Life of*, 103
Symeon of Durham, 66
Syxtus, St, Pope Gregory's request for relics of, 24n

Tamworth, 82, 118, 126; mint at?, 184
Tatian, *Diatesseron* of, known in England, 6n, 294n
Tertullian, on just wars in Old Testament, 276
Tetney, hoard of coins at, 185
thegns: celibate clergy entitled to rank of, 140; ceorls worthy to become, 119; town houses of, 121

Thelwall, 118
Theodore, archbishop of Canterbury: orders penance for killing in war, 280; penitential collection of, 16n, 25n, 26, 32, 61, 62–3; and validity of Irish orders, 52
Thetford, 126, 398; mint at, 184
Theuderic III, Merovingian king, 36
Theuderic IV, Merovingian king, 38
Thornaby on Tees, 'rune-stone' at, 165, 168
Totnes, 126n; mint at, 184
Towcester, 118
towns, 115–28; archaeological study of, 392–9
trade: with the continent, 116; in towns, 121, 122, 128
Trent valley, Grimston-hybrid place-names in, 154, 155, 159, 160, 162
Trier, bishopric of, 40
Trumhere, bishop of Mercians, 50

Uhtred, king of the Hwicce, 78
Ulfcytel and the Danes, in *ASC*, 225, 226
Ultán, Irish scribe at a cell of Lindisfarne, 56
Utrecht, 37, 41

Valerius Maximus, used by translator of Orosius, 239, 244, 246–7, 251
verse, oral and formulaic, 291–2
Vikings, raids by, 65, 66, 67, 72; *ASC* on, 79, 223, 225–6, 229; Burghal Hidage records answer to, 117; resistance to, 72; threat from and military obligations, 79–80, 83, 84; towns as product of resistance to, 119, 125; see also Danes
Vinnian, 61
Virgil, Irish bishop of Salzburg, 44–5
Virgil, poet of *Beowulf* acquainted with *Æneid* of, 283, 291
Völsung lays, cycle of, 289–90
Vopiscus, used by translator of Orosius?, 239

*Waldere*, 274
Wallingford, 82, 118, 121n, 126, 397
war, ethic of, in OE, 269–82
Wareham, 81–2, 126, 397
weights and measures, 143
Wessex: military obligations in, 69, 75–6, 80–2, 84; origins of, 396; towns in, 116
Whitby, Synod of (664), 12, 13, 38, 50
Wicklow Hundreds, on Suffolk–Essex border, 91n
*Widsith*, heroes of epic listed in, 284, 285
Wiglaf, king of Mercia, buried at Repton, 353, 388
Wihtberht, missionary, in Ireland, 50, 52
Wihtfrith, 50
Wihtred, king of Kent, 75, 79
Wilfrid, St, 38, 47

417